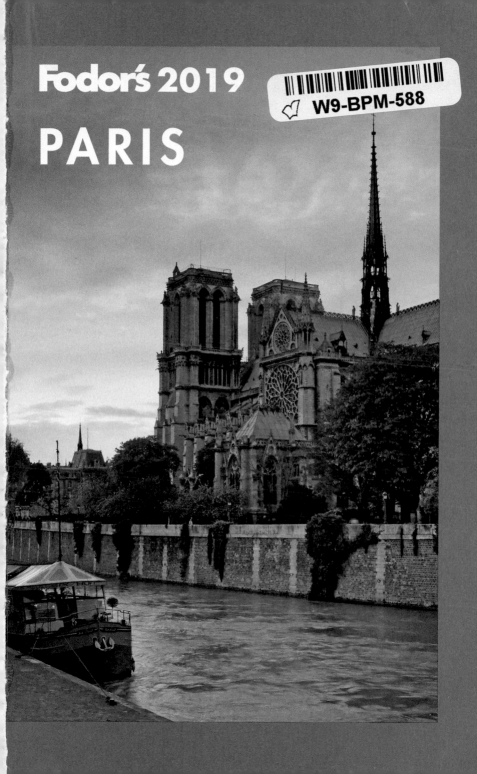

Fodor's 2019

PARIS

W9-BPM-588

WELCOME TO PARIS

Paris is one of the most beautiful cities on earth, a truth easily appreciated on a stroll that could yield one stunning vista after another, from the epic Eiffel Tower to the regal Jardin des Tuileries to the petite cafés bursting onto the sidewalks. Beyond the city's visual appeal, the cultural riches of the French capital are unsurpassed. Whether you opt to explore the historic, fashion-conscious, bourgeois, or bohemian and arty sides of Paris, one thing is certain: the City of Light will always enthrall.

TOP REASONS TO GO

★ **Iconic Landmarks:** From the Eiffel Tower to the Arc de Triomphe, Paris dazzles.

★ **Chic Shopping:** The Champs-Élysées and Rue St-Honoré are the ultimate shopaholic high.

★ **Heavenly Food:** Whether it's haute cuisine or baguettes, locals know how to eat.

★ **The Seine:** The river's bridges and islands reward exploration by foot or boat.

★ **Grand Museums:** From the mammoth Louvre to the petite Musée Rodin, art abounds.

★ **Majestic Churches:** Notre-Dame and Sacré-Coeur boldly mark the city's skyline.

20 ULTIMATE EXPERIENCES

Paris offers terrific experiences that should be on every traveler's list. Here are Fodor's top picks for a memorable trip.

1 Luxembourg Gardens

Bordered by Saint-Germain-des-Prés and the Latin Quarter, these charming gardens are the definition of a true Parisian park. Here, you can relax on a lawn chair in the sunshine or enjoy an impromptu picnic. *(Ch. 11)*

2 Eiffel Tower

Whether you head to the top or pose for a photo in front, the breathtaking Eiffel Tower is the ultimate symbol of Paris for most visitors. *(Ch. 3)*

3 Parisian Cuisine

From pastries and *macarons* to baguettes and crêpes, food in Paris is nothing short of sublime. *(Ch. 14)*

4 Basilique du Sacre-Couer

It's hard not to feel as though you're climbing up to heaven when you visit Sacred Heart Basilica, the white castle in the sky perched atop the city. *(Ch. 7)*

5 Marché aux Puces St-Ouen

The 150-year-old market is the world's largest and most famous flea market, selling everything from vintage couture to gilded mirrors and burnished silver. *(Ch. 16)*

6 The Seine

There's nothing like seeing Paris via a walk or boat trip on its main waterway. Along the tranquil Seine, historic bridges connect the city's most famous landmarks. *(Ch. 2)*

7 Champs-Élysées

A mecca for shoppers (both locals and visitors alike), the Champs-Élysées remains the most famous avenue in Paris—and, perhaps, the world. *(Ch. 4)*

8 Parisian Cafés

Still the center of social life for many Parisians, neighborhood cafés offer great food and coffee, and better people-watching. *(Ch. 14)*

9 Montmartre

Montmarte, and other neighborhoods like Canal St-Martin and the Latin Quarter, are more like charming villages filled with shops, eateries, and cobblestone streets. *(Ch. 7)*

10 Arc de Triomphe

This colossal monument to military victory is a major landmark of the city, with excellent views from the top of all of Paris. *(Ch. 4)*

11 Opéra Garnier

Home of the Phantom of the Opera and the inspiration for Edgar Degas's dancer paintings, the dazzling Palais Garnier is one location of the National Opera of Paris. *(Ch. 6)*

12 Centre Pompidou

One of modern Paris's more controversial buildings when it was built in 1977, this art complex now houses the city's modern art museum. *(Ch. 8)*

13 Cimetière du Pére-Lachaise

Perhaps the world's most famous cemetery, this oasis is the final resting place for notable figures like Marcel Proust, Oscar Wilde, Jim Morrison, and Gertrude Stein. *(Ch. 9)*

14 Musée Rodin

Once the sculptor's studio, this stately 18th-century mansion contains more than 6,000 of Rodin's sculptures, including his masterpieces *The Thinker* and *The Kiss*. *(Ch. 3)*

15 Versailles

The famous château was home to Louis XIV and Marie-Antoinette, and remains the grandest palace in France, from its dazzling Hall of Mirrors to its landscaped gardens. *(Ch. 19)*

16 Musée D'Orsay

Under the soaring roof of one of Paris's grand Beaux-Arts railway stations, the Musée d'Orsay contains the world's largest collection of Impressionist masterpieces. *(Ch. 11)*

17 Musée Picasso

Home to the world's largest public collection of Pablo Picasso works, the paintings, sculptures, and drawings here span the artist's entire career. *(Ch. 8)*

18 Jardin des Tuileries

This quintessential French garden was once where Paris's wealthiest came to stroll, and today is still one of the city's best walks. *(Ch. 5)*

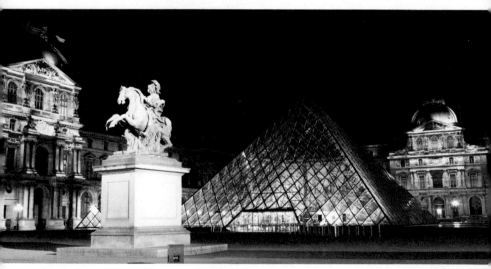

19 The Louvre

The world's greatest art museum—and the largest, with works from almost every civilization on earth—houses masterpieces like the *Mona Lisa* and the *Venus de Milo. (Ch. 5)*

20 Notre-Dame

This cathedral is the symbolic heart of Paris and, for many, of France itself. Don't miss the unforgettable view, framed by stone gargoyles, from the top. (Ch. 2)

Fodor's PARIS 2019

Editorial: Douglas Stallings, *Editorial Director*; Margaret Kelly, Jacinta O'Halloran, *Senior Editors*; Kayla Becker, Alexis Kelly, Amanda Sadlowski, *Editors*; Teddy Minford, *Content Editor*; Rachael Roth, *Content Manager*

Design: Tina Malaney, *Design and Production Director*; Jessica Gonzalez, *Production Designer*

Photography: Jill Krueger, *Senior Photo Editor*

Maps: Rebecca Baer, *Senior Map Editor*; David Lindroth and Mark Stroud, *Cartographers*

Production: Jennifer DePrima, *Editorial Production Manager*; Carrie Parker, *Senior Production Editor*; Elyse Rozelle, *Production Editor*

Business & Operations: Chuck Hoover, *Chief Marketing Officer*; Joy Lai, *Vice President and General Manager*; Stephen Horowitz, *Director of Business Development and Revenue Operations*; Tara McCrillis, *Director of Publishing Operations*; Eliza D. Aceves, *Content Operations Manager and Strategist*

Public Relations and Marketing: Joe Ewaskiw, *Manager*; Esther Su, *Marketing Manager*

Writers: Linda Hervieux, Jennifer Ladonne, Virgina Power, Jack Vermee

Editor: Amanda Sadlowski, Debbie Harmsen

Production Editor: Jennifer DePrima

ISBN 978-1-64097-064-9

ISSN 0149–1288

All details in this book are based on information supplied to us at press time. Always confirm information when it matters, especially if you're making a detour to visit a specific place. Fodor's expressly disclaims any liability, loss, or risk, personal or otherwise, that is incurred as a consequence of the use of any of the contents of this book.

SPECIAL SALES

This book is available at special discounts for bulk purchases for sales promotions or premiums. For more information, e-mail SpecialMarkets@fodors.com.

PRINTED IN THE UNITED STATES OF AMERICA

10 9 8 7 6 5 4 3 2 1

CONTENTS

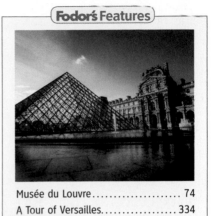

CONTENTS

MAPS

ABOUT THIS GUIDE

Fodor's Recommendations

Everything in this guide is worth doing—we don't cover what isn't—but exceptional sights, hotels, and restaurants are recognized with additional accolades. **Fodor's Choice★** indicates our top recommendations. Care to nominate a new place? Visit Fodors.com/contact-us.

Trip Costs

We list prices wherever possible to help you budget well. Hotel and restaurant price categories from **$** to **$$$$** are noted alongside each recommendation. For hotels, we include the lowest cost of a standard double room in high season. For restaurants, we cite the average price of a main course at dinner or, if dinner isn't served, at lunch. For attractions, we always list adult admission fees; discounts are usually available for children, students, and senior citizens.

Hotels

Our local writers vet every hotel to recommend the best overnights in each price category, from budget to expensive. Unless otherwise specified, you can expect private bath, phone, and TV in your room. *For expanded hotel reviews, visit Fodors.com.*

Top Picks	Hotels & Restaurants
★ **Fodor's**Choice	🏨 Hotel
Listings	⇗ Number of rooms
✉ Address	⫶❍⫶ Meal plans
✉ Branch address	✕ Restaurant
☎ Telephone	⚓ Reservations
🖷 Fax	🏛 Dress code
⊕ Website	▭ No credit cards
✉ E-mail	⑊ Price
🎟 Admission fee	**Other**
⊙ Open/closed times	⇨ See also
Ⓜ Subway	☞ Take note
⊹ Directions or Map coordinates	🏌 Golf facilities

Restaurants

Unless we state otherwise, restaurants are open for lunch and dinner daily. We mention dress code only when there's a specific requirement and reservations only when they're essential or not accepted. *For expanded restaurant reviews, visit Fodors.com.*

Credit Cards

The hotels and restaurants in this guide typically accept credit cards. If not, we'll say so.

EUGENE FODOR

Hungarian-born Eugene Fodor (1905–91) began his travel career as an interpreter on a French cruise ship. The experience inspired him to write *On the Continent* (1936), the first guidebook to receive annual updates and discuss a country's way of life as well as its sights. Fodor later joined the U.S. Army and worked for the OSS in World War II. After the war, he kept up his intelligence work while expanding his guidebook series. During the Cold War, many guides were written by fellow agents who understood the value of insider information. Today's guides continue Fodor's legacy by providing travelers with timely coverage, insider tips, and cultural context.

PARIS TODAY

Bienvenue à Paris! Or, welcome to Paris! Although it may seem as if time stands still in this city—with its romantic buildings, elegant parks, and sublime squares—there's an undercurrent of small but significant changes happening here that might not be immediately obvious.

City of the Future

While Paris may be one of the world's top destination among travelers, entrepreneurs have long shunned the City of Light as a tourist town rather than a cutting-edge capital. All that quickly changed after the upstart Emmanuel Macron won the presidency in May 2017 at the tender age of 39. The new president instantly began unfurling an ambitious agenda to overhaul the country's notoriously rigid labor laws, lower the sky-high taxes, and loosen visa rules to attract top talent in business and tech (and to lure back French talent who had fled to more convivial business climates). With British industry threatened by the Brexit vote to leave the European Union, Macron has set his sights on dethroning London as Europe's investment capital. Innovation has already come knocking, with new ventures like the gigantic Station F, an incubator with space for 1,000

start-ups and backed by Microsoft, Amazon, and Facebook. Paris has also begun making headlines for producing other highly valued start-ups like BlaBlaCar, a low-cost ride-sharing service, upping the talk from venture capitalists that Paris is in the midst of a business revolution. The news that France won its bid for the 2024 Summer Olympic Games injected another dose of optimism into the capital.

Technology

The recent wave of innovation in Paris hasn't been limited to start-ups. The contemporary art venue Gaîté Lyrique mixes innovation with art, and it's a quick walk from the wonky Musée des Arts et Métiers, a treasure trove of inventions like the first flying machine to cross the English Channel. Google has opened the Google Cultural Institute, which includes the permanent exhibit "Liquid Galaxy" at the Pavillon de l'Arsenal. In 2016, the Grand Palais become the first exhibition space to offer visitors glasses linked to earbuds that offers explanations of what's being viewed (some movie theaters now use the glasses to translate subtitles). Next, the Louvre raised the cool quotient for audioguides by switching to the Nintendo 3DS system. You can also rent bikes

WHAT'S HOT IN PARIS

In late 2017, the city announced ambitious plans to build three new bridges over the Seine. The move is a nod to the city's 18th-century *ponts* lined with merchants—think Florence's Ponte Vecchio—but these are being billed as bridges of the future. Not only would they be home to shops and offices, but also cafés, theaters, and gardens—and they'll be completely car-free.

The art world has been buzzing with the reopening of the Fondation Galeries Lafayette—rechristened Lafayette Anticipations—in March 2018 in a historic abode in the Marais, with 25,000 square feet over five stories and a glass exhibition tower shooting up from the central courtyard. Coming next is the much-anticipated Collection Pinault-Paris (opening spring 2019), showcasing the works of Gucci via an app, and the handy Smarter Paris app updates everything from transit info to maps in real-time, even when offline.

The Environment

Over at Paris City Hall, mayor Anne Hidalgo has been waging her own campaign to shake things up. The city's first female mayor enraged motorists in 2017 by closing the roadways hugging the banks of the Seine to traffic at all times (previously this had just been done on weekends). Benches and palm trees popped up on the previously bare cement terrain, and residents and visitors alike hailed the transformation. But with more cars idling on the surrounding streets, gridlock exploded, pollution ticked up, and legal challenges followed. Yet Hidalgo was unmoved in her goal of ending the city's dependence on cars. She also wants all public transportation to be electric by 2030—and a majority of Parisians support this initiative. To that end, in 2018 the city revamped—with some hiccups—its much-copied Velib' bike-share program, adding electric cycles to the regular bikes you can rent for short rides. Expansion also continued of the city's zero-emissions fleet of Autolib' electric cars that are also available to rent.

Have you ever imagined being able to stroll down a car-free Champs-Elysées? It happened on a Sunday in October 2017, and you can expect a repeat in 2018 and 2019.

Security

The year 2015 changed Paris forever, with the Charlie Hebdo attack in January followed by the devastating Bataclan massacre in November. Many Parisians wondered how life could ever return to normal. But rather than staying home and cowering to threats, Parisians took to the streets, filled café terraces, and lived their lives with the usual *joie de vivre*. While tourism did dip briefly, it came roaring back to set records in 2017, with overjoyed officials predicting 89 million visitors by the year's end. Of course, additional security in Paris is now simply a reality. Machine gun-toting soldiers patrol the streets, and there are longer waits at security checks for public buildings and airports. After the Bastille Day 2016 truck attack in Nice, concrete barriers were positioned to protect public spaces, and the feet of the Eiffel Tower are now encased in bulletproof glass.

---

billionaire François Pinault. The fashion world got its jewel in late 2017 with the opening of the Musée Yves Saint Laurent Paris, a tribute to the designer who revolutionized women's clothing. And the decorative arts palace attached to the Louvre broke all attendance records with its astounding Christian Dior retrospective; it was so popular that shortly after it closed in January 2018, officials announced it was henceforth to be called MAD—short for Musée des Arts Décoratifs.

Lording over the Place de la Concorde for more than two centuries, the Hôtel de Crillon reopened in 2017 after a sweeping, four-year renovation that transformed the regal palace's 125 rooms and suites (two of them designed by Karl Lagerfeld).

WHAT'S WHERE

1 **Ile de la Cité and Ile St-Louis.** Just a few steps from the "mainland," these small islands in the Seine are the heart of Paris. This is where you'll find Notre-Dame and Sainte-Chapelle.

2 **Around the Eiffel Tower.** With the Champ de Mars, Les Invalides, and the Seine nearby, many lovely strolls give you camera-ready views of Paris's ultimate monument.

3 **Champs-Élysées.** The Champs-Élysées and Arc de Triomphe are obvious stops for visitors, but several excellent museums here are also well worth checking out.

4 **Around the Louvre.** Anchored by the renowned museum, this neighborhood has ultrachic streets and *passages couverts* that attract shoppers as well as art lovers.

5 **The Grands Boulevards.** Use the Palais Garnier as your landmark and set out to do some power shopping. There are some good, small museums in the area, too.

6 **Montmartre.** Like a village within a city, Montmartre feels separate from the rest of Paris—but it's prime tourist territory, with Sacré-Coeur as its main attraction.

7 **The Marais.** Paris's old Jewish neighborhood is now one of the city's hippest

1

hoods. While here, visit the renovated Picasso Museum and linger at lovely Place des Vosges.

8 Eastern Paris. If it's new and happening, you'll find it out here. Neighborhoods like Canal St-Martin are full of trendy eateries, funky galleries, and edgy boutiques.

9 The Latin Quarter. Built around the fabled Sorbonne, the Latin Quarter has been the center of student life since 1257. It's also home to the Panthéon and Musée de Cluny.

10 St-Germain-des-Prés. The Musée d'Orsay is a must-see for fans of Impressionism, but make sure you leave time to amble through the charming Jardin du Luxembourg.

11 Montparnasse. Once the haunt of creative souls—Picasso and Hemingway included—Montparnasse is now known for its contemporary-art scene, as well as the Catacombs.

12 Western Paris. The Bois de Boulogne is one great reason to trek here. The popular park contains the kid-friendly Jardin d'Acclimatation and art-filled Fondation Louis Vuitton.

PARIS PLANNER

When to Go

Although the City of Light is magical all year round, summer is the most popular (and priciest) time to go. It used to be that Paris was largely deserted in August when locals fled to the coast or countryside, leaving a wake of closed shops and restaurants. But today it remains very much alive throughout the summer, with outdoor music festivals, open-air movie screenings, and fun activities like those available at the popular Paris Plages, the "beaches" on the Right Bank of the Seine and along the upper Canal St-Martin.

Nevertheless, the city is perhaps most appealing in late spring and early fall. June, when long, warm days translate into extended hours of sightseeing (the sun doesn't set until 10 pm), is particularly gorgeous. Ditto for September, which promises temperate weather, saner rates, and cultural events timed for the *rentrée* (or return), signifying the end of summer vacation. In the third weekend in September, scores of national buildings that are normally closed to the public open for visits during the annual Journées du Patrimoine (Patrimony Days).

Winter can be dark and cold, but it's also the best time to find cheap airfares and hotel deals. Spring tends to remain damp and chilly into May, when prices start rising in synch with the mercury in local thermometers.

Getting Around

Thanks to Baron Haussmann's mid-19th-century redesign, Paris is a compact wonder of wide boulevards, gracious parks, and leafy squares; and, without question, the best way to explore it is on foot.

When you want a lift, though, public transportation is easy and inexpensive. The *métro* (subway) will get you just about anywhere you want to go for €1.90 a ride (a *carnet*, or "pack" of 10 tickets, is €14.90); tickets also work on buses, trams, and the RER train line within Paris. If you're sticking to sites on or near the river, Batobus offers a convenient on-the-water alternative. A ticket for one day of unlimited hop-on/hop-off boat travel costs €17.

Paris is divided into 20 *arrondissements* (neighborhoods) spiraling out from the center of the city. The numbers reveal the neighborhood's location and its age, the 1er arrondissement at the city's heart being the oldest. The arrondissements in central Paris—the 1er to 8e—are the most visited. To help you navigate, download an app like Citymapper or Smart Paris, or pick up a copy of *Paris Pratique Par Arrondissement*, the essential map guide, available at newsstands and bookstores.

Saving Time and Money

Paris is one of the world's most visited cities—with the crowds to prove it—so it pays to be prepared. Buy tickets online when you can: most cultural centers and museums offer advance-ticket sales, and the small service fee you'll pay might be worth the time saved waiting in line. Investigate alternative entrances at popular sites, and check when rates are reduced, often during once-a-week evening openings. Also note that national museums are free the first Sunday of each month, including the Louvre, Musée d'Orsay, and Centre Pompidou.

A Paris Museum Pass (⊕ *www.paris-museumpass.com*) can save you money if you're planning on serious sightseeing, but it might be even more valuable because it allows you to bypass the lines. It's sold at the destinations it covers as well as at airports, major métro stations, and the tourism office in the Carrousel du Louvre. The two-, four-, and six-day passes cost €48, €62, and €74, respectively.

Stick to the omnipresent ATMs (but try to use indoor machines) for the best exchange rates; exchanging cash at your hotel or at a currency exchange outlet is never going to be to your advantage.

Hours

Paris is by no means a 24/7 city, so planning your days beforehand can save you aggravation. Museums are closed one day a week (usually Monday or Tuesday), and most stay open late at least one night each week, which is also the least crowded time to visit. Store hours are generally 9:30 or 10 am to 7 or 8 pm, Monday through Saturday, though smaller shops may close for several hours during the afternoon. After years of pressure from business leaders and workers to allow stores to open on Sundays, the government finally eased restrictions; shops are now permitted to open 12 Sundays per year at the owner's discretion rather than the previous five. Stores in tourist areas have long been exempt from these restrictions, so the best spots for Sunday shopping are the Champs-Élysées and the Marais where most retailers open around 2 pm.

Eating Out

Restaurants follow French mealtimes, serving lunch from noon to 2:30 pm and dinner from 7:30 or 8 pm. Some cafés serve food all day long. If you have your heart set on a specific restaurant, it's wise to reserve a table for dinner; top choices book up months in advance. When you're ready for the check, you must ask for it (it's considered rude to bring a bill unbidden). In cafés you'll get a register receipt with your order. *Service* (gratuity) is always included, but it's good form to leave something extra if you're satisfied with the service: a few cents for drinks, €1 for lunch, €3 at dinner. Leave 5% of the bill only in higher-end restaurants.

What to Wear

When it comes to clothing, the standard French look is dressier than the American equivalent. Athletic clothes are reserved for sports. Sneakers are not usually worn by adults, but if you pack yours, keep them for daytime only. Neat jeans are acceptable everywhere except at the top restaurants; check to see whether there's a dress code at any upscale places.

Paris Etiquette

The Parisian reputation for rudeness is undeserved. In fact, Parisians are sticklers for politeness and exchanging formal greetings is the rule. Informal American-style manners are considered impolite. Beginning an exchange with a simple "Do you speak English?" will get you on the right foot. Learning a few key French words will take you far. Offer a hearty *bonjour* (bohn-zhoor) when walking into a shop or café and an *au revoir* (o ruh-vwahr) when leaving, even if nobody seems to be listening (a chorus may reply). When speaking to a woman over age 16, use *madame* (ma-dam), literally "my lady." For a young woman or girl, use *mademoiselle* (mad-mwa-zel). A man of any age goes by *monsieur* (murh-syur). Always say please, *s'il vous plaît* (seel-voo-play), and thank you, *merci* (mehr-see).

UNDER-THE-RADAR PARIS

You've been to the Eiffel Tower and the Louvre, but have you ever learned to cook French pastries or celebrated Bastille Day like a real Parisian? On your next trip to Paris, try one of these suggestions and discover Paris's off-the-beaten-path activities, from hip market streets to hunting museums to hidden parks, and much more.

Go Swimming

Flooded with daylight, glass-roofed Piscine Pontoise—a model of Art Deco design tucked between Notre Dame and the Jardin des Plantes—is illuminated only by underwater lights in the evenings until 11:45 pm on weeknights. Opened in 1924, all three pools of the picturesque indoor-outdoor Butte-aux-Cailles complex are fed by an underground spring. Care to swim in the Seine? Afloat on the river (but not in it, whew!), the popular Piscine Josephine Baker is the next best thing, with a retractable roof that keeps sunbathers happy. The Piscine Molitor is open to guests at the MGallery Hotel only, but it may be worth the splurge for a dip in Paris's most glamorous pool.

Enjoy a Cocktail with a View

There has been an explosion of cocktail bars in Paris, but taking in panoramic views of the city while sipping your drink is still a tall order. Though at different ends of the glamour spectrum, two hotel bars boast to-die-for views. On the higher end, the spectacular Peninsula hotel's L'Oiseau Blanc offers 360° views from the restaurant, bar, and terrace. Across the river, the more modest Holiday Inn Notre Dame's 43 Up on the Roof bar is the sixth arrondissement's best-kept secret. Open every night until 11:30 pm, the terrace bar reveals the entire city in front of you.

Watch a Film at Historic Movie Theater

The Louxor cinema, a masterpiece of Egyptian-inspired Art Deco architecture is a designated historic monument situated in the scruffy, but up-and-coming Pigalle neighborhood. Louxor screens art-house films—many of them American—and offers a café-bar with a terrace and views of Sacré-Coeur. Dating from 1932, the illustrious Grand Rex on Grands-Boulevards boasts Europe's largest screening room and a Baroque-inspired decor, complete with frescoed ceilings and fountains. The Fondation Pathé near Place d'Italie is in a historic building—complete with sculptures by Rodin—restored with a shimmering 21st-century addition by Renzo Piano. The foundation contains a movie museum, featuring historic posters, cameras, and projectors, plus a small, state-of-the-art screening room.

Take a Cooking Class

Forget the trinkets and T-shirts; learning to cook a French specialty is a souvenir for a lifetime. Whether it's a featherweight *macaron* or buttery croissants, after a few hours at Le Foodist, you'll be ready to impress your friends with culinary skills acquired firsthand in Paris. Better yet, combine your lesson with a trip to a typical Parisian market then sit down to a meal of your own making or hone your cheese and wine pairing skills at an expert-led tasting. There's no limit to what you can learn at these lively and inspiring classes—all taught in English. At the École de Cuisine Alain Ducasse you can learn to make a baguette or the secrets of bistro or haute cuisine. Though pricier, the classes are also taught in English and are backed by a name that's synonymous with the best.

Dance the Night Away

Seasonal public balls are a long-established, deeply Parisian tradition that few tourists know about, let alone experience. To celebrate Bastille Day, two nights a year—on either July 13 or 14—every city hall in Paris and its suburbs hosts a *bal des pompiers* (firemen's ball), starting at 9 pm and lasting into the wee hours of the morning. Dancing, eating, drinking, and revelry (and sometimes a lighthearted striptease by the famously beefy firemen) are all part of the fun. Popularized in the Paris cabarets and suburban guinguettes of the 19th century, the *bal populaire* was a working-class pastime fueled by high spirits, plenty of wine, music, and dancing. Once a month at the marvelous 104 Centquatre, one of Paris's reigning contemporary arts centers, locals gather under garlands of light to dance to live music. The balls are free and have a different theme each month, listed on the Centquatre website.

Explore an Abandoned Railway

Part of a huge, many-year restoration project spearheaded by Paris City Hall, La Petite Ceinture (little belt), a 19-mile-long abandoned railway that rings the city, is Paris's final green frontier. A haven for biodiversity—with more than 200 plant and 70 animal species—the future of the Petite Ceinture is unclear. Mayor Hidalgo's plan to redevelop 10 kilometers (6 miles) of the space by adding restaurants, cinemas, housing, gardens, and green space by 2020 has been hotly contested by neighborhood organizations and conservation groups. Still, since 2007 portions of the line have been slowly reopened to the public for hiking and exploration. In the 13th arrondissement, you can reach the newest section open to the public at 60 rue Damesme; in the 16th, a larger green space, between the Porte d'Auteuil and Gare de la Muette, has elevators and wheelchair access, and in the 12th, a 600-foot-longnature trail can be accessed at 21 rue Rottembourg. Adventurers can hop in anywhere along the line to find the favorite lairs of Paris graffiti artists and hidden entrances to the catacombs.

Visit a Village Within the City

On any sunny day in the Mouzaïa (also known as the Quartier d'Amérique) the sound of birdsong fills the air as residents tend their luxuriant gardens. A slice of the countryside in Paris, charming Mouzaïa is one of Paris's last hidden neighborhoods, where some 250 unique cottages, dating from the late 19th and early 20th centuries, were built over Paris's old gypsum quarries. Originally built as some of the city's first low-income housing for laborers, these storybook one- and two-story cottages are now some of Paris's hottest real estate, populated by artists, writers, and even celebrities. These protected historic enclaves near the lovely Buttes-Chaumont park can be found along the rue de Mouzaïa and the rues du Général Brunet, de la Liberté and Bellevue, starting at the métro stop Botzaris.

PARIS WITH KIDS

Paris may be an adult playground, but there's no shortage of children's activities to keep the young ones busy—even many of the city's top attractions have carousels parked outside them in summer. Make sure to buy a *Pariscope* (found at most newsstands) and check the *enfants* section for current children's events.

Museums

Paris has a number of museums that cater to the young and young at heart. They're great places to occupy restless minds, especially if the weather is bad. The Parc de la Villette's **Cité des Sciences et de l'Industrie** is an enormous science center with a kids' area that's divided into two main sections: one for 2- to 7-year-olds, another for the 5 to 12 set. Interactive exhibits let inquisitive young visitors do everything from building a house to learning about communications through the ages. The **Musée de la Musique**, also in the Parc de la Villette, will appeal to more arts-minded children while the **Palais de la Découverte** has high-definition, 3-D exhibits covering subjects like chemistry, biology, meteorology, and physics. Many of the displays are in French, but that doesn't stop most kids from having a blast—the choice between this and the Louvre is a no-brainer. The **Musée de l'Homme** was previously an anthropological museum but a recent renovation has made it supremely kid-friendly, where little ones can shake hands with a Neanderthal man, sample some of 7,000 languages, and enjoy plenty of interactive exhibits.

Zoos

Visiting a zoo is usually a good way to get kids' attention, although you might want to keep in mind that most European ones aren't as spacious as their American counterparts. A part of the **Muséum National d'Histoire Naturelle** (with its own exceptional butterfly collection and Gallery of Paleontology and Comparative Anatomy with too many bones on display to count), the **Ménagerie** at the Jardin des Plantes is an urban zoo dating from 1794 and is home to more than 200 mammals, nearly 300 birds, 200 reptiles, and 300 insects. The city's largest zoo, the **Parc Zoologique** in the Bois de Vincennes, lets you observe animals in realistic-looking habitats. The **Musée de la Chasse et de la Nature** in the Marais is another place to get up close and personal with ferocious lions, tigers, and one in-your-face polar bear—the only catch being that these aren't alive. The impressive collection of taxidermy trophies takes children on a safari to discover man's relationship with animals.

Shows

What child could pass up the circus? There are several in the city, including perennial favorites **Espace Chapiteaux** at the Parc de la Villette and **Cirque d'Hiver de Paris** near Place République. For traditional entertainment, try **Les Guignols,** French puppet shows. The original Guignol was a marionette character created by Laurent Mourguet, supposedly in his own likeness, celebrating life, love, and wine; today, shows are primarily aimed at children, and are found in open-air theaters throughout the city in the warmer months. Check out the Marionettes des Champs-Élysées, Champ de Mars, Parc Montsouris, Parc des Buttes-Chaumont, Jardin du Luxembourg, and the Parc Floral in the Bois de Vincennes. Even if they don't understand French, kids are usually riveted.

Underground Paris

There's something about exploring underground that seems to fascinate kids, at least the older ones. **Les Égouts,** allows a peek into the storied Paris sewer tunnels that harbored revolutionaries on the run throughout the ages. At the redesigned **Catacombs,** in Montparnasse, dark tunnels filled with skulls and skeletons of 6 million Parisians are spookily titillating—provided you're not prone to nightmares. For some cheap underground entertainment without the ick factor, the **métro** itself can be its own sort of adventure, complete with fascinating station art such as the submarine decor at Arts-et-Metiers, the colorful Parisian timeline murals at Tuileries, or the Egyptian statues of the Louvre–Rivoli station. A good tip: métro Lines 1 and 14 feature conductorless trains that let you sit at the very front, and kids love the sensation that they're driving.

Active Options

Many kids are oddly thrilled at the prospect of climbing countless stairs just to get a cool view. The **Eiffel Tower** is the quintessential Paris climb (especially now that the first level boasts a dizzying glass floor), but **Notre-Dame** gets extra points for the gargoyles, and the **Arc de Triomphe** is a good bet, since it's at the end of the Champs-Élysées. Parks offer other opportunities for expending energy. In summer, kids can work off steam on trampolines or ride ponies at the **Jardin des Tuileries;** the **Jardin du Luxembourg** has a playground and a pond where they can rent miniature boats; and the **Bois de Boulogne** has real rowboats, bumper cars, and lots of wide-open spaces. For rainy-day rescues, La Galerie des Enfants at the **Pompidou Centre** has a children's play gallery with activities tied to the current exhibitions.

In winter, consider ice-skating. From mid-December through February several outdoor sites transform into spectacular rinks with twinkling lights, music, and rental skates available; the main one is at **Place de l'Hôtel de Ville,** in front of City Hall.

Sweet Treats

All that activity will no doubt make kids hungry, and luckily there's no shortage of special places to stop for a snack. Crêperies always aim to please and you'll find plenty along the main tourist streets. Also be on the look-out for hot chocolate—the French version is deliciously rich and thick, unlike what American children are usually used to. You'll also find plenty of places offering decadent ice cream. French children adore the pastel clouds of meringue that decorate almost every pâtisserie window—and, when in need, a chocolate croissant is never hard to find. After filling up, you can cap the day with perhaps the best treat of all, a **boat ride on the Seine.** It's the perfect way to see the sights while resting weary feet.

GREAT ITINERARIES

Paris is a treasure of neighborhoods and history, and a visit to this glorious city is never quite as simple as a quick look at a few landmarks. But if you only have a day to take it all in, there are some icons that you just can't miss. Over five days, you'll have the luxury to truly take in the sites and museums while leaving time for random exploring including sampling the foods and beverages that have put the capital on the gastronomic world map.

PARIS IN 1 DAY

Begin your day at the Trocadéro métro, where you can get the best views of the **Eiffel Tower** from the esplanade of the Palais de Chaillot. If you want to ride to the top, now is the best time to get in line (it opens at 9 am). Afterward, take a walk along the Seine, stopping to visit the sculpture gardens of the **Musée Rodin** (entrance to the gardens €4), and continuing on to the **Musée d'Orsay** to tackle the late-19th-century works of art and admire the gorgeous former train station.

If your feet are still happy, cross the gilded Pont Tsar Alexandre III to the **Champs-Élysées**, passing the Belle Époque art palaces known as the **Grand Palais** and **Petit Palais**. You can take Bus 73 (€1.90) from the **Assemblée Nationale** across the bridge to **Place de la Concorde** and all the way up **Avenue des Champs-Élysées** to the **Arc de Triomphe**. Open until 10:30 pm (11 pm from May to September), its panoramic viewing platform is ideal for admiring the City of Light.

Next, head to the most famous art museum in the world, the **Louvre**. With just one day in the city, you'll have to limit your time here, but grab a museum guide and hit up the Big Three: the *Mona Lisa*, Venus de Milo, and Winged Victory Of Samothrace. There should still be time to see **Notre-Dame Cathedral**, and, if it's before 6 pm, get a glimpse inside.

PARIS IN 5 DAYS

Day 1: Notre-Dame and the Latin Quarter

Start your day at Pont Neuf for excellent views off the western tip of Ile de la Cité, then explore the island's magnificent architectural heritage, including the **Conciergerie**, **Sainte-Chapelle**, and **Notre-Dame**. The brave can climb the corkscrew staircase to the towers for a gargoyle's-eye view of the city.

Take a detour to neighboring Ile St-Louis for lunch before heading into the medieval labyrinth of the **Latin Quarter**; its most valuable treasures are preserved in the **Musée de Cluny,** including the reconstructed ruins of 2nd-century Gallo-Roman steam baths. At the summit of the hill above the Sorbonne University is the imposing **Panthéon**, a monument (and mausoleum) of French heroes. Follow Rue Descartes to Rue Mouffetard for a café crème on one of the oldest market streets in Paris.

Day 2: Jardin des Tuileries, the Louvre, and the Musée d'Orsay

Begin at **Place de la Concorde**, where an Egyptian obelisk replaces the guillotine where Louis XVI and Marie-Antoinette met their bloody fate during the French Revolution, then escape the traffic in the formal **Jardin des Tuileries**, which once belonged to the 16th-century Tuileries Palace, destroyed during the Paris Commune of 1871. Pass through the small Arc du Carrousel to the modern glass pyramid that serves as the main entrance to the **Louvre**, the world's grandest museum, once a 12th-century fortress. You'll never be able to see it all, but take a few hours to explore and make sure you hit up all the essentials.

The **Musée d'Orsay** merits an afternoon gander and the short post-Louvre stroll to this museum on the Left Bank is just long enough to get some fresh air before feasting your eyes on the world's biggest collection of Impressionist and Postimpressionist masterpieces, housed in a building that's equally magnificent visually.

Day 3: Eiffel Tower, Champs-Élysées, and Arc de Triomphe

Begin your day at the Trocadéro métro, where you can get the best views of the **Eiffel Tower** from the esplanade of the Palais de Chaillot. Visit the **Musée de l'Homme,** with 120 mummies among its 30,000 prehistoric artifacts, and take advantage of the spectacular selfie ops of both the Tour Eiffel and the Seine.

Then meander over to Quai d'Orsay, near Invalides, stopping for a *plat du jour* along the way before crossing the Alexandre III bridge to the Grand Palais, where you can now sneak some rooftop peeks, and then visit its sister, the Petit Palais. From here, you can walk all the way up **Avenue des Champs-Élysées** (focus on the prize and not the chain stores that line the avenue) to the **Arc de Triomphe.** Open until 10:30 pm (11 pm from April to September), its panoramic viewing platform is ideal for admiring the City of Light.

Day 4: The Marais

In the 4th arrondissement, the hip Marais district just keeps getting hipper, and is the perfect neighborhood to spend a relaxing day filled with culture, food, and fashion. To the south you can find the **Hôtel de Sens,** home to King Henry IV's feisty ex-wife Queen Marguerite, and one of the few surviving examples of late-medieval architecture. Around the corner on Rue Charlemagne is a preserved section of the city's 12th-century fortifications built by King Philippe-Augustus. Cross busy Rue St-Antoine to Le Marais and enter the **Hôtel de Sully,** a fine example of the elegant private mansions built here by aristocrats in the early 17th century. Stop by any of the old aristocratic mansions in Le Marais that have been turned into museums, including the **Musée Carnavalet** and **Musée Picasso.**

Day 5: Versailles

On Day 5, head 20 km (12½ miles) southwest of Paris to the gilded palace and reminder of pre-Revolution indulgence that is **Versailles.** The estate is divided into four sections: the Palace with the King's Grand Apartments and the famous Hall of Mirrors, the Grand Trianon, Marie-Antoinette's Estate, and, of course, the spectacular gardens. Book an English tour, which includes the King's Apartments, Royal Chapel, and Opera, and make sure you get there by 9 am so you can be sure to see everything. The easiest (and least expensive) way to visit Versailles is by the 45-minute Paris RER train serviced from St-Michel–Notre-Dame, Musée d'Orsay, Invalides, and Tour Eiffel stations. Buy tickets (destination: Versailles Rive G) directly from the automatic ticket machines or from the booth.

FREE AND CHEAP

It's easy to break the bank in Paris, but those acquainted with the city know where to find the free (or almost free) stuff. Here are some tips.

Free Exhibits

Thanks to the city of Paris's dedication to promoting culture, access to the permanent collections in municipal museums is free, so you can learn about the city's rich history and revel in artworks without dropping a dime (although sometimes there is a charge for temporary exhibitions). The **Hôtel de Ville** (City Hall) in the Marais regularly runs exhibitions with a focus on Paris. Other free museums include **Maison de Balzac, Maison de Victor Hugo, Musée Cognacq-Jay, Musée d'Art Moderne de la Ville de Paris,** and the **Petit Palais,** also known as **Musée des Beaux Arts de la Ville de Paris.**

Free Music

Many of Paris's churches host free or almost-free concerts at lunchtime and in the evening, allowing you to enjoy fine classical music in an ethereal setting. Look for flyers posted around the city and outside the churches, or check weekly events listings. There are free organ recitals on Sunday at **Notre-Dame** and **Église St-Eustache,** both in the 1er arrondissement, at 4:30 and 5:30 pm respectively. Free concerts at **Église de la Madeleine** (*8e*), **Église St-Roch** (*1er*), the **American Church in Paris** (*7e*), **Église St-Merry** (*4e*), and **Église de la Trinité** (*9e*) are music to frugal ears, too. You can watch up-and-coming students perform in 300 concerts *entrée libre* at the **Conservatoire Nationale Supérieur de Musique. Radio France** also sponsors about 180 free concerts throughout the year (usually at 7 pm on Monday, with tickets given out 30 minutes beforehand in Hall B at the studio; reservations via the website are highly recommended). In summer and fall there are free concerts in the city's parks, including the **Jardin des Luxembourg** (classical music) and the **Parc de la Villette** (world music, pop, and jazz). During **Paris Plages,** in late summer, there are free nightly pop and rock concerts on the quays of the Seine. When the weather's nice you're also likely to find musicians along the quai of the **Canal St-Martin,** or in **Place des Vosges,** guitars in hand for spontaneous song.

Parks

If the hustle and bustle of Paris is getting to you, there are plenty of parks where you can kick back for free. Some host no- or low-cost activities and events: the **Parc de la Villette,** for one, shows free open-air movies in July and August as part of the Cinéma en Plein Air Festival. Parisians also like to recharge their batteries with an afternoon catnap in one of the handy reclined chairs scattered throughout the city's gardens. This is the cheapest option for relaxation, reading, and postcard writing—just make sure your possessions are secure if you're actually going to grab some shut-eye. Perennial favorites for parking yourself are the **Jardin du Luxembourg** and the **Jardin des Tuileries,** but one of the most serene venues, buffered from the traffic by the arcaded shops, is the garden at the **Palais Royal,** not far from the Louvre. Any perch along the Seine will also do in a pinch if the busy streets start to feel overwhelming: it's amazing how tranquil a spot by the water can be, so close to the frenetic workings of the city, especially if you find yourself on the incomparably charming **Ile de la Cité.**

Cheap Souvenirs

What souvenir retails for about €0.10 and makes a perfect memento for friends back home? The postcard, of course. Go retro and send some quintessential scenery home with a "J'aime Paris" scribbled on the back, or just bring back a little packet of choice images. For the best prices, check out the news kiosks along Rue de Rivoli and the Grands Boulevards. Keep an eye out for vintage postcards sold by the *bouquinistes* along the Seine and by collectors inside Passage des Panoramas. You can buy stamps at any *tabac* as well as at post offices. Alternatively, you can pop into a French pharmacy where you'll find more than a few products that are cheaper than back home, including some unique French beauty products.

(Almost) Free Sightseeing Tours

Some of the city's public bus routes are fantastically scenic; hop on the right one and you can get a great tour for just €1.90—sans squawking commentary. The **No. 29** route reaches from Gare St-Lazare, past the Opéra Garnier, to the heart of the Marais, crossing Place des Vosges before ending up at the Bastille. This is one of the few lines that runs primarily on small streets, not major arteries. Hop the **No. 69** bus at Champ de Mars (by the Tour Eiffel) and ride through parts of the Quartier Latin, across the bridge to the Rive Droite near the Louvre, and on to the Bastille. The **No. 72** bus follows the Seine from the Hôtel de Ville west past the Louvre and most of the big-name Rive Droite sights, also giving you views of the Rive Gauche, including the Tour Eiffel. Bus **No. 73** is the only line that goes along Avenue des Champs-Élysées, from the Arc de Triomphe through Place de la Concorde and ending at Musée d'Orsay. You can also take walking tours with the enthusiastic guides from **Paris Greeters** (⊕ *www.greeters.paris*), **Sandemans** (⊕ *www.newparistours.com*), or **City Free Tour** (⊕ *cityfreetour.com*)—all are free, though tips are appreciated.

Free Wine Tastings

Here's a tip for getting tipsy: wine stores often offer free or inexpensive wine tastings, generally on the weekends. Check out the regular offerings at **La Derniere Goutte** (6 *rue de Bourbon le Château, 6e, 01–43–29–11–62*) and the prestigious **Caves Taillevent** (228 *rue du Faubourg St-Honoré, 8e, 01–45–61–14–09*). Paris in spring becomes even more enticing with tastings at **Caves Augé** (116 *bd. Haussmann, 8e, 01–45–22–16–97*) each Saturday from 11 to 6 in April and May. **La Cave du Panthéon** (174 *rue St-Jacques, 5e, 01–46–33–90–35*), touted for its conviviality, is another destination where wine lovers congregate on Saturday afternoon to learn about—and indulge in—their favorite beverage.

BEST TOURS IN PARIS

Sometimes a guided tour is the way to go, even if you usually prefer to fly solo while traveling. Tours can be a great way to explore out-of-the-way neighborhoods, to get an insider's perspective on where locals eat and play, and to learn about interesting aspects of the city's history, inhabitants, or architecture. Whether you want a boat tour along the Seine or a more personal, interest-specific walk, you'll find it here.

Boat Tours

Batobus. Hop on and off at one of Batobus's eight stops, which include the Eiffel Tower, Musée d'Orsay, Notre-Dame, and the Champs-Élysées. A one-day pass for unlimited travel—boats are heated and have panoramic views but offer no commentary—is €17; a two-day pass is only €19. ⊠ *Port de la Bourdonnais, Eiffel Tower* ☎ *33/08–25–05–01–01* ⊕ *www. batobus.com* ⊠ *From €17.*

Green River Cruises. Whether it's a Sunday cruise or a candlelight happy hour along the Seine, the boat outings offered by Green River Cruises last from one to three hours. They're limited to 11 people maximum, providing a more intimate tour of the city. Champagne is included in some options, but you are welcome to bring your own wine and snacks. ⊠ *Bateau Play Time , 34 Quai d'Austerlitz, Montparnasse* ☎ *33/06–50–22–90–65* ⊕ *www. greenriver-paris.fr/en* ⊠ *From €34 per person.*

Walking Tours

Sight Seeker's Delight. This company's unique 2½- to 3-hour walking tours bring the city's various quarters to life with engaging information and personal insight from English-speaking guides. ⊠ *Paris* ☎ *33/07–63–07–09–68* ⊕ *www. sightseekersdelight.com* ⊠ *From €40.*

Wego Walking Paris. These 3½-hour walking tours are in English and begin next to Notre-Dame or at the Eiffel Tower, covering 25 attractions with lots of history and fun anecdotes. Often called the most entertaining tour in Paris, it's pay what you wish, or more accurately, you pay your guide what you think he or she deserves. ⊠ *1 Pont au Double, Ile de la Cité* ⊕ *www.wegowalking.com.*

Specialty Tours

Better Travel Photos Paris. Discover the City of Light through your camera lens while learning how to take skilled snaps under the advice of professional (and English-speaking) photographers. Itineraries range from 3½-hour to multiday tours, covering the Marais, Montmartre, and other classic Paris locations. ⊠ *Paris* ⊕ *www.bettertravelphotos.com* ⊠ *From €195 (or €80 each for a group of 3).*

Culinary Tours of Paris. Spend more than three hours discovering French food, wine, and culture with a French-American tour guide who has lived in Paris for nearly a decade. During the English-speaking tours, you'll dine at two or three different restaurants, with digestive walks of the neighborhoods in between destinations. Tour options focus on the Latin Quarter, Montmartre, or the French countryside (45 minutes east of the city). ⊠ *Paris* ⊕ *www.culinarytoursofparis.com* ⊠ *From €80.*

Midnight In Paris On Wheels. Take in the city's main monuments in a nocturnal escapade in a classic 2CV car. The tour guide will tailor the ride to your tastes, whether it be history or a desire to discover new areas. ⊠ *Paris* ☎ *33/06–51–19–24–88* ⊕ *www.midnightinparisonwheels. com/en* ⊠ *From €90.*

ILE DE LA CITÉ
AND ILE ST-LOUIS

Getting Oriented

BEST CAFÉS

La Charlotte de l'Isle. Sip tea (or lusciously thick hot chocolate) and sample tasty cakes at this atmospheric salon. ✉ 24 rue St-Louis-en-l'Ile, Île Saint-Louis ☎ 01–43–54–25–83 ⊕ www.lacharlottedelisle. fr ⊗ Closed Mon. and Tues. Ⓜ Pont Marie.

Le Saint-Régis. Wondering where locals take their coffee on touristy Ile St-Louis? Try this old-timer—it's open until 2 am daily. ✉ 6 rue Jean du Bellay, Île Saint-Louis ☎ 01–43–54–59–41 ⊕ www.cafesaintregisparis.com Ⓜ Pont Marie.

TOP REASONS TO GO

Notre-Dame. This gorgeous Gothic cathedral has welcomed visitors to Paris for centuries. Gaze at its famed rose windows, climb the bell tower to mingle with gargoyles, or amble around back to contemplate the awe-inspiring flying buttresses from Square Jean-XXIII. At the end of the plaza in front of the cathedral, down the stairs, is the interesting Crypte Archéologique, a museum that showcases the city's Roman ruins.

Sainte-Chapelle. Visit on a sunny day to best appreciate the exquisite stained glass in this 13th-century chapel built for King Louis IX.

Strolling the islands. Ile de la Cité is where Paris began. Start with the city's oldest bridge, the Pont Neuf (incongruously called the "new bridge") and give a nod to the statue of Henry IV, who once proudly said, "I make love, I make war, and I build." From here, cross to Place Dauphine and make your way to Ile St-Louis, one of the city's most exclusive enclaves.

Ile de la Cité and Ile St-Louis

2

ICE CREAM VS. GELATO

Amorino. Popping up all over—and winning converts faster than you can finish a double scoop—is the Amorino chain of gelaterias, which serves inventive frozen concoctions in the shape of a flower blossom. Popular flavors include rich *bacio* (dark chocolate with hazelnuts) and mascarpone with figs. ⊠ *47 rue St-Louis-en-l'Ile, Île Saint-Louis* ☎ *01–44–07–48–08* ⊕ *www.amorino.com* Ⓜ *Pont-Marie.*

Berthillon. Parisian ice cream is served at cafés all over town, but it's worth making a pilgrimage to the mecca of artisanal *crèmes glacées* to understand what all the fuss is about. The family-owned Berthillon shop features more than 30 flavors that change with the seasons, from mouth-puckering *cassis* (black currant) in summer to nutty *marron* (candied chestnut) in winter. ⊠ *31 rue St-Louis-en-l'Ile, Île Saint-Louis* ☎ *01–43–54–31–61* ⊕ *www.berthillon.fr* ⊟ *No credit cards* ⊘ *Closed Mon. and Tues.* Ⓜ *Pont-Marie.*

MAKING THE MOST OF YOUR TIME

This little area of Paris is easily walkable and packed with sights and stunning views, so give yourself as much time as possible to explore. With Notre-Dame, the Conciergerie, and Sainte-Chapelle, you could spend a day wandering, but the islands are easily combined with the St-Germain quarter. On warmer days, Rue de Buci is an ideal place to pick up a picnic lunch to enjoy in leafy Square du Vert-Galant at the tip of Ile de la Cité. If you have limited time in the area, make sure you visit Notre-Dame and go for a stroll.

GETTING HERE

Ile de la Cité and Ile St-Louis are in the 1er and 4e arrondissements (Boulevard du Palais is the dividing line between the 1er and 4e arrondissements on Ile de la Cité). If you're too far away to get here on foot, take the métro to St-Michel station or La Cité.

Sightseeing
★★★★
Dining
★★
Lodging
★★★
Shopping
★★
Nightlife
★

At the heart of Paris, linked to the banks of the Seine by a series of bridges, are two small islands: Ile St-Louis and Ile de la Cité. They're the perfect places to begin your visit, with postcard-worthy views all around. The Ile de la Cité is anchored by mighty Notre-Dame; farther east, the atmospheric Ile St-Louis is dotted with charming hotels, cozy restaurants, and small specialty shops.

ILE DE LA CITÉ

Updated by
Jack Vermee

At the western tip of Ile de la Cité is regal **Place Dauphine,** one of Paris's oldest squares. The impressive Palais de Justice (courthouse) sits between **Sainte-Chapelle,** the exquisite medieval chapel of saintly King Louis IX, and the **Conciergerie,** the prison where Marie-Antoinette and other bluebloods awaited their slice of history at the guillotine.

The Gothic powerhouse that is **Notre-Dame** originally loomed over a medieval huddle of buildings that were later ordered razed by Baron Georges-Eugène Haussmann, the 19th-century urban planner who transformed Paris into the city we see today. In front of the cathedral is Place du Parvis, the point from which all roads in France are measured. On the north side of the square is the **Hôtel-Dieu** (roughly translated as "general hospital"): it was immortalized by Balzac as the squalid last stop for the city's most unfortunate, but today houses a modern hospital. Just behind the cathedral lies Rue du Cloître-Notre-Dame, which cuts through the **Ancien Cloître Quartier,** on whose narrow streets you can imagine the medieval quarter as it once was, densely packed and teeming with activity. At 9–11 quai aux Fleurs, a plaque commemorates the abode that was the setting of the tragic, 12th-century love affair between the philosopher Peter Abélard and his young conquest, Héloïse.

At the eastern tip of Ile de la Cité is the **Mémorial des Martyrs de la Déportation,** all but hidden in a pocket-size park. A set of stairs leads down to this impressive and moving memorial, which commemorates the French citizens who died in Nazi concentration camps.

TOP ATTRACTIONS

FAMILY **Conciergerie.** Most of the Ile de la Cité's medieval structures fell victim to wunderkind urban planner Baron Haussmann's ambitious rebuilding program of the 1860s. Among the rare survivors are the jewel-like Sainte-Chapelle, a vision of shimmering stained glass, and the Conciergerie, the cavernous former prison where Marie-Antoinette and other victims of the French Revolution spent their final days. Constructed by Philip IV in the late 13th and early 14th centuries, the Conciergerie—which takes its name from the building's concierge or keeper—was part of the original palace of the kings of France before the royals moved into the Louvre around 1364. In 1391, it became a prison. During the French Revolution, Marie-Antoinette languished 76 days here awaiting her date with the guillotine. There is a re-creation of the doomed queen's sad little cell—plus others that are far smaller—complete with wax figures behind bars. In the chapel, stained glass, commissioned after the queen's death by her daughter, is emblazoned with the initials *M.A.* Outside you can see the small courtyard where women prisoners took meals and washed their clothes in the fountain (men enjoyed no similar respite). Well-done temporary exhibitions on the ground floor aim to please kids and adults alike; themes have included enchanted forests and Gothic castles. There are free guided tours (in French only) most days at 11 and 3. ⊠ *2 bd. du Palais, Ile de la Cité* ☎ *01–53–40–60–80* ⊕ *www.conciergerie.monuments-nationaux. fr* ⊠ *€9; €15 with joint ticket to Sainte-Chapelle* ☞ *Ticket window closes at 5:30* Ⓜ *Cité.*

> ### MONSIEUR GUILLOTIN
>
> Beheading by means of an ax or sword was a popular form of punishment long before the French Revolution, but it was Dr. Joseph-Ignace Guillotin who suggested there was a more humane way of decapitating prisoners. Not surprisingly, Dr. Guillotin's descendants changed their surname.

Mémorial des Martyrs de la Déportation (*Memorial of the Deportation*). On the east end of Ile de la Cité lies this stark monument to the more than 200,000 French men, women, and children who died in Nazi concentration camps during World War II. The evocative memorial, inaugurated by Charles de Gaulle in 1962, was intentionally designed to be claustrophobic. Concrete blocks mark the narrow entrance to the crypt, which contains the tomb of an unknown deportee killed at the Neustadt camp. A dimly lit narrow gallery studded with 200,000 pieces of glass symbolizes the lives lost, while urns at the lateral ends contain ashes from the camps. ⊠ *Square de l'Île de France, 7 quai de l'Archevêché, Ile de la Cité* ⊠ *Free* ☽ *Closed Mon.* Ⓜ *Cité, St-Michel.*

Fodor's Choice **Notre-Dame.** Looming above Place du Parvis, this Gothic sanctuary is the
★ symbolic heart of Paris and, for many, of France itself. Napoléon was crowned here, and kings and queens exchanged marriage vows before

its altar. Begun in 1163, completed in 1345, badly damaged during the Revolution, and restored in the 19th century by Eugène Viollet-le-Duc, Notre-Dame may not be the country's oldest or largest cathedral, but in beauty and architectural harmony it has few peers—as you can see by studying the front facade. Its ornate doors seem like hands joined in prayer, the sculpted kings above them form a noble procession, and the west rose window gleams with what seems like divine light.

The front facade has three main entrances: the Portal of the Virgin (left); the Portal of the Last Judgment (center); and the Portal of St. Anne (right). As you enter the nave, the faith of the early builders permeates the interior: the soft glow of the windows contrasts with the exterior's triumphant glory. At the entrance are the massive 12th-century columns supporting the towers. Look down the nave to the transepts—the arms of the church—where, at the south entrance to the choir, you'll glimpse the haunting 12th-century statue of Notre-Dame de Paris, *Our Lady of Paris*, for whom the cathedral is named. On the choir's south side is the Treasury, with its small collection of religious artifacts. On the north side is the north rose window, one of the cathedral's original stained-glass panels; at the center is an image of Mary holding a young Jesus. Biblical scenes on the choir's north and south screens depict the life of Christ and apparitions of him after the Resurrection. Behind the choir is the Pietà, representing the Virgin Mary mourning over the dead body of Christ.

The best time to visit is early morning, when the cathedral is brightest and least crowded. Audioguides are available at the entrance (€5); free guided tours in English run Monday, Tuesday, and Saturday at 2:30, and Wednesday, Thursday, and Friday at 2. A separate entrance, to the left of the front facade, provides access to the towers via 387 stone steps. These wind up to the bell tolled by the fictional Quasimodo in Victor Hugo's 1831 *Notre-Dame de Paris*. The famed gargoyles (technically chimeras since they lack functioning waterspouts) were 19th-century additions. Reserving a tower visit online is now obligatory; lines to climb the tower are shortest on weekday mornings. Down the stairs in front of the cathedral is the Crypte Archéologique, an archaeological museum offering a fascinating subterranean view of this area from the 1st century, when Paris was a Roman city called Lutetia, through medieval times. Note that Notre-Dame was one of the first buildings to make use of flying buttresses—exterior supports that spread the weight of the building and roof. People first thought they looked like scaffolding that hadn't been removed. By day, the most tranquil place to appreciate these and other architectural elements is Square Jean-XXIII, the lovely garden behind the cathedral. By night, Seine boat rides promise stellar views. ⊠ *6 parvis Notre-Dame–Place Jean-Paul II, Ile de la Cité* ☎ *01–42–34–56–10* ⊕ *www.notredamedeparis.fr* ✉ *Cathedral free; towers €10; crypt €8; treasury €4* ☉ *Crypt closed Mon.* Ⓜ *Cité.*

Fodor's Choice **Sainte-Chapelle.** Built by the obsessively pious Louis IX (1214–70), this
★ Gothic jewel is home to the oldest stained-glass windows in Paris. The chapel was constructed over three years, at phenomenal expense, to house the king's collection of relics acquired from the impoverished emperor of Constantinople. These included Christ's Crown of Thorns,

fragments of the Cross, and drops of Christ's blood—though even in Louis's time these were considered of questionable authenticity. Some of the relics have survived and can be seen in the treasury of Notre-Dame, but most were lost during the Revolution.

The narrow spiral staircase by the entrance takes you to the upper chapel where the famed beauty of Sainte-Chapelle comes alive: 6,458 square feet of stained glass are delicately supported by painted stonework that seems to disappear in the colorful light streaming through the windows. Deep reds and blues dominate the background, noticeably different from later, lighter medieval styles such as those of Notre-Dame's rose windows.

> ### THE FLOWER MARKET
>
> Every day of the week, you can find the Marché aux Fleurs (flower market) facing the entrance to the imposing Palais de Justice on Boulevard du Palais. It's a fragrant detour from the Ile de la Cité, and the Guimard-designed entrance to the Cité métro station seems to blend beautifully with the potted plants on display in open-air and covered pavilions. On Sunday, the place is chirping with birds and other small pets for sale.

The chapel is essentially an enormous magic lantern illuminating 1,130 biblical figures. Its 15 windows—each 50 feet high—were dismantled and cleaned with laser technology during a 40-year restoration, completed in 2014 to coincide with the 800th anniversary of St. Louis's birth. Besides the dazzling glass, observe the detailed carvings on the columns and the statues of the apostles. The lower chapel is gloomy and plain, but take note of the low, vaulted ceiling decorated with fleurs-de-lis and cleverly arranged Ls for "Louis." Audioguides (€3) are available, or you can download a free PDF guide from the website.

Sunset is the optimal time to see the rose window; however, to avoid waiting in killer lines, plan your visit for a weekday morning, the earlier the better. Come on a sunny day to appreciate the full effect of the light filtering through all that glorious stained glass. You can buy a joint ticket with the Conciergerie: lines are shorter if you purchase it there or online, though you'll still have to go through a longish metal-detector line to get into Sainte-Chapelle itself. The chapel makes a divine setting for classical concerts; check the schedule at www.classictic.com ⊠ *4 bd. du Palais, Ile de la Cité* ☏ *01–53–40–60–80* ⊕ *www.sainte-chapelle.fr* ☞ *€10; €15 with joint ticket to Conciergerie* ☞ *Ticket window closes 30 min before closing* Ⓜ *Cité.*

WORTH NOTING

Ancien Cloître Quartier. Hidden in the shadows of Notre-Dame is an evocative, often-overlooked tangle of medieval streets. Through the years lucky folks, including Ludwig Bemelmans (who created the beloved *Madeleine* books) and the Aga Khan have called this area home, but back in the Middle Ages it was the domain of cathedral seminary students. One of them was the celebrated Peter Abélard (1079–1142)—philosopher, questioner of the faith, and renowned declaimer of love poems. Abélard boarded with Notre-Dame's clergyman, Fulbert, whose

2

17-year-old niece, Héloïse, was seduced by the compelling Abélard, 39 years her senior. She became pregnant, and the vengeful clergyman had Abélard castrated; amazingly, he survived and fled to a monastery, while Héloïse took refuge in a nunnery. The poetic, passionate letters between the two cemented their fame as thwarted lovers, and their story inspired a devoted following during the romantic 19th century. They still draw admirers to the Père-Lachaise Cemetery, where they're interred ensemble. The clergyman's house at 10 rue Chanoinesse was redone in 1849; a plaque at the back of the building at 9–11 quai aux Fleurs commemorates the lovers. ⊠ *Rue du Cloître-Notre-Dame north to Quai des Fleurs, Ile de la Cité* Ⓜ *Cité.*

Place Dauphine. The Surrealists called Place Dauphine "le sexe de Paris" because of its suggestive V shape; however, its origins were much more proper. The pretty square on the western side of Pont Neuf was built by Henry IV, who named it as a homage to his son the crown prince (or dauphin) who became Louis XIII when Henry was assassinated. In warmer weather, treat yourself to a romantic meal on a restaurant terrace here—the square is one of the best places in Paris to dine *en plein air.* ⊠ *Ile de la Cité* Ⓜ *Cité.*

Square du Vert-Galant. The equestrian statue of the Vert Galant himself— amorous adventurer Henry IV—keeps a vigilant watch over this leafy square at the western end of the Ile de la Cité. The dashing but ruthless Henry, king of France from 1589 until his assassination in 1610, was a stern upholder of the absolute rights of monarchy and a notorious womanizer. He is probably best remembered for his cynical remark that *"Paris vaut bien une messe"* ("Paris is worth a Mass"), a reference to his readiness to renounce Protestantism to gain the throne of predominantly Catholic France. To ease his conscience, he issued the Edict of Nantes in 1598, according French Protestants (almost) equal rights with their Catholic countrymen. The square is a great place for a quai-side picnic. It's also the departure point for Vedette Pont Neuf tour boats (at the bottom of the steps to the right). ⊠ *Ile de la Cité* Ⓜ *Pont Neuf.*

ILE ST-LOUIS

Nearby Pont St-Louis, which always seems to be occupied by street performers, leads to the Ile St-Louis, one of the city's best places to wander. There are no cultural hot spots, just a few narrow streets that comprise one of the most privileged areas in Paris. Small hotels, eateries, art galleries, and shops selling everything from chocolate and cheese to silk scarves line the main street, Rue St-Louis-en-L'Ile. There were once two islands here, Ile Notre-Dame and Ile aux Vaches ("Cow Island," an erstwhile grazing pasture), both owned by the Church. Speculators bought the islands, joined them, and sold the plots to builders who created what is today some of the city's most elegant and expensive real estate. Baroque architect Louis Le Vau (who later worked on Versailles) designed fabulous private mansions for aristocrats, including the majestic Hôtel de Lauzun on lovely Quai d'Anjou.

St-Louis-en-L'Ile. You can't miss the unusual lacy spire of this church as you approach the Ile St-Louis; it's the only church on the island and there are no other steeples to compete with it. It was built from 1652 to 1765 according to the Baroque designs of architect François Le Vau, brother of the more famous Louis, who designed several mansions nearby—as well as the Palace of Versailles. St-Louis's interior was essentially stripped during the Revolution, as were so many French churches, but look for the odd outdoor iron clock, which dates from 1741. Check the church website for upcoming classical music events. ⊠ *19 bis, rue St-Louis-en-L'Ile, Île Saint-Louis* ☎ *01–46–34–11–60* ⊕ *www.saintlouisenlile.catholique.fr* Ⓜ *Pont Marie.*

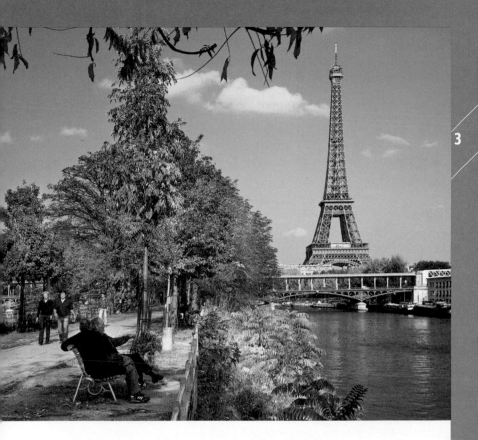

AROUND THE
EIFFEL TOWER

Getting Oriented

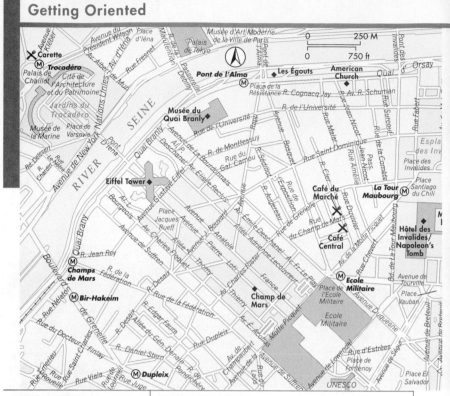

GETTING HERE

This neighborhood includes the 7e, 15e, and 16e arrondissements. The most romantic way to reach the Eiffel Tower is by boat. Alternately, you can head for RER C: Champs de Mars/ Tour Eiffel. For the best view, get off at the Trocadéro station (métro Line 9 or 6) and make the short walk over the Pont (bridge) d'Iéna to the tower. For the Musée Rodin, get off at Varenne (Line 13). Use this stop, or La Tour-Maubourg (Line 8), for Napoléon's Tomb and Hôtel des Invalides.

TOP REASONS TO GO

Eiffel Tower. No question, the ultimate symbol of France is worth a visit at least once in your life.

Musée Rodin. A must-see for fans of the master sculptor, this magnificent 18th-century *hôtel particulier* (private mansion) was Rodin's former workshop. The manicured garden is a perfect setting for his timeless works.

Napoléon's Tomb. The golden-domed Hôtel des Invalides is a fitting place for Napoléon's remains. Military history buffs will appreciate the impressive display of weaponry and armor in the adjoining Musée de l'Armée.

A boat ride. Whether you choose a guided Bateaux Mouches tour or a Batobus (water bus) trip, cruising the Seine is a relaxing way to see city highlights without traffic or crowds. Book a ride after dark when all of Paris is aglow.

Around the Eiffel Tower

3

MAKING THE MOST OF YOUR TIME

This neighborhood is home to one of the world's most iconic sites, the Eiffel Tower. Depending on the time of year, you can wait hours to ascend La Tour (it helps to buy your ticket online or come at night, when lines are shorter), but even if you stay firmly on the ground, it's worth a trip to see the landmark up close. Afterward, explore Rue St-Dominique's shops, bakeries, and restaurants. If you're up for a picnic, grab fixings on Rue Cler (between Rue de Grenelle and Avenue de La Motte-Piquet), a pedestrian-only market street; then head back to the park at the foot of the tower.

If you have a day to spare, visit the Musée Rodin. If you're pressed for time, do a quick tour of the garden, where some of the best-known sculptures can be seen. From here it's a short walk to Napoléon's over-the-top tomb at the Hôtel des Invalides, which also houses the Musée de l'Armée devoted to military history. To appreciate art from Asia, Africa, and Oceania, spend an hour or two in the Musée du Quai Branly.

BEST CAFÉS

Café Central. If it's apéritif time, this is the place to be. With soft lighting, loungy music, plus a generous selection of wines, cocktails, and beers, Café Central makes an ideal spot for an end-of-the-afternoon drink. ✉ *40 rue Cler, Eiffel Tower* ☎ *01–47–05–00–53* ⊕ *www. cafecentralparis.com* Ⓜ *École Militaire.*

Café du Marché. On the quaint Rue Cler, this small but busy café is popular with residents. Savor your morning café and croissant here, or enjoy an inexpensive prix-fixe lunch on the popular *terrasse.* ✉ *38 rue Cler, Eiffel Tower* ☎ *01–47–05– 51–27* Ⓜ *La Tour-Maubourg, École Militaire.*

Carette. Serving chic Parisians since 1927, this Art Deco tea salon on Place du Trocadéro is a hot spot for lunch or afternoon tea. ✉ *4 pl. du Trocadero, Eiffel Tower* ☎ *01–47–27– 98–85* ⊕ *www.carette-paris.fr* Ⓜ *Trocadéro.*

Sightseeing
★★★★★
Dining
★★★
Lodging
★★★★★
Shopping
★★★★
Nightlife
★★★

One of Paris's most upscale neighborhoods, the posh 7e arrondissement (where nearly every block affords a view of La Tour Eiffel) is home to the French *bourgeoisie* and well-heeled expats. Commanding the southwestern end of Paris, the Eiffel Tower was considered an iron-latticed monstrosity when it opened in 1889. Today it is a beloved icon, especially at night when thousands of twinkling lights sparkle at the top of every hour.

Updated by
Jack Vermee

There are other monumental sights here, too, notably the **Hôtel des Invalides,** a sprawling Baroque complex with a towering golden dome under which lies the enormous tomb of the pint-size dictator, Napoléon. Along the river, the **Palais Bourbon,** seat of the French Parliament, is an 18th-century homage to ancient Greek architecture. Nearby is the modern **Musée du Quai Branly,** built by star architect Jean Nouvel. Don't miss the **Musée Rodin,** where the master's sculptures ooze sensuality both outside in the garden and inside the elegant Hôtel Biron.

From the Eiffel Tower east, the walkway along the Seine will take you past **Les Égouts** (where you can embark on a subterranean tour of actual working sewers) and the **American Church.** For one of the best views in Paris, cross **Pont Alexandre III,** the city's most ornate bridge spanning the Seine from Invalides to the Grand Palais. Named for the Russian czar to celebrate Franco-Russian friendship, it was built between 1896 and 1900 and is bedecked with gilded sculptures, cherubs, and Art Nouveau lamps.

TOP ATTRACTIONS

FAMILY
Fodor'sChoice
★

Eiffel Tower (*Tour Eiffel*). The Eiffel Tower is to Paris what the Statue of Liberty is to New York and what Big Ben is to London: the ultimate civic emblem. French engineer Gustave Eiffel—already famous for building viaducts and bridges—spent two years working to erect this iconic monument for the World Exhibition of 1889.

Because its colossal bulk exudes such a feeling of permanence, you may have trouble believing that the tower nearly became 7,000 tons of scrap (it contains 12,000 pieces of metal and 2,500,000 rivets) when the concession expired in 1909. Only its potential use as a radio antenna saved the day; and it still bristles with a forest of radio and television transmitters. Given La Tour's landmark status, it is equally hard to believe that so many Parisians—including arbiters of taste like Guy de Maupassant and Alexandre Dumas—initially derided the 1,063-foot structure. (De Maupassant reputedly had lunch in the tower's restaurant every day because it was the only place in Paris from which the tower wasn't visible.)

Gradually, though, the Tour Eiffel became part of the city's topography, entering the hearts and souls of residents and visitors alike. Today it is most breathtaking at night, when every girder is highlighted in a sparkling display originally conceived to celebrate the turn of the millennium. The glittering light show was so popular that the 20,000 lights were reinstalled for permanent use in 2003. The tower does its electric dance for five minutes every hour on the hour until 1 am.

More recent enhancements are also noteworthy. A two-year, €30-million renovation of the first level, completed in 2014, added a vertigo-inducing "transparent" floor 187 feet above the esplanade, plus a pair of glass-facade pavilions, which hug the side of the tower and house interactive educational areas. A new miniturbine plant, four vertical-turbine windmills, and eco-friendly solar panels will minimize the tower's carbon footprint over time, too.

You can stride up 704 steps as far as the second level, but if you want to go to the top you'll have to take the elevator. (Be sure to look closely at the fantastic ironwork.) Although the view of the flat sweep of Paris at 1,000 feet may not beat the one from the Tour Montparnasse skyscraper, the setting makes it considerably more romantic—especially if you come in the late evening, after the crowds have dispersed. Beat the crushing lines by reserving your ticket online; you can also book a skip-the-line guided tour from one of many local companies (from €34). ⊠ *Quai Branly, Eiffel Tower* ☎ *08–92–70–12–39 (€0.35 per min)* ⊕ *www.toureiffel.paris* 🖲 *By elevator: 1st and 2nd levels €16, top €25. By stairs: €10 (1st and 2nd levels only). By stairs to 2nd level and elevator to the top: €19* ☉ *Closed last 2 wks in Jan. for annual maintenance* ☞ *Stairs close at 6 pm in off-season (Oct.–June)* Ⓜ *Trocadéro, Bir-Hakeim, École Militaire; RER: Champ de Mars–Tour Eiffel.*

Fodor's Choice
★ **Hôtel des Invalides.** The baroque complex known as Les Invalides (pronounced "lehz-ahn-vah- *leed*") is the eternal home of Napoléon Bonaparte (1769–1821) or, more precisely, the little dictator's remains, which lie entombed under the towering golden dome.

Louis XIV ordered the facility built in 1670 to house disabled soldiers (hence the name), and at one time 4,000 military men lived here. Today, a portion of it still serves as a veterans' residence and hospital. The Musée de l'Armée, containing an exhaustive collection of military artifacts from antique armor to weapons, is also here.

If you see only a single sight, make it the Église du Dome (one of Les Invalides' two churches) at the back of the complex. Napoléon's tomb was moved here in 1840 from the island of Saint Helena, where he died in forced exile. The emperor's body is protected by a series of no fewer than six coffins—one set inside the next, sort of like a Russian nesting doll—which are then encased in a sarcophagus of red quartzite. The bombastic tribute is ringed by statues symbolizing Napoléon's campaigns of conquest. To see more Napoléoniana, check out the collection in the Musée de l'Armée featuring his trademark gray frock coat and huge bicorne hat. Look for the figurines reenacting the famous coronation scene when Napoléon crowns his empress, Josephine. You can see a grander version of this scene by the painter David hanging in the Louvre.

The Esplanade des Invalides, the great lawns in front of the building, are favorite spots for pickup soccer, Frisbee games, sunbathing, and dog walking—despite signs asking you to stay off the grass. ■ TIP→ The best entrance to use is at the southern end, on Place Vauban (Avenue de Tourville); the ticket office is here, as is Napoléon's Tomb. There are automatic ticket machines at the main entrance on Place des Invalides. ⊠ *Pl. des Invalides, Eiffel Tower* ☎ *01–44–42–38–77* ⊕ *www.musee-armee.fr* ✉ *€12 with temporary exhibitions; €10 after 5 pm Apr.–Oct. and after 4 pm Nov.–Mar.* ☞ *Last admission 30 min before closing* Ⓜ *La Tour–Maubourg, Varenne.*

FAMILY **Musée du Quai Branly.** This eye-catching museum overlooking the Seine was built by star architect Jean Nouvel to house the state-owned collection of "non-Western" art, culled from the Musée National des Arts d'Afrique et d'Océanie and the Musée de l'Homme. Exhibits mix artifacts from antiquity to the modern age, such as funeral masks from Melanesia, Siberian shaman drums, Indonesian textiles, and African statuary. A corkscrew ramp leads from the lobby to a cavernous exhibition space, which is color coded to designate sections from Asia, Africa, and Oceania. The lighting is dim—sometimes too dim to read the information panels (which makes investing in the €5 audioguide a good idea).

Renowned for his bold modern designs, Nouvel has said he wanted the museum to follow no rules; however, many critics gave his vision a thumbs-down when it was unveiled in 2006. The exterior resembles a massive, rust-color rectangle suspended on stilts, with geometric shapes cantilevered to the facade facing the Seine and louvered panels on the opposite side. The colors (dark reds, oranges, and yellows) are meant to evoke the tribal art within. A "living wall" composed of some 150 species of exotic plants grows on the exterior, which is surrounded by a wild jungle garden with swampy patches—an impressive sight after dark when scores of cylindrical colored lights are illuminated. The trendy Les Ombres restaurant on the museum's fifth floor (separate entrance) has prime views of the Tour Eiffel—and prices to match. The budget-conscious can enjoy the garden at Le Café Branly on the ground floor. ⊠ *37 quai Branly, Eiffel Tower* ☎ *01–56–61–70–00* ⊕ *www.quaibranly.fr* ✉ *€10; €12 with temporary exhibits (free 1st Sun. of month)* ☉ *Closed Mon.* ☞ *Ticket office closes 1 hr before museum* Ⓜ *Alma-Marceau.*

FAMILY
Fodor's Choice
★

Musée Rodin. Auguste Rodin (1840–1917) briefly made his home and studio in the Hôtel Biron, a grand 18th-century mansion that now houses a museum dedicated to his work. He died rich and famous, but many of the sculptures that earned him a place in art history were originally greeted with contempt by the general public, which was unprepared for his powerful brand of sexuality and raw physicality. The reaction to this museum's new look was markedly different when it finally emerged from a three-year, tip-to-toe renovation in 2015. Everything from the building and grounds to Rodin's sculptures themselves was restored and re-presented. The reputed cost was €16 million; the overall effect remains nothing short of dazzling.

Most of Rodin's best-known sculptures are in the gardens. The front one is dominated by *The Gates of Hell* (circa 1880). Inspired by the monumental bronze doors of Italian Renaissance churches, Rodin set out to illustrate stories from Dante's *Divine Comedy*. He worked on the sculpture for more than 30 years, and it served as a "sketch pad" for many of his later works. Look carefully and you can see miniature versions of *The Kiss* (bottom right), *The Thinker* (top center), and *The Three Shades* (top center). Inside, look for *The Bronze Age,* which was inspired by the sculptures of Michelangelo: this piece was so realistic that critics accused Rodin of having cast a real body in plaster. In addition, the museum now showcases long-neglected models, plasters, and paintings, which offer insight into Rodin's creative process. Pieces by other artists, gleaned from his personal collection, are on display as well—including paintings by van Gogh, Renoir, and Monet. Antiquities Rodin collected (and was inspired by) have been removed from storage and given their own room. There's also a room devoted to works by Camille Claudel (1864–1943), his student and longtime mistress, who was a remarkable sculptor in her own right. Her torturous relationship with Rodin eventually drove her out of his studio—and out of her mind. In 1913 she was packed off to an asylum, where she remained until her death. An English audioguide (€6) is available for the permanent collection and for temporary exhibitions. Tickets can be purchased online for priority access (€1 service fee). If you wish to linger, the lovely Café du Musée Rodin serves meals and snacks in the shade of the garden's linden trees. ⊠ *77 rue de Varenne, Eiffel Tower* ☎ *01–44–18–61–10* ⊕ *www.musee-rodin.fr* ⟟ *€10; €4 temporary exhibitions (€13 for both museum and exhibitions); €4 gardens only (free 1st Sun. of month)* ⊙ *Closed Mon.* Ⓜ *Varenne.*

WORTH NOTING

American Church. Not to be confused with the American Cathedral, across the river at 23 avenue George V, this pretty neo-Gothic Protestant church was built between 1927 and 1931. It features a pair of Tiffany stained-glass windows—a rare find in Europe. Besides ecumenical services, the church hosts architectural tours, free classical and acoustic concerts, plus popular exercise classes (including yoga). You can check event listings and download a self-guided PDF tour at the church website. ✉ *65 quai d'Orsay, Eiffel Tower* ☎ *01–40–62–05–00* ⊕ *www.acparis.org* Ⓜ *Alma-Marceau; RER: Pont de l'Alma.*

FAMILY **Champ de Mars.** Flanked by tree-lined paths, this long expanse of grass lies between the Eiffel Tower and École Militaire. It was previously used as a parade ground and was the site of the world exhibitions in 1867, 1889 (when the tower was built), and 1900. Landscaped at the start of the 20th century, the park today is a great spot for temporary art exhibits, picnics, pickup soccer games, and outdoor concerts. You can also just sprawl on the center span of grass, which is unusual for Paris. There's a playground where kids can let off steam, too. Visiting during Bastille Day? If you can brave the crowds, arrive early to get a premier viewing position for the spectacular July 14th fireworks display, with the Eiffel Tower as a backdrop. Be vigilant at night. ✉ *Eiffel Tower* Ⓜ *École Militaire; RER: Champ de Mars–Tour Eiffel.*

FAMILY **Les Égouts** (*The Sewers*). Leave it to the French to make even sewers seem romantic. Part exhibit but mostly, well, sewer, the 1,640-foot stretch of tunnels provides a fascinating—and not too smelly—look at the underbelly of Paris. Visitors can stroll the so-called galleries of this city beneath the city, which comes complete with street signs mirroring those aboveground. Walkways flank tunnels of whooshing wastewater wide enough to allow narrow barges to dredge sand and sediment. Lighted panels, photos, and explanations in English detail the workings of the system. Immortalized as the escape routes of the Phantom of the Opera and Jean Valjean in *Les Misérables*, the 19th-century sewers have a florid real-life history. Since Napoléon ordered the underground network built to clean up the squalid streets, they have played a role in every war, secreting revolutionaries and spies and their stockpiles of weapons. Grenades from World War II were recovered not far from where the gift shop now sits. The display cases of stuffed toy rats and "Eau de Paris" glass carafes fold into the walls when the water rises after heavy rains. Buy your ticket at the kiosk on the Left Bank side of the Pont de l'Alma. Guided one-hour tours by friendly *égoutiers* (sewer workers) are available in French only; call or email ahead for details. ✉ *Opposite 93 quai d'Orsay, Eiffel Tower* ☎ *01–53–68–27–81* ⊕ *www.paris.fr* 🎟 *€5* ⊙ *Closed Thurs., Fri., and 2 wks in mid-Jan.* Ⓜ *Alma-Marceau; RER: Pont de l'Alma.*

Palais Bourbon. The most prominent feature of the Palais Bourbon—home of the Assemblée Nationale (or French Parliament) since 1798—is its colonnaded facade, commissioned by Napoléon to match that of the Madeleine, across the Seine. Jean-Pierre Cortot's sculpted pediment portrays France holding the tablets of Law, flanked by Force and Justice. Inside is an exquisite library with a soaring ceiling of cupolas painted by Delacroix. Unfortunately, guided tours have been discontinued, but that won't stop you from admiring the architecture and sculpture on display. ✉ *33 quai d'Orsay, Eiffel Tower* ☎ *01–40–63–60–00* ⊕ *www.assemblee-nationale.fr* Ⓜ *Assemblée Nationale.*

THE CHAMPS-ÉLYSÉES

Getting Oriented

GETTING HERE

This neighborhood includes the 8e and 16e arrondissements. For the top of the Champs-Élysées/Arc de Triomphe, take métro Line 1, 2, or 6, or the RER A, to Charles-de-Gaulle–Étoile. For the bottom of the avenue, near the Grand Palais, go to the Champs-Élysées–Clemenceau métro station on Line 1. For the Palais de Chaillot, use the Trocadéro métro station on Lines 6 and 9.

TOP REASONS TO GO

Avenue des Champs-Élysées. Splurge in the upscale boutiques on and around this fabled avenue, or simply practice the fine art of *lèche-vitrines* (literally "window licking," the French term for window-shopping).

Palais de Chaillot. A favorite of fashion photographers, this statue-lined plaza-terrace at Place du Trocadéro boasts the city's best view of the Eiffel Tower.

Musée Guimet. One of Paris's finest smaller museums has a world-class collection of art from all over Asia. Don't miss the rare Khmer sculptures from Cambodia.

Macarons **from Ladurée.** Is it worth lining up for 30 minutes to get a little taste of heaven? You decide. But rest assured: the round meringue cookies made by this famous pâtissier since 1862 are as scrumptious as ever.

The Champs-Élysées

4

BEST CAFÉS

Café La Belle Férronnière. A favorite of Parisians for morning *noisettes*, business lunches, and after-work *apéros* , this popular spot is a short walk from the Champs-Élysées. Settle in at a sidewalk table or retreat to the quieter interior. ✉ *53 rue Pierre Charron, Champs-Élysées* ☎ *01-42-25-03-82* Ⓜ *George V.*

Ladurée. With 50-plus locations worldwide, the most opulent branch of the Ladurée tea salon empire is worth the splurge. Reserve a table upstairs or grab a bite in the Art Nouveau bar in the back. ✉ *75 av. des Champs-Élysées, Champs-Élysées* ☎ *01-40-75-08-75* ⊕ *www. laduree.com* Ⓜ *George V.*

MAKING THE MOST OF YOUR TIME

This neighborhood is an essential stop for every first-time visitor to Paris, and returning travelers will find plenty to do, too. Leave yourself a full day to tour some of the museums around Place du Trocadéro before heading to the Champs-Élysées, worth a walk from end to end. Stop for lunch or dessert at one of the cafés or tea salons en route; then detour down Avenue Montaigne, Paris's answer to Rodeo Drive.

If your time is limited, you can just come for a stroll at night, when the Champs is alight: there are bars and nightclubs for all tastes, plus movie houses showing French films and English-language blockbusters (look for v.o., meaning *version originale,* if you prefer to see an undubbed one).

Sightseeing
★★★★★
Dining
★★★
Lodging
★★★★★
Shopping
★★★★
Nightlife
★★★★★

Make no mistake: the Champs-Élysées, while ceding some of its elegance in recent times, remains the most famous avenue in Paris—and, perhaps, the world. Like New York's Times Square or London's Piccadilly Circus, it is a mecca for travelers and locals alike. Some Parisians complain that fast-food joints and chain stores have cheapened Avenue des Champs-Élysées, but others are more philosophical, noting that there is something here for everyone. If you can't afford lunch at Ladurée, there's always McDonald's (and the view from its second floor is terrific).

Updated by
Jack Vermee

Anchoring the Champs is the **Arc de Triomphe,** Napoléon's monument to himself. At the other end, the exquisitely restored **Grand Palais** plays host to some of the city's grandest art exhibitions. Across the street, the permanent art collection is free at the **Petit Palais,** and there's also a quiet garden café. Between here and **Place du Trocadéro,** a busy traffic circle, you can find several museums housed in some of Paris's most impressive buildings. The **Palais de Chaillot** complex includes the **Cité de l'Architecture et du Patrimoine,** a must for architecture buffs, along with the anthropology-oriented **Musée de l'Homme.** Farther on, the **Musée Guimet** has a superlative Asian art collection, while the new **Musée Yves Saint Laurent** contains 13 rooms dedicated to the master couturier's groundbreaking designs. The **Musée d'Art Moderne de la Ville de Paris,** on Avenue du Président Wilson, contains a free permanent collection of 20th-century pieces. Contemporary-art lovers should also check out what's showing next door at the trendy **Palais de Tokyo.** These twin Art Nouveau buildings, constructed for the 1937 World's Fair, are notable for their monumental facades. Across the street is the **Palais Galliera:** framed by a lovely garden outside, it has a museum inside that focuses on fashion.

TOP ATTRACTIONS

Fodor'sChoice
★

Arc de Triomphe. Inspired by Rome's Arch of Titus, this colossal, 164-foot triumphal arch was ordered by Napoléon—who liked to consider himself the heir to Roman emperors—to celebrate his military successes. Unfortunately, Napoléon's strategic and architectural visions were not entirely on the same plane, and the Arc de Triomphe proved something of an embarrassment. Although the emperor wanted the monument completed in time for an 1810 parade in honor of his new bride, Marie-Louise, it was still only a few feet high, and a dummy arch of painted canvas was strung up to save face. Empires come and go, but Napoléon's had been gone for more than 20 years before the Arc was finally finished in 1836. A small museum halfway up recounts its history.

> **DID YOU KNOW?**
>
> The monument at Place de l'Alma, at the bottom of Avenues Montaigne and George V, along the Seine and just next to the Bateaux Mouches boarding dock, has become Princess Diana's unofficial shrine. Bouquets and messages are still placed here by her admirers—city workers regularly clean up flowers, graffiti, and photographs. The replica of the Statue of Liberty's flame predates Diana's car accident though: it was donated by Paris-based American companies in 1989 in honor of the bicentennial of the French Revolution.

The Arc de Triomphe is notable for magnificent sculptures by François Rude, including *The Departure of the Volunteers in 1792,* better known as *La Marseillaise,* to the right of the arch when viewed from the Champs-Élysées. Names of Napoléon's generals are inscribed on the stone facades—the underlined names identify the hallowed figures who fell in battle.

The traffic circle around the Arc is named for Charles de Gaulle, but it's known to Parisians as L'Étoile, or "the Star"—a reference to the streets that fan out from it. Climb the stairs to the top of the arch and you can see the star effect of the 12 radiating avenues and the vista down the Champs-Élysées toward Place de la Concorde and the distant Musée du Louvre.

■TIP→ France's Unknown Soldier is buried beneath the arch, and a commemorative flame is rekindled every evening at 6:30. That's the most atmospheric time to visit, but, to beat the crowds, come early in the morning or buy your ticket online.

⚠ Be wary of the traffic circle that surrounds the arch. It's infamous for accidents—including one several years ago that involved the French transport minister. Always use the underground passage from the northeast corner of the Avenue des Champs-Élysées. ⊠ *Pl. Charles-de-Gaulle, Champs-Élysées* ☎ *01–55–37–73–77* ⊕ *www.paris-arc-de-triomphe.fr* ⧮ *€12* ⟳ *Last admission 45 mins before closing* Ⓜ *Métro or RER: Charles-de-Gaulle–Étoile.*

4

NEED A
BREAK

✕ **L'Atelier Renault.** Leave it to the French to put a split-level restaurant in a car showroom, then make it as chic and high-tech as the Formula 1 racing cars on display. People-gazing from the second floor is not to be missed. ✉ *53 av. des Champs Élysées, Champs-Élysées* ☎ *01–76–84–14–14* ⊕ *www. atelier.renault.com* Ⓜ *Franklin-D.-Roosevelt.*

FAMILY **Avenue des Champs-Élysées.** Marcel Proust lovingly described the genteel elegance of the storied Champs-Élysées (pronounced "chahnz- *eleezay*," with an "n" sound instead of "m," and no "p") during its Belle Époque heyday, when its cobblestones resounded with the clatter of horses and carriages. Today, despite unrelenting traffic and the intrusion of chain stores and fast-food franchises, the avenue still sparkles. There's always something happening here: stores are open late (and many are open on Sunday, a rarity in Paris); nightclubs remain top destinations; and cafés offer prime people-watching, though you'll pay for the privilege—after all, this is Europe's most expensive piece of real estate. Along the 2-km (1¼-mile) stretch, you can find marquee names in French luxury, like Cartier, Guerlain, and Louis Vuitton. Car manufacturers lure international visitors with space-age showrooms. Old stalwarts, meanwhile, are still going strong—including the Lido cabaret and Fouquet's, whose celebrity clientele extends back to James Joyce. The avenue is also the setting for the last leg of the Tour de France bicycle race (the third or fourth Sunday in July), as well as Bastille Day (July 14) and Armistice Day (November 11) ceremonies. The Champs-Élysées, which translates to "Elysian Fields" (the resting place of the blessed in Greek mythology), began life as a cow pasture and in 1666 was transformed into a park by the royal landscape architect André Le Nôtre. Traces of its green origins are visible towards the Concorde, where elegant 19th-century park pavilions house the historic restaurants Ledoyen and Laurent. ✉ *Champs-Élysées* Ⓜ *Champs-Élysées–Clemenceau, Franklin-D.-Roosevelt, George V, Charles-de-Gaulle–Étoile.*

NEED A
BREAK

✕ **Publicis Drugstore.** A stone's throw from the Arc de Triomphe, this trendy spot—part mini department store, part brasserie—is stocked with an ever-changing array of upscale wares from designer handbags and diamond bracelets to fine wine and cigars. When you're done browsing, enjoy a quick bite at the on-site eatery (a prix-fixe menu is available) or stop by the bakery for food to take away. ✉ *133 av. des Champs-Élysées, Champs-Élysées* ☎ *01–44–43–75–07* ⊕ *www.publicisdrugstore.com* Ⓜ *Charles-de-Gaulle–Étoile.*

Cité de l'Architecture et du Patrimoine. The greatest gems of French architecture are represented at the City of Architecture and Heritage, which occupies the east wing of the Palais de Chaillot. Recipient of a recent €84-million renovation, the former French Monuments Museum contains some 350 plaster-cast reproductions spread out over 86,000 square feet. While it may seem odd to see a collection comprised entirely of copies, these are no ordinary ones: they include partial facades from some of the most important Gothic churches, a gallery of frescoes and windows (among them a stained-glass stunner from the famous

Chartres cathedral), plus an assembly of gargoyles practically leaping off the back wall of the soaring first-floor gallery. Video monitors with joysticks allow a 360-degree view of some of the grandest cathedrals. The upper-floor gallery is devoted to architecture since 1851, with a life-size replica of a postwar apartment in Marseille designed by the urban-planning pioneer Le Corbusier. It's well worth picking up the free English audiovisual guide. When you're ready for a break, the museum's small café offers a great view of the Eiffel Tower. ✉ *Palais de Chaillot, 1 pl. du Trocadéro, Champs-Élysées* ☎ *01-58-51-52-00* ⊕ *www.citedelarchitecture.fr* ⊠ *€8; €12 with temporary exhibits* ⊘ *Closed Tues.* Ⓜ *Trocadéro.*

Grand Palais. With its curved-glass roof and gorgeously restored Belle Époque ornamentation, you can't miss the Grand Palais whether you're approaching from the Seine or the Champs-Élysées. It forms an elegant duo with the Petit Palais across Avenue Winston Churchill: both stone buildings, adorned with mosaics and sculpted friezes, were built for the 1900 World's Fair, and, like the Eiffel Tower, were not intended to be permanent. The exquisite main exhibition space called Le Nef (or nave) hosts large-scale shows which focus on everything from jewelry to cars. The art-oriented shows staged here—including the annual FIAC, Paris's contemporary-art fair—are some of the hottest tickets in town. Previous must-sees included an Edward Hopper retrospective and *Picasso and the Masters*. To skip the long queue, booking an advance ticket online for an extra euro is strongly advised. ✉ *Av. Winston Churchill, Champs-Élysées* ☎ *01-40-13-48-00* ⊕ *www.grandpalais.fr* ⊠ *Around €15 (exhibitions vary)* ⊘ *Closed Tues.* Ⓜ *Champs-Élysées–Clemenceau.*

Musée d'Art Moderne de la Ville de Paris (*Paris Museum of Modern Art*). Although the city's modern art museum hasn't generated a buzz comparable to that of the Centre Georges Pompidou, visiting can be a more pleasant experience because it draws fewer crowds. The Art Nouveau building's vast, white-walled galleries make an ideal backdrop for temporary exhibitions of 20th-century art and postmodern installation projects. The permanent collection on the lower floor takes over where the Musée d'Orsay leaves off, chronologically speaking: among the earliest works are Fauvist paintings by Maurice Vlaminck and André Derain, followed by Pablo Picasso's early experiments in Cubism. Other highlights include works by Robert and Sonia Delaunay, Chagall, Matisse, Rothko, and Modigliani. ✉ *11 av. du Président Wilson, Champs-Élysées* ☎ *01-53-67-40-00* ⊕ *www.mam.paris.fr* ⊠ *Free; up to €12 for temporary exhibitions* ⊘ *Closed Mon.* Ⓜ *Alma-Marceau, Iéna.*

FAMILY **Musée de l'Homme.** After a raison d'être revamp and six years of renovation, Paris's storied anthropology museum, located in the west wing of the Palais de Chaillot, reopened its doors in late 2015. When President Jacques Chirac's legacy project (the Musée du Quai Branly, dedicated to the world's indigenous arts and cultures) pilfered half of this museum's pieces, few thought the rest would survive. But now it has come roaring back to life. Focused now on "science and human societies," the Musée de l'Homme has 33,368 square feet of sparkling exhibition space, where it displays more than 700,000 prehistoric artifacts and art objects. And it now does so using the most modern of museum tricks—including interactive displays, 3-D projections, and educational games—to help visitors understand the history of the human species. While you're admiring the 25,000-year-old Venus of Lespugue or comparing the skull of Cro-Magnon man with that of René Descartes, don't forget to look out the window: the view from the upper floors across to the Eiffel Tower and southern Paris is spectacular. ✉ *Palais de Chaillot, 17 Pl. du Trocadéro, Champs-Élysées* ☎ *01–44–05–72–72* ⊕ *www. museedelhomme.fr* 🖫 *€10 (€12 with temporary exhibitions)* ☞ *Closed Tues.* Ⓜ *Trocadéro.*

Fodor'sChoice **Musée Guimet.** The outstanding Musée Guimet boasts the western world's
★ biggest collection of Asian art, thanks to the 19th-century wanderings of Lyonnaise industrialist Émile Guimet. Exhibits, enriched by the state's vast holdings, are laid out geographically in airy, light-filled rooms. Just past the entry, you can find the largest assemblage of Khmer sculpture outside Cambodia. The second floor has statuary and masks from Nepal, ritual funerary art from Tibet, and jewelry and fabrics from India. Peek into the library rotunda, where Monsieur Guimet once entertained the city's notables under the gaze of eight caryatids atop Ionic columns; Mata Hari danced here in 1905. The much-heralded Chinese collection, made up of 20,000-odd objects, covers seven millennia, while the impressive Buddhist Pantheon features scores of Buddhas from China and Japan. Grab a free English-language audioguide and brochure at the entrance. If you need a pick-me-up, stop at the Salon des Porcelaines café on the lower level for a ginger milk shake. And don't miss the Guimet's adjunct space just up the street at 19 avenue d'Iéna. The Hôtel d'Heidelbach contains a Japanese garden and the museum's collection of Asian furniture; admission is free with a Musée Guimet ticket. ✉ *6 pl. d'Iéna, Champs-Élysées* ☎ *01 56 52–54–33* ⊕ *www.guimet.fr* 🖫 *€9; €12 with temporary exhibition* ⊙ *Closed Tues.* Ⓜ *Iéna, Boissiére.*

FAMILY **Palais de Chaillot.** This honey-color Art Deco cultural center on Place du Trocadéro was built in the 1930s to replace a Moorish-style building constructed for the 1878 World's Fair. Its esplanade is a top draw for camera-toting visitors intent on snapping the perfect shot of the Eiffel Tower. In the building to the left is the Cité de l'Architecture et du Patrimoine—billed as the largest architectural museum in the world—and the Théâtre National de Chaillot, which occasionally stages plays in English. Also here is the Institut Français d'Architecture, an organization and school. The twin building to the right contains the recently renovated Musée de l'Homme, a thoroughly modern anthropology museum. Sculptures and fountains adorn the garden leading to the Seine. ✉ *Pl. du Trocadéro, Champs-Élysées* Ⓜ *Trocadéro.*

Palais de Tokyo. The go-to address for some of the city's funkiest exhibitions, the Palais de Tokyo is a stripped-down venue that spotlights provocative, ambitious contemporary art. There is no permanent collection: instead, cutting-edge temporary shows are staged in a cavernous space reminiscent of a light-filled industrial loft. The programming extends to performance art, concerts, readings, and fashion shows. Night owls will appreciate the midnight closing. The museum's new Les Grands Verres restaurant and cocktail bar—serving an avant-garde take on traditional

4

French fare—is a haunt of hip locals, especially at lunch. Visit the offbeat gift shop for souvenirs that are as edgy and subversive as the exhibits. ✉ *13 av. du Président Wilson, Champs-Élysées* ☎ *01–81–97–35–88* ⊕ *www.palaisdetokyo.com* 🎫 *€12* ⊗ *Closed Tues.* Ⓜ *Iéna.*

✕ **Les Grands Verres.** Traditional French fare gets an avant-garde twist at the Palais de Tokyo, which has one of the most popular museum café-restaurants in town. Open daily from noon to 2 am, it's filled with hip locals—especially at lunch. ✉ *13 av. du Président Wilson, Champs-Élysées* ☎ *01–85–53–03–61* ⊕ *www.quixotic-projects.com/fr/venue/les-grands-verres* Ⓜ *Iéna.*

Fodor's Choice
★

Palais Galliera, Musée de la Mode. The city's Museum of Fashion occupies a suitably fashionable mansion—the 19th-century residence of Marie Brignole-Sale, Duchess of Galliera; and, having emerged from an extensive makeover in 2013, it is now more stylish than ever. Inside, temporary exhibitions focus on costume and clothing design (a reopening retrospective, for instance, honored the visionary Azzedine Alaïa). Covering key moments in fashion history and showcasing iconic French designers, the museum's collection includes 100,000 dresses and accessories that run the gamut from basic streetwear to haute couture. Details on shows (there are no permanent displays) are available on the museum website. Don't miss the lovely 19th-century garden that encircles the palace. ✉ *10 av. Pierre-1er-de-Serbie, Champs-Élysées* ☎ *01–56–52–86–00* ⊕ *www.palaisgalliera.paris.fr* 🎫 *€8 and up, depending on the exhibition* ⊗ *Closed Mon. and between exhibitions.* Ⓜ *Iéna.*

Petit Palais, Musée des Beaux-Arts de la Ville de Paris. The "little" palace has a small, overlooked collection of excellent paintings, sculpture, and objets d'art, with works by Monet, Gauguin, and Courbet, among others. Temporary exhibitions, beefed up in recent years (and occasionally free), are particularly good—especially those dedicated to photography. The building, like the Grand Palais across the street, is an architectural marvel of marble, glass, and gilt built for the 1900 World's Fair, with impressive entry doors and huge windows overlooking the river. Search directly above the main galleries for 16 plaster busts set into the wall representing famous artists. Outside, note two eye-catching sculptures: French World War I hero Georges Clemenceau faces the Champs-Élysées, while a resolute Winston Churchill faces the Seine. In warmer weather, head to the garden café with terrace seating. ✉ *Av. Winston Churchill, Champs-Élysées* ☎ *01–53–43–40–00* ⊕ *www.petitpalais.paris.fr* 🎫 *Free; €5–€15 for temporary exhibitions* ⊗ *Closed Mon.* Ⓜ *Champs-Élysées–Clemenceau.*

✕ **Le Jardin du Petit Palais.** The quiet little café hidden in the lush garden inside the Petit Palais is one of this quarter's best-kept secrets. ✉ *Av. Winston Churchill, Champs-Élysées* ☎ *01–40–07–11–41* ⊕ *www.petitpalais.paris.fr* ⊗ *Closed Mon.* Ⓜ *Champs-Élysées–Clemenceau.*

WORTH NOTING

FAMILY **Aquarium de Paris.** An aquarium and cinema may seem like a strange combination, but the two coexist nicely in this attractive space beneath the Trocadéro gardens. In addition to 10,000 fish and a giant tank of small sharks, it promises puppet and magic shows, along with workshops for children in animation, art, and dance (these are offered in French, but the staff speaks English). There are also kid-oriented films showing on one big screen and, for the grown-ups, feature films playing on a second. Check the website for times and activities. Book tickets online to avoid lines. ⊠ *5 av. Albert De Mun, Champs-Élysées* ☎ *01–40–69–23–23* ⊕ *www.cineaqua.com* ⊠ *€21* ⟲ *Last entry 1 hr before closing* Ⓜ *Trocadéro.*

La Maison Baccarat. Playing on the building's Surrealist legacy, designer Philippe Starck brought an irreverent *Alice in Wonderland* approach to the HQ and museum of the venerable Baccarat crystal firm: Cocteau, Dalí, Buñuel, and Man Ray were all frequent guests of the mansion's onetime owner, Countess Marie-Laure de Noailles. At the entrance, talking heads are projected onto giant crystal urns, and a lighted chandelier is submerged in an aquarium. Upstairs, the museum features masterworks created by Baccarat since 1764, including soaring candlesticks made for Czar Nicholas II and the perfume flacon Dalí designed for Schiaparelli. Don't miss the rotunda's "Alchemy" section by Gérard Garouste, showcasing the technical history of cutting, wheel engraving, enamelling, and gilding. If you're in the mood for shopping, contemporary crystal by top-name designers as well as stemware, vases, tableware, jewelry, chandeliers, and even furniture are sold in the on-site shop. Set aside a few moments to enjoy the little park just outside in the Place des États-Unis with impressive statues of Washington and Lafayette. ⊠ *11 pl. des États-Unis, Champs-Élysées* ☎ *01–40–22–11–00* ⊕ *www.baccarat.fr* ⊠ *€10* ⊘ *Closed Sun. and Mon.* Ⓜ *Iéna.*

Musée Yves Saint Laurent Paris. As elegant and stylish as the master couturier's groundbreaking designs, this new museum, opened in October 2017, is housed in the very mansion where Yves Saint Laurent did his work and entertained celebrity clients. More than 50 prototypes—including such landmarks as the Mondrian dress, the original pantsuit, and the woman's tuxedo—are on display at any one time, as are dozens of design drawings and a glittering array of jewelry. Thanks to its huge windows, the light-bathed upstairs atelier, stuffed with books and fabrics, offers an intimate glimpse into YSL's world. Be sure not to miss the touching short film detailing the relationship between Saint Laurent and his longtime partner Pierre Bergé. All of the exhibits have detailed English labeling, and there is a free English guide available at reception. ⊠ *5 av. Marceau, Champs-Élysées* ☎ *01–44–31–64–00* ⊕ *www.museeyslparis.com* ⊠ *€10* ⊘ *Closed Mon.* ⟲ *Last entry 45 min before closing* Ⓜ *Alma-Marceau.*

4

FAMILY **Palais de la Découverte** (*Palace of Discovery*). The Palace of Discovery, a popular science museum in the rear of the Grand Palais complex, has a wide variety of exhibits spread out over two floors under an elegant glass-and-iron roof. Subjects include astronomy, chemistry, biology, physics, and earth sciences. Free audioguides can be downloaded to your smart device, and there are plenty of buttons and levers to press and pull to keep little (and not so little) hands busy. This fun facility—a smaller cousin of the Cité des Sciences et de l'Industrie in Parc de la Villette—also features regularly scheduled demos and 3-D films, along with daily planetarium shows (in French only). ✉ *Av. Franklin-D.-Roosevelt, Champs-Élysées* ☏ *01–56–43–20–20* ⊕ *www. palais-decouverte.fr* 🎟 *€9; €12 with planetarium* ⊘ *Closed Mon.* Ⓜ *Champs-Élysées–Clemenceau.*

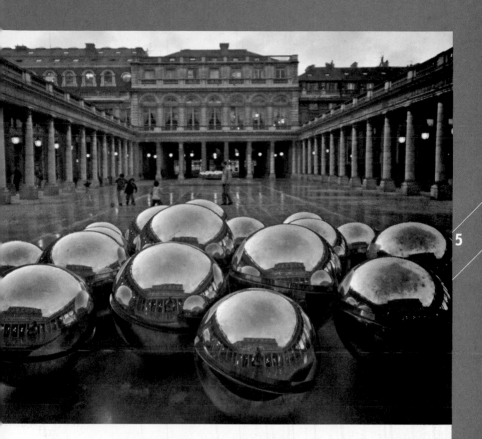

AROUND THE LOUVRE

Getting Oriented

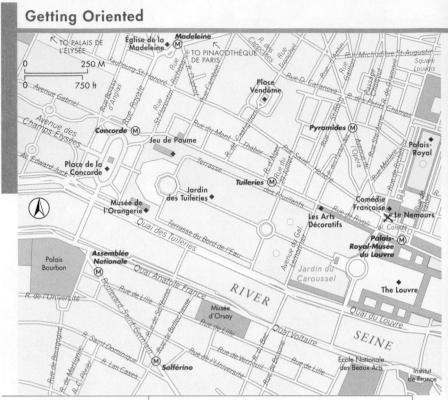

GETTING HERE	TOP REASONS TO GO

GETTING HERE

The neighborhoods in this chapter include the 1er and 2e arrondissements, from the Faubourg St-Honoré to Les Halles. If you're heading to the Louvre, take the métro Line 1 to the Palais-Royal–Musée du Louvre or Louvre–Rivoli stop. For the Tuileries, use the Tuileries stop on the same line. For Place de la Concorde, use the Concorde stop on Line 1, 8, or 12. This is a good starting point for a walk on Rue St-Honoré. If you're going to Les Halles, take Line 4 to Les Halles or Line 1 to Châtelet.

TOP REASONS TO GO

Musée du Louvre. The world's first great art museum—which displays such renowned works as the serenely smirking *Mona Lisa* and the statuesque Venus de Milo—deserves a long visit.

Tuileries to Place de la Concorde. For centuries, Parisians and visitors alike have strolled the length of this magnificent garden to the gold-tipped obelisk at Place de la Concorde.

Galerie Vivienne. The prettiest 19th-century glass-roofed shopping arcade left in Paris, this *passage* is worth a stop for shopping, lunch, or afternoon tea.

Palais-Royal. Visit these arcades and the romantic garden to understand why the French writer Colette called the view from her window "a little corner of the country."

Rue Montorgueil. This historic market street, lined with food shops and cafés, is at the heart of one of the city's trendiest neighborhoods.

Around the Louvre

BEST CAFÉS

Au Rocher de Cancale. As its impressive facade attests, this café has a special history. It opened in 1846, when Balzac was a regular and Rue Montorgueil was *the* place to buy oysters. ✉ *78 rue Montorgueil, Louvre* ☎ *01–42–33–50–29* Ⓜ *Les Halles.*

Le Fumoir. Equal parts café, bar, and restaurant, Le Fumoir is a timelessly popular place to sip coffee and read the paper, or enjoy an after-dinner drink. Reservations are recommended for dinner and Sunday brunch. ✉ *Pl. du Louvre, 6 rue de l'Amiral-Coligny, Louvre* ☎ *01–42–92–00–24* ⊕ *www.lefumoir.com* Ⓜ *Louvre-Rivoli.*

Le Nemours. Plan your day over a croissant and a *café crème* at this classic café with two long rows of tables overlooking lively Place Colette, just steps from the Palais-Royal and the Musée du Louvre. ✉ *2 pl. Colette, Louvre* ☎ *01–42–61–34–14* Ⓜ *Palais-Royal–Louvre.*

MAKING THE MOST OF YOUR TIME

Try to devote two days or more—one alone for the Louvre—to these vastly different neighborhoods. Along the narrow sidewalks of the Faubourg St-Honoré you'll find some of the finest Parisian boutiques. Place de la Concorde is the gateway to the Tuileries garden. At the eastern end, Les Halles (the old market district) is booming with shops and eateries popping up around cobbled Rue Montorgueil, where traffic is mercifully restricted.

If you're headed to the mammoth Musée du Louvre, it's best to have a game plan in mind. First step: buy your ticket online at ⊕ *www.louvre.fr.* If there is a crowd waiting to enter the Pyramide, use the entrance in the underground mall, the Carrousel du Louvre, 99 rue de Rivoli.

Sightseeing
★★★★
Dining
★★
Lodging
★★★★
Shopping
★★★★★
Nightlife
★★

The neighborhoods from the très chic Faubourg St-Honoré to trendy Les Halles are a study in contrasts, with the Louvre in the midst of the bustle. The posh Rue Faubourg St-Honoré, once the stomping ground of kings and queens, is now home to the French president and assorted foreign ambassadors. Beloved by fashionistas for three centuries, it is as popular today as it was when royal mistresses shopped here—which explains the plethora of high-end stores (almost every luxury brand is represented). Not surprisingly, ritzy restaurants and haute hotels are located here as well.

Updated by
Linda Hervieux

To the east, **Les Halles** (pronounced leh- *ahl*) has risen from its roots as a down-and-out market district to become one of the city's hottest, hippest neighborhoods. Vermin-infested cobbled streets have given way to trendy shops, cafés, and bars, centered on Rue Montorgueil; and a sweeping multiyear renovation of the former wholesale food market (which closed in 1969) gave a much-needed face-lift to the plaza aboveground and the vast shopping mall below.

Between Faubourg St-Honoré and Les Halles, you can find some of Paris's top draws—namely the mighty **Musée du Louvre** and, next door, the majestic **Jardin des Tuileries.** The garden is home to the **Musée de l'Orangerie,** with its curved galleries showcasing Monet's *Water Lilies,* while nearby **Les Arts Décoratifs** is a must for design buffs. In Place Colette, the stately theater, the **Comédie Française,** is still going strong after 400 years, and at the edge of the square is the psychedelic sculpture—doubling as a métro entrance—of the *kiosque des noctambules* (kiosk of the nightcrawlers), designed by artist Jean-Michel Othoniel. Hidden just off Place Colette is the **Palais-Royal,** a romantic garden ringed by arcades with boutiques selling everything from old-fashioned music boxes to fashion-forward frocks. A stone's throw away is **Galerie Vivienne,** an exquisitely restored 19th-century shopping arcade.

TOP ATTRACTIONS

Galerie Véro-Dodat. A lovely 19th-century passage that's been gorgeously restored, the Véro-Dodat has a dozen artsy boutiques selling objets d'art, textiles, furniture, and accessories. The headliner tenant is Christian Louboutin, at Rue Jean-Jacques Rousseau, whose red-soled stilettos are favored by Angelina, Madonna, and other members of the red-carpet set. On the opposite end, at the Rue du Bouloi entrance, star cosmetics-maker Terry De Gunzburg has a boutique, By Terry. ✉ *Main entrance at 19 rue Jean-Jacques Rousseau, Louvre* Ⓜ *Palais-Royal–Louvre.*

Galerie Vivienne. Considered the grande dame of Paris's 19th-century *passages couverts*—the world's first shopping malls—this graceful covered arcade evokes an age of gaslights and horse-drawn carriages. Once Parisians came to passages like this one to tred tiled floors instead of muddy streets and to see and be seen browsing boutiques under the glass-and-iron roofs. Today, the Galerie Vivienne still attracts unique retailers selling clothing, accessories, and housewares. La Marelle (No. 25) stocks secondhand designer labels, and wine merchant Legrand Filles & Fils (1 rue de la Banque) is the place for an upscale wine tasting. The Place des Victoires, a few steps away, is one of Paris's most picturesque squares. In the center is a statue of an outsized Louis XIV (1643–1715), the Sun King, who appears almost as large as his horse. ✉ *Main entrance at 4 rue des Petits-Champs, Louvre* Ⓜ *Palais-Royal–Louvre, Bourse.*

FAMILY
Fodor's Choice
★
Jardin des Tuileries. The quintessential French garden, with its verdant lawns, manicured rows of trees, and gravel paths, was designed by André Le Nôtre for Louis XIV. After the king moved his court to Versailles in 1682, the Tuileries became *the* place for stylish Parisians to stroll. (Ironically, the name derives from the decidedly unstylish factories, which once occupied this area: they produced *tuiles,* or roof tiles, fired in kilns called *tuileries.*) Monet and Renoir captured the garden with paint and brush, and it's no wonder the Impressionists loved it—the gray, austere light of Paris's famously overcast days make the green trees appear even greener.

The garden still serves as a setting for one of the city's loveliest walks. Laid out before you is a vista of must-see monuments, with the Louvre at one end and the Place de la Concorde at the other. The Eiffel Tower is on the Seine side, along with the Musée d'Orsay, reachable across a footbridge in the center of the garden. A good place to begin is at the Louvre end, at the Arc du Carrousel, a stone-and-marble arch ordered by Napoléon to showcase the bronze horses he stole from St. Mark's Cathedral in Venice. The horses were eventually returned and replaced here with a statue of a *quadriga,* a four-horse chariot. On the Place de la Concorde end, twin buildings bookend the garden. On the Seine side, the former royal greenhouse is now the exceptional Musée de l'Orangerie, home to the largest display of Monet's lovely *Water Lilies* series, as well as a sizable collection of early-20th-century paintings. On the opposite end is the Jeu de Paume, which has some of the city's best temporary photography exhibits.

Note that the Tuileries is one of the best places in Paris to take kids if they're itching to run around. There's a carousel, trampolines, and, in summer, an amusement park.

If you're hungry, look for carts serving gelato from Amorino or sandwiches from the chain bakery Paul at the eastern end near the Louvre. Within the gated part of the gardens are four cafés with terraces. Pavillon des Tuilleries near Place de la Concorde is a good place to stop for late-afternoon tea or an apéritif. ✉ *Bordered by Quai des Tuileries, Pl. de la Concorde, Rue de Rivoli, and the Louvre, Louvre* ☎ *01–40–20–90–43* 🖾 *Free* Ⓜ *Tuileries or Concorde.*

Les Arts Décoratifs. As the city's leading showcase of French design, Les Arts Décoratifs was rechristened the Musée des Arts Décoratifs—or MAD—in 2018 in an effort to better carve out a niche for itself in a city with many competitors for that title. Sharing a wing of the Musée du Louvre, but with a separate entrance and admission charge, MAD is actually three museums in one spread across nine floors. The stellar collection of decorative arts, fashion, and graphics includes altarpieces from the Middle Ages and furnishings from the Italian Renaissance to the present day. There are period rooms reflecting the ages, such as the early 1820s salon of the Duchesse de Berry (who actually lived in the building), plus several rooms reproduced from designer Jeanne Lanvin's 1920s apartment. Don't miss the gilt-and-green-velvet bed of the Parisian courtesan who inspired the boudoir in Émile Zola's novel *Nana*; you can hear Zola's description of it on the free English audioguide, which is highly recommended. The second-floor jewelry gallery is another must-see.

MAD is also home to an exceptional collection of textiles, advertising posters, films, and related objects that are shown in rotating exhibitions. The museum routinely makes headlines for crowd-pleasing temporary exhibits such as 2017's Christian Dior show that broke records for attendance. Before leaving, take a break at the restaurant Le Loulou, where an outdoor terrace is an ideal spot for lunch or afternoon tea. Shoppers should browse through the on-site boutique as well. Stocked with an interesting collection of books, paper products, toys, tableware, accessories, and jewelry, it is one of the city's best museum shops. If you're combining a visit here with the Musée du Louvre, note that the two close on different days, so don't come on Monday or Tuesday. If you're pairing it with the exquisite Nissim de Camondo, joint tickets are available at a reduced cost. ✉ *107 rue de Rivoli, Louvre* ☎ *01–44–55–57–50* ⊕ *madparis.fr* 🖾 *€11; €11 temporary exhibits; €13 joint ticket with Musée Nissim de Camondo* ☽ *Closed Mon.* Ⓜ *Palais-Royal–Louvre.*

Les Halles. For 800 years, Paris was fed by the acres of food halls overflowing with meats, fish, and vegetables that made up this district. Sensuously described in Émile Zola's novel *The Belly of Paris*, Les Halles was teeming with life—though not all of it good. Hucksters and the homeless shared these streets with prostitutes (who still ply their trade in diminishing numbers on nearby Rue St-Denis); and the plague of cat-size rats didn't cease until the market moved to the suburbs in

1969. Today, you can still see stuffed pests hanging by their tails in the windows of the circa-1872 shop Julien Aurouze (8 rue des Halles) whose sign, *Destruction des Animaux Nuisibles* (in other words, vermin extermination), says it all. All that remains of the 19th-century iron-and-glass market buildings, designed by architect Victor Baltard, is a portion of the superstructure on the southern edge of the Jardins des Halles. The Fontaine des Innocents, from 1550, at Rues Berger and Pierre Lescot, marks the site of what was once a vast cemetery before the bones were moved to the Catacombs.

After years of delays, Les Halles finally underwent one of the city's most ambitious public works projects: a sweeping €500 million renovation, completed in 2018, that has transformed the plaza, and the much-maligned underground concrete mall called the Forum des Halles, into a must-go destination. While the project was not without opponents, even famously grumpy Parisians were finally happy about the prospect of a prettier Les Halles—and a spruced-up train station below ground. (The metro and RER station at Les Halles is one of the city's busiest transport hubs.). In an echo of the past, a 48-foot iron-and-yellow glass canopy floats over the entrance, flooding light into the caverns below. Aboveground, a 10-acre park called the Jardin Nelson Mandela is dotted with trees, decorative pools, and play areas for kids. On the northern end, a redesigned Place René Cassin has tiered steps centered around *L'Ecoute*, Henri de Miller's giant head and hand sculpture. Looming behind is the magnificent church of St-Eustache, a Gothic gem. Movie buffs should check out the Forum des Images, which stages screenings of quirky or older films, often with notables on hand such as director Oliver Stone. Or sample some of the 7,000 films available for viewing on individual screens. To find it, enter the mall on the side of the church at the Porte St-Eustache.

The streets surrounding Les Halles have boomed in recent years with boutiques, bars, and restaurants galore that have sent rents skyrocketing. Historic Rue Montorgueil is home to food shops and cafés. Running parallel, Rue Montmartre, near the church, still has a few specialty shops selling foie gras and other delicacies, though these merchants, like the butchers and bakers before them, are slowly being pushed out by trendy clothing boutiques. ⊠ *Garden entrances on Rues Coquillière, Berger, and Rambuteau. Mall entrances on Rues Pierre Lescot, Berger, and Rambuteau, Louvre* ⊕ *www.forumdeshalles.com* Ⓜ *Les Halles; RER: Châtelet–Les Halles.*

Fodor's Choice ★ **The Louvre.** Simply put, the Louvre is the world's greatest art museum—and the largest, with 675,000 square feet of works from almost every civilization on earth. The *Mona Lisa* is, of course, a top draw, along with the Venus de Milo and Winged Victory. These and many more of the globe's most coveted treasures are displayed in three wings—the Richelieu, the Sully, and the Denon—which are arranged like a horseshoe. Nestled in the middle is I.M. Pei's Pyramide, the giant glass pyramid surrounded by a trio of smaller ones that opened in 1989 over the new entrance in the Cour Napoléon. To plot your course through the complex, grab a color-coded map at the information desk. For an excellent overview, book a 90-minute English-language tour (€12, daily at 11 and 2); slick Nintendo 3DS multimedia guides (€5; pay for it when you buy your ticket), available at the entrance to each wing, offer a self-guided alternative.

Having been first a fortress and later a royal residence, the Louvre represents a saga that spans nine centuries. Its medieval roots are on display below ground in the Sully wing, where vestiges of the foundation and moat remain. Elsewhere in this wing you can ogle the largest display of Egyptian antiques outside of Cairo, most notably the magnificent statue of Ramses II (salle 12). Upstairs is the armless Venus de Milo, a 2nd-century representation of Aphrodite (salle 7). Highlights of the wing's collection of French paintings from the 17th century onward include the *Turkish Bath* by Jean-August-Dominique Ingres (salle 60). American Cy Twombly's contemporary ceiling in salle 32 adds a 21st-century twist. In the Denon wing, climb the sweeping marble staircase (Escalier Daru) to see the sublime Winged Victory of Samothrace, carved in 305 BC. This wing is also home to the iconic, enigmatic *Mona Lisa* (salle 6); two other Da Vinci masterpieces hang in the adjacent Grand Galerie. The museum's latest architectural wonder is here as well—the 30,000-square-foot Arts of Islam exhibition space, which debuted in 2012. Topped with an undulating golden roof evoking a flowing veil, its two-level galleries contain one of the largest collections of art from the Islamic world. After admiring it, be sure to visit the Richelieu wing and the Cour Marly, with its quartet of horses carved for Louis XIV and Louis XV. On the ground floor, the centerpiece of the Near East Antiquities Collection is the Lamassu, carved 8th-century winged beasts (salle 4). The elaborately decorated Royal Apartments of Napoléon III are on the first floor. On the second floor, French and Northern School paintings include Vermeer's *The Lacemaker* (salle 38). Note that crowds are thinner on Wednesday and Friday nights, when the museum is open late. Save queue time by purchasing online tickets for an additional fee; admission includes some temporary exhibitions and entry within 48 hours to the charming Musée Eugène-Delacroix. If you arrive without a ticket, you can buy one at the kiosks or automatic machines in a newly renovated space below the Pyramid. Avoid crowds by using the lesser-known entrance through the underground mall, Carrousel du Louvre. ✉ *Palais du Louvre, Louvre* ☎ *01–40–20–53–17 for info* ⊕ *www.louvre.fr* 💶 *€15, includes entry to Musée Eugène Delacroix (free 1st Sun. of month, Oct. Mar.)* ☉ *Closed Tues* Ⓜ *Palais-Royal–Louvre, Louvre-Rivoli.*

Musée de l'Orangerie. In high season the lines can be long to see Claude Monet's huge, meditative *Water Lilies* (*Les Nymphéas*), displayed in two curved galleries designed in 1914 by the master himself. But they are well worth the wait. These works are the highlight of the Orangerie's small but excellent collection, which also features early-20th-century paintings by Renoir, Cézanne, and Matisse. Many hail from the private holdings of high-powered art dealer Paul Guillaume (1891–1934), among them Guillaume's portrait by Modigliani entitled *Novo Pilota* (*New Pilot*). Temporary exhibitions, such as 2017's Dada Africa, are typically quirky and well curated. Built in 1852 to shelter orange trees, the long rectangular building, a twin of the Jeu de Paume across the

Continued on page 84

MUSÉE DU LOUVRE

Try to wrap your mind around this: The Louvre has more than 37,000 pieces of art in its collection, representing nearly every civilization on earth, and more than 675,000 square feet of exhibition space. It's gone through countless cycles of construction and demolition, expansion and renovation, starting as a medieval fortress, then becoming a royal residence before opening its doors as the Museum Central des Arts at the end of the 18th century.

Left: Michelangelo's *Dying Slave*

Below: The Louvre's iconic *Pyramide*, designed by I. M. Pei.

Don't make the mistake of thinking that you'll be able to see the Louvre's entire collection in one visit and still enjoy—or remember—what you've seen. The three most popular artworks here are, of course, the *Mona Lisa*, the *Venus de Milo*, and *Winged Victory*. Beyond these must-sees, your best bet is to focus on highlights that interest you the most—and don't worry about getting lost because you're bound to stumble upon something interesting. Stop by the information desk for a free color-coded map. For help navigating the collection, rent an excellent Nintendo 3DS multimedia guide, or take a daily guided tour in English. The Louvre has three wings—the Richelieu, the Sully, and the Denon—arranged like a horseshoe, with I.M. Pei's striking *Pyramide* nestled outside in the middle.

RICHELIEU WING

COLLECTIONS
Near East Antiquities
French Painting
French Sculpture
Northern Schools
Decorative Arts

Below Ground & Ground Floor. Entering from the Pyramide, head upstairs to the sculpture courtyards, Cour Marly and Cour Puget. In Cour Marly you'll find the **Marley Horses** (see right). Salle 2 has fragments from Cluny, the powerful Romanesque abbey in Burgundy that dominated 11th-century French Catholicism. Salles 4–6 follows the evolution of French sculpture, and in Salles 7–10 you'll find funerary art. In Cour Puget, products from the Académie Royale, the art school of 18th-century France, fill Salles 25–33. Behind this is the Near East Antiquities Collection. Salle 3's centerpiece is the Codex of Hammurabi, an 18th-century BC black-diorite stela containing the world's oldest written code of laws. In Salle 4, you'll find **Lamassu** (see right).

First Floor. Head straight through Decorative Arts to see the magnificently restored **Royal Apartments of Napoléon III** (see right).

Second Floor. Much of this floor is dedicated to French and Northern School paintings. At the entrance is a 14th-century painting of John the Good—the oldest-known individual portrait from the north of Italy. In Salle 4 hangs *The Madonna of Chancellor Rolin,* by the 15th-century Early Netherlandish master Jan van Eyck (late 14th century–1441). Peter Paul Rubens's (1577–1640) the *Disembarkation of Marie de' Medici at the Port of Marseille* is in Salle 18. In Salle 31 are several paintings by Rembrandt van Rijn (1606–69), including **Bathsheba**, his largest nude. The masterpiece of the Dutch collection is Vermeer's **The Lacemaker** (see right).

TIPS

■ The 25 paintings by Rubens commisioned by Marie de Medici for the Luxembourg Palace in Salle 18 on the second floor each mark an event in the queen's life.

■ To see what's on the minds of the museum staff, check out the Painting of the Month in Salle 17, French section, on the 2nd floor.

■ Take a hot chocolate break in the Café Richelieu on the first floor, run by the upscale *confiseur* Angelina. There is an outdoor terrace in summer and a tempting lunch menu.

■ Save your ticket and duck out for lunch at one of the nearby cafés.

DON'T MISS

LAMASSU, 8TH CENTURY   SALLE 4

With their fierce beards and gentle eyes, these massive winged beasts are benevolent guardians straight from the dreamworld. Magical for children and adults, the strangely lifelike sculptures are located in the Near Eastern antiquities collection. The winged bull demigods are part of the Cour Khorsabad, a re-creation of the temple erected by Assyrian king Sargon II. ✛ *Richelieu, ground floor*

Lamassu

THE LACEMAKER, 1669–1671   SALLE 38

This is a small but justifiably famous gem of Dutch optical accuracy (and a must-see for fans of the movie and book, *Girl With a Pearl Earring*, to see how his style evolved over a 5-year period.) Here, Jan Vermeer (1632–75) painted the red thread in the foreground as a slightly blurred jumble, just as one would actually see it if focusing on the girl. The lacemaker's industriousness represents domestic virtue, but the personal focus of the painting is far more engaging than a simple morality tale. ✛ *Richelieu, second floor*

The Lacemaker

MARLY HORSES, 1699–1740   COUR MARLY

During the dramatic 1989 reorganization of the Louvre, two courtyards were elegantly glassed over to match the entrance pyramid. The dramatic glass-roofed Marly sculpture court houses several sculptures from Louis XIV's garden at Marly, including two magnificent winged horses by Antoine Coysevox. Later, the artist's nephew Guillaume Coustou created two accompanying earthbound horse sculptures for Louis XV; their fame was such that, during the Revolution, these sculptures were moved to the Tuileries gardens for public viewing. Now the four original horses greet visitors to the Richelieu Wing, ready to gallop off into the museum; replicas stand guard in the Tuileries. ✛ *Richelieu, lower ground floor*

The Marly Horses

ROYAL APARTMENTS
OF NAPOLÉON III, 1860s   SALLE 87

These dozen reception rooms, hung with crystal chandeliers, elaborate mirrors, and imperial velour, are a gilt-covered reminder that the Louvre was a palace for centuries, regally designed to impress. En route, you'll pass decorative items like the solid-crystal Restoration dressing table (Salle 77) that prepare you for the eye-popping luxury of the Second Empire. ✛ *Richelieu, first floor*

Royal Apartments of Napoléon

SULLY WING

Below Ground & Ground Floor. Start your visit with a journey to the roots of the Louvre—literally. From the *Pyramide* entrance, tour the 13th-century foundations of the original fortress and the Medieval Moat. In Salle 12 you'll find towering Ramses II. Check out the mummies in Salles 14 and 15, along with rare examples of Egyptian funerary art.

Upstairs, the north galleries of the Sully continue the ancient Iranian collection begun in the Richelieu Wing. Salle 16 has the 2nd-century BC **Venus de Milo** (see right), anchoring the Greek collection of Salles 7–17.

First Floor. The northern galleries of the first floor continue with the Decorative Arts collection including works from all over Europe, and connect with the Napoléon III apartments.

Second Floor. Sully picks up French painting in the 17th century where the Richelieu leaves off. The Académiciens are best exemplified by Nicolas Poussin (1594–1665, Salle 19), the first international painting star from France. The antithesis of this style was the candlelit modest work by outsider Georges de La Tour (Salle 28), as in his *Magdalene of Night Light.*

The Académie Royale defined the standards of painting through revolution, republic, and empire. Exoticism wafted in during the Napoleonic empire, as in the **Turkish Bath** (see right) painting of Jean-Auguste-Dominique Ingres (1780–1867). Fresh energy crackled into French painting in the 18th century. Antoine Watteau (1684–1721), was known for his theatrical scenes and *fêtes galantes*, portrayals of well-dressed figures in bucolic settings. In *Pilgrimage to the Island of Cythera* (Salle 36), he used delicate brushstrokes and soft tones to convey the court set, here depicted arriving on (or departing from) Cythera, the mythical isle of love.

TIPS

■ There is a little-known collection with Monet, Renoir, and Cezanne in Salle C on the second floor, the only Impressionist works in the Louvre.

■ There's a surprise in Salle 17 on the ground floor—the *Sleeping Hermaphrodite* by the entrance.

■ Be sure to look up as you make your way up Escalier Henri II. It took four years to complete this 16th-century vaulted ceiling.

■ Need a bathroom? There are some tucked between Salles 22 and 23 on the 1st floor. (And admire the colorful, 4,000-year-old Seated Scribe in Salle 22.)

■ For a breather, head to the bench in Salle 33 on the first floor and enjoy the sedate three-part ceiling by Georges Braque (1955) called *Les Oiseux* (The Birds).

DON'T MISS

RAMSES II, APPROX. 1200 BC — SALLE 12
The sphinx-guarded Egyptian Wing is the biggest display of Egyptian antiquities in the world after the Cairo museum—not surprising, considering that Egyptology as a Western concept was invented by a Frenchman, Champollion, founder of the Louvre's Egypt collection and translator of the hieroglyphics on the Rosetta Stone. This statue from the site of Tanis, presumed to be Ramses II, never fails to stop visitors' breath with its gleaming stone, beatific expression, and perfect proportions. ✛ *Sully, ground floor*

VENUS DE MILO, APPROX. 120 BC — SALLE 16
After countless photographs and bad reproductions, the original Aphrodite continues to dazzle. The armless statue, one of the most reproduced and recognizable works of art in the world, is actually as beautiful as they say. She was unearthed on the Greek island of Milos in the 19th century and sold for 6,000 francs to the French ambassador in Constantinople, who presented her to King Louis XVIII. ✛ *Sully, ground floor*

MEDIEVAL MOAT, 13TH CENTURY — MEDIEVAL LOUVRE
Wander around the perimeter of the solidly built original moat to reach the remarkable Salle Saint-Louis with its elegant columns and medieval artifacts. Keep an eye out for the parade helmet of Charles VI, which was dug up in 169 fragments and astonishingly reassembled. ✛ *Sully, lower ground floor*

THE TURKISH BATH, 1862 — SALLE 60
Though Jean-August-Dominique Ingres' (1780–1867) long-limbed women hardly look Turkish, they are singularly elegant and his polished immaculate style was imitated by an entire generation of French painters. This painting is a prime example of Orientalism, where Western artists played out fantasies of the Orient in their work. Popular as a society portrait painter, Ingres returned repeatedly to langorous nudes—compare the women of the *Turkish Bath* with the slinky figure in his *La Grande Odalisque*, in the Denon Wing. ✛ *Sully, second floor*

Ramses II

Venus de Milo

Medieval Moat

The Turkish Bath

5

IN FOCUS THE LOUVRE

THE DENON WING

COLLECTIONS

Ancient Egypt
Greek, Roman, & Etruscan
Antiquities
French Painting
Italian & Spanish Painting
Graphic Arts
Italian, Spanish, &
Northern Sculpture
African, Asian, Oceanic, &
American Arts
Arts of Islam

TIPS

■ Don't skip the coat check on the ground floor. Much of the museum is hot and stuffy.

■ Don't miss the glass case near *Winged Victory of Samothrace* on the first floor. It contains her two-fingered hand.

■ Need a bathroom? There are some tucked away at the end of the wing on the first floor near Salle 13.

Below Ground & Ground Floor. The stunning Arts of Islam wing with 30,000 square feet of gallery space is built into the Cour Visconti and topped with an undulating glass roof meant to evoke a floating head scarf. Here you'll find Europe's largest collection of treasures from across the Islamic world, including the Ottoman Empire. On the lower level, don't miss the Baptistery of Saint Louis, a 14th-century sculpted golden basin. The galleries to the south and east of the *Pyramide* entrance display early Renaissance Italian sculpture, including a 15th-century *Madonna and Child* by Florentine Dontallo (1386–1466). Drift upstairs to the Italian sculptures on the ground level, where you'll find the exquisite Michelangelo's *Slaves* (1513–15) in Salle 4.

First Floor. Walk up the marble Escalier Daru to discover the sublime **Winged Victory of Samothrace** (see right), cleaned in 2014. Then head to the stunning Galerie d'Apollon (Apollo Gallery). Built in 1661 but not finished until 1851, the hall was a model for Versailles's Hall of Mirrors.

Back out and into Paintings, you'll find four by Leonardo da Vinci (1452–1519). His enigmatic, androgynous St-John the Baptist hangs here, along with more overtly religious works such as the 1483 Virgin of the Rocks. Take a close look at the pretty portrait of La Belle Ferronnière, which Leonardo painted a decade before the **Mona Lisa** (see right); it will give you something to compare with Mona when you finally get to meet her in the Salle des Etats, near Salles 5 and 6. Head across to Salle 75 for an artistic 180°: the gleaming pomp and circumstance of a new empire with the **Coronation of Napoléon** (see right) by French classicist Jacques-Louis David (1748–1825).

In Salle 77 is the graphic 1819 **The Raft of the Medusa,** (see right) by Théodore Géricault (1791–1824).

DON'T MISS

MONA LISA, 1503   SALLE 7

The most famous painting in the world, *La Gioconda* (*La Joconde* in French) is tougher than she looks: the canvas was stolen from the Louvre by an Italian nationalist in 1911, recovered from a Florentine hotel, and survived an acid attack in 1956. She is believed to be the wife of Francesco del Giocondo, a Florentine millionaire, and was probably 24 when she sat for this painting; some historians believe the portrait was actually painted after her death. Either way, she has become immortal through da Vinci's ingenious "sfumato" technique, which combines glowing detail with soft, depth-filled brushwork. ✢ *Denon, first floor*

Mona Lisa

THE RAFT OF THE MEDUSA, 1819   SALLE 77

Théodore Géricault was inspired by the grim news report that survivors of a wrecked French merchant ship were left adrift on a raft without supplies. Géricault interviewed survivors, visited the morgue to draw corpses, and turned his painting of the disaster into a strong indictment of authority, the first time an epic historical painting had taken on current events in this way. Note the desperate energy from the pyramid construction of bodies on the raft and the manipulation of greenish light. ✢ *Denon, first floor*

The Raft of the Medusa

WINGED VICTORY OF SAMOTHRACE, 305 BC   STAIRS

Poised for flight at the top of the Escalier Daru, this exhilarating statue was found on a tiny Greek island in the northern Aegean. Depicted in the act of descending from Olympus, *Winged Victory*, or Nike, to the Ancient Greeks, was carved to commemorate the naval victory of Demetrius Poliorcetes over the Persians. ✢ *Denon, first floor*

Winged Victory of Samothrace

CORONATION OF NAPOLÉON, 1805   SALLE 75

Classicist Jacques-Louis David (1748–1825) was the ultimate painter-survivor: he began his career under the protection of the King, became official designer of the Revolutionary government, endured two rounds of exile, and became one of the greatest of Napoléon's painters. Here, David avoided the politically fraught moment of December 2, 1804—when Napoléon snatched the crown from the hands of Pope Pius VII to place it upon his own head—choosing instead the romantic moment when the new emperor turned to crown Joséphine. ✢ *Denon, first floor*

Detail from the Coronation of Napoléon

PLANNING YOUR VISIT

TOURS

Pick up a slick Nintendo 3DS multimedia guide at the entrance to each wing (€5); it has information on 250 artworks, four self-guided tours, and a GPS function so you can get your bearings.

There are 90-minute guided tours in English daily (€12, 11 am and noon). The meeting point is at "Accueil des Groups" under the pyramid. There are also free thematic leaflets to self-guide through a particular trail—some designed especially for kids. The Louvre has a phenomenal program of courses and workshops (mostly in French); see website for details.

ACCESSIBILITY

Wheelchair visitors or those with strollers can skip the long entry line and use the marvelous cylinder lift inside the entrance pyramid.

WITH KIDS

Begin your tour in the Sully Wing at the Medieval moat, which leads enticingly to the sphinx-guarded entrance of the Egyptian Wing, a must for mummy enthusiasts. For a more in-depth visit, you can reserve private kid-centric family tours such as the Paris Muse Clues. Don't forget the Tuileries is right next door (with carnival rides in summer).

ENTRY TIPS

You can order your ticket online (€15 plus €2 fee) at www.ticketlouvre.fr. Or save the fee and buy your ticket at the official Paris tourist office a short walk from the museum at 25 rue des Pyramides. See www.parisinfo.com for more information.

In high season, shorten your wait by avoiding the main entrance at the Pyramide and head for the entrance in the underground mall, Carrousel du Louvre. Automatic ticket machines are available. Note that crowds are thinner on Wednesday and Friday nights, when the museum is open late. Be sure to check the website for room closings; renovations are always taking place. Remember the Louvre is closed on Tuesday.

A WHIRLWIND TOUR

If you've come to Paris and feel you must go to the Louvre to see the Big Three—**Venus de Milo, Winged Victory,** and **Mona Lisa**—even though you'd rather be strolling along the Champs-Elysees, it can be done in an hour or less if you plan well. Start in Denon and head upstairs through Estruscan and Greek antiquities, walking down the long hall of sculptures until you see the Winged Victory in front of you. Take a right and head up the staircase through French painting to the Mona Lisa. Then go back down under the Pyramid to Sully to see the Venus de Milo.

✉ Palais du Louvre, Louvre/Tuileries
☎ 01-40-20-53-17 (information)
🌐 www.louvre.fr
🕐 Mon., Thurs., and weekends 9–6; Wed. and Fri. 9 am–9:45 pm; closed Tues.
Ⓜ Palais-Royal / Musée du Louvre

LOWER GROUND FLOOR

RICHELIEU

The Marly Horses

French Sculptures
17th-18th Cent.

Italian Sculptures
11th-15th Cent.

SULLY

Medieval Moat

Medieval Louvre

DENON

Arts of Islam

French Sculptures
500-1850

Mesopotamia

RICHELIEU

Near Eastern Antiquities

French Sculptures
1500-1850

Lamassu

GROUND FLOOR

Italian Sculptures
16th-19th Cent.;
Northern Sculptures
17th-19th Cent.

Pyramide

SULLY

Ramses II

Egyptian Antiquities

Venus de Milo

DENON

African Arts

Decorative Arts
500-1850

Etruscan and Roman Antiquities

RICHELIEU

Egyptian Antiquities

Objets d'Art
Napoléon III Apartments

Royal Apartmets of Napoleon III

FIRST FLOOR

Raft of the Medusa

Coronation of Napoléon

SULLY

Louvre History

U.S. and British Paintings

Mona Lisa

Winged Victory of Samothrace

DENON

Greek and Roman Antiquities
700 BC-400 AD

Spanish Paintings

Italian Paintings

French Paintings
19th Cent. (large)

Apollo Gallery

Northern Europe
1350-1850

RICHELIEU

Prints and Drawings
French 17th Cent.

The Lacemaker

SECOND FLOOR

French Paintings
1350-1850

SULLY

French Paintings
18th-19th Cent.

The Turkish Bath

DENON

French Paintings
19th Cent. (large)

garden, includes a portion of the city's 16th-century wall (you can see remnants on the lower floor). A small café and gift shop are here, too. ⊠ *Jardin des Tuileries at Pl. de la Concorde, Louvre* 🕾 *01–44–77–80–07* ⊕ *www.musee-orangerie.fr* 🎫 *€9; €16 joint ticket with Musée d'Orsay; €18.50 joint ticket with Giverny (open March-Nov.)* ⊙ *Closed Tues.* Ⓜ *Concorde.*

Fodor's Choice
★

Palais-Royal. The quietest, most romantic Parisian garden is enclosed within the former home of Cardinal Richelieu (1585–1642). It's the perfect place to while away an afternoon, cuddling with your sweetheart on a bench under the trees, soaking up the sunshine beside the fountain, or browsing the 400-year-old arcades that are now home to boutiques ranging from quirky (picture Anna Joliet's music boxes) to chic (think designs by Stella McCartney). One of the city's oldest restaurants is here, the haute-cuisine Le Grand Véfour, where brass plaques recall regulars like Napoléon and Victor Hugo. Built in 1629, the *palais* became royal when Richelieu bequeathed it to Louis XIII. Other famous residents include Jean Cocteau and Colette, who wrote of her pleasurable "country" view of the *province à Paris*. Today, the garden often plays host to giant-size temporary art installations sponsored by another tenant, the Ministry of Culture. The courtyard off Place Colette is outfitted with an eye-catching collection of squat black-and-white columns created in 1986 by artist Daniel Buren. ⊠ *Pl. du Palais-Royal, Louvre* Ⓜ *Palais-Royal–Louvre.*

Place de la Concorde. This square at the foot of the Champs-Élysées was originally named after Louis XV. It later became the Place de la Révolution, where crowds cheered as Louis XVI, Marie-Antoinette, and some 2,500 others lost their heads to the guillotine. Renamed Concorde in 1836, it got a new centerpiece: the 75-foot granite Obelisk of Luxor, a gift from Egypt quarried in the 8th century BC. Among the handsome 18th-century buildings facing the square is the Hôtel Crillon, which was originally built as a private home by Gabriel, the architect of Versailles's Petit Trianon. After a massive renovation that spanned four years, the Crillon's scaffolding came down in summer 2017 to reveal a stunning facelift. ⊠ *Rue Royale, Louvre* Ⓜ *Concorde.*

Place Vendôme. Jules-Hardouin Mansart, an architect of Versailles, designed this perfectly proportioned octagonal plaza near the Tuileries in 1702; and, to maintain a uniform appearance, he gave the surrounding *hôtels particuliers* (private mansions) identical facades. It was originally called Place des Conquêtes to extoll the military conquests of Louis XIV, whose statue on horseback graced the center until Revolutionaries destroyed it in 1792. Later, Napoléon ordered his likeness erected atop a 144-foot column modestly modeled after Rome's Trajan Column. But that, too, was toppled in 1871 by painter Gustave Courbet and his band of radicals. The Third Republic raised a new column and sent Courbet the bill, though he died in exile before paying it. The Ritz, a longtime tenant, picked up the tab for a 2016 renovation teamed with the hotel's own four-year clean-up. Chopin lived and died at No. 12, which is also where Napoléon III enjoyed trysts with his mistress; since 1902 it has been home to the high-end jeweler Chaumet. ⊠ *Pl. Vendôme, Louvre* Ⓜ *Tuileries.*

Fodor's Choice **Rue Montorgueil.** Rue Montorgueil was once the gritty oyster hub of Les
★ Halles. Now lined with food shops and cafés, the cobbled street whose
name translates to Mount Pride is the heart of one of the city's trendiest neighborhoods. History runs deep here. Monet captured the scene
in 1878 when Montorgueil was ablaze with tricolor flags during the
World's Fair (see it in the Musée d'Orsay). Honoré de Balzac and his
19th-century band of scribes frequented Au Rocher de Cancale at No.
78, whose famously crumbling facade has been painstakingly restored
with gilt panache. Other addresses have been around for centuries:
Stohrer at No. 51 has been baking elaborate pastries since 1730; and
L'Escargot Montorgueil at No. 38, a favorite of Charlie Chaplin, is still
graced by a giant golden snail. Relative newcomers include the luxury
Nuxe spa at Nos. 32 and 34. Browse the boutiques on Rue Montmartre,
which runs parallel, or shop for cookware at Julia Child's old haunt, E.
Dehillerin, still in business at 18–20 rue Coquillière. Rue Tiquetonne
is rife with bistros, and once-sleepy Rue St-Sauveur became a destina-
tion when the Experimental Cocktail Club (No. 37) moved in, joined
by other trendy eating and drinking spots. Even Rue St-Denis, once a
scruffy red-light district, is now a hipster fave with bar-restaurants like
Le Pas Sage at the entrance of the lovely covered arcade, Passage du
Grand Cerf. ⊠ *Rue Montorgueil, off Rue de Turbigo, Louvre* Ⓜ *Sentier,
Les Halles.*

St-Eustache. Built as the market neighborhood's answer to Notre-Dame,
this massive church is decidedly squeezed into its surroundings. Constructed between 1532 and 1640 with foundations dating to 1200, the
church mixes a Gothic exterior, complete with impressive flying buttresses, and a Renaissance interior. On the east end (Rue Montmartre),
Dutch master Rubens's *Pilgrims of Emmaus* (1611) hangs in a small
chapel. Two chapels to the left is Keith Haring's *The Life of Christ,* a
triptych in bronze and white-gold patina: it was given to the church
after the artist's death in 1990, in recognition of the parish's efforts to
help people with AIDS. On the Rue Montmartre side of the church, look
for the small door to Saint Agnes's crypt, topped with a stone plaque
noting the date, 1213, below a curled fish, an indication the patron
made his fortune in fish. ⊠ *2 impasse St-Eustache, Louvre* ⊕ *www.saint-
eustache.org for concert info* Ⓜ *Les Halles; RER: Châtelet–Les Halles.*

WORTH NOTING

Comédie Française. Refined productions by Molière and Racine, and
modern interpretations by masters such as Robert Wilson, are staged
regularly (though only in French) at the vintage venue where actress
Sarah Bernhardt began her career. Founded in 1680 by Louis XIV, the
theater finally opened its doors to the public in 1799. It nearly burned to
the ground a hundred years later. The current building dates from 1900.
⊠ *Salle Richelieu, 1 pl. Colette, Louvre* ⊕ *www.comedie-francaise.fr*
Ⓜ *Palais-Royal–Louvre.*

Église de la Madeleine. With its rows of uncompromising columns, this
enormous neoclassical edifice in the center of Place de la Madeleine
was consecrated as a church in 1842, nearly 78 years after construction

began. Initially planned as a Baroque building, it was later razed and begun anew by an architect who had the Roman Pantheon in mind. Interrupted by the Revolution, the site was razed yet again when Napoléon decided to make it into a Greek temple dedicated to the glory of his army. Those plans changed when the army was defeated and the emperor deposed. Other ideas for the building included making it into a train station, a market, and a library. Finally, Louis XVIII decided to make it a church, which it still is today. Classical concerts are held here regularly, some of them free. ☒ *Pl. de la Madeleine, Louvre* ☏ *01–44–51–69–00* ⊕ *www.eglise-lamadeleine.com* Ⓜ *Madeleine.*

Église St-Germain-l'Auxerrois. Founded in 500 AD, this grand church across from the Louvre's eastern end is one of the city's oldest. It was destroyed during the Norman siege in 885–886, rebuilt in the 11th century, and subsequently expanded until the current edifice was finished in 1580. The bell, named Marie, dates from 1527. ☒ *2 pl. du Louvre, Louvre* ☏ *01–42–60–13–96* ⊕ *www.saintgermainauxerrois.fr* ☉ *Closed Mon.* Ⓜ *Louvre-Rivoli.*

Jeu de Paume. This Napoléon III–era building at the north entrance of the Jardin des Tuileries began life in 1861 as a place to play *jeu de paume* (or "palm game"), a forerunner of tennis. It later served as a transfer point for art looted by the Germans during World War II. Now it displays some of the city's best photography, serving as an ultramodern, white-walled showcase for up-and-comers as well as icons such as Diane Arbus, Richard Avedon, Cindy Sherman, and Robert Frank. ☒ *1 pl. de la Concorde, Louvre* ☏ *01–47–03–12–50* ⊕ *www.jeudepaume. org* ☒ *€10* ☉ *Closed Mon.* Ⓜ *Concorde.*

Passage du Grand-Cerf. This stately glass-roofed arcade was built in 1825 and expertly renovated in 1988. Today it's home to about 20 shops, many of them small designers selling original jewelry, accessories, and housewares. If it's apéritif time, stop by the popular Le Pas Sage, with a wine bar and a restaurant flanking either side of the entrance at Rue St-Denis. ☒ *Entrances at 145 rue St-Denis and 8 rue Dussoubs, Louvre* Ⓜ *Étienne Marcel.*

FAMILY **Tour Jean Sans Peur.** This fascinating little tower is the only remnant of a sprawling complex built on the edge of the original city walls in 1369. It is named for Jean Sans Peur (John the Fearless), the Duke of Burgundy, who gained power in 1407 after ordering the assassination of his rival, the king's brother. In 1409, as civil war raged, he had the tower erected and put his bedroom on a high floor with a bird's-eye view of approaching enemies. Carved into the vaulted second-floor ceiling—a masterwork of medieval architecture—is an ornate sculpture of an oak tree entwined with plants representing the duke's family. Children (and curious adults) will enjoy the climb up to see the restored red-velvet-lined latrine, a state-of-the-art comfort in its time. Kitschy costumed mannequins and medieval-themed exhibits covering subjects from food to furniture to hygiene lend the tower added kid appeal. Be sure to ask for English information at the entry. ☒ *20 rue Étienne Marcel, Louvre* ☏ *01–40–26–20–28* ⊕ *www.tourjeansanspeur.com* ☒ *€6; €4 exhibits only* ☉ *Closed Mon. and Tues.* Ⓜ *Étienne Marcel.*

LES GRANDS BOULEVARDS

Getting Oriented

GETTING HERE	TOP REASONS TO GO
This neighborhood covers parts of the 2e, 3e, 8e, and 9e arrondissements. Take the métro to the Opéra station, named for the opulent opera house. Just behind it, you can find the department stores Galeries Lafayette and Au Printemps, each with three buildings (women's, men's, home) along Baron Haussmann's wide avenues known as the Grands Boulevards. If you're planning to visit the numerous small museums, take the métro to Parc Monceau.	**Les Grands Magasins.** Sample a new perfume under the magnificent dome at Galeries Lafayette; update your look, wander the sumptuous food halls, or gaze at Parisian rooftops from the 8th-floor outdoor restaurant terraces at Au Printemps. **Opéra Garnier.** It may not be haunted by the Phantom, but this 19th-century opera house still dazzles. Enjoy a ballet or an opera, take the guided tour, or simply ogle the halls bedecked in marble and gold leaf. **Parc Monceau.** Join the well-dressed children of well-heeled Parisians and frolic on some of the prettiest lawns in the city. **Les Passages Couverts.** Stroll the passages Jouffroy, Verdeau, and Panoramas to experience what the original shopping malls were like 200 years ago.

Les Grands Boulevards

6

BEST CAFÉS

Café de la Paix. Once described as the "center of the civilized world," this grand café was a meeting place for the Belle Époque's glitterati. It's an elegant spot to enjoy a drink (or meal) in the shadow of the Opéra Garnier. ✉ *5 pl. de l'Opéra, Grands Boulevards* ☎ *01–40–07–36–36* ⊕ *www. cafedelapaix.fr* Ⓜ *Opéra.*

Café Le Brebant. Night owls will love that this popular brasserie—a favorite of Parisian film folk—is open until 5 am daily. The rest of us can just enjoy the classic French fare, eye-popping decor, and friendly service. ✉ *32 bd. Poissonnière, Grands Boulevards* ☎ *01–47–70–01–02* Ⓜ *Grands Boulevards.*

Delaville Café. This edgy café is a favorite with locals. Open late, it's best for an evening apéritif and snack. ✉ *34 bd. de Bonne Nouvelle, Grands Boulevards* ☎ *01–48–24–48–09* ⊕ *www.delavillecafe.com* Ⓜ *Bonne Nouvelle.*

MAKING THE MOST OF YOUR TIME

If you're a serious shopper, plan on a day-long visit to this neighborhood, beginning with the department stores near the Opéra métro stop. Nearly every French chain has a shop dotting the boulevard, which changes names several times (Boulevard Haussmann, Montmartre, Poissonnière, de Bonne Nouvelle, etc.) as it stretches from west to east.

If shopping isn't your bag, plan on a long afternoon's visit: tour the Opéra Garnier and one or two museums, or bring a picnic lunch to lovely Parc Monceau on the western edge.

Sightseeing
★★★
Dining
★★★
Lodging
★★★★★
Shopping
★★★★★
Nightlife
★★★★★

In Belle Époque Paris, the Grands Boulevards were the place to see and be seen: in the cafés, at the opera, or in the ornate *passages couverts* (glass-roofed arcades that served as the world's first malls). If you close your eyes, you can almost imagine the Grands Boulevards immortalized on canvas by the Impressionists, with well-attired Parisians strolling wide avenues dotted with shops, cafés, and horse-drawn carriages—all set against a backdrop of stately Haussmannian buildings. Today, despite the chain stores, sidewalk vendors, and fast-food joints, the Grands Boulevards remain the city's shopping epicenter, home to the most popular department stores, Galeries Lafayette and Au Printemps, near Place de l'Opéra.

Updated by
Jack Vermee

Shopping aside, the Grands Boulevards are a cultural destination anchored by the magnificent **Opéra Garnier,** commissioned by Napoléon III. The neighborhood is also home to some of the city's best small museums, all former private collections housed in 19th-century *hôtels particuliers* (mansions) that alone are worth the trip. The exquisite **Musée Jacquemart-André** displays an impressive collection of Italian Renaissance art, while the jewel-box **Musée Nissim de Camondo** remembers one family's tragic end. The **Musée Cernuschi** has a dazzling array of Asian art, and the **Musée National Gustave-Moreau** is an offbeat tribute to the Symbolist master.

TOP ATTRACTIONS

Au Printemps. Encompassing a trio of upscale department stores (Printemps Mode, Printemps Beauté-Maison-Enfant, and Printemps Homme), this vast, venerable retailer has been luring shoppers since 1865. Besides the clothes, shoes, housewares, and everything else, there are appealing lunch options here. Two floors of the main building (Printemps Homme) have been completely renovated and are now home to Printemps du Goût, a celebration of French gourmet cuisine. If you are a do-it-yourself-er, you can find the best of French foodstuffs on the seventh floor. But if you want to eat in style while taking in spectacular views, either from inside via floor-to-ceiling windows or outside on the wrap-around terrace, continue on to the eighth floor, where four noted chefs and food artisans—master cheesemaker Laurent Dubois, chef pâtissier Christophe Michalak, artisanal baker Gontran Cherrier, and master chef Akrame—oversee a gourmet cornucopia. ⊠ *64 bd. Haussmann, Grands Boulevards* ☎ *01–42–82–50–00* ⊕ *www.printemps.com* Ⓜ *Havre-Caumartin, St-Lazare.*

FAMILY **Choco-Story Paris: Le Musée Gourmand du Chocolat.** Considering that a daily dose of chocolate is practically obligatory in Paris, it's hard to believe that this spot (opened in 2010) is the city's first museum dedicated to the sweet stuff. Exhibits on three floors tell the story of chocolate from the earliest traces of the "divine nectar" in Mayan and Aztec cultures, through to its introduction in Europe by the Spanish, who added milk and sugar to the spicy dark brew and launched a Continental craze. There are detailed explanations in English, with many for the kids. While the production of chocolate is a major topic, there is also a respectable collection of some 1,000 chocolate-related artifacts, such as terra-cotta Mayan sipping vessels (they blew into straws to create foam) and delicate chocolate pots in fine porcelain that were favored by the French royal court. Frequent chocolate-making demonstrations finish with a free tasting. ⊠ *28 bd. de Bonne Nouvelle, Grands Boulevards* ☎ *01–42–29–68–60* ⊕ *www.museeduchocolat.fr* ⊠ *€11; €14 with a cup of hot chocolate* Ⓜ *Bonne-Nouvelle, Strasbourg, St-Denis.*

Galeries Lafayette. The stunning Byzantine glass *coupole* (dome) of the city's most famous department store is not to be missed. Amble to the center of the main store, amid the perfumes and cosmetics, and look up. If you're not in the mood for shopping, visit the (free) first-floor Galerie des Galeries, an art gallery devoted to fashion, applied arts, and design; or have lunch at one of the restaurants, including a rooftop bar and restaurant in the main store. On your way down, the top floor of the main store is a good place to pick up interesting Parisian souvenirs. Across the street in Galeries Maison, the excellent Lafayette Gourmet food hall has one of the city's best selections of delicacies. Try a green-tea éclair from Japanese–French baker Sadaharu Aoki—and don't miss the Bordeauxthèque on Galeries Maison's first floor, where €30,000 bottles of wine are on display. ⊠ *35–40 bd. Haussmann, Grands Boulevards* ☎ *01–42–82–34–56* ⊕ *www.galerieslafayette.com* Ⓜ *Chaussée d'Antin, Havre-Caumartin.*

Fodor's Choice ★ **Musée Cernuschi.** Wealthy Milanese banker and patriot Enrico (Henri) Cernuschi fled to Paris in 1850 after the new Italian government collapsed, only to be arrested during the 1871 Paris Commune. He subsequently decided to wait out the unrest by traveling and collecting Asian art. Upon his return 18 months later, he had a special mansion built on the edge of Parc Monceau to house his treasures, notably a two-story bronze Buddha from Japan. Today, this well-appointed museum contains France's second-most-important collection of Asian art, after the Musée Guimet. Cernuschi had an eye not only for the bronze pieces he adored but also for Neolithic pottery (8000 BC), *mingqi* tomb figures (300–900 AD), and an impressive array of terra-cotta figures from various dynasties. A collection highlight is La Tigresse, a bronze wine vessel in the shape of a roaring feline (11th century BC) purchased after Cernuschi's death. Although the museum is free, there is a charge for temporary exhibitions: previous shows have featured Japanese drawings, Iranian sculpture, and Imperial Chinese bronzes. ✉ *7 av. Velasquez, Grands Boulevards* ☎ *01–53–96–21–50* ⊕ *www.cernuschi.paris.fr* ✉ *Free; €8 for temporary exhibitions* ⊘ *Closed Mon.* Ⓜ *Monceau.*

> ### DID YOU KNOW?
>
> The inspiration for the mysterious lake underneath the Opéra Garnier in *The Phantom of the Opera* was sparked when construction of the building was delayed while the marshy site was drained. Rumors of an underground river began to circulate, and from there it was a small leap for Gaston Leroux to invent the Phantom sailing on a subterranean waterway. In the movie version, a vengeful Phantom sent the opera's chandelier crashing into the audience, an idea also drawn from real life: in 1896 one of the counterweights of the 8-ton crystal chandelier fell, crushing a woman in her red velvet seat.

Fodor's Choice
★

Musée Jacquemart-André. Perhaps the city's best small museum, the opulent Musée Jacquemart-André is home to a huge collection of art and furnishings lovingly assembled in the late 19th century by banking heir Edouard André and his artist wife, Nélie Jacquemart. Their midlife marriage in 1881 raised eyebrows—he was a dashing bachelor and a Protestant, and she, no great beauty, hailed from a modest Catholic family. Still, theirs was a happy union fused by a common passion for art. For six months every year, the couple traveled, most often to Italy, where they hunted down works from the Renaissance, their preferred period. Their collection also includes French painters Fragonard, Jacques-Louis David, and François Boucher, plus Dutch masters Van Dyke and Rembrandt. The Belle Époque mansion itself is a major attraction. The elegant ballroom, equipped with collapsible walls operated by then-state-of-the-art hydraulics, could hold 1,000 guests. The winter garden was a wonder of its day, spilling into the *fumoir*, where André would share cigars with the *grands hommes* (important men) of the day. You can tour the separate bedrooms—his in dusty pink, hers in pale yellow. The former dining room, now an elegant café, features a ceiling by Tiepolo. Don't forget to pick up the free audioguide in English, and do inquire about the current temporary exhibition , which is usually top-notch. Plan on a Sunday visit and enjoy the popular brunch (€29.30) in the café from 11 to 2:30. Reservations are not accepted, so come early or late to avoid waiting in line. ✉ *158 bd. Haussmann, Grands Boulevards* ☎ *01–45–62–11–59* ⊕ *www.musee-jacquemart-andre.com* ✉ *€14; €3 for temporary exhibitions* Ⓜ *St-Philippe-du-Roule, Miromesnil.*

CLOSE UP

Paris's Covered Arcades

Before there were the *grands magas-ins,* there were the *passages couverts,* covered arcades that offered the early-19th-century Parisian shopper a hodgepodge of shops under one roof and a respite from the mud and grit of streets that did not have sidewalks. Until the rise of department stores in the latter part of the century, they would rule as the top places to wander, as well as shop. Technical and architectural wonders of the time, the vaulting structures of iron and frosted glass inspired artists and writers such as Émile Zola.

Of the 150 arcades built around Paris in the early 1800s, only about a dozen are still in business today, mostly in the 2e and 9e arrondissements. Two arcades still going strong are the fabulously restored **Galerie Vivienne** (*4 rue Petits Champs, 2e*) and the **Galerie Véro-Dodat** (*19 rue Jean-Jacques Rousseau, 1er*), both lined with unique and glamorous boutiques.

Three other modest passages enjoying a renaissance can be found end to end off the Grands Boulevards, east of Place de l'Opéra. Begin with the most refined, the **Passage Jouffroy**

(*10–12 bd. Montmartre, 9e*), which is home to the Musée Grévin and the well-regarded, budget-friendly Hôtel Chopin. There's an eclectic array of shops such as M.G.W. Segas at No. 34, where the three Segas brothers sell a wildly eccentric collection of furnishings and canes capped with animal heads and whatnot. You can outfit your dollhouse at Pain D'épices (No. 29), which stocks thousands of miniatures. Pop out at the northern end of Passage Jouffroy and cross Rue de la Grange-Batelière into the **Passage Verdeau** (*9e*), where you can pick up some antique candlesticks—or a cow skull—at the quirky, red-walled Valence gallery at No. 22. On the southern end of the Passage Jouffroy, across Boulevard Montmartre, is the **Passage des Panoramas** (*2e*). The granddaddy of the arcades, opened in 1800, became the first public space in Paris equipped with gaslights in 1817. A few philatelist shops remain, though the arcade is now dominated by restaurants, including two popular wine bar–bistros (Racines at No. 8 and Coinstot Vino at No. 26, bis), as well as Paris's original gluten-free restaurant (Noglu, at No. 16).

6

OFF THE BEATEN PATH

Musée National Gustave-Moreau. Visiting the quirky town house and studio of painter Gustave Moreau (1826–98) is well worth your time. With an eye on his legacy, Moreau—a high priest of the Symbolist movement—created an enchanting gallery to showcase his dark paintings, drawings, and sculpture. The recently refurbished first-floor rooms, closed to the public for more than a decade, now trace Moreau's "sentimental journey"; their walls are festooned with family portraits and works offered by close friends and allies like Chassériau, Fromentin, and Degas. The two light-flooded top floors house Moreau's vast workshops, where hundreds of paintings, watercolors, and more than 4,000 drawings give a broad overview of his techniques and subjects. Some of the pieces appear unfinished, such as *Unicorns* (No. 213) inspired by the medieval tapestries in the Musée de Cluny: Moreau refused to work on it further, spurning the wishes of a wealthy would-be patron. His interpretation of Biblical scenes and Greek mythology combine flights of fantasy with a keen use of color, shadow, and tracings influenced by Persian and Indian miniatures. There are wax sculptures and cupboards with sliding vertical doors containing small-format paintings. The Symbolists loved objects, and Moreau was no different. His cramped private apartment on the second floor is jam-packed with bric-a-brac, and artworks cover every inch of the walls. ⊠ *14 rue de la Rochefoucauld, Grands Boulevards* ☎ *01–48–74–38–50* ⊕ *www.musee-moreau.fr* ▨ *€5* ⊘ *Closed Tues.* Ⓜ *Trinité, St-Georges.*

Fodor's Choice
★
Opéra Garnier. Haunt of the Phantom of the Opera and the real-life inspiration for Edgar Degas's dancer paintings, the gorgeous Opéra Garnier is one of two homes of the National Opera of Paris. The building, the Palais Garnier, was begun in 1860 by then-unknown architect Charles Garnier, who finished his masterwork 15 long years later, way over budget. Festooned with (real) gold leaf, colored marble, paintings, and sculpture from the top artists of the day, the opera house was about as subtle as Versailles and sparked controversy in post-Revolutionary France. The sweeping marble staircase, in particular, drew criticism from a public skeptical of its extravagance. But Garnier, determined to make a landmark that would last forever, spared no expense. The magnificent grand foyer is one of the most exquisite salons in France. In its heyday, the cream of Paris society strolled all 59 yards of the vast hall at intermission, admiring themselves in the towering mirrors. To see the opera house, buy a ticket for an unguided visit, which allows access to most parts of the building, including a peek into the auditorium. There is also a small ballet museum with a few works by Degas and the tutu worn by prima ballerina Anna Pavlova when she danced her epic *Dying Swan* in 1905. To get to it, pass through the unfinished entrance built for Napoléon III and his carriage (construction was abruptly halted when the emperor abdicated in 1870). On the upper level, you can see a sample of the auditorium's original classical ceiling, which was later replaced with a modern version painted by a septuagenarian Marc Chagall. His trademark willowy figures encircling the dazzling crystal chandelier—today the world's third largest—shocked an unappreciative public upon its debut in 1964. Critics who fret that Chagall's masterpiece clashes with the fussy crimson-and-gilt decor can take some comfort in knowing that the original ceiling is preserved underneath, encased in a plastic dome.

The Opéra Garnier plays host to the Paris Ballet as well as a few operas each season (most are performed at the Opéra Bastille). If you're planning to see a performance, tickets cost €10–€231 and should be reserved as soon as they go on sale—typically a month ahead at the box office, earlier by phone or online; otherwise, try your luck last minute. To learn about the building's history, and get a taste of aristocratic life during the Second Empire, take an entertaining English-language tour (daily at 11 and 2:30) or rent an audioguide (€5) and proceed at your own pace. To complete the experience, dine at L'Opéra, the contemporary on-site restaurant run by chef Chihiro Yamazaki; or browse through the Palais Garnier gift shop for ballet-inspired wares, fine Bernardaud porcelain depicting the famous Chagall ceiling, and an exceptional selection of themed DVDs and books. ⊠ *Pl. de l'Opéra, Grands Boulevards*

☏ 08–92–89–90–90 (€0.35 per min), 01–71–25–24–23 from outside France ⊕ www.operadeparis.fr ▢ €11; €12 with temporary exhibition; €16 for tours Ⓜ Opéra.

FAMILY   **Parc Monceau.** This exquisitely landscaped park began in 1778 as the Duc de Chartres's private garden. Though some of the land was sold off under the Second Empire (creating the exclusive real estate that now borders the park), the refined atmosphere and some of the fanciful faux ruins have survived. Immaculately dressed children play under the watchful eye of their nannies, while lovers cuddle on the benches. In 1797 André Garnerin, the world's first-recorded parachutist, staged a landing in the park. The rotunda—known as the Chartres Pavilion—is surely the city's grandest public restroom: it started life as a tollhouse. ✉ Entrances on Bd. de Courcelles, Av. Velasquez, Av. Ruysdaël, Av. van Dyck, Grands Boulevards Ⓜ Monceau.

WORTH NOTING

Chapelle Expiatoire (Atonement Chapel). Commissioned in 1815, this neoclassical temple marks the original burial site of Louis XVI and Marie-Antoinette. After the deposed monarchs took their turns at the guillotine on Place de la Concorde, their bodies were taken to a nearby mass grave. A loyalist marked their place, and their remains were eventually retrieved by the dead king's brother, Louis XVIII, who moved them to the Basilica of St. Denis. He then ordered the monument (which translates to Expiatory, or Atonement, Chapel) built on this spot, in what is now the leafy Square Louis XVI off Boulevard Haussmann. Two massive white-marble sculptures by François Joseph Bosio show the king and queen being succored by angels, while stone tablets below are inscribed with the last missives of the doomed royals, including pleas to God to forgive their Revolutionary enemies. ✉ Square Louis-XVI, 29 rue Pasquier, Grands Boulevards ☏ 01–42–65–35–80 ⊕ www.chapelle-expiatoire-paris.fr ▢ €6 ⊘ Closed Sun., Mon., and Wed. in Oct.–Mar.; and Sun. and Mon. in Apr.–Sept. Ⓜ St-Augustin.

Fragonard Musée du Parfum. More of a showroom than a museum, the small exhibit run by parfumier Fragonard above its boutique on Rue Scribe is heavy on decorative objects associated with perfume, including crystal bottles, gloves, and assorted bibelots. The shop is a good place to find gifts, like body lotion made with royal jelly, myriad soaps, and, of course, perfume. True fragrance aficionados can double their pleasure by visiting the Théâtre Musée des Capucines-Fragonard, another minimuseum nearby at 39 boulevard des Capucines. ✉ 3–5 Sq. de l'Opéra Louis Jouvet, Grands Boulevards ☏ 01–40–06–10–09 ⊕ musee-parfum-paris.fragonard.com ▢ Free ⊘ Closed Sun. Ⓜ Opéra.

Hôtel Drouot. Hidden away in a small antiques district, not far from the Opéra Garnier, is Paris's central auction house. With everything from old clothes to haute-couture gowns and from tchotchkes to ornate Chinese lacquered boxes, rare books, and wine, Drouot sells it all. Anyone can attend the sales and viewings, which draw a mix of art dealers, ladies who lunch, and art amateurs hoping to discover an unknown masterpiece. Check the website to see what's on the block.

6

Don't miss the small galleries and antiques dealers in the Quartier Drouot, a warren of small streets around the auction house, notably on Rues Rossini and de la Grange-Batelière. ⊠ *9 rue Drouot, Grands Boulevards* ☎ *01–48–00–20–20* ⊕ *www.drouot.com* 🖭 *Free* ⊘ *Closed Sun.* Ⓜ *Richelieu-Drouot.*

Musée de la Vie Romantique. A visit to the charming Museum of Romantic Life, dedicated to novelist George Sand (1804–76), will transport you to the countryside. Occupying a pretty 1830s mansion in a tree-lined courtyard, the small permanent collection features drawings by Delacroix and Ingres, among others, though Sand is the undisputed star. Displays include glass cases stuffed with her jewelry and even a mold of the hand of composer Frédéric Chopin—one of her many lovers. The museum, about a five-minute walk from the Musée National Gustave-Moreau, is in a picturesque neighborhood once called New Athens, a reflection of the architectural tastes of the writers and artists who lived there. There is usually an interesting temporary exhibit here, too. The garden café (open mid-March to mid-October) is a lovely spot for lunch or afternoon tea. ⊠ *16 rue Chaptal, Grands Boulevards* ☎ *01–55–31–95–67* ⊕ *www.museevieromantique.paris.fr* 🖭 *Free; €5 temporary exhibits* ⊘ *Closed Mon.* Ⓜ *Blanche, Pigalle, St-Georges.*

FAMILY **Musée Grévin.** If you like wax museums, this one founded in 1882 ranks among the best. Pay the steep entry price and ascend a grand Phantom-of-the-Opera–like staircase into the Palais des Mirages, a mirrored salon from the 1900 Paris Exposition that transforms into a hokey light-and-sound show the kids will love (it was a childhood favorite of designer Jean-Paul Gaultier). From there, get set for a cavalcade of nearly 300 statues, from Elvis to Ernest Hemingway, Picasso to Barack Obama. Every king of France is here, along with Michael Jackson and George Clooney, plus scores of French singers and celebrities. ⊠ *Passage Jouffroy, 10 bd. Montmartre, Grands Boulevards* ☎ *01–47–70–85–05* ⊕ *www.grevin-paris.com/fr* 🖭 *From €18* Ⓜ *Grands Boulevards.*

Musée Nissim de Camondo. The story of the Camondo family is steeped in tragedy, and it's all recorded within the walls of this superb museum. Patriarch Moïse de Camondo, born in Istanbul to a successful banking family, built his showpiece mansion in 1911 in the style of the Petit Trianon at Versailles and stocked it with some of the most exquisite furniture, wainscoting, and bibelots of the mid-to-late 18th century. Despite his vast wealth and purported charm, his wife left him five years after their marriage. Then his son, Nissim, was killed in World War I. Upon Moïse's death in 1935, the house and its contents were left to the state as a museum named for his lost son. A few years later, daughter Béatrice, her husband, and two children were murdered at Auschwitz. No heirs remained and the Camondo name died out. Today, the house remains an impeccable tribute to Moïse's life. ⊠ *63 rue de Monceau, Grands Boulevards* ☎ *01–53–89–06–50* ⊕ *madparis.fr/francais/musees/musee-nissim-de-camondo* 🖭 *€9; €13 joint ticket with Musée des Arts Décoratifs* ⊘ *Closed Mon. and Tues.* Ⓜ *Villiers, Monceau.*

MONTMARTRE

Getting Oriented

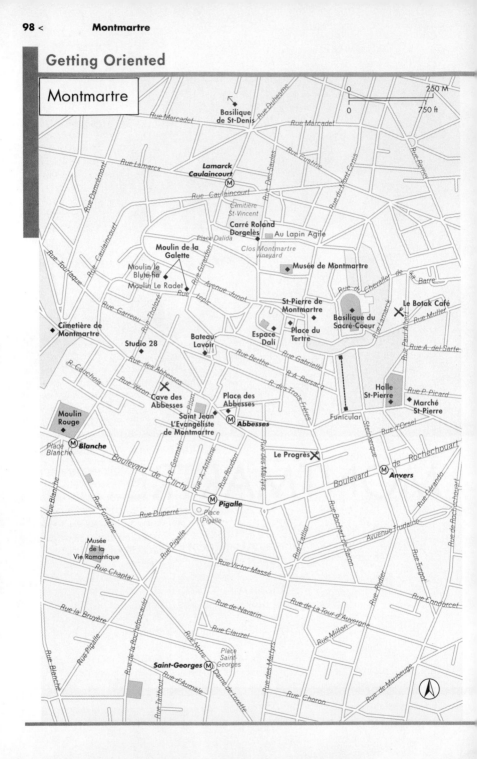

Montmartre

250 M
750 ft

Rue Marcadet
Basilique de St-Denis
Rue Marcadet
Rue Duhesme
Rue Marcadet
Rue Lamarcx
Rue Damrémont
Rue des Saules
Rue Cristino
Rue du Mont-Cenis
Rue Ramey
Lamarck Caulaincourt
Rue Caulaincourt
Cimetière St-Vincent
Carré Roland Dorgelès
Au Lapin Agile
Rue Toullaque
Rue Caulaincourt
Place Dalida
Clos Montmartre vineyard
Moulin de la Galette
Moulin le Blute-fin
Moulin Le Radet
Rue Lepic
Avenue Junot
Rue Girardon
Musée de Montmartre
Rue du Chevalier de la Barre
Rue du Mont-Cenis
Le Botak Café
St-Pierre de Montmartre
Basilique du Sacré-Coeur
Rue Muller
Rue Lamarck
Rue Paul-Albert
Cimetière de Montmartre
Rue Garreau
Rue Tholoze
Studio 28
Bateau-Lavoir
Espace Dalí
Place du Tertre
Rue A. del Sarte
R. Cauchois
Rue des Abbesses
Rue Berthe
Rue Gabrielle
R.A. Barsacq
Halle St-Pierre
Rue P. Picard
Rue Véron
Cave des Abbesses
Place des Abbesses
R. des Trois-Frères
Marché St-Pierre
Moulin Rouge
Saint Jean L'Evangéliste de Montmartre
Abbesses
Rue Steinkerque
Funicular
Rue d'Orsel
Place Blanche
Blanche
Boulevard de Clichy
Rue A-Antoine
Rue Ravignan
Rue des Martyrs
Le Progrès
Boulevard
de Rochechouart
Anvers
Rue Blanche
Rue Germain-Pilon
Rue Fontaine
Pigalle
Place Pigalle
Rue Duperré
Rue Houdon
Rue Frochot
Rue Jean-Baptiste Pigalle
Rue Bochart de Saron
Avenue Trudaine
Rue Gérando
Rue de Rochechouart
Musée de la Vie Romantique
Rue Pigalle
Rue Chaptal
Rue Victor Massé
Rue Laffitte
Rue Rodier
Rue Turgot
Rue la Bruyère
Rue de Navarin
Rue de La Tour d'Auvergne
Rue Condorcet
Rue Pigalle
Rue Notre-Dame-de-Lorette
Rue Clauzel
Rue Milton
Rue de la Rochefoucauld
Place Saint-Georges
Saint-Georges
Rue Choron
Rue Blanche
Rue Taitbout
Rue d'Aumale

TOP REASONS TO GO

Basilique du Sacré-Coeur. The best view of Paris is worth the climb—or the funicular ride—especially at twilight when the city lights create a magnificent panorama below the hill of Montmartre.

Place du Tertre. This bustling square beside Sacré-Coeur teems with crowds of tourists and hordes of street artists clamoring to paint them.

Place des Abbesses. Capture the village ambience that makes Montmartre special by exploring the tiny streets branching out from this picturesque square.

Carré Roland Dorgelès. Bring your camera to this little square overlooking a pair of classic Montmartre sights: the city's only vineyard and the famous Au Lapin Agile cabaret.

MAKING THE MOST OF YOUR TIME

Devote a day to this neighborhood if you want to see more than the obligatory Sacré-Coeur Basilica. If possible, avoid weekends, when the narrow—and extremely hilly—streets are jam-packed.

GETTING HERE

Montmartre is in the 18e arrondissement. Take Line 2 to Anvers métro station, and then take the funicular (one métro ticket) up to Sacré-Coeur. Or take Line 12 to Abbesses station and take your time wandering the cobbled streets and staircases that lead up to the basilica. For a scenic tour, hop the public bus, Montmartrobus (one métro ticket). An easy starting point is the métro station Jules-Joffrin (Line 12): the bus winds up the hilly streets, with a convenient stop at Sacré-Coeur. Alternatively, pile the kids onto Le Petit Train de Montmartre (€4.50–€6.50), a bus disguised as a minitrain that runs a circuit every 30 minutes (every hour in winter) from Place Blanche.

BEST CAFÉS

Cave des Abbesses. Locals head to this charming retro-looking *caviste* (wineshop) and wine bar for a glass of something special with a side of oysters, or perhaps La Grande Mixte, a platter of charcuterie, terrine, and cheese (€15). ⊠ *43 rue des Abbesses, Montmartre* ☎ *01–42–52–81–54* ⊘ *Closed Mon.* Ⓜ *Abbesses.*

Le Botak Café. On the eastern side of Sacré-Coeur, at the bottom of the stairs, you'll find the leafy Square Louise Marie and this little café, which serves a small, ever-changing menu of French home cooking. The daily lunch specials (€16 for two courses and a glass of wine) are a great deal, but service can sometimes be slow when it's busy. ⊠ *1 rue Paul Albert, Montmartre* ☎ *01–46–06–98–30* ⊘ *Closed Sun. nights in winter* Ⓜ *Anvers, Château Rouge.*

Le Progrès. This photo op–ready corner café draws a quirky mix of hipsters, artists, and discriminating tourists. The food is good and includes classics like steak tartare. ⊠ *7 rue des Trois Frères, Montmartre* ☎ *01–42–64–07–37* Ⓜ *Abbesses.*

7

Sightseeing
★★★★
Dining
★★★
Lodging
★★
Shopping
★★★
Nightlife
★

Montmartre has become almost too charming for its own good. Yes, it feels like a village (if you wander off the beaten path); yes, there are working artists here (though far fewer than there used to be); and yes, the best view of Paris is yours for free from the top of the hill (if there's no haze). That's why on any weekend day, year-round, you can find scores of visitors crowding these cobbled alleys, scaling the staircases that pass for streets, and queuing to see Sacré-Coeur, the "sculpted cloud," at the summit.

Updated by
Jack Vermee

If you're lucky enough to have a little corner of Montmartre to yourself, you'll understand why locals love it so. Come at nonpeak times, on a weekday, or in the morning or later in the evening. Stroll around **Place des Abbesses,** where the rustic houses and narrow streets escaped the heavy hand of urban planner Baron Haussmann. Until 1860 the area was, in fact, a separate village, dotted with windmills. Always a draw for bohemians and artists, many of whom had studios at what is now the **Musée de Montmartre** and the **Bateau-Lavoir,** Montmartre has been home to such painters as Suzanne Valadon and her son Maurice Utrillo, Picasso, van Gogh, Géricault, Renoir, and, of course, Henri de Toulouse-Lautrec, whose iconic paintings of the cancan dancers at the **Moulin Rouge** are now souvenir-shop fixtures. While you can still see shows at the Moulin Rouge in **Place Blanche** and the pocket-size cabaret **Au Lapin Agile,** much of the entertainment here is on the seedier side—the area around Pigalle is the city's largest red-light district, though it's far tamer than it used to be. **Boulevard de Clichy** was virtually an artists' highway at the turn of the 20th century: Degas lived and died at No. 6, and Picasso lived at No. 11. The *quartier* is a favorite of filmmakers (the blockbuster *Moulin Rouge* was inspired by it), and visitors still seek out Café des Deux Moulins at 15 rue Lepic, the real-life café (unfortunately with a remodeled look) where Audrey Tautou waited tables in 2001's *Amélie.* In 1928 **Studio 28** opened as the world's first cinema for experimental films.

TOP ATTRACTIONS

Fodor's Choice ★ **Basilique du Sacré-Coeur.** It's hard not to feel as though you're ascending to heaven when you visit Sacred Heart Basilica, the white castle in the sky, perched atop Montmartre. The French government commissioned it in 1873 to symbolize the return of self-confidence after the devastating years of the Commune and Franco-Prussian War, and architect Paul Abadie employed elements from Romanesque and Byzantine styles when designing it—a mélange many critics dismissed as gaudy. Construction lasted until World War I, and the church was finally consecrated in 1919. Many people now come to Sacré-Coeur to admire the superlative view from the top of its 271-foot-high dome. But if you opt to skip the climb up the spiral staircase, the view from the front steps is still ample compensation for the trip.

Inside, expect another visual treat—namely the massive golden mosaic set high above the choir. Created in 1922 by Luc-Olivier Merson, *Christ in Majesty* depicts Christ with a golden heart and outstretched arms, surrounded by various figures, including the Virgin Mary and Joan of Arc. It remains one of the largest mosaics of its kind. Also worth noting are the portico's bronze doors, decorated with biblical scenes; and the stained-glass windows, which were installed in 1922, destroyed by a bombing during World War II (there were miraculously no deaths), and rebuilt in 1946. In the basilica's 262-foot-high campanile hangs La Savoyarde, one of the world's heaviest bells, weighing about 19 tons.

The best time to visit Sacré-Coeur is early morning or early evening, and preferably not on a Sunday, when the crowds are thick. Photographers angling for the perfect shot of the church should aim for a clear blue-sky day or arrive at dusk, when the pink sky plays nicely with the lights of the basilica. If you're coming to worship, there are daily Masses.

■TIP➜ To avoid the steps, take the funicular, which costs one métro ticket each way. ⊠ *Pl. du Parvis-du-Sacré-Coeur, Montmartre* ☎ *01–53–41–89–00* ⊕ *www.sacre-coeur-montmartre.com* 🖃 *Basilica free, dome €6* Ⓜ *Anvers, plus funicular; Jules Joffrin plus Montmartrobus.*

Bateau-Lavoir (*Wash-barge*). The birthplace of Cubism isn't open to the public, but a display in the front window details this unimposing spot's rich history. Montmartre poet Max Jacob coined the name because the original structure here reminded him of the laundry boats that used to float in the Seine, and he joked that the warren of paint-splattered artists' studios needed a good hosing down (wishful thinking, since the building had only one water tap). It was in the Bateau-Lavoir that, early in the 20th century, Pablo Picasso, Georges Braque, and Juan Gris made their first bold stabs at Cubism, and Picasso painted the groundbreaking *Les Demoiselles d'Avignon* in 1906–07. The experimental works of the artists weren't met with open arms, even in liberal Montmartre. All but the facade was rebuilt after a fire in 1970. Like the original building, though, the current incarnation houses artists and their studios. ⊠ *13 pl. Émile-Goudeau, Montmartre* Ⓜ *Abbesses.*

Carré Roland Dorgelès. This unassuming square is a perfect place to take in two of Montmartre's most photographed sites: the pink-and-green Au Lapin Agile cabaret and Clos Montmartre, Paris's only working vineyard. While the former, famously painted by Camille Pissarro, still welcomes revelers after almost 160 years, the latter is closed to visits except during the annual Fête de Jardins (Garden Festival) weekend in September. The stone wall on the northwestern edge of the square borders the peaceful Cimetière St-Vincent, one of the neighborhood's three atmospheric cemeteries. ⊠ *Corner of Rue des Saulnes and Rue St-Vincent, Montmartre* Ⓜ *Lamarck-Caulaincourt.*

Halle St-Pierre. The elegant iron-and-glass 19th-century market hall at the foot of Sacré-Coeur stages dynamic exhibitions of *art brut* (raw art), or outsider and folk art. The international artists featured are contemporary in style and out of the mainstream. There's also a good bookstore and a café serving light, well-prepared dishes, such as savory tarts and quiches with salad on the side, plus homemade desserts. ⊠ *2 rue Ronsard, Montmartre* ☎ *01–42–58–72–89* ⊕ *www.hallesaintpierre. org* ✉ *Museum €9* ☉ *Closed Aug.* Ⓜ *Anvers.*

Moulin de la Galette. Of the 14 windmills (*moulins*) that used to sit atop this hill, only two remain. They're known collectively as Moulin de la Galette—the name being taken from the bread that the owners used to produce. The more storied of the two is Le Blute-Fin. In the late 1800s there was a dance hall on the site, famously captured by Renoir (you can see the painting in the Musée d'Orsay). A facelift restored the windmill to its 19th-century glory; however, it is on private land and can't be visited. Down the street is the other moulin, Le Radet. ⊠ *Le Blute-Fin, corner of Rue Lepic and Rue Tholozé, Montmartre* Ⓜ *Abbesses.*

Place des Abbesses. This triangular square is typical of the countrified style that has made Montmartre famous. Now a hub for shopping and people-watching, the *place* is surrounded by hip boutiques, sidewalk cafés, and shabby-chic restaurants—a prime habitat for the young, neo-bohemian crowd and a sprinkling of expats. Trendy streets like Rue Houdon and Rue des Martyrs have attracted small designer shops, a store specializing in Spanish *pata negra* ham, and even a cupcake shop. Many retailers remain open on Sunday afternoon. ⊠ *Intersection of Rue des Abbesses and Rue la Vieuville, Montmartre* Ⓜ *Abbesses.*

Place du Tertre. Artists have peddled their wares in this square for centuries. Busloads of tourists have changed the atmosphere, but if you come off-season—when the air is chilly and the streets are bare—you can almost feel what is was like when up-and-coming Picassos lived in the houses that today are given over to souvenir shops and cafés. ⊠ *East end of Rue Norvin, Pl. du Tertre, Montmartre* Ⓜ *Abbesses.*

NEED A BREAK

✕ **Le Rendez-Vous des Amis.** Friendly but not fancy, this watering hole—halfway up the hill to Sacré-Coeur—is a good place to stop for a *demi* (small draft beer) or a glass of wine. If you want a snack, order the *planche* (wooden board) with a selection of cheeses and charcuterie (€12). ⊠ *23 rue Gabrielle, Montmartre* ☎ *01–46–06–01–60* Ⓜ *Abbesses.*

CLOSE UP

A Scenic Walk in Montmartre

One of Paris's most charming walks begins at the Abbesses métro station (Line 12), which has one of only two remaining iron-and-glass Art Nouveau canopies designed by famed architect Hector Guimard. Explore the streets ringing **Place des Abbesses,** or begin the walk immediately by heading west along Rue des Abbesses. Turn right on Rue Tholozé and note the historic movie house, **Studio 28,** at No. 10. At the top of the street is **Le Blute-Fin,** a windmill portrayed in a well-known work by Renoir. A right on Rue Lepic takes you past the only other windmill still standing, **Le Radet.** Take a left here onto Rue Girardon, to **Place Dalida,** marked with a voluptuous bust of the beloved French singer who popularized disco. (Yolanda Gigliotti, aka Dalida, lived until her death in 1987 at 11 bis, rue d'Orchampt, one of the city's narrowest streets, opposite Le Radet.)

The stone house behind Dalida's bust is the 18th-century **Château des Brouillards,** whose name, Castle of the Mists, is taken from the light fog that used to cloak this former farmland. Detour down the romantic alley of the same name. Renoir is said to have lived in the château before moving to the small house across the way at No. 8. From Place Dalida, head down winding Rue de l'Abreuvoir, one of the most photographed streets in Paris. Residents used to walk their horses to the *abreuvoir,* or watering trough, at No. 15. Pissarro kept a pied-à-terre at No. 12. The stone-and-wood-beam house at No. 4 was once home to a historian of the Napoleonic wars whose family symbol was an eagle. Notice the wooden sundial with a rooster and the inscription:

"When you chime, I'll sing." At the pink-and-green **Maison Rose** restaurant, committed to canvas by resident artist Maurice Utrillo, turn left on Rue des Saules, where you'll find Paris's only working vineyard, **Clos de Montmartre.**

Across the street is the famous cabaret **Au Lapin Agile,** still going strong. On the opposite corner, a stone wall rings the **Cimetière Saint-Vincent,** one of the city's smallest cemeteries, where Utrillo is buried (to see it, walk west along Rue St-Vincent, take a right, then another quick right). Backtrack up Rue des Saules and take the first left onto Rue Cortot to the **Musée de Montmartre,** once home to a bevy of artists. Renoir rented a studio here to store his painting of Le Blute-Fin. A few doors down, at No. 6, the composer Erik Satie, piano player at Le Chat Noir nightclub, lived during a penniless period in a 6-by-4-foot flat with a 9-foot ceiling (plus skylight). At the corner of Rue Mont-Cenis, the white water tower Château d'Eau still services the neighborhood. Turn right to reach **Place du Tertre,** a lively square packed with tourists and street artists. Easily overlooked is **St-Pierre de Montmartre,** one of the city's oldest churches, founded in 1147. End your walk at the basilica **Sacré-Coeur,** and enjoy one of the best views of Paris from the city's highest point. This *butte,* or hilltop, has been famous since the 3rd century: St-Denis (the first bishop of Paris) was martyred here, and after his decapitation he was said to have walked miles while holding his own head. For an easy descent, take the funicular, which has been ferrying people up and down since 1900.

7

WORTH NOTING

OFF THE
BEATEN
PATH

Basilique de St-Denis. Built between 1136 and 1286, St-Denis Basilica is one of the most important Gothic churches in France. It was here, under dynamic prelate Abbé Suger, that Gothic architecture (typified by pointed arches and rib vaults) was said to have made its first appearance. The kings of France soon chose St-Denis as their final resting place, and their richly sculpted tombs—along with what remains of Suger's church—can be seen in the choir area at the east end. The basilica was battered during the Revolution; afterward, however, Louis XVIII reestablished it as the royal burial site by moving the remains of Louis XVI and Marie-Antoinette here to join centuries' worth of monarchial bones. The vast 13th-century nave is a brilliant example of structural logic; its columns, capitals, and vault are a model of architectural harmony. The facade, retaining the rounded arches of the Romanesque that preceded the Gothic period, is set off by a small rose window, reputedly the oldest in France. Check out the extensive archaeological finds, such as a Merovingian queen's grave goods. Guided tours in English are available by reservation; if you'd rather explore on your own, audioguides are available for €4.50. ⊠ *1 rue de la Légion d'Honneur, St-Denis* ☎ *01–48–09–83–54* ⊕ *www.saint-denis.monuments-nationaux.fr* 🔊 *€9* Ⓜ *Basilique de St-Denis.*

Cimetière de Montmartre. Overshadowed by better-known Père-Lachaise, this cemetery is just as picturesque. It's the final resting place of a host of luminaries, including painters Degas and Fragonard; Adolphe Sax, inventor of the saxophone; dancer Vaslav Nijinsky; filmmaker François Truffaut; and composers Hector Berlioz and Jacques Offenbach. The Art Nouveau tomb of novelist Émile Zola (1840–1902) lords over a lawn near the entrance—though Zola's remains were removed to the Panthéon in 1908. ⊠ *20 av. Rachel, Montmartre* Ⓜ *Blanche.*

Espace Dalí (*Dalí Center*). One of several museums dedicated to the Surrealist master, the permanent collection in this black-walled exhibition space includes about 300 works, mostly etchings and lithographs. Among the two dozen sculptures are versions of Dalí's melting bronze clock and variations on the Venus de Milo. Since he was a multimedia pioneer ahead of his time, there are videos with Dalí's voice, and temporary exhibits have included the mustachioed man's foray into holograms. There's plenty of information in English, and audioguides can be rented for €3.50. ⊠ *11 rue Poulbot, Montmartre* ☎ *01–42–64–40–10* ⊕ *www.daliparis.com* 🔊 *€12* Ⓜ *Abbesses.*

FAMILY **Marché St-Pierre.** This self-described "fabric kingdom" has been selling Parisians their curtains for more than 60 years. With five floors, it actually stocks a lot more than draperies, including bolts of fine silk, feather boas, and spangled cushions. Among the regulars here are the designers who create the famous windows at Hermès. The Marché anchors a fabric district that extends to the neighboring streets; each shop is a bit different from the next. ⊠ *2 rue Charles Nodier, Montmartre* ☎ *01–42–06–92–25* ⊕ *www.marchesaintpierre.com* ☉ *Closed Sun.* Ⓜ *Anvers.*

Moulin Rouge. When this world-famous cabaret opened in 1889, aristocrats, professionals, and the working classes all flocked in to ogle the scandalous performers (the cancan was considerably more kinky in Toulouse-Lautrec's day, when girls kicked off their knickers). There's not much to see from the outside except for tourist buses and sex shops; if you want to catch a show inside, ticket prices start at €112. Souvenir seekers should check out the Moulin Rouge gift shop (around the corner at 11 rue Lepic), which sells official merchandise, from jewelry to sculpture, by reputable French makers. ⊠ *82 bd. de Clichy, Montmartre* ☎ *01–53–09–82–82* ⊕ *www.moulinrouge.fr* Ⓜ *Blanche.*

> ## PICASSO LIVED HERE
>
> Montmartre is virtually littered with "Picasso Lived Here" plaques. The artist resided at three different addresses in the area: on Rue Gabrielle when he first arrived; at the Bateau-Lavoir; and at 11 boulevard de Clichy.

Musée de Montmartre. During its turn-of-the-20th-century heyday, this building—now home to Montmartre's historical museum—was occupied by painters, writers, and cabaret artists. Foremost among them was Pierre-Auguste Renoir, who painted *Le Moulin de la Galette* (an archetypal scene of sun-drenched revelers) while living here. Recapping the area's colorful past, the museum has a charming permanent collection, which includes many Toulouse-Lautrec posters and original Eric Satie scores. An ambitious renovation, completed in 2014, doubled its space by incorporating both the studio-apartment once shared by mother-and-son duo Suzanne Valadon and Maurice Utrillo (now fully restored) and the adjoining Demarne Hotel (which has been redesigned to house temporary exhibitions). The lovely surrounding gardens—named in honor of Renoir—have also been revitalized. An audioguide is included in the ticket price. ⊠ *12 rue Cortot, Montmartre* ☎ *01–49–25–89–39* ⊕ *www. museedemontmartre.fr* ⊡ *€10* Ⓜ *Lamarck–Caulaincourt.*

Saint Jean L'Evangéliste de Montmartre. This eye-catching church with a compact Art Nouveau interior was the first modern house of worship built in Paris (1897–1904) and the first to be constructed of reinforced cement. Architect Anatole de Baudot's revolutionary technique defied the accepted rules at the time with its use of unsupported masonry; critics, who failed to stop construction, feared the building would crumble under its own weight. Today the church attracts a steady flow of visitors curious about its unusual Moorish-inspired facade of redbrick and curved arches. Note the tiny clock at the top left of the bell tower and the handsome stained-glass windows. Free concerts and art exhibitions are staged in the church from time to time. ⊠ *19 rue des Abbesses, Montmartre* ☎ *01–46–06–43–96* ⊕ *www.saintjeandemontmartre.com* Ⓜ *Abbesses.*

St-Pierre de Montmartre. Tucked in the shadow of mighty Sacré-Coeur is one of the oldest churches in Paris. Built in 1147 on the site of a 5th-century temple to the god Mars, this small sanctuary with its impressive sculpted metal doors was once part of a substantial Benedictine abbey. Besides the church, all that remains is a small cemetery, now closed (you can see it through the ornate metal door on the left as you enter the courtyard). Renovated multiple times through the ages, St-Pierre combines various styles. Interior elements, such as the columns in the nave, are medieval; the facade dates to the 18th century, with renovations in the 19th century; and the stained-glass windows are 20th century. Maurice Utrillo's 1914 painting of the titular saint hangs in the Musée de l'Orangerie. ⊠ *2 rue du Mont Cenis, off pl. du Tertre, Montmartre* ☎ *01–46–06–57–63* ⊕ *www.saintpierredemontmartre.net* Ⓜ *Anvers.*

Studio 28. This little movie house has a distinguished history: when it opened in 1928, it was the first theater in the world purposely built for *art et essai,* or experimental film (Luis Buñuel and Salvador Dalí's *L'Age d'Or* caused a riot when it premiered here). Through the years artists and writers came to see "seventh art" creations by directors such as Jean Cocteau, François Truffaut, and Orson Welles. Today it's a repertory cinema, showing first-runs, just-runs, and previews—usually in their original language. Movies are screened from 3 pm daily, and tickets cost €9. In the back of the movie house is a cozy bar and café that has a quiet outdoor terrace decorated with murals of film stars. Oh, and those charmingly bizarre chandeliers in the *salle*? Cocteau designed them. ⊠ *10 rue Tholozé, Montmartre* ☎ *01–46–06–47–45* ⊕ *www.cinema-studio28.fr/en* 🎟 *Movie tickets €9* Ⓜ *Abbesses.*

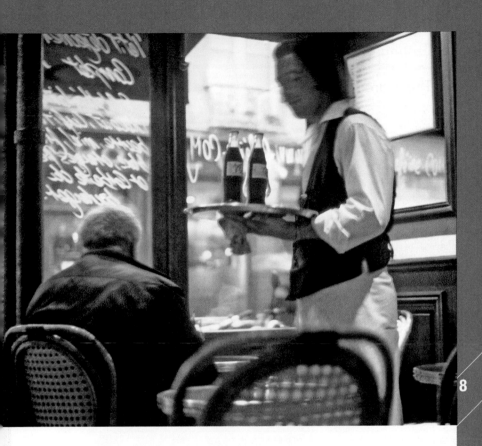

THE MARAIS

Getting Oriented

The Marais

GETTING HERE	TOP REASONS TO GO

The Marais includes the 3e and 4e arrondissements. It's a pleasant walk from the Beaubourg—the area around Centre Pompidou—into the heart of the Marais. Rue Rambuteau turns into Rue des Francs-Bourgeois, which runs right into Place des Vosges. If you're going by métro, the most central stop is St-Paul on Line 1. If you're going to the Pompidou, take Line 11 to Rambuteau. For the Musée Picasso, the closest stop is St-Sébastien–Froissart on Line 8. For the 3e arrondissement, get off at Arts et Métiers on Line 3 or 11, or Filles du Calvaire on Line 8.

Centre Pompidou. Paris's leading modern art museum is also a vast (and architecturally ambitious) arts center that presents films, theater, and dance performances.

Place des Vosges. The prettiest square in the French capital surrounds a manicured park, where inviting patches of grass are accessible to those needing a siesta.

Musée National Picasso-Paris. Spectacularly renovated, this museum is a must-see for fans of the Spanish master, who painted some of his best work while living in the city.

Jewish history tour. The old Jewish quarter has two world-class sites: Mémorial de la Shoah (the Holocaust Memorial) and the Musée d'Art et d'Histoire du Judaïsme.

No reason at all. Lose yourself in simple pleasures, like exploring the tiny streets near the Centre Pompidou or people-watching in a café on Rue Vieille du Temple.

BEST CAFÉS

Dame Tartine. Cafés abound around the Centre Pompidou, but this one—overlooking the Stravinsky fountain—is a good choice. You won't go wrong with any of the many *tartines* : toasts topped with delicious ingredients. ⊠ *2 rue Brisemiche, Marais Quarter* ☎ *01–77–18–88–59* Ⓜ *Rambuteau.*

La Tartine. This calm café on busy Rue de Rivoli is a local favorite with an impressive wine list. Try the €8 French onion soup or indulge in classic French dishes like *tartare de boeuf* or escargots. ⊠ *24 rue de Rivoli, Marais Quarter* ☎ *01–42–72–76–85* ⊕ *www. latartineparis.fr* Ⓜ *St-Paul.*

Le Loir dans la Théière. Sink into a shabby armchair at this popular tearoom, whose name translates to "the Dormouse in the Teapot" (from *Alice in Wonderland*). The savory tarts are stellar, but the real stars are desserts like the decadent chocolate crumble tart. ⊠ *3 rue des Rosiers, Marais Quarter* ☎ *01–42–72–90–61* ⊕ *www. leloirdanslatheiere.com* Ⓜ *St-Paul.*

MAKING THE MOST OF YOUR TIME

The Marais has something for everyone, and how much time you spend here depends on how much time you have in Paris. One day seems painfully short, but it would allow you to take a do-it-yourself walking tour, peeking into private courtyards and picnicking in the Place des Vosges as you proceed. Leave at least two days if your itinerary includes the Centre Pompidou and the Musée Picasso. In three days you could cover some of the smaller museums, which are well worth visiting as many are housed in exquisite mansions. If time permits, wander to the 3e arrondissement to see the charming streets, away from the crowds, or drop into the quirky science-centric Musée des Arts et Métiers. Sunday afternoon is a lively time to come because many shops are open, notably on Rue des Francs-Bourgeois. This neighborhood thrives after dark as well; business is brisk at cafés and bars—particularly those aimed at the gay community.

Sightseeing
★★★★★
Dining
★★★★
Lodging
★★★★
Shopping
★★★★★
Nightlife
★★★★

From swampy to swanky, the Marais has a fascinating history. Like an aging pop star, the *quartier* has remade itself many times, and today retains several identities. It's the city's epicenter of cool with hip boutiques, designer hotels, and art galleries galore; the hub of Paris's gay community; and, though fading, the nucleus of Jewish life. You could easily spend your entire visit to Paris in this neighborhood—there is that much to do.

Updated by
Jack Vermee

"Marais" means marsh, and that is exactly what this area was until the 12th century, when it was converted to farmland. In 1605 Henri IV began building the Place Royale (today's Place des Vosges, the oldest square in Paris), which touched off a building boom, and the wealthy and fabulous moved in. Despite the odors—the area was one of the city's smelliest—it remained the chic quarter until Louis XIV transferred his court to Versailles, trailed by dispirited aristocrats unhappy to decamp to the country. Merchants moved into their exquisite *hôtels particuliers* (private mansions), which are some of the city's best surviving examples of Baroque architecture. Here you can see the hodgepodge of narrow streets that so vexed Louis Napoléon and his sidekick, Baron Haussmann, who feared a redux of the famous *barricades* that Revolutionaries threw up to thwart the monarchy. Haussmann leveled scores of blocks like these, creating the wide, arrow-straight avenues that are a hallmark of modern Paris. Miraculously, the Marais escaped destruction, though much of it fell victim to neglect and ruin. Thanks to restoration efforts over the past half century, the district is enjoying its latest era of greatness, and the apartments here—among the city's oldest—are also the most in demand, with *beaucoup* charm, exposed beams, and steep crooked staircases barely wide enough for a supermodel. (Should you be lucky enough to find an elevator, don't expect it to fit your suitcase.) Notice the impressive *portes cochères,* the huge doors built to accommodate aristocratic carriages that today open into many sublime courtyards and hidden gardens.

The 4e arrondissement, the Marais's glitzier half, is sandwiched between two opposite poles—the regal **Place des Vosges** in the east and the eye-teasing modern masterpiece **Centre Pompidou** in the west. Between these points you'll find most of the main sites, including the **Musée Picasso,** and the **Maison Européenne de la Photographie,** which is the best place to see how the city evolved through the ages. To tour an exquisitely restored 17th-century hôtel particulier, visit the excellent **Musée Cognacq-Jay** or wander into the manicured back garden of the magnificent **Hôtel de Sully.** The quieter 3e arrondissement half of the Marais, around Rue de Bretagne, has become one of Paris's most in-demand areas to live—and one of the most interesting to explore. Here you'll find intriguing, off-the-tourist-track boutiques, bars, and galleries, plus sites such as the **Musée des Arts and Métiers,** Europe's oldest science museum.

Paris's **Jewish quarter** (the Pletzl, Yiddish for "little place") has existed in the Marais in some form since the 13th century, and it still thrives around Rue des Rosiers, even as hipster hangouts encroach on the traditional bakeries and delis. Not far away is the beating heart of the **gay Marais,** radiating out from Rue Vieille du Temple, along Rue St-Croix de la Bretonnerie to Rue du Temple; it's filled with trendy shops, cool cafés, and lively nightspots aimed at gays but welcoming to all.

TOP ATTRACTIONS

FAMILY
Fodor'sChoice
★

Centre Pompidou. Love it or hate it, the Pompidou is certainly a unique-looking building. Most Parisians have warmed to the industrial, Lego-like exterior that caused a scandal when it opened in 1977. Named after French president Georges Pompidou (1911–74), it was designed by then-unknowns Renzo Piano and Richard Rogers. The architects' claim to fame was putting the building's guts on the outside and color-coding them: water pipes are green, air ducts are blue, electrics are yellow, and things like elevators and escalators are red. Art from the 20th century to the present day is what you can find inside.

The Musée National d'Art Moderne (Modern Art Museum, entrance on Level 4) occupies the top two levels. Level 5 is devoted to modern art from 1905 to 1960, including major works by Matisse, Modigliani, Marcel Duchamp, and Picasso; Level 4 is dedicated to contemporary art from the '60s on, including video installations. The Galerie d'Enfants (Children's Gallery) on the mezzanine level has interactive exhibits designed to keep the kids busy. Outside, next to the museum's sloping plaza—where throngs of teenagers hang out (and where there's free Wi-Fi)—is the Atelier Brancusi. This small, airy museum contains four rooms reconstituting Brancusi's Montparnasse studios with works from all periods of his career. On the opposite side, in Place Igor-Stravinsky, is the Stravinsky fountain, which has 16 gyrating mechanical figures in primary colors, including a giant pair of ruby red lips. On the opposite side of Rue Rambuteau, on the wall at the corner of Rue Clairvaux and Passage Brantôme, is the appealingly bizarre mechanical brass-and-steel clock, *Le Défenseur du Temps*.

The Pompidou's permanent collection takes up a relatively small amount of the space when you consider this massive building's other features: temporary exhibition galleries, with a special wing for design and architecture; a highly regarded free reference library (there's often a queue of university students on Rue Renard waiting to get in); and the basement, which includes two cinemas, a theater, a dance space, and a small, free exhibition space.

On your way up the escalator, you'll have spectacular views of Paris, ranging from Tour Montparnasse, to the left, around to the hilltop Sacré-Coeur on the right. The rooftop restaurant, Georges, is a romantic spot for dinner. Be sure to reserve a table near the window. ⊠ *Pl. Georges-Pompidou, Marais Quarter* ☏ *01–44–78–12–33* ⊕ *www.centrepompidou.fr* 🖥 *Center access free, Atelier Brancusi free, museum and exhibits €14 (free 1st Sun. of month)* ⊘ *Closed Tues.* Ⓜ *Rambuteau.*

Église St-Merry. This impressive Gothic church, in the shadow of the Centre Pompidou, was completed in 1550. Notable features include the turret (it contains the oldest bell in Paris, cast in 1331) and an 18th-century pulpit supported on carved palm trees. There are free concerts here Saturday at 8 pm and Sunday at 4 pm. See the website for more information. ⊠ *76 rue de la Verrerie, Marais Quarter* ☏ *01–42–71–93–93* ⊕ *www.saintmerry.org* Ⓜ *Hôtel de Ville.*

Maison de Victor Hugo. France's most famous scribe lived in this house on the southeast corner of Place des Vosges between 1832 and 1848. It's now a museum dedicated to the multitalented author. In Hugo's apartment on the second floor, you can see the tall desk, next to the short bed, where he began writing his masterwork *Les Misérables* (as always, standing up). There are manuscripts and early editions of the novel on display, as well as others such as *Notre-Dame de Paris,* known to English readers as *The Hunchback of Notre-Dame.* You can see illustrations of Hugo's writings, including Bayard's rendering of the impish Cosette holding her giant broom (which has graced countless *Les Miz* T-shirts). The collection includes many of Hugo's own, sometimes macabre, ink drawings (he was a fine artist) and furniture from several of his homes. Particularly impressive is the room of carved and painted Chinese-style wooden panels that Hugo designed for the house of his mistress, Juliet Drouet, on the island of Guernsey, when he was exiled there for agitating against Napoléon III. Try to spot the intertwined Vs and Js (hint: look for the angel's trumpet in the left corner). The first floor is dedicated to temporary exhibitions that often have modern ties to Hugo's work. ⊠ *6 pl. des Vosges, Marais Quarter* ☏ *01–42–72–10–16* ⊕ *www. maisonsvictorhugo.paris.fr* 🖥 *Free; €5-€7 for temporary exhibitions* ⊘ *Closed Mon.* Ⓜ *St-Paul, Bastille.*

Maison Européenne de la Photographie (*Center for European Photography*). Much of the credit for the city's ascendancy as a hub of international photography goes to MEP and its former director, Jean-Luc Monterosso, who also founded Paris's hugely successful Mois de la Photo festival (a biennial event held in April of odd-numbered years). The MEP hosts up to four simultaneous exhibitions, changing about every three months. Shows feature an international crop of photographers and video artists. Works by superstar Annie Leibovitz or designer-photographer Karl Lagerfeld may overlap with a collection of self-portraits by an up-and-coming artist. MEP often stages retrospectives of the classics (by Doisneau, Cartier-Bresson, Man Ray, and others) from its vast private collection. Programs are available in English, and English-language tours are sometimes given; check the website for details. ✉ *5/7 rue de Fourcy, Marais Quarter* ☎ *01–44–78–75–00* ⊕ *www.mep-fr.org* 💶 *€9* ⊙ *Closed Mon., Tues., and between exhibitions* Ⓜ *St-Paul.*

Mémorial de la Shoah (*Memorial to the Holocaust*). The first installation in this compelling memorial and museum is the deeply moving Wall of Names, tall plinths honoring the 76,000 French Jews deported from France to Nazi concentration camps, of whom only 2,500 survived. Opened in 2005, the center has an archive on the victims, a library, and a gallery hosting temporary exhibitions. The permanent collection includes riveting artifacts and photographs from the camps, along with video testimony from survivors. The children's memorial is particularly poignant and not for the faint of heart—scores of back-lighted photographs show the faces of many of the 11,000 murdered French children. The crypt, a giant black marble Star of David, contains ashes recovered from the camps and the Warsaw ghetto. You can see the orderly drawers containing small files on Jews kept by the French police. (France only officially acknowledged the Vichy government's role in 1995.) The history of anti-Semitic persecution in the world is revisited as well as the rebounding state of Jewry today. There is a free guided tour in English the second Sunday of every month at 3. ✉ *17 rue Geoffroy l'Asnier, Marais Quarter* ☎ *01–42–77–44–72* ⊕ *www.memorialdelashoah.org* 💶 *Free* ⊙ *Closed Sat.* Ⓜ *Pont Marie, St-Paul.*

Musée Cognacq-Jay. One of the loveliest museums in Paris, this 16th-century rococo-style mansion contains an outstanding collection of mostly 18th-century artwork in its rooms of *boiserie* (intricately carved wood paneling). A tour through them allows a rare glimpse into the lifestyle of wealthy 19th-century Parisians. Ernest Cognacq, founder of the now closed department store La Samaritaine, and his wife, Louise Jay, amassed furniture, porcelain, and paintings—notably by Fragonard, Watteau, François Boucher, and Tiepolo—to create one of the world's finest private collections of this period. Some of the best displays are also the smallest, like the tiny enamel medallion portraits showcased on the second floor; or, on the third floor, the glass cases filled with exquisite inlaid snuff boxes, sewing cases, pocket watches, perfume bottles, and cigar cutters. Exhibits are labeled in French only, but free pamphlets and €5 audioguides are available in English. ✉ *8 rue Elzévir, Marais Quarter* ☎ *01–40–27–07–21* ⊕ *www.museecognacqjay.paris.fr* 💶 *Free; €6–€8 for temporary exhibitions* ⊙ *Closed Mon.* Ⓜ *St-Paul.*

Musée d'Art et d'Histoire du Judaïsme. This excellent museum traces the tempestuous history of French and European Jews through art and history. Housed in the refined 17th-century Hôtel St-Aignan, exhibits have good explanatory texts in English, but the free English audioguide adds another layer of insight; guided tours in English are also available on request (€4 extra). Highlights include 13th-century tombstones excavated in Paris; a wooden model of a destroyed Eastern European synagogue; a roomful of early paintings by Marc Chagall; and Christian

8

Boltanski's stark, two-part tribute to Shoah (Holocaust) victims in the form of plaques on an outer wall naming the (mainly Jewish) inhabitants of the Hôtel St-Aignan in 1939, and canvas hangings with the personal data of the 13 residents who were deported and died in concentration camps. The rear-facing windows offer a view of the Jardin Anne Frank. To visit it, use the entrance on Impasse Berthaud, off Rue Beaubourg, just north of Rue Rambuteau. ⊠ *71 rue du Temple, Marais Quarter* ☎ *01–53–01–86–60* ⊕ *www.mahj.org* 💳 *€10 with temporary exhibitions* ⊙ *Closed Mon.* Ⓜ *Rambuteau, Hôtel de Ville.*

FAMILY **Musée des Arts et Métiers.** Science buffs should not miss this cavernous museum, Europe's oldest dedicated to invention and technology. It's a treasure trove of wonkiness with 80,000 instruments, machines, and gadgets—including 16th-century astrolabes, Pascal's first mechanical calculator, and film-camera prototypes by the Frères Lumière. You can watch video simulations of groundbreaking architectural achievements, like the cast-iron dome, or see how Jacquard's mechanical loom revolutionized clothmaking. Kids will love the flying machines (among them the first plane to cross the English Channel), and the impressive display of old automobiles in the high-ceilinged chapel of St-Martin-des-Champs. Also in the chapel is a copy of Foucault's Pendulum, which proved to the world in 1851 that the Earth rotated (demonstrations are staged daily at noon and 5). The building, erected between the 11th and 13th centuries, was a church and priory. It was confiscated during the Revolution, and, after incarnations as a school and a weapons factory, became a museum in 1799. Most displays have information in English, but renting an English audioguide (€5) helps. If you're taking the subway here, check out the platform of métro Line 11 in the Arts and Métiers station—one of the city's most elaborate—made to look like the inside of a Jules Verne-style machine, complete with copper-color metal walls, giant bolts, and faux gears. ⊠ *60 rue Réaumur, Marais Quarter* ☎ *01–53–01–82–75* ⊕ *www.arts-et-metiers.net* 💳 *€8; €9 with temporary exhibitions* ⊙ *Closed Mon.* Ⓜ *Arts et Métiers.*

Fodor's Choice **Musée National Picasso-Paris.** This immensely popular museum rose
★ phoenixlike in late 2014, when it finally reopened after an ambitious (and often controversial) five-year makeover that cost an estimated €52 million. Home to the world's largest public collection of Picasso's inimitable oeuvre, it now covers almost 54,000 square feet in two buildings: the regal 17th-century Hôtel Salé and a sprawling new structure in the back garden that's dedicated to temporary exhibitions. Diego Giacometti's exclusively designed furnishings in the former are an added bonus.

The collection of 200,000-plus paintings, sculptures, drawings, documents, and other archival materials (much of it previously in storage for lack of space) spans the artist's entire career; and while it doesn't include his most recognizable works, it does contain many of the pieces treasured most by Picasso himself. The renovated museum (which now has more than double the dedicated public space) is split into three distinct areas. The first two floors cover Picasso's work from 1895 to 1972. The top floor illustrates his relationship to his favorite artists; landscapes, nudes, portraits, and still lifes taken from his private collection detail his "artistic dialogue" with Cézanne, Gauguin, Degas, Rousseau, Matisse,

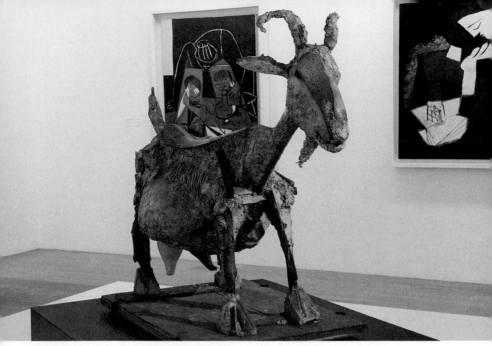

The Musée Picasso Paris highlights various works from Pablo Picasso, including his longtime devotion to sculpture.

Braque, Renoir, Modigliani, Miró, and others. The basement centers around Picasso's workshops, with photographs and engravings, paintings, and sculptures that document or evoke key pieces created at the Bateau Lavoir, Château de Boisgeloup, Grands-Augustins, the Villa La Californie, and his farmhouse, Notre-Dame-de-Vie, in Mougins. With plenty of multimedia components and special activities that cater to kids, this is ideal for both children and adult art lovers alike.

■ TIP➔ It's worth paying the extra €1 to buy tickets online well in advance of your planned visit. Also, try to avoid visiting on weekends, when the crowds are thickest. ⊠ 5 rue de Thorigny, Marais Quarter ☎ 01–85–56–00–36 ⊕ www.museepicassoparis.fr ☑ €13 (free 1st Sun. of month); €18 with audioguide ⊗ Closed Mon. Ⓜ St-Sébastien–Froissart.

FAMILY
Fodor's Choice
★

Place des Vosges. The oldest square in Paris and—dare we say it?—the most beautiful, Place des Vosges represents an early stab at urban planning. The precise proportions offer a placid symmetry, but things weren't always so calm here. Four centuries ago this was the site of the Palais des Tournelles, home to King Henry II and Queen Catherine de Medici. The couple staged regular jousting tournaments, and Henry was fatally lanced in the eye during one of them in 1559. Catherine fled to the Louvre, abandoning her palace and ordering it destroyed. In 1612 the square became Place Royale on the occasion of Louis XIII's engagement to Anne of Austria. Napoléon renamed it Place des Vosges to honor the northeast region of Vosges, the first in the country to pony up taxes to the Revolutionary government. At the base of the 36 redbrick-and-stone houses—nine on each side of the square—is an arcaded, covered walkway lined with art galleries, shops, and cafés. There's also an elementary school, a synagogue (whose barrel roof was designed by Gustav Eiffel), and several chic hotels. The formal, gated garden's perimeter is lined with chestnut trees; inside are a children's play area and a fountain. Aside from hanging out in the park, people come here to see the house of the man who once lived at No. 6—Victor Hugo, the author of *Les Misérables* and *Notre-Dame de Paris* (aka *The Hunchback of Notre-Dame*).

■**TIP➔** One of the best things about this park is that you're actually allowed to sit—or snooze or snack—on the grass during spring and summer. There is no better spot in the Marais for a picnic: you can pick up fixings at the nearby street market on Thursday and Sunday mornings (it's on Boulevard Richard Lenoir between Rues Amelot and St-Sabin). The most likely approach to Place des Vosges is from Rue de Francs-Bourgeois, the main shopping street. However, for a grander entrance walk along Rue St-Antoine until you get to Rue de Birague, which leads directly into the square. ⊠ *Off Rue des Francs-Bourgeois, near Rue de Turenne, Marais Quarter* Ⓜ *Bastille, St-Paul.*

3e arrondissement. The thick crowds that flock to Place des Vosges rarely venture to the other side of the Marais: the 3e arrondissement, which has morphed into one of the hottest neighborhoods in Paris. Good luck finding an apartment to rent here—most are small walk-ups with exposed wooden beams and lots of charm. But even if you can't move in, you can enjoy this trendy quartier like a local. First, head to Rue de Bretagne, the main drag. Stop for lunch at one of the food stalls in the Marché des Enfants Rouges (No. 39, open Tuesday through Sunday): it's the oldest covered market in Paris. Next, explore narrow side streets, like Rues Charlot, Debelleyme, and Poitou, lined with art galleries and small boutiques. Stop for a cup of Joe and a croissant at Poilâne (38 rue Debelleyme) or treat yourself to a gelato at Mary's (60 rue du Temple. Across the street is the 19th-century iron-and-glass Carreau du Temple, which, after a long-overdue renovation, reopened as a locally driven arts and sports community center. This is the site of the former Templar Tower, where Louis XIV and Marie-Antoinette were imprisoned before the king's date with the guillotine (Napoléon later razed it). For your evening apéritif, make a beeline for the buzzy Café Charlot, at 38 rue de Bretagne. If you're in the mood for couscous, try Chez Omar, a neighborhood institution at No. 47. ⊠ *Marais Quarter* Ⓜ *Arts et Métiers, Filles du Calvaire.*

WORTH NOTING

Agoudas Hakehilos Synagogue. Art Nouveau genius Hector Guimard built this unique synagogue (also called Synagogue de la Rue Pavée) in 1913 for a Polish-Russian Orthodox association. The facade resembles an open book: Guimard used the motif of the Ten Commandments to inspire the building's shape and its interior, which can only rarely be visited. Knock on the door and see if the caretaker will let you upstairs to the balcony, where you can admire Guimard's well-preserved decor. Like other Parisian synagogues, its front door was dynamited by Nazis on Yom Kippur, 1941. The Star of David over the door was added after the building was restored. ✉ *10 rue Pavé, Marais Quarter* ☎ *01–48–87–21–54* Ⓜ *St-Paul.*

Archives Nationales. Thousands of important historical documents are preserved inside the Hôtel de Soubise and Hôtel de Rohan—a pair of spectacular buildings constructed in 1705 as private homes. Fans of the decorative arts will appreciate a visit to the former, where the well-preserved private apartments of the Prince and Princess de Soubise are among the first examples of the rococo style, which preceded the more somber Baroque opulence of Louis XIV. The Hôtel de Soubise also has a museum that displays documents dating from 625 to the 20th century. Highlights include the Edict of Nantes (1598), the Treaty of Westphalia (1648), the wills of Louis XIV and Napoléon, and the Declaration of Human Rights (1789). Louis XVI's diary is also here, containing his sadly clueless entry for July 14, 1789—the day the Bastille was stormed and the French Revolution was launched. The Hôtel de Rohan, open to the public only during Patrimony Weekend in September, was built for Soubise's son, Cardinal Rohan. Before you leave, notice the medieval turrets in the courtyard: this is the Porte de Clisson, all that remains of a stately 14th-century mansion. ✉ *60 rue des Francs-Bourgeois, Marais Quarter* ☎ *01–40–27–60–96* ⊕ *www.archives-nationales.culture.gouv. fr* 🏛 *Hôtel de Soubise €5 (free 1st Sun. of month); €8 for temporary exhibitions* ⊘ *Closed Tues.* Ⓜ *Rambuteau.*

Hôtel de Sens. One of the few remaining structures in Paris from the Middle Ages, this little castle was most famously the home of Queen Margot, who took up residence here in 1605 after her marriage to Henry IV was annulled. Margot was known for her many lovers (she supposedly wore wigs made from locks of their hair) and reputedly ordered a servant beheaded in the courtyard after he ridiculed one of her companions. The street is said to be named after a fig tree she ordered cut down because it was inconveniencing her carriage. Perhaps for that reason there's a fig tree planted in the elegant rear garden, which is open to the public. Notice the cannonball lodged in the front facade commemorating a battle here during the three-day revolution in July 1830. Built for the archbishop of Sens in 1475, the castle was extensively renovated in the 20th century and is today home to the Bibliothèque Forney, a library that also stages temporary exhibitions drawn from its extensive collection of fine and graphic arts. ✉ *1 rue du Figuier, Marais Quarter* ☎ *01–42–78–14–60* 🏛 *Library free; free to €6 for exhibitions* ⊘ *Closed Sun. and Mon.* Ⓜ *Pont Marie.*

Hôtel de Ville. Overlooking the Seine, City Hall contains the residence and offices of the mayor. Reconstructed in 1873 after an attack by rioting crowds, it is one of Paris's most stunning buildings, made all the more dramatic by elaborate nighttime lighting. The adjoining public library stages frequent free exhibits celebrating famous photographers like Doisneau or Atget and their notable subjects, often the city herself (the entrance is on the side across from the department store BHV). Alas, the impressive interior of the main administrative building, with its lavish reception halls and staircases, is only open for independent visits during Patrimony Weekend in September. If your French is good,

8

however, free guided tours are given biweekly in summer, weekly in other seasons: call two months ahead for further information and reservations. The grand public square out front is always lively, playing host to events and temporary exhibitions. There's a carousel and a beach volleyball court (or similar) in summer, and an ice-skating rink (with skate rental available) in winter. ✉ *Pl. de l'Hôtel-de-Ville, Marais Quarter* ☎ *01–42–76–43–43 for tours* ⊕ *www.paris.fr* ✉ *Free* ⊙ *Closed weekends* ✐ *Access for visits at 29 rue de Rivoli* Ⓜ *Hôtel de Ville.*

La Gaîté Lyrique. One of Paris's newest contemporary-art venues combines innovative exhibits with live musical performances and a multimedia space that features a library, movies, and free video games. Think of it as a smaller, more interactive Centre Pompidou. La Gaîté Lyrique occupies three floors of a 19th-century theater—remnants of which are visible in the café upstairs. ✉ *3 bis, rue Papin, Marais Quarter* ☎ *01–53–01–52–00* ⊕ *www.gaite-lyrique.net* ✉ *Free; €5–€7 for temporary exhibitions; concert prices vary* ⊙ *Closed Mon.* Ⓜ *Réaumur-Sébastopol.*

FAMILY **Musée de la Chasse et de la Nature.** Mark this down as one of Paris's most bizarre—and fascinating—collections. The museum, housed in the gorgeous 17th-century Hôtel de Guénégaud, features lavishly appointed rooms stocked with animal- and hunt-themed art by the likes of Rubens and Gentileschi, plus antique weaponry and taxidermy animals. In a tribute to Art Nouveau, the decor includes chandeliers curled like antlers and matching railings. Older kids will appreciate the jaw-dropping Trophy Room with an impressive menagerie of beasts, not to mention the huge polar bear stationed outside. There is a lovely multimedia exhibit on the myth of the unicorn, as well as an interactive display of bird calls. Temporary exhibits and silent auctions take place on the first floor. ✉ *62 rue des Archives, Marais Quarter* ☎ *01–53–01–92–40* ⊕ *www.chassenature.org* ✉ *€8* ⊙ *Closed Mon.* Ⓜ *Rambuteau.*

Musée Pierre Cardin, Passé-Présent-Futur. Housed, appropriately, in a former necktie factory, this museum was opened in late 2014 by Cardin himself (then age 92). Covering three levels and six decades, it serves up the forward-thinking couturier's most memorable fashion statements. You'll see 200-plus designs—including the iconic "bubble dress"—as well as assorted accessories. ✉ *5 rue St-Merri , 4e, Marais Quarter* ☎ *01–42–76–00–57* ⊕ *www.pierrecardin.com/museum* ✉ *€25* ✐ *Closed Mon. and Tues.* Ⓜ *Hotel de Ville, Rambuteau.*

OFF THE BEATEN PATH

Nicolas Flamel's Home. Built in 1407 and reputed to be the oldest house in Paris (though other buildings also claim that title), this abode has a mystical history. Harry Potter fans should take note: this was the real-life residence of Nicolas Flamel, the alchemist whose sorcerer's stone is the source of immortality in the popular book series. A wealthy scribe, merchant, and dabbler in the mystical arts, Flamel willed his home to the city as a dormitory for the poor—on the condition that boarders pray daily for his soul. Today, the building contains apartments and a restaurant. ✉ *51 rue Montmorency, Marais Quarter* Ⓜ *Rambuteau.*

EASTERN PARIS

with Bastille, Canal St-Martin,
République, and Belleville

Getting Oriented

Eastern Paris

TOP REASONS TO GO

Canal St-Martin. This scenic canal is now one of the city's hottest, hippest hangouts—it's great for strolling, with plenty of galleries, shops, and cafés en route.

Place de la Bastille. The flashpoint of the French Revolution still draws agitators and their frequent, noisy demonstrations. It's also a nightlife hub and home to the Opéra Bastille.

Cimetière du Père-Lachaise. Fans of celebrities, from Frédéric Chopin to Oscar Wilde to Jim Morrison, come to pay tribute at their final resting place.

Parc de la Villette. As the site of the city's well-regarded science museum and planetarium, this is a good destination for both curious kids and grown-up science buffs.

Coulée verte René-Dumont/Promenade Plantée (Viaduc des Arts). An abandoned rail line has been turned into a tree-fringed walkway perched atop a brick viaduct that's bursting with boutiques.

BEST CAFÉS

Café A. The Maison de l'Architecture—a center for architectural advancement—occupies a onetime monastery near the Canal St-Martin. Inside its Renaissance courtyard, Café A offers a seasonal menu at prices that are reasonable for this ever-gentrifying area. ⊠ *148 rue du Faubourg St-Martin, Canal St-Martin* ☎ *09–81–29–83–38* ⊕ *www.cafea.fr* Ⓜ *Gare de l'Est.*

Café Charbon. This ultracool café is a neighborhood institution that stays open late every night of the week. ⊠ *109 rue Oberkampf, Oberkampf* ☎ *01–43–57–55–13* ⊕ *www. lecafecharbon.fr* Ⓜ *Parmentier, Menilmontant.*

Chez Prune. Grab an outdoor table at this hot spot on the Canal St-Martin and watch the world go by. ⊠ *36 rue Beaurepaire, Canal St-Martin* ☎ *01–42–41–30–47* ▭ *No credit cards* Ⓜ *Jacques Bonsergent, République.*

GETTING HERE

Eastern Paris includes the 10e, 11e, 12e, 19e, and 20e arrondissements. The Bastille métro stop, on Lines 1, 5, and 8, is a good place to start. For the Canal St-Martin, use the Place de la République stop (Lines 3, 5, 8, 9, 11) and walk along Rue Faubourg du Temple; use the Gare de l'Est stop (Lines 4, 5, 7) and walk along Rue des Récollets; or choose the Jaurès stop (Lines 2, 5, and 7 bis), take the Boulevard de Villette exit, and walk a mere 80 feet south. For Oberkampf, go to the Parmentier stop on Line 3 or the Oberkampf stop on Line 9. For the Cimetière du Père-Lachaise, take Line 2 or 3 to the eponymous stop.

MAKING THE MOST OF YOUR TIME

The Canal St-Martin is one of the most popular places in the city, particularly on Sunday afternoon, when the streets are closed to cars. Have lunch in a café, grab a Vélib' rental bike, and head to Parc de la Villette. A Sunday morning trip to the picturesque Marché d'Aligre is also recommended, even if you're not buying. The heaps of fresh produce and colorful flowers hawked by spirited vendors are worth seeing. On any day Place de la Bastille is a lively spot to stop for drinks or lunch; if time is limited, reserve this neighborhood for after dark, when the streets around Place de la Bastille and Oberkampf really come to life.

9

Sightseeing
★★
Dining
★★★★
Lodging
★★
Shopping
★★★★
Nightlife
★★★★★

Updated by
Jack Vermee

The Bastille used to be the star of this area, and a stop here—at the epicenter of the French Revolution—was obligatory. The small streets forking off Place de la Bastille still buzz at night, thanks to bars, music clubs, and the top-flight Opéra Bastille.

There are also noteworthy attractions, like the nearby **Coulée verte René-Dumont (Viaduc des Arts)**, an urban-renewal project that transformed an old elevated rail line into arcaded, design-focused studios and shops. Along the top, the Promenade Plantée makes for a lovely stroll through the 12e arrondissement, which includes stately apartment buildings and pretty Square Trousseau, gateway to the **Marché d'Aligre.** But today the neighborhoods farther afield are the real draw, having evolved into some of Paris's top destinations.

The **Canal St-Martin,** once the down-and-out cousin on the northern border, is now trend-spotting central, brimming with funky bars, cafés, art galleries, and boutiques. The scene is similar on Rues Oberkampf, St-Maur, and Jean-Pierre-Timbaud, where artists and small designers have set up shop, and where a substantial slice of the city's *bobo* (bourgeois-bohemian) contingent is buying up the no-longer-so-affordable apartments.

Continuing east, you'll find the city's largest cemetery, **Père-Lachaise,** with a roster of famous tenants. Not far away is the impressively wild **Parc Buttes-Chaumont,** with grassy fields, a small Greek-style temple, and sweeping hilltop views of Paris. It's the perfect place to eat a picnic lunch and let museum-weary kids blow off some steam. The eastern section is also home to two other popular parks: the **Parc de la Villette,** which contains a pair of engaging museums, and the **Bois de Vincennes,** home to the city's largest zoo.

To the south of the Bastille, the old wine warehouses at **Bercy** have become a veritable village of shops and restaurants bordering Parc de Bercy. Directly across the Seine is the **Bibliothéque Nationale François Mitterrand,** the National Library of France, a sprawling complex of modern glass towers opened in 1998.

TOP ATTRACTIONS

FAMILY **Bercy.** Tucked away south of the Gare de Lyon in the 12e arrondissement, blocks of stone warehouses that once stored wine are now home
to Bercy Village, a collection of boutiques and eateries that stay open
unusually late for Paris—many shops until 9 pm, Monday to Saturday;
some restaurants until 2 am daily (*28 rue François Truffaut* ☎ *08–
25–16–60–75* ⊕ *www.bercyvillage.com*). You can still see the old train
tracks used to transport the wine barrels from the provinces. Adjacent
to the shops is the tranquil Parc de Bercy, with lawns, ponds, and flower
beds crisscrossed by gravel paths, and the Jardin Yitzhak Rabin, a garden named for the late Nobel peace prize winner. Nearby, at 51 rue
de Bercy, a Cubist building by Frank Gehry houses the Cinémathèque
Française, a film buff's paradise, showing classic films, many in English; there are frequent homages to directors and actors, plus a cinema
bookshop and museum. ⊠ *Eastern Paris* Ⓜ *Cour St-Emilion, Bercy.*

NEED A BREAK

✕ **Pink Flamingo.** This American-owned pizzeria will deliver your pie
directly to the banks of the canal—they spot you thanks to the pink balloon
you're holding. ⊠ **67 rue Bichat, Canal St-Martin** ☎ **01–42–02–31–70**
⊕ **www.pinkflamingopizza.com** Ⓜ *Jacques Bonsergent, Colonel Fabien.*

Fodor's Choice ★ **Canal St-Martin.** This once-forgotten canal has morphed into one of
the city's trendiest places to wander. A good time to come is Sunday
afternoon, when the Quai de Valmy is closed to cars and some of the
shops are open. Rent a bike at any of the many Vélib' stations, stroll
along the banks, or go native and cuddle quai-side in the sunshine with
someone special.

In 1802 Napoléon ordered the 4.3-km (2.7-mile) canal dug as a source
of clean drinking water after cholera and other epidemics swept the city.
When it finally opened 23 years later, it extended north from the Seine
at Place de la Bastille to the Canal de l'Ourcq, near La Villette. Baron
Haussmann later covered a 1.6-km (1-mile) stretch of it, along today's
Boulevard Richard Lenoir. It nearly became a highway in the 1970s,
before the city's urban planners regained their senses. These days you
can take a boat tour from end to end through the canal's nine locks:
along the way, the bridges swing or lift open. The drawbridge with four
giant pulleys at Rue de Crimée, near La Villette, was a technological
marvel when it debuted in 1885.

In recent years gentrification has transformed the once-dodgy canal,
with artists taking over former industrial spaces and creating studios
and galleries. The bar and restaurant scene is hipster central, and small
designers have arrived, fleeing expensive rents in the Marais. To explore
this evolving *quartier,* set out on foot. Start on the Quai de Valmy at
Rue Faubourg du Temple (use the République métro stop). Here, at
Square Frédéric Lemaître facing north, there is a good view of one
of the locks (behind you the canal disappears underground). As you
head north, detour onto side streets like Rue Beaurepaire, a fashionista
destination with several "stock" (or surplus) shops for popular brands,
some open on Sunday. Rues Lancry and Vinaigriers are lined with bars,
restaurants, and small shops.

9

A swing bridge across the canal connects Lancry to the Rue de la Grange aux Belles, where you'll find the entrance to the massive Hôpital Saint-Louis, built in 1607 to accommodate plague victims and still a working hospital today. In front of you is the entrance to the chapel, which held its first Mass in July 1610, two months after the assassination of the hospital's patron, Henry IV. Stroll the grounds, flanked by the original brick-and-stone buildings with steeply sloping roofs. The peaceful courtyard garden is a neighborhood secret.

Back on Quai Valmy, browse more shops near the Rue des Récollets. Nearby is the Jardin Villemin, the 10e arrondissement's largest park (4½ acres) on the former site of another hospital. The nighttime scene, especially in summer, is hopping with twentysomethings spilling out of cafés and bars and onto the canal banks. If you've made it this far, reward yourself with a fresh taco or burrito at the tiny and authentically Mexican El Nopal taqueria at 3 rue Eugène Varlin. Farther up, just past Place Stalingrad, is the Rotonde de la Villette, a lively square with restaurants and twin MK2 cinemas on either side of the canal, plus a boat to ferry ticket holders across. Canauxrama (www.canauxrama.com) offers 2½-hour boat cruises through the locks (€18). Embarkation is at each end of the canal: at Bassin de la Villette or Port de l'Arsenal. ✉ *Canal St-Martin* Ⓜ *Jaurès (north end), République (south end), Gare de l'Est (middle).*

NEED A BREAK

✕ **Hôtel du Nord.** With a retro white facade, the Hôtel du Nord looks like a movie set—and indeed, it was famously used by Marcel Carné in his 1938 namesake film. The star, actress-icon Arletty, claimed to be unmoved by the romantic canal-side setting, uttering the memorable line "Atmosphere, atmosphere, I've had it with atmosphere!" Today the restaurant, beautifully restored, is a hipster favorite, though the food is not as fabulous as the ambience. ✉ *102 quai de Jemmappes, Canal St-Martin* ☎ *01–40–40–78–78* ⊕ *www.hoteldunord.org* Ⓜ *Jacques Bonsergent.*

Fodor's Choice **Cimetière du Père-Lachaise.** Bring a red rose for "the Little Sparrow" ★ Edith Piaf when you visit the cobblestone avenues and towering trees that make this 118-acre oasis of green perhaps the world's most famous cemetery. Named for Père François de la Chaise, Louis XIV's confessor, Père-Lachaise is more than just a who's who of celebrities. The Paris Commune's final battle took place here on May 28, 1871, when 147 rebels were lined up and shot against the Mur des Fédérés (Federalists' Wall) in the southeast corner. Aside from the sheer aesthetic beauty of the cemetery, the main attraction is what (or who, more accurately) is below ground.

Two of the biggest draws are Jim Morrison's grave (with its own guard to keep Doors fans under control) and the life-size bronze figure of French journalist Victor Noir, whose alleged fertility-enhancing power accounts for the patches rubbed smooth by hopeful hands. Other significant grave sites include those of 12th-century French philosopher Pierre Abélard and his lover Héloïse; French writers Colette, Honoré de Balzac, and Marcel Proust; American writers Richard Wright, Gertrude Stein, and Alice B. Toklas; Irish writer Oscar Wilde; French actress

DID YOU KNOW?

Many people take boat rides on the Seine, but there are also several companies that offer trips along the Canal St-Martin. Check out 🌐 *en.pariscanal.com* or 🌐 *www.canauxrama.com* for more information.

Famed cemetery Père-Lachaise is the final resting place for artists like Edith Piaf, Jim Morrison, Marcel Proust, Oscar Wilde, and many more.

Sarah Bernhardt; French composer Georges Bizet; Greek-American opera singer Maria Callas; Franco-Polish composer Frédéric Chopin; painters of various nationalities including Georges-Pierre Seurat, Camille Pissaro, Jean-Auguste-Dominique Ingres, Jacques-Louis David, Eugène Delacroix, Théodore Géricault, Amedeo Clemente Modigliani, and Max Ernst; French jazz violinist Stephane Grappelli; French civic planner Baron Haussmann; French playwright and actor Molière; and French singer Edith Piaf. (To visit the grave sites of a few other famous French men and women, head south to Cimetière du Montparnasse , north to Cimetière de Montmartre, or west to Passy Cemetery.)

■ TIP➜ Pinpoint grave sites on the website before you come, but buy a map anyway outside the entrances—you'll still get lost, but that's part of the fun. One of the best days to visit is on All Saints' Day (November 1), when Parisians bring flowers to adorn the graves of loved ones or favorite celebrities. ⊠ *Entrances on Rue des Rondeaux, Bd. de Ménilmontant, and Rue de la Réunion, Eastern Paris* ☎ *01–55–25–82–10* ⊕ *www.pere-lachaise.com* ✉ *Free* ⊙ *Closed after 6 pm.* Ⓜ *Gambetta, Philippe-Auguste, Père-Lachaise.*

FAMILY **Cité des Sciences et de l'Industrie** (*Museum of Science and Industry*). Occupying a colorful three-story industrial space that recalls the Pompidou Center, this ambitious science museum in Parc de la Villette is packed with things to do—all of them accessible to English speakers. Scores of exhibits focus on subjects like space, transportation, and technology. Hands-on workshops keep the kids entertained, and the planetarium is invariably a hit. Temporary exhibitions, like a recent exploration of cinematic special effects, are always multilingual and usually interactive.

✉ *Parc de la Villette , 30 av. Corentin-Cariou, Eastern Paris* ☏ *01–40–05–70–00, 01–85–53–99–74 Interactive Voice response* ⊕ *www.citesciences.fr* 🎫 *€12 (permanent and temporary exhibitions; planetarium)* ⊘ *Closed Mon.* Ⓜ *Porte de la Villette.*

Coulée Verte René-Dumont/Promenade Plantée (*La Coulée Verte*). Once a train line from the Paris suburbs to Bastille, this redbrick viaduct (often referred to as Le Viaduc des Arts) is now the green heart of the unpretentious 12e arrondissement. The rails have been transformed into a 4.5-km (2.8-mile) walkway lined with trees, bamboo, and flowers, offering a bird's-eye view of the stately Haussmannian buildings along Avenue Daumesnil. Below, the *voûtes* (arcades) have been transformed by the city into artisan boutiques, many focused on decor and design. All tenants are hand-picked. There are also temporary galleries showcasing art and photography. The Promenade, which gained fame as a setting in the 2004 film *Before Sunset,* was the inspiration for New York's High Line. It ends at the Jardin de Reuilly. From here you can continue your walk to the Bois de Vincennes. If you're hungry, grab a bite at L'Arrosoir, a cozy café under the viaduct at 75 avenue Daumesnil. ✉ *1–129 av. Daumesnil, Bastille* ☏ *01–86–95–95–07* ⊕ *www. leviaducdesarts.com* Ⓜ *Bastille, Gare de Lyon.*

Marché d'Aligre. Place d'Aligre boasts two of Paris's best markets: the lively outdoor Marché d'Aligre and the covered Marché Beauvau. Open every day but Monday, both are great places to pick up picnic essentials, which you can enjoy nearby in the small park at Square Trousseau or on the Promenade Plantée. The picturesque outdoor market has dozens of boisterous vendors, their stands laden with fresh fruits and vegetables, flower bouquets, and regional products such as jam, honey, and dried sausage. The best bargains are had just before closing time, and many vendors are happy to give you a taste of whatever they're selling. The covered market stocks everything from meats and cheeses to Belgian beer. Sunday morning, when the accompanying flea market is in full swing, is the liveliest time to visit. Don't forget your camera. Stop for a plate of *saucisse* and a glass of *rouge* (even on Sunday morning) at one of the city's quirkiest wine bars, Le Baron Rouge, 1 rue Théophile Roussel. ✉ *Pl. d'Aligre, Bastille* ⊕ *www.equipement. paris.fr/marche-couvert-beauvau-marche-d-aligre-5480* ⊘ *Closed Mon.* Ⓜ *Ledru-Rollin, Bastille.*

FAMILY **Musée de la Musique.** Parc de la Villette's music museum contains four centuries' worth of instruments from around the world—about 1,000 in total, many of them exquisite works of art. Their sounds and stories are evoked on numerous video screens and via commentary you can follow on headphones (ask for a free audioguide in English). Leave time for the excellent temporary exhibitions, like the recent one on the life and music of French chanteuse Barbara. On the plaza, adjacent to the museum, the outdoor terrace at Café des Concerts (☏ *01–42–49–74–74* ⊕ *www.cafedesconcerts.com*) is an inviting place to have a drink on a sunny day. ✉ *Parc de la Villette, 221 av. Jean-Jaurès, Eastern Paris* ☏ *01–44–84–44–84* ⊕ *www.philharmoniedeparis.fr/fr/musee-de-la-musique* 🎫 *€8; €11 with temporary exhibits* ⊘ *Closed Mon.* Ⓜ *Porte de Pantin.*

9

Opéra Bastille. Paris's main opera house opened its doors on July 14, 1989, to mark the bicentennial of the French Revolution. The fabulous acoustics of the steeply sloping, stylish auditorium have earned more plaudits than the modern facade designed by Uruguay-born architect Carlos Ott. If you want to see a show, reserve your ticket well in advance, or take your chances snagging a same-day seat just prior to the performance. Once the doors open, 32 standing-room-only tickets also go on sale for €5. Tickets for a 90-minute guided tour (in French only) cost €15. ⊠ *Pl. de la Bastille, Bastille* ☎ *08–92–89–90–90 for tickets and tour information (€0.35 per minute), 01–71–25–24–23 from outside of France* ⊕ *www.operadeparis.fr* ⊗ *Closed mid-July– Aug. Box office closed Sun. and after 6:30 pm, except 1 hr before curtain call)* Ⓜ *Bastille.*

FAMILY **Parc de la Villette.** This former abattoir is now an ultramodern, 130-acre park. With lawns and play areas, an excellent science museum, a music complex, and a cinema, it's the perfect place to entertain exhausted kids. You could easily spend a whole day here.

The park itself was designed in the 1980s by postmodern architecture star Bernard Tschumi, who melded industrial elements, children's games (don't miss the dragon slide), ample green spaces, and funky sculptures along the canal into one vast yet unified playground. Loved by picnickers, the lawns also attract rehearsing samba bands and pickup soccer players. In summer there are outdoor festivals and a free open-air cinema, where people gather at dusk to watch movies on a huge inflatable screen.

In cold weather you can visit an authentic submarine and the Espace Chapiteaux (a circus tent featuring contemporary acrobatic theater performances) before hitting the museums. The hands-on one at the Cité des Sciences et de l'Industrie is a favorite stop for families and a must for science fans; its 3-D Omnimax cinema (La Géode) is housed in a giant mirrored ball. Arts-oriented visitors of all ages will marvel at the excellent, instrument-filled Musée de la Musique. The park has even more in store for music lovers in the form of the Philharmonie de Paris, a striking 2,400-seat concert hall designed by Jean Nouvel.

All that's left of the slaughterhouse that once stood here is La Grande Halle, a magnificent iron-and-glass building currently used for exhibitions, performances, and trade shows. ⊠ *Parc de la Villette, 211 av. Jean Jaurès, Eastern Paris* ☎ *01–40–03–75–75* ⊕ *www.lavillette.com* Ⓜ *Porte de Pantin, Porte de la Villette.*

FAMILY **Parc des Buttes-Chaumont.** If you're tired of perfectly manicured Parisian parks with lawns that are off-limits to your weary feet, this place is for you. Built in 1863 on abandoned gypsum quarries and a former gallows, it was northern Paris's first park, part of Napoléon III's planned greening of the city (the emperor had spent years in exile in London, where he fell in love with the public parks). Today the lovely 61-acre hilltop expanse in the untouristy 19e arrondissement has grassy fields, shady walkways, waterfalls, and a picturesque lake dotted with swans. Rising from the lake is a rocky cliff you can climb to find a mini Greek-style temple and a commanding view of Sacré-Coeur Basilica. A favorite of families, the park also has pony rides and an open-air puppet theater—Guignol de Paris (€5; shows at 3:30 pm and 4:45 pm Wednesday and Saturday, and at 11:15 am, 3:30 pm, and 4:45 pm on Sunday, year-round)—not far from the entrance at the Buttes-Chaumont métro stop. When you've worked up an appetite, grab a snack at the Rosa Bonheur café (⊕ *www. rosabonheur.fr*), or reserve a table for weekend lunch at Le Pavillon du Lac restaurant (⊕ *www.lepavillondulac.fr*). Major renovation work that began in 2012 is almost finished, but expect some unsightly construction and limited access to certain areas. ⊠ *Entrances on Rue Botzaris or Rue Manin, Belleville* Ⓜ *Buttes-Chaumont, Botzaris, Laumière.*

> **DID YOU KNOW?**
>
> The Bastille prison is long gone, but you can still see remnants of it. The best place to look is in the Bastille métro station, where large stones are visible on the platform of Line 5 (direction Bobigny), with an explanation and artist's rendering of the prison. Another chunk of one of the towers, excavated during construction of the métro in 1898, sits nearby, unmarked, in the Square Henri-Galli at the edge of a small park: go to the intersection of Boulevard Henri IV and the quai of the same name.

Place de la Bastille. Almost nothing remains of the infamous Bastille prison, destroyed more than 225 years ago, though tourists still ask bemused Parisians where to find it. Until the late 1980s, there was little more to see here than a busy traffic circle ringing the Colonne de Juillet (July Column), a memorial to the victims of later uprisings in 1830 and 1848. The opening of the Opéra Bastille in 1989 rejuvenated the area, however, drawing art galleries, bars, and restaurants to the narrow streets, notably along Rue de Lappe—once a haunt of Edith Piaf—and Rue de la Roquette.

Before it became a prison, the Bastille St-Antoine was a defensive fortress with eight immense towers and a wide moat. It was built by Charles V in the late 14th century and transformed into a prison during the reign of Louis XIII (1610–43). Famous occupants included Voltaire, the Marquis de Sade, and the Man in the Iron Mask. On July 14, 1789, it was stormed by an angry mob that dramatically freed all of the remaining prisoners (there were only seven), thereby launching the French Revolution. The roots of the revolt ran deep. Resentment toward Louis XVI and Marie-Antoinette had been building amid a severe financial crisis. There was a crippling bread shortage, and the free-spending monarch was blamed. When the king dismissed the popular finance minister, Jacques Necker, enraged Parisians took to the streets. They marched to Les Invalides, helping themselves to stocks of arms, then continued on to the Bastille. A few months later, what was left of the prison was razed—and 83 of its stones were carved into miniature Bastilles and sent to the provinces as a memento (you can see one of them in the Musée Carnavalet, when it re-opens). The key to the prison was given to George Washington by Lafayette and has remained at Mount Vernon ever since. Today, nearly every major street demonstration in Paris—and there are many—passes through this square. ⊠ *Bastille* Ⓜ *Bastille.*

9

WORTH NOTING

Bibliothèque Nationale François Mitterrand. The National Library of France, across the sleek Simone de Beauvoir footbridge from Bercy Park, is a stark complex comprising four 22-story L-shape buildings representing open books. Commissioned by President Mitterrand, the €1 billion library was said to be the world's most modern when it opened in 1998—a reputation quickly sullied when it was discovered that miles of books and rare documents were baking in the glass towers, unprotected from the sun (movable shutters were eventually installed). Some of the most important printed treasures of France are stored here, though the majority of them are available only to researchers. Visitors can see the impressive 17th-century Globes of Coronelli, a pair of 2-ton orbs made for Louis XIV. There's a sunken center garden with tall trees (open to the public the first weekend in June) ringed by low-ceilinged reading rooms, which are nothing special. A first-floor gallery hosts popular temporary exhibitions on subjects such as the life of Casanova. Enter through the easternmost tower. ⊠ *Quai François Mauriac, Eastern Paris* ☎ *01–53–79–59–59* ⊕ *www.bnf.fr* ✉ *Globes gallery free; reading rooms €4; exhibitions €9; concerts and live performances €10* ⊗ *Closed Mon.* Ⓜ *Bibliothèque, Quai de la Gare.*

FAMILY **Bois de Vincennes.** Like the Bois de Boulogne to the west, this much-loved retreat on the city's eastern border was landscaped by Napoléon III. Its roots, however, reach back to the 13th century, when Philippe Auguste created a hunting preserve in the shadow of the royal Château de Vincennes, which once ranked as the largest château in Europe. In 1731 Louis XV created a public park here, and the *bois* (or wood) now features lush lawns, a flower garden, and summertime jazz concerts. Rowboats are for hire at a pair of lakes: Lac Daumesnil, which has two islands, and Lac des Minimes, which has three. For the kids, there are pony rides, a miniature train, and numerous play areas. Here, too, you'll find the stunning Palais de la Porte Dorée (home to an immigration museum and a tropical aquarium), the Parc Zoologique, the Hippodrome de Vincennes racetrack, two cafés, and, in spring, an amusement park. Bikes can be rented at the Château de Vincennes métro stop. ⊠ *Bois de Vincennes, Eastern Paris* Ⓜ *Château de Vincennes, Porte Dorée.*

Château de Vincennes. This imposing high-walled château, on the northern edge of the Bois de Vincennes, was France's medieval answer to Versailles. Built and expanded by various kings between the 12th and 14th centuries, it is now surrounded by a dry moat and dominated by a 170-foot keep (the last of nine original towers). The royal residence eventually became a prison holding convicts, notably of both sexes—and "the doors did not always remain closed between them," as one tour guide coyly put it. Inmates included the philosopher Diderot and the Marquis de Sade. Both the château and its cathedral, Sainte-Chapelle (designed in the style of the Paris church of the same name) have undergone a spectacular restoration, returning them to their previous glory. If you speak French, the free 90-minute tour is worthwhile; otherwise, consider spending €3 for the English audioguide. ⊠ *Av. de*

Paris, Eastern Paris ☎ *01–43–28–15–48* ⊕ *www.chateau-vincennes.fr* €9 Ⓜ *Château de Vincennes.*

OFF THE BEATEN PATH

Le 104. Le Cent Quatre takes its name from its address in a rough-around-the-edges corner of the 19e arrondissement, not far from the top of the Canal St-Martin. The former site of the city morgue, this cavernous art hub is home to an offbeat collection of performance venues, shops, and studios (artists of all genres compete for free studio space, and sometimes you can get a sneak peek of them at work). Contemporary art exhibits, some of which charge admission, are staged here, as are concerts. On-site you'll also find a restaurant, a café, a bookstore, a secondhand shop, and a play area for children. Check the website before going to see what's on. ⊠ *104 rue d'Aubervilliers, Eastern Paris* ☎ *01–53–35–50–00* ⊕ *www.104.fr* Free; prices for exhibits and concerts vary ⊘ Closed Mon. Ⓜ *Stalingrad.*

OFF THE BEATEN PATH

Musée Edith Piaf. Devotees will appreciate the tiny two-room apartment where the "little sparrow" lived for a year, when she was 28 years old and sang in the working-class cafés on Rue Oberkampf. The flat was obtained by Les Amis d'Edith Piaf in 1978 and is now a shrine to the petite crooner, whose life-size photo (she was just 4 feet, 9 inches tall) greets visitors at the door. The red walls are covered with portraits of Piaf done by her many artist friends, and her personal letters are framed. On display, you'll see her books and handbags, as well as a few dresses, her size 4 shoes, and a touching pair of old boxing gloves belonging to one of her great loves—champion pugilist Marcel Cerdan. (A reservation is required; no English spoken.) ⊠ *5 rue Crespin du Gast, Oberkampf* ☎ *01–43–55–52–72* Free, donations strongly encouraged ⊘ Closed Fri.–Sun. Ⓜ *Ménilmontant.*

FAMILY **Palais de la Porte Dorée.** If you're bound for the Bois de Vincennes, pay a visit to the Palais de la Porte Dorée. Built for the 1931 Colonial Exhibition, it's one of the best examples of Art Deco architecture in Paris. The ornate facade features bas-relief sculptures representing France's erstwhile empire. Inside, the elaborate marble, ornate metalwork, and original lighting are all beautifully maintained. Entry to the ground floor is free. On either end are furnished salons, one representing Asia, the other Africa (a Gucci commercial was filmed in the latter); peek into the central room, called the Forum, where restored Africa-inspired mosaics line the walls. The upper floors are occupied by the Cité Nationale de l'Historie de l'Immigration, a well-executed modern museum tracing the history of immigration in France. The basement contains L'Aquarium Tropical, a small but engaging aquarium with a pair of rare albino alligators plus many types of exotic marine life. ⊠ *293 av. Daumesnil, Eastern Paris* ☎ *01–53–59–58–60* ⊕ *www.palais-portedoree.fr* Ground floor free; museum €5; aquarium €5; combined ticket €8 (€1 or €2 more when there is a temporary exhibition) ⊘ Closed Mon. Ⓜ *Porte Dorée.*

FAMILY **Parc Floral de Paris.** A lake, a butterfly garden, and seasonal displays of blooms make the Bois de Vincennes's 70-acre floral park a lovely place to spend a summer afternoon. Kids will also enjoy the minigolf and game areas. The park hosts jazz concerts most weekends from

April through September, but other months many attractions are closed. ⊠ *Rte. de la Pyramide, Eastern Paris* ☎ *01–49–57–24–81* ⊕ *www.vin-cennes-tourisme.fr/Decouvrir/Parc-Floral* ⧉ *€3 May–Oct.; free rest of year* Ⓜ *Château de Vincennes.*

FAMILY **Pavillon de l'Arsenal.** If your knowledge of Paris history is *nul* (nil), stop here for an entertaining free tutorial. Built in 1879 as a private museum, the Pavillon today is a restored structure of glass and iron that show-cases the city's urban development through the ages. A giant model of Paris traces its evolution (with information in English). There are photos, maps, and videos, plus a giant digital interactive model detail-ing what Paris is predicted to look like in 2020. The standout, created in partnership with Google, is a floor mosaic made up of 48 LED screens that allows visitors at stationary consoles to explore the city via Google Maps. The Pavillon also has a café-bookstore and hosts frequent architecture-themed temporary exhibits. ⊠ *21 bd. Morland, Bastille* ☎ *01–42–76–33–97* ⊕ *www.pavillon-arsenal.com* ⧉ *Free* ⊗ *Closed Mon.* Ⓜ *Sully-Morland, Bastille.*

FAMILY **Piscine Josephine Baker.** This modern floating aquatic center, named after the much-beloved American entertainer, features a pool with a retract-able glass roof, two solariums, a steam room, Jacuzzis, and a gym. Check the opening hours and schedule of classes online. ⊠ *Porte de la Gare, 21 quai François Mauriac, Eastern Paris* ☎ *01–56–61–96–50* ⊕ *www.piscine-baker.fr* ⧉ *€4 for pool (€7 in summer); fees may apply for other activities* Ⓜ *Quai de la Gare, Bibilothèque.*

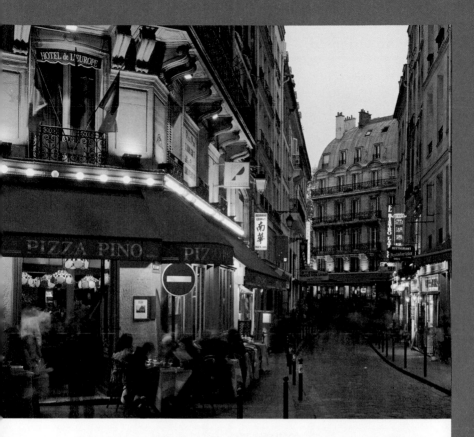

THE LATIN QUARTER

Getting Oriented

The Latin Quarter

TOP REASONS TO GO

Musée de Cluny. On the site of an ancient Roman bath, this former abbey is home to the famous *The Lady and the Unicorn* tapestries; the building, tranquil garden, and extensive collection have the hush of a medieval monastery.

Shakespeare & Company. This legendary English-language bookstore is more than a shopping destination; it's a meeting place for young expats and literature-loving travelers alike.

Rue Mouffetard. Whether you're a gastronome or just plain hungry, you'll be enthralled by the array of characteristically French edibles sold on this winding market street.

Jardin des Plantes. This garden is a great spot to enjoy a picnic or to rest your tired feet on one of the many shaded benches.

La Grande Mosquée de Paris. Relax with a little glass of mint tea in the leafy courtyard café at Paris's most beautiful mosque.

MAKING THE MOST OF YOUR TIME

The Quartier Latin is the perfect place to wander sans itinerary, though there is no shortage of sites worth seeing. Shopping here is generally more affordable (but less original) than in other neighborhoods, and there are lots of new- and used-book stores, many of which stock English-language titles. Pick up picnic supplies in the food shops along Rue Mouffetard or the open-air market at Place Monge (Wednesday, Friday, and Sunday until mid-afternoon), then savor your booty on a bench at the Jardin des Plantes. Linger over mint tea at the lovely Grande Mosquée de Paris or take in a terrific view from the roof of the Institut du Monde Arabe. Stroll the hilly streets around the Panthéon on your way to see the treasures at the Musée de Cluny. Finish with a sunset apéritif on one of the barge cafés (open spring to fall) along the Seine, across from Notre-Dame.

GETTING HERE

The Quartier Latin is in the 5e arrondissement. Take métro Line 4 to St-Michel to start exploring at the Lucifer-slaying fountain near Shakespeare & Company, across the Seine from Notre-Dame. Go to the Cluny stop on Line 10 if you're heading to the Musée de Cluny. The Place Monge stop on Line 7 puts you near the Panthéon and Rue Mouffetard, the Mosquée de Paris, and the Jardin des Plantes. Les Gobelins neighborhood straddles the 5e, 13e, and 14e arrondissements, but is considered part of the 5e because of the Manufacture des Gobelins.

BEST CAFÉS

Cave La Bourgogne. Settle in on the terrace of this old-school bistro for lunch, or join the locals at the zinc bar. ⊠ *144 rue Mouffetard, Latin Quarter* ☎ *01–47–07–82–80* Ⓜ *Censier-Daubenton.*

Les Patios. If you're young—or young at heart—come here to hang with the Sorbonne crowd. ⊠ *5 pl. de la Sorbonne, Latin Quarter* ☎ *01–43–54–34–43* Ⓜ *Cluny–La Sorbonne.*

10

Sightseeing
★★★★

Dining
★★★

Lodging
★★★★

Shopping
★★★

Nightlife
★★★

The Quartier Latin is the heart of student Paris—and has been for more than 800 years. France's oldest university, La Sorbonne, was founded here in 1257, and the neighborhood takes its name from the fact that Latin was the common language of the students, who came from all over Europe. Today the area is full of cheap and cheerful cafés, bars, and shops.

Updated by
Jack Vermee

The main drag, **Boulevard St-Michel,** is a busy street where bookshops have given way to chain clothing stores and fast-food joints—but don't let that stop you! There are (almost) as many French people wandering the streets here as there are tourists. At **Place St-Michel,** the symbolic gateway to the *quartier,* notice the 19th-century fountain depicting Saint Michael slaying the "great dragon," Satan—a symbolic warning to rebellious locals from Napoléon III. Today the fountain serves as a meeting spot and makes a rather fine metaphor for the boulevard it anchors: a bit grimy but extremely popular.

When you've had enough of the crowds, turn off the boulevard and explore the side streets, where you can find quirky boutiques and intimate bistros. Or stop for a *demi* (a half pint of draft beer) at one of the cafés on **Place de la Sorbonne,** ground zero for students (and their many noisy demonstrations). Around the winding streets behind the **Panthéon,** where French luminaries are laid to rest, you can still encounter plenty of academics arguing philosophy while sipping espresso, but today the 5e arrondissement is also one of Paris's most charming and sought-after (read: expensive) places to live.

Shop along **Rue Mouffetard** as Parisians do—all the while complaining about the high prices—for one of the best selections of runny cheeses, fresh breads, and charcuterie. Grab a seat in a bustling café, or follow the locals' lead and stand at the bar, where drinks are always cheaper. Film buffs won't have to look far to find one of the small cinema revival houses showing old American films in English (look for v.o., for *version originale*). Not far from le Mouffe is the gorgeous white **Grande**

Mosquée de Paris with its impressive minaret. Just beyond the mosque is the **Jardin des Plantes**—a large, if somewhat bland, botanical garden that is home to three natural history museums, most notably the **Grande Galerie de l'Évolution**. Inside, kids can marvel at enormous whale skeletons, along with all sorts of taxidermy. Some of Paris's most intriguing sites are in this neighborhood, including the **Musée de Cluny** and the innovative **Institut du Monde Arabe**. See ancient history mingle with modern life at the **Arènes de Lutèce**, a Roman amphitheater and favorite soccer pitch for neighborhood kids.

TOP ATTRACTIONS

FAMILY **Grande Galerie de l'Évolution** (*Great Hall of Evolution*). With a parade of taxidermied animals ranging from the tiniest dung beetle to the tallest giraffe, this four-story natural history museum in the Jardin des Plantes will perk up otherwise museum-weary kids. The flagship of three natural history museums in the garden, this restored 1889 building has a ceiling that changes color to suggest storms, twilight, or the hot savanna sun. Other must-sees are the gigantic skeleton of a blue whale and the stuffed royal rhino (he came from the menagerie at Versailles, where he was a pet of Louis XV). Kids 6 to 12 will enjoy La Galerie d'Enfants (The Children's Gallery): opened in 2010, it has bilingual interactive exhibits about the natural world. A lab stocked with microscopes often offers free workshops, and most of the staff speaks some English. Hang on to your ticket; it will get you a discount at the other museums within the Jardin des Plantes. ✉ *36 rue Geoffroy-St-Hilaire, Latin Quarter* ☎ *01–40–79–54–79* ⊕ *www.grandegaleriedelevolution.fr* ≊ *€10; €12 combined with Children's Gallery or temporary exhibitions; €14 for all three* ☉ *Closed Tues.* Ⓜ *Place Monge, Censier-Daubenton.*

FAMILY **Institut du Monde Arabe.** This eye-catching metal-and-glass tower by architect Jean Nouvel cleverly uses metal diaphragms in the shape of square Arabic-style screens to work like a camera lens, opening and closing to control the flow of sunlight. The vast cultural center's layout is intended to reinterpret the traditional enclosed Arab courtyard. Inside, there are various spaces—among them a museum that explores the culture and religion of the 22 Arab League member nations. With the addition of elements from the Louvre's holdings and private donors, the museum's impressive collection includes Islamic art, artifacts, ceramics, and textiles, which are displayed on four floors. There is also a performance space, a sound-and-image center, a library, and a bookstore. Temporary exhibitions usually have information and an audioguide in English. Glass elevators whisk you to the ninth floor,

10

where you can sip mint tea in the rooftop restaurant, Le Zyriab, while feasting on one of the best views in Paris. ⊠ *1 rue des Fossés-St-Bernard, Latin Quarter* ☎ *01–40–51–38–38* ⊕ *www.imarabe.org* ⊠ *€8* ⊙ *Closed Mon.* Ⓜ *Jussieu.*

FAMILY   **Jardin des Plantes** (*Botanical Gardens*). Opened in 1640 and once known
Fodor's Choice   as the Jardin du Roi (or King's Garden), this sprawling patch of green-
★   ery is a neighborhood gem. It's home to several gardens and various museums, all housed in 19th-century buildings whose original architecture blends glass with ornate ironwork. The botanical and rose gardens are impressive, and plant lovers won't want to miss the towering greenhouses (*serre* in French)—they are filled with one of the world's most extensive collections of tropical and desert flora. If you have kids, take them to the excellent Grande Galerie de l'Évolution or one of the other natural history museums here: the Galerie de Paléontologie, stocked with dinosaur and other skeletons, and the recently renovated, rock-laden Galerie de Minéralogie. If the kids prefer fauna, visit the Ménagerie, a small zoo founded in 1794 whose animals once fed Parisians during the 1870 Prussian siege. The star attractions are Nénette, the grande-dame orangutan from Borneo, and her swinging friends in the monkey and ape house. ∎TIP➔ If you need a break, there are three kiosk cafés in the Jardin. ⊠ *Entrances on Rue Geoffroy-St-Hilaire, Rue Cuvier, Rue de Buffon, and Quai St-Bernard, Latin Quarter* ☎ *01–40–79–56–01* ⊕ *www.jardindesplantes.net* ⊠ *Museums €7–€12; zoo €13; greenhouses €7; gardens free* ⊙ *Museums and greenhouses closed Tues.* Ⓜ *Gare d'Austerlitz, Jussieu; Place Monge, Censier-Daubenton for Grande Galerie de l'Évolution.*

Fodor's Choice   **Musée de Cluny** (*Musée National du Moyen-Age [National Museum of
★   the Middle Ages]*). Built on the ruins of Roman baths, the Hôtel de Cluny has been a museum since medievalist Alexandre Du Sommerard established his collection here in 1844. The ornate 15th-century mansion was created for the abbot of Cluny, leader of the mightiest monastery in France. Symbols of the abbot's power surround the building, from the crenellated walls that proclaimed his independence from the king, to the carved Burgundian grapes twining up the entrance that symbolize his valuable vineyards. The scallop shells (*coquilles St-Jacques*) covering the facade are a symbol of religious pilgrimage, another important source of income for the abbot; the well-traveled pilgrimage route to Spain once ran around the corner along Rue St-Jacques. The highlight of the museum's collection is the world-famous *La Dame à la Licorne* (*The Lady and the Unicorn*) tapestry series, woven in the 16th century, probably in Belgium, and now presented in refurbished surroundings. The vermillion tapestries (Room 13) are an allegorical representation of the five senses. In each, a unicorn and a lion surround an elegant young woman against an elaborate *millefleur* (literally, "1,000 flowers") background. The enigmatic sixth tapestry is thought to be either a tribute to a sixth sense, perhaps intelligence, or a renouncement of the other senses; "To my only desire" is inscribed at the top. The collection also includes the original sculpted heads of the *Kings of Israel and Judah* from Notre-Dame, decapitated during the Revolution and discovered in 1977 in the basement of a French bank. The *frigidarium* (Room 9) is

CLOSE UP

Literary Lion

The English-language bookstore **Shakespeare & Company** (*37 rue de la Bûcherie, 01–43–25–40–93* ⊕ *www.shakespeareandcompany. com*) is one of Paris's most eccentric and lovable literary institutions. Founded by George Whitman, the maze of new and used books has offered a sense of community (and often a bed) to wandering writers since the 1950s. The store takes its name from Sylvia Beach's original Shakespeare & Co., which opened in 1919 at 12 rue d'Odéon, welcoming the likes of Ernest Hemingway, James Baldwin, and James Joyce. Beach famously bucked the system when she published Joyce's *Ulysses* in 1922, but her original store closed in 1941. After the war Whitman picked up the gauntlet, naming his own bookstore after its famous predecessor.

When Whitman passed away in 2011, heavy-hearted locals left candles and flowers in front of his iconic storefront. He is buried in the literati-laden Père-Lachaise cemetery; however, his legacy lives on through his daughter Sylvia, who runs the shop and welcomes a new generation of Paris dreamers. Walk up the almost impossibly narrow stairs to the second floor and you'll still see laptops and sleeping bags tucked between the aging volumes and under dusty daybeds; it's sort of like a hippie commune. A revolving cast of characters helps out in the shop or cooks meals for fellow residents. They're in good company; Henry Miller, Samuel Beckett, and William Burroughs are among the famous writers to benefit from the Whitman family hospitality.

a stunning reminder of the city's cold-water Roman baths; the soaring space, painstakingly renovated, houses temporary exhibits. Also notable is the pocket-size chapel (Room 20) with its elaborate Gothic ceiling. Outside, in Place Paul Painlevé, is a charming medieval-style garden where you can see flora depicted in the unicorn tapestries. The free audioguide in English is highly recommended. For a different kind of auditory experience, check the event listings; concerts of medieval music are often staged Sunday afternoon and Monday at lunchtime (€7).

Note that extensive renovations, intended to vastly improve accessibility and transform the museum experience, are under way. They are slated to be complete sometime in 2020; in the interim, check the website for select exhibit closures. ⊠ *6 pl. Paul-Painlevé, Latin Quarter* ☎ *01–53–73–78–00* ⊕ *www.musee-moyenage.fr* ⊠ *€8 (free 1st Sun. of month); €9 during temporary exhibitions* ⊗ *Closed Tues.* Ⓜ *Cluny–La Sorbonne.*

NEED A BREAK

✕ **Place de la Contrescarpe.** This popular square behind the Panthéon attracts locals, students, and Hemingway enthusiasts (he once lived around the corner). It has a small-town feel during the day and a lively atmosphere after dusk when the bars and eateries fill up. ⊠ *Latin Quarter* Ⓜ *Place Monge.*

Panthéon. Rome has St. Peter's, London has St. Paul's, and Paris has the Panthéon, whose enormous dome dominates the Left Bank. Built as the

church of Ste-Geneviève, the patron saint of Paris, it was later converted to an all-star mausoleum for some of France's biggest names, including Voltaire, Zola, Dumas, Rousseau, and Hugo. Pierre and Marie Curie were reinterred here together in 1995. Begun in 1764, the building was almost complete when the French Revolution erupted. By then, architect Jacques-German Soufflot had died—supposedly

THE 13E ARRONDISSEMENT

The village-like neighborhood of La Butte aux Cailles (in the 13e arrondissement, south of Place d'Italie) is a fun destination with a hip crowd, not far from the Quartier Latin if you want a break from the tourists.

from worrying that the 220-foot-high dome would collapse. He needn't have fretted: the dome was so perfect that Foucault used it in his famous pendulum test to prove the Earth rotates on its axis. Time has taken its toll on the Panthéon, and the structure is now in the midst of an extensive, multiyear overhaul; however, the crypt and nave remain accessible to the public, and the famous pendulum has been returned to its place of honor. ⊠ *Pl. du Panthéon, Latin Quarter* ☎ *01–44–32–18–00* ⊕ *www. paris-pantheon.fr* ☕ *€9 (€12 with audioguide)* Ⓜ *Cardinal Lemoine; RER: Luxembourg.*

Fodor's Choice ★ **Rue Mouffetard.** This winding cobblestone street is one of the city's oldest and was once a Roman road leading south from Lutetia (the Roman name for Paris) to Italy. The upper half is dotted with restaurants and bars that cater to tourists and students; the lower half is the setting of a lively morning market, Tuesday through Sunday. The highlight of le Mouffe, though, is the stretch in between where the shops spill into the street with luscious offerings such as roasting chickens and potatoes, rustic *saucisson,* pâtés, and pungent cheeses, especially at Androuët (No. 134). If you're here in the morning, Le Mouffetard Café (No. 116) is a good place to stop for a Continental breakfast (about €10). If it's apéritif time, head to Place de la Contrescarpe for a cocktail, or enjoy a glass of wine at Cave La Bourgogne (No. 144). Prefer to just do a little noshing? Sample the chocolates at Mococha (No. 89) or the gelato at Gelati d'Alberto (No. 45). Note that most shops are closed Monday. ⊠ *Latin Quarter* Ⓜ *Place Monge, Censier-Daubenton.*

WORTH NOTING

FAMILY **Arènes de Lutèce** (*Lutetia Amphitheater*). This Roman amphitheater, designed as a theater and circus, was almost completely destroyed by barbarians in AD 280. The site was rediscovered in 1869, and you can still see part of the stage and tiered seating. Along with the remains of the baths at Cluny, the arena constitutes rare evidence of the powerful Roman city of Lutetia that flourished on the Rive Gauche in the 3rd century. It's a favorite spot for picnicking, pickup soccer, or *boules.* ⊠ *Entrances on Rues Monge, de Navarre, and des Arènes, Latin Quarter* ☎ *01–45–35–02–56* ☕ *Free* Ⓜ *Place Monge, Cardinal Lemoine, Jussieu.*

10

CLOSE UP

Hemingway's Paris

There is a saying: "Everyone has two countries, his or her own—and France." For the Lost Generation after World War I, these words rang particularly true. Lured by favorable exchange rates, free-flowing alcohol, and a booming arts scene, many American writers, composers, and painters moved to Paris in the 1920s and 1930s, Ernest Hemingway among them. He arrived in Paris with his first wife, Hadley, in December 1921 and headed for the Rive Gauche—the Hôtel de l'Angleterre, to be exact (still operating at 44 rue Jacob). To celebrate their arrival the couple went to the Café de la Paix for a meal they nearly couldn't afford.

Hemingway worked as a journalist and quickly made friends with expat writers such as Gertrude Stein and Ezra Pound. In 1922 the Hemingways moved to 74 rue du Cardinal Lemoine, a bare-bones apartment with no running water (his writing studio was around the corner, on the top floor of 39 rue Descartes). Then, in 1924, they and their baby son settled at 113 rue Notre-Dame des Champs. Much of *The Sun Also Rises*, Hemingway's first serious novel, was written at nearby café La Closerie des Lilas. These were the years in which he forged his writing style, paring his sentences down to the pith—as he noted in *A Moveable Feast*, "hunger was good discipline." There were

some especially hungry months when Hemingway gave up journalism for short-story writing, and the family was "very poor and very happy."

They weren't happy for long: in 1926, as *The Sun Also Rises* made him famous, Hemingway left Hadley. The next year, he wed his mistress, Pauline Pfeiffer, and moved to 6 rue Férou, near the Musée du Luxembourg.

For gossip and books, and to pick up his mail, Papa would visit Shakespeare & Company (then at 12 rue de l'Odéon). For cash and cocktails, Hemingway usually headed to the upscale Rive Droite. He collected the former at the Guaranty Trust Company, at 1 rue des Italiens. He found the latter, when he was flush, at the bar of the landmark Hôtel de Crillon, on Place de la Concorde next to the American Embassy, or, when poor, at the Caves Mura, at 19 rue d'Antin, or Harry's Bar, still in brisk business at 5 rue Daunou. Hemingway's loyal and legendary association with the Hôtel Ritz was sealed during the Liberation in 1944, when he strode in at the head of his platoon and "liberated" the joint by ordering martinis all around. Here Hemingway asked Mary Welsh to become his fourth wife, and here also, the story goes, a trunk full of notes regarding his first years in Paris turned up in the 1950s, giving him the raw material for writing *A Moveable Feast*.

La Grande Mosquée de Paris. This awe-inspiring white mosque, built between 1922 and 1926, has tranquil arcades and a minaret decorated in the style of Moorish Spain. Enjoy sweet mint tea and an exotic pastry in the charming courtyard tea salon or tuck into some couscous in the restaurant. Prayer rooms are not open to sightseers, but there are inexpensive—and quite rustic—hammams, or Turkish steam baths, with scrubs and massages offered to women and men on separate days (check website for times and prices). ⌧ *2 bis, pl. du Puits de l'Ermite,* *entrance to tea salon and restaurant at 39 rue Geoffroy St-Hillaire, Latin Quarter* ☎ *01–45–35–97–33* ⊕ *www.mosqueedeparis.net* ✉ *€3* ⊙ *Closed Fri. (open for worshippers only)* Ⓜ *Place Monge.*

La Sorbonne (*Paris IV*). Unless your French is good enough to justify joining a 90-minute group tour (€915 by reservation only), you can't get into the city's most famous university without a student ID—but it's still fun to hang out with the young scholars. Although La Sorbonne remains the soul of the Quartier Latin, it is only one of several campuses that make up the public Université de Paris. ⊠ *1 rue Victor Cousin, Latin Quarter* ☎ *01–40–46–22–11* ✍ *visites.sorbonne@ac-paris.fr for tour reservations* ⊕ *www.sorbonne.fr* ⊙ *Closed weekends* Ⓜ *Cluny–La Sorbonne.*

Le Musée de la Préfecture de Police. Crime buffs will enjoy this museum hidden on the second floor of the 5e arrondissement's police station. Although the exhibits are in French only, the photographs, letters, drawings, and memorabilia pertaining to some of the city's most sensational crimes are easy enough to follow. Among the 2,000-odd relics you'll find a guillotine, old uniforms, and remnants of the World War II occupation—including what's left of a firing post, German machine guns, and the star insignias worn by Jews. ⊠ *4 rue de la Montagne Ste-Geneviève, Latin Quarter* ☎ *01–44–41–52–50* ✉ *Free* ⊙ *Closed Sat. (except 3rd Sat. of month) and Sun.* Ⓜ *Maubert-Mutualité.*

Manufacture des Gobelins. Tapestries have been woven at this spot in southeastern Paris, on the banks of the long-covered Bièvre River, since 1662. The Galerie des Gobelins stages exhibitions on two light-flooded floors, highlighting tapestries, furnishings, timepieces, and other treasures mostly drawn from the state collection. Guided visits to the Manufacture (in French, by reservation only) allow a fascinating look at weavers—from students to accomplished veterans—as they work on tapestries and rugs that take years to complete. Also on-site is a highly selective school that teaches weaving, plus a workshop charged with repairing and restoring furnishings belonging to the French government, which are also stored here in a vast concrete warehouse. ⊠ *42 av. des Gobelins, Latin Quarter* ☎ *08–25–05–44–05 For reservations (€0.15/ min.)* ⊕ *www.mobiliernational.culture.gouv.fr* ✉ *€8 temporary exhibits (free 1st Sun. of month); €16 guided tour of workshops* ⊙ *Galerie closed Mon.* Ⓜ *Gobelins.*

Place St-Michel. This square was named for Gabriel Davioud's grandiose 1860 fountain sculpture of St. Michael vanquishing Satan—a loaded political gesture from Napoléon III's go-to guy, Baron Haussmann, who hoped St-Michel would quell the Revolutionary fervor of the neighborhood. The fountain is often used as a meeting point for both local students and young tourists. ⊠ *Latin Quarter* Ⓜ *Métro or RER: St-Michel.*

St-Étienne-du-Mont. This jewel box of a church has been visited by several popes, owing to the fact that Ste-Geneviève (the patron saint of Paris) was buried here before Revolutionaries burned her remains. Built on the ruins of a 6th-century abbey founded by Clovis, the first King of the Franks, it has a unique combination of Gothic, Renaissance, and early Baroque elements, which adds a certain warmth that is lacking in other

10

Parisian churches of pure Gothic style. Here you'll find the only rood screen left in the city—an ornate 16th-century masterwork of carved wood spanning the nave like a bridge, with a spiral staircase on either side. Observe the organ (dating from 1631, it is the city's oldest) and the marker in the floor near the entrance that commemorates an archbishop of Paris who was stabbed to death here by a defrocked priest in 1857. Guided tours are free, but a small offering is appreciated; call for times. ✉ *Pl. Ste-Geneviève, 30 rue Descartes, Latin Quarter* ☎ *01–43–54–11–79* ⊕ *www.saintetiennedumont.fr* Ⓜ *Cardinal Lemoine.*

St-Julien-le-Pauvre. This tiny shrine in the shadow of Notre-Dame is one of the three oldest churches in Paris. Founded in 1045, it became a meeting place for university students in the 12th century and was Dante's church of choice when he was in town writing his *Divine Comedy.* Today's structure dates mostly from the 1600s, but keep an eye out for older pillars, which crawl with carvings of demons. You can maximize your time inside by attending one of the classical or gospel concerts held here. Alternately, go outside and simply perch on a bench in the garden to relish the view of Notre-Dame. ✉ *1 rue St-Julien-le-Pauvre, Latin Quarter* ☎ *01–43–54–52–16* ⊕ *www.sjlpmelkites.fr* Ⓜ *St-Michel.*

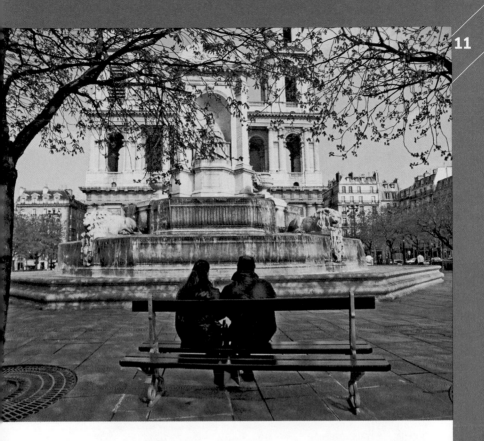

ST-GERMAIN-DES-PRÉS

Getting Oriented

St-Germain-des-Prés

TOP REASONS TO GO

Musée d'Orsay. The magnificent vaulted ceiling and abundant natural light inside this train station–turned–art museum are reminders of why the Impressionist painters thought *les gares* were the cathedrals of the 19th century.

Jardin du Luxembourg. Take in a puppet show, wander the tree-lined gravel paths, or simply laze by the fountain in one of the city's most elegant gardens.

Boulevard St-Germain. The main artery of this chic neighborhood is edged with shops and galleries. The top boutiques are clustered around Rue de Rennes.

Café life. This is prime people-watching territory. So pull up a seat at a comfy café, order a coffee, beer, or *boisson,* and prepare to watch the world go by.

MAKING THE MOST OF YOUR TIME

Aim for an early start—savor a *café crème* at a café along the river and get to the Musée d'Orsay early, when crowds are thinner. Leave some time for window-shopping around Boulevard St-Germain and Rue de Rennes on your way to the Jardin du Luxembourg. You might want to plan your visit on a day other than Monday, when the Orsay, many of the art galleries, and even some shops are closed.

GETTING HERE

The St-Germain neighborhood is in the 6e arrondissement and a bit of the 7e. To get to the heart of this area, take the Line 4 métro to St-Germain-des-Prés. For shopping, use this station or St-Sulpice. It's a short walk to the Jardin du Luxembourg, or take the RER B line to the Luxembourg station. For the Musée d'Orsay, take the Line 12 métro to Solferino or the RER C line to the Musée d'Orsay.

BEST CAFÉS

Café de la Mairie. Overlooking the St-Sulpice church, this retro café recalls the Latin Quarter of yesteryear before the proliferation of luxury boutiques and trendy eateries. ✉ *8 pl. St-Sulpice, St-Germain-des-Prés* ☎ *01–43–26–67–82* Ⓜ *St-Sulpice.*

Café du Métro. You can refuel at this friendly café-brasserie after a shopping spree around Rue de Rennes. Main menu items are pricey, but the free Wi-Fi compensates. ✉ *67 rue de Rennes, St-Germain-des-Prés* ☎ *01–45–48–58–56* ⊕ *www.cafedumetro.com* ⊙ *Closed Sun.* Ⓜ *St-Sulpice.*

La Palette. The terrace of this corner café, opened in 1902, is a favorite haunt of local gallery owners and Beaux Arts students. Light fare is available throughout the day. ✉ *43 rue de Seine, St-Germain-des-Prés* ☎ *01–43–26–68–15* ⊕ *www.cafelapaletteparis.com* Ⓜ *Mabillon, Odéon.*

Le Bar du Marché. Grab a sidewalk table—if you're lucky or stand at the bar, skip the food, and order an apéritif at this constantly packed little place. The feel is classic French with a splash of kitsch, right down to the waiters in overalls and berets. ✉ *75 rue de Seine, St-Germain-des-Prés* ☎ *01–43–26–55–15* Ⓜ *Mabillon.*

Sightseeing
★★★★★
Dining
★★★
Lodging
★★★★★
Shopping
★★★★★
Nightlife
★★

If you had to choose the most classically Parisian neighborhood, this would be it. St-Germain-des-Prés has it all: genteel blocks lined with upscale art galleries, storied cafés, designer boutiques, atmospheric restaurants, and a fine selection of museums. Cast your eyes upward after dark and you may spy a frescoed ceiling in a tony apartment. These historic streets can get quite crowded, especially in summer, so mind your elbows and plunge in.

Updated by
Virginia Power

This *quartier* is named for the oldest church in Paris, **St-Germain-des-Prés**, and it's become a prized address for Parisians and expats alike. Despite its pristine facade, though, this wasn't always silver-spoon territory. Claude Monet and Auguste Renoir shared a cramped studio at 20 rue Visconti, and the young Picasso barely eked out an existence in a room on Rue de Seine. By the 1950s St-Germain bars bopped with jazz, and the likes of Albert Camus, Jean-Paul Sartre, and Simone de Beauvoir puffed away on Gauloises while discussing the meaninglessness of life at Café Flore. Nearby in the 7e arrondissement, the star attraction is the **Musée d'Orsay,** home to a world-class collection of Impressionist paintings in a converted Belle Époque railway station on the Seine. It's famous for having some of Paris's longest lines, so a visit to the Orsay should be planned with care. There are also several smaller museums worth a stop, including the impressive **Musée Maillol,** a private collection in an elegant mansion dedicated to the work of sculptor Aristide Maillol. The **Musée Delacroix,** in lovely Place Furstenberg, is home to a small collection of the Romantic master's works. Not far away is the stately **Église St-Sulpice,** where you can see two impressive Delacroix frescoes.

Paris is a city for walking, and St-Germain is one of the most enjoyable places to practice the art of the *flâneur,* or stroll. Make your way to the busy crossroads of **Carrefour de Buci,** dotted with cafés, flower markets, and shops. Rue de l'Ancienne Comédie is so named because it was the first home of the legendary Comédie Française; it cuts through to busy Place de l'Odéon and Rue St-André des Arts. Along the latter you can

11

find the historic **Cour du Commerce St-André** (opposite No. 66), a charming cobbled passageway filled with cafés—including, halfway down on the left, Paris's oldest, Le Procope.

Make sure you save some energy for the exquisite **Jardin du Luxembourg**, a vintage French garden whose tree-lined paths have attracted fashionable fresh-air fans through the ages.

TOP ATTRACTIONS

FAMILY **Carrefour de Buci.** Just behind the neighborhood's namesake St-Germain church, this colorful crossroads (*carrefour* means "intersection") was once a notorious Rive Gauche landmark. During the French Revolution, the army enrolled its first volunteers here. It was also here that thousands of royalists and priests lost their heads during the 10-month wave of public executions known as the Reign of Terror. There's certainly nothing sinister about the area today, though; brightly colored flowers are for sale alongside take-out ice cream and other sweet treats. Devotees of the superb, traditional bakery Carton (6 rue de Buci) line up for fresh breads and pastries (try the *pain aux raisins, tuiles* cookies, and *tarte au citron*). ✉ *Intersection of Rues Mazarine, Dauphine, and de Buci, St-Germain-des-Prés* Ⓜ *Mabillon.*

Église St-Germain-des-Prés. Paris's oldest church was built to shelter a simple shard of wood, said to be a relic of Jesus' cross brought back from Spain in AD 542. Vikings came down the Seine and sacked the sanctuary, and Revolutionaries used it to store gunpowder. Yet the elegant building has defied history's abuses: its 11th-century Romanesque tower continues to be the central symbol of the neighborhood. The colorful 19th-century frescoes in the nave are by Hippolyte Flandrin, a pupil of the classical master Ingres; and the Saint Benoit chapel contains the tomb of philosopher René Descartes. Step inside for spiritual nourishment, or pause in the square to people-watch—there's usually a street musician tucked against the church wall, out of the wind. The church stages superb organ concerts and recitals. See the website for details. ✉ *Pl. St-Germain-des-Prés, St-Germain-des-Prés* ☎ *01–55–42–81–10* ⊕ *www.eglise-sgp.org* Ⓜ *St-Germain-des-Prés.*

Fodor'sChoice **Église St-Sulpice.** Dubbed the Cathedral of the Rive Gauche, this enormous 17th-century Baroque church has entertained some unlikely christenings—among them those of the Marquis de Sade and Charles Baudelaire—as well as the nuptials of novelist Victor Hugo. More recently, the church played a supporting role in the best-selling novel *The Da Vinci Code,* and it now draws scores of tourists to its obelisk (part of a *gnomon*, a device used to determine exact time and the equinoxes, built in the 1730s). Other notable features include the exterior's asymmetrical towers and two magnificent Delacroix frescoes, which can be seen in a chapel to the right of the entrance. In the square just in front, view Visconti's magnificent 19th-century fountain—it's especially beautiful at night. ✉ *Pl. St-Sulpice, 2 rue Palatine, St-Germain-des-Prés* ☎ *01–42–34–59–60* ⊕ *www.paris.catholique.fr/-saint-sulpice* Ⓜ *St-Sulpice, St-Germain-des-Pres, Mabillon.*

The cafés in St-Germain-des-Prés are perfect for people-watching along with coffee, dinner, or an apéro (cocktail).

Jardin du Luxembourg. Everything that is charming, unique, and befuddling about Parisian parks can be found in the Luxembourg Gardens: cookie-cutter trees, ironed-and-pressed walkways, sculpted flower beds, and immaculate emerald lawns meant for admiring, not necessarily for lounging. The tree- and bench-lined paths are a marvelous reprieve from the bustle of the two neighborhoods it borders: the Quartier Latin and St-Germain-des-Prés. Beautifully austere during the winter months, the garden grows intoxicating as spring brings blooming beds of daffodils, tulips, and hyacinths, and the circular pool teems with wooden sailboats nudged along by children. The park's northern boundary is dominated by the Palais du Luxembourg, which houses the Sénat (Senate), one of two chambers that make up the Parliament. The original inspiration for the gardens came from Marie de Medici, nostalgic for the Boboli Gardens of her native Florence; she is commemorated by the Fontaine de Medicis.

Les Marionettes du Théâtre du Luxembourg is a timeless attraction, where, on weekends at 11 and 3:15 and Wednesday at 3:15 (hours may vary), you can catch classic *guignols* (marionette shows) for €6.40. The wide-eyed kids might be the real attraction—their expressions of utter surprise, despair, and glee have fascinated the likes of Henri Cartier-Bresson and François Truffaut. The park also has a merry-go-round, swings, and pony rides; the bandstand hosts free concerts on summer afternoons.

As you stroll the paths, you might be surprised by a familiar sight: one of the original (miniature) casts of the Statue of Liberty was installed in the gardens in 1906. Check out the rotating photography exhibits hanging on the perimeter fence near the entrance on Boulevard St-Michel and Rue de Vaugirard. If you want to burn off that breakfast *pain au chocolat,* there's a well-maintained trail around the perimeter that is frequented by gentrified joggers. Gendarmes regularly walk the grounds to ensure park rules are enforced; follow guidelines posted on entry gates. ☒ *Bordered by Bd. St-Michel and Rues de Vaugirard, de Medicis, Guynemer, Auguste-Comte, and d'Assas, St-Germain-des-Prés* ⊕ *www.senat.fr/visite/jardin* ☒ *Free* ☽ *Closed dusk–dawn* Ⓜ *Odéon; RER: B Luxembourg.*

FAMILY
Fodor's Choice
★

Musée d'Orsay. Opened in 1986, this gorgeously renovated Belle Époque train station displays a world-famous collection of Impressionist and Postimpressionist paintings on three floors. To visit the exhibits in a roughly chronological manner, start on the first floor, take the escalators to the top, and end on the second. If you came to see the biggest names here, head straight for the top floor and work your way down. English audio guides and free color-coded museum maps (both available just past the ticket booths) will help you plot your route.

Galleries off the main alley feature early works by Manet and Cézanne in addition to pieces by masters such as Delacroix and Ingres. The Pavillon Amont has Courbet's masterpieces *L'Enterrement à Ornans* and *Un Atelier du Peintre.* Hanging in Salle 14 is Édouard Manet's *Olympia,* a painting that pokes fun at the fashion for all things Greek and Roman (his nubile subject is a 19th-century courtesan, not a classical goddess). Impressionism gets going on the top floor, with iconic works by Degas, Pissarro, Sisley, and Renoir. Don't miss Monet's series on the cathedral at Rouen and, of course, samples of his water lilies. Other selections by these artists are housed in galleries on the ground floor. On the second floor, you'll find an exquisite collection of sculpture as well as Art Nouveau furniture and decorative objects. There are rare surviving works by Hector Guimard (designer of the swooping green Paris métro entrances), plus Lalique and Tiffany glassware. Postimpressionist galleries include work by Van Gogh and Gauguin, while Neo-impressionist galleries highlight Seurat and Signac.

■**TIP**➜ To avoid the lines here, which are among the worst in Paris, book ahead online or buy a Museum Pass, then go directly to Entrance C. Otherwise, go early. Thursday evening the museum is open until 9:45 pm and less crowded. Don't miss the views of Sacré-Coeur from the balcony—this is the Paris that inspired the Impressionists. The Musée d'Orsay is closed Monday, unlike the Pompidou and the Louvre, which are closed Tuesday. ☒ *1 rue de la Légion d'Honneur, St-Germain-des-Prés* ☎ *01–40–49–48–14* ⊕ *www.musee-orsay.fr* ☒ *€12; €9 after 4:30, except Thurs. after 6 (free 1st Sun. of month)* ☽ *Closed Mon.* Ⓜ *Solférino; RER: Musée d'Orsay.*

Musée du Luxembourg. Located in the northwestern corner of the Luxembourg Gardens, this former orangery for the Palais du Luxembourg became the city's first public painting gallery in 1884. It now features excellent temporary exhibitions that are well worth a visit. ☒ *19 rue de Vaugirard, St-Germain-des-Prés* ☎ *01–40–13–62–00* ⊕ *www.museeduluxembourg.fr* ☒ *€13* Ⓜ *Rennes, St-Sulpice.*

WORTH NOTING

11

Cour du Commerce St-André. Like an 18th-century engraving come to life, this charming street arcade is a remnant of *ancien* Paris with its uneven cobblestones, antique roofs, and old-world facades. Famed for its rabble-rousing inhabitants—journalist Jean-Paul Marat ran the Revolutionary newspaper *L'Ami du Peuple* at No. 8, and the agitator Georges Danton lived at No. 20—it is also home to Le Procope, Paris's oldest café. The passageway contains a turret from the 12th-century wall of Philippe-Auguste, which is visible through the windows of Un Dimanche à Paris, a chocolate shop and pastry atelier at No. 4. ⊠ *Linking Bd. St-Germain and Rue St-André-des-Arts, St-Germain-des-Prés* Ⓜ *Odéon.*

École Nationale des Beaux-Arts. Occupying three large mansions near the Seine, the national fine arts school—today the breeding ground for painters, sculptors, and architects—was once the site of a convent founded in 1608 by Marguerite de Valois, the first wife of Henri IV. After the Revolution the convent was turned into a museum for works of art salvaged from buildings attacked by the rampaging French mobs. In 1816 the museum was turned into a school. Today its peaceful courtyards host contemporary installations and exhibits. ⊠ *14 rue Bonaparte, St-Germain-des-Prés* 🕾 *01–47–03–50–00* ⊕ *www.beauxartsparis.com* 🎫 *Free* ☉ *Closed weekends* ☞ *There are occasional temporary exhibits. Public access to the school is limited* Ⓜ *St-Germain-des-Prés.*

Institut de France. The Institut de France is one of the country's most revered cultural institutions, and its golden dome is one of the Rive Gauche's most impressive landmarks. The site was once punctuated by the Tour de Nesle (forming part of Philippe-Auguste's medieval fortification wall, the tower had many royal occupants—including Henry V of England). Then, in 1661, wealthy Cardinal Mazarin willed 2 million French *livres* (pounds) for the construction of a college here. It's also home to the Académie Française: the protectors of the French language. The edicts issued by this esoteric group of 40 *perpétuel* (lifelong) members are happily ignored by the French public. The interior is off-limits to visitors. ⊠ *Pl. de l'Institut, St-Germain-des-Prés* ⊕ *www.institut-de-france.fr* Ⓜ *Pont Neuf.*

Mairie du 6e. The *mairie* (town hall) of the 6e arrondissement often stages impressive free art exhibitions and other cultural offerings. Stop by the *accueil* (reception desk) on the ground floor to see what's on or to pick up information on other timely happenings around this artsy district. ⊠ *78 rue Bonaparte, St-Germain-des-Prés* 🕾 *01–40–46–75–06* ⊕ *www.mairie06.paris.fr* 🎫 *Free* ☉ *Closed Sun.* Ⓜ *Saint-Sulpice.*

Musée Delacroix. The final home of artist Eugène Delacroix (1798–1863) contains only a small collection of his sketches and drawings. But you can check out the lovely studio he had built in the large garden at the back to work on frescoes he created for St-Sulpice Church, where they remain on display today. The museum also plays host to temporary exhibitions, such as Delacroix's experiments with photography. France's foremost Romantic painter had the good luck to live on Place Furstenberg, one of the smallest, most romantic squares in

CLOSE UP

Dueling Cafés

Les Deux Magots (*6 pl. St-Germain-des-Prés*) and the neighboring **Café de Flore** (*172 bd. St-Germain*) have been duking it out on this bustling corner in St-Germain for more than a century. Les Deux Magots, the snootier of the two, is named for the two Chinese figurines, or *magots*, inside, and has hosted the likes of Oscar Wilde, Hemingway, James Joyce, and Richard Wright. Jean-Paul Sartre and Simone du Beauvoir frequented both establishments, though they are claimed by the Flore. The two cafés remain packed, but these days you're more likely to rub shoulders with tourists than with philosophers. Still, if you're in search of that certain je ne sais quoi of the Rive Gauche, you can do no better than to station yourself at one of the sidewalk tables—or at a window table on a wintry day—to watch the passing parade. Stick to a croissant and an overpriced coffee, or enjoy an early-evening apéritif; the food is expensive and nothing special.

Paris: seeing it is reason enough to come. ⊠ *6 rue Furstenberg, St-Germain-des-Prés* ☎ *01–44–41–86–50* ⊕ *www.musee-delacroix.fr* ⊠ *€7; €15 with admission to the Louvre within 48 hours* ⊙ *Closed Tues.* Ⓜ *St-Germain-des-Prés.*

Musée de la Monnaie. Louis XVI transferred the royal mint to this imposing mansion in the late 18th century. It was moved again (to Pessac, near Bordeaux) in 1973; however, weights and measures, medals, and limited-edition coins are still made here, and the site houses a museum devoted to currency. The Musée de la Monnaie has an extensive collection of coins and related artifacts, plus workshops where you can watch artisans in action as they mint, mold, sculpt, polish, and engrave using century-old techniques. Refreshed public spaces host cultural programs and temporary contemporary art exhibitions. The museum also has a three-star Guy Savoy restaurant (reservations required: reserv@guysavoy.com). ⊠ *11 quai de Conti, St-Germain-des-Prés* ☎ *01–40–46–56–66* ⊕ *www.monnaiedeparis.fr* ⊠ *€10* ⊙ *Closed Mon.* Ⓜ *Pont Neuf, Odéon.*

Musée National de la Légion d'Honneur (*Hôtel de Salm*). A must for military-history buffs, the National Museum of the Legion of Honor is dedicated to French and foreign military leaders. Housed in an elegant mansion just across from the Musée d'Orsay, it features a broad collection of military decorations, themed paintings, and video tributes to various luminaries—including U.S. general Dwight Eisenhower, a Légion member who led the Allied liberation of France in 1944. The palatial complex was completed in 1788 and acquired by the Legion of Honor in 1804. Admission includes an English audioguide. ⊠ *2 rue de la Légion d'Honneur, St-Germain-des-Prés* ☎ *01–40–62–84–25* ⊕ *www.legiondhonneur.fr* ⊠ *Free* Ⓜ *Solférino; RER: Musée d'Orsay.*

MONTPARNASSE

Getting Oriented

Montparnasse

TOP REASONS TO GO

Catacombs. History buffs, lovers of the macabre, and the just plain curious can make an unforgettable descent into Paris's underground bastion of bones. Claustrophobic folks, however, need not apply.

Fondation Cartier pour l'art contemporain. Connoisseurs of cutting-edge art will appreciate what's on view here. The building itself was designed by Jean Nouvel, the avant-garde darling of Paris architecture.

Fondation Henri Cartier-Bresson. Photography fans shouldn't miss the chance to see Cartier-Bresson's restored atelier, featuring a small collection of his work plus photographs from young artists.

The Tour Montparnasse. Even though this 680-foot black behemoth of a skyscraper is considered one of the biggest eyesores in Paris, its open-air roof terrace is still one of the best spots to see the City of Light.

BEST CAFÉS

La Rotonde Brasserie. A second home to foreign artists and political exiles in the '20s and '30s, La Rotonde has a less exotic but faithful clientele today. It's still a very pleasant place to have coffee or a quick bite on the sunny terrace. ⊠ *105 bd. Montparnasse, Montparnasse* ☎ *01–43–26–48–26* Ⓜ *Vavin.*

Le Lithographe. With its Art Nouveau decor, friendly waitstaff, and menu of fresh bistro food, this is the perfect place for a drink or meal after visiting the nearby Montparnasse Cemetery or Fondation Cartier. Homemade tapenade and toasted baguettes are served with drinks. ⊠ *234 bd. Raspail, Montparnasse* ☎ *01–77–13–26–08* ⊕ *www.lelithographe.fr* Ⓜ *Raspail.*

GETTING HERE

12

Montparnasse includes the 14e and 15e arrondissements. Take Line 4, 6, 12, or 13 to Montparnasse–Bienvenue for the Tour Montparnasse; walk along Boulevard du Montparnasse to reach the cafés. Take Line 4 or 6 to the Raspail métro stop for the Cimetière du Montparnasse or the Fondation Cartier. To visit the Catacombs, take the 4 or 6 line to Denfert-Rochereau. Other nearby métro stops include the Edgar Quinet stop on the 6 line and the Gaîté stop on the 13 line for the Fondation Henri Cartier-Bresson.

MAKING THE MOST OF YOUR TIME

If you can get to the top of the Tour Montparnasse on a clear day, you'll be rewarded with a vista unmatched in all of Paris. The viewing deck is open until 10:30 pm (11:30 on Friday and Saturday), so you can watch the lights sparkle on the Eiffel Tower at the top of the hour. The Catacombs and the Fondation Henri Cartier-Bresson are closed Monday. The Cimetière du Montparnasse is open daily.

Sightseeing
★★★
Dining
★★★
Lodging
★★
Shopping
★
Nightlife
★★

Once a warren of artists' studios and swinging cafés, much of Montparnasse was leveled in the 1960s to make way for a gritty train station and the Tour Montparnasse, Paris's only—and much maligned—skyscraper. Nevertheless, the neighborhood has maintained its reputation as a hub for its lively cafés and the kind of real-life vibe lost in some of the trendier sections of the city.

Updated by
Virginia Power

Despite its soulless modern architecture, the **Tour Montparnasse** has an upside—after all, the rooftop terrace provides a prime panoramic view of Paris. It's okay to feel smug during your ascent as you consider how savvy you've been to avoid the long lines at the Tour Eiffel; afterward, congratulate yourself with a fancy cocktail at Le Bar Américain on the 56th floor.

The other star attraction of Montparnasse is underground. The labyrinthine tunnels of the Paris **Catacombs** contain the bones of centuries' worth of Parisians, moved here when disease, spread by rotting corpses, threatened the city center.

The café society that flourished in the early 20th century—Picasso, Modigliani, Hemingway, Man Ray, and even Trotsky raised a glass here—is still evident along Boulevard du Montparnasse. The Art Deco interior of **La Coupole** attracts diners seeking piles of golden choucroute.

Along Boulevard Raspail you can see today's art stars at the **Fondation Henri Cartier-Bresson** and the **Fondation Cartier pour l'art contemporain,** or pay your respects to Baudelaire, Alfred Dreyfus, or Simone de Beauvoir in the **Cimetière du Montparnasse.**

TOP ATTRACTIONS

Cimetière du Montparnasse. Many of the neighborhood's most illustrious residents rest here, a stone's throw from where they lived and loved: Charles Baudelaire, Frédéric Bartholdi (who designed the Statue of Liberty), Alfred Dreyfus, Guy de Maupassant, and, more recently, photographer Man Ray, playwright Samuel Beckett, writers Marguerite Duras, Jean-Paul Sartre, and Simone de Beauvoir, actress Jean Seberg, and singer-songwriter Serge Gainsbourg. Opened in 1824, the ancient farmland is the second-largest burial ground in Paris and is spread over 47 acres—so if you go late in the day, give yourself plenty of time to get back to the gate before the exits are locked. (The largest cemetery in Paris is Cimetière du Père-Lachaise; *see* Eastern Paris.) ⊠ *Entrances on Rue Froidevaux, Bd. Edgar Quinet, Montparnasse* ⌚ *Free* ☉ *Closes dusk–dawn* ⌕ *Gates lock at 5:30 pm (around 6 to 6:30 pm mid-Mar.– late Oct.)* Ⓜ *Raspail, Edgar Quinet, Gaîté.*

FAMILY **Fondation Cartier Pour L'art Contemporain.** There's no shortage of museums in Paris, but this eye-catching gallery may be the city's premier place to view cutting-edge art. Funded by luxury giant Cartier, the foundation is at once an architectural landmark, a corporate collection, and an exhibition space. Architect Jean Nouvel's 1993 building is a glass house of cards layered seamlessly between the boulevard and the garden. The foundation regularly hosts *Soirées Nomades* (Nomadic Nights) featuring lectures, dance, music, film, or fashion on various evenings. Some are in English. Family tours and creative workshops for children ages 9 to 13 are available. There are free guided tours of exhibits at 6 pm Tuesday through Friday, depending on space. ⊠ *261 bd. Raspail, Montparnasse* ⌚ *01–42–18–56–50* ⊕ *www.fondationcartier.com* ⌚ *€11: €1 fee to purchase online* ☉ *Closed Mon.* Ⓜ *Raspail.*

Fondation Henri Cartier-Bresson. Photography has deep roots in Montparnasse, as great experimenters like Louis Daguerre and Man Ray lived and worked here. In keeping with this spirit of innovation, Henri Cartier-Bresson, legendary photographer and co-creator of the Magnum photo agency, launched this foundation with Martine Franck and their daughter Melanie. The restored 1913 artists' atelier holds three temporary exhibitions of contemporary photography each year. Be sure to go to the top floor to see a small gallery of Cartier-Bresson's own work. ⊠ *2 impasse Lebouis, Montparnasse* ⌚ *01–56–80–27–00* ⊕ *www.henricartierbresson.org* ⌚ *€8; free on Wed. 6:30 pm–8:30 pm* ☉ *Closed Mon. and Aug.* Ⓜ *Gaîté, Edgar Quinet.*

Fodor's Choice ★ **Les Catacombes.** This is just the thing for anyone with morbid interests: a descent through dark, clammy passages brings you to Paris's principal ossuary, which also once served as a hideout maze for the French Resistance. Bones from the defunct Cimetière des Innocents were the first to arrive in 1786, when decomposing bodies started seeping into the cellars of the market at Les Halles, drawing swarms of ravenous rats. The legions of bones dumped here are stacked not by owner but by type—rows of skulls, packs of tibias, and piles of spinal disks, often rather artfully arranged. Among the nameless 6 million or so are the bones of Madame de Pompadour (1721–64), laid to rest with the riffraff after a lifetime spent as the mistress of Louis XV. Unfortunately, one of the most interesting aspects of the catacombs is one you probably won't see: *cataphiles,* mostly art students, have found alternate entrances into its 300 km (186 miles) of tunnels and here they make art, party, and purportedly raise hell. Arrive early as the line can get long and only 200 people can descend at a time. Audioguides are available for €5. Not recommended for claustrophobes or young children. ⊠ *1 av. du Colonel Henri Roi-Tanguy, Montparnasse* ☎ *01–43–22–47–63* ⊕ *www.catacombes.paris.fr* ⊠ *€13* ⊘ *Closed Mon.* Ⓜ *Métro or RER: Denfert-Rochereau.*

Fodor's Choice **Musée Zadkine.** Sculptor Ossip Zadkine spent nearly four decades liv-
★   ing in this bucolic retreat near the Jardin du Luxembourg, creating
graceful, elongated figures known for their clean lines and simplified
features. Zadkine, a Russian-Jewish émigré, moved to Paris in 1910
and fell into a circle of avant-garde artists. His early works, influenced
by African, Greek, and Roman art, later took a Cubist turn, no doubt
under the influence of his friend, the founder of the Cubist movement:
Pablo Picasso. The museum displays a substantial portion of the 400
sculptures and 300 drawings bequeathed to the city by his wife, artist
Valentine Prax. There are busts in bronze and stone reflecting the range
of Zadkine's style, and an airy back room filled with lithe female nudes
in polished wood. The leafy garden is worth the trip alone: it contains
a dozen statues nestled in the trees, including *The Destroyed City,* a
memorial to the Dutch city of Rotterdam, destroyed by the Germans
in 1940. ⊠ *100 bis, rue d'Assas, Montparnasse* ☎ *01–55–42–77–20*
⊕ *www.zadkine.paris.fr* ⊠ *Free; €7 during temporary exhibitions*
⊘ *Closed Mon.* Ⓜ *Vavin, Notre-Dame-des-Champs; RER: Port Royal.*

Tour Montparnasse. A 40-second elevator ride gets you to the top of
one of continental Europe's tallest skyscrapers, where you can take in
the stupendous panoramic view of Paris and beyond from the glass-
enclosed observation deck on the 56th floor. On a clear day, you can see
for 40 km (25 miles). The more adventurous can climb another three
flights to the open-air roof terrace, complete with a seasonal champagne
bar so you can really celebrate the occasion. Built in 1973, the 680-
foot building attracts approximately one million gawkers each year.
Café 360 serves light refreshments year-round and temporary animated
events, such as sky-high trampoline jumping and rink roller skating,
are organized for the young (and young at heart). Purchase tickets in
advance to avoid lines. ⊠ *Rue de L'Arrivee, Montparnasse* ☎ *01–45–
38–52–56* ⊕ *www.tourmontparnasse56.com* ⊠ *€18* ⟳ *Last elevator 30
min before closing (10:30 pm–11:30 pm depending on day and season)*
Ⓜ *Montparnasse–Bienvenüe.*

WORTH NOTING

Closerie des Lilas. Now a popular and pricey bar-restaurant, the Closerie
remains a staple of all Parisian literary tours. Commemorative plaques
are bolted to the bar as if they were still saving seats for their former
clientele: an impressive list of literati including Zola, Baudelaire, Rim-
baud, Apollinaire, Beckett, and, of course, Hemingway. ("Papa" wrote
pages of *The Sun Also Rises* here and lived around the corner at 115
rue Notre-Dame-des-Champs.) Although the lilacs that once graced the
garden—and shaded such habitués as Ingres, Whistler, and Cézanne—
are gone, the terrace still opens onto a garden wall of luxuriant foliage. There is live music in the piano bar. ⊠ *171 bd. du Montparnasse,
Montparnasse* ☎ *01–40–51–34–50* ⊕ *www.closeriedeslilas.fr* Ⓜ *Vavin;
RER: Port Royal.*

Artists, Writers, and Exiles

Paris became a magnet for the international avant-garde in the mid-1800s and remained Europe's creative capital until the 1950s. It all began south of **Montmartre,** when Romantics, including writers Charles Baudelaire and George Sand (with her lover, Polish composer Frédéric Chopin), moved into the streets below Boulevard de Clichy. Impressionist painters Claude Monet, Edouard Manet, and Mary Cassatt had studios here, near Gare St-Lazare, so they could commute to the countryside. In the 1880s the neighborhood dance halls had a new attraction: the cancan, and in 1889 the **Moulin Rouge** cabaret was opened.

The artistic maelstrom continued through the Belle Époque and beyond. In the early 1900s Picasso and Braque launched Cubism from a ramshackle hillside studio, the **Bateau-Lavoir,** and a similar beehive of activity was established at the south end of the city in a curious studio building called La Ruche (the beehive, at the Convention métro stop). Artists from different disciplines worked together on experimental productions. In 1917 the modernist ballet *Parade* hit the stage, danced by impresario Sergei Diaghilev's Ballets Russes, with music by Erik Satie and costumes by Picasso—everyone involved was hauled off to court, accused of being cultural anarchists.

World War I shattered this creative frenzy, and when peace returned, the artists had moved. The narrow streets of **Montparnasse** had old buildings suitable for studios, and the area hummed with a wide, new, café-filled boulevard. At 27 rue Fleurus, Gertrude Stein held court with her partner, Alice B. Toklas. Picasso drew admirers to **La Rotonde,** and F. Scott Fitzgerald drank at the now-defunct Dingo.

The Spanish Civil War and World War II brought an end to carefree Montparnasse. But the literati reconvened in **St-Germain-des-Prés. Café de Flore** and **Deux Magots** had long been popular with an alternative crowd. Expat writers Samuel Beckett and Richard Wright joined existentialists Jean-Paul Sartre, Simone de Beauvoir, and Albert Camus in the neighborhood, drawn into the orbit of literary magazines and publishing houses.

Although Paris can no longer claim to be the epicenter of Western artistic innovation, pockets of outrageous creativity still bubble up. The galleries on Rue Louise Weiss in **Tolbiac** and the open-studio weekends in **Belleville** and **Oberkampf,** for instance, reveal the city's continuing artistic spirit; and the Ménilmontant district, where past arts icons rest in peace at the Père-Lachaise Cemetery, is considered a new mecca for creative souls.

Jardin Atlantique. Built above the tracks of Gare Montparnasse, this park nestled among tall modern buildings is named for its assortment of trees and plants typically found in coastal regions near the Atlantic Ocean. At the far end of the garden are small twin museums devoted to World War II: the **Mémorial du Maréchal-Leclerc,** named for the liberator of Paris, and the adjacent **Musée Jean-Moulin,** devoted to the leader of the French Resistance. Both feature memorabilia and share a common second floor showing photos and video footage (with English subtitles) of the final days of the war. Admission is free, though temporary exhibitions cost a few euros. In the center of the park, what looks like a quirky piece of metallic sculpture is actually a meteorological center, with a battery of flickering lights reflecting temperature, wind speed, and monthly rainfall. ✉ *1 pl. des Cinq-Martyrs-du-Lycée-Buffon, Montparnasse* ☎ *01– 40–64–39–44* ⊕ *www.museesleclercmoulin.paris.fr* ▤ *Free* ⊘ *Museum closed Mon. and Tues.* Ⓜ *Montparnasse–Bienveniie.*

Marché Edgar Quinet. To experience local living in one of the best ways, visit this excellent street market that sells everything from fresh fruit to wool shawls on Wednesday and Saturday. On Wednesday there are produce stands, but also inexpensive clothing, jewelry, and knickknacks. Saturday is a food lover's delight with multiple stands selling spices, olives, fish, cheese, meat, and other gastronomic delights. It's a good place to pick up lunch on the go before paying your respects at Cimetière du Montparnasse across the street. ✉ *Bd. du Edgar Quinet at métro Edgar Quinet, Montparnasse* ⊘ *Closed Sun.–Tues., Thurs. and Fri.* Ⓜ *Edgar Quinet.*

Place du 18-Juin-1940. At the busy intersection of Rue de Rennes and Boulevard du Montparnasse, this square commemorates an impassioned radio broadcast Charles de Gaulle made from London on June 18, 1940. In it he urged the French to resist Nazi occupiers (who had invaded the month prior), thereby launching the French Resistance Movement. It was also here that German military governor Dietrich von Choltitz surrendered to the Allies in August 1944, ignoring Hitler's orders to destroy the city as he withdrew. The square (in fact, a triangle) has been restored and is now a small but proper plaza, with a bench and fountain. ✉ *Montparnasse* Ⓜ *Montparnasse–Bienveniie.*

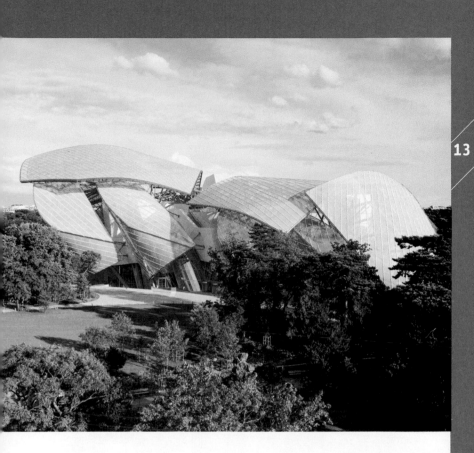

WESTERN PARIS

Getting Oriented

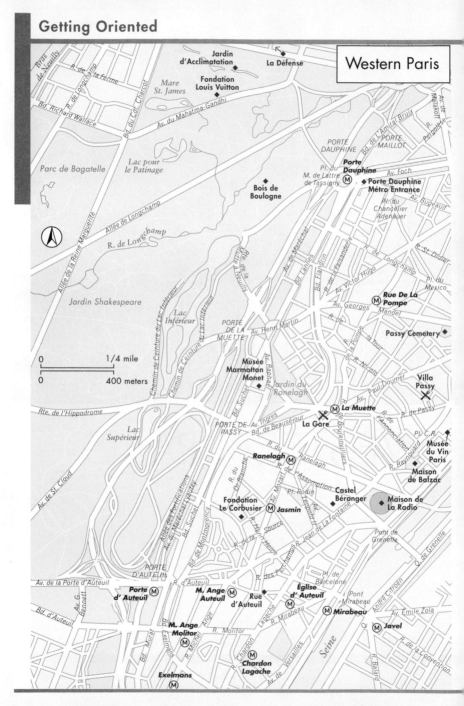

Western Paris

Jardin
d'Acclimatation
La Défense

Fondation
Louis Vuitton

Mare
St. James

Bras de Neuilly
R. du Cdt. Charcot
R. de Longchamp
R. de la Ferme
Bd. Richard Wallace

Av. du Mahatma-Gandhi

Parc de Bagatelle

Lac pour
le Patinage

Bois de
Boulogne

PORTE
DAUPHINE
PORTE
MAILLOT

Av. de l'Amiral Bruix
R. Perpignac
Av. de Malakoff

Porte
Dauphine
Pl. du
M. de Lattre
de Tassigny

Porte Dauphine
Métro Entrance

Av. Foch
Av. Bugeaud

Pl. du
Chancelier
Adenauer

Allée de Longchamp

R. de Longchamp

Allée de la Reine Marguerite

Jardin Shakespeare

Lac
Inférieur

PORTE
DE LA
MUETTE

Av. Henri Martin

Chemin de Ceinture du Lac Intérieur

Av. du Maréchal Maunoury

Av. Victor Hugo
Av. Georges Mandel
Av. Raymond Poincaré
Bd. Lannes
R. de Longchamp
R. St. Didier
Pl. du Mexico

Rue De Lá
Pompe

Passy Cemetery

0   1/4 mile
0   400 meters

Rte. de l'Hippodrome

Lac
Supérieur

Musée
Marmottan Monet

Jardin du
Ranelagh

Av. Raphaël
Bd. Suchet
Av. Ingres
Bd. de Beauséjour

R. de la Pompe
R. de la Tour
R. Nicolo
Av. Paul Doumer

Villa
Passy

La Muette

Av. de St. Cloud

PORTE DE
PASSY

La Gare

R. de Passy

Pl. C.R.

Musée
du Vin
Paris

Ranelagh

R. du
Dr. Blanche

R. du Ranelagh
R. Mozart
R. de l'Assomption

Av. Mozart

Maison
de Balzac

R. Raynouard

Castel
Béranger

Maison de
La Radio

Pont de
Grenelle

Fondation
Le Corbusier

Jasmin

Pl. Rodin

R. Jean de la Fontaine

Q. de Grenelle

Av. des fortifications
Bd. Suchet
Bd. Montmorency
R. Henri Heine
Av. du Maréchal Franchet

R. du Dr. Blanche
R. de la Source

PORTE
D'AUTEUIL

R. des Perchamps

Pl. de
Barcelone

R. de la Tour
Av. André Citroën
Q. de Grenelle

Av. de la Porte d'Auteuil

R. d'Auteuil

Porte
d' Auteuil

M. Ange
Auteuil

Rue
d'Auteuil

Église
d' Auteuil

Mirabeau

Av. Émile Zola

Javel

Av. G. Bennett
Bd. d'Auteuil

Bd. Murat
Bd. Exelmans

R. Michel Ange
R. Molitor

R. Mirabeau

M. Ange
Molitor

Chardon Lagache

R. de Versailles
R. Balard
R. de la Convention
Seine

Chardon
Lagache

Exelmans

TOP REASONS TO GO

Fondation Louis Vuitton. Contemporary art meets iconoclastic architecture at this new museum designed by Frank Gehry in a sculptural mix of wood, steel, and glass.

Musée Marmottan Monet. If you're a fan of Claude Monet, don't miss this gem of a museum tucked away deep in the 16e near the Jardin du Ranelagh.

Bois de Boulogne. Whether you spend your afternoon in a rowboat or wandering gardens filled with foliage, the Bois is a perfect escape from the city.

Jardin d'Acclimatation. There's not a child under the age of five who won't love this amusement park on the northern edge of the Bois de Boulogne.

MAKING THE MOST OF YOUR TIME

If this isn't your first time in Paris, or even if it is and you've had enough of the touristy central part of the city, this neighborhood is a great choice and can be treated like a day trip. Spend the morning admiring the Monets at the uncrowded Musée Marmottan Monet, then take in the Art Nouveau architecture on Rue Jean de la Fontaine; or while away the day in the leafy Bois de Boulogne.

GETTING HERE

Western Paris includes the 16e and 17e arrondissements. Take Line 9 to La Muette métro stop for the Musée Marmottan Monet, or to the Jasmin stop (also Line 9) to explore Rue Jean de la Fontaine. Take Line 6 to the Passy stop for the Musée du Vin or to reach the main drag, Rue de Passy; alternately, take Bus 72 from the Hôtel de Ville or 63 from St. Sulpice. For the main entrance of the Bois de Boulogne, take Line 2 to the Porte Dauphine stop or RER C to Avenue Foch. For the Jardin d'Acclimatation, enter the park from the Les Sablons or Porte Maillot métro stops on Line 1. If you're heading out to La Défense, it's the terminus of Line 1.

BEST CAFÉS

La Gare. Housed in a former train station, this restaurant-lounge is frequented by business types and chic youth alike. Sit on the large terrace or descend the wide staircase to a room bathed in natural light by day and warm golden tones at night. ✉ *19 chausée de la Muette, Western Paris* ☎ *01–42–15–15–31* ⊕ *www.restaurantlagare.com* Ⓜ *La Muette.*

Villa Passy. The courtyard of this bucolic café just off Rue de Passy may make you think you've stumbled into a small village. Sit outside on a cushioned banquette shaded by ivy and order the plat du jour, prepared with fresh market ingredients. ✉ *4 impasse des Carrières, opposite 31 rue de Passy, Western Paris* ☎ *01–45–27–68–76* ⊕ *http://la-villa-passy.lafourchette.rest* ◷ *No Sun. dinner. Closed Mon.* Ⓜ *Passy.*

13

Sightseeing
★★
Dining
★
Lodging
★
Shopping
★
Nightlife
–

Meet Paris at its most prim and proper. This genteel area is a study in smart urban planning, with classical architecture and newer construction cohabiting as easily as the haute bourgeoisie inhabitants mix with their expat neighbors. There's no shortage of celebrities seeking some peace and quiet here, but you're just as likely to find well-heeled families who decamped from the center of the city in search of a spacious apartment. Passy, once a separate village and home to American ambassadors Benjamin Franklin and Thomas Jefferson, was incorporated into the city in 1860 under Napoléon III.

Updated by
Jack Vermee

A walk along the main avenues gives you a sense of Paris's finest Art Nouveau and Modernist buildings, including **Castel-Béranger,** by Hector Guimard, and the **Fondation Le Corbusier** museum, a prime example of the titular architect's pioneering style (it was one of Le Corbusier's first Paris commissions). This neighborhood is also home to one of the city's best and most overlooked museums—the **Musée Marmottan Monet**—which has an astonishing collection of Impressionist art. Enjoy a *dégustation* (tasting) at the **Musée du Vin** or simply find a café on Rue de Passy and savor a moment in one of the city's most exclusive enclaves. For outdoor adventures, the **Bois de Boulogne** is the place to be, especially if you have kids in tow. At *le Bois,* you can explore the Pré Catelan and peacock-filled Bagatelle gardens, both meticulously landscaped and surrounded by woods. You can also admire contemporary art in the new **Fondation Louis Vuitton,** head to the old-fashioned amusement park at the Jardin d'Acclimatation, take a rowboat out on one of the park's two bucolic lakes, or rent a bike and hit 14 km (9 miles) of marked trails.

TOP ATTRACTIONS

FAMILY

Fodor's Choice

★

Bois de Boulogne. When Parisians want to experience the great outdoors without going too far from home, they head to the Bois de Boulogne. Once a royal hunting ground, the Bois is not a park in the traditional sense—more like a vast tamed forest where romantic lakes and wooded paths are complemented by formal gardens and family-friendly amusements. On nice days, it's filled with cyclists, rowers, rollerbladers, joggers, pétanque players, picnickers, and hordes of preschoolers. Art lovers are also flocking here thanks to the opening of the Fondation Louis Vuitton, a stunning exhibition space dedicated to contemporary art near the Jardin d'Acclimatation.

The Parc de Bagatelle is a floral garden with irises, roses, tulips, water lilies, and roaming peacocks that is at its most colorful between April and June. Pré Catelan contains one of Paris's largest trees: a copper beech more than 200 years old. Romantic Le Pré Catelan restaurant (three Michelin stars), where *le tout Paris* used to dine on the elegant terrace during the Belle Époque, still draws diners and wedding parties—especially on weekends. The Jardin Shakespeare inside the Pré Catelan has a sampling of the flowers, herbs, and trees mentioned in Shakespeare's plays, and it becomes an open-air theater for the Bard's works in spring. The Jardin d'Acclimatation, on the northern edge of the Bois, is an amusement park that attracts seemingly every local preschooler on summer Sunday afternoons. Boats or bikes can be rented for a few euros at Lac Inférieur. You can row or take a quick "ferry" to the island restaurant, Le Chalet des Iles. Two popular horse-racing tracks are also in the park: the Hippodrome de Longchamp and the Hippodrome d'Auteuil. Fans of the French Open can visit its home base, Stade Roland-Garros.

The main entrance to the Bois is off Avenue Foch near the Porte Dauphine métro stop on Line 2; it is best for accessing the Pré Catelan and Jardin Shakespeare, both located off the Route de la Grande-Cascade by the lake. For the Jardin d'Acclimatation and the Fondation Louis Vuitton, off Boulevard des Sablons, take Line 1 to Les Sablons or Porte Maillot, where you can walk or ride the Petit Train to the amusement park, which is next door to the foundation. The foundation also offers a €2-return-trip shuttle from Place de l'Étoile. The Parc de Bagatelle, off Route de Sèvres-à-Neuilly, can be accessed from either Porte Dauphine or Porte Maillot, though it's a bit of a hike. You'll want to leave the park by dusk, as the Bois—seedy and potentially dangerous after dark—turns into a distinctly "adult" playground. ⊠ *Western Paris* 📞 *01–53–64–53–80 for Parc de Bagatelle, 01–40–67–90–85 for Jardin d'Acclimatation* ⊕ *www.jardindacclimatation.fr* 🎫 *Parc de Bagatelle free except during exhibitions (€6 during exhibitions); Jardin Shakespeare free; Jardin d'Acclimatation €5 entry, €3 per person for rides* Ⓜ *Porte Dauphine for main entrance; Porte Maillot or Les Sablons for northern end; Porte d'Auteuil for southern end.*

Castel Béranger. It's a shame you can't go inside this house, which is considered the city's first Art Nouveau structure. Dreamed up in 1898 by Hector Guimard, the wild combination of materials and the grimacing

13

grillwork led neighbors to call it Castle *Dérangé* (Deranged). Yet the project catapulted the 27-year-old Guimard into the public eye, leading to his famous métro commission. After ogling the sea-inspired front entrance, go partway down the alley to admire the inventive treatment of the traditional Parisian courtyard, complete with a melting water fountain. A few blocks up the road at No. 60 is the Hotel Mezzara, designed by Guimard in 1911 for textile designer Paul Mezzara. You can trace Guimard's evolution by walking to the subtler Agar complex at the end of the block. Tucked beside the stone entrance at the corner of Rue Jean de la Fontaine and Rue Gros is a tiny café-bar with an Art Nouveau glass front and furnishings. ✉ *14 rue Jean de la Fontaine, Western Paris* Ⓜ *Ranelagh; RER: Maison de Radio France.*

Fondation Le Corbusier (*Le Corbusier Foundation*). Maison La Roche is a must-see for architecture and design lovers. Built as a private residence in 1923, it's a stellar example of Swiss architect Le Corbusier's innovative construction techniques based on geometric forms, recherché color schemes, and a visionary use of iron and concrete. The sloping ramp that replaces the traditional staircase is one of the most eye-catching features. Free, hour-long English tours are available at 4 pm every Tuesday, Thursday, and Friday, and must be reserved online. ✉ *8–10 sq. du Docteur Blanche, Western Paris* ☎ *01–42–88–75–72 Maison La Roche* ⊕ *www.fondationlecorbusier.fr* ✍ *€8; €15 for combined visit with Le Corbusier's studio-apartment* ◷ *Closed Mon. morning and Sun.* Ⓜ *Jasmin, Michel-Ange–Auteuil.*

Fodor'sChoice **Fondation Louis Vuitton.** Rising up out of the Bois de Boulogne like a
★ magnificent ship sporting billowing crystal sails, Frank Gehry's contemporary-art museum and cultural center is the most captivating addition to the Parisian skyline since the unveiling of the Centre Pompidou in 1977. Commissioned by Bernard Arnault (chairman and CEO of luxury-goods conglomerate LVMH), it houses Arnault's substantial private collection, including pieces by Pierre Huyghe, Gerhard Richter, Thomas Schütte, Ellsworth Kelly, Bertrand Lavier, Taryn Simon, Sarah Morris, and Christian Boltanski, among others. La Fondation Louis Vuitton also hosts extensive temporary exhibitions, like the mesmerizing light installations of Danish-Icelandic artist Olafur Eliasson. Le Frank, the pricey on-site restaurant overseen by Michelin-starred chef Jean-Louis Nomicos, is noted for its sophisticated mix of French and international cuisine. The museum is a 12-minute walk from Les Sablons métro on Line 1; alternatively, you can catch the Fondation shuttle (€2 for a return ticket), which leaves every 10–15 minutes from Avenue de Friedland at Place de l'Étoile. ✉ *8 av. du Mahatma Gandhi, Western Paris* ☎ *01–40–69–96–00* ⊕ *www.fondationlouisvuitton.fr* ✍ *€14, includes entrance to Jardin d'Acclimatation* ◷ *Closed Tues.* Ⓜ *Les Sablons.*

Fodor'sChoice **Musée Marmottan Monet.** This underrated museum boasts the largest col-
★ lection of Monet's work anywhere. More than 100 pieces, donated by his son Michel, occupy a specially built basement gallery in an elegant 19th-century mansion, which was once the hunting lodge of the Duke de Valmy. Among them you can find such works as the *Cathédrale de Rouen* series (1892–96) and *Impression: Soleil Levant* (*Impression: Sunrise,* 1872), the painting that helped give the Impressionist movement

its name. Other exhibits include letters exchanged by Impressionist painters Berthe Morisot and Mary Cassatt. Upstairs, the mansion still feels like a graciously decorated private home. Empire furnishings fill the salons overlooking the Jardin du Ranelagh on one side and the private yard on the other. There's also a captivating room of illuminated medieval manuscripts. To best understand the collection's context, pick up an English-language audioguide (€3) on your way in. ⊠ *2 rue Louis-Boilly, Western Paris* ☏ *01–44–96–50–33* ⊕ *www.marmottan.fr* ✉ *€11* ⊙ *Closed Mon.* Ⓜ *La Muette.*

13

WORTH NOTING

OFF THE
BEATEN
PATH

La Défense. First conceived in 1958, this Modernist suburb just west of Paris was inspired by Le Corbusier's dream of high-rise buildings, pedestrian walkways, and sunken vehicle circulation. Built as an experiment to keep high-rises out of the historic downtown, the Parisian business hub has survived economic uncertainty to become the city's prime financial district. Today 20,000 people live in the suburb, but 180,000 people work here, and many more come to shop in its enormous mall. Arriving via métro Line 1, you'll get a view of the Seine, then emerge at a pedestrian plaza studded with some great public art, including César's giant thumb, Joan Miró's colorful figures, and one of Calder's great red "stabiles." The Grande Arche de La Défense dominates the area: it was designed as a controversial closure to the historic axis of Paris (an imaginary line that runs through the Arc de Triomphe, the Arc du Carrousel, and the Louvre Pyramid). Glass-bubble elevators in a metal-frame tower whisk you a heart-jolting 360 feet to the viewing platform. ⊠ *Parvis de La Défense, Western Paris* ☏ *01–47–74–84–24* ⊕ *www.lagrandearche.fr/en* ✉ *Grande Arche €15* Ⓜ *Métro or RER: Grande Arche de La Défense.*

Maison de Balzac. Literature aficionados can visit the modest home of the great French 19th-century novelist Honoré de Balzac (1799–1850), which contains exhibits charting his tempestuous yet prolific career. Balzac penned nearly 100 novels and stories known collectively as *The Human Comedy,* many of them set in Paris. You can still feel his presence in his study and pay homage to his favorite coffeepot—his working hours were fueled by a tremendous consumption of the "black ink." He would escape his creditors by exiting the flat through a secret passage that led down to what is now the Musée du Vin. ⊠ *47 rue Raynouard, Western Paris* ☏ *01–55–74–41–80* ⊕ *www.maisondebalzac. paris.fr* ✉ *Free; around €6 for temporary exhibitions* ⊙ *Closed Mon.* Ⓜ *Passy, La Muette.*

Maison de la Radio. Headquarters to France's state broadcasting company, this imposing 1963 circular building is more than 500 yards in circumference. It's said to have more floor space than any other building in the country and features a 200-foot tower that overlooks the Seine. Radio France sponsors 100-plus concerts a year, including performances by its own Orchestre Philharmonique de Radio France and the Orchestre National de France. Though the concerts take place at venues throughout the city, a great number are held here, and they're generally either free of charge or inexpensive. French-only building tours are offered Tuesday and Thursday at 6 pm, and Saturday at 3 and 5 pm. ⊠ *116 av. du Président-Kennedy, Western Paris* ☎ *01–56–40–15–16 for tour and concert information* ⊕ *www.maisondelaradio. fr* 🖥 *€10 for tours* ☽ *Closed Sun.* Ⓜ *Ranelagh; RER: Maison de Radio France; Bus 22, 52, 72.*

Musée du Vin Paris. Oenophiles with some spare time will enjoy this quirky museum housed in a 15th-century abbey, a reminder of Passy's roots as a pastoral village. Though hardly exhaustive and geared to beginners, the small collection contains old wine bottles, glassware, and ancient wine-related pottery excavated in Paris. Wine-making paraphernalia shares the grotto-like space with hokey figures retired from the city's wax museum, including Napoléon appraising a glass of Burgundy. But you can partake in a thoroughly nonhokey wine tasting, or bring home one of the 200-plus bottles for sale in the tiny gift shop. Check online for a calendar of wine tastings and classes offered in English. You can book ahead for a casual lunch, too (restaurant open Tuesday through Saturday, noon to 3, reservations required). ⊠ *Rue des Eaux/5 sq. Charles Dickens, Western Paris* ☎ *01–45–25–63–26* ⊕ *www.museeduvinparis.com* 🖥 *€14 with a glass of wine; €25 with 3 wine tastings and lecture* ☽ *Closed Sun. and Mon.* Ⓜ *Passy.*

Passy Cemetery. Visiting graveyards in Paris can become addictive. The Passy Cemetery dates to 1821 and sits in the shadows of Trocadéro. Here you'll find the tombstones of famous aristocrats and artists such as composer Claude Debussy and Impressionist painters Édouard Manet and Berthe Morisot. ⊠ *2 rue du Commandant Schlœsing, Western Paris* ☎ *01–47–27–51–42* Ⓜ *Trocadéro.*

Porte Dauphine Métro Entrance. Visitors come here to snap pictures of the queen of subway entrances—one of the city's two remaining Art Nouveau canopied originals designed by Hector Guimard (the other is at the Abbesses stop on Line 12). A flamboyant scalloped "crown" of patina-painted panels and runaway metal struts adorns this whimsical 1900 creation. Porte Dauphine is the terminus of Line 2. The entrance is on the Bois de Boulogne side of Avenue Foch, so take the Boulevard de l'Amiral Bruix exit. ⊠ *Av. Foch, Western Paris* Ⓜ *Porte Dauphine.*

Rue d'Auteuil. This narrow shopping street escaped Haussmann's urban renovations and today still retains the country feel of old Auteuil, a sedate bourgeois enclave. Molière once lived on the site of No. 2, while Racine was on nearby Rue du Buis: the pair met up to clink glasses and exchange drama notes at the Mouton Blanc Inn, now a traditional brasserie, at No. 40. Numbers 19–25 and 29 are an interesting combination of 17th- and 18th-century buildings. At the foot of the street, the scaly dome of the Église Notre-Dame d'Auteuil (built in the 1880s) is an unmistakable small-time cousin of Sacré-Coeur in Montmartre. Rue d'Auteuil is at its liveliest on Wednesday and Saturday mornings, when a much-loved street market crams onto Place Jean-Lorraine. ⊠ *Western Paris* Ⓜ *Michel-Ange–Auteuil, Église d'Auteuil.*

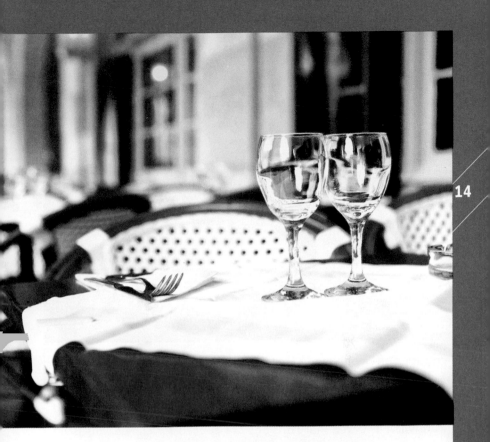

WHERE TO EAT

EAT LIKE A LOCAL

Parisians are many things, but above all, they are great eaters, and social ones at that. After that first flaky croissant and frothy café crème, the day revolves around what, when, and with whom the next meal will be. Given that Parisians are spoiled for choice, this is no surprise.

BREAD

One of the great mainstays of French food, not all bread in Paris is created equal. Many boulangeries still offer industrial baguettes (made from frozen dough) that go hard within the hour. Others offer traditional crusty loaves so glorious you will happily travel across town to get one. If you don't have the time to experiment, a good compromise is to buy at a reputable *épicerie* (gourmet grocer).

COFFEE

The café culture of Paris is as alive and well as ever, but with a new twist—better coffee. Many Parisians are no longer settling for any bitter brew served up in your corner café, and hip coffee houses featuring pedigreed baristas are popping up all over town, with an emphasis on carefully sourced beans roasted in-house or at least somewhere in Paris.

PASTRIES

What would Paris be without pastries, and what would a pastry be without Paris? The two go hand in hand, but like bread, the quality varies from indifferent to sublime. Pierre Hermé, the father of Paris's new wave pastry, is a great place to start, but you can't go wrong with any of the following: Sébastien Gaudard (whose shop, on the fabulous Rue des

Martyrs, is a dream), Jean-Paul Hévin, Jacques Genin (to be eaten only in the elegant tea salon on the premises), Eric Kayser, Pain de Sucre, and Blé Sucré. Several have multiple locations, making a stop easy.

CHEESE

No visit to France is complete without sampling a few of the country's some 625 unpasteurized cheeses, made from either sheep, goat, or cow's milk and best paired simply with a crusty baguette and a fresh green salad. Made in specific regions, often in optimal conditions for a very specific microbe (like the caves of Roquefort), you won't find their equivalent anywhere else.

CRÊPES

Paris's first street food, the humble crêpe, which hails from Brittany and Normandy, can still be found on city corners. There are two kinds: the savory *galette,* made with buckwheat flour and filled with ham, cheese, egg, veggies, and other hearty ingredients, and the sweet, tender crêpe, made with white flour and filled with nutella, jam, salted caramel, or simply lemon with a dusting of sugar.

CHOCOLATE

In the last few years, Paris has surpassed both Zurich and Brussels as the chocolate center of Europe. And Paris's 6e arrondissement has emerged as the epicenter, with no less than 15 truly world-class *chocolatiers* (many also *pâtissiers*) plying their yummy trade.

GOURMET ÉPICERIES

Derived from the disappearing local mom-and-pop shops (*traiteurs*) where you could pick up anything from a variety of homemade cold salads and pâtés to a goose breast stuffed with chestnuts, gourmet grocers are a fairly recent trend in Paris. From the chic Maison Plisson in the Marais to the Bon Marché's exceptional La Grande Épicerie, these are a great introduction to a wide range of top-quality French artisanal foods.

HAUTE GASTRONOMY

You can safely say that there is no city in the world that compares to Paris when it comes to fine dining. Palace hotel restaurants like Le Cinq at the Four Seasons George V, L'Ecrin at Hôtel de Crillon, La Scène at Hôtel Prince des Galles, and L'Abeille at the Shangri-La are just a few of the many haute dining experiences you can find in the city. Haute vegetarian is also well established, a trend initiated by Alain Passard at L'Arpège and extravagantly mastered by Alain Ducasse at the Plaza Athénée. For pure romance, try Yannick Alléno's sublime Pavillon Ledoyen and for a more modern stunner, Guy Savoy's sleek art-bedecked gem in La Monnaie de Paris took the Best Restaurant in the World prize in both 2016 and 2017.

Updated
by Jennifer
Ladonne

A new wave of culinary confidence has been running through one of the world's great food cities and spilling over both banks of the Seine. Whether cooking up *grand-mère*'s roast chicken and *riz au lait* or placing a whimsical hat of cotton candy atop wild-strawberry-and-rose ice cream, Paris chefs—established and up-and-coming, native and foreign—have been breaking free from the tyranny of tradition and following their passion.

Emblematic of the "bistronomy" movement is the proliferation of "gastrobistros"—often in far-flung or newly chic neighborhoods—helmed by established chefs fleeing the constraints of the star system or passionate young chefs unfettered by overblown expectations. Among the seasoned stars and exciting newcomers to the scene are Yannick Alléno, who left behind two Michelin stars at Le Meurice to open his locavore bistro Terroir Parisien at the Palais Brogniart and earned three stars at the storied Pavillon Ledoyen within his first year at the helm; David Toutain at the exceptional Restaurant David Toutain; Sylvestre Wahid at Brasserie Thoumieux; and Katsuaki Okiyama's Abri.

But self-expression is not the only driving force behind the current trend. A traditional high-end restaurant can be prohibitively expensive to operate. As a result, more casual bistros and cafés, which reflect the growing allure of less formal dining and often have lower operating costs and higher profit margins, have become attractive opportunities for even top chefs.

For tourists, this development can only be good news, because it makes the cooking of geniuses such as Joël Robuchon, Guy Savoy, Eric Frechon, and Pierre Gagnaire a bit more accessible (even if these star chefs rarely cook in their lower-price restaurants) and opens up a vast range of new possibilities for exciting dining.

Like the chefs themselves, Paris diners are breaking away from tradition with renewed enthusiasm. New restaurants, wine bars, and rapidly multiplying *épiceries* (gourmet grocers) and sandwich shops recognize that not everyone wants a three-course blowout every time they dine out. And because Parisians are more widely traveled than in the past, many ethnic restaurants—notably the best North African, Vietnamese–Laotian, Chinese, Spanish, and Japanese spots—are making fewer concessions to French tastes, resulting in far better food.

PLANNING

WINE BARS

For tantalizing wines, good food, and great value, look no farther than one of Paris's many wine bars. The past 10 years have seen an explosion of a new kind of *bar à vins,* or, more accurately, *cave à manger*—essentially amplified wineshops with a few tables, which serve a plate or two of regional cheeses or artisanal charcuterie to complement the wines. The new generation of *cavistes* stood apart as champions of natural wines, which are unfiltered, contain minimal or no added sulfites, and are often *bio* (organic) or grown biodynamically, that is, according to a specific set of agricultural guidelines. As the natural-wine movement dovetailed with the crusade toward simply prepared foods made from quality seasonal ingredients, the contemporary wine bar was born. Indeed, the food in a handful of wine bars now rivals that in the best Paris bistros—and can be a lot more affordable. Whatever the emphasis, the upward trajectory of the wine bar has had a major hand in reinvigorating Paris's wine-and-food scene.

Wine bars usually keep restaurant hours (noon to 2 pm and 7:30 to 11 pm); some combine with an épicerie, stay open all day, and close earlier in the evening; others offer a late-night scene. Although casual, most wine bars nowadays require reservations, so call in advance, especially if Sunday brunch is available—still a rarity in Paris. Look for the "wine bar" designation in our restaurant listings.

CHILDREN

Some restaurants provide booster seats, but don't count on them: be sure to ask when you confirm your reservation.

HOURS

Paris restaurants generally serve food from noon to 2 pm and from 7:30 or 8 pm to about 11 pm. Brasseries have longer hours and often serve all day and late into the evening; some are open 24 hours. Surprisingly, many restaurants close on Saturday as well as Sunday, and Monday closings are also not uncommon. July and August are common months for annual closings, but restaurants may also close for a week in February, around Easter, or at Christmas.

MENUS

All establishments must post menus outside so they're available to look over before you enter. Most have two basic types of menu: à la carte and fixed price (*prix fixe, le menu,* or *la formule*). Although it limits your choices, the prix fixe is usually the best value. If you feel like indulging, the *menu dégustation* (tasting menu), consisting of numerous small courses, lets you sample the chef's offerings.

14

ORDERING WINE

Most sommeliers are knowledgeable about their lists and can make appropriate suggestions after you've made your tastes and budget known. Simpler spots serve wine in carafes (*en carafe*, or *en pichet*). All restaurants sell wine by the glass, but prices can be steep; be sure to do the math.

RESERVATIONS

Restaurant staff will nearly always greet you with the phrase "*Avez-vous réservé?*" (Have you reserved?), and a confident "*Oui*" is the best answer, even in a neighborhood bistro. Although some wine bars do not take reservations—or take them online only—many do, so call and check.

SMOKING

Smoking is not allowed in restaurants, bars, and cafés but many places have added covered terraces for smokers.

TIPPING AND TAXES

According to French law, prices must include tax and tip (*service compris* or *prix nets*), but pocket change left on the table in cafés, or an additional 5% in better restaurants, is always appreciated. Beware of bills stamped "Service Not Included" in English or restaurants slyly using American-style credit-card slips, hoping that you'll be confused and add the habitual 15% tip.

WHAT IT COSTS

You'll be lucky to find a good bistro meal for €25 or less, even at lunch, so consider economizing on some meals to have more to spend on the others. Slurping inexpensive Japanese noodles on Rue Ste-Anne, grabbing a sandwich at a casual eatery, or having a picnic in a park will save euros for dinner. And, of course, if you've rented an apartment, you can shop at the city's wonderful markets and cook a few meals at "home."

WHAT IT COSTS			
	$	$$	$$$	$$$$
AT DINNER	under €18	€18–€24	€25–€32	over €32

Price per person for a main course at dinner, or if dinner is not served, at lunch, including tax (19.6%) and service.

WHAT TO WEAR

Casual dress is acceptable at all but the fanciest restaurants—this usually means stylish sportswear, which might be a bit dressier than in the United States. When in doubt, leave the T-shirts and sneakers behind.

RESTAURANT REVIEWS

Dining reviews have been shortened. For full information, visit Fodors. com. Reviews are in alphabetical order by neighborhood. Use the coordinates (✛ 1:B2) at the end of each review to locate a property on the corresponding map at the end of the chapter.

ILE DE LA CITÉ AND ILE ST-LOUIS

Ile de la Cité and Ile St-Louis are great for sightseeing, which is why much of the dining scene on these islands revolves around fast food and tourist traps. Luckily, a few long-established brasseries and inspired bistros on elegant Ile St-Louis—not to mention the legendary Berthillon, the city's great *glacier* (ice-cream maker)—more than compensate. Among the shops, épiceries, and ancient bookstores of Rue St-Louis en l'Ile, the island's central spine, you'll find enough quality dining to keep you satisfied at any time of the day.

ILE ST-LOUIS

$$ ✕**Brasserie de l'Isle Saint-Louis.** With its dream location on the tip of
BRASSERIE Ile St-Louis overlooking the Seine and Notre-Dame, you'd think this charming brasserie, like so many before it, would have succumbed to its own success. Yet it remains exactly what a decent neighborhood brasserie should be, with an authentic decor, efficiently friendly service, and solid brassiere fare. **Known for:** fantastic views of Notre Dame; coveted outdoor terrace by the Seine; decent prices, considering the location. ⑤ *Average main: €21* ⊠ *55 quai de Bourbon, 4e, Île Saint-Louis* ☎ *01-43-54-02-59* ⊕ *www.labrasserie-isl.fr* ۞ *Closed Wed.* Ⓜ *Pont Marie, Maubert-Mutualité, Sully-Morland* ✛ *4:E3.*

AROUND THE EIFFEL TOWER

Lively bistros and daring contemporary restaurants bring unexpected exuberance to the otherwise sedate streets around the Eiffel Tower. Because money is rarely an object in this area, you can find everything from top-notch contemporary restaurants that draw foodies to nostalgic bistros that appeal to aristocratic residents with comfort-food cravings.

$$ ✕**Afaria.** The otherwise unexciting 15th arrondissement is home to
BISTRO much-lauded chef Ludivine Merlin and his Basque-inspired recipes. Basque cooking is known for its bold flavors and generosity, and the choices at Afaria are no exception. **Known for:** laid-back, classic bistro atmosphere; artichoke terrine with smoked bacon and aged comté cheese; hazelnut soufflé with homemade dark-chocolate sorbet for dessert. ⑤ *Average main: €21* ⊠ *15 rue Desnouettes, 15e, Eiffel Tower* ☎ *01-48-42-95-90* ⊕ *www.restaurant-afaria.fr* ۞ *Closed Sun., Mon., and 2 wks at Christmas.* Ⓜ *Convention* ✛ *3:C6.*

$$$$ ✕**Au Bon Accueil.** To see what well-heeled Parisians like to eat these
BISTRO days, book a table at this chic little bistro run by Jacques Lacipière as soon as you get to town. The contemporary dining room is unusually comfortable, and the sidewalk tables have an Eiffel Tower view, but it's the excellent, well-priced *cuisine du marché* that has made this spot a hit. **Known for:** good value, three-course dinner menu; excellent price-to-quality ratio; scintillating views of the Eiffel Tower from the charming sidewalk terrace. ⑤ *Average main: €39* ⊠ *14 rue de Monttessuy, 7e, Eiffel Tower* ☎ *01-47-05-46-11* ⊕ *www.aubonaccueilparis. com* ۞ *Closed weekends and 3 wks in Aug.* Ⓜ *Métro or RER: Pont de l'Alma* ✛ *3:D1.*

14

$$$$
BRASSERIE

✕ **Brasserie Thoumieux.** When this old-world bistro was revived, much of its vintage character was thankfully preserved. Despite its location in the sedate 7e arrondissement, it has quickly became a place to be seen eating tasty versions of classic brasserie dishes a notch above the usual quality (albiet pricier). **Known for:** Angus burgers and Parmesan fries; old-school atmosphere; reservations taken exactly six days ahead of time. $ *Average main: €40* ✉ *79 rue St-Dominique, 7e, Eiffel Tower* ☎ *01–47–05–49–75* ⊕ *www.thoumieux.fr* Ⓜ *La Tour–Maubourg* ✛ *3:E1.*

$
CAFÉ
FAMILY

✕ **Café Coutume.** A lofty space between the Musée Rodin and the Bon Marché makes this the perfect pit stop between museum going and shopping. Look for healthy salads, sandwiches, snacks, desserts, and a delicious cup of any kind of coffee drink that takes your fancy. **Known for:** some of the finest coffee in town; healthy salads for lunch; prime location near major museums. $ *Average main: €8* ✉ *47 rue de Babylone, 7e, Eiffel Tower* ☎ *01–45–51–50–47* ⊙ *No dinner* Ⓜ *Saint-François Xavier, Sèvres-Babylone* ✛ *3:G3.*

$$$
BISTRO

✕ **D'Chez Eux.** The red-checked tablecloths and jovial maître d'hôtel at this authentic southwestern French bistro near the Invalides might seem like a tourist trap until you realize that it's just as popular with food-loving locals and top French politicians as it is with foreigners. Everything one the menu is hearty and delicious, if not especially refined—don't miss the gooey help-yourself chocolate mousse. **Known for:** spacious sidewalk terrace; famous "house-made" charcuterie; extremely generous portions. $ *Average main: €32* ✉ *2 av. de Lowendal, 7e, Eiffel Tower* ☎ *01–47–05–52–55* ⊕ *www.chezeux.com* ⊙ *Closed Aug.* Ⓜ *Varenne, École Militaire* ✛ *3:E3.*

$$$$
FRENCH FUSION
Fodor'sChoice
★

✕ **Hiramatsu.** In this Art Deco dining room near Trocadéro, Takashi Nakagawa continues his variations on the subtly Japanese-inspired French cuisine of restaurant namesake Hiroyuki Hiramatsu, who still sometimes works the kitchen. Luxury ingredients feature prominently in dishes such as thin slices of lamb with onion jam and thyme-and-truffle-spiked jus, or an unusual pot-au-feu of oysters with foie gras and black truffle. **Known for:** 90€ seven-course dinner menu, a steal for this quality; Scottish salmon marinated in fines herbs with caviar and leek mousse; staggering wine list. $ *Average main: €50* ✉ *52 rue de Longchamp, 16e, Eiffel Tower* ☎ *01–56–81–08–80* ⊕ *www.hiramatsu. co.jp/fr* ⊙ *No lunch. Closed weekends, 1 wk at Christmas, and Aug.* Ⓜ *Trocadéro* ✛ *1:B6.*

$$$$
MODERN FRENCH
Fodor'sChoice
★

✕ **L'Abeille.** Everything here, from the dove-gray decor to the sparkling silver, speaks of quiet elegance—all the better to savor Christophe Moret's masterful cuisine. Choices include a "harlequin" of yellow, red, and white beets with a ginger-tinged yogurt and aloe vera emulsion; Breton langoustine in a cinnamon-perfumed gelée, with grapefruit pulp and a ginger-and-Tahitian-vanilla-infused mayonnaise; and lightly caramelized scallops in an ethereal cloud of white-chocolate foam. **Known for:** some of the best service in town (including a jar of honey as a parting gift); relaxed, intimate dining; elegant decor overlooking interior garden. $ *Average main: €100* ✉ *Paris Shangri-La Hotel, 10 av. d'Iéna,*

French Restaurant Types

Bistro: The broadest category, a bistro can be a simple, relaxed restaurant serving traditional fare, one of the new "bistronomic" eateries, or a chic hot spot where dinner costs more than €50 per person. The bistro menu is fairly limited and usually changes with the season.

Brasserie: More informal than a bistro, the brasserie is large, lively, and always has a bar. Ideal for relatively quick meals, it often specializes in Alsatian fare, like *choucroute garnie* (a mixed meat dish with sauerkraut and potatoes) or seafood platters. With flexible hours (usually open all day and well into the night) and diverse menus, brasseries are an excellent choice if you're traveling with kids.

Café: Often an informal neighborhood hangout, the café may also be a showplace attracting a well-heeled crowd or one of the newer barista cafés serving up a virtuosic brew to a much more exacting standard. A limited menu of sandwiches, simple dishes, and classic desserts is usually available throughout the day. Beware of the prices: a half bottle of mineral water can cost €5 or more.

French Fusion: The French fusion restaurant has discernible influences of French cuisine and the cuisine of another region or country.

Haute French: Ambitious and expensive, the haute French restaurant is helmed by a pedigreed chef who prepares multicourse meals to be remembered.

Modern French: Although not necessarily super expensive or pretentious, the modern French restaurant boasts a creative menu showcasing a variety of culinary influences.

Wine Bar: A more recent phenomenon, the wine bar serves more than the usual three or four wines by the glass—and often with an emphasis on natural wines—along with traditional charcuterie or cheese, small dishes, or, more often nowadays, a full gourmet meal.

14

16e, Eiffel Tower ☎ *01–53–67–19–90* ⊕ *www.shangri-la.com* ⊗ *Closed Sun. and Mon. No lunch Sat.-Wed.* Ⓜ *Iéna* ✛ *1:C6.*

$$$$
BASQUE
✗ **L'Ami Jean.** If you love Yves Camdeborde's southwestern France–inflected cooking at Le Comptoir but can't get a table for dinner, head to this tavern-like Basque restaurant run by his longtime second-in-command, Stéphane Jégo. Jégo's style is remarkably similar to Camdeborde's because he uses the same suppliers and shares his knack for injecting basic ingredients with sophistication reminiscent of haute cuisine. You can go hearty with Spanish *piquillo* peppers stuffed with salt-cod paste or *poulet basquaise* (chicken stewed with peppers), or lighter with seasonal dishes that change weekly. **Known for:** convivial atmosphere (especially when rugby is on); a local favorite; seasonal market-driven menu. ⑤ *Average main: €39* ⊠ *27 rue Malar, 7e, Eiffel Tower* ☎ *01–47–05–86–89* ⊕ *www. lamijean.fr* ⊗ *Closed Sun., Mon., and Aug.* Ⓜ *Invalides* ✛ *3:E1.*

$$$$
MODERN FRENCH
Fodor's Choice
★
✗ **L'Arpège.** Breton-born Alain Passard, one of the most respected chefs in Paris, famously shocked the French culinary world by declaring that he was bored with meat. Though his vegetarianism is more lofty than practical—L'Arpège still caters to fish and poultry eaters—he does

EATING VEGETARIAN IN PARIS

Vegetarianism was once so uncommon in Paris that star chef Alain Passard caused a sensation when he declared a few years ago that he was bored with red meat and would be focusing on vegetables and fish. True to his word, Passard established a small farm outside Paris where he grows heirloom vegetables that are whizzed to his restaurant **L'Arpège** (*84 rue Varenne, 01–45–51–47–33*) by high-speed train. Customers pay the price; a simple yet sensational beet dish costs €45. Though Paris is hardly a vegetarian paradise, Passard's initiative seems to have rubbed off on other chefs in the 7e. **Le Violon d'Ingres** (*135 rue St-Dominique, 01–45–55–15–05*) and **L'Atelier de Joël Robuchon** (*5 rue Montalembert, 01–42–22–56–56*) both cater, with imagination, to vegetarians. Next door, in the 8e, Alain Ducasse's splendid dining room in Plaza Athénée (**Alain Ducasse at the Plaza Athénée**, *25 av. Montaigne, 01–53–67–65–00*) gives Arpège its first real Paris competition. The superstar-chef's stellar new menu puts grains, vegetables—sourced from Versailles's *jardin de la reine*—and fish front and center.

cultivate his own vegetables outside Paris and his dishes elevate the humblest vegetables to sublime heights. **Known for:** legendary Paris chef; one of Paris's rare three-star restaurants; redefining what a cook can do with simple vegetables. $ *Average main: €100* ⊠ *84 rue de Varenne, 7e, Eiffel Tower* ☎ *01–47–05–09–06* ⊕ *www.alain-passard. com* ☉ *Closed weekends* Ⓜ *Varenne* ✚ *3:G2.*

$$$$ ✕ **L'Astrance.** Pascal Barbot rose to fame thanks to his restaurant's rea-
MODERN FRENCH   sonable prices and casual atmosphere, but after the passage of several
Fodor's Choice   years, Astrance has become resolutely haute. His dishes often draw on
★   Asian ingredients, as in grilled lamb with miso-lacquered eggplant and a palate-cleansing white sorbet spiked with chili pepper and lemongrass. **Known for:** set menus that change daily; space that seats only 25 lucky diners a night; extraordinary wine list. $ *Average main: €120* ⊠ *4 rue Beethoven, 16e, Eiffel Tower* ☎ *01–40–50–84–40* ☉ *Closed weekends, Mon., and Aug.* Ⓜ *Passy* ✚ *1:B6.*

$$$$ ✕ **La Table d'Aki.** Set in a quiet, aristocratic *quartier* near the Musée
MODERN FRENCH   Rodin, La Table d'Akihiro might just be the most perfect little-gem res-
Fodor's Choice   taurant in all of Paris. Its simple elegance highlights the thrilling cuisine
★   centered on the sea. **Known for:** romantic ambience; perfectly prepared fish; open kitchen serving just 16 diners at a time. $ *Average main: €40* ⊠ *49 rue Vaneau, 7e, Eiffel Tower* ☎ *01–45–44–43–48* ☉ *Closed Sun., Mon., 2 wks in Feb., and Aug.* Ⓜ *Saint-François-Xavier* ✚ *3:G3.*

$$$ ✕ **La Table Lauriston.** This chic bistro near the Trocadéro has a win-
BISTRO   ning formula: top-notch ingredients, simply prepared and generously served. The trademark dish, a gargantuan rib steak, is big enough to silence even the hungriest Texan. **Known for:** favorite with local diners; friendly service; famously delicious (and giant) baba au rhum for dessert. $ *Average main: €26* ⊠ *129 rue de Lauriston, 16e, Eiffel Tower* ☎ *01–47–27–00–07* ⊕ *www.restaurantlatablelauriston.com* ☉ *Closed Sun. and 4 wks in Aug. No lunch Sat.* Ⓜ *Trocadéro* ✚ *1:A6.*

$ ✕ **Le Café Constant.** Parisians are a nostalgic bunch, which explains the
BISTRO popularity of this down-to-earth venue, a relatively humble bistro with
cream-color walls, red banquettes, and wooden tables. The menu reads
like a French cookbook from the 1970s—who cooks veal *cordon bleu*
these days?—but the dishes taste even better than before. **Known for:**
excellent prices, especially at lunch; classic bistro fare with a gourmet
twist; neighborhood favorite. $ *Average main: €17* ✉ *139 rue St-Dom-
inique, 7e, Eiffel Tower* ☎ *01–47–53–73–34* ⊕ *www.maisonconstant.
com* Ⓜ *École Militaire; Métro or RER: Pont de l'Alma* ✛ *3:D2.*

$$$$ ✕ **Le Jules Verne.** Alain Ducasse doesn't set his sights low, so it was no
MODERN FRENCH real surprise when he took over this prestigious dining room on the
second floor of the Eiffel Tower. Most accessible is the €105 lunch menu
(weekdays only), which brings you à la carte dishes in slightly smaller
portions. **Known for:** famous Eiffel Tower dining (with accompanying
views); lavishly priced dishes; reservations needed months in advance.
$ *Average main: €90* ✉ *Tour Eiffel, south pillar, Av. Gustave Eiffel,
7e, Eiffel Tower* ☎ *01–45–55–61–44* ⊕ *www.lejulesverne-paris.com*
🍽 *Jacket and tie* Ⓜ *Bir-Hakeim* ✛ *3:C2.*

$$ ✕ **Le Troquet.** A quiet residential street shelters one of the best-value
MODERN FRENCH bistros around: prix-fixe menus start at €31 at lunch and rise to €41
FAMILY for a six-course tasting menu (there are also à la carte selections), but
it's the quality, not quantity, here that counts. A changing roster of
dishes from the Basque and Béarn regions of southwestern France are
available. **Known for:** proximity to the Eiffel Tower; sampling of the
French classics; dessert soufflé du jour. $ *Average main: €21* ✉ *21 rue
François-Bonvin, 15e, Eiffel Tower* ☎ *01–45–66–89–00* ⊕ *www.restau-
rantletroquet.fr* ☉ *Closed Sun., Mon., 3 wks in Aug., 1 wk in May, and
1 wk at Christmas* Ⓜ *Ségur* ✛ *3:E5.*

$$$$ ✕ **Le Violon d'Ingres.** Following in the footsteps of Joël Robuchon and
MODERN FRENCH Alain Senderens, Christian Constant gave up the Michelin-star chase in
favor of relatively accessible prices and a packed dining room. Here, the
food is sophisticated and the atmosphere is lively; you can find signature
dishes like the almond-crusted sea bass with rémoulade (a buttery caper
sauce), alongside game and scallops (in season), and comforting desserts
like *pots de crème* and chocolate tart. **Known for:** few minutes' walk
to the Eiffel Tower; famous chef that actually cooks here; reservations
needed at least a week in advance. $ *Average main: €38* ✉ *135 rue
St-Dominique, 7e, Eiffel Tower* ☎ *01–45–55–15–05* ⊕ *www.maison
constant.com* Ⓜ *École Militaire* ✛ *3:D2.*

$$ ✕ **Les Cocottes de Christian Constant.** Chef Christian Constant has an
MODERN FRENCH unfailing sense of how Parisians want to eat these days, as proved by
this third addition to his mini restaurant empire near the Eiffel Tower.
At Les Cocottes, he's shifted the normally leisurely bistro experience
into high gear, which allows him to keep prices moderate. **Known for:**
cozy spot for elevated French comfort food; casual, child-friendly atmosphere; dishes served in cast-iron pots. $ *Average main: €20* ✉ *135 rue
St-Dominique, 7e, Eiffel Tower* ⊕ *www.maisonconstant.com* Ⓜ *École
Militaire; Métro or RER: Pont de l'Alma* ✛ *3:D2.*

$$$$ ✕ **LiLi.** The operatically beautiful LiLi, in the Peninsula Hotel, places
CANTONESE sophisticated Cantonese cuisine in its rightful place—the gastronomic

14

center of the world. The menu features all the classics, raised to the status of haute cuisine: small plates of dim sum (seafood, vegetable, or pork dumplings) alongside more substantial fare like fried rice studded with market-fresh vegetables, succulent Sichuan shrimp, and barbecued suckling pig. **Known for:** authentic peking duck; gourmet dim sum; cocktails at the Bar Kléber. $ *Average main: €36* ⊠ *The Peninsula Paris, 19 rue Kléber, 16e, Eiffel Tower* ☎ *01–58–12–67–50* ⊕ *paris.peninsula. com* Ⓜ *Kléber, Charles de Gaulle–Étoile* ✛ *1:C5.*

$$$$
FRENCH FUSION
Fodor's Choice
★

✕ **Restaurant David Toutain.** Although chef David's Toutain's approach may be exasperatingly conceptual for some, others find his earthy, surprising, and inspired concoctions utterly thrilling. Each dish is a lesson in contrasts—of temperature, texture, and flavor—as well as a feat of composition: briny oysters, brussels sprouts, and foie gras in a warm potato consommé; creamy raw oysters with tart kiwi and yuzu; crispy pork chips alongside velvety smoked potato puree. **Known for:** equally wonderful choices for vegetarians and carnivores; epitome of "seasonal" cuisine; plenty of avant-garde thrills. $ *Average main: €42* ⊠ *29 rue Surcouf, 7e, Eiffel Tower* ☎ *01–45–50–11–10* ⊕ *www. davidtoutain.com* ☽ *Closed weekends* Ⓜ *Invalides, La Tour–Maubourg* ✛ *3:E1.*

$$
FRENCH
Fodor's Choice
★

✕ **Savarin la Table.** This cozy restaurant has a laid-back contemporary vibe that belies the immense sophistication of the dishes created by Mehdi Kebboul and Hliza Ayun, young chefs trained in some of Paris's leading kitchens. Here adventurous diners are treated to dishes of rare creativity, with delectable options such as rabbit cake with piquillo peppers, chard and octopus, or succulent duck ravioli. **Known for:** romantic dining upstairs; excellent quality-to-price value; wonderful desserts. $ *Average main: €26* ⊠ *34 rue de Bourgogne, 7e, Eiffel Tower* ☎ *09–86–59–19–67* ☽ *Closed weekends* Ⓜ *Varenne, Solferino* ✛ *3:G2.*

THE CHAMPS-ÉLYSÉES

Style often wins out over substance around the Champs-Élysées, but a handful of restaurants continue to defy fashion. This part of Paris is home to many of the city's most ambitious chefs, whose restaurants are surrounded by palatial hotels, bourgeois apartments, embassies, and luxury boutiques. Some, such as Eric Frechon at Le Bristol's Epicure, offer sophisticated updates of French classics, whereas others, like Pierre Gagnaire, constantly push culinary boundaries in the manner of a mad scientist. A few solid bistros survive here, notably the Art Deco Chez Savy.

$$$$
MODERN FRENCH
Fodor's Choice
★

✕ **Alain Ducasse at the Plaza Athénée.** Set within the Plaza Athénée hotel, Alain Ducasse's three-star Paris flagship totally redefines French haute cuisine. Arguably the world's most visible chef, Ducasse surprises here, devoting himself entirely to vegetables, grains, and fish and mixing the most luxe with the humblest ingredients to sublime effect. **Known for:** gorgeous, uberopulent dining room; haute-vegetarian dining; consistent winner of three Michelin stars. $ *Average main: €125* ⊠ *Hôtel Plaza Athénée, 25 av. Montaigne, 8e, Champs-Élysées* ☎ *01–53–67–65–00*

A Cheese Primer

Their cuisine might be getting lighter, but the French aren't ready to relinquish their cheese. Some restaurants present a single, lovingly selected slice, whereas the more prestigious restaurants wheel in a trolley of specimens aged on the premises. Cheese always comes after the main course and before—or instead of—dessert.

Among the best bistros for cheese are **Astier,** where a giant basket of oozy wonders is brought to the table, and **Le Comptoir,** where a dazzling cheese platter is part of the five-course prix-fixe dinner, or **Le Bistro Paul Bert,** where an overflowing cheese board is left on your table for you to help yourself. A few *bars à fromages* are springing up, too: devoted to cheese the way *bars à vins* are dedicated to wine. **Fromagerie Cantin** (*12 rue du Champ de Mars, 01–45–50–43–94* ⊕ *www. cantin.fr*) is a terrific example.

Armed with these phrases, you can wow the waiter and work your way through the most generous platter.

Avez-vous le Beaufort d'été? Do you have summer Beaufort?

Beaufort is similar to Gruyère, and the best Beaufort is made with milk produced in summer, when cows eat fresh grass. Aged Beaufort is even more reminiscent of a mountain hike.

Je voudrais un chèvre bien frais/ bien sec. I'd like a goat cheese that's nice and fresh/nice and dry.

France produces many goat cheeses, some so fresh they can be scooped with a spoon, some tough enough to use as doorstops. It's a matter of taste, but hard-core cheese eaters favor drier specimens, which stick to the roof of the mouth and have a frankly goaty aroma.

C'est un St-Marcellin de vache ou de chèvre? Is this St-Marcellin made with cow's or goat's milk?

St-Marcellin is a more original choice than the ubiquitous *crottin de chèvre* (poetically named after goats' turds). Originally a goat cheese, today it's more often made with cow's milk. The best have an oozy center, though some like it dry as a hockey puck.

C'est un Brie de Meaux ou de Melun? Is this Brie from Meaux or Melun?

There are many kinds of Brie. Brie de Meaux is the best known, with a smooth flavor and runny center; the much rarer Brie de Melun is more pungent and saltier.

Je n'aime pas le Camembert industriel! I don't like industrial Camembert!

Camembert might be a national treasure, but most of it is industrial. Real Camembert has a white rind with rust-color streaks and a yellow center.

Avez-vous de la confiture pour accompagner ce brebis? Do you have any jam to go with this sheep's cheese?

In the Basque region berry jam is the traditional accompaniment for sharp sheep's-milk cheeses like Ossau-Iraty.

C'est la saison du Mont d'Or. It's Mont d'Or season.

This potent mountain cheese, also known as Vacherin, is produced only from September to March. It's so runny, it's eaten with a spoon.

14

⊕ *www.alain-ducasse.com* ⊘ *Closed weekends. No lunch Mon.–Wed.* 🏛 *Jacket required* Ⓜ *Alma-Marceau* ✛ *1:D6.*

$$$$
MODERN FRENCH
Fodor'sChoice
★

✕ **Alléno Paris au Pavillon Ledoyen.** Tucked away in a quiet garden across from the Petit Palais, Ledoyen—open since 1779—is a study in Empire-style elegance. Star chef Yannick Alléno injects the three-star dining room with a frisson of modernity by putting fresh farmhouse ingredients front and center in his €295, 10-course tasting extravaganza. **Known for:** one of the most romantic settings in Paris; lots of cool history (Napoléon and Josephine met here); langoustine tart with caviar. Ⓢ *Average main: €120* ⊠ *1 av. Dutuit, on Carré des Champs-Élysées, 8e,   Champs-Élysées* ☎ *01–53–05–10–01* ⊕ *www.yannick-alleno. com/restaurant/le-pavillon-ledoyen* ⊘ *Closed Sun. and Aug.* 🏛 *Jacket required* Ⓜ *Concorde, Champs-Élysées–Clemenceau* ✛ *1:F6.*

$$$
BISTRO

✕ **Chez Savy.** Just off glitzy Avenue Montaigne, Chez Savy's Art Deco cream-and-burgundy interior is blissfully intact, occupying its own circa-1930s microcosm. Fill up on rib-sticking specialties from the Aveyron region of central France—lentil salad with bacon, foie gras (prepared on the premises), perfectly charred lamb with featherlight shoestring frites, and pedigreed Charolais beef. **Known for:** good prices in a pricey neighborhood; authentic brasserie experience; competent, unpretentious service. Ⓢ *Average main: €30* ⊠ *23 rue Bayard, 8e, Champs-Élysées* ☎ *01–47–23–46–98* ⊕ *www.chezsavy.com* ⊘ *Closed weekends and Aug.* Ⓜ *Franklin-D.-Roosevelt* ✛ *1:E5.*

$$$$
BISTRO

✕ **Dominique Bouchet.** To taste the cooking of one of the city's revered chefs, head to Dominique Bouchet's elegant modern bistro, where contemporary art brightens cream-color walls. On the menu, refined French technique meets country-style cooking, as in leg of lamb braised in wine with roasted cocoa bean and potato puree, or a chocolate éclair with black cherries and ice cream. **Known for:** master chef of French technique; attentive service in a small dining room; well-deserved Michelin star. Ⓢ *Average main: €35* ⊠ *11 rue Treilhard, 8e, Champs-Élysées* ☎ *01–45–61–09–46* ⊕ *www.dominique-bouchet.com* ⊘ *Closed weekends and 3 wks in Aug.* Ⓜ *Miromesnil* ✛ *1:F3.*

$$$$
MODERN FRENCH

✕ **Epicure.** One of the more inventive young chefs in Paris, Eric Frechon is now the chef at Le Bristol Hotel's revered restaurant, quickly earning the three Michelin stars that he has retained ever since. Frechon creates masterworks—say, farmer's pork cooked "from head to foot" with truffle-enhanced crushed potatoes—that are both deeply satisfying and unpretentious. **Known for:** alfresco dining in a beautiful French garden in warm weather; superb French provencial dining room; relatively affordable lunch menu. Ⓢ *Average main: €110* ⊠ *Hôtel Bristol, 112 rue du Faubourg St-Honoré, 8e, Champs-Élysées* ☎ *01–53–43–43–00* ⊕ *www.lebristolparis.com* 🏛 *Jacket and tie* Ⓜ *Miromesnil* ✛ *1:F4.*

$$$$
MODERN FRENCH
Fodor'sChoice
★

✕ **Guy Savoy.** Within the beautifully restored La Monnaie (the old Paris mint), you'll find star chef Guy Savoy's hallowed dining room. The market-fresh menu retains the master's classics—artichoke soup with black truffles—with some new dishes like oysters pot-au-feu and sweet, bitter, and peppery roasted duck *paletot* that reveal the magnitude of his talent. **Known for:** gorgeous setting overlooking the Seine; intimate, art-filled dining rooms; one of Paris's most highly rated dining experiences outside a palace hotel. $ *Average main: €120* ✉ *18 rue Troyon, 17e, Champs-Élysées* ☎ *01–43–80–40–61* ⊕ *www.guysavoy.com* ⊘ *Closed Sun. and Mon., and 1 wk at Christmas. No lunch Sat.* 🏛 *Jacket required* Ⓜ *Charles-de-Gaulle–Étoile* ✛ *1:C3.*

$$$$
JAPANESE
✗ **Kifuné.** Some Japanese expats say you won't find anything closer to authentic Japanese cooking in Paris than the kitchen in Kifune. Sit at the bar to admire the sushi chef's lightning-quick skills or opt for a more intimate table for tasting the sublime crab-and-shrimp salad starter, or a deeply comforting miso soup with clams. **Known for:** small, intimate, and totally authentic; top-notch service; good-value lunch menu. $ *Average main: €35* ✉ *44 rue St-Ferdinand, 17e, Champs-Élysées* ☎ *01–45–72–11–19* ⊘ *Closed Sun. and Mon., 3 wks in Aug., and 1 wk in Dec.* Ⓜ *Argentine* ✛ *1:A3.*

$$$$
JAPANESE
✗ **Komatsubaki.** To savor the city's freshest sushi and other authentic Japanese specialities, head to Komatsubaki. It's run by Yoichi Kino, a 30-year master sushi chef whose family has specialized in smoked eel for generations, and Ryuma Takubo, who earned a Michelin star in Japan and specializes in the exquisite vegetarian cuisine favored by Japanese monks. **Known for:** high-end takeaway sushi; authentic dining experience on tatami mats; rare selection of wines, sakes, and teas. $ *Average main: €45* ✉ *3 rue d'Artois, 8e, Champs-Élysées* ☎ *01–42–25–26–78* ⊕ *www.komatsubaki-paris.com* ⊘ *Closed Mon.* Ⓜ *Saint-Philippe-du-Roule* ✛ *1:E4.*

$$$$
MODERN FRENCH
✗ **L'Arôme.** Eric Martins ran a popular bistro in the far reaches of the 15e arrondissement before opening this contemporary restaurant off the Champs-Élysées, and his background in haute cuisine makes this ambitious dining room an easy transition. The spot turns out seasonal dishes with a touch of finesse from the open kitchen. **Known for:** masterful wine pairings; Breton crab with avocado, Japanese rice and tomato gelée with smoked pepper; pricey fixe-prix menus (no à la carte). $ *Average main: €48* ✉ *3 rue St-Philippe du Roule, 8e, Champs-Élysées* ☎ *01–42–25–55–98* ⊕ *www.larome.fr* ⊘ *Closed weekends, and Aug.* Ⓜ *St-Philippe du Roule* ✛ *1:E4.*

$$$
SEAFOOD
✗ **L'Huîtrier.** If you have a single-minded craving for oysters, this is the place for you. The friendly owner will describe the many different kinds available, and you can follow with any of several daily fish specials—or opt for a full seafood platter for around €50. **Known for:** the freshest oysters around; good price-to-quality ratio for heaping seafood platters; lively ambience. $ *Average main: €28* ✉ *16 rue Saussier-Leroy, 17e, Champs-Élysées* ☎ *01–40–54–83–44* ⊕ *www.huitrier.fr* ⊘ *Closed Aug.* Ⓜ *Ternes* ✛ *1:C2.*

$$$$
MODERN FRENCH
✗ **La Cristal Room.** The success of this restaurant in the Baccarat museumboutique stems not only from the stunning decor—mirrors, patches of exposed-brick wall, and a stunning chandelier—but also from the culinary stylings of chef Mathieu Mécheri. The menu provides a taste of his ultrarefined style with dishes such as a velvety *velouté* of wild mushrooms, and sole *meunière* with grapefruit and an arugula flan. **Known for:** opulent dining room in a famous Paris mansion; fabulous bar with cocktail menu; affordable lunch menu. $ *Average main: €42* ✉ *11 pl.*

14

des États-Unis, 16e, Champs-Élysées ☎ *01–40–22–11–10* ⊕ *www.baccarat.fr* ⊘ *Closed Sun. and Mon.* Ⓜ *Kléber* ✢ *1:C5.*

$$$$ ✕ **Le Cinq.** Christian Le Squer is among the most famous and most
MODERN FRENCH respected chefs in Paris, as proved by his turn here at one of the city's
Fodor's Choice most deluxe dining rooms. You'll find all the luxury products you might
★ expect—caviar, truffles, game in season—along with a masterful touch
that often transforms homey Breton ingredients such as oysters or lamb
into imaginative tours de forces. **Known for:** Michelin-starred French
fine dining; famous flowery outdoor terrace; unfailingly accommodating
service. ⑤ *Average main: €110* ✉ *Hôtel Four Seasons George V, 31 av.
George V, 8e, Champs-Élysées* ☎ *01–49–52–70–00* ⊕ *www.fourseasons.com/paris* 🏛 *Jacket and tie* Ⓜ *George V* ✢ *1:D5.*

$$ ✕ **Le Hide.** Hide Kobayashi, known as "Koba," is one of several Japanese
BISTRO chefs in Paris who trained with some of the biggest names in French
Fodor's Choice cuisine before opening their own restaurants. Not surprisingly, this
★ great-value bistro near the Arc de Triomphe became instantly popular
with locals as well as visiting Japanese and Americans who follow the
food scene. **Known for:** chic, unpretentious dining room; stellar prices
for this pricey neighborhood; one of Paris's best prix-fixe menus. ⑤ *Average main: €20* ✉ *10 rue du Général Lanzerac, 8e, Champs-Élysées*
☎ *01–45–74–15–81* ⊕ *www.lehide.fr* ⊘ *Closed Sun., 2 wks in May, and
2 wks in Aug.* Ⓜ *Charles de Gaulle–Étoile* ✢ *1:B3.*

$$ ✕ **Le Petit Verdot du 17e.** Sandwich bars might be threatening the tradi-
BISTRO tional two-hour lunch, but that doesn't stop this old-fashioned neigh-
borhood bistro with its painted facade and wine-theme dining room
from flourishing. Business executives loosen their neckties to feast on
homemade pâté, plate-engulfing steak for two, or guinea hen with cabbage, along with one of 50 or so small-producer wines. **Known for:**
small and authentic space; generous plates at great prices; legendary
steak tartare. ⑤ *Average main: €18* ✉ *9 rue Fourcroy, 17e, Champs-
Élysées* ☎ *01–42–27–47–42* ⊘ *Closed Sun. No lunch Sat.* Ⓜ *Charles de
Gaulle–Étoile* ✢ *1:C2.*

$$$$ ✕ **Le Relais Plaza.** Parisian to its core, the Hotel Plaza Athénée's Art
FRENCH Deco dining room—including a mural that's a registered historic landmark—is a cherished neighborhood stalwart. Masterful updates of
French classics include dishes like warm salad of delicate greens, thin-
sliced artichokes, and Parmesan, flecked with shaved black truffles,
and house-made foie gras with slices of fresh figs and a rich dried-fruit
chutney. **Known for:** throwback Jazz nights every last Wednesday of
the month; exceptional dining room with historic Art Deco murals;
a favorite with the locals. ⑤ *Average main: €50* ✉ *Plaza Athénée, 21
av. Montaigne, 8e, Champs-Élysées* ☎ *01–53–67–64–00* ⊕ *www.alainducasse.com/en/restaurant/le-relais-plaza* Ⓜ *Alma-Marceau, Franklin
D. Roosevelt* ✢ *1:D6.*

$$$ ✕ **Mini Palais.** Inside the Grand Palais, Mini Palais is among Paris's most
MODERN FRENCH stylish dining rooms, but the menu is the real draw. The burger *de
magret et foie gras*, a flavorful mélange of tender duckling breast and
duck foie gras drizzled with truffled jus on a buttery brioche bun, under-
scores what's best about this place: a thoroughly modern cuisine with
an old-fashioned extravagance. **Known for:** soaring outdoor terrace

with views of the Petit Palais and Pont Alexandre III; late-night snacks; decent prices, considering the neighborhood. $ *Average main: €25* ⊠ *3 av. Winston Churchill, 8e, Champs-Élysées* ☎ *01–42–56–42–42* ⊕ *www.minipalais.com* Ⓜ *Champs-Élysées–Clemenceau* ✢ *1:F6.*

$$$$
MODERN FRENCH
Fodor's Choice
★
✕ **Pierre Gagnaire.** If you want to venture to the frontier of contemporary cooking—and if money is no object—dinner here is a must. Chef Pierre Gagnaire's work is at once intellectual and poetic, often blending three or four unexpected tastes and textures in a single dish. Just taking in the menu requires concentration (ask the waiters for help), so complex are the multiline descriptions about each dish's six or seven ingredients. **Known for:** consistently ranked among the world's best (and most expensive) restaurants; combines French technical mastery with cutting-edge techniques; complicated menu descriptions. $ *Average main: €130* ⊠ *6 rue de Balzac, 8e, Champs-Élysées* ☎ *01–58–36–12–50* ⊕ *www. pierre-gagnaire.com* ⊘ *Closed weekends and Aug.* Ⓜ *Charles de Gaulle–Étoile* ✢ *1:D4.*

$$$$
SEAFOOD
✕ **Rech.** Having restored the historic Paris bistros Aux Lyonnais and Benoît to their former glory, star chef Alain Ducasse turned his piercing attention to this seafood brasserie founded in 1925. His wisdom lies in knowing what not to change: the original Art Deco chairs in the main-floor dining room; seafood shucker Malec, who has been a fixture on this chic stretch of sidewalk since 1982; and the supersized éclair that's drawn in locals for decades. **Known for:** most delicate line-caught sole sautéed in butter; luminous dining room that is a lovely setting at lunch or dinner; Mediterranean-inspired dishes. $ *Average main: €33* ⊠ *62 av. des Ternes, 17e, Champs-Élysées* ☎ *01–45–72–29–47* ⊕ *www.restaurant-rech.fr* ⊘ *Closed Sun., Mon., and late July–late Aug.* Ⓜ *Ternes* ✢ *1:B3.*

$$$$
MODERN FRENCH
✕ **Taillevent.** Perhaps the most traditional of all Paris luxury restaurants, this grande dame basks in renewed freshness under brilliant chef Alain Solivérès, who draws inspiration from the Basque country, Bordeaux, and Languedoc for his daily menu. Traditional dishes such as scallops *meunière* (with butter and lemon) are matched with contemporary choices like a splendid spelt risotto with truffles and frogs' legs or pan-fried duck liver with caramelized fruits and vegetables. **Known for:** one of the oldest names in Paris for fine French dining; discrete hangout for Paris politicians; 19th-century salon turned winter garden. $ *Average main: €110* ⊠ *15 rue Lamennais, 8e, Champs-Élysées* ☎ *01–44–95–15–01* ⊕ *www.taillevent.com* ⊘ *Closed weekends and Aug.* 🎩 *Jacket and tie* Ⓜ *Charles de Gaulle–Étoile* ✢ *1:D4.*

AROUND THE LOUVRE

Home to the city's wholesale food market until the 1960s, Les Halles is still the place to go for late-night onion soup or steak frites, washed back with gulps of cheap and tasty red wine. The streets grow more subdued around the Louvre and Palais Royal, where you can slurp oysters at a classic brasserie or indulge in the more experimental haute cuisine at a foodie hangout.

$$$
BISTRO

✕ **Chez Georges.** If you were to ask Parisian bankers, aristocrats, or antiques dealers to name their favorite bistro for a three-hour weekday lunch, many would choose Georges. The traditional fare is very good—chicken-liver terrine, curly endive salad with bacon and a poached egg, steak with béarnaise—and the atmosphere is better, compensating for the steep prices. **Known for:** authentic brasserie, with authentic food to match; only top-quality products used, which accounts for the price; lively historic atmosphere. ⓢ *Average main: €32* ✉ *1 rue du Mail, 2e, Louvre* ☎ *01–42–60–07–11* ⊘ *Closed weekends, Aug., and 1 wk at Christmas* Ⓜ *Sentier* ✛ *2:C5.*

$$
WINE BAR
Fodor's Choice
★

✕ **Juvéniles.** A favorite with the French and the expat crowd, Juvéniles is the ideal kind of neighborhood outpost that mixes great dining with an inspired wine list, all at affordable prices. The lunch menu might start with velvety foie gras *maison* (paired with a crisp Riesling), followed by slow-braised beef with a tangy tarragon-and-dill sauce *ravigote*. **Known for:** prix-fixe lunch that's an outstanding bargain; bottles of wine also available to take home; small space so reserve in advance. ⓢ *Average main: €21* ✉ *47 rue de Richelieu, 1er, Louvre* ☎ *01–42–97–46–49* ⊘ *Closed Sun. No lunch Mon.* Ⓜ *Bourse, Pyramides* ✛ *2:B6.*

$$$
BISTRO

✕ **L'Ardoise.** Despite the updated chic decor, this tiny, reliably good bistro has not sacrificed substance to style. This is first-rate dining, and the three-course dinner menu (you can also order à la carte, but it's less of a bargain) tempts with original dishes like mushroom-and-foie-gras ravioli with smoked duck; farmer's pork with porcini mushrooms; and red mullet with creole sauce. Just as enticing are the desserts, such as a superb *feuillantine au citron*—caramelized pastry leaves filled with lemon cream and lemon slices—and a boozy baba au rhum. **Known for:** good-value prix-fixe menus at lunch and dinner; traditional fare with a contemporary twist; noisy crowds. ⓢ *Average main: €27* ✉ *28 rue du Mont Thabor, 1er, Louvre* ☎ *01–42–96–28–18* ⊕ *www.lardoise-paris. com* ⊘ *No lunch Sun.* Ⓜ *Concorde* ✛ *1:H6.*

$$$$
BISTRO

✕ **La Bourse et La Vie.** After a takeover by the French-trained American chef Daniel Rose, this bistro stalwart transformed from a duckling to a swan, with elegant revamps of its bistro decor and an upgrade on those deeply satisfying French comfort-food classics. The humble steak frites is a buttery, melt-in-the-mouth slab of beef ringed by a halo of perfectly crisp golden frites. **Known for:** hand-picked quality ingredients; one of the best tarte tatins in town; cozy interior. ⓢ *Average main: €35* ✉ *12 rue Vivienne, 2e, Louvre* ☎ *01–42–60–08–83* ⊕ *www.labourselavie. com* ⊘ *Closed weekends and Aug.* Ⓜ *Bourse* ✛ *2:C5.*

$$$
MODERN FRENCH
FAMILY

✕ **La Régalade Saint-Honoré.** After taking over the original La Régalade, chef Bruno Doucet kept some of what made the old restaurant so popular (country terrines, reasonably priced wines, convivial atmosphere). But he also had a few tricks under his toque, creating a successful haute-cuisine-meets-comfort-food destination with dishes like earthy morel mushrooms in a frothy cream for a starter, followed by the signature succulent caramelized pork belly over tender Puy lentils. **Known for:** grand-mère's creamy rice pudding for dessert; good-value prix-fixe menu for lunch and dinner; last-minute reservations sometimes possible. ⓢ *Average main: €25* ✉ *123 rue Saint-Honoré, 1er, Louvre* ☎ *01–42–21–92–40* Ⓜ *Louvre–Rivoli* ✛ *4:C1.*

$$$
MODERN FRENCH

⚔ **Le Georges.** One of those rooftop show-stopping venues so popular in Paris, Le Georges preens atop the Centre Georges Pompidou. Part of the Costes brothers' empire, the establishment trots out fashionable dishes such as sesame-crusted tuna and coriander-spiced beef fillet flambéed with cognac. **Known for:** stunning views of central Paris and beyond; cocktails on the terrace; hit-or-miss food except for the decadent desserts. ⑤ *Average main: €32* ✉ *Centre Pompidou, 6th fl., 19 rue Beaubourg, 4e, Louvre* ☎ *01–44–78–47–99* ⊕ *www.restaurantgeorgesparis. com* ☉ *Closed Tues.* Ⓜ *Rambuteau* ✥ *4:E1.*

$$$$
MODERN FRENCH
Fodor's Choice
★

⚔ **Le Grand Véfour.** Originally built in 1784, Le Grand Véfour has welcomed everyone from Napoléon to Colette to Jean Cocteau under its mirrored ceiling, and is still a contender for the most beautiful restaurant in Paris today. The rich and fashionable continue to gather here to swoon over two-Michelin-star chef Guy Martin's unique blend of sophistication and rusticity. **Known for:** ultimate place for romance; sumptuous historic décor that's remained unchanged for 200 years; outstanding cheese trolley. ⑤ *Average main: €130* ✉ *17 rue de Beaujolais, 1er, Louvre* ☎ *01–42–96–56–27* ⊕ *www.grand-vefour.com* ☉ *Closed weekends, Aug., and Christmas holidays* Ⓜ *Palais-Royal* ✥ *2:B6.*

14

$$
BISTRO

⚔ **Les Fines Gueules.** Invest in good ingredients and most of the work is done: that's the principle of this wine bar–bistro that's developed a loyal following. The products are treated simply, often serving high-quality meats and vegetables raw alongside a salad or sautéed potatoes. **Known for:** good selection biodynamic and natural wines; fresh and succulent steak tartare; intimate atmosphere. ⑤ *Average main: €20* ✉ *43 rue Croix des Petits Champs, 1er, Louvre* ☎ *01–42–61–35–41* ⊕ *www. lesfinesgueules.fr* Ⓜ *Palais-Royal* ✥ *2:C6.*

$$$$
BISTRO
Fodor's Choice
★

⚔ **Restaurant du Palais-Royal.** This stylish modern bistro serves stunning gastronomic cuisine to match its gorgeous location under the arcades of the Palais-Royal. Sole, scallops, and risotto—including a dramatic black-squid-ink-and-lobster version, or an all-green vegetarian one—are beautifully prepared, but the grilled suckling pig and roasted carrots is also popular with expense-account lunchers. **Known for:** peerless setting in the Palais Royal gardens; outdoor dining in the garden in warm weather; reservations needed well in advance. ⑤ *Average main: €35* ✉ *Jardins du Palais-Royal, 110 Galerie Valois, 1er, Louvre* ☎ *01–40–20–00–27* ⊕ *www.restaurantdupalaisroyal.com* ☉ *Closed Sun. and Mon.* Ⓜ *Palais-Royal* ✥ *2:B6.*

$$
MODERN FRENCH

⚔ **Willi's Wine Bar.** More a restaurant than a wine bar, this British-owned spot is a stylish haunt for Parisian and visiting gourmands who might stop in for a glass of wine at the oak bar or settle into the wood-beamed dining room. The selection of reinvented classic dishes changes daily. **Known for:** expat hangout; fine choice of wines by the glass; prix-fixe menu of reliably good food. ⑤ *Average main: €20* ✉ *13 rue des Petits-Champs, 1er, Louvre* ☎ *01–42–61–05–09* ⊕ *www.williswinebar.com* ☉ *Closed Mon. in Aug and Sun. year-round* Ⓜ *Bourse* ✥ *2:B6.*

$$$$
FRENCH FUSION
Fodor's Choice
★

⚔ **Yam'Tcha.** Inspired by Chinese cooking, many of the dishes here rely on brilliant flavor combinations and very precise cooking, like the roasted Challans duck (a cross between wild and domestic) with Sichuan-style eggplant. There's also a tea sommelier, who introduces diners to earthy or grassy flavors that complement the food. **Known for:** prix-fixe menus paired with rare teas; one of Paris's star chefs; close to the Louvre and the Centre Pompidou. ⑤ *Average main: €100* ⊠ *121 rue St. Honoré, 1er, Louvre* ☏ *01–40–26–08–07* ⊕ *www.yamtcha.com* ⊘ *Closed Sun., Mon., Christmas, and Aug. No lunch Tues.* Ⓜ *Louvre-Rivoli, Les Halles* ✛ *4:C1.*

$
JAPANESE

✕**Zen.** There's no shortage of Japanese restaurants around the Louvre, but this one is a cut above much of the competition. The menu has something for every taste, from warming ramen soups (part of a €12 lunch menu that includes five pork dumplings) to sushi and sashimi prepared with particular care. **Known for:** quick, good-value lunch; great for vegetarians; friendly, helpful service. ⑤ *Average main: €17* ⊠ *8 rue de l'Echelle, 1er, Louvre* ☏ *01–42–61–93–99* ⊘ *Closed 10 days in mid-Aug.* Ⓜ *Pyramides, Palais-Royal* ✛ *2:B6.*

LES GRANDS BOULEVARDS

One of Paris's most atmospheric, and up-and-coming, neighborhoods, it's also a culinary melting pot, with everything from the minuscule Japanese noodle shops lining Rue St-Anne, authentic 19th-century brasseries that evoke the old working-class *bouillons*, and Art Nouveau–style Belle Époque dining rooms, to a new generation of young, talented chefs cooking up some of the city's most exciting cuisine.

$
BISTRO
FAMILY

✕**Chartier.** This classic *bouillon* (a term referring to the Parisian soup restaurants popular among workers in the early 20th century) is a part of the Gérard Joulie group of bistros and brasseries, which discreetly updated the menu without changing the fundamentals. People come here more for the bonhomie and the stunning 1896 interior than the cooking, which could be politely described as unambitious—then again, where else can you find a plate of foie gras for €7? **Known for:** Paris's last truly authentic "bouillon"; 19th-century ambience; extensive menu with gentle prices. ⑤ *Average main: €12* ⊠ *7 rue du Faubourg-Montmartre, 9e, Grands Boulevards* ☏ *01–47–70–86–29* ⊕ *www.bouillon-chartier.com* Ⓜ *Montmartre* ✛ *2:C4.*

$$
BISTRO

✕**Chez Casimir.** This easygoing bistro, run by Breton chef Thierry Breton, is popular with polished Parisian professionals and hipster foodies alike. The affordable set dinner menu covers lentil soup with fresh croutons, braised endive and andouille salad, and roast lamb on a bed of Paimpol beans, along with 12 different cheeses to choose from. **Known for:** excellent value wines by the glass; sidewalk dining; daily-changing blackboard menu. ⑤ *Average main: €19* ⊠ *6 rue de Belzunce, 10e, Grands Boulevards* ☏ *01–48–78–28–80* ⊘ *No dinner weekends* Ⓜ *Gare du Nord* ✛ *2:E2.*

$$$
MODERN FRENCH
FAMILY

✕**Drouant.** Best known for the literary prizes awarded here since 1914, Drouant has shed its dusty image to become a forward-thinking restaurant. The playful menu revisits the French hors d'oeuvres tradition with starters that come as a series of four plates; diners can pick from themes such as French classics (like a deconstructed leek salad) or convincing minitakes on Thai and Moroccan dishes. **Known for:** France's most prestigious literary prize, the Prix Goncourt, awarded here; good for same-day reservations; elegant atmosphere. $ *Average main: €25* ✉ *16–18 pl. Gaillon, 2e, Grands Boulevards* ☎ *01–42–65–15–16* ⊕ *www.drouant.com* Ⓜ *Pyramides* ✛ *2:B5.*

$ ✕ **Echo Deli.** Parisians flock to the newly hip Sentier neighborhood for
CONTEMPORARY a taste of this chic coffeeshop's fresh and imaginative California-style
Fodor's Choice cuisine. Eggs are served in the most delicious ways: scrambled with
★ cheese, scallions, and hot sauce; in a slow-cooked congee of wild-mushrooms and whole brown rice; or with thick slices of multigrain bread, avocado, and anchovies. **Known for:** delicious Saturday and Sunday brunch; vegetarian, vegan, and gluten-free options; great coffee and other hot drinks. $ *Average main: €12* ✉ *95, rue d'Aboukir, 2e, Grands Boulevards* ⊕ *www.echo-paris.com* ☽ *Closed Mon. and Tues.* Ⓜ *Bonne Nouvelle, Strasbourg-Saint-Denis, Sentier* ✛ *2:D5.*

$$$$ ✕ **Frenchie.** A brick-and-stone-walled bistro on a pedestrian street near
BISTRO Rue Montorgueil, Frenchie has quickly became one of the most packed
Fodor's Choice bistros in town, with tables booked months in advance, despite two
★ seatings each evening. This success is due to the good-value, five-course dinner menu (prix fixe only); boldly flavored dishes such as calamari gazpacho with squash blossoms, and melt-in-the-mouth braised lamb with roasted eggplant and spinach are excellent options. **Known for:** casual laid-back atmosphere that belies the ultrasophisticated dishes; extensive and original wine list; graciously accommodating to vegetarians. $ *Average main: €34* ✉ *5 rue du Nil, 2e, Grands Boulevards* ☎ *01–40–39–96–19* ⊕ *www.frenchie-restaurant.com* ☽ *Closed weekends, 2 wks in Aug., and 10 days at Christmas. No lunch Mon.–Wed.* Ⓜ *Sentier* ✛ *2:D5.*

$ ✕ **Frenchie Bar à Vins.** If this weren't one of Paris's outstanding wine bars,
WINE BAR the wait and metal tractor seats might be a deterrent. Yet wine lovers
Fodor's Choice would be hard-pressed to find a better venue for sampling a great list of
★ French wines and inspired selections from Italy and Spain—every one of them sold by the bottle or glass—with superb tapas to match. **Known for:** choice selection of natural wines from France and Europe; rare expertise in natural, organic, and biodynamic wines; long waits unless you get there right when they open (7 pm). $ *Average main: €17* ✉ *6 rue du Nil, 2e, Grands Boulevards* ☎ *No phone* ⊕ *www.frenchie-restaurant. com* ☽ *Closed weekends. No lunch* Ⓜ *Sentier* ✛ *2:D5.*

$ ✕ **Frenchie To Go.** The third outpost in Frenchie's Rue du Nil empire,
MODERN FRENCH Frenchie To Go capitalizes on three of the latest Paris food trends:
FAMILY breakfast, fast food, and takeaway. The hot dogs and tasty pastrami (almost unheard of in Paris) are meticulously sourced, as is pretty much everything else—Brittany lobster for the lobster rolls and line-caught hake for the scrumptious fish-and-chips. **Known for:** good value for top-quality ingredients; quick breakfasts or take-out lunches; homemade ginger beer. $ *Average main: €10* ✉ *9 rue du Nil, 2e, Louvre* ☎ *01–40–39–96–19* ⊕ *www.frenchietogo.com* Ⓜ *Sentier* ✛ *2:D5.*

$$$ ✕ **Goupil le Bistro.** The best Paris bistros emit an air of quiet confidence,
BISTRO and this is certainly the case with Goupil, a triumph despite its out-of-the-way location not far from the Porte Maillot conference center. The

tiny open kitchen works miracles with seasonal ingredients, transforming mackerel into luxury food (on buttery puff pastry with mustard sauce) and panfrying monkfish to perfection with artichokes and chanterelles. **Known for:** more gourmet than its casual appearance suggests; daily-changing blackboard menu; outdoor dining in warm weather. ⑤ *Average main: €26* ✉ *4 rue Claude Debussy, 17e, Grands Boulevards* ☎ *01–45–74–83–25* ⊘ *Closed weekends and 3 wks in Aug.* Ⓜ *Porte de Champerret* ✛ *1:B1.*

$$
BRASSERIE

✕ **Lazare.** With so many of Paris's fabled brasseries co-opted by upscale chains, the news that three-star Michelin chef Eric French was opening a modern take on the traditional brasserie in the St-Lazare train station was met with curiosity and joy. Though prices are commensurate with his status, Frechon doesn't skimp on the classics: steak tartare, escargots, and charcuterie all make memorable appearances. **Known for:** quick dining before catching a train; can usually snag a seat sans reservation; classic brasserie atmosphere and cooking. ⑤ *Average main: €24* ✉ *108 rue Saint-Lazare, 8e, Grands Boulevards* ☎ *01–45–23–42–06* ⊕ *www.lazare-paris.fr* Ⓜ *St-Lazare* ✛ *1:H3.*

$$$
WINE BAR

✕ **Racines.** Originally a *cave à manger* (a wine bar/bistro) serving natural wines and top-quality French fare, the foodie world rejoiced when adulated chef Simone Tondo took the helm and introduced a small but stellar menu of Italian comfort dishes mixed with classic French stalwarts The old tile floors, wood tables, and location in the atmospheric Passage des Panoramas, Paris's oldest covered arcade, only add to the ambience. It's utterly packed at mealtimes, so be sure to reserve in advance. **Known for:** wonderful atmosphere in a historic passage; hard-to-find Italian wines; homemade tagliatelli with slow-cooked beef. ⑤ *Average main: €26* ✉ *8 passage des Panoramas, 2e, Grands Boulevards* ☎ *01–40–13–06–41* ⊕ *www.racinesparis.com* ⊘ *Closed weekends, 3 wks in Aug., and at Christmas* Ⓜ *Grands Boulevards, La Bourse* ✛ *2:C4.*

$
FRENCH
Fodor'sChoice
★

✕ **Rrraw.** Just when Paris thought its already phenomenal chocolate scene couldn't get any better, chocolatier Frédéric Marr opened this chic chocolate factory and boutique. Now the words "healthy" and "chocolate" appear together in the organic, non-dairy, vegan (and yes, tasty) chocolates made here from unheated raw beans in order preserve all the nutrients, subtle flavors, and (minimal) natural sugars. **Known for:** amazing chocolate you can watch be made on the premises; vegan, gluten-free, organic, and low sugar products; delicious hot chocolate. ⑤ *Average main: €6* ✉ *8 rue de Mulhouse , 2e, Grands Boulevards* ☎ *01–45–08–84–04* ⊕ *www.rrraw.fr* ⊘ *Closed Sun. and Mon.* Ⓜ *Bonnes Nouvelle* ✛ *2:D5.*

$$$$
MODERN FRENCH
Fodor'sChoice
★

✕ **Saturne.** It's no surprise that chef Sven Chartier, a veteran of famous produce-centric restaurants L'Arpège and Racines, would focus his restaurant around seasonal, locally sourced veggies, along with the freshest seafood and pedigreed meats. Dishes tend to be fresh and minimally cooked, featuring unusual pairings of vegetables and greens that are sophisticated to the point of cerebral. **Known for:** Michelin-starred prixe-fixe menu; all-natural wines; organic ingredients only. ⑤ *Average main: €35* ✉ *17 rue Notre-Dame des Victoires, 2e, Grands Boulevards*

☎ *01–42–60–31–90* ⊕ *www.saturne-paris.fr* ☉ *Closed weekends* Ⓜ *Bourse* ✛ *2:B1.*

MONTMARTRE

Perched above central Paris, Montmartre is buzzing with a hip vibe. Idyllic as the portrayal of Montmartre might seem in Jean-Pierre Jeunet's film *Amélie*, it's surprisingly close to reality. Though decidedly out of the way, Montmartre is still one of the most desirable areas in Paris, seamlessly blending the trendy and the traditional. The less picturesque neighborhood around Gare du Nord and Gare de l'Est is making its mark on the culinary scene: besides classic brasseries, tucked-away bistros, and the city's most authentic Indian restaurants, you'll find a new generation of cafés and gastrobistros exploding onto the scene.

14

$ ✕ **Bal Café.** Set in a bright, modern space on a tiny street in the lower
CAFÉ reaches of Montmartre, the popular Bal Café caters to a diverse clientele
FAMILY who come for the great coffee, delicious homey food, lively crowd, and
Fodor's Choice the art gallery–bookstore. British–French-inspired cuisine with far-flung
★ influences (like kedgeree, a Scottish–Indian rice-and-smoked-haddock dish), tender pancakes, fried eggs with ham and roasted tomatoes, and buttery scones with jam represent some the best comfort food in town. **Known for:** great brunches and reliably good coffee; art gallery on the premises; outdoor terrace on a quiet passageway. ⑤ *Average main: €12* ✉ *6 impasse de la Défense, 18e, Montmartre* ☎ *01–44–70–75–51* ⊕ *www.le-bal.fr* ☉ *Closed Mon. and Tues. No dinner Sun.* Ⓜ *Place de Clichy* ✛ *2:A1.*

$ ✕ **Café Lomi.** A trailblazer on the Paris gastro-coffee scene, Café Lomi
CAFÉ first supplied expertly roasted single-origin coffees to the first wave of barista cafés and top restaurants. Now Lomi's industrial-chic loft is equal parts roaster, café, workshop, and pilgrimage stop for hard-core coffee lovers, serving up a range of splendid brews along with a menu of warm and cold dishes and a hearty brunch on weekends. **Known for:** industrial-chic space; coffee roasted on the premises; consistently excellent brews. ⑤ *Average main: €8* ✉ *3 ter rue Marcadet, 18e, Montmartre* ☎ *09–80–39–56–24* ⊕ *www.cafelomi.com* ☉ *Closed 3 wks in Aug.* Ⓜ *Marcadet-Poissonnière* ✛ *2:E1.*

$$$ ✕ **Guilo Guilo.** Already a star in Kyoto, Eiichi Edakuni created a sensa-
JAPANESE tion with his first Parisian restaurant, where 20 diners seated around the black horseshoe bar can watch him at work each night. The €55 set menu is a bargain given the quality and sophistication of the food. **Known for:** reliably good Japanese cuisine with French accents; signature foie-gras sushi; buzzy, sometimes chaotic atmosphere. ⑤ *Average main: €27* ✉ *8 rue Garreau, 18e, Montmartre* ☎ *01–42–54–23–92* ☉ *Closed Sun. and Mon. No lunch* Ⓜ *Abbesses* ✛ *2:B1.*

$$$ ✕ **L'Arcane.** Once a well-guarded foodie secret, a Michelin star brought
FRENCH this cozy restaurant tucked behind the Sacré-Coeur richly deserved
Fodor's Choice acclaim. Now the intimate 14-seat dining room is packed with diners
★ enjoying impeccable contemporary French cuisine that's gorgeously presented and full of flavor. **Known for:** three-course "surprise" menu; location near the Sacré-Coeur; online reservations needed. ⑤ *Average main:*

€26 ⊠ 9 *rue Lamarck , 18e, Montmartre ⊕ www.restaurantlarcane.com*
⊘ *Closed Sun. and Mon. No lunch Tues.* Ⓜ *Lamarck-Cauliancourt.*

$$$
BRASSERIE
FAMILY

✕ **La Mascotte.** Though everyone talks about the "new Montmartre," exemplified by a wave of chic residents and throbbingly cool cafés and bars, it's good to know that the old Montmartre is alive and well at the untrendy-and-proud-of-it Mascotte. This old-fashioned café-brasserie—which dates from 1889, the same year that saw the opening of the Tour Eiffel and the Moulin Rouge—is where you can find neighborhood fixtures such as the drag queen Michou (of the nearby club Chez Michou), who always wears blue. **Known for:** copious oyster and seafood platters; sidewalk dining in summer; typically Belle Époque Montmartre atmosphere. Ⓢ *Average main: €26 ⊠ 52 rue des Abbesses, 18e, Montmartre* ☎ *01–46–06–28–15 ⊕ www.la-mascotte-montmartre. com* Ⓜ *Abbesses* ✛ *2:B1.*

$
CAFÉ
FAMILY
Fodor's Choice
★

✕ **Soul Kitchen.** Run by three friendly young women, the snug Soul Kitchen unites a pleasantly homey decor and welcoming atmosphere with the kind of Anglo-French all-organic comfort food that soothes body and soul. Choose from gruyère mac and cheese, chèvre and leek tarts, house-made foie gras, and a pastry counter laden with treats like homemade scones, cheesecake, tiramisu, and rich mousse au chocolat. **Known for:** charming atmosphere; delicious coffee and fresh juices; range of homemade dishes and desserts made fresh daily. Ⓢ *Average main: €12 ⊠ 33 rue Lamarck, 18e, Montmartre* ☎ *01–71–37–99–95* ⊘ *Closed Mon.* Ⓜ *Lamarck-Caulaincourt* ✛ *2:C1.*

THE MARAIS

The once-run-down Marais is now the epitome of chic, but you can still find reminders of its down-to-earth past along Rue des Rosiers, where falafel shops and Eastern European delis jostle with designer boutiques. Truly ambitious restaurants are few and far between in the Marais, but picturesque old bistros, like Benoît and the wonderful Café des Musées, and smaller veggie-centric eateries are popping up all over. A brand-new generation of barista cafés serving gourmet snacks for breakfast and lunch have created their own niche, answering a need for better coffee and faster sit-down dining. The popular Breizh Café attracts young and old alike with its inexpensive and authentic *galettes* (buckwheat crêpes) made with quality ingredients and served with a crisp, delicious *cidre* from Normandy or Brittany.

$$
BISTRO

✕ **Au Bourguignon du Marais.** The handsome, contemporary look of this Marais bistro and wine bar is the perfect backdrop for traditional fare and excellent Burgundies served by the glass and bottle. Unusual for Paris, food is served nonstop from noon to 11 pm, and you can drop by just for a glass of wine in the afternoon. **Known for:** traditional bistro atmosphere; hearty Burgundian cuisine; sidewalk dining with nice views of the Marais. Ⓢ *Average main: €22 ⊠ 52 rue François-Miron, 3e, Marais Quarter* ☎ *01–48–87–15–40* Ⓜ *St-Paul* ✛ *4:F2.*

$$$$
BISTRO

✕ **Benoît.** Without changing the vintage 1912 setting, superchef Alain Ducasse and Thierry de la Brosse of L'Ami Louis have subtly improved the menu here, with dishes such as marinated salmon, frogs' legs in a morel-mushroom cream sauce, and an outstanding cassoulet served in a cast-iron pot. It's a splurge to be here, so go all the way and top off your meal with the caramelized tarte tatin or a rum-doused baba. **Known for:** glorious Marais setting overlooking the Seine with equally romantic interior; affordable prix-fixe lunch menu; charming outdoor terrace in warm weather. $ *Average main: €38* ⊠ *20 rue St-Martin, 4e, Marais Quarter* ☎ *01–42–72–25–76* ⊕ *www.benoit-paris.com* ☾ *Closed Aug. and 1 wk in Feb.* Ⓜ *Châtelet* ✛ *4:D1.*

$ ✕ **Breizh Café.** Eating a crêpe in Paris might seem a bit clichéd, until
FRENCH you venture into this modern offshoot of a Breton crêperie. The plain,
FAMILY pale-wood decor is refreshing, but what really makes the difference are
Fodor's Choice the ingredients—farmers' eggs, unpasteurized Gruyère, shiitake mush-
★ rooms, Valrhona chocolate, homemade caramel, and extraordinary
butter from a Breton dairy farmer. **Known for:** some of the best crêpes in Paris; adventurous ingredients; Cancale oysters also on the menu. $ *Average main: €12* ⊠ *109 rue Vieille du Temple, 3e, Marais Quarter* ☎ *01–42–72–13–77* ⊕ *www.breizhcafe.com* ☾ *Closed Mon., Tues., and Aug.* Ⓜ *St-Sébastien–Froissart* ✛ *4:F1.*

$ ✕ **Bubar.** In summer look for the crowd spilling out the front of this
WINE BAR signless wine bar in the Marais named for Jean-Louis, the bartender (*bubar* or *barbu* is French slang for "bearded"). The wine menu—with many selections available by the glass—features French wines and small-batch vintages from South Africa, Chile, and Argentina. **Known for:** low-lit, almost clandestine atmosphere; wines to discover, guided by a knowledgeable and generous owner; bring your own snacks policy. $ *Average main: €12* ⊠ *3 rue des Tournelles, 4e, Marais Quarter* ☎ *01–40–29–97–72* ☾ *No lunch* Ⓜ *Bastille* ✛ *4:G2.*

$ ✕ **Café des Musées.** A true neighborhood haunt, this bustling little bistro
BISTRO near the Musée Picasso offers a convivial slice of Parisian life at a good value. Here traditional French bistro fare is adapted to a modern audience, and the best choices are the old tried-and-trues: hand-cut *tartare de boeuf*; rare entrecôte served with a side of golden-crisp frites and homemade béarnaise; and the classic parmentier with pheasant instead of the usual ground beef. **Known for:** reliable bistro fare; warm and friendly service; proximity to Marais museums. $ *Average main: €17* ⊠ *49 rue de Turenne, 3e, Marais Quarter* ☎ *01–42–72–96–17* ⊕ *www. lecafedesmusees.fr* Ⓜ *St-Paul* ✛ *4:G1.*

$ ✕ **Cantine Merci.** On the lower garden level of a chic concept store resides
MODERN FRENCH the perfect spot for a quick and healthy lunch between bouts of shopping. Highlights include a small soup menu, a risotto of the day, and hearty vegetarian salads. **Known for:** quick lunchtime spot; fresh juices and mint iced tea; rosé by the glass. $ *Average main: €17* ⊠ *111 bd. Beaumarchais, 3e, Marais Quarter* ☎ *01–42–77–79–28* ⊕ *www.merci-merci.com* ☾ *Closed Sun. No dinner* Ⓜ *St-Sébastien–Froissart* ✛ *4:G1.*

$ ✕ **La Caféothèque.** This was Paris's first coffee bar, founded by former
CAFÉ Guatemalan ambassador to France-turned coffee ambassador Gloria
Fodor's Choice Montenegro. With three spacious rooms, any coffee preparation under
★ the sun, and a daily special brew chosen from among dozens of varieties of meticulously sourced beans from plantations around the globe, this place is a Paris institution. **Known for:** rigorously sourced, hard-to-find

14

beans; excellent coffee of the day; all roasting done in-house. ⑤ *Average main: €4* ✉ *52 rue de l'Hotel de Ville, 4e, Marais Quarter* ☎ *01–53–01–83–84* ⊕ *www.lacafeotheque.com* Ⓜ *Pont Marie, St-Paul* ✛ *4:E2.*

$$
BISTRO

✕ **L'Ambassade d'Auvergne.** The rare authentic Parisian bistro that refuses to change, Les Ambassade claims one of the city's great restaurant characters: the maître d' Francis Panek, with his handlebar mustache and gravelly voice. Settle into the dining room in an ancient Marais house to try rich, rib-sticking dishes from the Auvergne, a sparsely populated region in central France. **Known for:** copious quantities of classic French cuisine; excellent price-to-quality ratio; chocolate mousse for dessert. ⑤ *Average main: €20* ✉ *22 rue du Grenier St-Lazare, 3e, Marais Quarter* ☎ *01–42–72–31–22* ⊕ *www.ambassade-auvergne.com* Ⓜ *Rambuteau* ✛ *4:E1.*

$
MIDDLE EASTERN
FAMILY
Fodor's Choice
★

✕ **L'As du Fallafel.** If you're looking for one of the cheapest and tastiest meals in Paris, look no further than the fantastic falafel stands on the pedestrian Rue de Rosiers. L'As (the Ace) is widely considered the best of the bunch, which accounts for the lunchtime line that extends down the street. **Known for:** the best, freshest, and most heaping falafel sandwich in town; fast take-out or seated service at lunch; shawarma sandwiches. ⑤ *Average main: €10* ✉ *34 rue des Rosiers, 4e, Marais Quarter* ☎ *01–48–87–63–60* ⊘ *Closed Sat. No dinner Fri.* Ⓜ *St-Paul* ✛ *4:F2.*

EASTERN PARIS

Head over to the up-and-coming Canal St-Martin to watch Parisian *bobos,* or *bourgeois-bohemian,* in action. The area is home to fashion designers, artists, and media folk who make the most of the waterside cafés on sunny days. The bistro scene gets interesting east of the Bastille, where lower rents have encouraged young chefs to set up shop. Around Père Lachaise the selection thins, but wander a little farther to multicultural Belleville to find an intriguing mix of Chinese and North African eateries alongside some superb gastrobistros from a handful of gifted young chefs.

BASTILLE

$$$$
BISTRO

✕ **Au Trou Gascon.** This elegant establishment off Place Daumesnil—off the beaten tourist track but worth the trip—offers a refined take on the cuisine of Gascony, a region renowned for its ham, foie gras, lamb, and duck. Most popular with the regulars are the surprisingly light cassoulets (all the meats are grilled before going into the pot) with big white Tarbais beans and a superb duck or goose confit. **Known for:** gourmet take on the rich gastronomy of southwest France; time-honored specialty of roasted milk-fed lamb; splurge-worthy wine list. ⑤ *Average main: €35* ✉ *40 rue Taine, 12e, Bastille* ☎ *01–43–44–34–26* ⊕ *www. alaindutournier.com/wp/autrougascon* ⊘ *Closed weekends, Aug., and 1 wk in Jan.* Ⓜ *Daumesnil* ✛ *4:H4.*

$$
BRASSERIE
FAMILY

✕ **Bofinger.** One of the oldest, loveliest, and most popular brasseries in Paris has improved in recent years, so stake out one of the tables, which are dressed in crisp white linen under a glowing Art Nouveau glass cupola, and enjoy classic brasserie fare. Stick to trademark dishes such as the seafood, choucroute, steak tartare, or smoked haddock with spinach, as the seasonal specials can be hit-or-miss. **Known for:** authentic Belle Époque decor; mile-high seafood plates; convenient setting between Bastille and the Marais. $ *Average main: €20* ⊠ *5–7 rue de la Bastille, 4e, Bastille* ☎ *01–42–72–87–82* ⊕ *www.bofingerparis. com* Ⓜ *Bastille* ✛ *4:H2.*

$ ✕ **Jacques Genin Salon de Thé.** Master chocolatier-pâtissier Jacques Genin
FRENCH deserves the Legion d'honneur for his efforts to restore great traditional
Fodor'sChoice French pastries to their classic form, particularly the august mille-feuille.
★ Genin's stripped-down version disposes with the usual bells and whistles—fresh fruit, custard, chocolate—to achieve a scintillating clarity: layers of lightly caramelized *pâte feuilletée*, a buttery puff pastry, and an ethereal, barely sweet pastry cream in either vanilla, caramel, or praline. **Known for:** sinful chocolat chaud; some of the city's best chocolate, caramels, and pastries; bittersweet hot chocolate. $ *Average main: €8* ⊠ *133 rue de Turenne, 3e, Bastille* ☎ *01–45–77–29–01* ⊕ *jacquesgenin. fr* ☺ *Closed Mon.* Ⓜ *Filles du Calvaire* ✛ *2:G6.*

$ ✕ **Le Baron Rouge.** This proletarian wine bar near the Place d'Aligre mar-
WINE BAR ket is a throwback to another era, with a few tables and giant barrels
Fodor'sChoice along the walls for filling and refilling your take-home bottles. A fun
★ time to come is Sunday morning (yes, morning) when it's packed with locals who have just been to the market and want to linger over good food and that first glass of the day. **Known for:** wine by the barrel with refills to take home; authentic neighborhood atmosphere; oysters on a winter evening. $ *Average main: €11* ⊠ *1 rue Théophile Roussel, 12e, Bastille* ☎ *01–43–43–14–32* Ⓜ *Ledru-Rollin* ✛ *4:H3.*

$$$ ✕ **Le Bistrot Paul Bert.** The Paul Bert delivers everything you could want
BISTRO from a traditional Paris bistro (faded 1930s decor, thick steak with real
Fodor'sChoice frites, and good value), so it's no wonder its two dining rooms fill every
★ night with a cosmopolitan crowd. The impressively stocked wine cellar helps, as does the heaping cheese cart, the laid-back yet efficient staff, and hearty dishes such as monkfish with white beans and duck with pears. **Known for:** excellent, and abundant, cheese trolley; delicious dessert soufflés; sidewalk seating in summer. $ *Average main: €25* ⊠ *18 rue Paul Bert, 11e, Bastille* ☎ *01–43–72–24–01* ☺ *Closed Sun. and Mon.* Ⓜ *Rue des Boulets* ✛ *4:H3.*

$ ✕ **Mokonuts.** One of the city's best examples of the casual gourmet
CONTEMPORARY coffeeshops popping up around Paris, Mokonuts is run by a talented
Fodor'sChoice husband-and-wife team who create delicious dishes and pastries that
★ are as pleasing to the eye as they are to the palate. At lunch, locals elbow their way in for a variety of gourmet salads, sandwiches, and hot dishes. **Known for:** excellent coffee; late hours for a café (open until 6 pm); small space so it gets crowded fast. $ *Average main: €12* ⊠ *5 rue Saint-Bernard, Oberkampf* ☎ *09–80–81–82–85* ☺ *No dinner* Ⓜ *Faidherbe-Chaligny, Ledru-Rollin* ✛ *4:H3.*

$$ ✕ **Septime.** With amazing food and a convivial, unpretentious atmo-
BISTRO sphere, Septime has become one of the hottest tickets in town. Seasonal ingredients, inventive pairings, and excellent natural wines bring in diners as do the sophisticated dishes like creamy gnochetti in an orange-rind-flecked Gouda sauce sprinkled with coriander flowers. **Known for:** exceptional Parisian bistro; one-Michelin star; reservations needed far

14

in advance. $ *Average main: €23* ✉ *80 rue de Charonne, 11e, Bastille* ☎ *01–43–67–38–29* ⊕ *www.septime-charonne.fr* ⊙ *Closed weekends. No lunch Mon.* Ⓜ *Ledru Rollin, Charonne* ✛ *4:E4.*

$$$
MODERN
ARGENTINE
✕ **Unico.** An architect and a photographer, both Parisians born in Argentina, teamed up to open one of Bastille's hottest restaurants—literally hot, too, since the Argentinean meat served here is grilled over charcoal. Whichever cut of beef you choose (the ultimate being *lomo*, or fillet), it's so melt-in-your-mouth that the sauces served on the side seem almost superfluous. **Known for:** tender Argentinian beef, aged and grilled; chic retro atmosphere; excellent value prix-fixe menus. $ *Average main: €30* ✉ *15 rue Paul-Bert, 11e, Bastille* ☎ *01–43–67–68–08* ⊕ *www. resto-unico.com* ⊙ *Closed Sun. No lunch Mon.* Ⓜ *Faidherbe–Chaligny* ✛ *4:H3.*

BELLEVILLE

$
VIETNAMESE
✕ **Dong Huong.** While not quite a secret, these two undecorated dining rooms on a Belleville side street can be hard to find, but this is where Chinese and Vietnamese locals come for a reassuring bowl of *pho* (noodle soup) or plate of grilled lemongrass-scented meat with rice. Spicy, peanut-y *saté* soup is a favorite, and at this price, you can also spring for a plate of crunchy imperial rolls, to be wrapped in accompanying lettuce and mint. **Known for:** authentic Asian cuisine; good prices; exceptionally fresh bo bun. $ *Average main: €11* ✉ *14 rue Louis-Bonnet, 11e, Belleville* ☎ *01–43–32–25–74* ⊙ *Closed Tues. and 3 wks in Aug.* Ⓜ *Belleville* ✛ *2:H4.*

$$
BISTRO
FAMILY
Fodor's Choice
★
✕ **Le Baratin.** This place has been around for more than 20 years, but that hasn't stopped it from being one of the more sought-after and reliable out-of-the-way bistros in Paris. The key to its success is the combination of fresh, comforting cooking and a lovingly selected list of organic and natural wines from small producers. **Known for:** artisanal charcuterie; late hours; affordable lunch menu. $ *Average main: €23* ✉ *3 rue Jouye Rouve, 20e, Latin Quarter* ☎ *01–43–49–39–70* ⊙ *No lunch Sat. Closed Sun., Mon., and Aug.* Ⓜ *Pyrénées, Belleville* ✛ *2:H3.*

CANAL ST-MARTIN

$$
MODERN FRENCH
Fodor's Choice
★
✕ **Abri.** This tiny storefront restaurant's immense popularity has much to do with the fresh and imaginative food, the friendly servers, and great prices. The lauded Japanese chef works from a small open kitchen behind the zinc bar, putting forth skillfully prepared dishes like lemon-marinated mackerel topped with microthin slices of beet with honey vinaigrette, or succulent duck breast with vegetables au jus. **Known for:** daily changing menu inventive French-Japanese cuisine; casual atmosphere and great prices; need to make reservations weeks in advance. $ *Average main: €23* ✉ *92 rue du Faubourg-Poissonnière, 10e, Canal St-Martin* ☎ *01–83–97–00–00* ⊙ *Closed Sun., Mon., 1 wk at Christmas, and Aug.* Ⓜ *Poissonnière, Cadet* ✛ *2:D3.*

$
CAFÉ
FAMILY
Fodor's Choice
★
✕ **Holybelly.** A welcome addition to the Canal St-Martin area, this spacious, modern coffee bar caters to Paris's blossoming breakfast and brunch scene with a menu of American-style classics. Homemade granola, pancakes topped with fruit, and eggs and bacon are served up all-day long, accompanied by hearty sandwiches, healthy salads

(with kale!), and homemade desserts. **Known for:** wonderful coffee; lively, friendly atmosphere; spacious enough to accommodate groups. ⑤ *Average main: €12* ✉ *19 rue Lucien Sampaix, 10e, Canal St-Martin* ☎ *09–73–60–13–64* ☻ *Closed Tues. and Wed. No dinner* Ⓜ *Jacques Bonsergent* ⊹ *2:F4.*

$ **✕ Jeanne A.** This six-table épicerie-bistro–wine bar–traiteur on a pretty
WINE BAR cobbled street is just the thing for an uncomplicated lunch, dinner, or afternoon snack. Whether you desire a great glass of wine and a plate of charcuterie and cheese or a full meal, the classic French fare here is always excellent. **Known for:** rotisserie chicken; good breakfast spot; secluded table great for large parties. ⑤ *Average main: €16* ✉ *42 rue Jean-Pierre-Timbaud, 11e, Canal St-Martin* ☎ *01–43–55–09–49* ⊕ *www.jeanne-a-comestibles.com* Ⓜ *Parmentier, Oberkampf* ⊹ *2:H5.*

$$$$ **✕ Le Chateaubriand.** A chef who once presented a single, peeled apple
MODERN FRENCH pip (really) on a plate (at the museum restaurant Le Transversal outside Paris) has no ordinary approach to food. Self-taught Basque cook Inaki Aizpitarte is undeniably provocative, but he gets away with it because (a) he's young and extremely cool and (b) he has an uncanny sense of which unexpected ingredients go together, as in a combination of oysters and lime zest in chicken stock. **Known for:** inventive but approachable cuisine; lively and hip crowd; one-Michelin star. ⑤ *Average main: €45* ✉ *129 av. Parmentier, 11e, Canal St-Martin* ☎ *01–43–57–45–95* ⊕ *www.lechateaubriand.net* ☻ *Closed Sun., Mon., and 1 wk at Christmas. No lunch* Ⓜ *Goncourt* ⊹ *2:H5.*

$$ **✕ Le Dauphin.** Avant-garde chef Inaki Aizpitarte transformed a dowdy
WINE BAR café into a sleek, if chilly, all-marble watering hole for late-night cuisinistas. Honing his ever-iconoclastic take on tapas, the dishes served here are a great way to get an idea of what all the fuss is about. **Known for:** late-night revelry; superb wines by the glass; tapas by a star chef. ⑤ *Average main: €20* ✉ *131 av. Parmentier, 11e, Canal St-Martin* ☎ *01–55–28–78–88* ⊕ *www.restaurantledauphin.net* ☻ *Closed Sun., Mon., and 1 wk at Christmas. No lunch Tues.* Ⓜ *Parmentier* ⊹ *2:H5.*

$$ **✕ Le Galopin.** Across from a pretty square on the border of two up-
BISTRO and-coming neighborhoods, this light-drenched spot is one of Paris's
Fodor's Choice standout gastrobistros. By adhering to a tried-and-true formula—
★ meticulously sourced produce, natural wines, open kitchen—dishes here are small wonders of texture and flavor. **Known for:** daily changing, market-fresh gastronomic menu; hip, laid-back atmosphere; veggie-centric dishes. ⑤ *Average main: €22* ✉ *34 rue Sainte-Marthe, 10e, Canal St-Martin* ☎ *01–42–06–05–03* ⊕ *www.le-galopin.com* ☻ *Closed weekends. No lunch Mon.–Wed.* Ⓜ *Goncourt, Belleville, Colonel Fabien* ⊹ *2:H3.*

$$ **✕ Le Servan.** Here an impressive but unfussy gastronomic menu features
MODERN FRENCH Asian-inflected dishes that express the food's far-flung influences. A
Fodor's Choice starter of "zakouskis," several small dishes that may include deep-fried
★ giblets, fresh radishes with anchovy butter, or herb-infused cockles, warms you up for a sublime entrée of whole lacquered quail, cod with spicy black-bean reduction, or crispy melt-in-your mouth pork on a bed of braised leeks. **Known for:** great-value lunch menu; accommodating to vegetarians; lovely, intimate setting. ⑤ *Average main: €20* ✉ *32 rue*

14

Saint-Maur, 11e, Canal St-Martin ☏ *01–55–28–51–82* ⊕ *www.leservan.com* ☉ *Closed weekends. No lunch Mon.* Ⓜ *Voltaire, Rue Saint-Maur, Parmentier* ✛ *4:H2.*

$ ✕ **Ten Belles.** Canal St-Martin's first seriously good coffee bar, the tiny
CAFÉ   Ten Belles is where pedigreed baristas cater to a hip crowd of good brew connoisseurs. Sandwiches, soups, and an irresistible assortment of snacks and sweets all come from the ladies at the Bal Café. **Known for:** reliably good coffee; homemade everything; small space. Ⓢ *Average main: €6* ⊠ *10 rue de la Grange aux Belles, 10e, Canal St-Martin* ☏ *01–42–40–90–78* ⊕ *www.tenbelles.com* ☉ *No dinner* Ⓜ *Jacques Bonsergent, République* ✛ *2:G4.*

RÉPUBLIQUE

$$ ✕ **Astier.** There are three good reasons to go to Astier: the generous
BISTRO   cheese platter plunked on your table atop a help-yourself wicker tray,
FAMILY   the exceptional wine cellar with bottles dating back to the 1970s, and the French bistro fare (even if portions seem to have diminished over the years). Dishes like marinated herring with warm potato salad, sausage with lentils, and baba au rhum are classics on the frequently changing set menu, which includes a selection of no less than 20 cheeses. **Known for:** same-day reservations possible; traditional atmosphere; excellent choice for authentic French cooking. Ⓢ *Average main: €21* ⊠ *44 rue Jean-Pierre Timbaud, 11e, République* ☏ *01–43–57–16–35* ⊕ *www.restaurant-astier.com* Ⓜ *Parmentier* ✛ *2:H5.*

$ ✕ **Au Passage.** This *bistrot à vins* has the lived-in look of a longtime
WINE BAR   neighborhood hang-out—which it was until two veterans of the raging Paris wine-bar scene reinvented the place, keeping the vintage, laid-back atmosphere and adding a serious foodie menu that's one of the best deals in town. A blackboard lists a selection of tapas, including several house-made pâtés, fresh tomato or beet salads, a superb seafood carpaccio, and artisanal charcuterie and cheeses. **Known for:** gastronomy on a budget; friendly, low-key vibe; roasted lamb haunch to share. Ⓢ *Average main: €15* ⊠ *1 bis, passage Saint-Sébastien, 11e, République* ☏ *01–43–55–07–52* ⊕ *www.restaurant-aupassage.fr* ☉ *Closed Sun. No lunch* Ⓜ *Saint-Ambroise, Saint-Sebastien–Froissart, Richard Lenoir* ✛ *2:H6.*

LATIN QUARTER

Thanks to its student population, the Latin Quarter caters to those on a budget with kebab shops, crêpe stands, fast-food joints, and no-nonsense bistros. Look beyond the pedestrian streets such as Rue de la Huchette and Rue Mouffetard for less touristy eateries preferred by locals. As you might expect in an area known for its *gauche caviar* (wealthy intellectuals who vote Socialist), the Latin Quarter brims with atmospheric places to linger over a tiny cup of black coffee.

$$ ✕ **Kitchen Ter(re).** Michelin-starred chef William Ledeuil flexes his genius
FRENCH   for France-meets-Asia flavors at this chic address—his third—a few
Fodor's Choice   blocks from the Île Saint-Louis and Notre Dame. Ledeuil is known and
★   loved for his fearless pairings of bold and subtle flavors, like veal tartar pasta with crunchy peanuts and pungent bonito flakes or Thai beef soup with luscious Iberian ham, mushrooms, and sweet pear. **Known**

for: Asian-inflected contemporary French cuisine; excellent value lunch menus; easy walk to many tourist sites. $ *Average main: €22* ⊠ *26 bd. Saint-Germain, 5e, Latin Quarter* ☎ *01–42–39–47–48* ⊕ *www.zekitchengalerie.fr/kitchenterre* ☾ *Closed Sun., Mon., and 1st wk of Jan.* Ⓜ *Cardinal Lemoine* ✛ *4:E4.*

$$ ✕ **L'Avant-Goût.** Arnaud Van Santen
BISTRO belongs to a generation of gifted
FAMILY bistro chefs who have rejected the pressure-cooker world of haute cuisine in favor of something more personal and democratic. Typical of his market-inspired cooking is his signature pot-au-feu *de cochon aux épices*, in which spiced pork stands in for the usual beef, and the bouillon is served separately. **Known for:** family-friendly atmosphere; excellent-value prix-fixe menus and à la carte options; strong local following. $ *Average main: €21* ⊠ *26 rue Bobillot, 13e, Latin Quarter* ☎ *01–53–80–24–00* ⊕ *www.lavantgout. com* ☾ *Closed Sun. and Mon.* Ⓜ *Place d'Italie* ✛ *4:G6.*

$$ ✕ **L'Ourcine.** Sylvain Danière knows what it takes to open a popular bis-
BISTRO tro: choose an obscure location in a residential neighborhood, decorate it simply but cheerfully, work extremely hard, set competitive prices, and constantly reinvent your menu. The real key ingredient is talent, though, and Danière has plenty of it, as demonstrated by his updated duckling *au sang* (in blood sauce) with celery-root puree, and a popular *crémeux au chocolat* (chocolate pudding) to finish things off. **Known for:** popularity with the locals; modern takes on French classics; good value, ever-changing blackboard menu. $ *Average main: €20* ⊠ *92 rue Broca, 13e, Latin Quarter* ☎ *01–47–07–13–65* ⊕ *www.restaurant-lourcine.fr* ☾ *Closed Sun., Mon., 3 wks in Aug., 1 wk at Christmas, and 1 wk in Feb.* Ⓜ *Les Gobelins* ✛ *4:G6.*

$$$$ ✕ **La Tour d'Argent.** You can't deny the splendor of this legendary
MODERN FRENCH Michelin-starred restaurant's setting overlooking the Seine; if you don't
Fodor's Choice want to splurge on dinner, treat yourself to the three-course lunch menu
★ for €85. This entitles you to succulent slices of one of the restaurant's numbered ducks (the great duck slaughter began in 1919 and is now well past the millionth mallard, as your certificate will attest). **Known for:** duck in all its glorious forms; one of the city's best wine lists; fabulous Seine-side setting with glorious views. $ *Average main: €105* ⊠ *15–17 quai de la Tournelle, 5e, Latin Quarter* ☎ *01–43–54–23–31* ⊕ *www.latourdargent.com* ☾ *Closed Sun., Mon., and Aug.* 🎩*Jacket and tie* Ⓜ *Cardinal Lemoine* ✛ *4:E4.*

$$ ✕ **Le Balzar.** Regulars grumble about the uneven cooking at Le Balzar,
BRASSERIE but they continue to come back because they can't resist the waiters' wry
FAMILY humor and the dining room's amazing people-watching possibilities.

PARIS CAFÉ CULTURE

The café capital of the world is making room for the new barista cafés sweeping cities across the globe. For discerning coffee lovers this is good news indeed. Scattered throughout Paris's most compelling neighborhoods, most of the new cafés have a character all their own and, alongside superb gastronomic coffee, offer a selection of top-notch snacks or even meals.

Some of the very best include Bal Café, Café Coutume, Holybelly, La Caféothèque, Télescope, and Ten Belles.

14

The restaurant attracts politicians, writers, tourists, and local eccentrics—and remains one of the city's classic brasseries: the perfect stop before or after a film in a local art-house cinema. **Known for:** standard French bistro menu; famous patrons; drinks on the terrace. $ *Average main: €23* ⊠ *49 rue des Écoles, 5e, Latin Quarter* ☎ *01–43–54–13–67* ⊕ *www.brasseriebalzar.com* Ⓜ *Cluny–La Sorbonne* ✛ *4:C4.*

$$$
BISTRO
FAMILY
Fodor's Choice
★

✕ **Le Buisson Ardent.** This charming Quartier Latin bistro with woodwork and murals dating from 1925 is always packed and boisterous. A glance at the €39.90 set menu—a bargain €28 at lunch for three courses—makes it easy to understand why. **Known for:** authentic Parisian bistro atmosphere; excellent value daily prix-fixe menu; fresh twist on French classics. $ *Average main: €26* ⊠ *25 rue Jussieu, 5e, Latin Quarter* ☎ *01–43–54–93–02* Ⓜ *Jussieu* ✛ *4:E4.*

$$
MODERN FRENCH

✕ **Le Pré Verre.** Chef Jean-François Paris knows his cassia bark from his cinnamon thanks to a long stint in Asia. He opened this lively bistro with its purple-gray walls and photos of jazz musicians to showcase his culinary style, rejuvenating archetypal French dishes with Asian and Mediterranean spices. **Known for:** well-priced wines by the glass; unbeatable prix-fixe lunch menu; trademark spiced suckling pig. $ *Average main: €20* ⊠ *8 rue Thénard, 5e, Latin Quarter* ☎ *01–43–54–59–47* ⊕ *www.lepreverre.com* ⊙ *Closed Sun., Mon., and 1 wk at Christmas* Ⓜ *Maubert–Mutualité* ✛ *4:D4.*

$$
WINE BAR
Fodor's Choice
★

✕ **Les Papilles.** Part wineshop and épicerie, part restaurant, Les Papilles has a winning formula—pick any bottle off the well-stocked shelf and pay €7 corkage to drink it with your meal. You can also savor one of several superb wines by the glass at your table while enjoying the excellent set menu of dishes made with top-notch, seasonal ingredients. **Known for:** lively, authentic atmosphere; market menu that changes daily; excellent wines by the glass or bottle. $ *Average main: €18* ⊠ *30 rue Gay-Lussac, 5e, Latin Quarter* ☎ *01–43–25–20–79* ⊕ *www.lespapillesparis.fr* ⊙ *Closed Sun., Mon., last wk of July, and 2 wks in Aug.* Ⓜ *Cluny–La Sorbonne* ✛ *4:C5.*

$$$$
ECLECTIC
Fodor's Choice
★

✕ **Sola.** This foodie sanctuary is where dishes like miso-lacquered foie gras or sake-glazed suckling pig—perfectly crisp on the outside and melting inside—pair traditional Japanese and French ingredients to wondrous effect. The three-course set weekday lunch menu offers a choice of fish or meat and finishes with some stunning confections, and the four-course dinner menu (with an option to add a pairing of four glasses of wine or sake) is an excellent value for what you're getting. **Known for:** beautiful atmosphere in a 17th-century building; contemporary French-Japanese cooking at its finest; traditional Japanese dining downstairs. $ *Average main: €35* ⊠ *12 rue de l'Hôtel Colbert, 5e, Latin Quarter* ☎ *01–43–29–59–04* ⊕ *www.restaurant-sola.com* ⊙ *Closed Sun. and Mon.* Ⓜ *Maubert–Mutualité* ✛ *4:D3.*

$$$$
MODERN FRENCH
Fodor's Choice
★

✕ **Ze Kitchen Galerie.** The name of this contemporary bistro might not be inspired, but the cooking shows creativity and a sense of fun. From a deliberately deconstructed menu featuring raw fish, soups, pastas, and grills, consider the roast and confit duck with a tamarind-and-sesame condiment and foie gras, or the lobster with mussels, white beans, and Thai herbs. **Known for:** perfect location near the Seine; exquisitely presented French-Asian fusion dishes; locally sourced vegetables and spices. ⑤ *Average main: €39* ✉ *4 rue des Grands-Augustins, 6e, Latin Quarter* ☎ *01–44–32–00–32* ⊕ *www.zekitchengalerie.fr* ⊘ *Closed weekends* Ⓜ *St-Michel* ✛ *4:C2.*

ST-GERMAIN-DES-PRÉS

St-Germain is enjoying a revival as a foodie haunt, with Yves Camdeborde's Le Comptoir du Relais Saint-Germain the perfect example of the kind of market-inspired bistro that Parisians (and foreigners) adore. The neighborhood's old leftist roots and new bobo sensibility blend together nicely in eateries that are down-to-earth yet reflect a discerning touch. You'll find everything from top Paris chefs (Darroze, Robuchon) to neighborhood favorites so good (Semilla, Fish) that they draw Parisians from bordering arrondissements—and that's saying a lot.

$$
BISTRO

✕ **Boucherie Roulière.** If it's steak you're craving, put your faith in Jean-Luc Roulière, a fifth-generation butcher who opened this long, narrow bistro near St-Sulpice church. Partner Franck Pinturier is from the Auvergne region, which is also known for its melt-in-the-mouth meat, so start with truffle-scented ravioli or a rich marrow bone before indulging in a generous slab of Limousin or Salers beef, excellent veal kidney, or, for the meat-shy, perhaps lobster or sea bass. **Known for:** great for large groups; superb price-to-quality ratio; all things meat. ⑤ *Average main: €23* ✉ *24 rue des Canettes, 6e, St-Germain-des-Prés* ☎ *01–43–26–25–70* ⊕ *www.boucherie-rouliere.fr* ⊘ *Closed Aug.* Ⓜ *Mabillon* ✛ *4:B3.*

$$
CAFÉ

✕ **Café de Flore.** Picasso, Chagall, Sartre, and de Beauvoir, attracted by the luxury of a heated café, worked and wrote here in the early 20th century. Today you'll find more tourists than intellectuals, and prices are hardly aimed at struggling artists, but the outdoor terrace is great for people-watching and popular with Parisians. **Known for:** excellent people-watching; old-world atmosphere; legendary setting on a pretty square across from Paris's oldest church. ⑤ *Average main: €22* ✉ *172 bd. St-Germain, 6e, St-Germain-des-Prés* ☎ *01–45–48–55–26* Ⓜ *St-Germain-des-Pres* ✛ *4:A3.*

$
BISTRO
FAMILY

✕ **Eggs & Co.** With a cheerfully bright and tiny, wood-beamed dining room—there's more space in the loftlike upstairs—this spot is devoted to the egg in all its forms. Whether you like yours baked with smoked salmon, whisked into an omelet with truffle shavings, or beaten into fluffy pancakes, there will be something for you on the blackboard menu. **Known for:** great breakfast and brunch spot; quick, healthy shopping break; cheerful, child-friendly atmosphere. ⑤ *Average main: €12* ✉ *11 rue Bernard Palissy, 6e, St-Germain-des-Prés* ☎ *01–45–44–02–52* ⊕ *www.eggsandco.fr* Ⓜ *St-Germain-des-Prés* ✛ *4:A3.*

$$
BISTRO
Fodor's Choice
★

✕ **Fish La Boissonerie.** A perennial favorite, expats and locals prize this lively, unpretentious bistro for its friendly atmosphere, consistently good food, solid wine list, and English-speaking staff—a quartet sorely lacking in the neighborhood. Dishes like velvety black squid-ink risotto, roasted cod with tender braised fennel, and crispy pumpkin tempura always hit the spot, especially when followed by decadent molten chocolate cake, honey-roasted figs, or banana-bread pudding. **Known for:** convivial atmosphere; excellent selection of natural wines; good-value menu. ⑤ *Average main: €22* ✉ *69 rue de Seine, 6e, St-Germain-des-Prés* ☎ *01–43–54–34–69* Ⓜ *St-Germain-des-Prés, Odéon* ✛ *4:B3.*

$$$$ ✕ **Gaya Rive Gauche.** If you can't fathom paying upward of €200 per person to taste the cooking of Pierre Gagnaire (the city's most avant-garde
MODERN FRENCH chef) at his eponymous restaurant, book a table at his fashionable fish restaurant. At Gaya Rive Gauche, Gagnaire uses seafood as a palette for his creative impulses. **Known for:** intimate, cozy atmosphere; fresh, artfully presented seafood; lobster poached in verveine, with fregula pasta and apricot. ⑤ *Average main: €38* ✉ *44 rue du Bac, 7e, St-Germain-des-Prés* ☎ *01–45–44–73–73* ⊕ *www.pierre-gagnaire.com* ◷ *Closed Sun. and Mon.* Ⓜ *Rue du Bac* ✛ *3:H2.*

$$$$ ✕ **Hélène Darroze.** The most celebrated female chef in Paris is now cooking at the Connaught in London, but her St-Germain dining room
MODERN FRENCH is still the setting for her sophisticated take on southwestern French food. Darroze's intriguingly modern touch comes through in such dishes as a sublime duck-foie-gras confit served with an exotic-fruit chutney or a blowout of roast wild duck stuffed with foie gras and truffles. **Known for:** foie gras with wild strawberry and beetroot gelée; affordable eight-course tapas lunch menu; vegetarian and gluten-free options. ⑤ *Average main: €65* ✉ *4 rue d'Assas, 6e, St-Germain-des-Prés* ☎ *01–42–22–00–11* ⊕ *www.helenedarroze.com* ◷ *Closed Sun. and Mon.* Ⓜ *Sèvres-Babylone* ✛ *4:A4.*

$$ ✕ **Huîtrerie Régis.** It's all about oysters at this bright 14-seat restaurant
SEAFOOD with crisp white tablecloths and pleasant service, popular with the area's chic set. If you find yourself puzzling over the relative merits of *fines de claires, spéciales,* and *pousses en claires,* you can always go with the €30 prix fixe that includes a glass of Charentais, a dozen No. 3 (medium) oysters, and coffee—or ask the knowledgeable waiters for advice. **Known for:** setting in the heart of Saint-Germain shopping; freshness and variety of oysters; fruit pie for dessert. ⑤ *Average main: €24* ✉ *3 rue de Montfaucon, 6e, St-Germain-des-Prés* ☎ *01–44–41–10–07* ◷ *Closed early July–early Sept.* Ⓜ *Mabillon* ✛ *4:B3.*

$$$ ✕ **KGB.** After extravagant success with his Asian-infused cuisine at Ze
MODERN FRENCH Kitchen Galerie, master-chef William Ledeuil extended his artistry to annex KGB (Kitchen Galerie Bis) just down the street, this time with a different focus and gentler prices. For starters, the "zors-d'oeuvres" of two, four, or six minidishes—think cubes of foie gras *mi-cuit* (half-cooked) in duck consommé, tender pork wontons in coconut milk with a hint of galanga—allow for a deeper exploration of what makes Ledeuil's cooking so alluring. **Known for:** a taste of master-chef William Ledeuil's cooking at gentler prices; small plates perfect for sharing; casual chic setting. ⑤ *Average main: €31* ✉ *25 rue des Grands Augustins, 6e, St-Germain-des-Prés* ☎ *01–46–33–00–85* ⊕ *www.zekitchen-galerie.fr* ◷ *Closed Sun., Mon., and Aug.* Ⓜ *Odéon, St-Michel* ✛ *4:C3.*

$$ ✕ **La Ferrandaise.** Portraits of cows adorn the stone walls of this bistro
BISTRO near the Luxembourg Gardens, hinting at the kitchen's penchant for meaty cooking (Ferrandaise is a breed of cattle). Still, there's something for every taste on the market-inspired menu, which always lists three

meat and three fish mains. **Known for:** decent prices for this area; daily blackboard menu; prix-fixe options only. $ *Average main: €24* ✉ *8 rue de Vaugirard, 6e, St-Germain-des-Prés* ☎ *01–43–26–36–36* ⊕ *www. laferrandaise.com* ⊗ *Closed Sun. and 3 wks in Aug. No lunch Mon. and Sat.* Ⓜ *Odéon; RER: Luxembourg* ✛ *4:C4.*

$$$$
BISTRO

✗ **Lapérouse.** Émile Zola, George Sand, and Victor Hugo were regulars here, and the restaurant's mirrors still bear diamond scratches from the days when mistresses would double-check their jewels' value. It's hard not to fall in love with this storied 17th-century Seine-side town house with a warren of woodwork-graced salons, though the cuisine, a mix of traditional and modern, can be hit-or-miss. **Known for:** charming historic setting; location right on the Seine; high romance factor. $ *Average main: €50* ✉ *51 quai des Grands Augustins, 6e, St-Germain-des-Prés* ☎ *01–43–26–68–04* ⊕ *www.laperouse.com* ⊗ *Closed Sun. No lunch.* Ⓜ *St-Michel* ✛ *4:C2.*

$$
BISTRO

✗ **Le Comptoir du Relais Saint-Germain.** Run by legendary bistro chef Yves Camdeborde, this tiny Art Deco hotel restaurant is booked up well in advance for the single dinner sitting featuring five courses of haute-cuisine fare. On weekdays from noon to 6 and weekends until 10, a brasserie menu is served; reservations are not accepted, resulting in long lines and brisk service. **Known for:** lively in the day, romantic at night; daily blackboard "menu du jour"; sidewalk dining. $ *Average main: €22* ✉ *9 carrefour de l'Odéon, 6e, St-Germain-des-Prés* ☎ *01–44–27–07–50* ⊕ *www.hotel-paris-relais-saint-germain.com* Ⓜ *Odéon* ✛ *4:B3.*

$$
BISTRO

✗ **Le Timbre.** The meaning of Le Timbre ("postal stamp") really does describe this intimate space, where a spare but constantly changing seasonal menu concentrates on market fresh ingredients, offering meat and seafood dishes alongside plenty of hearty vegetables. You'll find *filet de boeuf d'Aubrac* (a pedigreed cow from southwest France) with potato terrine and Pardailhan turnips, scallops with cauliflower puree, or sweetbreads with pears and celery. **Known for:** reasonable prices; traditional brasserie cuisine; small space so expect crowds. $ *Average main: €20* ✉ *3 rue Ste-Beuve, 6e, St-Germain-des-Prés* ☎ *01–45–49–10–40* ⊕ *www.restaurantletimbre.com* ⊗ *Closed Sun., Mon., Aug., and 1 wk at Christmas* Ⓜ *Vavin* ✛ *4:A5.*

$$$$
BISTRO

✗ **Les Bouquinistes.** Expect to hear more English than French in the cheery, contemporary dining room of this bistro, with its closely packed tables looking out onto the Seine. But luckily the sophisticated seasonal cuisine—such as snails and mussels with gnocchi, followed by British Hereford beef with squash-stuffed rigatoni and a caramel crème brûlée—is as authentic as you could hope for. **Known for:** views of the river and Notre Dame; international crowd; gluten-free options. $ *Average main: €38* ✉ *53 quai des Grands-Augustins, 6e, St-Germain-des-Prés* ☎ *01–43–25–45–94* ⊕ *www.lesbouquinistes.com* ⊗ *Closed Aug.* Ⓜ *St-Michel* ✛ *4:C2.*

$$$
FRENCH
Fodor's Choice
★

✗ **Quinsou.** The serious, unpretentious, and mightily creative cuisine here has quickly catapulted Quinsou to culinary fame. An emphasis on first-rate growers and suppliers puts vegetables in the limelight, though fish, shellfish, and game make a welcome appearance in the few market-fresh dishes that grace the daily menu . **Known for:** highly

14

original seasonal cuisine; warm and welcoming service; good value prix-fixe menus. $ *Average main: €32* ✉ *33 rue de l'Abbé Grégoire, 6e, St-Germain-des-Prés* ☎ *01–42–22–66–09* ⊕ *quinsou.business.site* ⊘ *Closed Sun. and Mon. No lunch Tues.* Ⓜ *Rennes, Saint-Placide* ✛ *3:H4.*

$$$
BISTRO
Fodor's Choice
★

✕ **Semilla.** The duo behind the popular neighborhood bistro Fish and the excellent wineshop La Dernière Goutte have poured their significant expertise into this laidback bistro in the heart of tony St-Germain-des-Prés. Its sophisticated cuisine, superb wines by the bottle or glass, and total lack of pretension have quickly made Semilla the toast of the town. **Known for:** convivial dining room with a lively, appreciative crowd; great options for vegetarians; open kitchen with plenty of bistro classics. $ *Average main: €25* ✉ *54 rue de Seine, 6e, St-Germain-des-Prés* ☎ *01–43–54–34–50* Ⓜ *Odéon, St-Germain-des-Prés* ✛ *4:B3.*

$$$
JAPANESE

✕ **Yen.** If you're having what is known in French as a *crise de foie* (liver crisis), the result of overindulging in rich food, this chic Japanese noodle house with a summer terrace and a VIP room upstairs is the perfect antidote. The blond-wood walls soothe the senses, the staff is happy to explain proper slurping technique, and the soba (buckwheat noodles), served in soup or with a restorative broth for dipping, will give you the courage to face another round of caramelized foie gras. **Known for:** authentic Japanese noodles; artisanal sake and other Japanese spirits; light, delicious tempura. $ *Average main: €31* ✉ *22 rue St-Benoît, 6e, St-Germain-des-Prés* ☎ *01–45–44–11–18* ⊘ *Closed Sun. and 2 wks in Aug.* Ⓜ *St-Germain-des-Prés* ✛ *4:A2.*

> ## MONTPARNASSE OYSTERS
>
> Ever since the first trains from Brittany brought oyster-loving settlers to Montparnasse, the neighborhood has had a proud seafood tradition. The best oysters come from Normandy, Brittany, or Marennes-Oléron on the Atlantic coast. The knobbly shelled *creuses* are more common than the rounder *plates,* which are beloved by connoisseurs. Oysters can be dressed with vinegar and shallots, but a squeeze of lemon—or nothing at all—is probably the best accompaniment. Scoop the raw oyster from its shell with a small fork, slurp the juice, and chew a little before swallowing the taste of the sea.

MONTPARNASSE

It's hard not to feel part of the café culture in Montparnasse. Along the broad boulevards you can find some of the city's classic brasseries. As storied as they are, many have been bought by chains and drained of the true charm that once attracted artists, politicians, and intellectuals. Though authentic brasseries can still be found—like Le Dôme—some of the area's best food is found at small bistros on narrow side streets.

$$$
BISTRO
Fodor's Choice
★

✕ **L'Assiette.** David Rathgeber spent 12 years working for celebrity-chef Alain Ducasse before taking over this landmark restaurant, where he has created his own menu and welcomed a devoted clientele. Expect bourgeois classics with a subtle modern touch, perhaps white tuna steak with spinach, lemon, capers, and croutons, and crème caramel with salted butter—all executed with the precision you would expect of a Ducasse veteran. **Known for:** reliably excellent food; generous portions and good price-to-quality ratio; famous cassoulet. $ *Average main: €27* ✉ *181 rue du Château, 14e, Montparnasse* ☎ *01–43–22–64–86* ⊕ *www.restaurant-lassiette.com* ⊘ *Closed Mon., Tues., Aug., and 1 wk at Christmas* Ⓜ *Pernety, Mouton-Duvernet* ✛ *3:H6.*

$$
BISTRO

✕ **La Cerisaie.** If you can nab a seat in this unremarkable yellow-and-red dining room (be sure to call ahead), you'll be rewarded with food prepared with such attention to detail that it will restore your faith in humanity. Since the chef is from southwest France, foie gras makes several appearances on the chalkboard menu, as does a delicious cassoulet, but you can also find freshly caught fish and perhaps farmer's pork straight from Gascony, a rarity in Paris. **Known for:** skillfully prepared southwest France specialties; intimate dining room; daily blackboard menu. $ *Average main: €18* ✉ *70 bd. Edgar Quinet, 14e, Montparnasse* ☎ *01–43–20–98–98* ⊕ *www.restaurantlacerisaie.com* ⊘ *Closed weekends, mid-July–mid-Aug., and 1 wk at Christmas* Ⓜ *Edgar Quinet* ✛ *4:A6.*

$$$
BRASSERIE
FAMILY

✕ **La Coupole.** This world-renowned cavernous spot with Art Deco murals practically defines the term *brasserie*. It's been popular since Jean-Paul Sartre and Simone de Beauvoir were regulars, and it's still great fun. Today it attracts a mix of bourgeois families, tourists, and lone diners treating themselves to a dozen oysters. **Known for:** classic brasserie menu; no reservations needed; historic setting. $ *Average main: €26* ✉ *102 bd. du Montparnasse, 14e, Montparnasse* ☎ *01–43–20–14–20* ⊕ *www.lacoupole-paris.com* Ⓜ *Vavin* ✛ *4:A6.*

$
MODERN FRENCH
FAMILY

✕ **La Crêperie Josselin.** With lacy curtains, beamed ceilings, and murals, this is the closest you'll get to an authentic Breton crêperie without heading to the coast. Tuck into a hearty buckwheat galette, perfectly crisped on the edges and filled with, perhaps, a classic combo of country ham, egg, cheese, and mushrooms, accompanied by a pitcher of refreshing dry Breton cider. **Known for:** authentic Breton crêpes; quick and efficient service; perfect for families. $ *Average main: €10* ✉ *67 rue du Montparnasse, 14e, Montparnasse* ☎ *01–43–20–93–50* ⊘ *Closed Mon., Tues., Aug., and 2 wks in Jan.* ▭ *No credit cards* Ⓜ *Vavin, Edgar Quinet* ✛ *3:H6.*

$$$$
BRASSERIE

✕ **Le Dôme.** Now a fancy fish brasserie serving seafood delivered fresh from Normandy every day, this restaurant began as a dingy meeting place for exiled artists and intellectuals like Lenin and Picasso. Try the sole *meunière* or the bouillabaisse, the ingredients of which are on display in their raw form in the restaurant's fish shop next door. **Known for:** heaping seafood platters; authentic ambience; great oysters. $ *Average main: €36* ✉ *108 bd. Montparnasse, 14e, Montparnasse* ☎ *01–43–35–25–81* ⊕ *www.restaurant-ledome.com* ⊘ *Closed Sun. and Mon. in July and Aug.* Ⓜ *Vavin* ✛ *4:A6.*

14

WESTERN PARIS

Change comes slowly to this old bourgeois neighborhood bordering the Bois de Boulogne. It's full of Paris stalwarts, where families have gathered over generations, and you can find some wonderful deeply Parisian bistros and brasseries. Avoid anything looking too chic or polished, where you'll very often pay high prices for mediocre fare.

$$$$
FRENCH
Fodor'sChoice
★

✕ **Comice.** The culinary experience here is a progression of delights, from your first luscious sip of carrot velouté to a light-as-air chocolate souflé contrasted with a zesty yuzu *macaron*. In between, dishes like butter-poached lobster, with sweet potato, spinach and shallot; or fois gras en terrine with quince, walnuts, and dates—all meticulously sourced from the finest producers around France—surprise, comfort, and deeply satisfy. **Known for:** fantastic four-course lunch menu; beautiful, serene setting; excellent wine list, of mostly natural wines. $ *Average main:* €44 ⊠ *31 ave de Versailles, 15e, Western Paris* ☎ *01–42–15–55–70* ⊕ *www.comice.paris* ⊘ *Closed Sun. and Mon. No lunch Tues. and Wed.* Ⓜ *Mirabeau, Javel* ✛ *3:A3.*

$$$$
MODERN FRENCH
Fodor'sChoice
★

✕ **Le Pré Catelan.** Live a Belle Époque fantasy by dining beneath the chestnut trees on the terrace of this fanciful landmark *pavillon* in the Bois de Boulogne. Each of chef Frédéric Anton's dishes is a variation on a theme, such as *l'os à moelle*: bone marrow prepared two ways, one peppered and the other stuffed with porcini and cabbage, both braised in a concentrated meat jus. **Known for:** three Michelin stars; splendid "country" setting in the Bois de Boulogne; elegant service. $ *Average main: €120* ⊠ *Rte. de Suresnes, 16e, Western Paris* ☎ *01–44–14–41–14* ⊕ *www.restaurant-precatelan.com* ⊘ *Closed Sun., Mon., 2 wks in Feb., 3 wks in Aug., and 1 wk in late Oct.–early Nov.* 🎩 *Jacket and tie* Ⓜ *Porte Dauphine* ✛ *1:A3.*

WHERE TO EAT AND STAY IN PARIS

Hôtel Saint-Louis en L'Isle, 4:E3

Hôtel Seven, 4:D6

Hôtel Taylor, 2:F5

Hôtel Thérèse, 2:B6

Hôtel Tiquetonne, 2:D6

Hôtel Valadon Colors, 3:E2

Hôtel Verneuil, 4:A2

Hôtel Westminster, 2:A5

Jays Paris, 1:B5

L'Hôtel, 4:B2

La Maison Champs Elysées, 1:E5

La Maison Favart, 2:B4

La Réserve, 1:F5

Le 123 Hotel, 1:E4

Le Citizen Hôtel, 2:G4

Le Général Hôtel, 2:G5

Le Konfidentiel, 2:C6

Le Royal Monceau Raffles Paris, 1:D3

Le Sezz, 3:A3

Le Walt, 3:E3

Les Jardins du Luxembourg, 4:C5

Les Jardins du Marais, 4:H1

Marignan, 1:E5

Meliá Vendome Boutique Hotel, 1:H5

Mon Hotel, 1:B4

Park Hyatt Paris Vendôme, 2:A5

Pavillon de la Reine, 4:G2

Pershing Hall, 1:D5

Port-Royal Hôtel, 4:C6

Relais Christine, 4:C2

Renaissance Paris Arc de Triomphe, 1:C3

Renaissance Paris Hôtel Le Parc Trocadéro, 1:A5

Renaissance Paris Vendôme, 2:A6

Ritz, 2:A5

Saint James Paris, 1:A5

Shangri-La Hotel Paris, 1:C6

Standard Design Hôtel, 4:H2

Villa Brunel, 1:B3

W Paris-Opéra, 2:A4

15

WHERE TO STAY

Updated
by Jennifer
Ladonne

If your Parisian fantasy involves romantic evenings in a historic grand-dame or a chic boutique hotel that pampers you in high style, here's some good news: you don't have to be wealthy to make your dreams come true. With more than 2,000 hotels, the City of Light gives visitors classy options in all price ranges, and a place with plenty of charm is practically a given.

In terms of location and price, there are more hotels on the *Rive Droite* (the Right Bank) offering formal luxury with premium service than on the *Rive Gauche* (the Left Bank), where the hotels are frequently smaller though richer in charm. The Rive Droite's 1er, 8e, and 16e arrondissements are still the most exclusive, and the prices there reflect that. Paris's famed palace hotels—10 hotels in the city that are considered better than a five-star—charge more than €1,000 a night for a standard room, and the high-end competition is heating up. On both sides of the Seine, Paris is in the throes of a lodging renaissance in both established and up-and-coming neighborhoods, with everything from chic new boutique hotels to deluxe five-star dwellings. Major landmark luxury hotels are rising to the occasion with lavish renovations; two of the city's most legendary hotels, the Ritz and the Hôtel de Crillon underwent four-year refurbishments in recent years, and the legendary Lutetia reopened in 2018 after a five-year facelift. All this is good news for high rollers, especially when you factor in extraordinary newer lodgings like the Paris Peninsula and the small but exquisite La Réserve.

But those on a budget should fear not, because less expensive alternatives can be found in the fashionable Marais (the 3e and 4e arrondissements), as well as the Latin Quarter (5e arrondissement), along with a slew of newcomers that have laid their cornerstones in the newly chic 2e (Sentier). The Rive Gauche's 6e arrondissement (Saint Germain) is another hotbed for stylish hotels, and choices on all budgets can be found in the 5e and 7e. Everything from excellent budget deals to splendid designer spaces can also be found slightly off-the-beaten track in the 10e, 13e, and 20e arrondissements. Wherever possible, in the more expensive neighborhoods we've located budget hotels—check out the handful of budget-priced sleeps in the shadow of Notre-Dame, St-Germain-des-Prés, and the Louvre.

As for the environment inside your room, change is in the air—literally. Enforcement of the no-smoking law is taken very seriously, with few hotels risking the ire of guests well aware of the laws. Amenities have improved, with virtually every hotel now equipped with cable TV (meaning CNN and BBC news in English), high-definition screens, minibars, in-room safes, and free wireless Internet access. Another recent change is the increasing availability of air-conditioning in both hotels and restaurants—a godsend in the *canicules* (dog days) of July and August. One thing that hasn't changed, however, is the lack of elbow room. Indoor spaces—from bed- and bathrooms to elevators—may feel cramped to those not used to life on a European scale. If you're flush and looking for enough room to spread out multiple suitcases, be sure to book a suite; they can be found in virtually any hotel, from the most modest boutique to the palaces.

15

PLANNING

BREAKFAST

Almost all Parisian hotels charge extra for breakfast, with per-person prices ranging from €12 to more than €50. If you decide to eat elsewhere, inform the staff so breakfast won't be charged to your bill. Occasionally, Continental breakfast—coffee, baguette, croissant, jam, and butter—will be included in the hotel rate, especially with an online booking directly from the hotel.

CHECKING IN

Typical check-in and checkout times are 2 through 4 pm and noon, respectively, although some properties allow check-in as early as noon and require checkout as early as 11 am. Many flights from North America arrive early in the morning, but having to wait six hours for a room after arriving jet-lagged at 8 am isn't the ideal way to start a vacation. Alert the hotel of your early arrival; while you may not be able to get into your room, you can usually arrange for baggage storage, especially at the larger establishments.

CHILDREN

Most hotels in Paris allow children under the age of 12 to stay in their parents' room at no extra charge. Hotel rooms are often on the small side, unable to accommodate cots or cribs, so inquire about connecting rooms, suites, and floors with strategically placed doors to create private corridors for larger families and groups. In the last few years, almost all of the big luxury hotels have gone the extra mile to attract parents with young children, offering child-friendly activities like swimming lessons or playtime, while mom and dad enjoy the spa.

HOTEL FEATURES

In France, the "first floor" is the floor above the ground floor (*rez-de-chaussée*). The number of rooms listed at the end of each review reflects those with private bathroom (which means they have a shower or a

WHERE SHOULD I STAY?

	Neighborhood Vibe	Pros	Cons
St-Germain and Montparnasse (6e, 14e, 15e)	The center of café culture and the emblem of the Rive Gauche. The mood is leisurely; attractions are easy to access.	A safe, historic area with chic fashion boutiques, famous cafés and brasseries, pretty parks, and lovely side streets; lively all day.	Overdeveloped. Noisy along main streets; the busy commercial area around the Tour Montparnasse is devoid of charm.
The Latin Quarter (5e, 6e)	The historic student quarter of the Rive Gauche. Full of narrow, winding streets, major parks, museums and monuments like the Panthéon.	Plenty of cheap eats and sleeps, discount book and music shops, and noteworthy open-air markets; safe area for walks day and night.	Lacking in métro stations around the Panthéon; student pubs can be noisy in summer; hotel rooms tend to be smaller.
Marais and Bastille (3e, 4e, 11e)	Museums, chic shops, and bustling cafés line the narrow streets of the Marais, home to Jewish and gay communities. Farther east are stylish cocktail bars and edgy boutiques.	Excellent shopping, museum-going, and café culture in the active Marais; bargains aplenty at Bastille hotels; several boutique designer hotels in both areas.	Overcrowded. The Marais's narrow sidewalks are always packed on weekends and in summer, and rooms don't always come cheap; always noisy around the gritty boulevards of Place de la Bastille.
Montmartre and northeast Paris (18e, 19e, 20e)	The Rive Droite's hilltop district is known for winding streets leading up from the racy Pigalle district to the stark-white Sacré-Coeur Basilica.	Amazing views of Paris; romantic cobblestone streets; easy access to Roissy-Charles de Gaulle airport; authentic Parisian neighborhoods.	Inconvenient. Steep staircases can be challenging; few métro stations; Pigalle and Barbès area can be unsafe, especially late at night.
Champs-Élysées and Western Paris (8e, 16e, 17e)	The Triangle D'Or (Golden Triangle) and famous avenues are lively 24/7 with nightclubs, cinemas, and shops, all aimed at the moneyed jet set.	Home to many of the city's famous palace and five-star hotels and haute-couture boutiques, with no shortage of luxurious rooms and designer goods.	Expensive. The sky-high prices of this neighborhood, along with its commercial, touristy tendencies, lure pickpockets.
Around the Eiffel Tower (7e, 15e)	The impressive Eiffel Tower and sweeping Champs de Mars sit next to the Seine River.	Safe and quiet, this Rive Gauche area of Paris has picture-perfect views at every turn.	Residential. With fewer shops and restaurants, this district is quiet at night; longer distances between métro stations.
Louvre, Les Halles, Ile de la Cité (1er, 2e, 8e)	The central district around the Tuileries, Louvre, and Place de la Concorde is known for sightseeing and shopping; Les Halles is a buzzing commercial hub.	Excellent for getting around Paris on foot, bus, or métro. Safe, attractive district close to the Seine, museums, monuments, and shops of all types.	Noisy. The main artery of Rue de Rivoli can be loud with traffic during the day; restaurants cater to tourists; a pickpocket's mecca.
Opéra and Grands Boulevards (9e, 10e)	The newly chic historic district centered on the Garnier Opera House and Bourse (Stock Exchange) is a popular district for its lively streets and important sites.	Perfect for walking tours, the area has unique Parisian finds, distinct neighborhoods like Canal St-Martin and Belleville, and les Grands Magasins (department stores).	Crowded. Tourists and locals keep districts full of pietons, cars, buses, trucks, taxis, and scooters; be extra alert in areas near major train stations.

tub, but not necessarily both). In budget hotels, tubs don't always have fixed curtains or showerheads; how the French rinse themselves with the handheld nozzle without flooding the entire bathroom remains a cultural mystery. Moderately priced places that expect guests to share toilets or bathrooms are pretty much extinct, but be sure you know what facilities you are getting when you book a budget hotel.

HOTEL QUALITY

Note that the quality of accommodations can vary from room to room. If you don't like the room you're given, ask to see another. The French star ratings can be misleading: official stars are granted for specific amenities and services rather than for ambience, style, or overall comfort, so you may find that a two-star hotel eclipses a three-star establishment. Many hotels prefer to remain "under-starred" for tax reasons.

LODGING STRATEGY

Where should you stay? With hundreds of Paris hotels, it may seem like a daunting question. But don't worry—our expert writers and editors have done most of the legwork. The 100-plus selections here represent the best and newest properties this city has to offer. Pick an area of town that appeals to you, and find a review quickly in the listings, which are arranged by neighborhood and then alphabetically.

15

RESERVATIONS

Make reservations as far in advance as possible, especially for May, June, September, October, and around the holidays. Booking online works, but calling directly, or checking up on your online reservation, may be the easiest and most effective way to make contact and communicate your needs. Be sure to specify arrival and departure dates, room size (single or double), room type (standard, deluxe, or suite), the number of people in your party, and whether you want a bathroom with a shower or bathtub (or both). Double-check if breakfast, Internet, and taxes are included. Ask if a deposit is required and what penalties you may be liable for if you cancel. Always request a confirmation number to verify your reservation upon arrival and be sure to get a receipt sent to you via email, which makes it easy to verify that your requests have been noted in writing.

WHAT IT COSTS

Often a hotel in a certain price category will have a few less expensive rooms; it's worth asking. In the off-season—late July, August, November, early December, and late January—rates can be considerably lower. Be sure to check online specials and weekend package deals, and whether there are better rates if you're staying a week or longer. There's a nominal city *taxe de séjour* ranging between €0.83 and €4.40 per person, per night, based on the hotel's star rating. Sometimes this tax is included in the room price, sometimes not.

If you're staying in Paris for more than just a few days, you might want to look into the increasingly popular option of renting an apartment. Not only does this often save in nightly costs, but with your own kitchen you can cook some of your own meals.

WHAT IT COSTS			
$	$$	$$$	$$$$
FOR TWO PEOPLE	under €121	€121–€175	€176–€250	over €250

Prices in the reviews are the lowest cost of a double standard room in high season.

HOTEL REVIEWS

In alphabetical order by neighborhood. Hotel reviews have been shortened. For full information, visit Fodors.com. Use the coordinate (✛ 1:B2) at the end of each review to locate a property on the corresponding map at the end of the chapter.

ILE DE LA CITÉ AND ILE ST-LOUIS

Paris's islands give a good representation of the city's long and fascinating history. On Ile de la Cité—home of the glorious 13th-century Sainte-Chapelle and the foreboding Conciergerie, Marie-Antoinette's final home—you'll find some surprising lodging opportunities, including a tiny hotel tucked into the Hôtel Dieu, the city's oldest hospital. Ile St-Louis's elegant streets and leafy riverside walks inspire romance, and so do its small hotels and many elegant, if pricey, rentals.

$$
HOTEL
Hôtel Hospitel. Wake up to the bells of Notre Dame at this tiny convenience hotel tucked away in the Hôtel Dieu, Paris's oldest working hospital. **Pros:** two steps from Notre Dame; easy walk to Saint Germain, the Latin Quarter, the Marais, and Les Halles; views of the cathedral from rooms' skylights. **Cons:** bells can be noisy; exceedingly basic; hospital setting not for everyone. ⓢ *Rooms from: €150* ✉ *1 pl. du Parvis de Notre-Dame, Ile de la Cité* ☎ *01–44–32–01–00* ⊕ *www.hotel-hospitel. fr* ⌐ *14 rooms* Ⓜ *Cité, Hotel de Ville* ✛ *4:D3.*

$$$
HOTEL
Hôtel Saint-Louis en l'Isle. The location on the exceptionally charming Ile St-Louis is the real draw of this five-story hotel, which retains many of its original 17th-century stone walls and wooden beams. **Pros:** romantic location; ancient architectural details; friendly staff. **Cons:** location is a bit far from the sights; métro stations are not so convenient; small rooms. ⓢ *Rooms from: €205* ✉ *75 rue St-Louis-en-l'Ile, 4e, Île Saint-Louis* ☎ *01–46–34–04–80* ⊕ *www.saintlouisenlisle.com* ⌐ *20 rooms* ⦿ *No meals* Ⓜ *Pont Marie* ✛ *4:E3.*

AROUND THE EIFFEL TOWER

Hotel rooms with views of Paris's reigning icon come at a premium, but your chances of finding a room with a view are best in this quiet, primarily residential neighborhood. If you don't find one, no worries, there are gorgeous views to be had from every street corner.

$$$
HOTEL
FAMILY
Eiffel Seine Hôtel. This tiny boutique hotel minutes from the Eiffel Tower mixes contemporary amenities and designer furnishings with Art Nouveau flourishes. **Pros:** very close to the Eiffel Tower and Champs

de Mars; easy métro access; reasonable rates. **Cons:** long walk from popular sights; minimal space in standard rooms; street noise in some rooms facing river. $ *Rooms from: €250* ✉ *3 bd. de Grenelle, 15e, Eiffel Tower* ☎ *01–45–78–14–81* ⊕ *www.hoteleiffelseineparis.com* ⤴ *45 rooms* ⦿ *No meals* Ⓜ *Bir-Hakeim* ✢ *3:B3.*

$$$
HOTEL
Fodor's Choice
★
🏨 **Hôtel de Londres Eiffel.** Prices at this small, boutique hotel in an upscale neighborhood are fairly reasonable considering all you get—top-notch service, stylish homey decor, a lively neighborhood, and some spectacular views. **Pros:** excellent service; just steps from the Eiffel Tower; quaint setting. **Cons:** rooms on the small side; food not permitted in rooms; not super close to métro. $ *Rooms from: €225* ✉ *1 rue Augereau, 7e, Eiffel Tower* ☎ *01–45–51–63–02* ⊕ *www.hotel-paris-londres-eiffel.com* ⤴ *30 rooms* ⦿ *No meals* Ⓜ *La Tour-Maubourg, École Militaire* ✢ *3:D2.*

$$$$
HOTEL
🏨 **Hôtel du Cadran.** A well-located convenience hotel—actually two buildings run by the same management—Hôtel du Cadran's contemporary design appeals as much to business travelers as to urban creative types on a budget. **Pros:** bright, whimsical rooms; large closets and windows; convenient to Rue Cler, Eiffel Tower, and Les Invalides. **Cons:** two seperate buildings means you have to cross the street; lacks traditional Parisian charm; petite bathrooms. $ *Rooms from: €280* ✉ *16 rue Valadon, 7e, Eiffel Tower* ☎ *01–47–53–89–85* ⊕ *www.hotelvaladon. com* ⤴ *53 rooms* ⦿ *No meals* Ⓜ *École Militaire* ✢ *3:E2.*

$$
HOTEL
🏨 **Hôtel du Champ de Mars.** Around the corner from picturesque Rue Cler, this charming, affordable hotel welcomes guests with a Provence-inspired lobby and huge picture windows overlooking a quiet street. **Pros:** good value; walking distance to Eiffel Tower, Les Invalides, and Rodin Museum; free Wi-Fi. **Cons:** small rooms compared to larger hotels; no air-conditioning; inconsistent service. $ *Rooms from: €150* ✉ *7 rue du Champ de Mars, 7e, Eiffel Tower* ☎ *01–45–51–52–30* ⊕ *www.hote
lduchampdemars.com* ⤴ *25 rooms* ⦿ *No meals* Ⓜ *École Militaire* ✢ *3:E2.*

$$$
HOTEL
FAMILY
Fodor's Choice
★
🏨 **Hotel Eiffel Blomet.** Named for the cabaret a few doors down where Josephine Baker once sang, this handsome Art Deco hotel comes with a luxurious pool, hammam, and sauna. **Pros:** great pool, steam room, and sauna; chic rooms; good value. **Cons:** off-the-radar neighborhood; not that close to the Eiffel Tower; average breakfast. $ *Rooms from: €200* ✉ *78 rue Blomet, 15e, Eiffel Tower* ☎ *01–53–68–70–00* ⊕ *www. hoteleiffelblomet.com* ⤴ *87 rooms* ⦿ *No meals* Ⓜ *Vaugirard, Volon-taires* ✢ *3:D6.*

$$$$
HOTEL
🏨 **Hôtel Eiffel Trocadéro.** A curious blend of Second Empire and rococo styling awaits guests in this hotel on a quiet corner just off Place Trocadéro. **Pros:** views of Eiffel Tower from upper floors; upscale residential district convenient to métro; organic breakfast buffet. **Cons:** no full-service restaurant; long walk to city center; basic rooms feel cramped. $ *Rooms from: €270* ✉ *35 rue Benjamin-Franklin, 16e, Eiffel Tower* ☎ *01–53–70–17–70* ⊕ *www.hoteleiffeltrocadero.com* ⤴ *17 rooms* ⦿ *No meals* Ⓜ *Trocadéro* ✢ *3:A1.*

$$$$
HOTEL
🏨 **Hôtel Le Bellechasse.** If you like eclectic modern interior design, this tiny boutique hotel right around the corner from the popular Musée d'Orsay is a good choice for its access to the major sites. **Pros:** central

15

location near top museums; one-of-a-kind style; helpful staff. **Cons:** steep rates; street-facing rooms can be noisy; open bathrooms lack privacy. ⑤ *Rooms from: €350* ✉ *8 rue de Bellechasse, 7e, Eiffel Tower* ☎ *01–45–50–22–31* ⊕ *www.lebellechasse.com* ⋟ *33 rooms* ❙❁❙ *No meals* Ⓜ *Solferino* ✛ *3:H1.*

$$$
HOTEL
⛆ **Hôtel Le Tourville.** This cozy, contemporary haven near the Eiffel Tower, Champs de Mars, and Invalides is a comfortable base for exploring Paris. **Pros:** convenient location near métro; friendly service; free Wi-Fi in all rooms. **Cons:** small standard rooms; air-conditioning only during summer months; no restaurant. ⑤ *Rooms from: €250* ✉ *16 av. de Tourville, 7e, Eiffel Tower* ☎ *01–47–05–62–62* ⊕ *www.paris-hotel-tourville.com* ⋟ *30 rooms* ❙❁❙ *No meals* Ⓜ *École Militaire* ✛ *3:E3.*

$$$$
HOTEL
Fodor's Choice
★
⛆ **Le Cinq Codet.** Set in a 1930's former France Telecom exchange, the Art Deco–era building's streamlined contours create the ideal setting for spaces that mix modern elegance with high-tech advances, while making the most of some very Parisian views of nearby Invalides and the Eiffel Tower a few blocks away. **Pros:** fabulous courtyard cocktail bar; exceptional terraces with views; some of the chicest rooms in Paris. **Cons:** in a quiet part of the 7e; not a lot of nearby nightlife; not all rooms have terraces. ⑤ *Rooms from: €279* ✉ *5 rue Louis Codet, 7e, Eiffel Tower* ☎ *01–53–85–15–60* ⊕ *www.le5codet.com* ⋟ *57 rooms* ❙❁❙ *No meals* Ⓜ *École Militaire, Varenne* ✛ *3:E3.*

$$$$
HOTEL
Fodor's Choice
★
⛆ **Le Narcisse Blanc.** The superb five-star Le Narcisse Blanc covers all the bases in luxury accommodations with a top-notch gastronomic restaurant and a full-service Carita spa, all in a Haussmann-era mansion in an elegant neighborhood. **Pros:** glorious Art Deco–inspired pool, sauna, and steam room; Eiffel Tower views; lots of luxury for the price. **Cons:** hard to book during fashion weeks; neighborhood quiet at night; 15-minute walk to the Eiffel Tower. ⑤ *Rooms from: €425* ✉ *19 bd. de la Tour-Maubourg, 7e, Eiffel Tower* ☎ *01–40–60–44–32* ⊕ *www. lenarcisseblanc.com* ⋟ *37 rooms* ❙❁❙ *No meals* Ⓜ *La Tour-Maubourg, Assemblée Nationale* ✛ *3:F1.*

$$$$
HOTEL
⛆ **Le Walt.** The convenient location stands out at this boutique hotel in the chic district between the Eiffel Tower and Les Invalides. **Pros:** great location; friendly staff; free Wi-Fi. **Cons:** on a busy street; no hotel restaurant; some complaints about noisy doors in hallways. ⑤ *Rooms from: €320* ✉ *37 av. de la Motte Picquet, 7e, Eiffel Tower* ☎ *01–45–51–55–83* ⊕ *www.lewaltparis.com* ⋟ *25 rooms* ❙❁❙ *No meals* Ⓜ *École Militaire* ✛ *3:E3.*

$$$$
HOTEL
Fodor's Choice
★
⛆ **Shangri-La Hotel Paris.** Displaying French elegance at its best, this impressively restored 19th-century mansion gazing across the Seine at the Eiffel Tower was once the stately home of Prince Roland Bonaparte, grandnephew of the emperor himself, and his gilded private apartments have been transformed into La Suite Impériale. **Pros:** some of the best views in Paris; excellent dining; fabulous pool. **Cons:** astronomical rates; pool only open until 9 pm; expensive breakfast. ⑤ *Rooms from: €1100* ✉ *10 av. Iéna, 16e, Eiffel Tower* ☎ *01–53–67–19–98* ⊕ *www. shangri-la.com* ⋟ *101 rooms* ❙❁❙ *No meals* Ⓜ *Iéna* ✛ *1:B6.*

CHAMPS-ÉLYSÉES

The land of the palace hotel, the elegant area around the Golden Triangle is catnip for hedge-fund millionaires and international royalty. A good half of Paris's eight palace hotels are clustered here, starting with Le Bristol—a Paris legend—and including the Plaza Athénée, the superb Georges V, and Paris's newest palace, the Peninsula.

$$$$
HOTEL
⚏ Buddha-Bar Hotel Paris. True to the sleek and chic DNA of the Buddha-Bar franchise, this glamorous boutique hotel, set in an 18th-century mansion just minutes from prime shopping and museums, is a heady cocktail of stylish Asian design, lavish finishes, and contemporary art. **Pros:** exemplary service; great spa and fitness center; excellent Sunday brunch. **Cons:** decor is not for conservative tastes; pricey; rooms often booked up. Ⓢ *Rooms from: €420* ⊠ *4 rue d'Anjou, 8e, Champs-Élysées* ☎ *01–83–96–88–88* ⊕ *www.buddhabarhotelparis.com* ⇝ *56 rooms* ⧖ *Breakfast* Ⓜ *Madeleine* ✛ *1:H5.*

$$$$
HOTEL
⚏ Champs-Élysées Plaza Hotel and Wellness. Discreet, contemporary elegance sums up this graciously renovated seven-story town house steps from the hustle and bustle of the Champs-Élysées. **Pros:** extremely elegant rooms; friendly, attentive service; central location. **Cons:** small spa; gym only has five machines; limited breakfast buffet. Ⓢ *Rooms from: €440* ⊠ *35 rue de Berri, 8e, Champs-Élysées* ☎ *01–53–53–20–20* ⊕ *www.champs-elysees-plaza.com* ⇝ *35 rooms* ⧖ *No meals* Ⓜ *St-Philippe-du-Roule, George V* ✛ *1:E4.*

$$$$
HOTEL
FAMILY
Fodor's Choice
★
⚏ Four Seasons Hôtel George V Paris. As poised and polished as the day it opened in 1928, this superb hotel's original plaster detailing and 17th-century tapestries have been restored, the bas-reliefs regilded, and the marble-floor mosaics rebuilt tile by tile, adding up to an opulence rarely equalled in the city. **Pros:** some of the best dining in the city; courtyard dining in summer; indoor swimming pool. **Cons:** several blocks from the nearest métro; definitely for the one percent; lacks the intimacy of smaller boutique hotels. Ⓢ *Rooms from: €1100* ⊠ *31 av. George V, 8e, Champs-Élysées* ☎ *01–49–52–70–00* ⊕ *www.fourseasons.com/paris* ⇝ *244 rooms* ⧖ *No meals* Ⓜ *George V* ✛ *1:D5.*

$$$
HOTEL
⚏ Hidden Hotel. The rough-hewn-wood facade heralds the eco-friendly theme of this under-the-radar boutique hotel a block from the Arc de Triomphe, and the interior follows through with handcrafted glass, wood, stone, and ceramic decor. **Pros:** a block from main métro line and Champs-Élysées; organic toiletries in recycled packaging; free Wi-Fi. **Cons:** rooms on the small side; open-plan bathrooms offer little privacy; separate entrance and breakfast area for some rooms isn't intimate. Ⓢ *Rooms from: €224* ⊠ *28 rue de l'Arc de Triomphe, 17e, Champs-Élysées* ☎ *01–40–55–03–57* ⊕ *www.hidden-hotel.com* ⇝ *35 rooms* ⧖ *No meals* Ⓜ *Ternes* ✛ *1:B3.*

$$
HOTEL
FAMILY
Fodor's Choice
★
⚏ Hôtel Bradford Élysées. One of the Astotel group's popular Paris lodgings, this welcoming hotel follows a winning formula: annex a historic building, create attractive spaces in cheerful colors, offer plenty of perks (free drinks, snacks, and newspapers) and service that goes the whole nine yards, all for a reasonable price. **Pros:** lots of freebies, including lobby snack and complementary minibar; some rooms have period details; bargain prices. **Cons:** not in a central neighborhood; decor not

15

to all tastes; a métro ride to many sights. Ⓢ *Rooms from: €145* ✉ *10 rue Saint-Philippe du Roule , 8e, Champs-Élysées* ☎ *01–45–63–20–20* ⊕ *www.astotel.com/hotel/bradford-elysees* ☞ *50 rooms* ⑩ *No meals* Ⓜ *Saint-Philippe-du-Roule, Franklin D. Roosevelt* ✛ *1:E4.*

$$$$
HOTEL

▦ **Hôtel Daniel.** A contemporary antidote to the minimalist trend, the Daniel is decorated in rich fabrics and antique furnishings from France, North Africa, and the Far East. **Pros:** intimate atmosphere; luxurious decor; close to the Champs-Élysées. **Cons:** across from a noisy bar; expensive rates; inconsistent customer service. Ⓢ *Rooms from: €420* ✉ *8 rue Frédéric Bastiat, 8e, Champs-Élysées* ☎ *01–42–56–17–00* ⊕ *www.hoteldanielparis.com* ☞ *26 rooms* ⑩ *No meals* Ⓜ *St-Philippe-du-Roule* ✛ *1:E4.*

$$$$
HOTEL

▦ **Hôtel de Sers.** Built for the Marquis de Sers with a horse-drawn-carriage entrance, inner courtyard, expansive salons, and monumental staircase, this beautiful structure was transformed into a hotel in 1935. **Pros:** convenient central location in the Golden Triangle; many dining options nearby; soothing Turkish bath and fitness room. **Cons:** basic rooms a bit small; no formal spa; on the expensive side. Ⓢ *Rooms from: €500* ✉ *41 av. Pierre 1er de Serbie, 8e, Champs-Élysées* ☎ *01–53–23–75–75* ⊕ *www.hoteldesers-paris.fr* ☞ *52 rooms* ⑩ *No meals* Ⓜ *Alma-Marceau, George V* ✛ *1:D5.*

$$
HOTEL

▦ **Hôtel Ekta.** Two top-tier Paris designers transformed a humdrum 1960s office building into one of the city's liveliest fashion-centric boutique hotels. **Pros:** great location; in-room tea and coffee; charming garden. **Cons:** some rooms tiny; small bathrooms; air-conditioned only after May 1. ⓈNYC *Rooms from: €140* ✉ *52 Rue Galilée, 8e, Champs-Élysées* ☎ *01–53–76–09–05* ⊕ *www.hotelekta.com* ☞ *25 rooms* Ⓜ *George V* ✛ *1:C5.*

$$$$
HOTEL

▦ **Hôtel Fouquet's Barrière.** Steps away from one of the world's most famous streets, this luxury hotel adjacent to the legendary Fouquet's Brasserie at the corner of the Champs-Élysées and Avenue George V is recognizable by its uniformed valets, parked sports cars, and elegant Haussmannian entryway. **Pros:** many rooms overlook the Champs-Élysées; very close to métro; beautiful spa and pool. **Cons:** expensive; bars can get overcrowded; corporate events give the place a business-hotel feel. ⓈRooms from: €1000 ✉ *46 av. George V, 8e, Champs-Élysées* ☎ *01–40–69–60–00* ⊕ *www.lucienbarriere.com* ☞ *114 rooms* ⑩ *No meals* Ⓜ *George V* ✛ *1:D4.*

$$$
HOTEL
FAMILY
Fodor's Choice
★

▦ **Hôtel Keppler.** Like your own classy pied-à-terre, the Keppler—set on a quiet street not far from the Champs-Éysées—combines traditional French and contemporary style for a comfy, lived-in elegance that invites total relaxation. **Pros:** luxurious common spaces; great in-hotel bar; elegant neighborhood. **Cons:** some rooms quite small; a walk to the nearest métro; no spa. ⓈRooms from: €250 ✉ *10 rue Kepler, 16e, Champs-Élysées* ☎ *01–47–20–65–05* ⊕ *www.keppler.fr* ☞ *44 rooms* ⑩ *No meals* Ⓜ *George V* ✛ *1:C5.*

$$$$
HOTEL

▦ **Hôtel Lancaster.** Once a Spanish nobleman's town house, this luxurious retreat dating to 1889 dazzles with its elegant decor, lush courtyard, and acclaimed restaurant. **Pros:** steps away from the Champs-Élysées and five minutes from métro; excellent seasonal menus at La Table du

Lancaster; peaceful street. **Cons:** size of rooms varies greatly; decor looks tired; no spa. Ⓢ *Rooms from: €400* ⊠ *7 rue de Berri, 8e, Champs-Élysées* ☎ *01–40–76–40–76* ⊕ *www.hotel-lancaster.fr* ⤳ *56 rooms* ⓘⓄⓘ *No meals* Ⓜ *George V* ✛ *1:D4.*

$$$$
HOTEL
FAMILY
Fodor's Choice
★
🛉 **Hôtel Le Bristol.** The historic Bristol ranks among Paris's most exclusive hotels and has numerous accolades to prove it, as does its Michelin-starred restaurant. **Pros:** rooftop pool with views of Sacré-Coeur; on luxury shopping street; one of the best restaurants in Paris. **Cons:** a few blocks from the nearest métro; old-fashioned atmosphere may not be for everyone; very expensive rates. Ⓢ *Rooms from: €950* ⊠ *112 rue du Faubourg St-Honoré, 8e, Champs-Élysées* ☎ *01–53–43–43–00* ⊕ *www. lebristolparis.com* ⤳ *188 rooms* ⓘⓄⓘ *No meals* Ⓜ *Miromesnil* ✛ *1:F4.*

$$
HOTEL
Fodor's Choice
★
🛉 **Hôtel Le 123 Elysées.** Italian marble, exposed brick, rough concrete, and sleek wood mix with leather, feathers, Swarovski crystals, and fiber-optic fairy lights to give this boutique hotel a genuinely eclectic atmosphere. **Pros:** chic decor; near luxury shopping; hotel bar open daily. **Cons:** service can be impolite; no on-site restaurant; some rooms quite small for the price. Ⓢ *Rooms from: €155* ⊠ *123 rue du Faubourg St-Honoré, 8e, Champs-Élysées* ☎ *01–53–89–01–23* ⊕ *www.astotel. com/hotel/hotel-le-123-elysees/overview* ⤳ *41 rooms* ⓘⓄⓘ *No meals* Ⓜ *St-Philippe du Roule, Franklin-D.-Roosevelt* ✛ *1:E4.*

$$$$
HOTEL
FAMILY
Fodor's Choice
★
🛉 **Hôtel Plaza Athénée.** Distinguished by the scarlet flowers cascading over its elegant facade, this glamorous landmark hotel sits on one of the most expensive avenues in Paris. **Pros:** Eiffel Tower views; great restaurant and bar; Dior Institute spa. **Cons:** attracts oligarchs; exorbitant prices; small fitness room. Ⓢ *Rooms from: €1100* ⊠ *25 av. Montaigne, 8e, Champs-Élysées* ☎ *01–53–67–66–65* ⊕ *www.dorchestercollection. com/en/paris/hotel-plaza-athenee* ⤳ *208 rooms* ⓘⓄⓘ *No meals* Ⓜ *Alma-Marceau* ✛ *1:D6.*

$$$$
HOTEL
FAMILY
🛉 **Hôtel Raphael.** This discreet palace-like hotel was built in 1925 to cater to travelers spending a season in Paris, so every space is generously sized for long, lavish stays. **Pros:** a block from the Champs-Élysées and Arc de Triomphe; rooftop garden terrace; intimate hotel bar frequented by locals. **Cons:** decor can feel worn and dowdy; some soundproofing issues; neighborhood far from the action. Ⓢ *Rooms from: €650* ⊠ *17 av. Kléber, 16e, Champs-Élysées* ☎ *01–53–64–32–00* ⊕ *www.leshotels-baverez.com* ⤳ *83 rooms* ⓘⓄⓘ *No meals* Ⓜ *Kléber* ✛ *1:C4.*

$$$
HOTEL
🛉 **Hotel Vernet.** Originally opened in the waning years of the Belle Époque, a glamorous centenary update capitalized on this classy boutique hotel's larger volumes and beautiful bones while adding all the 21st-century luxuries. **Pros:** larger than average rooms; beautiful stained-glass ceilings designed by G. Eiffel; quiet street close to sights and shopping. **Cons:** coffee machines only in Deluxe rooms; extras can be pricey; in-hotel dining quite expensive. Ⓢ *Rooms from: €250* ⊠ *25 rue Vernet, 8e, Champs-Élysées* ☎ *01–44–31–98–00* ⊕ *www.hotelvernet-paris.fr* ⤳ *50 rooms* ⓘⓄⓘ *No meals* Ⓜ *George V, Étoile* ✛ *1:C4.*

$$$$
HOTEL
🛉 **La Maison Champs Elysées.** A 10-minute walk from the city's most famous avenue, this chic boutique hotel in the heart of the Golden Triangle lures an art-minded fashion crowd with an eclectic twist on a historical Haussmannian *belle demeure*. **Pros:** quiet street close to

15

métro; excellent location near the Grand and Petit Palais; unique decor. Cons: some rooms seem tired; no fitness center; expensive bar. ⑤ *Rooms from: €380* ✉ *8 rue Jean Goujon, 8e, Champs-Élysées* ☎ *01–40–74–64–65* ⊕ *www.lamaisonchampselysees.com* ↝ *57 rooms* ⅋⦶ *No meals* Ⓜ *Franklin-D.-Roosevelt* ✛ *1:E5.*

$$$$
HOTEL
Fodor's Choice
★

⛭ **La Réserve.** Set in a splendid 19th-century mansion just steps from the presidential palace and the American Embassy, this aristocratic lodging vies for the most elegant small hotel in Paris. Pros: top-notch spa with pool; splendid views over the Champs-Élysées and Eiffel Tower; excellent dining. Cons: very expensive; can be snobby; out-of-the-way neighborhood. ⑤ *Rooms from: €750* ✉ *42 av. Gabriel, 8e, Champs-Élysées* ☎ *01–58–36–60–60* ⊕ *www.lareserve-paris.com* ↝ *40 rooms* ⅋⦶ *No meals* Ⓜ *Franklin-D.-Roosevelt* ✛ *1:F5.*

$$$$
HOTEL
FAMILY

⛭ **Le Royal Monceau Raffles Paris.** The glamorous Royal Monceau Raffles offers tons of luxury, great dining, and an artsy atmosphere along with a hefty dose of cool. Pros: ethereal spa and fitness center; chic private apartments; nice terrace garden. Cons: hefty prices; away from the heart of Paris; fitness room is small. ⑤ *Rooms from: €780* ✉ *37 av. Hoche, 8e, Champs-Élysées* ☎ *01–42–99–88–00* ⊕ *www.leroyalmonceau.com* ↝ *149 rooms* ⅋⦶ *No meals* Ⓜ *Charles-de-Gaulle-Étoile* ✛ *1:D3.*

$$$$
HOTEL

⛭ **Marignan.** Set smack dab in the middle of Paris's Golden Triangle, just off the Champs-Élysées, this sleek five-star hotel is a paragon of contemporary style that includes fine in-hotel dining and some breathtaking terrace views. Pros: stellar views from upper terraces; prices good for this standard of luxury; great location. Cons: a few rooms on the smaller side; not all rooms have great views; lack of outlets in bathrooms. ⑤ *Rooms from: €350* ✉ *12 rue de Marignan, 8e, Champs-Élysées* ☎ *01–40–76–34–56* ⊕ *www.hotel-marignan.com* ↝ *50 rooms* ⅋⦶ *No meals* Ⓜ *Franklin-D.-Roosevelt* ✛ *1:E5.*

$$$
HOTEL

⛭ **Mon Hotel.** The contemporary design, modern comforts, and close proximity to the Arc de Triomphe and Champs-Élysées—a 10-minute walk away—are big draws at this stylish boutique hotel. Pros: unique contemporary styling; convenient to the métro; quiet residential street. Cons: some rooms have limited closet space; no extra beds for children; breakfast costs extra. ⑤ *Rooms from: €204* ✉ *1–5 rue d'Argentine, 16e, Champs-Élysées* ☎ *01–45–02–76–76* ⊕ *www.monhotel.fr* ↝ *36 rooms* ⅋⦶ *No meals* Ⓜ *Argentine* ✛ *1:B4.*

$$$$
HOTEL
FAMILY
Fodor's Choice
★

⛭ **The Peninsula Paris.** After a €900-million renovation that restored the luster of this gem dating to 1908, the lavishly appointed Peninsula raises the bar for luxury hotels in Paris. Pros: world-class dining; fabulous spa and pool; amazing views from higher floors. Cons: price out of reach for most; not centrally located; stuffy neighborhood. ⑤ *Rooms from: €795* ✉ *19 av. Kléber, Champs-Élysées* ☎ *01–58–12–28–88* ⊕ *paris.peninsula.com* ↝ *200 rooms* ⅋⦶ *No meals* Ⓜ *Kléber, Etoile* ✛ *1:C5.*

$$$$
HOTEL

⛭ **Renaissance Paris Arc de Triomphe.** This American-style hotel catering to corporate executives is located in a predominantly business district between the Arc de Triomphe and Place des Ternes. Pros: walking distance to métro; spacious rooms; good discounts with Marriott points. Cons: neighborhood lacks character; filled with business conferences; rather unfriendly service. ⑤ *Rooms from: €440* ✉ *39 av. de Wagram,*

17e, Champs-Élysées ☎ *01–55–37–55–37* ⊕ *www.marriott.fr/hotels/ travel/parwg-renaissance-paris-arc-de-triomphe-hotel* ⤢ *138 rooms* ⦿| *No meals* Ⓜ *Ternes* ✛ *1:C3.*

AROUND THE LOUVRE

Besides a central location starting at Paris's Rive Droite, this neighborhood's many attractions, from the stately Palais Royal gardens to its wealth of fine museums, makes the area around the Louvre a great place to hang your hat. Hotels in the neighborhood run the gamut from stylishly refurbished 18th-century mansions to colorful and reasonably priced boutique hotels.

$$$$
HOTEL
Fodor'sChoice
★

⊡ Grand Hotel du Palais Royal. Despite its splashy name, this gracious five-star hotel, housed in an 18th-century mansion just steps from the Palais Royal gardens, keeps a surprisingly relaxed profile, focusing less on flagrant luxury and more on the essentials that make a hotel truly grand—service, quality, comfort, refinement, and quiet. **Pros:** top-notch service; an island of quiet and calm in a bustling neighborhood; steps from the Louvre, Palais Royal, and many other sights. **Cons:** not all rooms come with balconies; no pool; small fitness room. Ⓢ *Rooms from: €300* ⊠ *4 rue de Valois, 1er, Louvre* ☎ *01–42–96–15–35* ⊕ *www. grandhoteldupalaisroyal.com* ⤢ *68 rooms* ⦿| *No meals* Ⓜ *Palais Royal–Musée du Louvre* ✛ *2:B6.*

$$$$
HOTEL
FAMILY

⊡ Hôtel Brighton. A few of the city's most prestigious hotels face the Tuileries or Place de la Concorde, but the 19th-century Brighton occupies the same prime real estate and offers a privileged stay for a fraction of the price. **Pros:** convenient central location; friendly service; breakfast buffet (free for kids under 12). **Cons:** some areas in need of repair; variable quality in decor between rooms; no restaurant for lunch or dinner. Ⓢ *Rooms from: €290* ⊠ *218 rue de Rivoli, 1er, Louvre* ☎ *01–47–03–61–61* ⊕ *www.paris-hotel-brighton.com* ⤢ *62 rooms* ⦿| *No meals* Ⓜ *Tuileries* ✛ *2:A6.*

$$$
HOTEL

⊡ Hôtel Britannique. Open since 1861 and a stone's throw from the Louvre, the romantic Britannique blends courteous English service with old-fashioned French elegance near the banks of the Seine. **Pros:** on calm side street; less than a block from the métro/RER station; excellent service from friendly staff. **Cons:** small rooms; soundproofing could be better; decor a bit stodgy. Ⓢ *Rooms from: €238* ⊠ *20 av. Victoria, 1er, Louvre* ☎ *01–42–33–74–59* ⊕ *www.hotel-britannique.fr* ⤢ *39 rooms* ⦿| *No meals* Ⓜ *Châtelet* ✛ *4:D1.*

$$$
HOTEL

⊡ Hôtel Crayon. Managed by artists, this hotel near the Louvre and Palais-Royal distinguishes itself with an eclectic pop-art decor—expect an unusual canvas of local and international guests that's just as colorful. **Pros:** bright decor; very friendly staff; central location. **Cons:** small bathrooms; basement breakfast area; lobby lounge lacks any coziness and warmth. Ⓢ *Rooms from: €188* ⊠ *25 rue du Bouloi, 1er, Louvre* ☎ *01–42–36–54–19* ⊕ *www.hotelcrayon.com* ⤢ *26 rooms* ⦿| *No meals* Ⓜ *Louvre* ✛ *4:C1.*

15

$$ ⌧ **Hôtel du Continent.** You'd be hard-pressed to find a budget hotel this
HOTEL stylish anywhere in Paris, let alone in an upscale neighborhood close to
Fodor's Choice many of the city's top attractions. **Pros:** superfriendly staff; all modern
★ amenities; location, location, location. **Cons:** no lobby; tiny bathrooms;
bold decor not for everyone. ⑤ *Rooms from: €150 ⊠ 30 rue du Mont-
Thabor, 1e, Louvre ☎ 01–42–60–75–32 ⊕ www.hotelcontinent.com
↩ 25 rooms ⦿ No meals Ⓜ Concord, Tuileries ✛ 1:H6.*

$$$$ ⌧ **Hotel Konfidentiel.** Sleep beneath the preguillotined head of Marie-
HOTEL Antoinette or amid the turmoil of the French Revolution in one of the
FAMILY six individually themed rooms here. **Pros:** next to the Louvre; comfort-
able rooms; friendly staff. **Cons:** can feel a bit enclosed; showers only in
bathrooms (no tubs); unreliable Wi-Fi. ⑤ *Rooms from: €370 ⊠ 64 rue
de l'Arbre Sec, 1er, Louvre ☎ 01–55–34–40–40 ⊕ www.konfidentiel-
paris.com ↩ 6 rooms ⦿ No meals Ⓜ Louvre–Rivoli ✛ 2:C6.*

$$$$ ⌧ **Hotel La Tamise.** This intimate 19-room hotel was once a stately home
HOTEL owned by a noble French family, which, in 1878, was converted to a
Fodor's Choice hotel favored by aristocrats, and later fashion icons. **Pros:** in the heart of
★ Paris on a quiet street; just steps from superlative shopping; old-world
elegance and comfort. **Cons:** small lobby; no balconies; limited views
of the Tuileries. ⑤ *Rooms from: €260 ⊠ 4 rue d'Alger , 1e, Louvre
☎ 01–40–41–14–14 ⊕ www.paris-hotel-la-tamise.com ↩ 19 Ⓜ Tuile-
ries, Concord ✛ 2:A6.*

$$$$ ⌧ **Hôtel Le Pradey.** Offering Pierre Marcolini chocolates and Hermès
HOTEL and Nux toiletries, this compact boutique hotel near the Tuileries has
a luxe feel. **Pros:** choice of copious breakfast buffet or quick coffee
and croissant; designer touches throughout; double doors for sound-
proofing in suites. **Cons:** smaller rooms lack closet space; rooms vary
greatly in style; nondescript entry and lackluster service result in luke-
warm welcome. ⑤ *Rooms from: €390 ⊠ 5 rue St-Roch, 1e, Louvre
☎ 01–42–60–31–70 ⊕ www.lepradey.com ↩ 28 rooms ⦿ No meals
Ⓜ Tuileries ✛ 2:A6.*

$$ ⌧ **Hôtel Louvre Sainte-Anne.** Walk to many major sites from this small,
HOTEL low-key budget property exceptionally located between the Opéra and
the Louvre. **Pros:** convenient location; free Wi-Fi; helpful reception.
Cons: very small rooms and dull decor; district can feel very un-Parisian;
subterranean breakfast area slightly claustrophobic. ⑤ *Rooms from:
€163 ⊠ 32 rue Ste-Anne, 1er, Louvre ☎ 01–40–20–02–35 ⊕ www.
paris-hotel-louvre.com ↩ 20 rooms ⦿ No meals Ⓜ Pyramides ✛ 2:B5.*

$$$$ ⌧ **Hôtel Meurice.** Since 1835, the Meurice has welcomed royalty and
HOTEL celebrities from the Duchess of Windsor to Salvador Dalí—who both
FAMILY resided in the grande-dame establishment—and Paris's first palace hotel
Fodor's Choice continues to please with service, style, and views. **Pros:** stunning art
★ and architecture; views over the Tuileries gardens; central location convenient to métro and major sites. **Cons:** popularity makes the public
areas not very discreet; front-desk service at times inattentive; incredibly expensive. ⑤ *Rooms from: €1295 ⊠ 228 rue de Rivoli, 1er, Louvre
☎ 01–44–58–10–09 ⊕ www.dorchestercollection.com ↩ 208 rooms
⦿ No meals Ⓜ Tuileries, Concorde ✛ 2:A6.*

$$$ ⌧ **Hôtel Thérèse.** Tucked away from the traffic and crowds of Avenue
HOTEL de l'Opéra, Hôtel Thérèse, named after the wife of Louis XIV, is a

Apartment Rentals

If you favor extra space plus that special feeling of living like a local, try renting a Paris apartment. Rentals can also offer savings, especially for groups.

Check out the **Paris Tourism Office** website (⊕ *www.parisinfo.com*) for reputable agency listings. Policies differ, but you can expect a minimum required stay from three to seven days; a refundable deposit payable on arrival; possibly an agency fee; and maid and linen service.

The following is a list of property hunters, good-value and luxury apartments, and apartment services. **Paris Perfect** (⊕ *www.parisperfect.com*) manages more than 100 apartments around Paris, mostly on the Left Bank in the upscale 7th arrondissement. Apartments come in a range of sizes and are designed to feel like your very own chic pied-à-terre; many come with Eiffel Tower views. Luxury services, like concierge and gourmet food tours, are often available. **Catta-lan Johnson** (☎ *01–45–74–87–77*, ⊕ *www.cattalanjohnson.com*) is an established French fee-based real estate agent highly specialized in rental properties. The multilingual staff has a citywide inventory of furnished apartments available for one week

to a few years. **Citadines Apart Hotel** (☎ *01–41–05–79–05* ⊕ *www. citadines.fr*) is a chain of apartment-style hotel accommodations. They're somewhat generic, but offer many services and good value for short stays. **Home Rental** (☎ *01–42–25–65–40* ⊕ *www.home-rental.com*) has been in business since 1992 and rents furnished studios to six bedrooms with a one-week minimum stay, short or long term, with no agency fees. Maid service, cable, and wireless Internet are included. **Lodgis Paris** (☎ *01–70–39–11–11* ⊕ *www.lodgis.com*) has one of the largest selections in Paris; however, the agency fee makes it cheaper per diem to rent for more than one week. **Paris Attitude** (☎ *01–42–96–31–46* ⊕ *www.parisattitude.com*) offers a large selection of furnished rentals of studios to five bedrooms from a week to a year. **Paris Vacation Apartments** (☎ *06–63–60–67–14* ⊕ *www. parisvacationapartments.com*) specializes in luxury rentals, with all-inclusive prices by the week. **Paris-Hospitality** (☎ *01–47–83–75–91* ⊕ *www.parisattitude.com*) lists 350 apartments in prime locations throughout Paris for short- or long-term visits. Concierge services are available.

15

---

stone's throw from regal sites like the Louvre, Palais Royal, and the historic Comédie Française theater. **Pros:** excellent location on quiet street; free Wi-Fi; breakfast can be served in room. **Cons:** rooms are relatively small for price; breakfast area located in basement; no restaurant or gym. ⑤ *Rooms from: €210* ✉ *5/7 rue Thérèse, 1er, Louvre* ☎ *01–42–96–10–01* ⊕ *www.hoteltherese.com* ⇆ *40 rooms* ⦿ *No meals* Ⓜ *Pyramides* ✥ *2:B6.*

$$$$ ⚿ **Mandarin Oriental Paris.** Of Paris's palace hotels—the highest designa-
HOTEL tion—the Mandarin Oriental is among the most contemporary, with a soaring marble entryway and a sleek, luxe style that makes a welcome contrast to the historic grande dames. **Pros:** impressive pool; many rooms with terraces; child-friendly, with babysitting services. **Cons:** not

much variation in standard rooms; noise from courtyard during special events; very pricey. ⑤ *Rooms from: €975* ✉ *251 rue de St-Honore, 1e, Louvre* ☎ *01–70–98–78–88* ⊕ *www.mandarinoriental.com/paris* ⤴ *138 rooms* ⍾ *No meals* Ⓜ *Tuileries, Concorde* ✛ *1:H5.*

$$$$
HOTEL

⌖ **Meliá Vendôme.** In a prestigious quarter a few minutes from the Jardin des Tuileries, Place de la Concorde, Opéra Garnier, and the Louvre, the Meliá Vendôme has handsome and spacious rooms in attractive contemporary tones that exude an understated elegance. **Pros:** outstanding location in the city center; near world-class shopping; elegant, immaculate rooms. **Cons:** expensive breakfast; no spa or pool; in-room cooling system unreliable. ⑤ *Rooms from: €370* ✉ *8 rue Cambon, 1e, Louvre* ☎ *01–44–77–54–00* ⊕ *www.melia.com/en/hotels/france/paris/melia-vendome-boutique-hotel/index.html* ⤴ *83 rooms* ⍾ *No meals* Ⓜ *Concorde, Madeleine* ✛ *1:H5.*

$$$$
HOTEL
FAMILY

⌖ **Renaissance Paris Vendôme.** Hiding behind a classic 19th-century facade is a fresh, contemporary hotel with subtle 1930s influences. **Pros:** posh location; trendy restaurant; full-service spa and fitness room. **Cons:** lacks authentic French character; public lounges noisy at times; packed with business groups. ⑤ *Rooms from: €620* ✉ *4 rue du Mont Thabor, 1er, Louvre* ☎ *01–40–20–20–00* ⊕ *www.marriott.com* ⤴ *97 rooms* ⍾ *No meals* Ⓜ *Tuileries* ✛ *2:A6.*

$$$$
HOTEL
Fodor's Choice
★

⌖ **The Ritz.** In novels, songs, and common parlance, there's not a word that evokes the romance and luxury of Paris better than the Ritz. **Pros:** spacious swimming pool; superlative selection of bars and restaurants; top-notch service. **Cons:** easy to get lost in the vast hotel; paparazzi magnet; astronomical prices. ⑤ *Rooms from: €1000* ✉ *15 pl. Vendôme, 1er, Louvre* ☎ *01–43–16–30–30* ⊕ *www.ritzparis.com* ⤴ *143 rooms* ⍾ *No meals* Ⓜ *Opéra* ✛ *2:A5.*

LES GRANDS BOULEVARDS

This bustling historic district is tops for travelers on a budget. Central to métro lines, the antiques district, and leafy neighborhoods like Parc Monceau and Canal St-Martin, there's plenty to explore on foot and a quick métro ride gets you to most other Paris neighborhoods in a jiffy.

$$$$
HOTEL

⌖ **Hôtel Banke.** In a stately bank building dating from the early 20th century, this interesting hotel lies in the heart of the Opéra district, which is full of shops and theaters. **Pros:** great location; excellent service; free Internet access. **Cons:** pricey restaurant; cramped gym; several blocks from the nearest métro. ⑤ *Rooms from: €301* ✉ *20 rue LaFayette, 9e, Grands Boulevards* ☎ *01–55–33–22–25* ⊕ *www.hotelbanke.com* ⤴ *91 rooms* ⍾ *No meals* Ⓜ *Opéra* ✛ *2:B4.*

$$
HOTEL

⌖ **Hôtel Chopin.** A unique mainstay of the district, the Chopin, set within the magnificent historic Passage Jouffroy, recalls its 1846 birth date with a creaky-floored lobby, aged woodwork, and its own homey charm. **Pros:** unique location; close to major métro station; great nightlife district. **Cons:** thin walls; single rooms are very small; few amenities. ⑤ *Rooms from: €132* ✉ *10 bd. Montmartre, 46 passage Jouffroy, 9e, Grands Boulevards* ☎ *01–47–70–58–10* ⊕ *www.hotelchopin.fr* ⤴ *36 rooms* ⍾ *No meals* Ⓜ *Grands Boulevards* ✛ *2:C4.*

$$$$ HOTEL Fodor's Choice ★ ▦ **Hôtel de Nell.** Tucked in a picturesque corner of a chic, up-and-coming neighborhood ripe for exploration, the serenely beautiful Hôtel de Nell offers contemporary luxury with clean lines and uncluttered spaces. **Pros:** great dining and bar on premises; interesting neighborhood to explore; beautiful rooms. **Cons:** area deserted at night; far from the major Paris attractions; no formal spa. *⑤ Rooms from: €350 ⊠ 9 rue du Conservatoire, 9e, Grands Boulevards ☎ 01–44–83–83–60 ⊕ www. hoteldenell.com ⬎ 33 rooms* ⦿*No meals* Ⓜ *Bonne Nouvelle* ⊹ *2:D4.*

$$$$ HOTEL ▦ **Hôtel de Noailles.** With a nod to the work of postmodern designers like Putman and Starck, this stylish boutique hotel is both contemporary and cozy. **Pros:** 15- to 20-minute walk to the Louvre and Opéra; a block from the airport bus; free Wi-Fi. **Cons:** no interesting views; some bathrooms in need of renovation; small elevator. *⑤ Rooms from: €345 ⊠ 9 rue de la Michodière, 2e, Grands Boulevards ☎ 01–47–42–92–90 ⊕ www.hotelnoailles.com ⬎ 56 rooms* ⦿*No meals* Ⓜ *Opéra* ⊹ *2:B5.*

$$$ HOTEL Fodor's Choice ★ ▦ **Hotel des Grands Boulevards.** Amid the hustle and bustle of the Grands Boulevards may not seem like the most serene or desirable place to lay your head, but this Revolution-era sanctuary tucked back in a vibrant up-and-coming neighborhood is an island of calm—and a very chic one at that. **Pros:** beautifully designed rooms; chic on-site cocktail bar and restaurant; lots of outdoor spaces and some fabulous private terraces. **Cons:** balconies can be noisy; not every room has a balcony; some rooms quite tiny. *⑤ Rooms from: €200 ⊠ 17 Boulevard Poissonnière, 2e, Grands Boulevards ☎ 01–85–73–33–33 ⬎ 50 rooms* Ⓜ *Bonne Nouvelle, Grands Boulevards* ⊹ *2:D4.*

15

$$ HOTEL Fodor's Choice ★ ▦ **Hôtel du Temps.** This stylish hotel is perfect for visitors looking for bargain lodgings in a crossroads neighborhood ripe for exploration. **Pros:** friendly service; close to métro; terrific neighborhood. **Cons:** tiny bathrooms; rooms facing Rue La Fayette can be noisy; bathrooms not that private. *⑤ Rooms from: €160 ⊠ 11 rue de Montholon, 9e, Grands Boulevards ☎ 01–47–70–37–16 ⊕ hotel-du-temps.fr ⬎ 23 rooms* ⦿*No meals* Ⓜ *Cadet, Poissonière* ⊹ *2:D3.*

$$$ HOTEL ▦ **Hôtel George Sand.** This family-run hotel, where the 19th-century writer George Sand once lived, feels fresh and modern while preserving some of its original architectural details. **Pros:** near two famous department stores; historic atmosphere; simple but comfortable rooms. **Cons:** noisy street; can hear métro rumble on lower floors; some rooms are quite small. *⑤ Rooms from: €250 ⊠ 26 rue des Mathurins, 9e, Grands Boulevards ☎ 01–47–42–63–47 ⊕ www.hotelgeorgesand.com ⬎ 20 rooms* ⦿*No meals* Ⓜ *Havre Caumartin* ⊹ *1:H4.*

$$ HOTEL ▦ **Hôtel Gramont Opéra.** Near the Opéra Garnier and some of the city's best department stores, this family-owned boutique hotel has lots of little extras that make it a great value. **Pros:** good breakfast buffet with eggs made to order; personalized and professional service; connecting rooms for families. **Cons:** singles have no desk; small bathrooms; elevator doesn't go to top-floor rooms. *⑤ Rooms from: €133 ⊠ 22 rue Gramont, 2e, Grands Boulevards ☎ 01–42–96–85–90 ⊕ www.hotel-gramont-opera.com ⬎ 25 rooms* ⦿*No meals* Ⓜ *Quatre-Septembre* ⊹ *2:B4.*

$$
HOTEL
⊞ **Hôtel Langlois.** This darling hotel gained a reputation as one of the more atmospheric budget sleeps in the city, although rates have since crept up. **Pros:** excellent views from the top floor; close to department stores and Opéra Garnier; historic decor. **Cons:** noisy street; a bit out of the way; some sagging furniture and worn fabrics. ⑤ *Rooms from:* €162 ✉ 63 rue St-Lazare, 9e, Grands Boulevards ☎ 01–48–74–78–24 ⊕ www.hotel-langlois.com ⟲ 27 rooms* ¶◉¶ No meals Ⓜ Trinité ✦ 2:A3.*

$$$$
HOTEL
⊞ **Hôtel Westminster.** On one of the most prestigious streets in Paris, between the Opéra and Place Vendôme, this mid-19th-century inn happily retains its old-world feel. **Pros:** prestigious location near major sights; soothing steam room; popular jazz bar. **Cons:** a bit old-fashioned; some rooms overlook an air shaft; poor bathroom plumbing. ⑤ *Rooms from:* €297 ✉ 13 rue de la Paix, 2e, Grands Boulevards ☎ 01–42–61–57–46 ⊕ www.warwickhotels.com/westminster ⟲ 102 rooms* ¶◉¶ No meals Ⓜ Opéra ✦ 2:A5.*

$$$
HOTEL
Fodor'sChoice
★
⊞ **The Hoxton Paris.** After wowing guests in London and Amsterdam, the Hoxton chain of trendsetting hotels applied their winning urban-chic formula to Paris: find a cool neighborhood, pare down, and tune in. **Pros:** cool neighborhood with lots to explore; historic mansion setting; wonderful bar scene. **Cons:** off-the-radar-neighborhood is not for everyone; average dining; most affordable rooms are very no-frills. ⑤ *Rooms from:* €200 ✉ 30–32 rue du Sentier, 2e, Grands Boulevards ☎ 01–85–65–75–00 ⊕ www.thehoxton.com ⟲ 172 rooms Ⓜ Grands Boulevards, Bonne Nouvelle ✦ 2:D5.*

$$$$
HOTEL
⊞ **La Maison Favart.** An atmospheric indoor pool, relaxing sauna, and around-the-clock concierge are some of the reasons this jewel-box hotel is fast becoming a popular choice for travelers. **Pros:** lovely rooms and interior design; spacious bathrooms; central location within walking distance of the sights. **Cons:** high demand for best rooms; impractical use of space in some rooms and bathrooms; no spa. ⑤ *Rooms from:* €340 ✉ 5 rue de Marivaux, 2e, Grands Boulevards ☎ 01–42–97–59–83 ⊕ www.lamaisonfavart.com ⟲ 39 rooms* ¶◉¶ No meals Ⓜ Quatre-Septembre ✦ 2:B4.*

$$$
HOTEL
⊞ **Le Swann Hôtel.** This delightful modern *hôtel littéraire* pays homage to France's greatest literary lion, Marcel Proust. **Pros:** not far from the big department stores; close to public transport; views from some rooms. **Cons:** some street noise; most rooms on the small size; bathrooms are minuscule. ⑤ *Rooms from:* €190 ✉ 15 rue de Constantinople, 8e, Grands Boulevards ☎ 01–45–22–80–80 ⊕ www.hotel-leswann.com ⟲ 81 rooms* ¶◉¶ No meals Ⓜ Europe, Villiers, Rome ✦ 1:G2.*

$$$$
HOTEL
Fodor'sChoice
★
⊞ **Park Hyatt Paris Vendôme.** Understated luxury with a contemporary Zen vibe differentiates this Hyatt from its more classic neighbors between Place Vendôme and Opéra Garnier. **Pros:** stylish urban-chic design; the latest technology; only in-suite spas in Paris. **Cons:** as part of the Hyatt chain, it can feel anonymous; many corporate events held here; very expensive. ⑤ *Rooms from:* €850 ✉ 3–5 rue de la Paix, 2e, Grands Boulevards ☎ 01–58–71–12–34 ⊕ www.hyatt.com/en-US/hotel/france/park-hyatt-paris-vendome/parph ⟲ 148 rooms* ¶◉¶ No meals Ⓜ Concorde, Opéra ✦ 2:A5.*

$$$$ ⚡ **W Paris-Opéra.** Located near Opéra Garnier, this 91-room hotel—
HOTEL the first W in France—feels part Moulin Rouge, part art gallery, with
cheeky and irreverent touches strewn throughout. **Pros:** coveted location in historic 19th-century building; excellent restaurant; cutting-edge
rooms with comfortable beds. **Cons:** fee for Wi-Fi; rooms and public
spaces feel claustrophobic; noisy neighborhood. $ *Rooms from: €490*
✉ *4 rue Meyerbeer, 9e, Grands Boulevards* ☎ *01–77–48–94–94* ⊕ *www.*
wparisopera.com ⟿ *91 rooms* ❘❍❘ *No meals* Ⓜ *Chaussée d'Antin–La*
Fayette ✛ *2:A4.*

MONTMARTRE

Like a village unto itself, off-the-beaten-path Montmartre and its
equally picturesque hotels provide a homey retreat after a day of sightseeing. There's much to explore here, and the old cobbled streets and
hidden historic corners harbor lodgings as varied as old, gated mansions
and quaint mom-and-pop hotels.

$ ⚡ **Ermitage Hôtel Sacré Coeur.** It's definitely a hike from the nearest métro
HOTEL station, but this family-run hotel in a Napoléon III–era building has a
friendly vibe and is filled with mirrored armoires, elegant chandeliers,
and other antiques. **Pros:** charming neighborhood; quiet district; warm
welcome from staff. **Cons:** no credit cards accepted; no facilities; handheld showers. $ *Rooms from: €110* ✉ *24 rue Lamarck, 18e, Mont-*
martre ☎ *01–42–64–79–22* ⊕ *www.ermitagesacrecoeur.fr* ⟿ *5 rooms*
❘❍❘ *Breakfast* Ⓜ *Lamarck–Caulaincourt* ✛ *2:C1.*

$$ ⚡ **Hotel Terrass.** If you feel like being away from it all, but in a reason-
HOTEL ably priced, fairly self-sufficient setting with a good on-site restaurant
FAMILY and a chic bar with stupendous views, this is the place. **Pros:** panoramic
Fodor's Choice views of all Paris; awesome terrace bar; welcoming common areas with
★ complimentary coffee. **Cons:** basic rooms are small; restaurant could
be better; some street noise. $ *Rooms from: €140* ✉ *12–14 rue Joseph*
de Maistre, 18e, Montmartre ☎ *01–46–06–72–85* ⊕ *www.terrass-hotel.*
com ⟿ *92 rooms* ❘❍❘ *No meals* Ⓜ *Blanche, Abbesses* ✛ *2:A1.*

THE MARAIS

A major shopping Mecca and the center of gay and Jewish life, the
trendy Marais is a vibrant and stylish mosaic in motion. Here elegant
grande-dame hotels abut hidden gardens and small boutique hotels har-
bor chic cocktail bars where guests can blend in with trendsetting locals.

$$$$ ⚡ **Hôtel Bourg Tibourg.** Scented candles and subdued lighting announce
HOTEL the blend of romance and contemplation cultivated by the Hôtel Bourg
Tibourg. **Pros:** in the heart of the trendy Marais; moderate prices; great
nightlife district. **Cons:** rooms tend to be small and poorly lit; no hotel
restaurant; lounge area gets crowded. $ *Rooms from: €290* ✉ *19 rue*
du Bourg Tibourg, 4e, Marais Quarter ☎ *01–42–78–47–39* ⊕ *bourgti-*
bourg.com ⟿ *30 rooms* ❘❍❘ *No meals* Ⓜ *Hôtel de Ville* ✛ *4:E2.*

$$$ ⚡ **Hôtel Caron.** On a relatively quiet side street, this contemporary bou-
HOTEL tique bed-and-breakfast may be petite, but many thoughtful extras
make it as accommodating as bigger hotels. **Pros:** excellent location

15

in center of Paris; friendly staff; great amenities. **Cons:** only enough storage for small suitcases; no hotel restaurant or bar; tight space in bathrooms. $ *Rooms from:* €249 ⊠ *3 rue Caron, 4e, Marais Quarter* ☎ *01–40–29–02–94* ⊕ *www.hotelcaron.com* ⇆ *18 rooms* ⦿| *No meals* Ⓜ *St-Paul* ✛ *4:G2.*

$$ ▦ **Hôtel Caron de Beaumarchais.** For that traditional French feeling, book

HOTEL   a room at this intimate, affordable, romantic hotel—the theme is the

Fodor's Choice   work of former next-door-neighbor Pierre-Augustin Caron de Beau-

★   marchais, a supplier of military aid to American revolutionaries and the playwright who penned *The Marriage of Figaro* and *The Barber of Seville*. **Pros:** cozy Parisian decor of yesteryear; breakfast in bed served until noon; excellent location within easy walking distance of major monuments. **Cons:** small rooms with few amenities; busy street of bars and cafés can be noisy; may feel old-fashioned for younger crowd. $ *Rooms from:* €175 ⊠ *12 rue Vieille-du-Temple, 4e, Marais Quarter* ☎ *01–42–72–34–12* ⊕ *www.carondebeaumarchais.com* ⇆ *19 rooms* ⦿| *No meals* Ⓜ *Hôtel de Ville* ✛ *4:F2.*

$$$ ▦ **Hôtel de la Bretonnerie.** In a 17th-century *hôtel particulier* (town house)

HOTEL   on a side street in the Marais, this small hotel with exposed wooden beams and traditional styling sits a few minutes from the Centre Pompidou and the numerous bars and cafés of Rue Vieille du Temple. **Pros:** typical Parisian character; moderate prices; free Wi-Fi access. **Cons:** quality and size of the rooms vary greatly; no air-conditioning; rooms facing street can be noisy. $ *Rooms from:* €185 ⊠ *22 rue Ste-Croix-de-la-Bretonnerie, 4e, Marais Quarter* ☎ *01–48–87–77–63* ⊕ *www.hotelparismaraisbretonnerie.com* ⇆ *29 rooms* ⦿| *No meals* Ⓜ *Hôtel de Ville* ✛ *4:E1.*

$$$$ ▦ **Hôtel Duo.** For this hotel in the heart of the trendy Marais district,

HOTEL   architect Jean-Philippe Nuel was commissioned to bring things up to date with bold colors and dramatic lighting; some rooms still have the original 16th-century beams but the overall feel is casual urban chic. **Pros:** central location near shops and cafés; walking distance to major monuments; good amenities. **Cons:** noisy neighborhood; service not always delivered with a smile; small standard rooms and bathrooms. $ *Rooms from:* €300 ⊠ *11 rue du Temple, 4e, Marais Quarter* ☎ *01–42–72–72–22* ⊕ *www.duoparis.com* ⇆ *58 rooms* ⦿| *No meals* Ⓜ *Hôtel de Ville* ✛ *4:E1.*

$$$ ▦ **Hôtel Jules & Jim.** In the less-traveled corner of the trendy Marais dis-

HOTEL   trict, this contemporary boutique hotel feels almost like an art gallery.

Fodor's Choice   **Pros:** bright and modern; stylish design; close to public transportation.

★   **Cons:** the small "Jules" rooms are best for those traveling light or staying just one night; no restaurant; no in-room coffeemakers. $ *Rooms from:* €240 ⊠ *11 rue des Gravilliers, 3e, Marais Quarter* ☎ *01–44–54–13–13* ⊕ *www.hoteljulesetjim.com* ⇆ *22 rooms, 1 duplex* ⦿| *No meals* Ⓜ *Arts et Métiers* ✛ *2:F6.*

$$$$ ▦ **Maison Breguet.** This classy addition to the Parisian five-star scene

HOTEL   is chic, well-located, and full of lovely surprises—including an eight-

FAMILY   person "maisonette" and a super-stylish restaurant and bar. **Pros:** walk-

Fodor's Choice   ing distance of the Marais, Bastille, Canal St-Martin, and the hip 11th

★   arrondissement,; small but nice pool; great in-house restaurant, bar, and dining terrace. **Cons:** views aren't amazing; not a budget hotel; spa treatments in-room only. $ *Rooms from: €280* ⊠ *8 rue Breguet, 11e, Marais Quarter* 🕾 *01–58–30–32–31* ⊕ *www.maisonbreguet.com* ⟿ *62 rooms* ¶○¶ *No meals* Ⓜ *Bastille, Richard Lenoir* ✛ *4:H2.*

$$$$
HOTEL

🔲 **Pavillon de la Reine.** Hidden off regal Place des Vosges behind a stunning garden courtyard, this enchanting château has gigantic beams, chunky stone pillars, and a weathered fireplace that speaks to its 1612 origins. **Pros:** historic character; quiet setting; free bicycles for guests. **Cons:** expensive for the area and the size of the rooms; the nearest métro is a few blocks away; no uniform theme for interior design. $ *Rooms from: €440* ⊠ *28 pl. des Vosges, 3e, Marais Quarter* 🕾 *01–40–29–19–19* ⊕ *www.pavillon-de-la-reine.com* ⟿ *54 rooms* ¶○¶ *No meals* Ⓜ *Bastille, St-Paul* ✛ *4:G2.*

EASTERN PARIS

15

Neighborhoods in the east of Paris—Bastille, République, Oberkampf, and hip Canal St-Martin—are quintessentially young, vibrant, fun, and eclectic. Among the many bars and bistros you'll find everything from stylish boutique hotels to sleek eco-centric sanctuaries. These neighborhoods can be lively at night, so look for lodgings tucked away on a smaller street, especially near the Bastille, or book a courtyard-facing room.

BASTILLE

$$
HOTEL

🔲 **Hôtel Bastille de Launay.** The no-frills decor might seem spartan at first, but this tidy boutique hotel also offers modern amenities like free Wi-Fi, a perfect location a few blocks from the regal Place des Vosges, and outstanding prices for the area. **Pros:** homey touches; attentive service; reasonably spacious for the neighborhood. **Cons:** tiny elevator; some small rooms; basic bathrooms. $ *Rooms from: €153* ⊠ *42 rue Amelot, 11e, Bastille* 🕾 *01–47–00–88–11* ⊕ *www.bastilledelaunay-hotel-paris.com* ⟿ *35 rooms* ¶○¶ *No meals* Ⓜ *Chemin Vert* ✛ *4:H1.*

$$
HOTEL
Fodor's Choice
★

🔲 **Hôtel Mama Shelter.** Close to Père-Lachaise in the up-and-coming 20e arrondissement, this large hotel has a fun and funky interior designed by Philippe Starck. **Pros:** trendy design without designer prices; cool vibe; entertainment center in each room. **Cons:** 10-minute walk to métro; nearby club can be noisy; small rooms. $ *Rooms from: €159* ⊠ *109 rue de Bagnolet, 20e, Bastille* 🕾 *01–43–48–48–48* ⊕ *www.mamashelter.com* ⟿ *172 rooms* ¶○¶ *No meals* Ⓜ *Gambetta* ✛ *2:H3.*

$$
HOTEL
FAMILY
Fodor's Choice
★

🔲 **Hotel Whistler.** If proximity to the Gare du Nord is what you're after, or if you'd like to discover an authentic Paris neighborhood full of locals-only treasures, look no further than this stylish, travel-themed boutique hotel. **Pros:** close to transport to anywhere in Paris; excellent prices; fun design. **Cons:** busy area around the train station; not in the heart of Paris; cheaper rooms on the small side. $ *Rooms from: €159* ⊠ *36 rue de Saint-Quentin, 10e, Eastern Paris* 🕾 *01–53–20–09–09* ⊕ *www.whistlerparis.com* ⟿ *31 rooms* ¶○¶ *No meals* Ⓜ *Gare du Nord, Gare du l'Est* ✛ *2:E2.*

CANAL ST-MARTIN

$$
HOTEL
Fodor's Choice
★

Ⓘ **Hôtel Fabric.** This urban-chic hotel tucked away on an old artisan street is fully in tune with the pulse of the lively Oberkampf neighborhood, close to fabulous nightlife, cocktail bars, restaurants, bakeries, and shopping (and the Marais and Canal St-Martin). **Pros:** all-you-can-eat breakfast for €17; lots of great sightseeing within walking distance; warm and helpful staff. **Cons:** rooms can be noisy; very popular so book well in advance; might be too party-focused for some. Ⓢ *Rooms from: €153* ✉ *31 rue de la Folie Méricourt, 11e, Canal St-Martin* ☎ *01–43–57–27–00* ⊕ *www.hotelfabric.com* ➥ *33 rooms* ⦿ *No meals* Ⓜ *Saint-Ambroise, Oberkampf* ✛ *2:H6.*

$$
HOTEL

Ⓘ **Hôtel Taylor.** Tucked away on a tiny one-way street between République and Canal St-Martin, Hôtel Taylor offers large rooms (by Parisians standards) at affordable prices in the edgy 10e arrondissement. **Pros:** close to the métro; Wi-Fi available in rooms; larger than average rooms. **Cons:** bathrooms and some rooms need refurbishment; street can seem intimidating at night; open-plan bathrooms. Ⓢ *Rooms from: €152* ✉ *6 rue Taylor, 10e, Canal St-Martin* ☎ *01–42–40–11–01* ⊕ *www.paris-hotel-taylor.com* ➥ *54 rooms* ⦿ *No meals* Ⓜ *République* ✛ *2:F5.*

$$$
HOTEL
Fodor's Choice
★

Ⓘ **Le Citizen Hôtel.** Boasting direct views over the historic Canal St-Martin and a setting close to the Marais, Le Citizen features a minimalist-chic decor, high-tech touches like loaner iPads, and a cool eastern Paris vibe. **Pros:** trendy neighborhood; cool perks; friendly, attentive staff. **Cons:** smallest rooms are best for one person; noisy street; about 20 minutes by métro from the main attractions. Ⓢ *Rooms from: €199* ✉ *96 quai de Jemmapes, 10e, Canal St-Martin* ☎ *01–83–62–55–50* ⊕ *www.lecitizenhotel.com* ➥ *12 rooms* ⦿ *Breakfast* Ⓜ *Jacques-Bonsergent* ✛ *2:G4.*

RÉPUBLIQUE

$$$$
HOTEL

Ⓘ **Le Général Hôtel.** Designer Jean-Philippe Nuel applied his sleek styling to Le Général, one of Paris's first affordable, high-design hotels. **Pros:** friendly service; smart design; in popular nightlife district. **Cons:** noisy neighborhood; not within easy walking distance of major tourist attractions; basic breakfast. Ⓢ *Rooms from: €300* ✉ *5–7 rue Rampon, 11e, République* ☎ *01–47–00–41–57* ⊕ *www.legeneralhotel.com* ➥ *46 rooms* ⦿ *No meals* Ⓜ *République; Oberkampf* ✛ *2:G5.*

PÈRE LACHAISE

$$$
B&B/INN
FAMILY
Fodor's Choice
★

Ⓘ **Eden Lodge.** Set back in a hidden tree-shaded courtyard off an uninspiring street minutes from Père Lachaise cemetery, no lodging in the capital is quite as unobtrusively fabulous as this trailblazing, 100% sustainable, five-room eco-lodge. **Pros:** 100% sustainable; tons of great restaurants in the neighborhood; lovely terraces in all rooms. **Cons:** low-key neighborhood; no in-house bar; not on the prettiest street. Ⓢ *Rooms from: €225* ✉ *175 rue de Charonne, Père Lachaise* ☎ *01–43–56–73–24* ⊕ *www.edenlodgeparis.net* ➥ *5 rooms* ⦿ *Free Breakfast* Ⓜ *Père Lachaise, Charonne* ✛ *4:H3.*

LATIN QUARTER

Leafy and bookish, this quiet *quartier* at the heart of the city retains all the charm of Old Paris, as do its hotels, which tend to be smaller, family-owned establishments or budget chains with character.

$$$$ **The Five Hôtel.** Small is beautiful at this design hotel on a quiet street
HOTEL near the Rue Mouffetard market and the Latin Quarter. **Pros:** unique design; personalized welcome; quiet side street. **Cons:** most rooms are too small for excessive baggage; the nearest métro is a 15-minute walk; most rooms only have showers. $ *Rooms from: €255* ✉ *3 rue Flatters, 5e, Latin Quarter* ☎ *01–43–31–74–21* ⊕ *www.thefivehotel.com* ⌕ *25 rooms* ⦶ *No meals* Ⓜ *Gobelins* ✛ *4:D6.*

$$ **Hôtel Collège de France.** Exposed stone walls, wooden beams, and
HOTEL medieval artwork echo the style of the Musée Cluny, two blocks from this charming, family-run hotel. **Pros:** walk to Rive Gauche sights; free Wi-Fi; ceiling fans. **Cons:** thin walls between rooms; no air-conditioning; old-fashioned bathrooms. $ *Rooms from: €140* ✉ *7 rue Thénard, 5e, Latin Quarter* ☎ *01–43–26–78–36* ⊕ *www.hotel-collegedefrance.com* ⌕ *29 rooms* ⦶ *No meals* Ⓜ *Maubert–Mutualité, St-Michel, Cluny–La Sorbonne* ✛ *4:D4.*

$$ **Hôtel des Grandes Écoles.** Distributed among a trio of three-story build-
HOTEL ings set back in a quiet cobbled courtyard, Madame Le Floch's rooms have a distinct grandmotherly vibe because of their flowery wallpaper and lace bedspreads, but they're spacious for this part of Paris. **Pros:** close to Latin Quarter nightlife spots; lovely courtyard; good value. **Cons:** uphill walk from the métro; walls are thin, meaning some internal noise; few amenities (and no television in room). $ *Rooms from: €160* ✉ *75 rue du Cardinal Lemoine, 5e, Latin Quarter* ☎ *01–43–26–79–23* ⊕ *www.hotel-grandes-ecoles.com* ⌕ *51 rooms* ⦶ *No meals* Ⓜ *Cardinal Lemoine* ✛ *4:E5.*

$$$$ **Hôtel des Grands Hommes.** The "great men" this hotel honors with its
HOTEL name rest in peace within the towering Panthéon monument across the street. **Pros:** major Latin Quarter sights within walking distance; comfortable and attractive rooms; lovely views from many rooms. **Cons:** closest métro is a 10-minute walk; neighborhood can be loud after dark; high price for this area. $ *Rooms from: €300* ✉ *17 pl. du Panthéon, 5e, Latin Quarter* ☎ *01–46–34–19–60* ⊕ *www.hoteldesgrandshommes.com* ⌕ *30 rooms* ⦶ *No meals* Ⓜ *RER: Luxembourg* ✛ *4:D4.*

$$$ **Hôtel Henri IV Rive Gauche.** About 50 paces from Notre-Dame and the
HOTEL Seine, this elegant hotel has identical, impeccable rooms with beige and
FAMILY rose linens and framed prints of architectural drawings. **Pros:** comfortable decor; close to major sights and RER station; friendly reception staff. **Cons:** on a busy street full of late-night bars; single rooms are small; furnishings showing their age. $ *Rooms from: €230* ✉ *9–11 rue St-Jacques, 5e, Latin Quarter* ☎ *01–46–33–20–20* ⊕ *www.henri-paris-hotel.com* ⌕ *23 rooms* ⦶ *No meals* Ⓜ *St-Michel* ✛ *4:D3.*

$$$ **Hôtel La Manufacture.** Just behind Place d'Italie and a short stroll from
HOTEL both the Jardin des Plantes and Rue Mouffetard, La Manufacture's lesser-known location makes you feel like a *vrai* (real) Parisian. **Pros:** easy access to major métro and bus lines; safe, nontouristy district; bright breakfast room. **Cons:** street noise; a long stroll to the center of

15

Paris; small rooms. $ *Rooms from: €180* ✉ *8 rue Philippe de Champagne, 13e, Latin Quarter* ☎ *01–45–35–45–25* ⊕ *www.hotel-la-manufacture.com* ↻ *57 rooms* ⦿*No meals* Ⓜ *Place d'Italie* ✛ *4:G6.*

$$$ 🛗 **Hotel Monge.** Chic, cozy, and welcoming, you couldn't land in a more
HOTEL charming—and reasonably priced—small boutique hotel in Paris. **Pros:**
Fodor's Choice excellent neighborhood close to sights and legendary markets; great
★ views from balconies; lovely spa. **Cons:** not all rooms have balconies; open-design showers; quiet neighborhood with few restaurants.
$ *Rooms from: €250* ✉ *55 rue Monge, 5e, Latin Quarter* ☎ *01–43–54–55–55* ⊕ *www.hotelmonge.com* ↻ *30 rooms* ⦿*No meals* Ⓜ *Jussieu, Cardinal Lemoine, Place Monge* ✛ *4:E5.*

$$$ 🛗 **Hôtel Notre Dame Saint-Michel.** If you love the quirky and eclectic fash-
HOTEL ions of Christian Lacroix and don't mind hauling your bags up some
steps, this unique boutique hotel overlooking Notre-Dame may be for
you. **Pros:** beautiful design by Christian Lacroix; stunning views of the
cathedral and river; comfortable beds. **Cons:** stairs can be tricky with
large bags; no minibar in rooms; some low ceilings. $ *Rooms from:*
€180 ✉ *1 quai Saint-Michel, 5e, Latin Quarter* ☎ *01–43–54–20–43*
⊕ *www.hotelnotredameparis.com* ↻ *26 rooms* ⦿*No meals* Ⓜ *St-Michel* ✛ *4:D3.*

$$$$ 🛗 **Hôtel Résidence Henri IV.** This small hotel on a quiet cul-de-sac is perfect
HOTEL for travelers—especially those with children—who need a home base
FAMILY where they can kick back, make their own meals, and feel at home. **Pros:**
handy kitchenettes; close to Latin Quarter attractions; charming rooms.
Cons: closest métro is a few blocks away; some rooms on the small side;
decor a bit dated. $ *Rooms from: €299* ✉ *50 rue des Bernadins, 5e,*
Latin Quarter ☎ *01–44–41–31–81* ⊕ *www.residencehenri4.com* ↻ *8*
rooms, 5 apartments ⦿*No meals* Ⓜ *Maubert–Mutualité* ✛ *4:D4.*

$$$ 🛗 **Hôtel Saint-Jacques.** Quaint is the word that springs to mind at this
HOTEL well-located Latin Quarter hotel, bedecked with faux-marble trompe-
l'oeil, Renoiresque murals on walls and ceilings, and all those cozy
details that remind you of a classic Parisian living room. **Pros:** unique
Parisian decor; close to Latin Quarter sights; free Wi-Fi. **Cons:** busy
street makes it noisy in summer; thin walls between rooms; decor needs
some refurbishment. $ *Rooms from: €230* ✉ *35 rue des Écoles, 5e,*
Latin Quarter ☎ *01–44–07–45–45* ⊕ *www.hotelrelaissaintjacques.com*
↻ *38 rooms* ⦿*No meals* Ⓜ *Maubert–Mutualité* ✛ *4:D4.*

$$$ 🛗 **Hotel Seven.** The "seven" may refer to the level of heaven you'll find
HOTEL at this wacky boutique hotel, but most likely it means the seven suites,
where a team of designers and artists were let loose to riff on imaginative themes like Secret Agent, Sublime, and Nuit Chic. **Pros:** fun design
elements; copious breakfast buffet; quiet location near Mouffetard market street. **Cons:** small closets; several blocks to closest métro; expensive
for so few amenities. $ *Rooms from: €203* ✉ *20 rue Berthollet, 5e,*
Latin Quarter ☎ *01–43–31–47–52* ⊕ *www.sevenhotelparis.com* ↻ *35*
rooms ⦿*No meals* Ⓜ *Censier–Daubentin* ✛ *4:D6.*

ST-GERMAIN-DES-PRÉS

True to its Rive Gauche bourgeois-bohemian vibe, lodgings here are an eclectic bunch. You'll find everything from posh L'Hôtel (Oscar Wilde's final dwelling) to smaller hotels with loads of character as well as some good budget options.

$$$$
HOTEL
FAMILY

Artus Hôtel. One of the best things about this comfortable six-story hotel is that it's smack in the middle of Rue de Buci in the lively St-Germain-des-Prés district. **Pros:** helpful concierge; excellent location on a market street; kid-friendly vibe. **Cons:** rooms are small and dated for the price; neighborhood is quite busy; Mad Men-esque decor not for everyone. $ *Rooms from: €300* ✉ *34 rue de Buci, 6e, St-Germain-des-Prés* ☎ *01–43–29–07–20* ⊕ *www.artushotel.com* ➹ *27 rooms* ¶⊙ *No meals* Ⓜ *Mabillon* ✢ *4:B3.*

$$$$
HOTEL

Hôtel Bel Ami. A short stroll from the famous Café de Flore, the Bel Ami hides its past as an 18th-century textile factory behind low-slung furnishings, computer stations, and flat-screen TVs. **Pros:** central St-Germain-des-Prés location; feels completely up-to-date; spacious fitness center and spa. **Cons:** some guests report loud noise between rooms; pretty pricey; books up quickly. $ *Rooms from: €590* ✉ *7–11 rue St-Benoît, 6e, St-Germain-des-Prés* ☎ *01–42–61–53–53* ⊕ *www. hotelbelami-paris.com* ➹ *108 rooms* ¶⊙ *No meals* Ⓜ *St-Germain-des-Prés* ✢ *4:B2.*

$$$$
HOTEL
FAMILY

Hôtel d'Aubusson. The showpiece at this 17th-century town house in the heart of St-Germain-des-Prés is the stunning front lobby, spanned by massive beams and a gigantic stone fireplace reminiscent of French aristocratic homes of yore. **Pros:** central location near shops and a market street; spacious rooms; on-site café and popular jazz club. **Cons:** some rooms lack character; street and bar can be noisy; very touristy. $ *Rooms from: €450* ✉ *33 rue Dauphine, 6e, St-Germain-des-Prés* ☎ *01–43–29–43–43* ⊕ *www.hoteldaubusson.com* ➹ *49 rooms* ¶⊙ *No meals* Ⓜ *Odéon* ✢ *4:C2.*

$$$$
HOTEL
Fodor's Choice
★

Hôtel de l'Abbaye. An 18th-century convent, this atmospheric hotel on a tranquil side street near St-Sulpice welcomes you with a cobblestone ante-courtyard, lovely rooms, and a spacious garden terrace. **Pros:** tranquil setting; upscale neighborhood; good value packages. **Cons:** rooms differ greatly in size and style; some bathrooms are quite small; old-fashioned decor a bit somber. $ *Rooms from: €280* ✉ *10 rue Cassette, 6e, St-Germain-des-Prés* ☎ *01–45–44–38–11* ⊕ *www.hotelabbayeparis. com* ➹ *44 rooms* ¶⊙ *Breakfast* Ⓜ *St-Sulpice* ✢ *4:A4.*

$$$$
HOTEL

Hôtel Duc de Saint-Simon. For pure French flavor, including rooms decorated in floral chintz, head to this intimate hotel in a hidden location between Boulevard St-Germain and Rue du Bac. Four of the antiques-filled rooms have spacious terraces overlooking the courtyard. **Pros:** upscale neighborhood close to St-Germain-des-Prés; historic character; friendly service. **Cons:** rooms in the annex are smaller and have no elevator; cramped bathrooms; no room service. $ *Rooms from: €295* ✉ *14 rue St-Simon, 7e, St-Germain-des-Prés* ☎ *01–44–39–20–20* ⊕ *www.hotelducdesaintsimon.com* ➹ *34 rooms* ¶⊙ *No meals* Ⓜ *Rue du Bac* ✢ *3:H2.*

15

$$$
HOTEL
Fodor'sChoice
★

⊡ **Hôtel Millésime.** The graceful stone archway of this 17th-century city mansion in St-Germain-des-Prés was the original entrance to the Saint Germain Abbey, but now leads to a captivating boutique hotel that's the height of Left Bank style. **Pros:** upscale shopping nearby; complimentary mobile phone for use throughout your stay; beautiful chic décor. **Cons:** ground-floor rooms can be noisy; elevator stops at the fourth floor; some rooms quite small. ⑤ *Rooms from: €240* ⊠ *15 rue Jacob, 6e, St-Germain-des-Prés* ☎ *01–44–07–97–97* ⊕ *www.millesimehotel.com* ⌁ *20 rooms* ⃝ *No meals* Ⓜ *St-Germain-des-Prés* ✦ *4:B2.*

$$$$
HOTEL

⊡ **Hôtel Odéon Saint-Germain.** Exposed stone walls and original wooden beams give this 16th-century building typical Rive Gauche character, and designer Jacques Garcia's generous use of striped taffeta curtains, velvet upholstery, and plush carpeting imbues it with the distinct luxury of St-Germain-des-Prés. **Pros:** free Internet; luxuriously appointed rooms; in an upscale shopping district near Jardin Luxembourg. **Cons:** small rooms a challenge for those with extra-large suitcases; tiny elevator; prices high for room size and average service. ⑤ *Rooms from: €260* ⊠ *13 rue St-Sulpice, 6e, St-Germain-des-Prés* ☎ *01–43–25–70–11* ⊕ *www.hotelparisodeonsaintgermain.com* ⌁ *27 rooms* ⃝ *No meals* Ⓜ *Odéon* ✦ *4:B3.*

$$$$
HOTEL
Fodor'sChoice
★

⊡ **Hôtel Recamier.** This discreet boutique hotel in a quiet corner overlooking Eglise St-Sulpice is perfect if you're seeking a romantic and cozy hideaway in the sought-after St-Germain-des-Prés district. **Pros:** peaceful garden courtyard; free Wi-Fi and computer station; well-appointed bathrooms. **Cons:** small closets and bathrooms; room service only until 11 pm; no fitness area, spa, or restaurant. ⑤ *Rooms from: €272* ⊠ *3 bis, pl. St-Sulpice, 6e, St-Germain-des-Prés* ☎ *01–43–26–04–89* ⊕ *www. hotelrecamier.com* ⌁ *24 rooms* ⃝ *No meals* Ⓜ *Mabillon* ✦ *4:B3.*

$$$
HOTEL

⊡ **Hôtel Relais Saint-Sulpice.** Sandwiched between St-Sulpice and the Jardin du Luxembourg, this little hotel wins accolades for its location. **Pros:** chic location; close to two métro stations; bright breakfast room and courtyard. **Cons:** some smallish rooms; noise from the street on weekend evenings; poorly designed lighting. ⑤ *Rooms from: €250* ⊠ *3 rue Garancière, 6e, St-Germain-des-Prés* ☎ *01–46–33–99–00* ⊕ *www. relais-saint-sulpice.com* ⌁ *26 rooms* ⃝ *No meals* Ⓜ *St-Germain-des-Prés, St-Sulpice* ✦ *4:B3.*

$$$$
HOTEL
Fodor'sChoice
★

⊡ **Hôtel Verneuil.** Steps away from the Musée d'Orsay and the Louvre sits an intimate and tastefully decorated boutique hotel in the heart of St-Germain. **Pros:** generous morning buffet; near-it-all location on Left Bank; welcoming service. **Cons:** sometimes touristy; no restaurant; no gym or spa. ⑤ *Rooms from: €290* ⊠ *8 rue de Verneuil, 7e, St-Germain-des-Prés* ☎ *01–42–60–82–14* ⊕ *www.hotel-verneuil-saint-germain.com* ⌁ *26 rooms* ⃝ *No meals* Ⓜ *Rue de Bac* ✦ *4:A2.*

$$$$
HOTEL
Fodor'sChoice
★

⊡ **L'Hôtel.** There's something just a bit playful in the air at this sumptuously beautiful boutique hotel, thanks to its history as an 18th-century *pavillon d'amour* (inn for trysts) and as the place where Oscar Wilde died in 1900 (Room 16 to be exact). **Pros:** funky history; elegant bar and restaurant; romantic swimming pool in the basement. **Cons:** some rooms are on the small side; opulent decor not for everyone; only a few rooms have a terrace. ⑤ *Rooms from: €420* ⊠ *13 rue des Beaux-Arts,*

6e, St-Germain-des-Prés ☎ *01–44–41–99–00* ⊕ *www.l-hotel.com* ↘ *20 rooms* ⦿ *No meals* Ⓜ *St-Germain-des-Prés* ✛ *4:B2.*

$$$$
HOTEL
Fodor's Choice
★

☲ **Relais Christine.** You'll find discrete old-world service and tranquility at this venerable (some parts date to the 13th century), five-star hotel set back off a quiet street among its own flagstone courtyard and gardens. **Pros:** lovely spa; beautiful decor; historic character. **Cons:** some duplex rooms have stairs; only four rooms have garden access; small bathtubs. Ⓢ *Rooms from: €375* ✉ *3 rue Christine, 6e, St-Germain-des-Prés* ☎ *01–40–51–60–80* ⊕ *www.relais-christine.com* ↘ *46 rooms* ⦿ *No meals* Ⓜ *Odéon* ✛ *4:C2.*

MONTPARNASSE

Once the famous (or infamous) stomping grounds for the likes of Hemingway, Picasso, Henry Miller, Anaïs Nin, Sartre, and so on— some of whom still remain in the sprawling *cimetière*—Montparnasse has all the trappings of a truly Parisian neighborhood: lively markets, old-fashioned brasseries, and pretty parks. Here you'll find anonymous chain hotels, charming mom-and-pop stops, and everything in between. Focus your search in the more residential areas away from the large boulevards or near the quiet Luxembourg Garden or the Montparnasse cemetery for a real dip into Parisian life.

15

$$$$
HOTEL

☲ **Apostrophe Hotel.** Those enamored of the artistic and literary history of Paris's Left Bank will appreciate this whimsical family-run hotel between Montparnasse and Luxembourg Garden. **Pros:** very friendly multilingual staff; quiet street in charming area; close to métro. **Cons:** limited closet space; little privacy with bathrooms opening up directly to rooms; no restaurant or bar. Ⓢ *Rooms from: €260* ✉ *3 rue de Chevreuse, 6e, Montparnasse* ☎ *01–56–54–31–31* ⊕ *www.apostrophe-hotel.com* ↘ *16 rooms* ⦿ *No meals* Ⓜ *Vavin* ✛ *4:A6.*

$$
HOTEL

☲ **Hôtel Lenox-Montparnasse.** Set in a typical 19th-century Haussmannian building on a small street lined with restaurants and cafés, this six-story hotel gets points for its proximity to the Jardin du Luxembourg and Saint-Germain, as well as for small perks like free Wi-Fi and in-room coffee and tea. **Pros:** lively district close to Montparnasse and St-Germain-des-Prés; well-stocked honesty bar; friendly, multilingual staff. **Cons:** standard rooms are small; noisy street; attracts business clientele. Ⓢ *Rooms from: €166* ✉ *15 rue Delambre, 14e, Montparnasse* ☎ *01–43–35–34–50* ⊕ *www.paris-hotel-lenox.com* ↘ *52 rooms* ⦿ *No meals* Ⓜ *Vavin* ✛ *4:A6.*

$$$
HOTEL

☲ **Hôtel Le Sainte-Beuve.** On a tranquil street between the Jardin du Luxembourg and Montparnasse's cafés and brasseries sits this pleasant six-story hotel. **Pros:** stylish decor; good location without the tourist crowds; close to major métro lines. **Cons:** 20-minute walk to the Latin Quarter or St-Germain-des-Prés; small rooms and elevator; unremarkable service. Ⓢ *Rooms from: €200* ✉ *9 rue Ste-Beuve, 6e, Montparnasse* ☎ *01–45–48–20–07* ⊕ *www.hotelsaintebeuve.com* ↘ *22 rooms* ⦿ *No meals* Ⓜ *Vavin* ✛ *4:A5.*

$$ ▥ **Hôtel Max.** A sleek Scandinavian design with lively splashes of color,
HOTEL bright comfortable rooms, and a warm and welcoming atmosphere
FAMILY make this 19-room hotel one of Paris's best-kept secrets. **Pros:** excellent
Fodor'sChoice prices; intimate feel; quiet residential neighborhood. **Cons:** rooms on the
★ small side; a walk or métro ride to most sights; no bathtubs. $⑤ Rooms
from: €126 ⊠ 34 rue d'Alési, Montparnasse ☎ 0–43–27–60–80 ⊕ www.
hotel-max.fr ↩ 19 rooms ⦿�‖ No meals Ⓜ Alésia ✣ 4:A6.$

$ ▥ **Hôtel Raspail-Montparnasse.** Montparnasse was the art capital of the
HOTEL world in the '20s and '30s, and this hotel captures some of that spirit
FAMILY by naming its rooms after artists who lived in the neighborhood while
Fodor'sChoice also providing excellent service at hard-to-beat prices. **Pros:** some rooms
★ have balconies and/or views of the Eiffel Tower; many markets and cafés
nearby; friendly staff. **Cons:** traffic noise on first floor; some rooms
small; not all rooms have Eiffel Tower views. $⑤ Rooms from: €107
⊠ 203 bd. Raspail, 14e, Montparnasse ☎ 01–43–20–62–86 ⊕ www.
hotelraspailmontparnasse.com ↩ 38 rooms ⦿�‖ No meals Ⓜ Vavin
✣ 4:A6.$

WESTERN PARIS

Hidden away behind the locked gates and grand Haussmann-era build-
ings of this leafy enclave bordering the Bois de Boulogne are the well-
heeled Parisians—diplomats, low-profile French movie stars, and other
Paris aristocracy. Lodgings reflect the more discrete nature of this neigh-
borhood, and what you lose in proximity to central Paris you'll more
than gain in elegance and quiet.

$$$$ ▥ **Renaissance Paris Le Parc Trocadéro Hotel.** This spacious and historic
HOTEL urban retreat in an upscale neighborhood, now part of the Marriott
FAMILY chain, was once the home of Alfred Nobel (who would go on to estab-
lish the famous peace prize). **Pros:** near métro stations; 24-hour fitness
center and room service; quiet area. **Cons:** hosts large groups; long
walk from center of Paris; service could be better. $⑤ Rooms from: €299
⊠ 55–57 av. Raymond-Poincaré, 16e, Western Paris ☎ 01–44–05–66–
66 ⊕ www.marriott.com/hotels/travel/parsp-renaissance-paris-le-parc-
trocadero-hotel ↩ 122 rooms ⦿�‖ No meals Ⓜ Trocadéro ✣ 1:A5.$

$$$$ ▥ **Saint James Paris.** Beyond a stone gateway you'll pass a beautiful
HOTEL fountain on your way into a grand foyer—this renovated 19th-century
mansion feels like a countryside château nestled in the heart of the
busy metropolis. **Pros:** beautiful decor and spacious rooms; generous
breakfast served in-room or in the restaurant; wellness spa. **Cons:**
expensive rates; residential area quiet at night; far from all the major
sights. $⑤ Rooms from: €495 ⊠ 43 av. Bugeaud, 16e, Western Paris
☎ 01–44–05–81–81 ⊕ www.saint-james-paris.com ↩ 49 rooms ⦿�‖ No
meals Ⓜ Porte Dauphine, Victor Hugo, Rue de la Pompe ✣ 1:A5.$

SHOPPING

Updated
by Jennifer
Ladonne

Nothing, but nothing, can push you into the current of Parisian life faster than a few hours of shopping. Follow the lead of locals, who slow to a crawl as their eyes lock on a tempting display. Window-shopping is one of this city's greatest spectator sports; the French call it *lèche-vitrine*—literally, "licking the windows"—which is fitting because many of the displays look good enough to eat.

Store owners here play to sophisticated audiences with voracious appetites for everything from spangly flagship stores to minimalist boutiques to under-the-radar spots in 19th-century glass-roofed *passages*. Parisians know that shopping isn't about the kill, it's about the chase: walking down cobblestone streets looking for items they didn't know they wanted, they're casual yet quick to pounce. They like being seduced by a clever display and relish the performance elements of browsing. Watching them shop can be almost as much fun as shopping yourself.

And nowhere is the infamous Parisian "attitude" more palpable than in the realm of fine shopping—the more *haute* the more hauteur.

Parisians are a proud bunch, and they value decorum. So dress to impress—and remember your manners. You must say *bonjour* upon entering a shop and *merci, au revoir* when leaving, even if it's to no one in particular. Think of it more as announcing your coming and going. Beyond this, protocol becomes less prescribed and more a matter of good judgment. If a salesperson is hovering, there's a reason; let him or her help you. To avoid icy stares, confidence and politeness go a long way.

As for what to buy, the sky's the limit in terms of choices. If your funds aren't limitless, however, take comfort in knowing that treasures can be found on a budget. And if you do decide to indulge, what better place to make that once-in-a-blue-moon splurge? When you get home and friends ask where you got those to-die-for shoes, with a shrug you'll casually say, "These? Oh ... I bought them in Paris."

PLANNING

DUTY-FREE

A value-added tax (or T.V.A.) of 20% is imposed on most consumer goods, and the rate can be as high as 33% for certain luxury items. To qualify for a refund, you must have bought more than €175 of goods in the same store on the same day and have stayed three months or less in the EU at the time of purchase. In 2014, the new PABLO reimbursement system was introduced: now, instead of lengthy paper applications, retailers provide computer-generated forms with a barcode and the PABLO logo, which must be scanned in the airport at a designated PABLO terminal before you check in for your outbound flight. Refunds are processed more quickly, and funds are directly credited to your credit card or bank account.

FOOD MARKETS

The city's open-air food markets attract the entire spectrum of Paris society, from the splendid matron with her minuscule dog in tow, to the mustachioed regular picking up his daily baguette. Although some markets are busier than others, there's not one in Paris that doesn't captivate the senses. Each season has its delicacies: *fraises des bois* (wild strawberries) and tender asparagus in spring, squash blossoms and fragrant herbs in summer, saffron-tinted chanterelles in autumn, bergamot oranges in late winter. Year-round you can find pungent *lait cru* (unpasteurized) cheeses, charcuterie, and wild game and fish. Many of the better-known open-air markets are in areas you'd visit for sightseeing. While most of the produce is direct from Rungis, the largest international food wholesaler in the world, organic markets (*marchés bio*) are gaining traction in the city. These are where you're most likely to find actual growers and producers, most notably at the Marché Raspail, Marché Batignolles, and Marché Richard Lenoir. To get a list of market days in your area, ask your concierge or check the markets section on the website ⊕ *www.paris.fr/marches*.

If you're unused to the metric system, it may be helpful to know that *une livre* is French for a pound; *une demi-livre* is a half pound. For cheese or meats, *un morceau* will get you a piece, *une tranche* a slice.

Most markets are open from 8 am to 1 pm three days a week year-round (usually the weekend and one weekday) on a rotating basis.

STORE HOURS

Store hours can be tricky in Paris. Aside from department stores, which keep slightly longer hours and usually shut their doors late on Thursday, shops tend to open around 10 am and close around 7 pm. It's not unusual to find a "back at 3" sign taped on the doors of smaller boutiques at lunchtime. Plan to do most of your foraging between Tuesday and Saturday, as the majority of shops, excluding the two major department stores, Printemps and Galeries Lafayette, are closed Sunday and some on Monday as well. You can find areas—particularly the Marais and tourist-oriented Champs-Élysées—where stores are open on Sunday. However, if you're making a special trip somewhere, it's wise to check hours online or call ahead.

16

■TIP→ Galeries Lafayette and Printemps each offer 10%-off discount cards to foreign visitors. Some items marked with a red dot, usually designer clothing and sale merchandise, are excluded. To get a card, go to the welcome desk on the main floor of either store. Remember to bring a passport or driver's license.

SHOPPING IN PARIS

Reviews are alphabetical by neighborhood.

CHAMPS-ÉLYSÉES

Step into your Chanel suit, gird your loins, and plunge into Paris's most desirable (and most daunting) hunting grounds, where royals, jet-setters, starlets, and other glitterati converge in pursuit of the high life. This elegant triangle—bordered by Avenues Montaigne, George V, and Champs-Élysées, with Rue François 1er in between—is home to almost all the luxury Goliaths with a few lesser worthies added in.

BEAUTY

Guerlain. This opulent address is a fitting home for Paris's first—and most famous—perfumer. Still the only Paris outlet for legendary perfumes like Shalimar and L'Heure Blue, it has added several new signature scents (including Myrrhe et Délires and Cuir Beluga). Personalized bottles in several sizes can be filled on demand, or, for a mere €30,000, a customized scent can be blended just for you. Sybarites will also appreciate Guerlain's makeup, scented candles, and redesigned spa featuring its much-adored skin-care line. There's an elegant gourmet restaurant for lunch or tea, too. ⊠ *68 av. des Champs-Élysées, 8e, Champs-Élysées* ☎ *01–45–62–52–57* ⊕ *www.guerlain.com* Ⓜ *Franklin-D.-Roosevelt.*

Parfums de Nicolaï. This perfumerie is run by Guerlain family member Patricia de Nicolaï. Children's, women's, and men's scents are on offer (including some unisex), as are sprays for the home and fragrant candles. ⊠ *69 av. Raymond Poincaré, 16e, Louvre* ☎ *01–44–55–02–00* ⊕ *www.pnicolai.com* Ⓜ *Victor-Hugo.*

CHILDREN'S CLOTHING

Fodor's Choice
★
Bonpoint. Outfit the prince or princess in your life at Bonpoint (yes, royalty *does* shop here). The prices are high, but the quality is exceptional, and the adorable miniduds couldn't be more stylish: picture a perfect hand-smocked Liberty-print dress, a velvety lambskin vest, or a double-breasted cashmere sweater for Little Lord Fauntleroy. The Avenue Raymond Poincaré boutique is one of more than a dozen citywide. ⊠ *64 av. Raymond Poincaré, 16e, Champs-Élysées* ☎ *01–47–27–60–81* ⊕ *www.bonpoint.com* Ⓜ *Trocadéro.*

FAMILY
Fodor's Choice
★
Petit Bateau. This children's clothing store provides a fundamental part of the classic French wardrobe from cradle to teen and beyond. The signature T-shirt—cut close to the body, with smallish shoulders—works equally well with school uniforms or vintage Chanel. Thanks to timeless designs, the high-grade cotton clothes remain wardrobe staples year after year; however, lines in cotton-silk or cotton-cashmere and

popular collaborations with chic designers like Christian Lacroix or Inès de la Fressange mean there's now even more in store. There are boutiques in all the major shopping neighborhoods. Stock up: if you can find this brand back home, the prices are sure to be higher. ✉ *116 av. des Champs-Élysées, 8e, Champs-Élysées* ☎ *01–40–74–02–03* ⊕ *www. petit-bateau.fr* Ⓜ *George V.*

CLOTHING

Fodor's Choice
★
Balenciaga. This venerable Paris house rose to fashion stardom under the brilliant Nicolas Ghesquière, whose architectural volumes and structural technique revolutionized the label. His abrupt departure in 2012 opened the door for American wunderkind Alexander Wang's brief tenure. A frisson of delight rocked the fashion world when it was announced, in late 2015, that underdog designer Demna Gvasalia, previously of Margiela and the ultracool insider label Vetements, would take the helm. The risk paid off immediately—his rigorously experimental streetwear-influenced designs, which use 3D printing technology, are edgy, innovative, and surprisingly elegant. ✉ *10 av. George V, 8e, Champs-Élysées* ☎ *01–47–20–21–11* ⊕ *www.balenciaga.com* Ⓜ *Alma-Marceau.*

Balmain. Slinky silhouettes, bare midriffs, sequins, crystals, frills, and furbelows, not to mention plenty of silver, patent leather, and cutouts: in other words, Balmain is not for shrinking violets. This may sound like a break from the couture house's ultrafeminine backstory (a favorite of '50s Hollywood idols), but in the hands of wunderkind Olivier Rousteing being feminine translates to being at home in your skin first, then dressing it up—his glamorous, highly Instagrammable flights of fancy are catnip for models, singers, and reality stars. The elegantly minimal boutique in the heart of the Golden Triangle carries the full collection and is a lovely backdrop for these opulent streetwear-meets-boudoir fashions. ✉ *44 rue François 1er, 8e, Champs-Élysées* ☎ *01–47–20–57–58* ⊕ *www.balmain.com* Ⓜ *Franklin D. Roosevelt, George V.*

Fodor's Choice
★
Céline. Reinvigorated by Michael Kors in the late 1990s, Céline got another much-needed jolt when Phoebe Philo arrived in 2008 and began dazzling the critics with her focused approach. Philo singlehandedly redefined the codes of fashion for professional women, garnering a huge and fiercely loyal following for her streamlined, minimal designs, featuring flowing pants; long, unstructured jackets; and the Cabas bag. LVMH announced in January 2018 that she'd be succeeded by Hedi Slimane, who left Saint Laurent in 2016 after rocking (or rock 'n' rolling) the label to its core. As of this writing, it remains to be seen what he does with one of fashion's most beloved labels. ✉ *53 av. Montaigne, 8e, Champs-Élysées* ☎ *01–40–70–07–03* ⊕ *www.celine. com* Ⓜ *Franklin-D.-Roosevelt.*

Fodor's Choice
★
Chanel. Elegant, modern looks with sex appeal and lasting value are Chanel's stock in trade. Although the spectacularly beautiful Avenue Montaigne flagship takes shoppers' breath away, the heart of this revered fashion house—helmed by the one-and-only Karl Lagerfeld— is still the boutique at 31 rue Cambon, where Chanel once perched high up on the mirrored staircase watching audience reactions to her

16

collection debuts. Great investments include all of Coco's favorites: the perfectly tailored suit, a lean soigné dress, or a quilted bag with a gold chain. Handbags, jewelry, shoes, and accessories are all found at the fabulous 42 avenue Montaigne boutique, opposite the flagship store. ✉ *51 av. Montaigne, 8e, Champs-Élysées* ☎ *01–44–50–73–00* ⊕ *www. chanel.com* Ⓜ *Franklin-D.-Roosevelt.*

FodorsChoice
★

Dior. Following in John Galliano's outsized footsteps, Raf Simons did a brilliant job of redefining the label, but himself decamped in late 2015, leaving the door open for Maria Grazia Chiuri, Dior's first female designer for a label that's traditionally defined the feminine. Chiuri proved herself quickly, starting with the runaway success of her "We Should All Be Feminists" T-shirt and gorgeous flower-strewn collections that she calls both "feminine and feminist." Now one of fashion's major darlings, Chiuri's collections are hotly anticipated each season and her Avenue Montaigne boutique is an absolute must while in Paris. ✉ *30 av. Montaigne, 8e, Champs-Élysées* ☎ *01–40–73–73–73* ⊕ *www.dior. com* Ⓜ *Franklin-D.-Roosevelt.*

Dolce & Gabbana. Dolce & Gabbana offers a sexy, young-Italian-widow vibe with a side of moody boyfriend. Svelte silk dresses, sharply tailored suits, and plunging necklines are made for drama. Women's clothes are at the Avenue Montaigne location; men's are at 3 rue Faubourg St-Honoré. ✉ *54 av. Montaigne, 8e, Champs-Élysées* ☎ *01–42–25–68–78* ⊕ *www.dolcegabbana.com* Ⓜ *Alma-Marceau.*

Le66. Finding just the right totally chic, totally black anything is a breeze here. This up-to-the-second concept store, composed of three boutiques on two levels (including shoes, jewelry, accessories, and menswear), lines up all the top names that you know, along with those that you may not but should. Diffusion lines of the major labels mingle with Acne, Marni, Helmut Lang, Rimowa, Alexander Wang, Damir Doma, and nearly 200 others, all hand-picked to ensure fabulousness. If pressed for time, it's a good bet for all-around satisfaction. ✉ *66 av. des Champs-Élysées, 8e, Champs-Élysées* ☎ *01–53–53–33–80* ⊕ *www. le66.fr* Ⓜ *Franklin-D.-Roosevelt.*

Maison Ullens. A glam Golden Triangle location, a Rem Koolhaas–designed boutique, sumptuous clothes—the Belgian label's first Paris outpost hits all the marks and then some. Founded in 2013, Maison Ullens puts the focus on luxe fabrics and skins in classic-chic designs with plenty of staying power. It has everything you need for après-ski or weekends on Capri. ✉ *4 rue de Marignan, 8e, Champs-Élysées* ☎ *01–47–20–23–56* ⊕ *www.maisonullens.com* Ⓜ *Franklin-D.-Roosevelt.*

Marni. Marni started out as a little Italian label that put a quirky spin on classic styles, employing retro-ish prints and colors (think citron yellow or seaweed green) and funky fabrics (such as rubberized cotton and filmy silks). Now it has evolved into a major player on the edgy fashion scene. Each season has something new to say—whether it's an inventive take on bold ethnic prints, ingenious knits, or eloquent color schemes. Sought-after shoes and jewelry never make it to sale time. ✉ *57 av. Montaigne, 8e, Champs-Élysées* ☎ *01–56–88–08–08* ⊕ *www. marni.com* Ⓜ *Franklin-D.-Roosevelt.*

Nina Ricci. Creative director Guillaume Henry, who lately resurrected the venerable Paris label Carven, brought a welcome edginess to this archly feminine line. Ricci's airy white-on-white Avenue Montaigne boutique is one of Paris's dreamiest, high on the must-visit list. But, alas, the designer's Fall 2018 collection will be his last for Ricci. Stay tuned in the never-ending saga of fashion's swinging doors! ⊠ *39 av. Montaigne, 8e, Champs-Élysées* ☎ *01–83–97–72–12* ⊕ *www.ninaricci. com* Ⓜ *Franklin-D.-Roosevelt.*

Prada. Prada spins gold out of fashion straw. Knee-length skirts, peacock colors, cardigan sweaters, geometric prints: the waiting lists cross continents. Shoes, bags, and other accessories for men and women perennially become cult items. ⊠ *10 av. Montaigne, 8e, Champs-Élysées* ☎ *01–53–23–99–40* ⊕ *www.prada.com* Ⓜ *Alma-Marceau.*

Réciproque. Paris's largest, most exclusive consignment store carries everything from furs and jewelry to evening gowns and lingerie. Almost any coveted designer you can think of is represented, and the savings are significant; prices, however, aren't as cheap as you might expect, and there's not much in the way of service or space. The six shops that comprise Réciproque (individually dedicated to women's clothing, menswear, accessories, and the like) are clustered together on Rue de la Pompe; all are closed Sunday and Monday. ⊠ *92, 93, 95, and 97 rue de la Pompe, 16e, Champs-Élysées* ☎ *01- 47–04–30–28* ⊕ *www. reciproque.fr* Ⓜ *Rue de la Pompe.*

16

HOME DECOR

Maison de Baccarat. This museum and crystal store was once the home of Marie-Laure de Noailles, known as the Countess of Bizarre. Philippe Starck revamped the space with his signature cleverness—yes, that's a chandelier floating in an aquarium and, yes, that crystal arm sprouting from the wall alludes to Jean Cocteau (a friend of Noailles). Follow the red carpet to the jewelry room, where crystal baubles hang from bronze figurines, and to the immense table stacked with crystal items for the home, and don't miss the drop-dead gorgeous Crystal Room restaurant, recently reopened after a colorful redesign by interiors star Jacques Grange and a new menu by two-star chef Guy Martin of Le Grand Véfour. ⊠ *11 pl. des États-Unis, 16e, Champs-Élysées* ☎ *01–40–22–11–00* ⊕ *www.baccarat.com* Ⓜ *Iéna.*

JEWELRY AND ACCESSORIES

Fodor'sChoice
★

Dior Joaillerie. When Victoire de Castellane was signed to create Dior's first line of fine jewelry, she brought a big dollop of wit and panache to the venerable brand. After her romance with death heads, the young designer has returned to what she does best—utterly flamboyant gems in raucous colors, but with a new delicacy and finesse that places her designs at the pinnacle of high jewelry. ⊠ *34 av. Montaigne, 8e, Champs-Élysées* ☎ *01–47–23–52–39* ⊕ *www.dior.com* Ⓜ *Franklin-D.-Roosevelt.*

SHOES, HANDBAGS, AND LEATHER GOODS

Berluti. Berluti has been making exquisite and expensive men's shoes for more than a century. "Nothing is too beautiful for feet" is Olga Berluti's motto; she even exposes her creations to the moonlight to give them an extra-special patina. One model is named after Andy

Warhol; other famous clients of the past include the Duke of Windsor, Fred Astaire, and James Joyce. ⊠ *26 rue Marbeuf, 8e, Champs-Élysées* ☎ *01–53–93–97–97* ⊕ *www.berluti.com* Ⓜ *Franklin-D.-Roosevelt.*

Giuseppe Zanotti Design. Every pair of shoes here is fetish worthy, if not downright dangerous. Mile-high spike heels, buckle stilettos, slinky python booties, and jewel-encrusted black-satin pumps beg to be noticed. More toned-down models, like over-the-knee leather flats, and even sneakers, can be had, too. ⊠ *12 av. Montaigne, 8e, Champs-Élysées* ☎ *01–47–20–07–85* ⊕ *www.giuseppezanotti.com* Ⓜ *Franklin-D.-Roosevelt.*

Jimmy Choo. This is the place for vampy stilettoes, strappy flats, and butch biker boots. Recent *Belle de Jour*–inspired kitten heels are a nice respite from the famous mile-high styles that put Choo on the map. Beautiful bags, clutches, and small leather items in animal print, reptile, and metallics are deservedly popular. ⊠ *34 av. Montaigne, 8e, Champs-Élysées* ☎ *01–47–23–03–39* ⊕ *www.jimmychoo.com* Ⓜ *Franklin-D.-Roosevelt.*

Fodor's Choice ★ **Louis Vuitton.** Louis Vuitton has spawned a voracious fan base from Texas to Tokyo with its mix of classic leather goods and saucy revamped versions orchestrated by Marc Jacobs. His 2013 exit left tall boots to fill, but Nicholas Ghesquière—a daring designer who single-handedly resurrected the Balenciaga label—has done an admirable job. Melding his signature edgy modernism with vintage touches and colors, Ghesquière is taking the legendary luxe label to a glorious new level. ⊠ *101 av. des Champs-Élysées, 8e, Champs-Élysées* ☎ *01–53–57–52–00* ⊕ *www.louisvuitton.com* Ⓜ *George V.*

Fodor's Choice ★ **Renaud Pellegrino.** Just steps away from the Arc de Triomphe, Renaud Pellegrino is a black-book address for style icons like Catherine Deneuve and Paloma Picasso, who eschew status labels in favor of individuality and staying power. A black lace-over-leather bag or an azure tote with tiny silver grommets brings glamour to daytime looks, and a Mondrian-esque patchwork of silk-satin adds magnificence to evening wear. ⊠ *8 av. Victor Hugo, 16e, Louvre* ☎ *01–42–61–75–32* ⊕ *www.renaudpellegrino.com* Ⓜ *Charles-de-Gaulle - Étoile.*

AROUND THE LOUVRE

The flagship stores of big luxury brands rub elbows here with independent boutiques and concept stores notable for their fashion cachet. The fabulous Rue St-Honoré—a bastion of Parisian chic—is the area's retail spine, but the Marché St-Honoré and the Faubourg provide tempting detours. Whatever you do, don't miss the gorgeous Palais-Royal gardens, where flashy fashion stars mix with the discrete purveyors of handmade gloves.

BEAUTY

Anne Sémonin. Anne Sémonin sells skin-care products made out of seaweed and trace elements, as well as essential oils that are popular with fashion models. ⊠ *2 rue des Petits-Champs, 2e, Louvre* ☎ *01–42–60–94–66* ⊕ *www.annesemonin.com* Ⓜ *Palais-Royal–Louvre.*

Annick Goutal. Annick Goutal sells its own line of signature scents, which come packaged in gilded gauze purses. Gardenia, Passion, Petite Chérie, and l'Eau d'Hadrien are perennial favorites. ✉ *14 rue de Castiglione, 1er, Louvre* ☎ *01–42–60–52–82* ⊕ *www.annickgoutal.com* Ⓜ *Concorde.*

By Terry. This small, refined store is the brainchild of Terry de Gunzburg, Yves Saint Laurent's former director of makeup, whose brand of ready-to-wear cosmetics is a favorite of French actresses and socialites. Upstairs, specialists create what de Gunzburg calls *haute couleur*: exclusive made-to-measure makeup tailored for each client (it's very expensive; book far in advance). ✉ *36 Galerie Véro-Dodat, 1er, Louvre* ☎ *01–44–76–00–76* ⊕ *www.byterry.com* Ⓜ *Palais-Royal–Louvre.*

Ex Nihilo. Find your perfect fragrance from a selection of base perfumes developed by a prominent Paris nose and delivered via a futuristic glass orb. The individual scents—including orange blossom, lychee, peach, and moss—can be worn as originally formulated, or you can pop up to the "sensorial boudoir" to have a customized blend created while you wait. Your precious elixir deserves a handcrafted flacon topped by a lid of onyx, mother of pearl, horn, or leather (diamonds and sapphires are available, too). ✉ *352 rue St-Honoré, 1er, Louvre* ☎ *01–40–15–93–77* ⊕ *www.ex-nihilo-paris.com* Ⓜ *Tuileries.*

Fodor's Choice **Guerlain.** The world's oldest perfumer has introduced a gorgeous new
★ Parisian flagship, just blocks from its very first shop founded by Pierre-François Guerlain in 1828. The new outpost, specializing in the art of perfumery, is a sumptuous affair and offers more personalized services and customization than ever before. A tablet helps you define your olfactory profile and experts are on hand to guide you in a private consultation in a special room decked out in blushing velvets; or you can have a private consultation with a house "nose" to design your own. If those options are out of your price range, as they are for most mortals, you can still personalize any of the perfumer's 110 fragrances from the "perfume bar," choosing from several crystal bottles and the color of your label and ribbons. ✉ *356 rue Saint Honoré, 1e, Louvre* ☎ *01–42–60–68–61* ⊕ *www.guerlain.com* Ⓜ *Tuileries, Pyramides.*

Jovoy. Representing 100 artisanal perfumers, Jovoy is not only Paris's largest independent purveyor of fragrances, but also the world's. Owner François Hénin can often be found in the shop expounding on the unique qualities and fascinating histories of the fragrances, some of which date back hundreds of years. Many are exclusive to the boutique. The shop also carries fragrances for the home and a range of beautifully packaged scented candles. ✉ *4 rue de Castiglione, 1er, Louvre* ☎ *01–40–20–06–19* ⊕ *www.jovoyparis.com* Ⓜ *Tuileries, Concorde.*

Fodor's Choice **Les Salons du Palais-Royal Serge Lutens.** Every year Shiseido's creative
★ genius, Serge Lutens, dreams up two new fragrances, which are then sold exclusively in this boutique. Each is compellingly original, from the strong *somptueux* scents (often with musk and amber notes) to intense florals (Rose de Nuit). Bottles can be etched and personalized for sumptuous gifts. ✉ *Jardins du Palais-Royal, 142 Galerie de Valois, 1er, Louvre* ☎ *01–49–27–09–09* ⊕ *www.sergelutens.com* Ⓜ *Palais-Royal–Louvre.*

16

Nose. This concept store offers a personalized service to help you find your ideal fragrance. A bilingual specialist takes you through a seven-step diagnostic to identify your olfactory profile—then the smelling begins. With all there is to choose from, one never leaves unsatisfied. Hard-to-locate lines of luxe body lotions, face serums, bath gels, scented candles, and yummy laundry soaps are also stocked. Fans can keep up with promotions and in-store events via the monthly "noseletter." ✉ *20 rue Bachaumont, 2e, Louvre* ☎ *01–40–26–46–03* ⊕ *www.nose.fr* Ⓜ *Etienne Marcel.*

BOOKS AND STATIONERY

Librarie Galignani. Dating back to 1520s Venice, this venerable book-store opened in Paris in 1801 and was the first to specialize in English-language books. Its present location, across from the Tuileries Garden on Rue de Rivoli, opened in 1856, and the wood bookshelves, creaking floors, and hushed interior provide the perfect atmosphere for perusing Paris's best collection of contemporary and classic greats in English and French, plus a huge selection of gorgeous art books. ✉ *224 rue de Rivoli, 1er, Louvre* ☎ *01–42–60–76–07* ⊕ *www.galignani.com* Ⓜ *Tuileries.*

W. H. Smith. This bookseller carries a multitude of travel and language books, cookbooks, plus fiction for adults and children. It also has the best selection of foreign magazines and newspapers in Paris (which you're allowed to flip through without interruption—many magazine dealers in France aren't so kind). ✉ *248 rue de Rivoli, 1er, Louvre* ☎ *01–44–77–88–99* ⊕ *www.whsmith.fr* Ⓜ *Concorde.*

CLOTHING

& Other Stories. H&M's latest upmarket "style-lab" covers all the major fashion bases while appealing to women of different tastes and ages. Unlike the minimalist COS—another H&M spawn—& Other Stories offers the kind of au courant looks and well-made basics that are beloved by urban sophisticates who wouldn't be caught dead buying the parent brand but still want style on a budget. The shoe collection downstairs is a serious draw all on its own. Accessories, lingerie, and makeup are also available. ✉ *277 rue St-Honoré, 8e, Louvre* ☎ *01–53–32–85–05* ⊕ *www.stories.com* Ⓜ *Concorde.*

Fodor's Choice ★ **Acne Studios.** Justly famous for their sexy, derriere-shaping jeans, the Swedish label for men and women daringly mixes genders and genres in body-hugging or oversized asymmetric styles that rival some of the best catwalk looks. Standout shoes, boots, and accessories—all exhibiting the brand's underplayed cool—are sold here, too. ✉ *124 Galerie de Valois, 1er, Louvre* ☎ *01–42–60–16–62* ⊕ *www.acnestudios.com* Ⓜ *Palais-Royal–Louvre.*

Agnès b. Agnès b embodies the quintessential French approach to easy but stylish dressing. There are many branches, and the clothes are also sold in department stores, but for the fullest range go to Rue du Jour, where Agnès takes up much of the street (women's and children's wear are at No. 6, menswear at No. 3). For women, classics include sleek black-leather jackets, flattering black jersey separates, and trademark wide-stripe T-shirts. Children love the two-tone T-shirts proclaiming their age. And the stormy-gray velour or corduroy suits you see on those slouchy, scarf-clad men? Agnès b. ⊠ *3 and 6 rue du Jour, 1er, Louvre* ☎ *01–42–33–04–13* ⊕ *www.agnesb.eu* Ⓜ *Châtelet–Les Halles.*

Fodor's Choice ★ **Alexander McQueen.** The first Paris flagship of this lauded label, which won global fame for designing the Duchess of Cambridge's wedding gown, is glorious to behold. The late McQueen's codes—tons of lace, gossamer fabrics, tartans, death's heads, and voluminous silhouettes— are all lavishly on display. But, while staying true to his vision, creative director Sarah Burton isn't as intent on pushing the boundaries as she is on creating her own magic in lavish gowns and dramatic ready-to-wear. Shoes, accessories, and surprisingly affordable jewelry to go with the garments are available as well. ⊠ *372 rue St-Honoré, 1er, Louvre* ☎ *01–70–80–78–00* ⊕ *www.alexandermcqueen.com* Ⓜ *Tuileries.*

Fodor's Choice ★ **Chloé.** Much like the clothes it sells, Chloé's flagship boutique is softly feminine and modern without being stark. Housed in an 18th-century mansion, its creamy-marble floors, gold sconces, and walls in the brand's signature rosy beige are the perfect backdrop for designer Clare Waight Keller's beautifully tailored yet fluid designs. Visitors are met with the kind of sincere attention that is all but extinct in most high-end Paris shops. Whether it's for a handbag or a whole new wardrobe, VIP rooms and professional stylists are available to assist anyone who calls for an appointment. ⊠ *253 rue St-Honoré, 1e, Louvre* ☎ *01–55–04–03–30* ⊕ *www.chloe.com* Ⓜ *Franklin-D.-Roosevelt.*

16

Claudie Pierlot. This designer is deservedly lauded for her smart, urban clothes that unite youthful chic with solid designs; they also successfully transition over several seasons. The irresistible combination of classic looks, good tailoring, and affordability keeps loyal fans coming back year after year. ⊠ *1 rue du 29 Juillet, 1er, Louvre* ☎ *01–42–60–01–19* ⊕ *www.claudiepierlot.com* Ⓜ *Étienne Marcel.*

Cotélac. Cotélac gives feminine shapes a bohemian edge in earthy tones from azure to deep aubergine. The figure-skimming and frillier separates beg to be layered. ⊠ *284 rue St-Honoré, 1er, Louvre* ☎ *01–47–03–21– 14* ⊕ *www.cotelac.fr* Ⓜ *Tuileries.*

Didier Ludot. The incredibly charming Didier Ludot inspired a fervent craze for vintage couture, and riffling through his racks of French-made pieces from the '20s to the '80s can yield wonderful Chanel suits, Balenciaga dresses, and Hermès scarves. Ludot has two boutiques in Galerie Montpensier: No. 20 houses his amazing vintage couture collection, while No. 24 has vintage ready-to-wear and accessories. ⊠ *Jardins du Palais-Royal, 20–24 Galerie Montpensier, 1er, Louvre* ☎ *01–42–96– 06–56* ⊕ *www.didierludot.fr* Ⓜ *Palais-Royal–Louvre.*

Gabrielle Geppert. Gabrielle Geppert's twin vintage shops (Nos. 32 and 33), under fashion-forward arcades of the Palais-Royal, assemble the greatest hits from the '60s to the '80s from the likes of Dior, Hermès, YSL, Mugler, and Aläia (picture anything from a 1960s jet-beaded mini-dress to an '80s disco number) at Nos. 32 and 33. ⊠ *32–33 Galerie Montpensier, 1er, Louvre* ☎ *01–42–61–53–52* ⊕ *www.gabriellegeppert. com* Ⓜ *Palais-Royal–Louvre.*

Loris Azzaro. When Azzaro saw his 1970s designs, now collector's items, worn by stars like Nicole Kidman and Liz Hurley, he decided to update his best sellers. He's a master of the dramatic dress: picture floor-length columns with jeweled collars and sheer gowns with strategically placed sequins. ⊠ *65 rue de Faubourg St-Honoré, 8e, Louvre* ☎ *01–42–66– 92–98* ⊕ *www.azzaro-couture.com* Ⓜ *Concorde.*

Fodor's Choice
★
Louis Vuitton. The Paris-based luxury leather goods and fashion house par excellence opened this outstanding new venue in late 2017, resplendent in an 18th-century mansion on the elegant Place Vendôme. Part fashion boutique, part art gallery, the impeccable restoration kept the original woodwork, gilding, and stone, adding contemporary chrome, glass, and colorful artworks from more than 30 contemporary artists and sculptors. Covering three floors, the grand Place Vendôme store contains the entire Vuitton collection, including high jewelry and watches, bags and accessories, fashion, luggage, and some fabulous home furnishings on the top floor. The perfect backdrop for creative director Nicolas Ghesquière's forward-thinking styles that mine the last several centuries of fashion for inspiration. ⊠ *356 rue Saint Honoré, 1er, Louvre* ☎ *01–81–70–23–00* ⊕ *www.louisvuitton.com.*

Lucien Pellat-Finet. Lucien Pellat-Finet does cashmere that shakes up the traditional world of cable knits: here, sweaters for men, women, and children come in punchy colors and cheeky motifs. A psychedelic marijuana leaf may bounce across a sky-blue crewneck; a crystal-outlined skull could grin from a sleeveless top. The cashmere is wonderfully soft—and the prices are accordingly high. ⊠ *2 rue d'Aboukir, 2e, Louvre* ☎ *01–42–22–22–77* ⊕ *www.lucienpellat-finet.com* Ⓜ *Tuileries.*

Maison Martin Margiela. This famously elusive Belgian designer has earned a devoted following for his avant-garde styling and for his innovative technique, from spiraling seams to deconstructed shirts. Women's fashion is sold at 25 bis, rue de Montpensier, menswear at No. 23 (Passage Potier). Look for Ligne 6—Margiela's cool, secondary line of more casual (and less expensive) clothes for women—in his store at 22 place du Marché St-Honoré. ⊠ *23 and 25 bis, rue de Montpensier, 1er, Louvre* ☎ *01–40–15–07–55* ⊕ *www.maisonmartinmargiela.fr* Ⓜ *Palais-Royal–Louvre.*

Maje. The popular label brings a certain ease to looking great. The designs are original, up-to-the-moment, and not wildly expensive— that's why Maje has expanded exponentially. Seasonal collections include minis in every form; lean, peg-leg trousers in denim and leather; and some of the best outerwear around. ⊠ *267 rue St-Honore, 2e, Louvre* ☎ *01–42–96–84–93* ⊕ *www.maje.com* Ⓜ *Palais-Royal–Louvre.*

Marc Jacobs. His singular take on 20th-century American classics—from flapper-style (big flowers, unstructured lines, drop waists, flounces) to 1960s prom (empire waists, copious tulle) with a bit of motorcycle chic thrown in and more recently the exaggerated silhouettes of the 1980s—has made Marc Jacobs the darling of American style. Metallics appear in most every collection, as do breezy, feminine fabrics, big shoulders, and lots of layers. Since closing his secondary line, Marc by Marc Jacobs, and consolidating everything under the Marc Jacobs

Jardin du Palais-Royal

Paris's secret oasis no more. With the arrival of Rick Owens and Stella McCartney, the palace and gardens of the Jardin du Palais-Royal officially joined the ranks of fashion hot spots. Not that it ever lacked allure; those in the know have come here for fabulous shoes, artisanal perfumes, and vintage haute couture for years. Shopping in Paris is no common experience, but shopping at the Palais-Royal—under its neat rows of lime and chestnut trees and vaulted arcades—is almost worship.

Entering the gardens from Rue St-Honoré, you'll see the Colonnes de Buren, a series of sculpted columns, covering the first inner courtyard. Galerie de Montpensier is the long arcade to your left; Galerie de Valois flanks the gardens to your right.

GALERIE DE VALOIS
No. 156: **Pierre Hardy:** head-turning heels that tantalize while they flatter, with some of Paris's best bags to match (☎ 01–42–60–59–75).

No. 142: **Les Salons du Palais-Royal Serge Lutens:** perfumes and exclusive scents from the titular "nose" par excellence are sold in this jewel-like boutique (☎ 01–49–27–09–09).

Nos. 130–133: **Rick Owens:** over-the-top rock-star glamour with

an avant-garde edge, he makes serious fashion waves worldwide (☎ 01–40–20–42–52).

Nos. 128–129: **Maison Fabre:** proving that practice makes perfect, this enterprise has been crafting some of the most beautiful gloves in the world since 1924 (☎ 01–42–60–75–88).

No. 124: **Acne Studios:** Swedish design for men and women who demand it all—style, fit, comfort, and plenty of cool (☎ 01–42–60–16–62).

Nos. 114–121: **Stella McCartney:** McCartney has A-List cred, and her wearable-yet-sexy separates are a must in any well-appointed wardrobe (☎ 01–47–03–03–80).

GALERIE DE MONTPENSIER
No. 28: **Epice:** jaunty, color-saturated scarves in blends of linen, cashmere, silk, and wool beloved by Parisian women (☎ 01–49–26–07–07).

Nos. 31–34: **Gabrielle Geppert:** vintage haute couture at its best: why buy a knockoff when you can have the original? Bags, jewelry, and sunglasses, too (☎ 01–42–61–53–52).

Nos. 20–24: **Didier Ludot:** vintage French pieces from the '20s to the '80s—look for couture, ready-to-wear, or tempting accessories (☎ 01–42–96–06–56).

16

label, the boutique exited its lovely boutique at the Palais Royal and decamped to this sleek new address. ⊠ *368 rue Saint-Honoré, 1e, Louvre* ☎ *01–40–20–11–30* ⊕ *www.marcjacobs.com* Ⓜ *Tuileries.*

Miu Miu. This Faubourg St-Honoré boutique dispenses with the designer's Modernist ethos in favor of a neo-Baroque sensibility—and it influences everything from the velvet wallpaper to, perhaps, a lavish pair of ruby slippers. Although the shoes and accessories scream glitz, the clothes still have a sleek refinement, with the designer's notorious tension between minimalism and opulence. ⊠ *92 rue du Faubourg St-Honoré, 8e, Louvre* ☎ *01–58–62–53–20* ⊕ *www.miumiu.com* Ⓜ *Miromesnil.*

Rick Owens. Rick Owens expertly finessed the jump from L.A. rock-star chic to Paris offbeat elegance. Lately defined more by glamour than grunge, his lush fabrics and asymmetrical designs have evolved to a new level of artistry—and wearability. Owens still loves a paradox (shrouding while revealing), and mixes high luxury with a bit of the tooth and the claw. You'll also find shoes, furs, jewelry, and accessories. ✉ *130–133 Galerie de Valois, 1er, Louvre* ☎ *01–40–20–42–52* ⊕ *www. rickowens.eu* Ⓜ *Palais-Royal–Louvre.*

Saint Laurent. Yves Saint Laurent revolutionized women's wear in the 1970s, putting pants in couture shows for the first time. His safari jackets, "le smoking" suits, Russian-boho collections, and tailored *Belle de Jour* suits are considered fashion landmarks. Taking the helm in 2012, Hedi Slimane caused a major stir, renaming the brand, moving its headquarters, and bringing his own street-smart L.A. chic while nose-tweaking fashion journalists. In the ever-evolving game of musical chairs shaking up the major fashion houses, Anthony Vaccarello took the reins in spring 2017, keeping the sexy, streetsmart look and adding his signature razor-sharp styling with plenty of metallics, feathers, and beading. The menswear shop, at No. 32 rue du Faubourg St-Honoré, features new and sleekly beautiful riffs on Saint Laurent's classic satin-lapel tuxes. ✉ *38 and 32 rue du Faubourg St-Honoré, 8e, Louvre* ☎ *01–42–65–74–59* ⊕ *www.ysl.com* Ⓜ *Concorde.*

Stella McCartney. Since launching her own label in 2001, Stella McCartney has steadily built on her success. Season after season, she channels the prevailing mood into innovative takes on classics like the boyfriend blazer, the silk sheath, and the cigarette jean. The clothes flatter real women, and the steep prices can be justified by their staying power (and the fact that nothing was killed in the making). ✉ *114–121 Galerie de Valois, 1er, Louvre* ☎ *01–47–03–03–80* ⊕ *www.stellamccartney.com* Ⓜ *Palais-Royal–Louvre.*

Vanessa Bruno. Expect a new brew of feminine dressing from Vanessa Bruno: some androgynous pieces (skinny pants) plus delicacy (filmy tops) with a dash of whimsy (lace insets). Separates are coveted for their sleek styling, gorgeous colors, and unerring sexiness. Wardrobe staples include perfectly proportioned cotton tops and sophisticated dresses. Athé, the diffusion line, flies off the racks, so if you see something you love, grab it. Bruno's shoes and accessories are the cherry on the cake: her iconic sequin-striped totes inspired an army of knockoffs. ✉ *100 rue Vieille du Temple, 3rd, Marais Quarter* ☎ *01–42–61–44–60* ⊕ *www. vanessabruno.fr* Ⓜ *Saint-Paul.*

Yohji Yamamoto. A master of the drape, fold, and twist, Yohji Yamamoto made his name in the 1980s. The design legend favors predominantly black clothes that are both functional and edgy. A canny fashion investment, these pieces never go out of style. You'll find ready-to-wear for men and women at the Louvre boutique, along with the Y's casual line. ✉ *25 rue du Louvre, 1er, Louvre* ☎ *01–42–21–42–93* ⊕ *www. yohjiyamamoto.co.jp* Ⓜ *Étienne Marcel.*

DEPARTMENT STORES

BHV. Short for Bazar de l'Hôtel de Ville, BHV houses an enormous basement hardware store that sells everything from doorknobs to cement mixers and has to be seen to be believed. The fashion offerings for men, women, and kids have been totally revamped, with many of the top labels and a fabulous, not-too-crowded lingerie department on the fifth floor. But BHV is most noteworthy for its high-quality home-decor items, electronics, stationery, and office supplies. If you're looking for typically French household goods (like those heavy, gold-rimmed café sets, gorgeous French linens, or Savon de Marseille), this is your ticket. The extensive men's store is across the street at 36 rue de la Verrerie. ✉ *52–64 rue de Rivoli, 4e, Louvre* ☎ *09–77–40–14–00* ⊕ *www.bhv.fr* Ⓜ *Hôtel de Ville.*

FNAC. Parisians flock to FNAC—the high-profile French "cultural" department store—for a huge selection of music and books, as well as photo, TV, and audio equipment. This centrally located branch is among the biggest. ✉ *Forum des Halles, 1er, Louvre* ☎ *08–25–02–00– 20* ⊕ *www.fnac.com* Ⓜ *Les Halles.*

FOOD AND TREATS

Jean-Paul Hévin. Forty masterful varieties of chocolate and some of the best pastries in Paris earned Jean-Paul Hévin his world-class chocolatier status. Devotees will be pleased to know that there's also an outpost near the Luxembourg Gardens at 3 rue Vavin. ✉ *231 rue St-Honoré, 1er, Louvre* ☎ *01–55–35–35 96* ⊕ *www.jeanpaulhevin.com* Ⓜ *Tuileries.*

Ladurée. Founded in 1862, Ladurée oozes period atmosphere—even at the big Champs-Élysées branch (No. 75)—but nothing beats the original tearoom on Rue Royale, with its pint-size tables and frescoed ceiling. Ladurée claims a familial link to the invention of the *macaron* and appropriately, there's a fabulous selection of these lighter-than-air cookies. Classic flavors include pistachio, salted caramel, and coffee; others, like violet–black currant, chestnut, and lime basil, are available seasonally. When you've worked your way through the macaron menu, try a cup of the famously rich hot chocolate with a flaky mille-feuille. Unfortunately, service has lagged at all three of the tearooms in recent years (including the charming upstairs room at 21 rue Bonaparte), and the crowded room feels ever more like an ersatz tourist destination than the historic tearoom that it is. Still, Ladurée's stylish boxes filled with sweet treats make memorable gifts. ✉ *16 rue Royale, 8e, Louvre* ☎ *01–42–60–21–79* ⊕ *www.laduree.com* Ⓜ *Madeleine.*

HOME DECOR

A. Simon. This is where Parisian chefs come for their kitchen needs— from plates and glasses to pans and wooden spoons. The quality is excellent and the prices reasonable. ✉ *48 rue Montmartre, 2e, Louvre* ☎ *01–42–33–71–65* Ⓜ *Étienne Marcel.*

Astier de Villatte. Come here for tongue-in-chic interpretations of 18th-century table settings and furniture; live out your Baroque or Empire fancies with milk-white china sets and lots of mahogany. Moody candles and incense complete the atmosphere. ✉ *173 rue St-Honoré, 1er, Louvre* ☎ *01–42–60–74–13* ⊕ *www.astierdevillatte.com* Ⓜ *Tuileries.*

16

E. Dehillerin. Never mind the creaky stairs: E. Dehillerin has been around for almost 200 years and clearly knows its business. The huge range of professional cookware in enamel, stainless steel, or fiery copper is gorgeous. During her years in Paris, Julia Child was a regular here. ⊠ *18–20 rue Coquillière, 1er, Louvre* ☎ *01–42–36–53–13* ⊕ *www.ede-hillerin.fr* Ⓜ *Les Halles.*

Gien. Gien has been making fine china since 1821. The *faience* spans traditional designs—such as those inspired by Italian majolica, blue-and-white delftware, and French toile—as well as contemporary looks. ⊠ *18 rue de l'Arcade, 8e, Louvre* ☎ *01–42–66–52–32* ⊕ *www.gien.com* Ⓜ *Madeleine.*

La Chalcographie du Louvre. More than 13,000 prints from the Louvre's collection can be had at the museum's own print shop for a relatively minor investment. The most popular images are in stock, easy to view, and can walk right out with you. ⊠ *Louvre museum store, 1er, Louvre* ☎ *01–40–20–59–35* ⊕ *www.chalcographiedulouvre.com* Ⓜ *Palais-Royal–Louvre.*

JEWELRY AND ACCESSORIES

Fodor's Choice ★ **Cartier.** Cartier flashes its jewels at more than half a dozen boutiques in the city. Longtime favorites such as the Trinity rings and Tank watches compete for attention with the newer Panthère, Love, and Caresse d'Orchidées collections. ⊠ *23 pl. Vendôme, 1er, Louvre* ☎ *01–44–55–32–20* ⊕ *www.cartier.fr* Ⓜ *Tuileries, Concorde.*

Dary's. This wonderful, family-run cavern teeming with artists, actors, models, and jewelry lovers offers an Ali Baba–ish shopping experience. You'll need to take your time though, because the walls are filled with row upon row of antique jewels from every era, more modern secondhand jewelry, and drawer upon drawer of vintage one-of-a-kinds. ⊠ *362 rue St-Honoré, 1er, Louvre* ☎ *01–42–60–95–23* ⊕ *www.darys-bijouterie-paris.fr* Ⓜ *Tuileries.*

LINGERIE

Fodor's Choice ★ **Alice Cadolle.** Selling lingerie to Parisians since 1889, Alice Cadolle offers some of the city's most sumptuous couture undergarments. Ready-to-wear bras, corsets, and sleepwear fill the Rue Cambon boutique; made-to-measure service is provided at 255 rue St-Honoré. ⊠ *4 rue Cambon, 1er, Louvre* ☎ *01–42–60–94–22* ⊕ *www.cadolle.com* Ⓜ *Concorde.*

Fodor's Choice ★ **Chantal Thomass.** The legendary lingerie diva is back with a *Pillow Talk–*meets–Louis XIV–inspired boutique. This is French naughtiness at its best, striking the perfect balance between playful and seductive. Sheer silk negligees edged in Chantilly lace and lascivious bra-and-corset sets punctuate the signature line. ⊠ *211 rue St-Honoré, 1er, Louvre* ☎ *01–42–60–40–56* ⊕ *www.chantalthomass.fr* Ⓜ *Tuileries.*

Fifi Chachnil. Fifi Chachnil channels the 1950's pinup babe, with a fondness for quilted-satin bed jackets, cropped angora sweaters, and lace-edged lingerie in candyland colors. The look is cheerfully sexy, with checkered push-up bras, frilled white knickers, and peach-satin corsets. The Saint-Germain boutique (34 rue de Grenelle) is a sweet little boudoir and at the Jean-Jacques Rousseau shop you can see the atelier where the lingerie is handmade. ⊠ *68 rue Jean-Jacques Rousseau, 1er, Les Halles* ☎ *01–42–21–19–93* ⊕ *www.fifichachnil.com* Ⓜ *Etienne Marcel, Les Halles.*

Princesse Tam Tam. This shop is the go-to for affordable and beguiling bra-and-panty sets that combine sex appeal and playfulness. Designed for mileage as much as allure, the softer-than-soft cotton wrap tops and nighties, lace-edged silk tap pants, camisoles, slips, and adorable separates for the boudoir are comfortable *and* comely. ⊠ *5 rue Montmartre, 1er, Louvre* ☎ *01–45–08–50–69* ⊕ *www.princessetamtam.com* Ⓜ *Les Halles.*

MARKETS

Rue Montorgueil. This old-fashioned market street has evolved into a chic bobo zone; its stalls now thrive amid stylish cafés and the oldest oyster counter in Paris. ⊠ *1er, Louvre* Ⓜ *Châtelet–Les Halles.*

SHOES, HANDBAGS, AND LEATHER GOODS

Causse. This place dates back to a time when the quality of the gloves said it all. Supple python or cherry-lacquered lambskin may not have been the rage in 1892 when this eminent glove maker was founded, but its 125 years in the business add up to unparalleled style and fit. ⊠ *12 rue de Castiglione, 1er, Louvre* ☎ *01–49–26–91–43* ⊕ *www.caussegantier.fr* Ⓜ *Tuileries.*

16

Christian Louboutin. These shoes carry their own red carpet with them, thanks to their trademark crimson soles. Whether tasseled, embroidered, or strappy, in Charvet silk or shiny patent leather, the heels are always perfectly balanced. No wonder they set off such legendary legs as Tina Turner's and Gwyneth Paltrow's. The men's shop is next door at No. 17, and the women's pop-up store (Christian Louboutin Beauté, featuring his cosmetics line) is around the corner at Galerie Véro-Dodat. The glamorous No. 68 rue du Faubourg St-Honoré boutique carries a full line of women's shoes and accessories. ⊠ *19 rue Jean-Jacques Rousseau, 1er, Louvre* ☎ *08–00–94–58–04* ⊕ *www.christianlouboutin.com* Ⓜ *Palais-Royal–Louvre.*

Goyard. These colorful totes are the choice of royals, blue bloods, and the like (clients have included Sir Arthur Conan Doyle, Gregory Peck, and the Duke and Duchess of Windsor). Parisians swear by their durability and longevity; they're copious enough for a mile-long baguette, and durable enough for a magnum of Champagne. What's more, they easily transition into ultrachic beach or diaper bags. ⊠ *233 rue St-Honoré, 1er, Louvre* ☎ *01–42–60–57–04* ⊕ *www.goyard.com* Ⓜ *Tuileries.*

Hermès. The go-to for those who prefer their logo discrete yet still crave instant recognition, Hermès was established as a saddlery in 1837; then went on to create the eternally chic Kelly (named for Grace Kelly) and Birkin (named for Jane Birkin) handbags. The silk scarves are legendary for their rich colors and intricate designs, which change yearly. Other accessories are also extremely covetable: enamel bracelets, dashing silk-twill ties, and small leather goods. During semiannual sales, in January and July, prices are slashed by up to 50%, and the crowds line up for blocks. ⊠ *24 rue du Faubourg St-Honoré, 8e, Louvre* ☎ *01–40–17–46–00* ⊕ *www.hermes.com* Ⓜ *Concorde.*

Lancaster. A household name in France for 100 years, Lancaster has a reputation for style and craftsmanship. Its bags are chic and sporty, with an emphasis on practicality; and all the classic models are available in this spaceship-modern boutique. Look for the popular cross-body Besace bag (it's made of patent leather or soft cowhide and comes in a rainbow of colors), along with exclusive designs sold only here, some in genuine reptile. Lovely leather covers and bags for every mobile device are here, too. ⊠ *422 rue St-Honoré, 8e, Louvre* ☎ *01–42–28–88–88* ⊕ *www.lancaster.com* Ⓜ *Concorde.*

Maison Fabre. Until you've eased into an exquisite pair of gloves hand-crafted by Fabre, you probably haven't experienced the sensation of having a second skin far superior to your own. Founded in 1924, this is one of Paris's historic *gantiers*. Styles range from classic to haute: picture elbow-length croc leather, coyote-fur mittens, and peccary driving gloves. ⊠ *128–129 Galerie de Valois, 1er, Louvre* ☎ *01–42–60–75–88* ⊕ *www.maisonfabre.com* Ⓜ *Palais-Royal–Louvre.*

Moynat. Designed to evoke a wheel, as in "we're going places, baby," this gleaming boutique showcases the new Moynat, while evoking the brand's 19th- and early-20th-century glory days, when Pauline Moynat was the queen of luggage design. Women's bags are sleek, expertly engineered, and exceedingly beautiful (the reversible leather tote in either bone/coral or mocha/taupe is an instant classic). Men's briefcases are convex on one side to avoid bumping legs: an ingenious design that harkens back to the advent of automobile travel, when Moynat's trunks were curved to hug a car roof. Crocodile bags, silk scarves, and a thriving bespoke service are cherries on the cake. ⊠ *348 rue St-Honoré, 1er, Louvre* ☎ *01–47–03–83–90* ⊕ *www.moynat.com* Ⓜ *Tuileries.*

Perrin. As much as we love a stylish clutch, after a cocktail or two it's likely to end up anywhere. Luckily, this fifth-generation leather goods specialist dispenses with the problem by adding a nifty handhold, in metal, leather, or other luxury skins, to its superchic version. Looking for something larger? The irresistible Baggala hobo bag comes in calf or matte crocodile; and the Bavolet, in red-and-gold python, is a sure showstopper. Gloves, sunglasses, and little leather items are also sold. ⊠ *3 rue d'Alger, 1er, Louvre* ☎ *01–42–36–53–54* ⊕ *www.perrinparis. com* Ⓜ *Tuileries.*

Pierre Hardy. With Vivier and Louboutin, Pierre Hardy completes the triumvirate of anointed Paris shoe designers. Armed with a pedigree— Dior, Hermès, Balenciaga—Hardy opened his own boutique in 2003 and made serious waves. Luxe bags are ever popular, and the shoes are unmistakable: sky-scraping platforms and wedges or demure kitten heels double as sculpture with breathtaking details and luscious colors. Movie stars are regularly seen sporting Hardy's popular (and expensive) sneakers. His new jewelry line features sexy, wearable baubles, perfect for a day-to-evening look. ⊠ *Palais-Royal Gardens, 156 Galerie de Valois, 1er, Louvre* ☎ *01–42–60–59–75* ⊕ *www.pierrehardy.com* Ⓜ *Palais-Royal–Louvre.*

Roger Vivier. Known for decades for his Pilgrim-buckle shoes and inventive heels, Roger Vivier's name is being resurrected through the creativity of über-Parisienne Inès de la Fressange and the expertise of shoe designer Gherardo Felloni. The results are easily some of the best shoes in town: leather boots that mold to the calf perfectly, towering rhinestone-encrusted or feathered platforms for evening, and vertiginous crocodile pumps. ⊠ *29 rue du Faubourg St-Honoré, 8e, Louvre* ☎ *01–53–43–00–85* ⊕ *www.rogervivier.com* Ⓜ *Concorde.*

SHOPPING GALLERIES

Galerie Véro-Dodat. Built in 1826, this beautifully restored, glass-ceilinged gallery has painted medallions and copper pillars, plus boutiques selling antiques, contemporary art, accessories, and more. Christian Louboutin is an anchor tenant. At what is now the Café de l'Époque, just at the gallery's entrance, mentally troubled French writer Gérard de Nerval took his last drink before heading to Châtelet to hang himself. ⊠ *19 rue Jean-Jacques Rousseau, 1er, Louvre* Ⓜ *Palais-Royal–Louvre.*

Fodor's Choice ★ **Galerie Vivienne.** Located between the Bourse and the Palais-Royal, Galerie Vivienne is the most glorious glass-capped arcade in Paris. The 19th-century beauty is home to an array of interesting boutiques as well as a lovely tearoom (A Priori Thé) and a terrific wineshop (Cave Legrand Filles et Fils). ⊠ *4 rue des Petits-Champs, 2e, Louvre* ⊕ *www.galerie-vivienne.com* Ⓜ *Palais-Royal–Louvre, Bourse.*

Passage du Grand-Cerf. Opened in 1825, this pretty *passage couvert* has regained the interest of Parisians. La Parisette, a small boudoir-pink space at No. 1, sells fun accessories, and Marci Noum, at No. 4, riffs on street fashion. Silk bracelets, crystals, and charms can be nabbed at Eric & Lydie and Satellite. ⊠ *Entrances at 145 rue St-Denis and 8 rue Dussoubs, 2e, Louvre* Ⓜ *Étienne Marcel.*

LES GRANDS BOULEVARDS

From the venerable old boutiques on Rue de la Paix to Paris's great *grands magasins* on Boulevard Haussmann (namely Galeries Lafayette and Au Printemps), there's no shortage of shopping opportunities here. Once you add in the area's elegant covered passages, there is enough to keep you busy for a weekend, if not an entire week.

BARGAIN SHOPPING

Monoprix. With branches throughout the city, this is *the* French dime store par excellence, stocking everyday items like French cosmetics, groceries, toys, kitchen wares, and more. It also has a line of stylish, inexpensive, basic wearables for the whole family—particularly adorable kids' clothes—and isn't a bad place to stock up on French chocolate, jams, or *confit de canard* at reasonable prices. ⊠ *21 av. de l'Opéra, 1er, Grands Boulevards* ☎ *01–42–61–78–08* ⊕ *www.monoprix.fr* Ⓜ *Opéra.*

BEAUTY

Make Up For Ever. Poised at the back of a courtyard, this store is a must-stop for makeup artists, models, actresses, and divas of all stripes. The riotous color selection includes hundreds of hues for foundation, eye shadow, powder, and lipstick. ⊠ *5 rue de la Boétie, 8e, Grands Boulevards* ☎ *01–53–05–93–30* ⊕ *www.makeupforever.fr* Ⓜ *St-Augustin.*

16

CLOTHING

Anouschka. Anouschka has set up shop in her apartment (by appointment only, Monday to Saturday) and has rack upon rack of vintage clothing dating from the 1930s to the '80s. It's the perfect place to find a '50s cocktail dress in mint condition or a mod jacket for him. A former model herself, she calls this a "designer laboratory," and teams from top fashion houses often pop by looking for inspiration. ✉ *6 av. du Coq, 9e, Grands Boulevards* ☎ *01–48–74–37–00* Ⓜ *St-Lazare, Trinité.*

Charvet. The Parisian equivalent of a Savile Row tailor, Charvet is a conservative, aristocratic institution. It's famed for made-to-measure shirts, exquisite ties, and accessories; for garbing John F. Kennedy, Charles de Gaulle, and the Duke of Windsor; and for its regal address. Although the exquisite silk ties, in hundreds of colors and patterns, and custom-made shirts for men are the biggest draw, refined pieces for women and girls, as well as adorable miniatures for boys, round out the collection. ✉ *28 pl. Vendôme, 1er, Grands Boulevards* ☎ *01–42–60–30–70* Ⓜ *Opéra.*

Eric Bompard. This cashmere shop provides stylish Parisians with luxury cashmeres in every color, style, and weight; yarns range from light as a feather to a hefty 50-ply for the jaunty caps. The store caters to men and women (there are some kids' models, too). Styles are updated seasonally yet tend toward the classic. ✉ *75 bd. Haussmann, 8e, Grands Boulevards* ☎ *01–42–68–00–73* ⊕ *www.eric-bompard.com* Ⓜ *Miromesnil.*

DEPARTMENT STORES

Au Printemps. A retail institution, Au Printemps is made up of three major stores: Printemps Maison (with home furnishings on four refurbished floors), Printemps Homme (featuring six levels of menswear plus two levels for the gourmet shopping area, Printemps du Goût, which opened in January 2018), and fashion-focused Printemps Mode (which has everything à la mode, from couture to teen trends). While in the Printemps Mode building, be sure to check out the newly enlarged beauty area—the largest in Paris—with the Nuxe spa, hair salons, and seemingly every beauty product known to woman under one roof. The luxurious Printemps du Louvre—in the Carrousel du Louvre, at the underground entrance to the museum, across from I.M. Pei's inverted pyramid—carries fine leather goods, accessories, watches, and beauty products; fittingly, it also hosts revolving art exhibitions. ✉ *64 bd. Haussmann, 9e, Grands Boulevards* ☎ *01–42–82–50–00* ⊕ *www.printemps.com* Ⓜ *Havre-Caumartin, St-Lazare.*

Galeries Lafayette. This mammoth department store is one of those places that you wander into unawares, leaving hours later a poorer and humbler person. Inside its flagship building at 40 boulevard Haussmann, a Belle Époque stained-glass dome caps the world's largest perfumery. The store bulges with thousands of designers, and 25-minute fashion shows are held Friday at 3 pm in the upstairs café to showcase their wares (reservations are a must: email *fashionshow@galerieslafayette.com; admission €12*). Another big draw is the comestibles department, stocked with everything from herbed goat cheese to Iranian caviar. Just across the street at 35 boulevard Haussmann is Galeries Lafayette Maison, which focuses on goods for the fashionable home. The Montparnasse branch is a pale shadow of the Boulevard Haussmann behemoths. ⊠ *35–40 bd. Haussmann, 9e, Grands Boulevards* ☏ *01–42–82–34–56* ⊕ *www.galerieslafayette.com* Ⓜ *Chaussée d'Antin, Havre-Caumartin.*

FOOD AND TREATS

À la Mère de Famille. This enchanting shop dates from 1761 and is the oldest continuously open confectionary in Paris. Though it has gone the way of the chain, with multiple boutiques in Paris, À la Mère de Famille retains its authenticity and is well versed in French regional specialties as well as old-fashioned bonbons, chocolates, marzipan, ice creams, and more. ⊠ *35 rue du Faubourg-Montmartre, 9e, Grands Boulevards* ☏ *01–47–70–83–69* ⊕ *www.lameredefamille.com* Ⓜ *Cadet.*

Fauchon. The most iconic of Parisian food stores is expanding globally, but its flagship is still behind the Madeleine church. Established in 1886, Fauchon sells renowned pâté, honey, jelly, tea, and private-label Champagne. Expats come for hard-to-find foreign foods (think U.S. pancake mix or British lemon curd), while those with a sweet tooth make a beeline to the pâtisserie for airy, ganache-filled *macarons*. There's also a café for a quick bite. Be prepared, though: prices can be eye-popping—marzipan fruit for €100 a pound? ⊠ *26 pl. de la Madeleine, 8e, Grands Boulevards* ☏ *01–70–39–38–00* ⊕ *www.fauchon.com* Ⓜ *Madeleine.*

HOME DECOR

Christofle. Founded in 1830, Christofle has fulfilled all kinds of silver wishes, from a silver service for the Orient Express to a gigantic silver bed. Come for timeless table settings, vases, jewelry boxes, and more. ⊠ *24 rue de la Paix, 2e, Grands Boulevards* ☏ *01–42–65–62–43* ⊕ *www.christofle.com* Ⓜ *Opéra.*

JEWELRY AND ACCESSORIES

Alexandre Reza. One of Paris's most exclusive jewelers, Alexandre Reza is first and foremost a gemologist. He travels the world looking for the finest stones and then works them into stunning pieces, many of which are replicas of jewels of historical importance. ⊠ *21 pl. Vendôme, 1er, Grands Boulevards* ☏ *01–42–61–51–21* ⊕ *www.alexandrereza.com* Ⓜ *Opéra.*

Chanel Jewelry. Chanel Jewelry feeds off the iconic design elements of the pearl-draped designer: witness the quilting (reimagined for gold rings), camellias (now brooches), and shooting stars (used for her first jewelry collection in 1932, now appearing as diamond rings). ⊠ *18 pl. Vendôme, 1er, Grands Boulevards* ☏ *01–40–98–55–55* ⊕ *www.chanel. com* Ⓜ *Tuileries, Opéra.*

Dinh Van. Just around the corner from Place Vendôme's titan jewelers, Dinh Van thumbs its nose at in-your-face opulence. The look here is refreshingly spare. Best sellers include a hammered-gold-orb necklace and leather-cord bracelets joined with geometric shapes in white or yellow gold, some with pavé diamonds. ⊠ *16 rue de la Paix, 2e, Grands Boulevards* ☏ *01–42–61–74–49* ⊕ *www.dinhvan.com* Ⓜ *Opéra.*

16

MARKETS

Rue Lévis. This market, near Parc Monceau, has Alsatian specialties and a terrific cheese shop. ⊠ *17e, Grands Boulevards* ⊙ *Closed Sun. afternoon and Mon.* Ⓜ *Villiers.*

SHOPPING GALLERIES

Passage des Panoramas. Built in 1799, Passage des Panoramas is the city's oldest extant arcade and has become a foodie paradise, with no less than a dozen gourmet destinations, including a chic non-gluten restaurant (Noglu) and a two-Michelin star dining room (Passage 53). ⊠ *11 bd. Montmartre, 2e, Grands Boulevards* Ⓜ *Opéra, Grands Boulevards.*

Passage Jouffroy. Passage Jouffroy is full of eclectic shops selling toys, Asian furnishings, cinema posters, and more. Pain D'épices, at No. 29, specializes in dollhouse decor. ⊠ *10–12 bd. Montmartre, 9e, Grands Boulevards* Ⓜ *Grands Boulevards.*

Passage Verdeau. Across from Passage Jouffroy, Passage Verdeau has shops carrying antique cameras, comic books, and engravings. Au Bonheur des Dames, at No. 8, has all things embroidery. ⊠ *4–6 rue de la Grange Batelière, 9e, Grands Boulevards* Ⓜ *Grands Boulevards.*

TOYS

Fodor's Choice
★
Pain d'Epices. This shop has anything you can imagine for the French home (and garden) in miniature, including Lilliputian croissants, wine decanters, and minuscule instruments in their cases. Build-it-yourself dollhouses include a 17th-century town house and a boulangerie storefront. Upstairs are do-it-yourself teddy-bear kits and classic toys. ⊠ *29 passage Jouffroy, 9e, Grands Boulevards* ☎ *01–47–70–08–68* ⊕ *www. paindepices.fr* Ⓜ *Grands Boulevards.*

FAMILY
Fodor's Choice
★
Village JouéClub. Le Passage des Princes—one of the city's historic covered *passages*—is home to Paris's most comprehensive toy store. Part of a large French chain, the two-level Village JouéClub carries all the usual suspects (Barbie, Disney, Hello Kitty, and the like) plus the better traditional European brands, including Vilac, Moulin Roty, and L'Atelier du Bois. It's made up of more than 10 "shops," each of which is dedicated to a different age group or toy genre. You'll find virtually every kind of plaything here, so be prepared to linger. ⊠ *5 bd. des Italiens, 2e, Grands Boulevards* ☎ *01–53–45–41–41* ⊕ *www.villagejoueclub.com* Ⓜ *Richelieu–Drouot.*

WINE

Lavinia. Lavinia has the largest selection of wine in one spot in Europe—more than 6,000 wines and spirits from all over the world, ranging from the simple to the sublime. There are expert English-speaking sommeliers on-site to help you sort it all out, as well as a wine-tasting bar, a bookshop, and a restaurant. ⊠ *3–5 bd. de la Madeleine, 1er, Grands Boulevards* ☎ *01–42–97–20–20* ⊕ *www.lavinia.fr* Ⓜ *St-Augustin.*

Les Caves Augé. One of the best wineshops in Paris, Les Caves Augé has been in operation since 1850. It's just the ticket, whether you're looking for a rare vintage, a select Bordeaux, or a seductive Champagne for a tête-à-tête. English-speaking experts are on hand to guide you through an excellent selection of small-producer, organic, and natural wines and select grower-producer Champagnes. ⊠ *116 bd. Haussmann, 8e, Grands Boulevards* 🕾 *01–45–22–16–97* ⊕ *www.cavesauge.com* Ⓜ *St-Augustin.*

MONTMARTRE

To avoid an uphill climb, the Abbesses métro stop on Rue de la Vieuville is a good starting point for serious shoppers. From here, descend picturesque Rue des Martyrs all the way down to Notre-Dame-de-Lorette: the route promises a cornucopia of captivating boutiques that sell everything from chic antiques and offbeat fashion to gourmet food.

CLOTHING

A.P.C. Stock. A.P.C. opened its surplus store steps away from Sacré-Coeur. No need to wait for sales; funky classics can always be found here for a whopping 50% off. ⊠ *20 rue André del Sarte, 18e, Montmartre* 🕾 *01–42–62–10–88* ⊕ *www.apc.fr* Ⓜ *Château Rouge.*

Spree. When Spree first opened, its mission was to give young designers a venue; it has since branched out to include fashion elites like Margiela, Isabel Marant, Golden Goose, and Christian Wijnants. The expertly chosen inventory seems almost curated. A great selection of accessories and jewelry, along with cool furniture and a revolving exhibition of artwork by international artists, complete the gallery feel. ⊠ *16 rue la Vieuville, 18e, Montmartre* 🕾 *01 42–23–41–40* ⊕ *www.spree.fr* Ⓜ *Abbesses.*

MARKETS

Fodor's Choice ★ **Marché aux Puces St-Ouen** (*Clignancourt*). This picturesque market on the city's northern boundary still lures crowds on weekends from 9 to 6 and Monday from 10 to 5, but its once-unbeatable prices are now a relic. Packed with antiques booths and *brocante* stalls, the century-old, miles-long labyrinth has been undergoing a mild renaissance lately: witness Village Vintage's recently opened warehouses filled with midcentury-modern pieces at 77 rue des Rosiers, plus other buzzworthy shops and galleries (some of which keep weekend-only hours). Destination eateries—including Philippe Starck's popular Ma Cocotte and the chic new MOB Hotel—also attract a hip Paris contingent. Arrive early to pick up the best loot, then linger over a meal or apéro. Be warned, though: if there's one place in Paris where you need to know how to bargain, this is it! If you're arriving by métro, walk under the overpass and take the first left at the Rue de Rosiers to reach the center of the market. Note that stands selling dodgy odds and ends (think designer knockoffs and questionable gadgets) set up around the overpass. These blocks are crowded and gritty; be careful with your valuables. ⊠ *18e, Montmartre* ⊕ *www.marcheauxpuces-saintouen.com* Ⓜ *Porte de Clignancourt, Garibaldi, Mairie de Saint-Ouen.*

THE MARAIS

The Marais has stolen the show as the city's hippest shopping destination—and for sheer volume it can't be beat. Rue des Francs Bourgeois and Rue Vieille de Temple form the central retail axis from which the upper and lower Marais branch out. The newest frontier is its northeastern edge (the *haut* Marais), which is known for ultrastylish boutiques, vintage stores, and design ateliers.

ANTIQUES AND COLLECTIBLES

Village St-Paul. This clutch of streets, in the beautiful historic netherworld tucked between the fringes of the Marais and the banks of the Seine, has many antiques shops. ⊠ *Enter from Rue St-Paul, 4e, Marais Quarter* ⊕ *www.levillagesaintpaul.com* Ⓜ *St-Paul.*

BARGAIN SHOPPING

L'Habilleur. L'Habilleur is a favorite with the fashion press and anyone looking for a deal. For women there's a great selection from designers like Harley of Scotland, Roberto Collina, and Natural Selection. Men can find elegant suits from Paul Smith at slashed prices. ⊠ *44 rue de Poitou, 3e, Marais Quarter* ☎ *01–48–87–77–12* Ⓜ *St-Sébastien–Froissart.*

Fodor's Choice ★ **Merci.** Paris's favorite concept store assembles fashions for men and women, home furnishings (including those irresistible French bed and bath linens) vintage, jewelry, and housewares plucked straight from top-tier French, European, and American designers. Every two months the store features a new design concept in the main entrance, with themes that range from Merci en Rose (featuring all things pink) to American Surf & Skate. The store's three cafés make lingering among Paris's fashion elite a pleasure. ⊠ *111 bd. Beaumarchais, 3e, Marais Quarter* ☎ *01–42–77–00–33* ⊕ *www.merci-merci.com* Ⓜ *St-Sebastien–Froissart.*

Zadig & Voltaire Stock. Here you'll find new unsold stock from last season. There's a great selection of beautiful cashmere sweaters, silk slip dresses, rocker jeans, and leather jackets, all in their signature luscious colors, for 40%–70% off. ⊠ *22 rue Bourg Tibourg, 4e, Marais Quarter* ☎ *01–44–59–39–62* ⊕ *www.zadig-et-voltaire.com* Ⓜ *Hôtel de Ville.*

BEAUTY

L'Artisan Parfumeur. L'Artisan Parfumeur is known for its own brand of scents for the home plus perfumes with names like Mûre et Musc (Blackberry and Musk). It also carries sumptuous shower gels, body lotions, and candles in the popular fragrances. ⊠ *32 rue du Bourg Tibourg, 4e, Marais Quarter* ☎ *01–48–04–55–66* ⊕ *www.artisanparfumeur.com* Ⓜ *Hôtel de Ville.*

BOOKS AND STATIONERY

Comptoir de l'Image. This is where designers John Galliano, Marc Jacobs, and Emanuel Ungaro stock up on old copies of *Vogue, Harper's Bazaar,* and *The Face.* You'll also find trendy magazines like *Dutch, Purple,* and *Spoon,* plus designer catalogs from the past and rare photo books. Don't go early: whimsical opening hours tend to start after lunch. ⊠ *44 rue de Sévigné, 3e, Marais Quarter* ☎ *01–42–72–03–92* Ⓜ *St-Paul.*

CHILDREN'S CLOTHING

FAMILY **Bonton.** Bonton takes the prize for most-coveted duds among those who like to think of children as fashion accessories. (Moms may find some useful wardrobe pointers, too.) Sassy separates in saturated colors layer beautifully, look amazing, and manage to be perfectly kid-friendly. Bonton sells toys and furniture, too. ⊠ *5 bd. des Filles du Calvaire, 3e, Marais Quarter* ☎ *01–42–72–34–69* ⊕ *www.bonton.fr* Ⓜ *Filles du Calvaire.*

CLOTHING

Abou d'Abi Bazar. A one-stop outfitter, Abou d'Abi Bazar organizes its collection of up-to-the-moment designers on color-coordinated racks that highlight the asymmetrical design of this opulent boutique. Artsy and bohemian all at once, there is plenty to covet here, from frothy Isabel Marant silk-organza blouses to sumptuous cashmere-blend tunics and satin shirtwaist dresses. Reasonably priced picks make it a desirable destination. ✉ *33 rue du Temple, 4e, Marais Quarter* ☎ *01–44–61–37–24* ⊕ *www.aboudabibazar.com* Ⓜ *Hôtel de Ville, Rambuteau.*

AB33. AB33 is like a sleek boudoir—complete with comfy chair and scented candles—and the clothes here are unabashedly feminine. Separates in luxury fabrics from top designers, irresistible silk lingerie, dainty jewelry, and a selection of accessories celebrate that certain French je ne sais quoi. ✉ *33 rue Charlot, 3e, Marais Quarter* ☎ *01–42–71–02–82* ⊕ *www.ab33.fr* Ⓜ *Filles du Calvaire.*

The Broken Arm. Like the ready-made Duchamp "artwork" for which it is named, The Broken Arm projects a minimalist cool that puts the concept back in concept store. A hypercurated selection of A-list brands for men and women includes vivid separates from the likes of Phillip Lim, Raf Simons, and the sublime Christophe Lemaire. A choice selection of objects and accessories (books, hats, shoes, jewelry, vases, leather goods) elevates the everyday to art. ✉ *12 rue Perrée, 3e, Marais Quarter* ☎ *01–44–61–53–60* ⊕ *www.the-broken-arm.com* Ⓜ *Temple.*

Comptoir des Cotonniers. Comfortable, affordable, au courant clothes make this chain popular. Its reputation is built on smart, wearable styles that stress ease over fussiness. Separates in natural fibers—cotton, silk, and cashmere blends—can be light and breezy or cozy and warm, but they are always soft, flattering, and in a range of beautiful colors. ✉ *33 rue des Francs-Bourgeois, 4e, Marais Quarter* ☎ *01–42–76–95–33* ⊕ *www.comptoirdescotonniers.com* Ⓜ *St-Paul.*

COS. COS—which stands for Collection of Style—is the H&M group's answer to fashion sophisticates, who flock here in droves for high-concept, minimalist designs with serious attention to quality tailoring and fabrics at a reasonable price. Classic accessories and shoes look more expensive than they are. ✉ *4 rue des Rosiers, 4e, Marais Quarter* ☎ *01–44–54–37–70* ⊕ *www.cosstores.com* Ⓜ *St-Paul.*

Free 'P' Star. Don't let the chaos at Free 'P' Star discourage you—there's gold in them there bins. Determined seekers on a budget can reap heady rewards, at least according to the young hipsters who flock here for anything from a floor-sweeping peasant skirt to a cropped chinchilla cape. A second Marais branch—at 61 rue de la Verrerie—is equally stuffed to the gills. Happy hunting! ✉ *52 rue de la Verrerie, 4e, Marais Quarter* ☎ *01–42–76–03–72* ⊕ *www.freepstar.com* Ⓜ *Hôtel de Ville.*

FrenchTrotters. The flagship store features an understated collection of contemporary French-made classic clothes and accessories for men and women that emphasize quality fabrics, style, and cut over trendiness. You'll also find a handpicked collection of exclusive collaborations with cutting-edge French brands (like sleek leather-and-suede booties by Avril Gau for FrenchTrotters), as well as FrenchTrotters' namesake label, and a limited selection of housewares for chic Parisian apartments. ✉ *128 rue Vieille du Temple, 3e, Marais Quarter* ☎ *01–44–61–00–14* ⊕ *www. frenchtrotters.fr* Ⓜ *St-Sébastien–Froissart, Filles du Calvaire.*

L'Eclaireur. This Rue de Sevigné boutique is Paris's touchstone for edgy, up-to-the-second styles. L'Eclaireur's knack for uncovering new talent and championing established visionaries is legendary—no surprise after 30 years in the business. Hard-to-find geniuses, like leather wizard Isaac Sellam and British prodigy Paul Harnden, cohabit with luxe labels such as Ann Demeulemeester, Haider Ackermann, and Gucci. ✉ *40 rue de Sevigné, 3e, Marais Quarter* ☎ *01–48–87–10–22* ⊕ *www. leclaireur.com* Ⓜ *St-Paul.*

Fodor'sChoice ★ **Lemaire.** Even during his time as creative director at Hermès, Christophe Lemaire kept his own eponymous label, designed with his wife Sarah-Linh Tran. Their refined little boutique in the fashionable Haut Marais is Lemaire's sole dedicated outpost in Paris and remains an absolute fashion mecca season after season. The chicest Parisiens flock here for a choice line of beautifully tailored minimalist designs in classic neutrals and dreamy hues. The boutique also carries the designers' choice selection of shoes and leather goods. ✉ *28 rue de Poitou, 3e, Marais Quarter* ☎ *01–44–78–00–09* ⊕ *www.lemaire.fr* Ⓜ *Filles du Calvaire.*

Majestic Filatures. Wearing a Majestic cashmere-cotton-blend T-shirt, dress, cardigan, or blazer is like spending the day cocooned in your favorite jammies. Fans have been known to buy five pairs of the silky-soft leggings in one go, just to be sure never to run out. The fact that you'll look totally stylish is just gilding the lily. ✉ *7 rue des Francs Bourgeois, 4e, Marais Quarter* ☎ *01–57–40–62–34* ⊕ *www.majestic-filatures.com* Ⓜ *St-Paul.*

Paule Ka. This house of fashion has that movie-star glamour down pat: for daytime, perfectly cut silk shirtdresses with matching coats; for evening, gemstone-studded gowns and furs. Both Hepburns (Audrey and Katherine) could have made this their second home. ✉ *20 rue Malher, 4e, Marais Quarter* ☎ *01–40–29–96–03* ⊕ *www. pauleka.com* Ⓜ *St-Paul.*

Pretty Box. The owners of Pretty Box have scoured Europe for unique pieces from the '20s through the '80s. Women love the superstylish belts, shoes, and bags—many in reptile—sold here for a fraction of what they'd cost new, along with an eccentric selection of cool separates and Betty Page–era lingerie. The men's collection includes vintage French military coats, sharkskin suits, and a gaggle of riotously patterned shirts. ✉ *46 rue de Saintonge, 3e, Marais Quarter* ☎ *01–48–04–81–71* Ⓜ *St-Sébastien–Froissart.*

Studio W. If you're nostalgic for the days of Studio 54, sashay over to Studio W, where a rare Loris Azzaro gold-chain top or a plunging Guy Laroche beaded couture dress in crimson mousseline has Liza and Bianca written all over them. With plenty of jewelry, shoes, bags, and even gloves to match, this elegant boutique is a must-see for fashion divas who don't mind spending a little more for sublimity. ✉ *21 rue du Pont aux Choux, 3e, Marais Quarter* ☎ *01–44–78–05–02* Ⓜ *St.-Sébastien–Froissart.*

Vintage Clothing Paris. It's worth a detour to the Marais's outer limits to visit Vintage Clothing Paris, where the racks read like an A-list of designer greats—Yves Saint Laurent, Margiela, Valentino, Comme des Garçons, and Mugler, just to name a few. Brigitte Petit's minimalist shop is the fashion insider's go-to spot for rare pieces that stand out in a crowd, like a circa-1985 Alaïa suede skirt with peekaboo grommets and a jaunty Yves Saint Laurent Epoch Russe hooded cape. ⊠ *10 rue de Crussol, 11e, Marais Quarter* ☎ *06–03–00–64–78* ⊕ *www.vintage-clothingparis.com* Ⓜ *Filles du Calvaire, Oberkampf.*

Zadig & Voltaire. Zadig & Voltaire rocks the young fashionistas by offering street wear at its best: racy camisoles, cashmere sweaters in gorgeous colors, cropped leather jackets, and form-fitting pants to cosset those tiny French derrieres. Branches abound in every chic corner of Paris. ⊠ *42 rue des Francs Bourgeois, 3e, Marais Quarter* ☎ *01–44–54–00–60* ⊕ *www.zadig-et-voltaire.com* Ⓜ *St-Paul.*

FOOD AND TREATS

Izraël. This place isn't called the *"épicerie du monde"* for nothing. Izraël is a one-stop shop for any spice under the sun, plus those hard-to-find items you'd otherwise spend days tracking down. Bins overflowing with every variety of candied fruit, nuts, beans, olives, pickles, and preserved fish give this tiny shop the air of an exotic bazaar. You'll also find all manner of canned goods, candies, rare spirits, and baking necessities. ⊠ *30 rue François Miron, 4e, Marais Quarter* ☎ *01–42–72–66–23* Ⓜ *St-Paul.*

Jacques Genin. Genin offers the essence of great chocolate: not too sweet, with handpicked seasonal ingredients for the velvety ganaches. The tea salon is a great spot to sample one of Genin's masterful takes on classic French pastries and a voluptuous *chocolat chaud.* ⊠ *133 rue de Turenne, 3e, Marais Quarter* ☎ *01–45–77–29–01* ⊕ *www.jacquesgenin.fr* Ⓜ *Filles du Calvaire, Oberkampf.*

Le Palais des Thés. White tea, green tea, black tea, tea from China, Japan, Indonesia, South America, and more: you can expect a comprehensive tea experience here. Try one of the flavored varieties such as Hammam, a traditional Turkish recipe with date pulp, orange flower, rose, and red berries. ⊠ *64 rue Vieille du Temple, 3e, Marais Quarter* ☎ *01–48–87–80–60* ⊕ *www.palaisdesthes.com* Ⓜ *St-Paul.*

Mariage Frères. Mariage Frères, with its colonial *charme* and wooden counters, has 100-plus years of tea purveying behind it. Choose from more than 450 blends from 32 countries, not to mention teapots, teacups, books, and tea-flavor biscuits and candies. High tea and light lunches are served here and at several other Paris locations. ⊠ *30 rue du Bourg-Tibourg, 4e, Marais Quarter* ☎ *01–42–72–28–11* ⊕ *www.mariagefreres.com* Ⓜ *Hôtel de Ville.*

Méert. The first Paris offshoot of the famous patisserie and tea salon in Lille (one of France's oldest) specializes in the *gauffre*, a delicate waffle handmade in the original 19th-century molds and wrapped in gilt-paper packages. Native to Belgium and northern France, Méert's version is treasured for its light cream center perfumed with Madagascar vanilla. There are also chocolates, pastries, and flavored *guimauves*,

16

the airy French marshmallows. ⊠ *16 rue Elzévir , 3e, Marais Quarter* ☎ *01–49–96–56–90* ⊕ *www.meert.fr* Ⓜ *St-Paul.*

HOME DECOR

Empreints. The raison d'être of the organization Métiers d'Art is to reward and promote French *savoir faire*—the traditional expertise of France's many fine craftspeople and artists passed down from generation to generation. To this end—and to the delight of local bobos (short for *bourgeois-bohème* or bourgeois-bohemians) decorating their Marais lofts—Métiers d'Art opened the capital's first crafts "concept store," which assembles the work of dozens of craftspeople and artists on four floors, including impeccably crafted glassware, porcelain, jewelry, leather goods, furnishings, housewares, fine art, and much more. It's an excellent place for a souvenir of French *art de vivre.* ⊠ *5 rue de Picardie, 3e, Marais Quarter* ☎ *01–40–09–53–80* ⊕ *www.empreintes-paris.com* Ⓜ *Temple, République, Filles du Calvaire.*

Le Monde Sauvage. Le Monde Sauvage is a must-visit for home accessories. Expect reversible silk bedspreads in rich colors, velvet throws, hand-quilted bed linens, silk floor cushions, colorful rugs, and the best selection of hand-embroidered curtains in silk, cotton, linen, or velvet. ⊠ *21 rue Sévigné, 4e, Marais Quarter* ☎ *01–44–61–02–61* ⊕ *www.lemondesauvage.com* Ⓜ *St-Paul.*

Muji. *Kanketsu* (simplicity) is the guiding philosophy at Muji, and the resulting streamlined designs are all the rage in Europe. Must-haves include a collection of mini-necessities—travel essentials, wee office gizmos, purse-size accoutrements, plus the best notebooks and pens around. They're so useful and adorable you'll want them all. ⊠ *47 rue des Francs Bourgeois, 4e, Marais Quarter* ☎ *01–49–96–41–41* ⊕ *www.muji.eu* Ⓜ *St-Paul.*

Sentou. Sentou knocked the Parisian world over the head with its fresh designs. Avant-garde furniture, rugs, and a variety of home accessories line the cool showroom. Look for the April Vase (old test tubes linked together to form different shapes) or the oblong suspended crystal vases and arty tableware. ⊠ *29 rue Francois Miron, 4e, Marais Quarter* ☎ *01–42–78–50–60* ⊕ *www.sentou.fr* Ⓜ *St-Paul.*

Van der Straeten. Paris designer Hervé van der Straeten started out creating jewelry for Saint Laurent and Lacroix, designed a perfume bottle for Christian Dior, and then moved on to making rather baroque and often wacky furniture. In his loft gallery-cum-showroom, furniture, lighting, jewelry, and startling mirrors are on display. ⊠ *11 rue Ferdinand Duval, 4e, Marais Quarter* ☎ *01–42–78–99–99* ⊕ *www.vanderstraeten.fr* Ⓜ *St-Paul.*

JEWELRY AND ACCESSORIES

Fodor's Choice
★

Hod. This understated boutique saves the razzle-dazzle for its wares—an outstanding selection of contemporary pieces by Europe's finest young designers. Look for Ileana Makri's delicately bejeweled cat's eye, snake, or winsome feathers; Honorine Jewel's finely wrought golden insect rings, necklaces, and bracelets; and Venessa Arizaga's protection necklaces with a tiny leather purse for your secret lucky charms. Hod has styles for all tastes and budgets. ⊠ *104 rue Vieille du Temple, 3e, Marais Quarter* ☎ *09–53–15–83–34* ⊕ *www.hod-boutique.com* Ⓜ *Filles du Calvaire.*

SHOES, HANDBAGS, AND LEATHER GOODS

Fodor's Choice ★ **Isaac Reina.** It takes up to several days of painstaking work to create one of Isaac Reina's refined, beautifully crafted handbags, satchels, totes, backpacks, and small leather goods. Meticulous detailing and gorgeous finishes are just some of the trademarks of this Barcelona native's elegant designs, all handcrafted in Paris in his sleek boutique near the Musée Picasso. These luxury bags are for people who appreciate superlative quality but don't care to flash a logo. ⊠ *12 rue de Thorigny, 3e, Marais Quarter* ☎ *01–42–78–81–95* ⊕ *www.isaacreina. com* Ⓜ *Saint-Paul, Chemin Vert.*

K. Jacques. K. Jacques has shod everyone from Brigitte Bardot to Drew Barrymore. The famous St-Tropez–based maker of strappy leather-soled flats has migrated to the big time while still keeping designs classic and comfortable. From gladiator style to lightweight cork platforms, metallics to neutrals, these are perennial favorites. ⊠ *16 rue Pavée, 4e, Marais Quarter* ☎ *01–40–27–03–57* ⊕ *www.kjacques.fr* Ⓜ *St-Paul.*

Mademoiselle Chapeau. Hats are back and this is the only hat maker in Paris where you can see jaunty cloches, fedoras, and flat-topped straw boaters being made with the centuries-old techniques in the on-site atelier. Classic models in straw, wool, rabbit felt, or silk in a huge range of colors come in a dozen styles, from a charming pillbox to an elegant wide-brim model so light and graceful it could easily pair with an evening suit or wedding gown. ⊠ *15 rue des Tournelles, 4e, Marais Quarter* ☎ *01–72–60–77–68* ⊕ *www.mademoisellechapeaux. com* Ⓜ *Bastille, Saint-Paul.*

Miguel Lobato. This is a sweet little boutique with accessories for the woman who wants it all. Beautiful high heels by Lanvin, Chloé, and Pierre Hardy and fabulous bags by Martin Margiela, Jil Sander, and Proenza Schouler are just a start. ⊠ *6 rue Malher, 4e, Marais Quarter* ☎ *01–48–87–68–14* Ⓜ *St-Paul.*

Fodor's Choice ★ **WHITE bIRD.** Irresistable is the word for this scintillating collection of jewels by an assemblage of top-echelon international designers that range from the daintiest of diamond rings, bracelets, and necklaces, to brilliantly colored stones in edgy settings. This spare boutique, a stone's throw from concept store Merci, may be tiny, but it's had a big impact on fashion jewelry in Paris. If you're looking for a piece to be worn every day or a statement piece that goes from day to night, this is your place. Trunk shows and openings are held at WHITE bIRD's first and larger boutique at 38 rue du Mont Thabor just off the Rue Saint-Honoré. ⊠ *7 bd. des Filles du Calvaire, 3e, Marais Quarter* ☎ *01–40–24–27–17* ⊕ *www.whitebirdjewellery.com* Ⓜ *Filles du Calvaire.*

16

EASTERN PARIS

"Off the beaten track" aptly describes the up-and-coming neighborhoods of eastern Paris, which are dotted with galleries, vintage shops, and funky boutiques. Low-key cool reigns here, so you won't encounter the high-wattage, high-profile designers that vie for attention elsewhere. Instead, local hipster shops ensure a few choice finds that will be seen on you and only you.

BASTILLE
CLOTHING

Isabel Marant. This rising design star is a honeypot of bohemian rock-star style. Her separates skim the body without constricting: layered miniskirts, loose peekaboo sweaters ready to slip from a shoulder, and super fox-fur jackets in lurid colors. Look for the secondary line, Étoile, for a less expensive take. ⊠ *16 rue de Charonne, 11e, Bastille* ☎ *01–49–29–71–55* ⊕ *www.isabelmarant.com* Ⓜ *Ledru-Rollin.*

Sessùn. Designer Emma François's main inspiration is traveling to faraway places, where she picks up ideas for the textures, prints, and colors for her versatile collection of fashion staples. Separates range from neutral basics—a lace inset top or camisole, a wraparound jumpsuit, a knitted cape—to brilliantly colored or natty print sweaters, trousers, blouses, and blazers. The collection is completed with a gently priced line of shoes, boots, scarves, and accessories. The Rue de Charonne concept store, the largest of the three Paris shops, also has a gallery featuring the work of French artists and artisans and a selection of handmade textiles, housewares, and jewelry. ⊠ *34 rue de Charonne, 11e, Bastille* ☎ *01–48–06–55–66* ⊕ *boutique.sessun.com/fr* Ⓜ *Bastille.*

HOME DECOR

Fodor's Choice
★
Borgo delle Tovaglie. This Naples-based label's soaring new concept store eschews sterile minimalism for an opulence well suited to its lavish Italian linen sheets and pillows. Crafted by hand in yummy colors that change with the seasons, they can be paired with a chic array of dishes, candles, and other treasures for the home. Linger at the stylish bistro—a neighborhood hipster hangout—for an espresso, a glass of wine, or a plate of Italian charcuterie. ⊠ *4 rue du Grand Prieuré, 11e, Oberkampf* ☎ *09–82–33–64–81* ⊕ *www.borgodelletovaglie.com* Ⓜ *Oberkampf.*

JEWELRY AND ACCESSORIES

Fodor's Choice
★
Yves Gratas. With a knack for pairing gems of varying sizes, brilliance, and texture, Yves Gratas allows each stone to influence the design. Whether it's a spectacular necklace of sapphire beads to be worn long or doubled, or a simple agate sphere tipped in gold and dangling like a tiny planet, these stellar jewels feel like one organic whole. If you're in the Marais, this shop (located just across the "border" in the Oberkampf neighborhood) deserves a detour. ⊠ *9 rue Oberkampf, 11e, Oberkampf* ☎ *01–49–29–00–53* ⊕ *www.yvesgratas.com* Ⓜ *Filles du Calvaire, Oberkampf.*

MARKETS

Marché Bastille. Paris's largest market is as much an event as a place to shop. Blocks of specialized stalls—including ones devoted to rare wines, regional cheeses, game, seafood, and flowers—cater to scores of Parisian chefs and epicures. It's open Thursday and Sunday 7–3. ⊠ *Bd. Richard Lenoir, between Rues Amelot and St-Sabin, 11e, Bastille* Ⓜ *Ledru-Rollin.*

Marché d'Aligre. Arguably the most authentic local market, Marché d'Aligre is open 7:30–1:30 Tuesday through Friday and 7:30–2:30 on weekends. Don't miss the covered hall on Place d'Aligre, where you can stop by a unique olive-oil boutique for bulk and prebottled oils from top producers—among many other irresistible specialty stores. The area is now lined with hip cafés, bars, and restaurants. ⊠ *Pl. d'Aligre, 12e, Bastille* Ⓜ *Ledru-Rollin, Bastille.*

SHOES

Fodor's Choice ★ **Amélie Pichard.** You'll feel positively cinematic sporting the shoes of this wildly creative young designer, whose career was jump-started in 2014 by a collaboration with her idol Pamela Anderson. Whether in zebra stripe, scarlet suede, or pink patent leather, the shoes, boots, bags, and small leather goods are always thrilling, showing loads of glamour and more than a hint of daring. You'll also find tartan, faux fur or crocodile, and basket weave. Pichard's adorable boutique is on a cobbled street just off the lucrative shopping fields of the Rue de Charonne. ⊠ *34 rue de Lappe, 11e, Bastille* ☎ *01-71-20-94-08* ⊕ *www.ameliepichard.com* Ⓜ *Bastille, Charonne, Ledru-Rollin.*

Fodor's Choice ★ **La Botte Gardiane.** Craftsmanship and style that won't wreck your budget—that's the trademark of this artisan bootmaker that hails from the Camargue, a wild area of Provence where gypsies and cowboys require durable boots to rustle the wild horses. That doesn't mean the boutique is short on chic. La Botte Gardiane has impeccably made and beautifully classic full-length boots, slouchy booties, chukkas, espadrilles, and strappy sandals in suede, python, shearling, and the supplest calf leather from the tanner that supplies Hermès. Look for styles for men, women, and kids. ⊠ *25 rue de Charonne, 11e, Bastille* ⊕ *www.labottegardiane.com* Ⓜ *Bastille, Charonne.*

CANAL ST-MARTIN

BOOKS AND STATIONERY

Fodor's Choice ★ **Artazart.** The best design bookstore in France carries tomes on everything from architecture to tattoo art: there are sections dedicated to photography, fashion, graphic art, typography, illustration, package design, color, and more. ⊠ *83 quai de Valmy, 10e, Canal St-Martin* ☎ *01-40-40-24-00* ⊕ *www.artazart.com* Ⓜ *République.*

CLOTHING

Antoine & Lili. This bright, fuchsia-color store is packed with an international assortment of eclectic objects and items from Antoine & Lili's own clothing line. There's an ethnic-rummage-sale feel, with old Asian posters, small lanterns, and basket upon basket of inexpensive doodads, baubles, and trinkets for sale. The clothing itself has simple lines, and there are always plenty of raw-silk pieces to pick from. ⊠ *95 quai de Valmy, 10e, Canal St-Martin* ☎ *01-40-37-41-55* ⊕ *www.antoineetlili. com* Ⓜ *Jacques-Bonsergent.*

FAMILY
Fodor's Choice ★ **Centre Commercial.** This store's A-list fashion credentials come with a big bonus—everything here is ethically and ecologically sourced. Peruse racks of men's and women's wear from handpicked European and U.S. labels; then head to the stellar shoe department to complete your look. Beneath glass skylights as clear as your conscience, you'll also find a fine selection of natural candles, leather goods, and jewelry. The kids' store just around the corner (22 rue Yves Toudic) is one of the city's best, with toys, decor, and color-coordinated togs that express canalside

16

cool. ✉ *2 rue de Marseille, 10e, Canal St-Martin* ☎ *01–42–02–26–08* ⊕ *www.centrecommercial.cc* Ⓜ *Jacques Bonsergent.*

Des Petits Hauts. This poetic brand charmed its way into the local fashion idiom with chic yet beguilingly feminine styles. Fabrics are soft, and styles are casual with a tiny golden star sewn into each garment for good luck. ✉ *21 rue Beaurepaire, 10e, Canal St-Martin* ☎ *01–75–44–05–83* ⊕ *www.despetitshauts.com* Ⓜ *République.*

HOME DECOR

Idé Co. Little items for the home in a riot of colors are sold at Idé Co. But you'll also find fabulous rubber jewelry and funky stuff for kids big and small. ✉ *19 rue Beaurepaire, 10e, Canal St-Martin* ☎ *01–42–01–00–11* ⊕ *www.idecoparis.com* Ⓜ *République.*

La Trésorerie. No place outfits chic Canal St-Martin lofts better than this soaring eco-friendly boutique. Housed in a historic treasury, it assembles the crème de la crème of French and European kitchen and dining ware, linens, bath products, small furnishings, hardware, lighting, paint, and more. Local hipsters come to La Trésorerie's bright, Scandinavian-style café for all things fresh, organic, and yummy. ✉ *11 rue du Château d'Eau, 10e, Canal St-Martin* ☎ *01–40–40–20–46* ⊕ *www.latresorerie. fr* Ⓜ *Jacques Bonsergent.*

JEWELRY AND ACCESSORIES

Médecine Douce. Sculptural pieces that combine leather, suede, rhinestones, agate, or resin with whimsical themes can be found at Médecine Douce. The wildly popular lariat necklace can be looped and dangled according to your mood du jour. ✉ *10 rue de Marseille, 10e, Canal St-Martin* ☎ *01–82–83–11–53* ⊕ *www.bijouxmedecinedouce. com* Ⓜ *République.*

Viveka Bergström. Forget traditional costume jewelry—these baubles just want to have fun! Whether it's a bracelet of gigantic rhinestones, a ring of fluorescent pink resin, or a pair of floating angel wings on a necklace, each Viveka Bergström piece has an acute sense of style while not taking itself too seriously. ✉ *23 rue de la Grange aux Belles, 10e, Canal St-Martin* ☎ *01–40–03–04–92* ⊕ *www.viveka-bergstrom. blogspot.fr* Ⓜ *République.*

SHOES, HANDBAGS, AND LEATHER GOODS

Jamin Puech Inventaire. These are last season's models, but no one will guess; savings are 30% to 60%. ✉ *61 rue d'Hauteville, 10e, Canal St-Martin* ☎ *01–40–22–08–32* ⊕ *www.jamin-puech.com* Ⓜ *Poisonnière.*

Patricia Blanchet. Do not hesitate to run for that taxi in a pair of super-chic pumps, flats, or yummy booties from Patricia Blanchet, which are neither too high nor too low but just the right height. Though the designer doesn't swerve from her five or six basic styles, her beautifully hued leathers, including metallics and exotic skins like pony and stingray, change with the season. Booties may come with metallic piping or colorful insets and cutouts, and are cut low for a sexy peek at the ankle. ✉ *20 rue Beaurepaire, 10e, Canal St-Martin* ☎ *01–42–02–35–85* ⊕ *www.patriciablanchet.com* Ⓜ *République.*

LATIN QUARTER

Considering this fabled *quartier* is home to the Sorbonne and historically one of Paris's intellectual-bohemian centers, it's not surprising that it has a rich selection of bookstores—not just for students but for collectors and bargain hunters, too. Gastronomes, meanwhile, flock in to shop at the outstanding charcuteries and fromageries along Rue Mouffetard.

BOOKS AND STATIONERY

Abbey Bookshop. Paris's Canadian bookstore has books on Canadian history as well as new and secondhand Québécois and English-language novels. The Canadian Club of Paris also organizes regular poetry readings and literary conferences here. ⊠ *29 rue de la Parcheminerie, 5e, Latin Quarter* ☎ *01–46–33–16–24* ⊕ *www.abbeybookshop.wordpress. com* Ⓜ *Cluny–La Sorbonne.*

Shakespeare & Company. This sentimental Rive Gauche favorite is named after the bookstore whose American owner, Sylvia Beach, first published James Joyce's *Ulysses.* Nowadays it specializes in expat literature. Although the eccentric and beloved owner, George Whitman, passed away in 2011, his daughter Sylvia has taken up the torch and made huge changes, including opening an on-site café. You can still count on a couple of characters lurking in the stacks, a sometimes spacey staff, the latest titles from British presses, and hidden secondhand treasures in the odd corners and crannies. Check the website for readings and workshops throughout the week. ⊠ *37 rue de la Bûcherie, 5e, Latin Quarter* ☎ *01–43–25–40–93* ⊕ *www.shakespeareandcompany.com* Ⓜ *St-Michel.*

HOME DECOR

Avant-Scène. Head to Avant-Scène for original, poetic furniture. Owner Elisabeth Delacarte commissions limited-edition pieces from artists like Mark Brazier-Jones, Franck Evennou, Elizabeth Garouste, and Hubert Le Gall. ⊠ *4 pl. de l'Odéon, 6e, Latin Quarter* ☎ *01–46–33–12–40* ⊕ *www.avantscene.fr* Ⓜ *Odéon.*

MARKETS

Rue Mouffetard. This colorful market street near the Jardin des Plantes reflects its multicultural neighborhood: vibrant, with a laid-back feel that still smacks of old Paris. It's best on weekends. ⊠ *5e, Latin Quarter* Ⓜ *Monge.*

ST-GERMAIN-DES-PRÉS

Ever since Yves Saint Laurent arrived in the 1960s, the Rive Gauche has been synonymous with iconoclastic style. Trendsetting stores line a jumble of streets in the 6e arrondissement, and exciting boutiques await between Place de l'Odéon and Église St-Sulpice. In the 7e arrondissement, don't miss Rue du Bac and that jewel of a department store, Le Bon Marché. St-Germain-des-Prés is also known for its chocolate shops.

16

ANTIQUES AND COLLECTIBLES

Fodor'sChoice **Carré Rive Gauche.** Head to the streets between Rue du Bac, Rue de
★ l'Université, Rue de Lille, and Rue des Sts-Pères to to unearth museum-
quality pieces. The more than 100 shops in this association of galleries
and antique dealers are marked with a small, blue square banner on
their storefronts. ⊠ *Between St-Germain-des-Prés and Musée d'Orsay,
7e, St-Germain-des-Prés* ⊕ *www.carrerivegauche.com* Ⓜ *St-Germain-
des-Prés, Rue du Bac.*

FAMILY **Deyrolle.** This fascinating 19th-century taxidermist has long been a stop
Fodor'sChoice for curiosity seekers. A 2008 fire destroyed what was left of the original
★ shop, but it has been lavishly restored and remains a cabinet of curi-
osities par excellence. Create your own box of butterflies or metallic
beetles from scores of bug-filled drawers or just enjoy the menagerie
that includes stuffed zebras, monkeys, lions, bears, and more. Also in
stock: collectible shells, corals, and crustaceans, plus a generous library
of books and posters that once graced every French schoolroom. There
is a line of cool wallpaper murals, too. ⊠ *46 rue du Bac, 7e, St-Germain-
des-Prés* ☎ *01–42–22–30–07* ⊕ *www.deyrolle.com* Ⓜ *Rue du Bac.*

BEAUTY

Fodor'sChoice **Buly 1803.** Although it only opened in 2014, you can be forgiven for
★ thinking Buly 1803 is an antique apothecary—all those jars overflowing
with exotic herbs, powders, and elixirs are used to re-create 200-year-
old recipes for its all-natural skin-care line. Deliciously smelling hand,
body, and face products come in scents like rose, Scottish moss, and
tuberose. Or you can pick up one of the dozen or so other lovely scents.
All the products are organic, beautifully packaged, and impossibly chic.
The adorable new Marais branch, at 45 rue de Saintonge, includes
an authentic Italian café, ⊠ *6 rue Bonaparte, 6e, St-Germain-des-Prés*
☎ *01–43–29–02–50* ⊕ *www.buly1803.com* Ⓜ *St-Germain-des-Prés.*

Editions de Parfums Frédéric Malle. This perfumerie is based on a simple
concept: take the nine most famous noses in France and have them
edit singular perfumes. The result? Exceptional, highly concentrated
fragrances. Le Parfum de Thérèse, for example, was created by famous
Dior nose Edmond Roudnitska for his wife. Monsieur Malle has
devised high-tech ways to keep each smelling session unadulterated.
At the Rue de Grenelle store, individual scents are released in glass
columns—just stick your head in and sniff. A second boutique at 140
avenue Victor Hugo has a glass-fronted "wall of scents," which mists
the air with a selected fragrance at the push of a button. ⊠ *37 rue
de Grenelle, 7e, St-Germain-des-Prés* ☎ *01–42–22–76–40* ⊕ *www.
fredericmalle.com* Ⓜ *Rue du Bac.*

Shu Uemura. Japanese make-up artist Shu Uemura founded this brand,
which has enhanced those whose faces are their fortune for decades.
Models swear by the cleansing oil; free samples are proffered. A
huge range of colors, every makeup brush imaginable, and the no-
pinch eyelash curler keep fans coming back. ⊠ *176 bd. St-Germain,
6e, St-Germain-des-Prés* ☎ *01–45–48–02–55* ⊕ *www.shuuemura.fr*
Ⓜ *St-Germain-des-Prés.*

BOOKS AND STATIONERY

Taschen. Perfect for night owls, Taschen is open until midnight on Friday and Saturday. The Starck-designed shelves and desks hold glam titles on photography, fine art, design, fashion, and fetishes. ✉ *2 rue de Buci, 6e, St-Germain-des-Prés* ☎ *01–40–51–79–22* ⊕ *www.taschen. com* Ⓜ *Mabillon.*

CHILDREN'S CLOTHING

FAMILY **Pom d'Api.** Pom d'Api lines up footwear for babies and preteens in quality leathers and vivid colors. Expect well-made, eye-catching fashion—bright fuchsia sneakers and leopard suede boots, as well as classic Mary Janes in shades of silver, pink, and gold. There are also utility boots for boys and sturdy rain gear. ✉ *28 rue du Four, 6e, St-Germain-des-Prés* ☎ *01–45–48–39–31* ⊕ *www.pomdapi.fr* Ⓜ *St-Germain-des-Prés.*

CLOTHING

Antik Batik. It's hard to resist Antik Batik's wonderful line of ethnically inspired clothes. There are rows of beaded and sequined dresses, Chinese silk tunics, short fur jackets and fur-lined anoraks, flowing organza separates, and some of Paris's most popular sandals and giant scarves. ✉ *26 rue St-Sulpice, 6e, St-Germain-des-Prés* ☎ *01–44–07–68–53* ⊕ *www.antikbatik.fr* Ⓜ *Odéon, Marais.*

16

A.P.C. The A.P.C. brand may be antiflash and minimal, but a knowing eye can always pick out its jeans in a crowd. The clothes here are rigorously well made and worth the investment in lasting style. Prime wardrobe pieces include dark indigo and black denim, zip-up cardigans, peacoats, and streamlined ankle boots. ✉ *38 rue Madame, 6e, St-Germain-des-Prés* ☎ *01–42–22–12–77* ⊕ *www.apc.fr* Ⓜ *St-Sulpice.*

Carven. Daringly original designs that are sexy yet wearable account for Carven's steady rise into the fashion stratosphere. Artistic director Guillame Henry was tapped in 2014 to revive the label; however, in fall 2017, Serge Ruffieux from Dior began bringing his own ingenue-meets-grandma take to the brand's meticulous tailoring and sleek silhouettes. ✉ *34 rue St-Sulpice, 6e, St-Germain-des-Prés* ☎ *09–60–45–47–04* ⊕ *www.carven.com* Ⓜ *St-Sulpice, Odéon.*

Fodor's Choice **Inès de la Fressange.** Paris's number one style icon now brings her legendary chic to an eponymous boutique in the heart of St-Germain-des-Prés. Along with her limited-edition fashions, de la Fressange introduces a line of wearable shoes (including sexy over-the-knee boots and dainty stilettos), plus handbags, accessories, and lingerie. You'll also discover long tables loaded with handpicked housewares and stationery from the tastemaker's favorite French brands. ✉ *24 rue de Grenelle, 7e, St-Germain-des-Prés* ☎ *01–45–48–19–06* ⊕ *www.inesdelafressange.fr* Ⓜ *St-Sulpice, Sèvres-Babylone.*

Karl Lagerfeld. The titular designer's own chiseled profile is a key design element in his St-Germain flagship store. Inside, look for two recently launched lines: Lagerfeld, featuring "everyday" clothes for the urban man, and Karl Lagerfeld Paris (KLP), a ready-to-wear collection for men and women. The latter is aimed at fashion-conscious twenty- and thirty-somethings who want to strut their stuff (think body-slimming jackets, lace-inset tops, and skin-tight jeans, mostly in black, white, and gray).

The store also stocks eyewear, accessories, bags, shoes, fragrances, and—you guessed it—Lagerfeld's signature fingerless leather gloves. ✉ *194 bd. St-Germain, 7e, St-Germain-des-Prés* ☎ *01–42–22–74–99* ⊕ *www.karl.com* Ⓜ *Rue du Bac.*

Maje Stock. This stock store is a prized listing in every chic Parisian's little black book. Shimmy into a pair of leather jeans, don a sheer silk blouse, and top off your outfit with a belted cashmere jacket. Back home, no one will know they're from last season. ✉ *9 rue du Cherche-Midi, 6e, St-Germain-des-Prés* ☎ *01–45–44–21–20* ⊕ *fr.maje.com* Ⓜ *St-Sulpice.*

Sonia Rykiel. Sonia Rykiel has been designing insouciant knitwear since the 1960s. Sweaters drape and cling by turns and her color combinations (she's partial to stripes) are lovely. Opulent silks, furs, accessories dotted with rhinestones, and soft leather bags punctuate the collection. Sonia by Sonia Rykiel—a smart and playful secondary line that targets a slightly younger crowd—is sold at the 4 rue de Grenelle boutique. ✉ *175 bd. St-Germain, 6e, St-Germain-des-Prés* ☎ *01–49–54–60–60* ⊕ *www.soniarykiel.com* Ⓜ *St-Germain-des-Prés.*

Tara Jarmon. The bases here are covered when it comes to that coveted French élan: sleek designs, excellent quality, luxe fabrics, and prices well within the stratosphere. With styles that vie with the high-profile designers, and accessories to match, this label is fast becoming the chic Parisian's wardrobe essential. ✉ *18 rue du Four, 6e, St-Germain-des-Prés* ☎ *01–46–33–26–60* ⊕ *www.tarajarmon.com* Ⓜ *Mabillon, Saint-Germain-des-Prés.*

DEPARTMENT STORES

Fodor'sChoice **Le Bon Marché.** Founded in 1852, Le Bon Marché has emerged as the
★ city's chicest department store. Long a hunting ground for linens and other home items, it has been undergoing a multimillion-euro facelift that brings fashion to the fore. The fact that this department store isn't nearly as crowded as those near the Opéra is an added bonus. On the ground floor of the main building, look for makeup, perfume, and accessories; this is where celebs duck in for essentials while everyone pretends not to notice. On the floor above, you can do laps through labels chichi (Givenchy, Stella McCartney, Lanvin) and überhip (Martin Margiela, Comme des Garçons, Ann Demeulemeester). The next floor up is home to streetwise designers, edgy secondary lines, plus French favorites, including Athé by Vanessa Bruno, Zadig & Voltaire, Tsumori Chisato, Isabel Marant's Étoile, and Majestic. Under the newly restored glass ceiling, the gleaming Le Soulier shoe department assembles the crème de la crème of European shoes. Meanwhile, the refurbished menswear department, Balthazar, has consumed the entire basement level. Across the street, the spanking new home store in the sister building is a great place to stock up on French linens, porcelain, cookware, and luggage, or just relax over tea or a gourmet lunch in the soaring atrium restaurant. Before leaving, be sure to visit the spectacularly renovated La Grande Épicerie and *cave* (wine shop): it's the haute couture of grocery stores. Artisanal jams, olive oils, and much more make great gifts, and the luscious pastries, fruit, and huge selection of prepared foods

beg to be chosen for a snack. ⊠ *24 rue de Sèvres, 7e, St-Germain-des-Prés* ☎ *01–44–39–80–00* ⊕ *www.lebonmarche.com* Ⓜ *Sèvres-Babylone.*

FOOD AND TREATS

Christian Constant. Chocolatier Christian Constant is deservedly praised for his exquisite ganaches, perfumed with jasmine, ylang-ylang, or verveine. ⊠ *37 rue d'Assas, 6e, St-Germain-des-Prés* ☎ *01–53–63–15–15* ⊕ *www.christianconstant.fr* Ⓜ *St-Placide.*

Debauve & Gallais. The two former chemists who founded Debauve & Gallais in 1800 became the royal chocolate purveyors and were famed for their "health chocolates," made with almond milk. Test the benefits yourself with ganache, truffles, or *pistoles* (flavored dark-chocolate disks). ⊠ *30 rue des Sts-Pères, 7e, St-Germain-des-Prés* ☎ *01–45–48–54–67* ⊕ *www.debauve-et-gallais.fr* Ⓜ *St-Germain-des-Prés.*

Henri Le Roux. The originator of the renowned *caramel au beurre salé*, Henri Le Roux pairs a Breton pedigree with Japanese flair. Brilliant confections result. You can also satisfy your sweet tooth in stores at 52 rue St-Dominique (7e) and 24 rue des Martyrs (9e). ⊠ *1 rue de Bourbon le Château, 6e, St-Germain-des-Prés* ☎ *01–82–28–49–80* ⊕ *www. chocolatleroux.com* Ⓜ *St-Germain-des-Prés.*

Jean-Charles Rochoux. Rochoux makes three superb collections of artisanal chocolates: the Ephemeral, with fresh fruit; Made-to-Measure, with animals and figurines; and the Permanent Collection of everyday favorites. ⊠ *16 rue d'Assas, 6e, St-Germain-des-Prés* ☎ *01–42–84–29–45* ⊕ *www.jcrochoux.com* Ⓜ *Rennes.*

La Maison du Chocolat. This is chocolate's gold standard. The silky ganaches are renowned for subtlety and flavor. See the website for a full list of locations. ⊠ *19 rue de Sèvre, 6e, St-Germain-des-Prés* ☎ *01–45–44–20–40* ⊕ *www.lamaisonduchocolat.fr* Ⓜ *Sèvres-Babylone.*

Patrick Roger. Paris's bad-boy chocolatier likes to shock with provocative shapes and wicked humor. Everything is sinfully good. The Boulevard St-Germain shop is one of six citywide. ⊠ *108 bd. St-Germain, 6e, St-Germain-des Prés* ☎ *01 43 29–38–42* ⊕ *www. patrickroger.com* Ⓜ *Odéon.*

Pierre Hermé. Hermé may be Paris's most renowned pâtissier. Sample the peerless cakes and cookies, or savor the chocolate delights (classic varieties, like the dark-chocolate and orange-rind batons, are perennial favorites). Hermé offers a scrumptious, zesty lemon pound cake preboxed and dense enough to survive the trip home... maybe. There are more than 10 Paris locations. ⊠ *72 rue Bonaparte, 6e, St-Germain-des-Prés* ☎ *01–43–54–47–77* ⊕ *www.pierreherme.com* Ⓜ *Odéon.*

Pierre Marcolini. Sourcing his star ingredient from independent farmers, Pierre Marcolini proves it's all in the bean. His specialty *saveurs du monde* collection of Belgian chocolates are each made with a single cacao from a single location, such as Madagascar or Ecuador, thus each with a distinct flavor. ⊠ *89 rue de Seine, 6e, St-Germain-des-Prés* ☎ *01–44–07–39–07* ⊕ *www.marcolini.com* Ⓜ *Mabillon.*

Richart. How do I love thee? The ways are too numerous to count. At Richart, inspired chocolates dazzle the eye and elevate the

16

The interior of the Galeries Lafayette department store—especially the ceiling—almost outshines the fabulous merchandise.

palate. In addition to the Boulevard St-Germain boutique, there's another at 27 rue Bonaparte (6e). ✉ *258 bd. St-Germain, 6e, St-Germain-des-Prés* ☎ *01–45–55–66–00* ⊕ *www.chocolats-richart. com* Ⓜ *St-Germain-des-Prés.*

Tomat's. Tucked into a courtyard, this luxe épicerie carries the full line of Huilerie Artisanale J. Leblanc et Fils oil—15 varieties pressed the old-fashioned way, with a big stone wheel, from olives, hazelnuts, pistachios, or grape seeds. You can also buy aged vinegars, *fleur de sel* (unprocessed sea salt), foie gras, and other regional French delicacies, plus the tools to serve them with. ✉ *12 rue Jacob, 6e, St-Germain-des-Prés* ☎ *01–44–07–36–58* ⊕ *www.tomats.net* Ⓜ *Mabillon, St-Germain-des-Prés.*

HOME DECOR

Alexandre Biaggi. Alexandre Biaggi specializes in 20th-century Art Deco and also commissions pieces from such talented designers as Patrick Naggar and Hervé van der Straeten. ✉ *14 rue de Seine, 6e, St-Germain-des-Prés* ☎ *01–44–07–34–73* ⊕ *www.alexandrebiaggi.com* Ⓜ *St-Germain-des-Prés.*

Fodor's Choice
★ **Cire Trudon.** This company has illuminated the great palaces and churches of Paris since the 1600s. Nowadays it provides the atmosphere for tony restaurants and exclusive soirées. The all-vegetal, atmospherically scented candles come in elegant black glass, pillars of all sizes, or busts of clients past—like Napoléon and Marie-Antoinette. ✉ *78 rue de Seine, 6e, St-Germain-des-Prés* ☎ *01–43–26–46–50* ⊕ *www.ciretrudon. com* Ⓜ *Odéon.*

Conran Shop. The brainchild of British entrepreneur Terence Conran, this shop carries expensive contemporary furniture, beautiful bed linens, and items for every other room in the house—all marked by a balance of utility and not-too-sober style. Conran makes even shower curtains fun. ⊠ *117 rue du Bac, 7e, St-Germain-des-Prés* ☎ *01–42–84–10–01* ⊕ *www.conranshop.fr* Ⓜ *Sèvres-Babylone.*

Fodor's Choice ★ Diptyque. A Paris mainstay since 1961, Diptyque's flagship shop is famous for its candles, eaux de toilette, and body fragrances in a huge range of sophisticated scents like myrrh, fig tree, wisteria, and quince. They're delightful but not cheap; the candles, for instance, cost nearly $1 per hour of burn time. ⊠ *34 bd. St-Germain, 6e, St-Germain-des-Prés* ☎ *01–43–26–77–44* ⊕ *www.diptyqueparis.fr* Ⓜ *Maubert–Mutualité.*

R&Y Augousti. The Paris-based husband-and-wife team of Ria and Yiouri Augousti take such materials as shagreen, nacre, and palm wood to make furniture and other objects for the home. ⊠ *103 rue du Bac, 7e, St-Germain-des-Prés* ☎ *01–42–22–22–21* ⊕ *www.augousti.com* Ⓜ *Sèvres-Babylone.*

Zuber. Have you always wanted to imitate the grand homes of Paris? Here's your chance. Zuber has operated nonstop for more than two centuries as the world's oldest producer of prestige hand-printed wallpapers, renowned for their magnificent panoramic scenes. Warning: with only one scene produced per year, the wait can be nearly a decade long. Opulent Restoration-era wallpapers (including metallics, silks, velvets, and pressed leather) make modern statements and can be purchased in 32-foot rolls for slightly less than a king's ransom. ⊠ *12 rue des Saints-Pères, 6e, St-Germain-des-Prés* ☎ *01–42–77–95–91* ⊕ *www.zuber.fr* Ⓜ *St-Germain-des-Prés.*

JEWELRY AND ACCESSORIES

Adelline. Entering this jewelry shop is like landing in Ali Baba's cave: each piece is more gorgeous than the last, and the bounty of beautiful shapes and styles satisfies a large range of tastes (and budgets). Cabochon rings can be pebble-size or rock-like, jeweled cuffs sport diamonds in a web of gold, and simple cord-and-gem bracelets cannot fail to make a statement. ⊠ *54 rue Jacob, 6e, St-Germain-des-Prés* ☎ *01–47–03–07–18* ⊕ *www.adelline.com* Ⓜ *St-Germain-des-Prés.*

Agatha. This chain is the perfect place to buy a moderately priced piece of fun jewelry. Agatha's line of earrings, rings, hair accessories, bracelets, necklaces, watches, brooches, and pendants is ultrapopular with Parisians. Styles change quickly, but classics include charm bracelets and fine gold necklaces with whimsical pendants. ⊠ *45 rue Bonaparte, 6e, St-Germain-des-Prés* ☎ *01–46–33–20–00* ⊕ *www.agatha.fr* Ⓜ *St-Germain-des-Prés.*

Alexandra Sojfer. The proprietress of this legendary little store is the queen of walking sticks (the late president François Mitterrand bought his here). Alexandra Sojfer also carries an amazing range of umbrellas, parasols, small leather goods, and other accessories for men and women. ⊠ *218 bd. St-Germain, 7e, St-Germain-des-Prés* ☎ *01–42–22–17–02* ⊕ *www.alexandrasojfer.com* Ⓜ *Rue du Bac.*

16

Arthus-Bertrand. Dating back to 1803, Arthus-Bertrand has glass show-cases full of designer jewelry and numerous objects to celebrate births. ✉ *54 rue Bonaparte, 6e, St-Germain-des-Prés* ☎ *01–49–54–72–10* ⊕ *www.arthus-bertrand.com* Ⓜ *St-Germain-des-Prés.*

LINGERIE

Fodor's Choice ★ **Sabbia Rosa.** You could easily walk straight past this discreet, boudoir-like boutique. It is, however, one of the world's finest lingerie stores and the place where actresses Catherine Deneuve and Isabelle Adjani (along with others who might not want to reveal their errand) buy superb French silks. ✉ *71–73 rue des Sts-Pères, 6e, St-Germain-des-Prés* ☎ *01–45–48–88–37* Ⓜ *St-Germain-des-Prés.*

MARKETS

Boulevard Raspail. The city's major *marché biologique*, or organic mar-ket, is on Boulevard Raspail between Rue du Cherche-Midi and Rue de Rennes. Bursting with produce, fish, and eco-friendly products, it's open every Sunday from 9 to 3. The market also operates on Tuesday and Friday, selling nonorganic products from 7 to 2:30. ✉ *6e, St-Germain-des-Prés* Ⓜ *Rennes.*

Rue de Buci. Vendors at this market often tempt you with tastes of their wares: slices of sausage, slivers of peaches. It's closed Sunday afternoon and Monday. ✉ *6e, St-Germain-des-Prés* Ⓜ *Odéon.*

SHOES, HANDBAGS, AND LEATHER GOODS

Fodor's Choice ★ **Avril Gau.** After designing a dozen collections for Chanel, Gau struck out on her own, opening her neo-Baroque boutique on the charming Rue des Quatre Vents. Gau takes her inspiration from glamorous French movie icons, dreaming up styles that are elegant and sexy without being trashy. Sleek pumps, wedge booties, ballerina flats, and riding boots (all in the finest quality calf, reptile, and lambskin) are as classy as they come. Bags share the spotlight, with updated riffs on the classics. ✉ *17 rue des Quatre Vents, 6e, St-Germain-des-Prés* ☎ *01–43–29–49–04* ⊕ *www.avrilgau.com* Ⓜ *Odéon.*

Fodor's Choice ★ **Jamin Puech.** Nothing's plain Jane at Jamin Puech, which thinks of its bags not just as a necessity, but as jewelry. Beaded bags swing from thin link chains; fringes flutter from dark embossed-leather totes; and small evening purses are covered with shells, oversize sequins, or hand-dyed crochet. The collections fluctuate with the seasons but never fail to be whimsical, imaginative, and highly coveted. ✉ *43 rue Madame, 6e, St-Germain-des-Prés* ☎ *01–45–48–14–85* ⊕ *www.jamin-puech.com* Ⓜ *St-Sulpice.*

Fodor's Choice ★ **Jérôme Dreyfuss.** The newest star in the city's handbag universe has cap-tivated *le tout Paris* with his artsy take on hobo, Birkin, and messenger bags. Unique styles (like the twee-mini) are impossibly cute, and you may need to take out a second mortgage to tote around a luxe matte-python model. A line of gorgeous, high-heeled footwear is equally chic. ✉ *4 rue Jacob, 6e, St-Germain-des-Prés* ☎ *01–43–54–70–93* ⊕ *www. jerome-dreyfuss.com* Ⓜ *St-Germain-des-Prés.*

Robert Clergerie. Robert Clergerie knows that shoes make the woman. Styles combine visionary design, first-rate craftsmanship, and wearability with rare staying power. Plus, they're still a relative bargain on this side of the Atlantic. ⊠ *5 rue du Cherche-Midi, 6e, St-Germain-des-Prés* ☎ *01–45–48–75–47* ⊕ *www.robertclergerie.com* Ⓜ *St-Sulpice.*

Fodor's Choice
★ **Tila March.** Fame came quickly to this ex-fashion editor, whose wildly successful first handbag collection was snatched up by celebs such as Sienna Miller, Kirsten Dunst, and Scarlett Johansson. March uses velvety nubuck in a range of saturated colors—aubergine, olive, brick, taupe, and more—along with sleek matte crocodile to craft everything from large totes (like her handy Daisy bag) to tiny evening bags. With sleekly sophisticated shoes to match, it's not just a boutique—it's a destination. ⊠ *24 rue St-Sulpice, 6e, St-Germain-des-Prés* ☎ *01–43–26–69–20* ⊕ *www.tilamarch.com* Ⓜ *Odéon, St-Sulpice.*

Fodor's Choice
★ **Verbreuil.** The classic-contemporary handbags here are for women whose sense of style transcends any logo. Refined, discrete, and meticulously crafted down to the finest detail, each of the four styles—in calf, crocodile, and shagreen, with luxe variations for evening—will add infinite style and elegance to any outfit. ⊠ *4 rue de Fleurus, 6e, St-Germain-des-Prés* ☎ *01–45–49–22–69* ⊕ *www.verbreuil.com* Ⓜ *Vavin, St-Sulpice.*

WINE

Fodor's Choice
★ **La Dernière Goutte.** This inviting *cave* (literally wine store or wine cellar) focuses on wines by small French producers. Each is handpicked by the owner, along with a choice selection of estate Champagnes, Armagnac, and the classic Vieille Prune (plum brandy). The friendly English-speaking staff makes browsing a pleasure. ■ **TIP→ Don't miss the Saturday afternoon tastings with the winemakers.** ⊠ *6 rue de Bourbon le Château, 6e, St-Germain-des-Prés* ☎ *01–46–29–11–62* Ⓜ *Odéon.*

Ryst-Dupeyron. This shop specializes in fine wines and liquors, with Port, Calvados, and Armagnacs that date from 1878. Looking for a great gift idea? Find a bottle from the year of a friend's birth and have it labeled with your friend's name. Personalized bottles can be ordered and delivered on the same day. ⊠ *79 rue du Bac, 7e, St-Germain-des-Prés* ☎ *01–45–48–80–93* ⊕ *www.maisonrystdupeyron.com* Ⓜ *Rue du Bac.*

MONTPARNASSE

The legendary Rue d'Alésia alone lands this neighborhood on the Paris shopping radar. If you're willing to dig a little, a thrilling afternoon can be had seeking out the many bargains here—from steeply discounted designer clothes, shoes, and accessories to housewares and kids' togs. Just roll up your sleeves and dive in.

BARGAIN SHOPPING

Rue d'Alésia. This street in the 14e arrondissement is the main place to find stores selling last season's fashions at a discount. Items for sale include designer clothes, shoes, and accessories. Be forewarned: most of the stores on this street are much more downscale than their elegant sister shops. Dressing rooms are not always provided. ⊠ *14e, Montparnasse* Ⓜ *Alésia.*

16

MARKETS

Les Puces des Vanves. This small flea market, on the southern side of the city, is a hit with the fashion and design set. It specializes in easily portable items (like textiles or clothing) and collectible objects that include books, posters, postcards, and glassware. With tables sprawling along both sides of the sidewalk, there's an extravagant selection—just be sure to bargain with vendors. It's open on weekends from 8 to 1, but come early for the real deals: good stuff goes fast, and stalls are liable to pack up before noon. ⊠ *Av. de le Porte de Vanves and Av. Marc Sangnier, 14e, Montparnasse* ⊕ *www.pucesdevanves.fr* Ⓜ *Porte de Vanves.*

NIGHTLIFE

Updated
by Jennifer
Ladonne

You haven't seen the City of Lights until you've seen the city at night. Throngs pour into popular streets, filling the air with the melody of engaged conversation and clinking glasses. This is when locals let down their hair and reveal their true bonhomie, laughing and dancing, flirting and talking. Parisians love to savor life together: they dine out, drink endless espressos, offer innumerable toasts, and are often so reluctant to separate that they party all night.

Parisians go out weekends and weeknights, late and early. They tend to frequent the same places once they've found spots they like: it could be a wine bar, a corner café, a hip music club, or, more and more, a chic cocktail bar in an out-of-the-way neighborhood. A wise way to spend an evening is to pick an area in a neighborhood that interests you, then give yourself time to browse. Parisians also love to bar-hop, and the energy shifts throughout the evening, so be prepared to follow the crowds.

PLANNING

GETTING PAST THE BOUNCER

It shouldn't surprise any nightlife lover that the more *branché* (literally, "plugged-in" or trendy) the spot, the knottier the door-entry issue will be. Most bars aren't a problem, but when it comes to clubbing, don't assume you're going to get in just because you show up. This is particularly true at the hot spots near the Champs-Élysées. Although a limo at your disposal and global fame aren't essential to pass muster, you absolutely must have a cocky yet simultaneously polite attitude—and look fabulous. Having a high female quotient in your party definitely helps. Solo men—or, worse, groups of men—are going to have a tougher time, unless they are high rollers and have reserved a table (bottle purchase *obligatoire*).

HOURS

Most bars stay open until between midnight and 2 am, with no specific last call; however, wine bars and hotel bars tend to close earlier. Clubs usually stay open until 4 am, although more dance clubs are staying open until dawn or beyond (some even serve breakfast). Many drinking establishments are closed Sunday night, so check before heading out on the town. If you want to hit bars at a relatively quiet hour, go for an apéritif around 6 pm. The more earnest places offer drink specials at this time, and it's also when Parisians congregate to make late-night plans. Do be aware that some spots are better for *apéro* hour than others. Apéritifs are typically sipped while seated at café tables or on a terrace if weather permits.

LATE-NIGHT TRANSPORTATION

The métro runs until 12:40 am Sunday through Thursday; however, there is service on Friday night, Saturday night, and nights before holidays until 2:15 am, when the last train on each line reaches its terminus. After that, you can try a cab, but it can be extremely difficult to find one after midnight or anytime when there's a chance of rain. Taxi stands are plagued with long lines of prospective passengers waiting for a limited number of vehicles, and even calling one on weekends can be a frustrating exercise. Following serious protests by Paris cabbies, the city government has been trying to crack down on smartphone car-hire services, like Uber and its French counterpart Chauffeur Privé, with varying degrees of success. For now, though, these are still thriving; apps can be downloaded at ⊕ *www.uber.com/cities/paris* and ⊕ *www.chauffeur-prive.com*, respectively. As long as you're in the Wi-Fi zone, cars usually arrive in less than 10 minutes—and drivers will go anywhere in or outside Paris without sizing you up first and deciding whether they feel like it. Another alternative is the Noctilien, the sometimes rowdy night-bus system. And if you're having a lot of fun, you can always wait until the métro starts running again at 5:30 am.

WHAT TO WEAR

Despite their reputation for flair, Parisians generally adhere to a conservative-elegant style, although, depending on the venue, you may see some more glitzy attire. Sandals are almost unheard-of for men, and neither sex would ever wear sweatpants on a night out, with the rare exception of designer versions at dance club. If you want to blend in (and get into clubs), dress the part. Men, you can wear jeans, but leave the sneakers at your hotel and try adding a blazer. Ladies, dressing up doesn't necessarily mean donning a dress—Parisian girls manage to look hip in jeans, high-heeled boots, and stylish tops.

BARS

Paris bars run the gamut from the toniest hotel lounge to the tiniest neighborhood *troquet*, where old-timers gather for a chat over their morning *petit blanc*.

Hotel bars were once considered the aristocrats of the genre. Some mix historic pedigrees with a hushed elegance, but these days even the palaces are seeking a more modern edge. A few still represent the chicest spots for the fashion set and frequent high-roller visitors to Paris, but breathtaking prices and stiff competition among increasingly imaginative and atmospheric cocktail bars means a hotel bar had better be special to be worth the price (and many are: the Hemingway Bar at the Ritz and Les Ambassadeurs at Hotel de Crillon are two of the city's best).

The cocktail bar scene has absolutely exploded in Paris and is now grabbing the spotlight in terms of where to drink in the city. Parisian cocktail bars rival anywhere else in the world, and, as in other places, they focus on mixed drinks—although most offer everything from locally crafted beer to small-producer Champagnes. The new cocktail bars run the gamut from dauntingly elegant hotel lounges to designer dives, and they attract a diverse crowd willing to shell out anywhere from €7 to €25 a libation. Once called barmen, the new curators of cocktails are "mixologists," and the best of the lot garner fame and a following among devoted enthusiasts. Drinks are crafted, ingredients are sourced, the booze is barrel-aged or infused, syrups are house-made, and the ice is artisanal.

Wine bars (*caves à manger*) are different from regular bars in that they also serve food, from simple snacks like cheese and charcuterie to full meals, plus handpicked wines that are often "natural" or *biodynamique*. Wine bars keep mealtime hours and close earlier than proper bars—somewhere between 11 and midnight. Be warned, though: many establishments calling themselves wine bars or *bars à vins* are in fact full-fledged restaurants, with no bar to speak of.

CABARETS

Paris's cabarets range from vintage venues once haunted by Picasso and Piaf to those sinful showplaces where *tableaux vivants* offer acres of bare flesh. Some of these places, like the Lido, are more Vegas than the petticoat vision re-created by Hollywood in Baz Luhrmann's *Moulin Rouge*—but the rebirth of burlesque is making some of the old-school venues and racier versions like the lascivious Crazy Horse more popular. Although you can dine at many cabarets, food isn't the attraction. Prices range from about €50 (admission plus one drink) to more than €200 (dinner plus a show) and can go as high as €300 for the works. At all but a handful of specific cabarets on specific nights, the clientele tends overwhelmingly to be visitors, middle-aged and older, from either the French countryside or abroad.

CLUBS

Paris's hyped *boîtes de nuit*—more often referred to as simply *boîtes* (nightclubs)—tend to be expensive and exclusive. If you're friends with a regular or relatively famous, you'll have an easier time getting through the door. Cover charges at some can be upwards of €25, with drinks at the bar starting at €10 for a beer. Others are free to enter, but getting past the doorman can still be problematic. Locals looking to dance generally stick to the more laid-back clubs, where the cover ranges from free (usually on slower weekdays) to €20, and the emphasis is on the dancing, music, and offbeat atmosphere (think on a barge or under a bridge). Club popularity depends on the night or event, as Parisians are more loyal to certain DJs than venues and often hit two or three spots before ending up at one of the many after-parties, which can last until noon the next day.

GAY AND LESBIAN

These bars and clubs—mostly concentrated in the Marais and Les Halles—include some of the hipper addresses in the city. Keep in mind, however, that many of these spots fall in and out of favor at lightning speed. The best way to find out what's hot is by perusing the gay and lesbian magazine *Têtu* (available at newsstands and online at ⊕ *www. tetu.com*) or *2X*, the free "agenda" that can be found in any of the venues listed here. Paris's gay, lesbian, bi, and trans tourist office (⊕ *www. centrelgbtparis.org*) is another good resource, as is the civic-run nightlife website (⊕ *www.parisnightlife.fr/en*).

PUBS

Pubs wooing English-speaking clients with selections of British and Irish beers exist in Paris. They're often good places to watch an important soccer match.

NIGHTLIFE IN PARIS

Reviews are alphabetical by neighborhood.

CHAMPS-ÉLYSÉES

17

As the sun sets, Paris's most elegant neighborhood comes to life. Join the fashionistas for a *coupe de Champagne* in an opulent hotel bar, spend a night clubbing with the international jet set, or indulge in a bit of over-the-top French "culture" at a cabaret.

BARS

Bar Anglais. You might find diplomats and other dignitaries discussing state affairs at this rich red den of masculinity in L'Hôtel Raphael, a stone's throw from the Arc de Triomphe. The hotel's Rooftop Bar, a well-guarded Parisian secret, was voted the best bar in Europe in recent years. ⊠ *17 av. Kléber, 16e, Champs-Élysées* ☎ *01–53–64–32–00* ⊕ *www.leshotelsbaverez.com* Ⓜ *Kléber, Champs-Élysées–Etoile.*

Blind Bar, Maison Champs Élysées. This romantic spot in the ultrachic Maison Champs Élysées offers a wood fire in winter and a quiet terrace in warmer months. Its impressive range of Champagnes and impeccable cocktails is well worth the stellar prices. The separate all-black cigar bar is one of the remaining few in Paris. ⊠ *8 rue Jean Goujon, 8e, Champs-Élysées* ☎ *01–40–74–64–65* ⊕ *www.lamaisonchampselysees. com* Ⓜ *Franklin-D.-Roosevelt, Champs-Élysées–Clémenceau.*

Buddha Bar. While it may be past its prime with Parisians, visitors can't get enough of the high-camp towering gold Buddha that presides over this bar's giant palm fronds, red satin walls, and colorful chinoiserie. A themed dining room serves pan-Asian fare. There's also an upscale speakeasy, Le Secret 8, which you access by answering a daily riddle on the bar's Facebook page and getting a password (only 25 are given out per day). ⊠ *8 rue Boissy d'Anglas, 8e, Champs-Élysées* ☎ *01–53–05–90–00* ⊕ *www.buddhabar.com* Ⓜ *Concorde.*

Fodor's Choice **Le Bar Botaniste.** The Shangri-La Hotel's opulent bar, inspired by eccen-
★ tric botanist Prince Roland Bonapart (nephew to Napoleon), serves
up a dazzling menu of imaginative cocktails spiked with plant and
flower essences and fruit nectars. ⊠ *10 av. d'Iéna, 16e, Champs-Élysées*
☎ *01–53–67–19–98* ⊕ *www.shangri-la.com* Ⓜ *Iéna.*

Le Bar at George V. An ultraluxe, clubby hideaway in the Four Seasons
Hotel, Le Bar at George V is perfect for stargazing from the plush
wine-red armchairs, Cognac in hand. Its charm still lures the glitterati, especially during fashion weeks. Be sure to notice the hotel's signature—and stunning—flower arrangements. ⊠ *31 av. George V, 8e,
Champs-Élysées* ☎ *01–49–52–70–00* ⊕ *www.fourseasons.com/paris/
dining/lounges/le_bar* Ⓜ *George V.*

Le Bar at the Hôtel Plaza Athénée. This hotel bar *par excellence* has a
clubby feel that lures a younger fashion crowd. Lounge in leather chairs
under an Yves Klein–blue ceiling installation while sipping stylish cocktails, like the signature Rose Royal (Champagne, raspberry, and a splash
of Cognac). Mood lighting and music spun by a live DJ Thursday
through Saturday set the tone for a glam late-night rendezvous. ⊠ *25 av.
Montaigne, 8e, Champs-Élysées* ☎ *01–53–67–66–00* ⊕ *www.dorches-
tercollection.com* Ⓜ *Alma–Marceau.*

Fodor's Choice **Le Bar du Bristol.** Apparently not satisfied with its usual rich and powerful
★ clientele, this tony spot is now vying for the impossibly hip too. Along
with enticing cocktails and rarified spirits, Le Bar promises exceptional
wines and tapas. Weekdays from 7 pm to 9:30 pm, it also showcases
curated art videos on its behind-the-bar mirror screen. Chic Paris DJs
heat up the scene between 9:30 pm and 2 am on Friday and Saturday.
⊠ *112 rue du Faubourg St-Honoré, 8e, Champs-Élysées* ☎ *01–53–43–
43–00* ⊕ *www.lebristolparis.com* Ⓜ *Miromesnil.*

Le Marta Paris. Swanky décor and luscious drinks are drawing the cocktail cognoscenti to this intimate lounge hidden away in the legendary
Le Fouquet's Hotel. If you prefer daylight, the hotel offers two other
superchic bars: Le Joy and L'Escadrille. ⊠ *Le Fouquet's Paris, 46 av.
George V, 8e, Champs-Élysées* ☎ *01–40–69–60–00* ⊕ *www.hotelsbarri-
ere.com* Ⓜ *Georges V.*

Fodor's Choice **Les Ambassadeurs.** Within the Crillon Hotel is this over-the-top bar that
★ makes use of the soaring room's original 18th-century gilding, sump-
tuous velvet seating, glorious chandeliers, and a golden bar to create
an atmosphere of unparalleled opulence. An eclectic cocktail list and
a scintillating selection of champagnes add to the extravagance. ⊠ *10
pl. de la Concorde, Champs-Élysées* ☎ *01–44–71–15–00* ⊕ *www.rose-
woodhotels.com/en/hotel-de-crillon* Ⓜ *Place de la Concorde.*

No Comment. Housed in a former swinger's club, this nightclub boasts
that it has retained the libertine vibe without the libertine ways. Only
the trendiest seem to go—and get in. ⊠ *36 rue de Ponthieu, 8e, Champs-
Élysées* ☎ *06–88–74–59–86* Ⓜ *Saint-Philippe du Roule.*

Publicis Drugstore. Open daily until 2 am, this bustling, phantasmagorical,
multilevel, bar-brasserie–hipster shop is just across the street from the Arc
de Triomphe. ⊠ *133 av. des Champs-Élysées, 8e, Champs-Élysées* ☎ *01–
44–43–79–00* ⊕ *www.publicisdrugstore.com* Ⓜ *Charles de Gaulle–Étoile.*

Fodor'sChoice ★ **Saint James Club Paris.** Like a library room out of *Harry Potter,* the bar at the Saint James Club Paris—complete with 5,000 leather-bound volumes and a cozy fireplace—is studiously inviting. It's very French, and open to nonmembers only after 7 pm or during Sunday brunch. The owners are a venerable old Bordeaux family; accordingly, you'll find a respectable selection of Champagnes and wines. ✉ *43 av. Bugeaud, 16e, Champs-Élysées* ☎ *01–44–05–81–81* ⊕ *www.saintjamesclub.com* Ⓜ *Porte Dauphine.*

CABARET

Fodor'sChoice ★ **Crazy Horse.** This world-renowned cabaret has elevated the striptease to an art form. Founded in 1951, it's famous for gorgeous dancers and naughty routines characterized by lots of humor and very little clothing. What garments there are have been dazzlingly designed by the likes of Louboutin and Alaïa and shed by top divas (including Dita von Teese). Reserved seats for the show start at €85. ✉ *12 av. George V, 8e, Champs-Élysées* ☎ *01–47–23–32–32* ⊕ *www.lecrazyhorseparis. com* Ⓜ *Alma–Marceau.*

Lido. The legendary Lido now adds a modern-day dose of awe-inspiring stage design to the cabaret's trademark style. The 100-minute productions—still featuring those beloved Bluebell Girls and 12 "Lido boys"—run at 9 pm and 11 pm, 365 days a year. Dinner for Two packages for the earlier show include the Soirée Etoile (€170), Soirée Champs-Elysées (€195), and the Soirée Triomphe (€300). If you're on a budget, €115 gets you a ticket plus half a bottle of bubbly. Yes, those prices are per person, but this is Paris nightlife as it's meant to be experienced. It's best to book your tickets in advance by phone, online, or on-site. ✉ *116 bis, av. des Champs-Élysées, 8e, Champs-Élysées* ☎ *01–40–76–56–10* ⊕ *www.lido.fr* Ⓜ *George V.*

CLUBS

Fodor'sChoice ★ **Manko.** This is a lavish spot for fashionistas and upscale revelers seeking chic thrills. Outrageous weekend cabarets, themed party nights, and a *branché* vibe—plus some very spiffy cocktails—put this happening club high on Paris's nightclub A-list. ✉ *15 ave Montaigne, 8e, Champs-Élysées* ☎ *01–82–28–00–15* ⊕ *www.manko-paris.com* Ⓜ *Alma-Marceau, Champs-Élysées Clemenceau.*

Fodor'sChoice ★ **Zig Zag.** With a state-of-the-art sound system, a glam location, and a riotous dance floor with room for 1,200 revelers, Zig Zag is hugely popular. Join the enthusiastic crowd gyrating to electrobeats from DJs or live bands ensconced on an illuminated stage highlighted by two giant screens, or observe the action from the wraparound balcony. ✉ *32 rue Marbeuf, 8e, Champs-Élysées* ☎ *06–35–25–03–61* ⊕ *zigzagclub.fr* Ⓜ *Franklin-D.-Roosevelt.*

JAZZ CLUBS

Jazz Club Etoile. This moody club at the Méridien Hotel hosts a roster of top-billed international musicians in a classy set of rooms. Check out the Sunday afternoon jazz brunch buffet and the interior garden. ✉ *Méridien Hotel, 81 bd. Gouvion–St-Cyr, 17e, Champs-Élysées* ☎ *01–40–68–30–42* ⊕ *www.jazzclub-paris.com* Ⓜ *Porte Maillot.*

17

AROUND THE LOUVRE

The cocktail craze has taken off in this atmospheric neighborhood, where dusky speakeasies and cozy hotel bars provide the perfect prelude to an evening of jazz or dancing until dawn at hip all-night clubs.

BARS

Fodor's Choice
★ **Ballroom du Beef Club.** Unmarked black door, basement setting, pressed-tin ceilings, atmospheric lighting—did anyone say "speakeasy"? All this and luscious libations draw a sophisticated crowd that appreciates the extra touches that make this cocktail bar a standout. ☒ *58 rue Jean-Jacques-Rousseau, 1er, Louvre* ☎ *09–54–37–13–65* Ⓜ *Les Halles, Palais Royal–Musée du Louvre.*

Bar 8. Ever since the monolithic marble bar at the Mandarin Oriental Hotel opened its doors, it has been the "in" game in town. There's an extensive Champagne menu, and the terrace is especially busy during fashion weeks. ☒ *251 rue Saint-Honoré, 1er, Louvre* ☎ *01–70–98–78–88* ⊕ *www.mandarinoriental.com* Ⓜ *Concorde, Tuileries.*

Bar 228. Hôtel Meurice converted its ground-floor Fontainebleau library into the intimate Bar 228, with wood paneling and huge murals depicting the royal hunting forests of Fontainebleau. Its loyal fashion crowd is continually wooed by Philippe Starck's decor updates and lubricated with the bar's famous Bellinis. Try the Meurice Millennium cocktail, made with Champagne, rose liqueur, and Cointreau. ☒ *228 rue de Rivoli, 1er, Louvre* ☎ *01–44–58–10–66* ⊕ *www.dorchestercollection.com* Ⓜ *Tuileries.*

Chacha Club. Behind a nondescript facade you'll find a 1930s-style bar-club-restaurant arranged like a private home, with a series of rooms on three floors—including a special smoking lounge—and lots of corners where the casually stylish cool cats of Paris get cozy until the wee hours. ☒ *47 rue Berger, 1er, Louvre* ☎ *01–40–13–12–12* Ⓜ *Louvre–Rivoli.*

Fodor's Choice
★ **Experimental Cocktail Club.** Fashioned as a speakeasy on a tiny brick-paved street, the Experimental Cocktail Club seems like it should be lighted by gas lamps. The show is all about the *alcool*; colorful, innovative cocktails like the Lemon Drop are mixed with aplomb by friendly (and attractive) bartenders. By 11 pm it's packed with a diverse mix of locals, professionals, and fashionistas, who occasionally dress up like characters from a Toulouse-Lautrec painting on special costume nights. ☒ *37 rue Saint-Sauveur, 2e, Louvre* ☎ *01–45–08–88–09* Ⓜ *Réamur–Sébastopol.*

The Hemingway Bar & the Ritz Bar. Literature lovers, cocktail connoisseurs, and other drink-swilling devotees still flock to the iconic Hemingway Bar & the Ritz Bar inside the Ritz Hotel. Drinks come with a rose, and bartenders will mix you a bespoke drink according to your personality and preferences. ☒ *15 pl. Vendôme, 1er, Louvre* ⊕ *www.ritzparis.com* Ⓜ *Opéra.*

Hôtel Costes. Despite years on the scene, Hôtel Costes still draws big names—and not just during fashion weeks. Expect to cross paths with anyone from Rihanna to Leonardo DiCaprio, as long as you make it past the chilly greeting of the statuesque hostess. Dressing to kill is strongly advised, especially for newcomers; otherwise, expect all the tables to be suddenly reserved. ✉ *239 rue St-Honoré, 1er, Louvre* ☎ *01–42–44–50–50* ⊕ *hotelcostes.com* Ⓜ *Tuileries.*

Jefrey's. A custom-DJ'd music track, enticing love seats, and inventive cocktails make this an easy choice for an intimate evening in sophisticated surroundings. Need further incentive to return? Jefrey's lets you keep your bottle stored on the shelf, with your name on it, for next time. ✉ *14 rue Saint-Sauveur, 2e, Louvre* ☎ *01–42–33–60–77* ⊕ *www. jefreys.fr* Ⓜ *Étienne Marcel.*

L'Assaggio Bar. At this bar, in Chanel's old neighborhood, you can order tea and *macarons* until midnight—in addition to cocktails. ✉ *33–37 rue Cambon, 1e, Louvre* ☎ *01–44–58–44–58* ⊕ *www.castille.com* Ⓜ *Concorde, Madeleine.*

Le Café Noir. Parisians from *bobos* (bourgeois-bohemians) to *pompiers* (firefighters) are lured to Le Café Noir's elegantly worn digs. In addition to cool drinks and friendly staff, the place features a pipe-smoking papier-mâché fish and a vintage leopard-print-covered motorbike. (The restaurant with the same name is unrelated.) ✉ *65 rue Montmartre, 2e, Louvre* ☎ *01–40–39–07–36* ⊕ *www.cafenoirparis.fr* Ⓜ *Étienne Marcel.*

Le Fumoir. Fashionable neighborhood gallery owners and young professionals meet for late-afternoon wine, early-evening cocktails, or dinner at this oh-so-reliably ultrachic charmer across from the Louvre. It features a superstocked bar in the front, an ample multilingual library in the back, and chessboards for the clientele to use while sipping martinis. ✉ *6 rue de l'Amiral-Coligny, 1er, Louvre* ☎ *01–42–92–00–24* ⊕ *www. lefumoir.com* Ⓜ *Louvre.*

CLUBS

Kong. This club is glorious not only for its panoramic skyline views but also for its exquisite manga-inspired decor and kooky, disco-ball-and-kid-sumo-adorned bathrooms. On weekends, top-shelf DJs keep patrons dancing. ✉ *1 rue du Pont Neuf, 1er, Louvre* ☎ *01–40–39–09–00* ⊕ *www.kong.fr* Ⓜ *Pont Neuf.*

VIP Room. Although it's no longer on the Champs-Élysées, this temple of bling still attracts hot DJs, beautiful people, and yes, VIPs. Check the website for info on the latest soirée: usually R&B–hip-hop–Top 40 crowd pleasers. There's a gift shop, a ground-floor café, and a pricey Italian restaurant on the top floor. Be sure to dress to impress. ✉ *188 bis, rue de Rivoli, 1er, Louvre* ☎ *01–58–36–46–00* ⊕ *www.viproom. com* Ⓜ *Palais Royal.*

GAY AND LESBIAN

Banana Café. This place draws a trendy, scantily clad mixed crowd and offers show tunes in the cellar, where dancing on tables is the norm. A very happy happy hour, lasting from 6 to 11 pm, primes the audience for the incomparable banana "go-go boys" nightly show. ✉ *13 rue de la Ferronnerie, 1er, Louvre* ☎ *01–42–33–35–31* ⊕ *www.bananacafeparis. com* Ⓜ *Châtelet–Les Halles.*

17

Le Dépôt. A cruising bar and club, Le Dépôt has the largest back room in Europe. The ever-popular Gay Tea Dance spices up Sunday afternoon. ✉ *10 rue aux Ours, 3e, Louvre* ☎ *01–44–54–96–96* ⊕ *www.ledepot-paris.com* Ⓜ *Étienne Marcel.*

Le Duplex. Young tortured-artist types flock here to enjoy the frequent art exhibitions, alternative music, and mood-inspiring ambient lighting. ✉ *25 rue Michel-Le-Comte, 3e, Louvre* ☎ *01–42–72–80–86* ⊕ *www. leduplex.com* Ⓜ *Rambuteau.*

JAZZ CLUBS

Duc des Lombards. Located in a famously bopping neighborhood, the Duc's cozy interior and top-class jazz acts make it one of the city's most popular small venues. It's best to purchase advance tickets online (go to *bons plans* for discounted tickets). ✉ *42 rue des Lombards, 1er, Louvre* ☎ *01–42–33–22–88* ⊕ *www.ducdeslombards.com* Ⓜ *Châtelet–Les Halles.*

Le Sunset-Sunside. This two-part club hosts French and American jazz musicians: the Sunside upstairs is devoted mostly to acoustic jazz, while the Sunset downstairs features everything from electronic jazz, fusion, and groove to classic and swing. Jam sessions have been known to last well into the wee hours. ✉ *60 rue des Lombards, 1er, Louvre* ☎ *01–40–26–46–60* ⊕ *www.sunset-sunside.com* Ⓜ *Châtelet–Les Halles.*

LES GRANDS BOULEVARDS

An assortment of well-established British-Irish pubs and clubs brings an Anglo-inflected nuance to this many-faceted neighborhood that bustles by day and empties out at night.

BARS

Barramundi. The city's nouveau-riche chill to electro-lounge tunes and world music here, drinking in Barramundi's cool golden ambience as they sip cold tropical drinks at the long copper bar. ✉ *3 rue Taitbout, 9e, Grands Boulevards* ☎ *01–47–70–21–21* ⊕ *www.barramundi.fr* Ⓜ *Richelieu–Drouot.*

Corcoran's Irish Pub. This roomy pub, with several locations in central Paris, has an ample menu, a gorgeous bar, plus old-timey photos and quotations on the walls—such as "He who opens his mouth most is the one who opens his purse least." Conversation turns to dancing at night with a regulated guy-to-girl ratio, so men shouldn't try coming alone. ✉ *23 bd. Poissonière, 2e, Grands Boulevards* ☎ *01–40–39–00–16* ⊕ *www.corcoransirishpub.fr* Ⓜ *Grands Boulevards.*

Fodor'sChoice ★ **Delaville Café.** With its huge, heated sidewalk terrace, Belle Époque mosaic-tile bar, graffitied walls, and swishy lounge, Delaville Café boasts a funky ambience. Hot Paris DJs ignite the scene Thursday to Saturday, so arrive early on weekends if you want a seat. ✉ *34 bd. Bonne Nouvelle, 10e, Grands Boulevards* ☎ *01–48–24–48–09* ⊕ *delavillecafe.com* Ⓜ *Bonne Nouvelle, Grands Boulevards.*

Duke's Bar. A favorite not only for its prestigious location between Opéra and Place Vendôme, but also for its worn-leather chairs and English-private-club feel, the Westminster Hotel's bar offers drinks like the "James Bond" and "Duke's Martini." At times you get the feeling that Mr. Hercule

Poirot is lurking just behind that wing chair. ✉ *13 rue de la Paix, 2e, Grands Boulevards* ☎ *01–42–61–55–11* ⊕ *www.leceladon.com* Ⓜ *Opéra.*

Harry's Bar. Also known as Harry's New York Bar, this cozy, wood-paneled hangout decorated with dusty college pennants is popular with expats and American-loving French people who welcome the ghosts of Ernest Hemingway and F. Scott Fitzgerald, who drank themselves unconscious here. Founded in 1911, Gershwin composed *An American in Paris* in the piano bar downstairs and the Bloody Mary is said to have originated on-site. ✉ *5 rue Daunou, 2e, Grands Boulevards* ☎ *01–42–61–71–14* Ⓜ *Opéra.*

Le Bar Long. At the Royal Monceau's innovative bar your mixologist will fix your drink right next to you at the illuminated, Philippe Stark–designed bar. The collection of glasses on the walls isn't just decoration—you may choose which to drink from. A light tapas menu is served between 6 and 11 pm. ✉ *37 av. Hoche, 8e, Grands Boulevards* ☎ *01–42–99–88–00* ⊕ *www.leroyalmonceau.com* Ⓜ *Ternes.*

Le Truskel. What looks, sounds, and feels like an English pub but kicks booty like a punk club? Le Truskel. The basement showcases gigs by the globe's hottest new alternative acts, while a loud, happy Parisian rocker crowd staggers around the roomy bar. ✉ *12 rue Feydeau, 2e, Grands Boulevards* ☎ *01–40–26–59–97* ⊕ *www.truskel.com* Ⓜ *Bourse.*

CLUBS

Le Rex. Open Wednesday through Sunday, this temple of techno and house is popular with students. One of France's most famous DJs, Laurent Garnier, is sometimes at the turntables. ✉ *5 bd. Poissonnière, 2e, Grands Boulevards* ☎ *01–42–36–10–96* ⊕ *rexclub.com* Ⓜ *Grands Boulevards.*

Silencio. David Lynch named his nightclub after a reference in his Oscar-nominated hit, *Mulholland Drive.* Silencio, which hosts concerts, films, and other performances, is open only to members and their guests until midnight; after that everyone is allowed. Guest DJs spin until 4 am Tuesday through Thursday, and until 6 am on Friday and Saturday. ✉ *142 rue Montmartre, 2e, Grands Boulevards* ☎ *01–40–13–12–33* ⊕ *www.silencio-club.com* Ⓜ *Bourse, Sentier.*

JAZZ CLUBS

Fodor's Choice
★

New Morning. At New Morning—the premier spot for serious fans of avant-garde jazz, folk, and world music—the look is spartan, and the mood reverential. ✉ *7 rue des Petites-Ecuries, 10e, Grands Boulevards* ☎ *01–45–23–51–41* ⊕ *www.newmorning.com* Ⓜ *Château d'Eau.*

MONTMARTRE

Vestiges of this *quartier*'s absinthe-tinged heyday, immortalized by Toulouse-Lautrec and Renoir, still endure in the cabarets and clubs that extend from the heights of Montmartre down to louche Pigalle's newly vibrant cocktail bar and dance scene.

BARS

Café la Fourmi. One of Pigalle's trendiest addresses, Café la Fourmi has a funky, spacious bar-café where cool locals party. ⊠ *74 rue des Martyrs, 18e, Montmartre* ☎ *01–42–64–70–35* Ⓜ *Pigalle.*

Fodor'sChoice ★ **Dirty Dick.** An updated version of the classic tiki lounge, this stylish option in the hip Pigalle neighborhood comes complete with lurid lighting, life-size totems, and retro rattan furniture. All the exotic drinks you'd expect at a Polynesian beach hut (or '60s motel lounge) are here—including fruity cocktails, a range of rums, and punch bowls with names like Amazombie. ⊠ *10 rue Frochot, 9e, Montmartre* ☎ *01–48–78–74–58* Ⓜ *Pigalle.*

Fodor'sChoice ★ **Glass.** Masquerading as a dive in Pigalle's rapidly gentrifying red-light district, this dark, candlelighted space is actually a shrine to urban cool. Hipsters party to a DJ while knocking back sophisticated cocktails, artisanal beers, and frosty margaritas from the frozen-drinks machine. It might also be the only place in Paris to find a boilermaker (a beer and a shot). Gourmet hot dogs help fuel the late-night party scene. ⊠ *9 rue Frochot, 9e, Montmartre* ☎ *06–25–16–72–17* ⊕ *www.glassparis. com* Ⓜ *Pigalle.*

Le Rendez-Vous des Amis. This makes an intriguing midway breather if you climb the hill of Montmartre by foot. Le Rendez-Vous des Amis has a jovial staff, eclectic music, and a century's worth of previous patrons immortalized in photos. ⊠ *23 rue Gabrielle, 18e, Montmartre* ☎ *01–46–06–01–60* Ⓜ *Abbesses.*

Le Sancerre. Café by day, Le Sancerre turns into an essential watering hole for Montmartrois and artists at night, with Belgian beers on tap and an impressive list of cocktails. Locals love its traditional old-school vibe. ⊠ *35 rue des Abbesses, 18e, Montmartre* ☎ *01–42–58–08–20* Ⓜ *Abbesses.*

Fodor'sChoice ★ **Paname Brewing Company.** One of Paris's first and best microbreweries on the city's relatively new brewery scene (Paris has always been more of a wine city, of course), Paname offers six masterful craft beers and a fabulous terrace on a plum spot facing the Canal de la Villette. ⊠ *41 bis, quai de la Loire, Montmartre* ☎ *01–40–36–43–55* ⊕ *www.paname-brewingcompany.com* Ⓜ *Crimée, Laumière, Ourcq.*

CABARET

Fodor'sChoice ★ **Au Lapin Agile.** An authentic survivor from the 19th century, Au Lapin Agile considers itself the doyen of cabarets. Founded in 1860, it inhabits the same modest house that was a favorite subject of painter Maurice Utrillo. It became the home-away-from-home for Braque, Modigliani, Apollinaire, and Picasso—who once paid for a meal with one of his paintings, then promptly exited and painted another that he named after this place. There are no topless dancers; this is a genuine French cabaret with songs, poetry, and humor (in French) in a publike setting. Entry is €28. ⊠ *22 rue des Saules, 18e, Montmartre* ☎ *01–46–06–85–87* ⊕ *www.au-lapin-agile.com* Ⓜ *Lamarck–Caulaincourt.*

Michou. The always-decked-out-in-blue owner, Michou, presents an over-the-top show here. It features *tranformiste* men on stage in extravagant drag, performing with high camp for a radically different cabaret experience. Dinner shows are €110 and €140, or you can watch from the bar for €40, which includes a drink. ✉ *80 rue des Martyrs, 18e, Montmartre* ☎ *01–46–06–16–04* ⊕ *www.michou.com* Ⓜ *Pigalle.*

Moulin Rouge. When it opened in 1889, the Moulin Rouge lured Parisians of all social stripes—including, of course, the famous Toulouse-Lautrec, who immortalized the venue and its dancers in his paintings. Although shows are no longer quite so exotic (no elephants or donkey rides for the ladies), you will still see the incomparable French cancan. It's the highlight of what is now a classy version of a Vegas-style revue, starring 100 dancers, acrobats, ventriloquists, and contortionists, and more than 1,000 costumes. Dinner starts at 7, revues at 9 and 11 (arrive 30 minutes early). Men are expected to wear a jacket. Prices range from €115 for just a revue to €240 for a luxe dinner and a show. ✉ *82 bd. de Clichy, 18e, Montmartre* ☎ *01–53–09–82–82* ⊕ *www.moulinrouge.fr* Ⓜ *Blanche.*

THE MARAIS

A first-class shopping destination by day, by night this superchic neighborhood draws a diverse and trendy crowd for its *branché* cocktail bars and the city's most vibrant gay and lesbian scene.

BARS

Andy Wahloo. With a hip crowd and an Andy Warhol–meets-*Casablanca* decor, here you can relax on oversize paint-can stools beneath high-kitsch silk-screened Moroccan coffee ads, and listen to funky Arabic Raï remixes. Dancing to DJs starts later in the night. ✉ *69 rue des Gravilliers, 3e, Marais Quarter* ☎ *01–42–71–20–38* ⊕ *andywahloo-bar.com* Ⓜ *Arts et Métiers.*

Auld Alliance. You'll feel like an honorary Highlander at Auld Alliance, where Scottish shields adorn the walls and the bar staff (who don kilts for special events) serve 120-plus types of whiskey. Scottish beer and pub grub, including a haggis burger, are also available. It's a great place to catch televised soccer or rugby matches, and, on occasion, live music. ✉ *80 rue François Miron, 4e, Marais Quarter* ☎ *01–48–04–30–40* ⊕ *www.theauldalliance.com* Ⓜ *St-Paul.*

Bar at the Hotel Jules & Jim. The look here is something between a chic contemporary Paris apartment and a low-key lounge. Enjoy a cocktail over a good book from the bar library, or relax with a smooth drink in front of the outdoor fireplace. ✉ *11 rue des Gravilliers, 3e, Marais Quarter* ☎ *01–44–54–13–13* ⊕ *www.hoteljulesetjim.com* Ⓜ *Arts et Métiers, Rambuteau.*

Fodor'sChoice
★ **Candelaria.** Steamy Candelaria is a taquería by day and a cocktail lounge by night. The tang of tequila hangs in the air at this hip hideaway, where deftly crafted drinks are poured for a contented crowd. ✉ *52 rue de Saintonge, 3e, Marais Quarter* ☎ *01–42–74–41–28* ⊕ *www.candelariaparis.com* Ⓜ *Filles du Calvaire.*

Grazie. Equal parts cocktail bar and gourmet pizzeria, this stylish offspring of the übercool concept store Merci promises top-quality libations and stone-oven-baked pizza. The decor is industrial-rustic, with

17

pressed-tin ceilings and a corrugated-iron bar, all enhanced by mood lighting. It's jam-packed with neighborhood hipsters, so reservations are a must. ⊠ *91 bd. Beaumarchais, 3e, Marais Quarter* 🕾 *01–42–78– 11–96* ⊕ *www.graziegrazie.fr* Ⓜ *Saint-Sébastien–Froissart.*

La Belle Hortense. This spot is heaven for anyone who ever wished they had a book in a bar (or a drink in a bookstore). The *bar litteraire* is the infamous spot where gal-about-town Catherine M. launched her *vie sexuelle* that became a bawdy bestseller. ⊠ *31 rue Vieille-du-Temple, 4e, Marais Quarter* 🕾 *01–48–04–74–60* Ⓜ *St-Paul.*

Fodor's Choice
★
Le Mary Celeste. Half-price oysters at happy hour (6–7 pm) aren't the only reason this refreshingly unpretentious cocktail bar is wildly popular. One of a trilogy of superhip watering holes (including Candelaria and Glass) opened by a trio of expat restaurateurs, its craft cocktails, microbrews, natural wines, and standout tapas menu deliver the goods and then some. If you're planning to dine, reserve ahead online. ⊠ *1 rue Commines, 3e, Marais Quarter* ⊕ *www.quixotic-projects.com/venue/ mary-celeste* Ⓜ *Saint-Sébastian–Froissart.*

Le Trésor. Located on a tiny street that's a tad separated from the some-times-madding crowd of the Marais, this large, lively space has mis-matched baroque furnishings and a chill vibe. ⊠ *7 rue du Trésor, 4e, Marais Quarter* 🕾 *01–42–71–35–17* Ⓜ *St-Paul.*

Little Red Door. Behind the red door, you'll discover a dark, cozy lounge that has style, sophistication, and atmosphere without the attitude. Creative cocktails—supplemented by artisanal beers and well-chosen wines by the glass (the last of which aren't always easy to come by in a cocktail bar)—can be enjoyed from a cushy velour barstool or cubby-hole alcove. ⊠ *60 rue Charlot, 3e, Marais Quarter* 🕾 *01–42–71–19–32* ⊕ *www.lrdparis.com* Ⓜ *Filles du Calvert.*

Max y Jeremy. An almost-too-cool crew can be found in Max y Jeremy's red ember-like interior, drinking cocktails and eating the sultry bite-sized *pintxos* of Basque country. There's a distinct party atmosphere here, which can spill into the street, especially in summer. ⊠ *6 rue Dupuis, 3e, Marais Quarter* 🕾 *01–42–78–00–68* ⊕ *www.maxyjeremy. com* Ⓜ *Temple.*

Fodor's Choice
★
Sherry Butt. On a quiet street close to the Bastille, Sherry Butt's relaxed loftlike atmosphere, imaginative drinks, whiskey flights, and tasty bar menu draw a lively crowd that appreciates meticulously crafted cocktails. A DJ spins on weekends. ⊠ *20 rue Beautreillis, 4e, Marais Quarter* 🕾 *09– 83–38–47–80* ⊕ *www.sherrybuttparis.com* Ⓜ *Bastille, Sully-Morland.*

GAY AND LESBIAN

Café Cox. "Le Cox" is a prime gay pickup joint. The café is known for its live DJ sets; and the extended Sunday happy hour—from 6 pm to 2 am—is a rollicking good time. ⊠ *15 rue des Archives, 4e, Marais Quarter* 🕾 *01–42–72–08–00* ⊕ *www.cox.fr* Ⓜ *Hôtel de Ville.*

Open Café. Drawing everyone from suits to punks, this spot is less of a hook-up spot than neighboring Café Cox. Relaxed and always packed, it has a disco-café vibe. ⊠ *17 rue des Archives, 4e, Marais Quarter* 🕾 *01–42–72–26–18* ⊕ *www.opencafe.fr* Ⓜ *Hôtel de Ville.*

Raidd Bar. The ever-popular Raidd has a darker downstairs bar and potent drinks. The men are hot, and so is the steamy shower show presented after 11 pm—not for timid voyeurs. ✉ *23 rue du Temple, 3e, Marais Quarter* ☎ *01–42–77–04–88* ⊕ *www.raiddbar.com* Ⓜ *Hôtel de Ville, St-Paul.*

So What! This happening lesbian bar in the heart of the gay district welcomes all comers (including small groups of men). The DJ in the tiny basement cooks on Friday and Saturday nights. ✉ *30 rue du Roi de Sicile, 4e, Marais Quarter* ☎ *01–42–71–24–59* Ⓜ *St-Paul.*

Tango. Carefully safeguarding its dance-hall origins, Tango lures a friendly mixed crowd of gays, lesbians, and "open-minded" heteros. Late-night music is mostly French and American pop, but the DJ plays classic *chansons* (French torch songs) before midnight—so arrive early to waltz and swing. ✉ *13 rue au Maire, 3e, Marais Quarter* ☎ *01–42–72–17–78* ⊕ *www.boite-a-frissons.fr* Ⓜ *Arts et Métiers.*

3W Kafé. 3W, as in "Women With Women," is a pillar of the Paris lesbian scene. ✉ *8 rue des Ecouffes, 4e, Marais Quarter* ☎ *01–48–87–39–26* Ⓜ *St-Paul.*

EASTERN PARIS

Young and hip—from the colorful cafés and bars surrounding Place de la Bastille to the newly chic 20e arrondissement, with Oberkampf's artsy cocktail clubs and Canal St-Martin's trendy watering holes in between—there's enough here for a week of stellar nights out.

BASTILLE/NATION

CLUBS

Fodor's Choice
★
Concrete. On a barge moored in the Seine, superhip Concrete is one of Paris's preeminent hard-core dance venues and a trailblazer on the techno scene. The club goes full tilt until the wee hours on Friday and Saturday nights; it also opens on alternate Sundays, when you can party from 7 am to 2 am accompanied by live acts—heavy on the techno—and Paris's hottest DJs. ✉ *69 port de la Rapée, Bastille* ☎ *No phone* ⊕ *www.concreteparis.fr* Ⓜ *Gare de Lyon, Gare d'Austerlitz.*

Le Balajo. A casual dance club in an old ballroom, Le Balajo has been around since 1936. Latin groove, funk, and R&B disco are the standards, with old-style musette Monday afternoon, salsa on Tuesday and Thursday nights, and rock on Wednesday night. Friday and Saturday are ladies' nights, with free entry before 12:30 am. ✉ *9 rue de Lappe, 11e, Bastille* ☎ *01–47–00–07–87* ⊕ *www.balajo.fr* Ⓜ *Bastille.*

BERCY/TOLBIAC

BARS

Folie en Tête. Folie en Tête or "Crazy in the Head," is a former mainstay of Paris's '70s punk scene. The comfortable interior is decorated with percussion instruments, comic books, and old skis. It's known for world music and jazz, not to mention the traffic light in the toilet that lets you know when it's safe to enter. ✉ *33 rue de la Butte aux Cailles, 13e, Eastern Paris* ☎ *01–45–80–65–99* ⊕ *lafolieentete.wix.com/lesite* Ⓜ *Corvisart, Place d'Italie.*

17

CLUBS

Le Djoon. This is not the place to stand around. Le Djoon attracts a devoted dance crowd, and DJs (inspired by the '80s New York house scene) mix afro, disco, and funk. It's a taxi-ride away from everywhere, but a fun diversion from the normally cramped clubs. It's open Friday and Saturday from 11:30 to 5 am, Thursday from 10 to 1 am. ✉ *22 bd. Vincent Auriol, 13e, Eastern Paris* ☎ *01–45–70–83–49* ⊕ *www.djoon. com* Ⓜ *Quai de la Gare.*

Fodor's Choice
★

Le Petit Bain. There's something about dancing on the water that gets this cool, casual crowd revved up for the live concerts and DJ nights set on a huge barge moored on the Seine. Eclectic sounds include alternative, electro, rock, and folktronica plus a program of cultural events. It's also great place to go just for watching the sun set on the river over a nice drink. ✉ *7 Port de la Gare, 13e, Bercy* ☎ *01–43–49–68–92* ⊕ *www. petitbain.org* Ⓜ *Quay de la Gare.*

CANAL ST-MARTIN

BARS

Chez Prune. Epitomizing the effortless cool of this arty neighborhood, Chez Prune is a lively golden getaway. It offers the designers, architects, and journalists who gather here a prime terrace for gazing out at the arched footbridges and funkier locals of Canal St-Martin. ✉ *36 rue Beaurepaire, 10e, Canal St-Martin* ☎ *01–42–41–30–47* Ⓜ *République, Jacques Bonsergent.*

Hôtel du Nord. This hotel—which starred in the classic Marcel Carné film of the same name—has been spiffed up but still maintains its cool with a vibrant lounge-bar (and restaurant) scene in the buzz-worthy Canal St-Martin district. ✉ *102 quai de Jemmapes, 10e, Canal St-Martin* ☎ *01–40–40–78–78* ⊕ *www.hoteldunord.org* Ⓜ *Goncourt.*

La Patache. Among the bars and eateries lining Rue Lancry, you'll find La Patache. It has a wide selection of wines and a retro-inspired ambience fueled by a jukebox and candlelight that illuminates the vintage photos on the wall. ✉ *60 rue Lancry, 10e, Canal St-Martin* ☎ *01–42–08–14–35* Ⓜ *Jacques-Bonsergent.*

CLUBS

La Java. The spot where Piaf and Chevalier made their names has reinvented itself as a dance club with an emphasis on rock–pop, soul, and electro. It also hosts inexpensive performances by up-and-coming bands. ✉ *105 rue du Faubourg du Temple, 10e, Canal St-Martin* ☎ *01–42–02–20–52* ⊕ *www.la-java.fr* Ⓜ *Belleville, Goncourt.*

Le Gibus. This is one of Paris's most famous music venues. More than 6,500 concerts (put on by the likes of Iggy Pop, The Clash, and The Police) have packed in fans for 30-plus years. Today the Gibus's cellars are *the* place for electro, techno, and hip-hop. ✉ *18 rue du Faubourg du Temple, 11e, Canal St-Martin* ☎ *01–47–00–78–88* ⊕ *www.gibus. fr* Ⓜ *République.*

OBERKAMPF

BARS

Café Charbon. Neighborhood bohos are seduced by Café Charbon's warm, wooden, Belle Époque charm and floor-to-soaring-ceiling mirrors. ✉ *109 rue Oberkampf, 11e, Oberkampf* ☎ *01–43–57–55–13* Ⓜ *Rue St-Maur, Parmentier.*

Favela Chic. This popular Latin cocktail bar took the scene early, forging Oberkampf's hip reputation. Back behind courtyard gates you'll find caipirinhas and mojitos, guest DJs presenting an eclectic mix of samba, soul, and hip-hop, and a nonstop dance scene. ✉ *18 rue du Faubourg du Temple, 11e, Oberkampf* ☎ *01–40–21–38–14* ⊕ *favelachic.com* Ⓜ *République.*

CLUBS

Le Nouveau Casino. You'll find this concert hall and club tucked behind the Café Charbon. Pop and rock concerts prevail during the week, with revelry on Friday and Saturday from midnight until dawn. Hip-hop, house, disco, and techno DJs are the standard. ✉ *109 rue Oberkampf, 11e, Oberkampf* ☎ *01–43–57–57–40* ⊕ *www.nouveau-casino.fr* Ⓜ *Parmentier.*

Pop-In. On a back street just off the Boulevard Beaumarchais (which links the Bastille to République), this dark, hard-partying boho playhouse has a pronounced English-rocker feel. ✉ *105 rue Amelot, 4e, Oberkampf* ☎ *01–48–05–56–11* ⊕ *popin.fr* Ⓜ *St-Sebastien–Froissart.*

PÈRE-LACHAISE

BARS

Mama Shelter. Hip Parisians make the pilgrimage to visit the Island Bar at this hotel, the happeningest spot around. Beautiful people flock in for solid cocktails, foosball, and even an adjacent pizza bar. It's always packed, but lines are out the door Thursday through Saturday, when DJs and other international artists perform. ✉ *109 rue de Bagnolet, 20e, Eastern Paris* ☎ *01–43–48–48–48* ⊕ *www.mamashelter.com* Ⓜ *Alexandre Dumas.*

CLUBS

Le Bellevilloise. This multiuse exhibition space in a hip, up-and-coming neighborhood functions as a bar, dance club, restaurant, and performance venue, with concerts and burlesque shows. ✉ *19–21 rue Boyer, 20e, Eastern Paris* ☎ *01–46–36–07–07* ⊕ *www.labellevilloise.com* Ⓜ *Gambetta, Ménilmontant.*

LATIN QUARTER

The smoke may have cleared from the jazz clubs in the city's historically bohemian quarter, but the atmosphere's still hopping.

BARS

Polly Maggoo. This convivial hangout is legendary as the student rioters' unofficial HQ during the May '68 uprising and is named after the satirical French art-house movie about a supermodel. Weekends are wild, with drinks at the wacky tile bar and live Latin music that keeps the party thumping until morning. ✉ *3–5 rue du Petit Pont, 5e, Latin Quarter* ☎ *01–46–33–33–64* Ⓜ *St-Michel.*

CABARET

Paradis Latin. Occupying a building that's attributed to Gustav Eiffel, Paradis Latin peppers its quirky show with acrobatics and eye-popping lighting effects, making this the liveliest and trendiest cabaret on the Left Bank. Prices range from €65 (for the show only) to €190 (with the top-of-line dinner option and wine added in). ✉ *28 rue du Cardinal Lemoine, 5e, Latin Quarter* ☎ *01–43–25–28–28* ⊕ *www.paradislatin. com* Ⓜ *Cardinal Lemoine.*

JAZZ CLUBS

Caveau de la Huchette. One of the few surviving cellar clubs from the 1940s, Caveau de la Huchette boasts the "best boppers" in the city and packs 'em in for swing dancing and Dixieland tunes. It's a killer jazz spot for everyone but claustrophobics. The music continues till dawn Thursday to Saturday. ✉ *5 rue de la Huchette, 5e, Latin Quarter* ☎ *01–43–26–65–05* ⊕ *www.caveaudelahuchette.fr* Ⓜ *St-Michel.*

ST-GERMAIN-DES-PRÉS

Exclusivity is the theme in the bobo (*bourgeois-bohème*) left bank, where "private" clubs draw celebs and fashionistas, and stylish cocktail bars cater to an urbane mix of students, gallerists, expats, and urban sophisticates.

BARS

Alcazar. Sir Terence Conran's makeover of a 17th-century Parisian *jeu de paume* court features a stylish mezzanine-level bar under a greenhouse-glass roof. DJs and "sound designers" spin mixes into the wee hours Thursday through Saturday. ✉ *62 rue Mazarine, 6e, St-Germain-des-Prés* ☎ *01–53–10–19–99* ⊕ *www.alcazar.fr/en* Ⓜ *Odéon.*

Bar du Marché. Waiters wearing red overalls and revolutionary "Gavroche" hats serve drinks every day of the week at this local institution (they demonstrate particular zeal around happy hour). With bottles of wine at about €25, it draws a quintessential Rive Gauche mix of expats, fashion-house interns, and even some professional rugby players. Sit outside on the terrace and enjoy the prime corner location. ✉ *75 rue de Seine, 6e, St-Germain-des-Prés* ☎ *01–43–26–55–15* Ⓜ *Mabillon, Odéon.*

Chez Georges. Chez Georges has been serving red wine, pastis, and beer for the past 60-odd years in pretty much the same *caveau* that still packs in devotees today. Older students and locals fill sofas and crowd around tiny, candle-topped tables in the cellar bar before grinding to pulsing world music all night. ✉ *11 rue de Canettes, 6e, St-Germain-des-Prés* ☎ *01–43–26–79–15* Ⓜ *Mabillon.*

Compagnie des Vins Surnaturels. After jump-starting the Paris cocktail bar scene, the partners behind the Experimental Cocktail Club and the Ballroom du Beef Club applied the same winning formula to this hybrid wine bar–nightclub. Plush surroundings, an extensive wine list, and upscale nibbles draw a crowd of hip young Parisians who can hone their wine-tasting skills on classics in every price range. Natural-wine aficionados should head to a full-fledged wine bar; though solid, the wine list here does not deliver as promised. ⊠ *7 rue Lobineau, 6e, St-Germain-des-Prés* ☎ *06–14–76–81–08* ⊕ *compagniedesvinssurnaturels.com* Ⓜ *Odéon, Mabillon.*

L'Hôtel. The hushed baroque bar at L'Hôtel is ideal for a discreet rendezvous. Designed in typically jaw-dropping Jacques Garcia style, the hideaway evokes the decadent spirit of one-time resident Oscar Wilde. ⊠ *13 rue des Beaux-Arts, 6e, St-Germain-des-Prés* ☎ *01–44–41–99–00* ⊕ *www.l-hotel.com* Ⓜ *St-Germain-des-Prés.*

Prescription Cocktail Club. This club is brought to you by the owners of popular cocktail bars in London, New York, and Paris—including the Ballroom du Beef Club and the Experimental Cocktail Club. So rest assured: the atmosphere will be stylish (think upholstered chairs, dim lighting, and vintage touches), the crowd hip, and the drinks tasty. Located in fashionable St-Germain-des-Prés, it's a good after-shopping apéro or dinner option. ⊠ *23 rue Mazarine, 6e, St-Germain-des-Prés* ☎ *01–46–34–67–73* ⊕ *www.prescriptioncocktail-club.com* Ⓜ *Odéon.*

CLUBS

Le Montana. It's notoriously difficult to get past the doorman at Le Montana, a sleek club owned by French nightlife king André (Le Baron). A Studio 54 vibe, Vincent Darré decor, and enormous cocktails make it popular among models, actors, artists, and Parisian playboys. ⊠ *28 rue St-Benoît, 6e, St-Germain-des-Prés* ☎ *01–44–39–71–00* Ⓜ *St-Germain-des-Prés, Mabillon.*

JAZZ CLUBS

Fodor'sChoice
★

Café Laurent. Bookcases on the wall and the glossy central piano recall this jazz bar's earlier incarnation as the Café Tabou, when Paris's postwar artists and intellectuals argued and partied the night away to the strains of New York jazz. Nowadays, its plush seating and low lights still draw a crowd of diehard jazz lovers. ⊠ *33 rue Dauphine, 6e, St-Germain-des-Prés* ☎ *01–43–29–43–43* ⊕ *www.hoteldaubusson.com/en/cafe-laurent.html* Ⓜ *Saint-Germain-des-Prés, Mabillon, Pont Neuf.*

MONTPARNASSE

Immortalized in the 1920s by the likes of F. Scott Fitzgerald and Pablo Picasso, the cafés and bars in this quiet corner of the city still radiate atmosphere. Whether sipping a sidecar at Hemingway's beloved La Closerie des Lilas or slurping oysters at one of the quarter's storied brasseries, you can't help but fall under Paris's spell here.

BARS

La Closerie des Lilas. La Closerie's swank "American-style" bar lets you drink in the swirling action of the adjacent restaurant and brasserie at a piano bar adorned with plaques honoring former habitués like

Man Ray, Jean-Paul Sartre, Samuel Beckett, and Ernest Hemingway, who talks of "the Lilas" in *A Moveable Feast.* ⊠ *171 bd. du Montparnasse, 6e, Montparnasse* ☎ *01–40–51–34–50* ⊕ *www.closeriedeslilas. fr* Ⓜ *Montparnasse.*

Le Rosebud. Step through the Art Nouveau front door of Jean-Paul Sartre's one-time haunt and you're instantly immersed in the dark, moody, fourth dimension of Old Montparnasse, where white-jacketed servers and red-lacquered tables transport you into the past. ⊠ *11 bis, rue Delambre, 14e, Montparnasse* ☎ *01–43–35–38–54* Ⓜ *Vavin.*

PERFORMING ARTS

Updated
by Jennifer
Ladonne

The performing arts scene in Paris runs the gamut from highbrow to lowbrow, cheap (or even free) to break-the-bank expensive. Venues are indoors and outdoors, opulent or spartan, and dress codes vary accordingly. Regardless of the performance you choose, it's probably unlike anything you've seen before. Parisians have an audacious sense of artistic adventure and a stunning eye for scene and staging. An added bonus in this city of classic beauty is that many of the venues themselves—from the opulent interiors of the Opéra Garnier and the Opéra Royal de Versailles to the Art Deco splendor of the Théâtre des Champs-Élysées—are a feast for the eyes.

One thing that sets Paris apart in the arts world is the active participation of the Ministry of Culture, which sponsors numerous concert halls and theaters, like the Comédie Française, that tend to present less commercial, though artistically captivating, productions. Other venues with broader appeal are known for sold-out shows and decade-long runs.

Most performances are in French, although you can find English theater productions. English-language movies are often presented undubbed, with subtitles. Of course, you don't need to speak the language to enjoy opera, classical music, dance, or the circus.

PLANNING

FESTIVALS

The music and theater season generally runs from September to June, but summer is packed with all sorts of performing arts festivals.

Days Off Festival. Held over 10 days in early July at the Philharmonie de Paris, this festival focuses on pop-rock, with some jazz and electro thrown in for good measure. Headliners like Rufus Wainwright and Blur frontman Damon Albarn lure Parisians away from their offices. Tickets can cost as much as €50, but some are *gratis*. ✉ *221 av. Jean-Jaurès, 19e, Eastern Paris* ☎ *01–44–84–44–84* ⊕ *www.daysoff.fr* Ⓜ *Porte de Pantin.*

Festival d'Automne à Paris. Since 1972, the Paris Autumn Festival has featured a packed program that includes contemporary dance, theater, music, the visual arts, and film. From September to December, 100,000 fans attend 50 productions from more than a dozen countries. They're staged in assorted venues in and around the city, and tickets cost €8 to €35. ✉ *Paris* ☎ *01–53–45–17–00* ⊕ *www.festival-automne.com.*

Festival d'Ile de France. In September and October, this fête takes you (and 25,000 other festival goers) to extraordinary venues in Paris and the surrounding region—among them churches, old warehouses, and historical sites. The 30-plus concerts on the program range from world to pop, and Baroque to classical. Tickets cost €6 to €26; they can be purchased online or, depending on availability, 45 minutes before showtime. ✉ ☎ *01–58–71–01–01* ⊕ *www.iledefrance.fr/competence/festival-ile-france.*

Festival Paris l'Été. Held throughout Paris from mid-July to mid-August, the Quartier d'Été festival attracts international stars of dance, world music, theater, and the circus. Prices for concert tickets typically range from €8 to €20, but half of the performances are free. ✉ *Paris* ☎ *01–44–94–98–00* ⊕ *www.parislete.fr.*

Fête de la Musique. Also known as World Music Day, Fête de la Musique is an international festival founded in 1981 by French minister of culture Jack Lang. On June 21 (the summer solstice), free concerts by amateurs and professionals alike are performed on city streets and in village squares throughout France. In Paris, it's an all-night party and a great opportunity to join in the fun, hear some great music, and blend in like a Parisian. ⊕ *www.fetedelamusique.culturecommunication.gouv.fr.*

Jazz à la Villette. The annual Jazz à la Villette Festival is held at various Parc de La Villette venues, including the Philharmonie de Paris and Trabendo, over 10 days in early September. You'll pay €8 to €33 for tickets; check the website for detailed information. ✉ *211 av. Jean Jaurès, 19e, Eastern Paris* ☎ *01–40–03–75–75* ⊕ *jazzalavillette.com/fr* Ⓜ *Porte de Pantin.*

Orangerie du Parc de Bagatelle. The Chopin Festival and the Solistes Festival strike musical high notes in the Orangerie du Parc de Bagatelle, one of Paris's most beautiful gardens. The former runs from mid-June through mid-July; the latter is held on three consecutive weekends in September. Tickets will set you back €21 to €35. ✉ *Parc de Bagatelle, Allée de Longchamp, 16e, Western Paris* ☎ *01–53–64–53–80* ⊕ *www.frederic-chopin.com* ⊕ *www.ars-mobilis.com* Ⓜ *Porte Maillot, then Bus 244.*

Parc Floral. Free outdoor classical concerts, staged weekends at 4 pm from August to mid-September, draw fans to the Parc Floral in Bois de Vincennes (entrance to the park is €6). This is also the spot that hosts the Paris Jazz Festival each weekend in June and July. ✉ *12e, Eastern Paris* ☎ *01–43–28–41–59* ⊕ *www.vincennes.fr* ⊕ *www.parisjazzfestival. fr* Ⓜ *Château de Vincennes.*

18

Rock-en-Seine. This rock festival, which runs each August on the outskirts of Paris, is one of the largest of its kind in France; past headliners include Lana Del Rey, Arcade Fire, Cypress Hill, and the Foo Fighters. A three-day pass is €119. ⊠ *Domaine National de St-Cloud, Parc de St-Cloud, Saint-Cloud* ⊕ *www.rockenseine.com* Ⓜ *Boulogne-Pont de Saint-Cloud.*

TICKET PRICES AND DISCOUNTS
As anywhere, it's best to buy tickets in advance.

Events range in price from about €5 for standing room at the Opéra Bastille to upward of €180 for an elaborate National Ballet production. Most performances, however, are in the €10 to €35 range. Discounts are often available for limited-visibility seats or for students and senior citizens. Movies cost €6.50 to €12, but many cinemas have reduced rates for matinees or for people under a certain age (18 or 26, depending on the venue).

Half-price tickets are also obtainable from many theaters during the first week of each new show's run, and inexpensive tickets can often be bought last minute.

FNAC. FNAC sells tickets online and in its 10 city stores, including one on the Champs-Élysées. ⊠ *Galerie du Claridge, 74 av. des Champs-Élysées, 8e, Champs-Élysées* ☎ *08–25–02–00–20 €0.18 per min* ⊕ *www.fnactickets.com* Ⓜ *George V.*

Le Kiosque Théâtre. Half-price tickets for same-day theater performances are available at Le Kiosque Théâtre's Madeleine location. See the website for information on outlets in Place Raoul Dautry (Montparnasse) and Place des Ternes (Les Grands Boulevards). ⊠ *Across from 15 pl. de la Madeleine, 7e, Louvre* ⊕ *www.kiosquetheatre.com* Ⓜ *Madeleine.*

WHERE TO GET INFO
Detailed entertainment listings in French can be found in the weekly magazines *Pariscope* and *L'Officiel des Spectacles,* available at newsstands and in bookstores; in the Wednesday entertainment insert *Figaroscope,* in the *Figaro* newspaper (⊕ *evene.lefigaro.fr*); and in the weekly *À Nous Paris,* distributed free in the métro. The webzine *Paris Voice* () offers superb highlights in English. Most performing arts venues also have their own websites, and many include listings as well as other helpful information in English.

The website of the Paris Tourist Office (⊕ *www.parisinfo.com*) has theater and music ⊕ *www.parisvoice.com* listings in English.

ARTS CENTERS

Fodor's Choice ★ **Atelier des Lumières.** An abandoned iron foundry in the hip 11th arrondissement is the soaring backdrop for this feast for the eyes and the senses, where visitors are invited to enter into the great masterpieces of 19th and 20th-century painting (many found in famous Parisian museums). Over 100 video projectors cast vivid scenes of gorgeously colored artwork on the walls, ceilings, and floors, accompanied by a dynamic soundtrack, for total immersion into a 30-minute explosion of color and sound. ⊠ *38–40 rue Saint-Maur, 11e, Père Lachaise*

☎ *01-80-98-46-00* ⊕ *www.atelier-lumieres.com/fr/votre-visite/horaires-et-acces* 🎟*€15* Ⓜ *Voltaire, Rue Saint-Maur, Père Lachaise.*

La Seine Musicale. Rising up from the Seine like a futuristic ocean liner, Le Seine Musicale answers Paris's desire to compete as one of the world's prime music destinations. The structure's two state-of-the-art concert halls, the largest with a seating capacity of 6,000, feature a range of musical performances, from classical to the legends of jazz and rock (Bob Dylan played the inaugural concert). Behind the sleek mirrored facade—whose solar panels generate enough power to dramatically illuminate the building at night—lies a jazz club, three restaurants, art galleries, and outdoor gardens offering panoramic views of Paris. The 28-acre island on the Seine is technically in Boulogne-Billancourt, a suburb of Paris, but is easily reached by metro or bus. ✉ *Île Seguin, Western Paris* ☎ *01–74–34–54–00* ⊕ *www.laseinemusicale.com* Ⓜ *Pont de Sèvres, Brimborion, Musée de Sèvres.*

Le Lucernaire. Occupying an abandoned factory, Le Lucernaire wins a standing ovation as far as cultural centers are concerned. With three theaters staging a total of six performances per day, three movie screens, a bookstore, photography exhibitions, a lively restaurant-bar, and the equally lively surrounding neighborhood of Vavin, it caters to young intellectuals. ✉ *53 rue Notre-Dame-des-Champs, 6e, Montparnasse* ☎ *01–45–44–57–34* ⊕ *www.lucernaire.fr* Ⓜ *Notre-Dame-des-Champs.*

Fodor's Choice
★

Opéra Garnier. The magnificent, magical former haunt of the Phantom of the Opera, painter Edgar Degas, and any number of legendary opera stars still hosts performances of the Opéra de Paris, along with a fuller calendar of dance performances (the theater is the official home of the Ballet de l'Opéra National de Paris). The grandest opera productions are usually mounted at the Opéra Bastille, whereas the Garnier now presents smaller-scale works such as Mozart's *La Clemenza di Tito* and *Così Fan Tutte.* Tickets generally go on sale at the box office a month before any given show, earlier by phone and online; you must appear in person to buy the cheapest tickets. Last-minute returned or unsold tickets, if available, are offered an hour prior to a performance. The box office is open Monday to Saturday 11:30–6:30 and one hour before curtain; however, you should get in line up to two hours in advance. You can also check the website at noon on certain Wednesdays for flash sales of sold-out shows. Venue visits (€12) and guided tours in English (€15.50) are available and can be reserved online; check the website for details. ✉ *Pl. de l'Opéra, 9e, Grands Boulevards* ☎ *08–92–89–90–90 (€0.34 per min), 01–71–25–24–23 from outside France* ⊕ *www.operadeparis.fr* Ⓜ *Opéra.*

Fodor's Choice
★

Opéra Royal de Versailles. The most lavish opera house in France (and perhaps in all of Europe) hosts an impressive yearly calendar of major operas, ballets, recitals, and musical theater by world-class French and international performers. The intimate 652-seat theater has excellent acoustics and provides an ideal setting for works by big-name composers, with an emphasis on the Baroque and classical periods. Finished in 1770—just in time for the marriage ceremonies of the young dauphin (later King Louis XVI) and 14-year-old Marie-Antoinette—the

18

structure's stunning neoclassical decor is crafted entirely of gilded and faux-marbled wood. A regular program of smaller concerts is also held in the splendid Hall of Mirrors (Galerie des Glaces) and at the Royal Chapel, where recitals might feature a 300-year-old royal organ. Although it's recommended to buy tickets online one to two months in advance (up to six months ahead for star performers), they can be purchased at the box office on the evening of the performance depending on availability. ⊠ *Place d'Armes, Versailles* ✛ *By commuter train (SNCF) from Paris Gare Montparnasse or Paris Gare Saint Lazare to Gare Versailles Chantiers or Rive Droite* ☎ *01–30–83–78–89* ⊕ *www. chateauversailles-spectacles.fr* Ⓜ *RER C: Gare Versailles Rive Gauche.*

Philharmonie de Paris. Designed by French architect Jean Nouvel, this is one of the world's finest and most expensive auditoriums. It can accommodate 2,400 music lovers, and the adjustable modular seating means you'll be able to see the stage no matter where you sit. Since the hall is home to the Orchestre de Paris, concerts are mostly classical; however, programming includes guest artists and, on weekends, pop, jazz, and world music performances appeal to patrons with more diverse tastes—and smaller budgets. Part of the same complex (formerly known as the Cité de la Musique), **Philharmonie 2** features a 1,000-seat concert hall and a 250-seat amphitheater. Designed by Christian de Portzamparc, they present an eclectic range of concerts (some of which are free) in a postmodern setting. The Philharmonie de Paris is a 45-minute métro ride from downtown. If you're driving, there are 600 parking spaces available. ⊠ *221 av. Jean Jaurès, 19e, Eastern Paris* ☎ *01–44–84–44–84* ⊕ *www.philharmoniedeparis.fr* Ⓜ *Porte de Pantin.*

Théâtre des Champs-Élysées. This was the scene of 1913's infamous Battle of the Rite of Spring, when police had to be called in after the audience ripped up seats in outrage at Stravinsky's *Le Sacre du Printemps* score and Nijinsky's choreography. Today Théâtre des Champs-Élysées is elegantly restored and worthy of a visit if only for the architecture (it's one of Paris's most striking examples of Art Deco). The theater also hosts first-rate opera and dance performances, along with orchestral, chamber, and Sunday morning concerts. ⊠ *15 av. Montaigne, 8e, Champs-Élysées* ☎ *01–49–52–50–50* ⊕ *www.theatrechampselysees.fr* Ⓜ *Alma-Marceau.*

CIRCUSES

Italian Antonio Franconi helped launch the first Cirque Olympique (considered the start of the modern circus) in Paris in 1783, and the French have been hooked ever since. Circus acts are cherished as high art for all ages here. The city boasts a 19th-century permanent circus theater and sprouts tents in every major park to present spectacles from the sublime to the quirky.

Cirque d'Hiver Bouglione. Cirque d'Hiver Bouglione brings together two famous circus institutions: the beautiful Cirque d'Hiver hall, constructed in 1852, and the Bouglione troupe, known for its rousing assembly of acrobats, jugglers, clowns, trapeze artists, tigers, and house cats that leap through rings of fire. Shows run mid-October to March, with a new production each season. ⊠ *110 rue Amelot, 11e, République* ☎ *01–47–00–28–81* ⊕ *www.cirquedhiver.com* Ⓜ *Filles du Calvaire.*

Cirque National Alexis Gruss. Founded in 1854, Cirque National Alexis Gruss remains true to the *Cirque à l'Ancienne* philosophy, serving up a traditional circus with showy horseback riders, trapeze artists, and clowns. The large-scale production runs mid-October through mid-March, with performances on Thursday, Friday, and Saturday at 4 or 8 pm, and on Sunday at 4 pm. Tickets cost €20 to €75. ⊠ *Carrefour des cascades, Porte de Passy, 16e, Western Paris* ☎ *01–45–01–71–26* ⊕ *www.alexis-gruss.com* Ⓜ *Ranelagh.*

Espace Chapiteaux. Parc de la Villette is home to Espace Chapiteaux: a circus-tent complex that hosts guest troupes several times a year, as well as students from the National Circus Arts Center. ⊠ *211 av. Jean-Jaurès, 19e, Eastern Paris* ☎ *01–40–03–75–75* ⊕ *www.villette. com* Ⓜ *Porte de Pantin.*

FAMILY **Théâtre Équestre Zingaro.** Ready for a variation on the circus theme? If you're lucky enough to be visiting during the two months Zingaro performs at home (usually in late fall), you'll have the chance to witness a truly unique spectacle. Since 1985, France's foremost horse whisperer, who goes by the name of Bartabas, has created captivating equestrian shows that mix theater, dance, music, and poetry. The 500-seat theater-in-the-round on the outskirts of Paris is part of a caravan, where trainers and their families, 45 horses, and Bartabas himself live and work. The horses perform in close proximity to the audience in astonishing displays of choreography and acrobatic skill. If you can't make it for Zingaro, there is a consolation prize: in 2003, Bartabas created the Académie du Spectacle Équestre at the royal stables of Versailles (Grandes Écuries). Audiences can catch a show there on weekends (Saturday at 6 pm, Sunday at 3 pm) and on certain weekdays during school holidays. Expect to pay €21 to €42 for tickets. ⊠ *176 av. Jean Jaurès, Aubervilliers* ☎ *01–39–02–62–75* ⊕ *www.bartabas.fr* Ⓜ *Fort d'Aubervilliers.*

CONCERTS

There's something majestic about listening to classical music under the airy roof of a medieval church, where many free or almost-free lunchtime and evening concerts are performed. Check weekly listings and flyers posted at the churches for information.

Many museums also host concerts; tickets, affordably priced, are usually sold separately from admission. The Auditorium du Louvre, for instance, presents chamber music or piano solos on Wednesday evening, performances by promising new musicians on Thursday afternoon, and either classic pieces or specially commissioned contemporary ones on Friday evening. The Musée de Cluny stages medieval music concerts between September and June, including *l'Heure Musicale* on Sunday at 4 and Monday at 12:30; the Musée d'Orsay, meanwhile, often offers small-scale concerts in its lower-level auditorium.

Fodor's Choice
★
L'Olympia. Paris's legendary music hall hosts an eclectic roster of performances that cover such far-flung genres as gospel, jazz, French *chanson*, and rock. Edith Piaf rose to fame after a series of Olympia concerts and Jeff Buckley's famous *Live at the Olympia* was recorded here. Now everyone from Leonard Cohen to Lady Gaga has been in on the action. ⊠ *28 bd. des Capucines, 9e, Grands Boulevards* ☎ *08–92–68–33–68 €0.34 per min* ⊕ *en.olympiahall.com* Ⓜ *Madeleine, Opéra.*

Fodor's Choice
★
La Cigale. Artists like Maurice Chevalier and Arletty were once a staple of this small concert hall in the storied Pigalle neighborhood before cabaret and vaudeville moved in. Today it's one of Paris's top pop and contemporary music venues, featuring such acts as Adele and Coldplay. ⊠ *120 bd. de Rochechouart, 18e, Montmartre* ☎ *01–49–25–89–99* ⊕ *www.lacigale.fr* Ⓜ *Pigalle, Anvers.*

Fodor's Choice
★
Salle Cortot. This acoustic jewel was built in 1929 by Auguste Perret, who promised to construct "a concert hall that sounds like a Stradivarius." Tickets for jazz and classical concerts can only be bought from the box office 30 minutes beforehand; otherwise, go online to ⊕ *www. fnactickets.com* or ⊕ *www.concertclassic.com.* Free student recitals are offered at 12:30 on Tuesday and Thursday from October to April and on some Wednesday afternoons from January to May. ⊠ *78 rue Cardinet, 17e, Grands Boulevards* ☎ *01–47–63–47–48* ⊕ *www.sallecortot. com* Ⓜ *Malesherbes.*

Salle Gaveau. The 1,020-seat Salle Gaveau is a perfectly appointed gold-and-white hall with remarkable acoustics and a distinctly Parisian allure. It hosts chamber music, orchestral, piano, and vocal recitals. ⊠ *45–47 rue la Boétie, 8e, Champs-Élysées* ☎ *01–49–53–05–07* ⊕ *www.sallegaveau.com* Ⓜ *Miromesnil.*

Salle Pleyel. Once one of Paris's major classical music venues, these days Salle Pleyel's packed concert calendar mostly focuses on contemporary music, entertainment, and events, as well as hosting the annual César Awards, France's answer to the Oscars. Tickets range from €10–€80. ⊠ *252 rue du Faubourg St-Honoré, 8e, Concorde* ☎ *01–42–56–13–13* ⊕ *www.sallepleyel.fr* Ⓜ *Ternes.*

DANCE

Classical ballets are staged in various historic venues, including the gorgeous Opéra Garnier. More avant-garde or up-and-coming choreographers tend to show their works off in the smaller performance spaces of the Bastille and the Marais or in the theaters of nearby suburbs. And of course there's the Centre National de Danse, which aims to make dance accessible to all.

Centre National de la Danse. Occupying a former administrative center in the suburb of Pantin, this space is dedicated to supporting professional dancers by offering classes, rehearsal studios, and a multimedia dance library. A regular program of free and reasonably priced performances, expositions, screenings, and conferences is also open to the public from October to July. ⊠ *1 rue Victor Hugo, Pantin* ☎ *01–41–83–98–98* ⊕ *www.cnd.fr* Ⓜ *Hoche; RER: Pantin.*

Maison des Arts de Créteil. This popular dance venue just outside Paris often attracts top-notch international and French companies, such as Blanca Li and Bill T. Jones; it also hosts the cutting-edge EXIT Festival, which runs over 10 days from the end of March. ✉ *1 Pl. Salvador Allende, Créteil* ☎ *01–45–13–19–19* ⊕ *www.maccreteil.com* Ⓜ *Créteil-Préfecture.*

Théâtre de la Bastille. An example of the innovative activity in the Bastille area, Théâtre de la Bastille has an enviable record as a launch pad for tomorrow's modern-dance stars. ✉ *76 rue de la Roquette, 11e, Bastille* ☎ *01–43–57–42–14* ⊕ *www.theatre-bastille.com* Ⓜ *Bastille.*

Théâtre de la Cité Internationale. In the heart of the Cité Internationale Universitaire de Paris, this complex includes three theaters, an international student residence community, and a park. It hosts young, avant-garde companies; however, its future is unclear given the university's proposed budget cuts. ✉ *17 bd. Jourdan, 14e, Montparnasse* ☎ *01–43–13–50–50* ⊕ *www.theatredelacite.com* Ⓜ *RER: Cité Universitaire.*

Théâtre de la Ville. At *the* top spot for contemporary dance, you'll find French and international troupes choreographed by the world's best—like William Forsythe and Anne-Teresa de Keersmaeker's Rosas company. Concerts and theatrical performances are also part of the season. Book early; shows sell out quickly. ✉ *2 pl. du Châtelet, 4e, Marais Quarter* ☎ *01–42–74–22–77* ⊕ *www.theatredelaville-paris.com* Ⓜ *Châtelet.*

> **PUPPET SHOWS**
>
> On most Wednesday, Saturday, and Sunday afternoons, the Guignol—the French equivalent of Punch and Judy—can be seen launching their hilarious puppet battles in most of Paris's larger parks. The Marionettes du Luxembourg ⊕ *www.marionnettes-duluxembourg.fr/acceuil.html* in the Luxembourg Gardens and the Théâtre de Guignol des Champs-Élysées ⊕ *www.theatreguignol.fr* are probably Paris's most famous, but you'll also find a popular Guignol theater at the lovely Parc Floral in the Bois de Vincennes. Entrance is usually €4.50 to €5; performances are in French.

18

FILM

The French call films the *septième art* (seventh art) and discuss the latest releases with the same intensity as they do gallery openings or theatrical debuts. Most theaters run English-language films undubbed, with subtitles, which are indicated with v.o., meaning *version originale*; films that are dubbed are v.f. (*version française*). Paris's legendary art house cinemas were traditionally clustered around Saint-Germain and the Latin Quarter; though many have closed, you'll still find neighborhood cinemas showing French independent films. Visitors who don't speak fluent French but still want that Parisian experience should check out Lost in Frenchlation (⊕ *www.lostinfrenchlation.com*, which organizes weekend screenings of recently released French films with English subtitles. First-run cinemas are clustered around the principal tourist areas, such as the Champs-Élysées, Boulevard des Italiens near the Opéra, Bastille, Châtelet, and Odéon. For listings online check ⊕ *www.allocine. fr* or ⊕ *www.offi.fr/cinema.*

Cinéma des Cinéastes. Catch previews of feature films, as well as documentaries, shorts, children's movies, and rarely shown flicks at Cinéma des Cinéastes. It's an old cabaret transformed into a movie house and wine bar. Tickets for matinées are only €6. ⊠ *7 av. de Clichy, 17e, Montmartre* ☎ *08-92-68-97-17 €0.34 per min* ⊕ *www.cinema-descineastes.fr* Ⓜ *Place de Clichy.*

Fodor's Choice   **Cinémathèque Française.** This is a mecca for cinephiles brought up on Federico Fellini, Igmar Bergman, and Alain Resnais known for its superb, ★ and exhaustive, retrospectives of world cinema past and present. Its spectacular home—in the former American Center, designed by Frank Gehry—includes elaborate museum exhibitions plus three cinemas and a video library. ⊠ *51 rue de Bercy, 12e, Bastille* ☎ *01-71-19-33-33* ⊕ *www.cinematheque.fr* Ⓜ *Bercy.*

La Géode. It's hard to miss La Géode—a steel globe with a 118-foot diameter in Parc de La Villette. The theater screens wide-angle Omnimax films—including kid-friendly documentaries—on a gigantic spherical surface. ⊠ *At Cité des Sciences et de l'Industrie, Parc de La Villette, 26 av. Corentin Cariou, 19e, Eastern Paris* ☎ *01-40-05-79-99* ⊕ *www. lageode.fr* Ⓜ *Porte de La Villette.*

Le Balzac. This theater often presents directors' talks before film screenings and features live music for silent classics. Every Saturday night, in partnership with the National Conservatory of Music, it hosts a free 20-minute concert before the movie in the main cinema. ⊠ *1 rue Balzac, 8e, Champs-Élysées* ☎ *01-45-61-10-60* ⊕ *www.cinemabalzac. com* Ⓜ *George V.*

Le Desperado. You can watch *version originale* American classics and cult films for €8 on Le Desperado's two screens. ⊠ *23 rue des Écoles, 5e, Latin Quarter* ☎ *01-43-25-72-07* Ⓜ *Maubert-Mutualité.*

Le Forum des Images. The Forum organizes thematic viewings in five state-of-the-art screening rooms, often presenting discussions with directors or film experts beforehand. Archival films and videos, workshops, and lectures are also on the schedule here. Movies cost €6, but roundtables and discussions are free; you can download the Forum app for smartphones. ⊠ *Forum des Halles, 2 rue du Cinéma, Louvre* ☎ *01-44-76-63-00* ⊕ *www.forumdesimages.fr* Ⓜ *Châtelet–Les Halles (St-Eustache exit).*

Fodor's Choice   **Le Grand Rex.** Since it opened in 1932, the Grand Rex—a designated ★ historic landmark—has been Europe's largest cinema, with 2,800 seats in its main auditorium and Paris's largest screen. The cinema's history is almost as colorful as its superb Art Deco architecture, considered some of the finest in the city. The Rex shows a large roster of international films, many in English, screened in either the orginal language or subtitled or dubbed in French. ⊠ *1 bd. Poissonnière, 2e, Grands Boulevards* ☎ *01-45-08-93-89* ⊕ *www.legrandrex.com* Ⓜ *Bonne Nouvelle, Grands Boulevards.*

Fodor's Choice **Le Louxor.** First opened in 1921, Le Louxor has since been returned to its
★ original Egyptian-themed splendor. Now the city's grandest cinema, this
Art Deco beauty is gorgeously appointed—all in rich ocher with jewel-
tone velvet seating—and shows a roster of contemporary international
art films in three cinemas. Have a drink at the top-floor bar or balcony
for spectacular views of the neighborhood and Sacré Coeur. ⊠ *170 bd.
Magenta, 10e, Montmartre* 🕾 *01–44–63–96–96* ⊕ *www.cinemalouxor.
fr* Ⓜ *Barbès–Rochechouart.*

MK2 Bibliothèque. This slick, 20- *salle* cineplex in the shadow of Mitterrand's National Library has trademark scarlet-red chairs—they fit
two people without a divider, so the experience is sort of like watching a movie at home on your couch. MK2 Bibliothèque also contains
two restaurants, plus shops selling gifts and DVDs. ⊠ *128–162 av. de
France, 13e, Eastern Paris* 🕾 *08–92–69–84–84 €0.60 per min* ⊕ *www.
mk2.com* Ⓜ *Quai de la Gare, Bibliothèque.*

Parc de La Villette. In July and August, Parc de La Villette shows free
open-air movies. Most people pack a picnic; you can also rent deck
chairs and blankets for €7 by the entrance. ⊠ *In Prairie du Triangle at
Parc de La Villette, 221 av. Jean-Jaurès, 19e, Eastern Paris* 🕾 *01–40–
03–75–75* ⊕ *www.villette.com* Ⓜ *Porte de Pantin, Porte de La Villette.*

Saint-André des Arts. One of a number of popular cinemas near the Sorbonne, Saint-André des Arts is also one of the best cinemas in Paris. It
hosts an annual festival devoted to a single director (like Bergman or
Tarkovski) and shows indie films every day at 1 pm. Some of the latter
are part of "Les Découvertes de Saint-André" series, which focuses
on the work of young filmmakers; these screenings are followed by a
discussion (check the website for details). ⊠ *30 rue St-André des Arts,
6e, Latin Quarter* 🕾 *01–43–26–48–18* ⊕ *cinesaintandre.fr* Ⓜ *St-Michel.*

UGC Ciné-Cité Bercy. This mammoth 18-screen complex is in the Bercy
Village shopping area. For sound and seating, it's one of the best. ⊠ *2
cour Saint Emilion, 12e, Bastille* 🕾 *01–76–64–79–64* ⊕ *www.ugc.fr*
Ⓜ *Cour Saint Emilion.*

18

OPERA

Opéra Bastille. This mammoth ultramodern facility, designed by architect
Carlos Ott and inaugurated in 1989, long ago took over the role of Paris's
main opera house from the Opéra Garnier (although both operate under
the same Opéra de Paris umbrella). Like the building, performances tend
to be on the avant-garde side—you're as likely to see a contemporary
adaptation of *La Bohème* as you are to hear Kafka set to music. Tickets
for Opéra de Paris productions run €15–€230 and generally go on sale at
the box office a month before shows, earlier by phone and online. Once
the doors open, "standing places" can be purchased for €5 from vending
machines in the lobby, but you'll need coins or a credit card (no bills)
and patience to snag one, as the lines are long. The opera season usually
runs September through July; the box office is open Monday through
Saturday 11:30–6:30 and one hour before curtain call. If you just want to
look around inside, you can also buy tickets for a 90-minute guided tour

(€15). ⊠ *Pl. de la Bastille, 12e, Eastern Paris* ☎ *08–92–89–90–90 (€0.34 per min), 01–71–25–24–23 from outside France, 01–40–01–19–70 for tours* ⊕ *www.operadeparis.fr* Ⓜ *Bastille.*

Fodor'sChoice
★
Opéra Comique. Opéra Comique—France's third-oldest theatrical institution—is a gem of an opera house whose reputation was forged by its former director, enfant terrible Jérôme Savary. As well as staging operettas, the hall hosts modern dance, classical concerts, and vocal recitals. Tickets usually range from €6 to €120 and can be purchased at the theater, online, or by phone. ⊠ *1 pl. Boieldieu, 2e, Grands Boulevards* ☎ *08–25–01–01–23 € 0.15 per min* ⊕ *www.opera-comique. com* Ⓜ *Richelieu-Drouot.*

THEATER

Parisians love the theater, and with nearly 140 theater venues, there's no hiding that Paris is on-par with both London and New York. But because shows are mostly in French, with a few rare exceptions, Anglophone theater buffs rarely get to take advantage of the cultural wealth. Enter **Theatre in Paris** (⊕ *www.theatreinparis.com*), an organization that has created a system of easily visible English surtitles that appear just above the stage's proscenium; now theater-lovers have access to a wide range of productions in a dozen or more historic venues around Paris. English-language theater groups playing in various venues throughout Paris and its suburbs include the **International Players** (⊕ *www.internationalplayers.co.uk*). Broadway-scale singing-and-dancing musicals are generally staged at either the Palais des Sports or the Palais des Congrès.

Ateliers Berthier. The outlying atelier for the more illustrious Théâtre de l'Odéon is in the 17e, a bit off the beaten path; the upside is that on Sunday it often has a 3 pm matinee in addition to the evening show (usually at 8 pm). ⊠ *1 rue André Suarès, 17e, Grands Boulevards* ⊹ *Corner of Bd. Berthier* ☎ *01–44–85–40–00* ⊕ *www.theatre-odeon. eu* Ⓜ *Porte de Clichy.*

Café de la Gare. This spot offers a fun opportunity to experience a particularly Parisian form of entertainment, the *café-théâtre*—part satire, part variety revue, jazzed up with slapstick humor and performed in a café salon. You'll need a good grasp of French slang and current events to keep up with the jokes. There's no reserved seating; doors open 15 minutes before showtime. ⊠ *41 rue du Temple, 4e, Marais Quarter* ☎ *01–42–78–52–51* ⊕ *www.cdlg.org* Ⓜ *Hôtel de Ville.*

Casino de Paris. Once a favorite of the immortal Serge Gainsbourg, Casino de Paris has a horseshoe balcony, a cramped but cozy music-hall feel, and performances by everyone from Dora the Explorer to the Scissor Sisters. This is where Josephine Baker performed in the early '30s with her leopard, Chiquita. ⊠ *16 rue de Clichy, 9e, Grands Boulevards* ☎ *08–92–69–89–26 €0.40 per min* ⊕ *www.casinodeparis.fr* Ⓜ *Trinité.*

Comédie des Champs-Élysées. Next door to the Théâtre des Champs-Élysées, the Comédie des Champs-Élysées offers intriguing productions in its small theater. ⊠ *15 av. Montaigne, 8e, Champs-Élysées* ☎ *01–53–23–99–19* ⊕ *www.comediedeschampselysees.com* Ⓜ *Alma-Marceau.*

Fodor'sChoice
★ **Comédie Française.** Founded in 1680, Comédie Française is the most hallowed institution in French theater. It specializes in splendid classical French plays by the likes of Racine, Molière, and Marivaux. Buy tickets at the box office, by telephone, or online. If the theater is sold out, the Salle Richelieu offers steeply discounted last-minute tickets an hour before the performance. ✉ *Salle Richelieu, Pl. Colette, 1er, Louvre* ☎ *08–25–10–16–80* €*0.15 per min* ⊕ *www.comedie-francaise. fr* Ⓜ *Palais-Royal–Musée du Louvre.*

La Cartoucherie. This multitheater complex in a former munitions factory lures cast and spectators into an intimate theatrical world. Go early for a simple meal; actors often help serve "in character." Detailed information for each venue is available at the website. ✉ *In Bois de Vincennes, Rte. du Champ de Manoeuvre, 12e, Eastern Paris* ☎ *01–43–74–24–08 Théâtre du Soleil, 01–43–74–99–61 Théâtre de l'Aquarium, 01–43–28–36–36 Théâtre de la Tempête, 01–48–08–39–74 Théâtre de l'Epée de Bois* ⊕ *www.cartoucherie.fr* Ⓜ *Château de Vincennes, then shuttle bus or Bus 112.*

Le Manoir de Paris. Let yourself be enchanted (and frightened) as 35 talented performers bring Paris legends to life. When you walk through this mansion, the history of the Bloody Baker, the Phantom of the Opera, and Catherine de Medici's hired assassin are acted out—on you! If you're in Paris during Halloween, this is just about the best game in town. On holiday weekends, you could wait hours to get in, but the tour-style performance itself lasts less than 60 minutes. ✉ *18 rue de Paradis, 10e, Eastern Paris* ☎ *06–70–89–35–87* ⊕ *www.lemanoirdeparis.fr* Ⓜ *Poissonniere, Gare de l'Est.*

Odéon–Théâtre de l'Europe. The former home of the Comédie Française now focuses on pan-European theater, offering a variety of European-language productions for no more than €40. ✉ *Pl. de l'Odéon, 6e, St-Germain-des-Prés* ☎ *01–44–85–40–00* ⊕ *www.theatre-odeon.eu* Ⓜ *Odéon.*

Théâtre Darius Milhaud. This theater stages classics by Camus and Baudelaire, as well as occasional shows for children. ✉ *80 allée Darius Milhaud, 19e, Eastern Paris* ☎ *01–42–01–92–26* ⊕ *www.theatredariusmilhaud.fr* Ⓜ *Porte de Pantin.*

Théâtre de la Huchette. This tiny Rive Gauche venue has been staging the titanic Romanian-French writer Ionesco's *The Bald Soprano* and *The Lesson* since 1957: it holds the world record for a nonstop theater run with 18,200 performances viewed by more than 2 million people. Other productions are also mounted, and for €38 you can see two shows in one day (single tickets cost €26). ✉ *23 rue de la Huchette, 5e, Latin Quarter* ☎ *01–43–26–38–99* ⊕ *www.theatre-huchette.com* Ⓜ *St-Michel.*

Théâtre de la Renaissance. Belle Époque superstar Sarah Bernhardt (who was the manager from 1893 to 1899) put Théâtre de la Renaissance on the map. Big French stars often perform here. Note that the theater is on the second floor, and there's no elevator. ✉ *20 bd. Saint-Martin, 10e, Canal St-Martin* ☎ *01–42–02–47–35* ⊕ *www.theatredelarenaissance. com* Ⓜ *Strasbourg–Saint-Denis.*

Théâtre des Abbesses. Part of the Théâtre de la Ville, Théâtre des Abbesses is a 400-seat venue in Montmartre. It features lesser-known theater acts, musicians, and up-and-coming choreographers, who often make it onto the program in the Théâtre de la Ville the following year. ✉ *31 rue des Abbesses, 18e, Montmartre* ☎ *01–42–74–22–77* ⊕ *www.theatredelaville-paris.com/aux-abbesses* Ⓜ *Abbesses.*

Théâtre des Bouffes du Nord. Welcome to the wonderfully atmospheric, slightly decrepit home of Peter Brook. The renowned British director regularly delights with his quirky experimental productions in French and, sometimes, English. ✉ *37 bis, bd. de la Chapelle, 10e, Stalingrad* ☎ *01–46–07–34–50* ⊕ *www.bouffesdunord.com* Ⓜ *La Chapelle.*

Théâtre du Palais-Royal. Located in the former residence of Cardinal Richelieu, this plush 716-seat, Italian-style theater is bedecked in gold and purple. It specializes in lighter fare, like comedies and theatrical productions aimed at the under-12 set. ✉ *38 rue de Montpensier, 1er, Louvre* ☎ *01–42–97–40–00* ⊕ *theatrepalaisroyal.com* Ⓜ *Palais-Royal.*

Théâtre Mogador. One of Paris's most sumptuous theaters features musicals and other productions with a pronounced popular appeal (think *Cats* or *Holiday on Ice*). ✉ *25 rue de Mogador, 9e, Grands Boulevards* ☎ *01–53–32–32–32* ⊕ *www.stage-entertainment.fr/theatre-mogador* Ⓜ *Trinité.*

Théâtre National de Chaillot. Housed in an imposing neoclassic building overlooking the Eiffel Tower, Théâtre National de Chaillot has a trio of theaters and a total of 1,600 seats. It's dedicated to experimental, world, and avant-garde drama, dance, and music or a mix of all three. Major names in dance—like the Ballet Royal de Suède and William Forsythe's company—visit regularly. There are programs for children too. ✉ *1 pl. du Trocadéro, 16e, Eiffel Tower* ☎ *01–53–65–30–00* ⊕ *theatre-chaillot.fr* Ⓜ *Trocadéro.*

18

SIDE TRIPS FROM PARIS

Updated by
Linda Hervieux

With so much to see in Paris, it may seem hard to justify a side trip. But just outside the city lies the rest of the fabled region known as Ile-de-France: there, along with gorgeous countryside and quiet towns, you can find spectacular Versailles, the immense Chartres cathedral, and a little region unto itself where a mouse named Mickey is king.

Plan to spend an entire day (at least) at **Versailles,** perusing the manicured gardens that make up one of the largest parks in Europe, and touring the palace, which includes the Hall of Mirrors and Marie-Antoinette's private retreat in an enclave of the royal park. The charming town of **Chartres** is a lovely day or half-day outing from Paris. Its main attraction is Cathédrale de Chartres, an awe-inspiring Gothic church that looms like a great fantasy ship on the horizon and is world renowned for its stained-glass windows. **Disneyland Paris** arrived in 1992, but the magic was slow to take effect. The resort opened with the uninspiring name of EuroDisney and further baffled the French, for whom no meal is complete without wine, with its ban on alcohol. After the ban was lifted in the park's sit-down restaurants and the site's name was changed, Disneyland Paris became France's leading tourist attraction, drawing sellout crowds of Europeans seeking a kitschy glimpse of the American Dream—and of American families stealing a day from their museum schedule.

PLANNING

Traveling to Chartres, Disneyland Paris, and Versailles from Paris is easy. Although each side trip is within an hour's drive, we strongly recommend taking the train from the city rather than renting a car. If Disneyland is your destination and you don't plan to visit Paris, there are shuttle buses that will take you directly from the airports to the park.

The château of Versailles is closed Monday. Disneyland Paris gets extremely crowded on summer weekends, so plan your trip during the week, and early, if possible.

Paris Day Trips

DINING AND LODGING PRICE CATEGORIES (IN EUROS)			
	$	**$$**	**$$$**	**$$$$**
Restaurants	under €18	€18–€24	€25–€32	over €32
Hotels	under €106	€106–€145	€146–€215	over €215

Restaurant prices are the average cost of a main course at dinner or, if dinner is not served, at lunch. Hotel prices are the lowest cost of a standard double room in high season

VISITOR INFORMATION

Special *forfait* tickets, combining travel and admission, are available for several regional tourist destinations (including Versailles). For general information on the area, check the website of Espace du Tourisme d'Ile-de-France (⊕ *www.visitparisregion.com*), or visit one of its kiosks; you'll find them at the Charles de Gaulle airport, Orly airport, Galeries Lafayette (Homme), Versailles, and Disneyland. Further information on Disneyland can be obtained from the Disneyland Paris reservations office.

VERSAILLES

Fodor'sChoice   *16 km (10 miles) west of Paris.*

★   It's hard to tell which is larger at **Château de Versailles**—the world-famous château that housed Louis XIV and 20,000 of his courtiers, or the mass of tour buses and visitors standing in front of it. The grandest palace in France remains one of the marvels of the world. But this edifice was not just home to the Sun King, it was also the new headquarters of the French government (from 1682 to 1789 and again from 1871 to 1879). To accompany the palace, a new city—in fact, a new capital—had to be built from scratch. Tough-thinking town planners took no prisoners, dreaming up vast mansions and avenues broader than the Champs-Élysées.

GETTING HERE AND AROUND

Versailles has three train stations, but its Rive Gauche *gare*—on the RER-C line from Paris, with trains departing from Austerlitz, St-Michel, Invalides, and Champ-de-Mars—provides the easiest access and puts you within a five-minute walk of the château (45 mins, €3.55).

Visitor Information Versailles Tourist Office. ⊠ *2 av. de Paris* ☎ *01–39–24–88–88* ⊕ *www.versailles-tourisme.com.*

EXPLORING

Fodor'sChoice   **Château de Versailles.** A two-century spree of indulgence by the consecu-

★   tive reigns of three French kings produced two of the world's most historic landmarks: gloriously, the Palace of Versailles and, momentously, the French Revolution. Less a monument than a world unto itself, Versailles is the king of palaces. The end result of countless francs, 40 years, and 36,000 laborers, it was Louis XIV's monument to himself—the Sun King. Construction of the sprawling palace and gardens, which Louis personally and meticulously oversaw, started in 1661 and took 40 years to complete. Today the château seems monstrously big, but it wasn't large enough for the army of 20,000 noblemen, servants, and hangers-on who moved in with Louis. A new city—a new capital, in fact—had to be constructed from scratch to accommodate them.

One of the palace highlights is the dazzling **Galerie des Glaces** (Hall of Mirrors). Lavish balls were once held here, as was a later event with much greater world impact: the signing of the Treaty of Versailles, which put an end to World War I on June 28, 1919. The **Grands Appartements** (State Apartments) are whipped into a lather of decoration, with painted ceilings, marble walls, parquet floors, and canopy beds topped with ostrich plumes. The **Petits Appartements** (Private Apartments), where the royal family and friends lived, are on a more human scale, lined with 18th-century gold and white rococo boiseries. The **Opéra Royal**, the first oval hall in France, was designed for Louis XV and inaugurated in 1770 for the marriage of 15-year-old Louis XVI to 14-year-old Austrian archduchess Marie-Antoinette. Considered the finest 18th-century opera house in Europe at the time (with acoustics to match), it is now a major venue for world-class performers. Completed in 1701 in the Louis XIV style, the **Appartements du Roi** (King's Apartments) comprise a suite of 15 rooms set in a "U" around the east facade's Marble Court. The **Chambre de la Reine** (Queen's Bed Chamber)—once among the world's most opulent—was updated for Marie-Antoinette in the chicest style of the late 18th century. The superb **Salon du Grand Couvert**, antechamber to the Queen's Apartments, is the place where Louis XIV took his supper every evening at 10 o'clock. The sumptuously painted walls and ceilings, tapestries, woodwork, and even the furniture have been returned to their original splendor, making this the only one of the queen's private rooms that can be seen exactly as it was first decorated in the 1670s. The park and gardens are a great place to stretch your legs while taking in details of André Le Nôtre's formal landscaping.

Versailles's royal getaways are as impressive in their own right as the main palace. A charmer with the ladies (as Louis's many royal mistresses would attest), the Sun King enjoyed a more relaxed atmosphere in which to conduct his dalliances away from the prying eyes of the court at the **Grand Trianon.** But Versailles's most famous getaway, the **Hameau de la Reine,** was added under the reign of Louis XVI at the request of his relentlessly scrutinized wife, Marie-Antoinette. Seeking to create a simpler "country" life away from the court's endless intrigues, between 1783 and 1787, the queen had her own rustic hamlet built in the image of a charming Normandy village, complete with a mill and dairy, roving livestock, and delightfully natural gardens. One of the most visited monuments in the world, Versailles is almost always teeming, especially in the summer; try to beat the crowds by arriving at 9 am, and buying your ticket online. ✉ *Pl. d'Armes* ☎ *01–30–83–78–00* ⊕ *www.chateauversailles.fr* ✉ *€18, all-attractions pass €20, Marie-Antoinette's Domain €12, park free (weekend fountain show €10, Apr.–Oct.)* ⊘ *Closed Mon.*

Musée Lambinet. Around the back of Notre-Dame, on Boulevard de la Reine (note the regimented lines of trees), are the elegant Hôtel de Neyret and the Musée Lambinet, a sumptuous mansion from 1751, with collections of paintings, weapons, fans, and porcelain (including the Madame du Barry "Rose"). A tearoom—open Thursday, Saturday, and Sunday afternoons—provides an elegant way to refresh after an intensive round of sightseeing. ✉ *54 bd. de la Reine* ☎ *01–30–97–28–75* ⊕ *culture-lambinet.versailles.fr* ✉ *€5* ⊘ *Closed Fri.*

Notre-Dame. If you have any energy left after exploring Louis XIV's palace and park, a tour of Versailles—a textbook 18th-century town—offers a telling contrast between the majestic and the domestic. From the front gate of Versailles's palace turn left onto Rue de l'Independence-Américaine and walk over to Rue Carnot past the stately Écuries de la Reine—once the queen's stables, now the regional law courts—to octagonal place Hoche. Down Rue Hoche to the left is the powerful Baroque facade of Notre-Dame, built from 1684 to 1686 by Jules Hardouin-Mansart as the parish church for Louis XIV's new town. ✉ *Versailles* ⊕ *notredameversailles.org.*

Continued on page 342

VERSAILLES

Revised by Linda Hervieux

Louis XIV's Hall of Mirrors

A two-century spree of indulgence in the finest riches of the age by the consecutive reigns of three French kings produced two of the world's most historic artifacts: gloriously, the Palace of Versailles and, momentously, the French Revolution.

Less a monument than an entire world unto itself, Versailles is the king of palaces. The end result of 380 million francs, 36,000 laborers, and enough paintings, if laid end to end, to equal 7 miles of canvas, it was conceived as the ne plus ultra expression of monarchy by Louis XIV. As a child, the king had developed a hatred for Paris (where he had been imprisoned by a group of nobles known as the Frondeurs), so, when barely out of his teens, he cast his cantankerous royal eye in search of a new power base. Marshy, inhospitable Versailles was the stuff of his dreams. Down came dad's modest royal hunting lodge and up, up, and along went the minion-crushing, Baroque palace we see today.

Between 1661 and 1710, architects Louis Le Vau and Jules Hardouin Mansart designed everything his royal acquisitiveness could want, including a throne room devoted to Apollo, god of the sun (Louis was known as *le roi soleil*). Convinced that his might depended upon dominating French nobility, Louis XIV summoned thousands of grandees from their own far-flung châteaux to reside at his new seat of government. In doing so, however, he unwittingly triggered the downfall of the monarchy. Like an 18th-century Disneyland, Versailles kept its courtiers so richly entertained they all but forgot the murmurs of discontent brewing back home.

As Louis XV chillingly foretold, "After me, the deluge." The royal commune was therefore shocked— shocked!—by the appearance, on October 5, 1789, of a revolutionary mob from Paris ready to sack Versailles and imprison Louis XVI. So as you walk through this awesome monument to splendor and excess, give a thought to its historic companion: the French Revolution. A tour of Versailles's grand salons inextricably mixes pathos with glory.

CROWNING GLORIES: TOP SIGHTS OF VERSAILLES

Seducing their court with their self-assured approach to 17th- and 18th-century art and decoration, a trinity of French kings made Versailles into the most vainglorious of châteaux.

Galerie des Glaces (Hall of Mirrors). Of all the rooms at Versailles, none matches the magnificence of the Galerie des Glaces (Hall of Mirrors). Begun by Mansart in 1678, this represents the acme of the Louis Quatorze (Louis-XIV) style. Measuring 240 feet long, 33 feet wide, and 40 feet high, it is ornamented with gilded candlesticks, crystal chandeliers, and a coved ceiling painted with Charles Le Brun's homage to Louis XIV's reign.

In Louis's day, the Galerie was laid with priceless carpets and filled with orange trees in silver pots. Nighttime galas were illuminated by 3,000 candles, their blaze doubled in the 17 gigantic mirrors that precisely echo the banner of windows along the west front. Lavish balls were once held here, and you can still get the full royal treatment at the Serenade Royale. This reenacts one of Louis XIV's grand soirées with dancers in period costumes. The 45-minute spectacle is held every Saturday at 6:30, 6:50, 7:10, 7:30, and 7:50 pm (€21-€42 ⊕ www.chateauversailles-spectacles.fr ☎ 01–30–83–78–98).

The Grands Appartements (State Apartments). Virtual stages for ceremonies of court ritual and etiquette, Louis XIV's first-floor state salons were designed in the Baroque style on a biceps-flexing scale meant to one-up the lavish Vaux-le-Vicomte château recently built for Nicolas Fouquet, the king's finance minister.

Flanking the Hall of Mirrors and retaining most of their bombastic Italianate Baroque decoration, the Salon de la Guerre (Salon of War) and the Salon de la Paix (Salon of Peace) are ornately decorated with gilt stucco, painted ceilings, and marble sculpture. Perhaps the most extravagant is the Salon d'Apollon (Apollo Chamber), the former throne room.

Versailles from the outside

Detail of the ceiling

Hall of Mirrors

Inside the Apollo Chamber

Hall of Battles

Appartements du Roi (King's Apartments). Completed in 1701 in the Louis-XIV style, the king's state and private chambers comprise a suite of 15 rooms set in a "U" around the east facade's Marble Court. Dead center across the sprawling cobbled forecourt is Louis XIV's bedchamber—he would awake and rise (just as the sun did, from the east) attended by members of his court and the public. Holding the king's chemise when he dressed soon became a more definitive reflection of status than the possession of an entire province. Nearby is Louis XV's magnificent Cabinet Intérieur (Office of the King), shining with gold and white boiseries; in the center is the most famous piece of furniture at Versailles, Louis XV's roll-top desk, crafted by Oeben and Riesener in 1769.

Louis XIV

IN FOCUS VERSAILLES

19

King's Apartments

VINTAGE BOURBON

Versailles was built by three great kings of the Bourbon dynasty. Louis XIV (1638–1715) began its construction in 1661. After ruling for 72 years, Louis Quatorze was succeeded by his great grandson, Louis XV (1710–74), who added the Royal Opera and the Petit Trianon to the palace. Louis XVI (1754–93) came to the throne in 1774 and was forced out of Versailles in 1789, along with Marie Antoinette, both guillotined three years later.

Chambre de la Reine (Queen's Bedchamber). At one time the most opulent bedroom in the world, this was initially created for Marie Thérèse, first wife of Louis XIV, to be part of the Queen's Apartments. For Marie Antoinette, however, the entire room was glammed up with silk wall-hangings covered with Rococo motifs that reflect her love of flowers. Legend has it that the gardens directly beyond these windows were replanted daily so that the queen could enjoy a fresh assortment of blossoms each morning. The bed, decked out with white ostrich plumes *en panache*, was also redone for Louis XVI's queen. Nineteen royal children were born in this room.

Queen's Bedchamber

Petits Appartements (Small Apartments). As styles of decor changed, Louis XIV's successors felt out of sync with their architectural inheritance. Louis XV exchanged the heavy red-and-gilt of Italianate Baroque for lighter, pastel-hued Rococo. On the top floor of the palace, on the right side of the central portion, are the apartments Louis XV commissioned to escape the wearisome pomp of the first-floor rooms. Here, Madame de Pompadour, mistress of Louis XV and famous patroness of the Rococo style, introduced grace notes of intimacy and refinement. In so doing, she transformed the daunting royal apartments into places to live rather than pose.

Parc de Versailles. Even Bourbon kings needed respite from Versailles's endless maze, hence the creation of one of Europe's largest parks. The sublime 250-acre grounds (☎01–30–83–77–88 for guided tour) is the masterpiece of André Le Nôtre, presiding genius of 17th-century classical French landscaping. Le Nôtre was famous for his "green geometries": ordered fantasies of clipped yew trees, multicolored flower beds (called *parterres*), and perspectival allées cleverly punctuated with statuary, laid out between 1661 and 1668. The spatial effect is best admired from inside the palace, views about which Le Nôtre said, "Flowers can only be walked on by the eyes."

Ultimately, at the royal command, rivers were diverted—to flow into more than 600 fountains—and entire forests were imported to ornament the park, which is centered around the mile-long Grand Canal. As for the great fountains, their operation costs a fortune in these democratic days, and so they perform only on weekends and some holidays (10-6) from April through mid-October and Tuesdays mid-May to mid-June; admission to the park during this time is €8. The park is open daily 7 am–8:30 pm in summer and 8–6 in winter.

LIGHTING UP THE SKY

The largest fountain at Versailles, the Bassin de Neptune, becomes a spectacle of rare grandeur during the Grandes Eaux Nocturnes, a light show to the strains of Baroque music, held Saturdays from the end of June through August at 9 pm, with fireworks at 11. Tickets are €23, €19 ages 6–17, and free for children under 6. ⊕ www.chateauversailles-spectacles.fr ☎01–30–83–78–98.

Dauphin's Apartments

Bassin de Neptune

Chapel and Opéra Royal: In the north wing of the château are three showpieces of the palace. The solemn white-and-gold Chapelle was completed in 1710—the king and queen attended daily mass here seated in gilt boxes. The Opéra Royal (Opera House), entirely constructed of wood painted to look like marble, was designed by Jacques-Ange Gabriel for Louis XV in 1770. Connecting the two, the 17th-century Galeries have exhibits retracing the château's history.

Opéra Royal

VERSAILLES: FIRST FLOOR, GARDENS & ADJACENT PARK

TO ↗
THE TRIANONS

Fountain of Autumn

Fountain of Summer

LATONA FOUNTAIN & PARTERRE

BOSQUET DES ROCAILLES

BATHS OF APOLLO

WATER PARTERRE

SOUTH PARTERRE

NORTH PARTERRE

Hall of Mirrors

Pyramid & Bathing Nymphs

Queen's Bed Chamber

State Apartments

King's Apartments

Hall of Battles

Royal Courtyard

Small Courtyard

Opera House

Opera Courtyard

Chapel

SOUTH WING

Prince's Courtyard

Chapel Courtyard

NORTH WING

LET THEM EAT CRÊPE: MARIE ANTOINETTE'S ROYAL LAIR

Was Marie Antoinette a luxury-mad butterfly flitting from ball to costume ball? Or was she a misunderstood queen who suffered a loveless marriage and became a prisoner of court etiquette at Versailles? Historians now believe the answer was the latter and point to her private retreats at Versailles as proof.

R.F.D. VERSAILLES?

Here, in the northwest part of the royal park, Marie Antoinette (1755–93) created a tiny universe of her own: her comparatively dainty mansion called Petit Trianon and its adjacent "farm," the relentlessly picturesque Hameau ("hamlet"). In a life that took her from royal cradle to throne of France to guillotine, her happiest days were spent at Trianon. For here she could live a life in the "simplest" possible way; here the queen could enter a salon and the game of cards would not stop; here women could wear simple gowns of muslin without a single jewel. Toinette only wanted to be queen of Trianon, not queen of France. And considering the horrible, chamber-pot-pungent, gossip-infested corridors of Versailles, you can almost understand why.

TEEN QUEEN

From the first, Maria-Antonia (her actual name) was ostracized as an outsider, "l'Autrichienne"—the Austrian "bitch." Upon arriving in France in 1770—at a mere 14 years of age—she was married to the Dauphin, the future King Louis XVI. But shamed by her initial failure to deliver a royal heir, she grew to hate overcrowded Versailles and escaped to the Petit Trianon. Built between 1763 and 1768 by Jacques-Ange Gabriel for Madame de Pompadour, this bijou palace was a radical statement: a royal residence designed to be casual and unassuming. Toinette refashioned the Trianon's interior in the sober Neoclassical style.

Hameau

Queen's House

Temple of Love

Petit Trianon

"THE SIMPLE LIFE"

Just beyond Petit Trianon lay the storybook Hameau, a mock-Norman village inspired by the peasant-luxe, simple-life daydreams caught by Boucher on canvas and by Rousseau in literature. With its water mill, thatched-roof houses, pigeon loft, and vegetable plots, this make-believe farm village was run by Monsieur Valy-Busard, a farmer, and his wife, who often helped the queen—outfitted as a Dresden shepherdess with a Sèvres porcelain crook—tend her flock of perfumed sheep.

As if to destroy any last link with reality, the queen built nearby a jewel-box theater (open by appointment). Here she acted in little plays, sometimes essaying the role of a servant girl. Only the immediate royal family, about seven or so friends, and her personal servants were permitted entry; disastrously, the entire officialdom of Versailles society was shut out—a move that only served to infuriate courtiers. This is how fate and destiny close the circle. For it was here at Trianon that a page sent by Monsieur de Saint-Priest found Marie-Antoinette on October 5, 1789, to tell her that Paris was marching on an already half-deserted Versailles.

Was Marie Antoinette a political traitor to France whose execution was well merited? Or was she the ultimate fashion victim? For those who feel that this tragic queen spent—and shopped—her way into a revolution, a visit to her relatively modest Petit Trianon and Hameau should prove a revelation.

Marie Antoinette

LES BEAUX TRIANONS

A mile from the château, the Grand Trianon was created by Hardouin Mansart in 1687 as a retreat for Louis XIV; it was restored in the early 19th century, with Empire-style salons. It's a memorable spot often missed by foot-weary tourists exhausted by the château, but well worth the effort. A special treat is Marie Antoinette's hideaway nearby, the Petit Trianon, presumably restored to how she left it before being forced to Paris by an angry mob of soon-to-be revolutionaries.

Place du Marché-Notre-Dame. This lively square in the heart of the Notre-Dame neighborhood is home to the largest market in the region, far outstripping anything in Paris. Outdoors, stalls offer a veritable cornucopia of fresh fruits, vegetables, herbs, and spices; meanwhile, the four historic halls (dating to the reign of Louis XV and rebuilt in 1841) brim with every gourmet delight—foie gras, fine wines, seafood, game, prepared delicacies, cheese from every corner of France—providing a sensory experience that will overwhelm even the most jaded foodie. The open-air market runs three half-days a week (Tuesday, Friday, and Sunday 7–2), but the covered food halls are open every day except Monday, from early morning until 7:30 pm (closing is at 2 on Sunday). If you're in the mood for more shopping, the town's marvelous antiques district begins at the northwest corner of the market square and extends along the cobbled streets to the charming Passage de la Geôle. ⊠ *Versailles.*

WHERE TO EAT

$$$$
MODERN FRENCH
Fodor's Choice
★

✕**Gordon Ramsay au Trianon.** Worldwide chef sensation Gordon Ramsay brings his conversation-worthy cuisine to this Versailles berth. Picture exemplary entrées like ravioli of langoustines and lobster cooked in a Riesling bisque with Petrossian caviar and lime consommé, or Périgord foie gras done "2 ways," roasted with a beetroot tart and pressed with green apple and Sauternes. **Known for:** stellar cuisine from a star chef; more casual Véranda outpost next-door; good option for French teatime. Ⓢ *Average main: €80* ⊠ *1 bd. de la Reine* ☎ *01–30–84–50–18* ⊕ *www.trianonpalace.fr/savourer/gastronomie/gordon-ramsay-au-trianon* ☉ *Closed Sun., Mon., and late July–late-Aug.* 🏛 *Jacket required.*

$$$$
MODERN FRENCH
Fodor's Choice
★

✕**L'Angelique.** Régis Douysset's refined yet unfussy French cuisine attracts the Versailles gourmet crowd. A seasonally changing menu offers a good balance of seafood and game: picture a delicate perch fillet with spaghetti *de mer* (in a shellfish bouillon) or venison shoulder with grilled turnips and a spätzle of girolle mushrooms. **Known for:** some of the best food in Versailles; historic 17th-century setting; swoon-worthy desserts. Ⓢ *Average main: €39* ⊠ *27 av. de Saint-Cloud* ☎ *01–30–84–98–85* ⊕ *www.langelique.fr* ☉ *Closed Sun. and Mon., 1 wk at Christmas, 1 wk in Feb., and 2 wks in Aug.*

$$$$
MODERN FRENCH
Fodor's Choice
★

✕**La Table du 11.** With a Michelin star in his pocket, rising chef Jean-Baptiste Lavergne-Morazzani has answered the city's dire need for top-quality and well-priced dining at La Table du 11. A small menu features the freshest market dishes: maybe line-caught daurade with candied citrus, Argentine beef with roasted pumpkin and velvety buratina cheese, and a spectacular cheese plate for dessert. **Known for:** excellent traditional French cuisine; affordable prix-fixe menus; charming ambience. Ⓢ *Average main: €44* ⊠ *8 rue de la Chancellerie* ☎ *09–83–34–76–00* ⊕ *www.latabledu11.com* ☉ *Closed Sun. and Mon.*

WHERE TO STAY

$ **Le Cheval Rouge.** Built in 1676, this unpretentious option is in a corner
HOTEL of the market square, close to the château and strongly recommended if
you plan to explore the town on foot. **Pros:** great setting in town center;
good value for Versailles. **Cons:** bland public areas; some rooms still need
renovating. $Rooms from: €94 ⊠ 18 rue André-Chénier ☎ 01–39–50–
03–03 ⊕ www.chevalrougeversailles.fr ⇄ 40 rooms ✺ No meals.

$$$ **L'Orangerie White-Palacio.** Across a charming garden from the main
B&B/INN house, this pretty cottage offers two quiet and comfortable suites with
private bathrooms, a common kitchen, and full garden access for meals
or relaxation. **Pros:** friendly, helpful host; very close to main sights.
Cons: cold breakfast; hand-held shower in bath. $Rooms from: €165
⊠ 37 av. de Paris, Quartier Saint-Louis ☎ 09–53–61–07–57 ⊕ www.l-
orangerie-versailles.fr ⇄ 2 rooms ✺ Breakfast.

$$$ **Trianon Palace Versailles.** Like a modern-day Versailles, this deluxe
HOTEL turn-of-the-20th-century hotel is a creamy white creation of imposing
size, filled with soaring rooms (including the historic Salle Clemenceau,
site of the 1919 Versailles Peace Conference). **Pros:** palatial glamour;
wonderful setting right by château park; Gordon Ramsay's on-site
restaurant. **Cons:** lacks a personal touch; glamorous setting not for
everyone; newer rooms not as glitzy. $Rooms from: €180 ⊠ 1 bd. de
la Reine ☎ 01–30–84–50–00 ⊕ www.trianonpalace.fr ⇄ 199 rooms
✺ No meals.

NIGHTLIFE AND PERFORMING ARTS

Académie Equestre de Versailles. On most weekends (and on certain weekdays during school holidays), you can watch 28 elegant white horses
and their expert riders perform balletic feats to music in a dazzling
hour-long show directed by the great equine choreographer Bartabas. If
you can't make the show staged in the converted 17th-century Manège
(riding school), opt for a tour of the aptly named Grandes Écuries
(grand stables), which take place Sunday at 10:30 am. Located opposite the palace, the structure was built for Louis XIV's royal cavalry.
⊠ Av. Rockefeller ☎ 01–39–02–62–75 ⊕ www.bartabas.fr ⊠ Shows
€25, stables visit €15.

Centre de Musique Baroque. An accomplished dancer, Louis XIV was also
a great music lover who bankrolled the finest musicians and composers
of the day—Lully, Charpentier, Rameau, Marais. So it's only fitting that
France's foremost institute for the study and performance of French
Baroque music should be based at Versailles. An excellent program of
concerts is presented in the château's Opéra Royal and chapel; the latter
are free of charge. ⊠ Versailles ☎ 01–39–20–78–10 ⊕ www.cmbv.fr.

Fodor's Choice **Opéra Royal du Château de Versailles.** One of the most beautiful opera
★ houses in Europe was built for 14-year-old Marie-Antoinette on the
occasion of her marriage to Louis XVI, and entering this extravagantly
gilded performance hall from the hewn-stone passageway can literally
take your breath away. But the beauty is not just skin-deep—the intimate 700-seat venue is blessed with rich acoustics. Home to the Royal

19

Opera, it hosts a world-class roster of orchestral and chamber concerts, as well as modern dance and ballet performances. For arts lovers, this spot alone will justify the quick trip from Paris. ⊠ *Château de Versailles* ☎ *01–30–83–78–89* ⊕ *www.chateauversailles-spectacles.fr.*

SHOPPING

Aux Colonnes. This charming, highly rated *confiserie* (candy shop) offers a cornucopia of chocolates and traditional French sweets. ⊠ *14 rue Hoche* ⊕ *www.auxcolonnes.com* ☉ *Closed Mon.*

Fodor'sChoice
★

La Cour des Senteurs. At the threshold of Versailles's Old Town, the beautiful Cour des Senteurs—Courtyard of Fragrances—celebrates the town's status as the birthplace of the modern perfumer. Tiny **Maison des Parfums** charmingly recounts the history of perfume with a timeline and interactive displays, while the **Inédite Toile de Jouy** boutique features the store's famous cotton decorated with country scenes on a range of table linens, handbags, clothing, jewelry, and more—all made in France. **Atelier Saveurs Versailles** offers inspiration in the art of the French dinner table, with a curated selection of dishes and elegant tableware by homegrown designers, along with a small épicerie carrying gourmet groceries. For a quick bite or afternoon tea, grab an outdoor table at Salon Sur Cour. ⊠ *8 rue de la Chancellerie.*

Les Délices du Palais. Everyone heads here to pick up homemade pâté, cold cuts, cheese, salad, and other picnic essentials. ⊠ *4 rue du Maréchal-Foch* ⊕ *www.charcuterie-lesdelicesdupalais.com* ☉ *Closed Mon.*

CHARTRES

88 km (55 miles) southwest of Paris.

If Versailles is the climax of French secular architecture, Chartres is its religious apogee. All the descriptive prose and poetry that have been lavished on this supreme cathedral can only begin to suggest the glory of its 12th- and 13th-century statuary and stained glass, somehow suffused with burning mysticism and a strange sense of the numinous. Chartres is more than a church—it's a nondenominational spiritual experience. If you arrive in summer from Maintenon across the edge of the Beauce, the richest agrarian plain in France, you can see Chartres's spires rising up from oceans of wheat. The whole town, however, is worth a leisurely exploration. Ancient streets tumble down from the cathedral to the river, lined most weekends with *bouquinistes* selling old books and prints. The streets are especially busy each year on August 15, when pilgrims and tourists flock in for the Procession du Vœu de Louis XIII commemorating the French monarchy's vow to serve the Virgin Mary.

GETTING HERE AND AROUND

Both Transilien and main-line (Le Mans–bound) trains leave Paris's Gare Montparnasse for Chartres (50–70 mins, €15). The train station on Place Pierre-Sémard puts you within walking distance of the cathedral.

Visitor Information **Chartres Tourist Office.** ⊠ *8 rue de la Poissonnerie* ☎ *02–37–18–26–26* ⊕ *www.chartres-tourisme.com.*

EXPLORING

Fodor'sChoice
★

Cathédrale Notre-Dame (*Chartres Cathedral*). Worship on the site of the Cathédrale Notre-Dame, better known as Chartres Cathedral, goes back to before the Gallo-Roman period—the crypt contains a well that was the focus of druid ceremonies. In the late 9th century Charles II (aka "the Bald") presented Chartres with what was believed to be the tunic of the Virgin Mary, a precious relic that went on to attract hordes of pilgrims. The current cathedral, the sixth church on the spot, dates mainly to the 12th and 13th centuries and was erected after the previous building, dating to the 11th century, burned down in 1194. A well-chronicled outburst of religious fervor followed the discovery that the Virgin Mary's relic had miraculously survived unsinged. Motivated by this "miracle," princes and paupers, barons and bourgeoisie gave their money and their labor to build the new cathedral. Ladies of the manor came to help monks and peasants on the scaffolding in a tremendous resurgence of religious faith that followed the Second Crusade. Just 25 years were needed for Chartres Cathedral to rise again, and it has remained substantially unchanged ever since. As spiritual as Chartres is, the cathedral also had its more earthbound uses. Look closely and you can see that the main nave floor has a subtle slant. It was designed to provide drainage because this part of the church was often used as a "hostel" by thousands of overnighting pilgrims in medieval time.

Worship on the site of the Cathédrale Notre-Dame, better known as Chartres Cathedral, goes back to before the Gallo-Roman period—the crypt contains a well that was the focus of druid ceremonies. In the late 9th century Charles II (aka "the Bald") presented Chartres with what was believed to be the tunic of the Virgin Mary, a precious relic that went on to attract hordes of pilgrims. The current cathedral, the sixth church on the spot, dates mainly to the 12th and 13th centuries and was erected after the previous building, dating to the 11th century, burned down in 1194. A well-chronicled outburst of religious fervor followed the discovery that the Virgin Mary's relic had miraculously survived unsinged. Motivated by this "miracle," princes and paupers, barons and bourgeoisie gave their money and their labor to build the new cathedral. Ladies of the manor came to help monks and peasants on the scaffolding in a tremendous resurgence of religious faith that followed the Second Crusade. Just 25 years were needed for Chartres Cathedral to rise again, and it has remained substantially unchanged ever since. As spiritual as Chartres is, the cathedral also had its more earthbound uses. Look closely and you can see that the main nave floor has a subtle slant. It was designed to provide drainage because this part of the church was often used as a "hostel" by thousands of overnighting pilgrims in medieval time.

19

Guided tours in English are offered at noon and 2:45, Monday through Saturday, Easter to mid-October. For a bird's-eye view, book a tour of the towers. Guided tours of the **Crypte** start from the Maison de la Crypte opposite the south porch. ⊠ *16 cloître Notre-Dame* ☎ *02–37–21–75–02* ⊕ *www.chartres-tourisme.com* ⊠ *Crypt €4, towers €6, tours €10.*

Chartres en Lumières. If you need an incentive to linger here until dusk, "Chartres en Lumières" (Chartres's festival of lights) provides it: 28 of the city's most revered monuments, including the glorious Notre-Dame Cathedral, are transformed into vivid light canvases. Thematically based on the history and purpose of each specific site, the animated projections are organized into a city walk that covers a wide swath of the Old Town's cobbled streets and bridges. The spectacle is free and occurs nightly from sunset to 1 am from mid-April through mid-October. A train tour of the illuminated city operates several times a night in summer. ⊠ *Chartres* ⊕ *www.chartresenlumieres.com.*

Musée des Beaux-Arts (*Fine Arts Museum*). Just behind the famed cathedral, the town art museum is housed in a handsome 18th-century building that once served as the bishop's palace. Its varied collection includes Renaissance enamels, a portrait of Erasmus by Holbein, tapestries, armor, and some fine (mainly French) paintings from the 17th, 18th, and 19th centuries. There's also a room devoted to the forceful 20th-century landscapes of Maurice de Vlaminck, who lived in the region. ⊠ *29 cloître Notre-Dame* ☎ *02–37–90–45–80* ⊠ *€4* ⊗ *Closed Mon. and Tues.*

WHERE TO EAT AND STAY

$ × **Esprit Gourmand.** On a picturesque street close to the cathedral, this quaint bistro is a lifesaver in a town sorely lacking in quality dining. The traditional French favorites it serves—like roast *poulet* with buttery potatoes, sautéed filet of dorade with grilled vegetables, and braised pork that's crisp on the outside and meltingly tender inside—are perennial crowd pleasers. **Known for:** classic French bistro dishes; garden terrace for outdoor dining; small space so reservations recommended. ⑤ *Average main: €18* ⊠ *6 rue du Cheval-Blanc* ☎ *02–37–36–97–84* ⊗ *Closed Mon. and Tues. No dinner Sun.*

FRENCH
FAMILY
Fodor's Choice
★

$$ × **Les Feuillantines.** The adventurous cuisine served at Les Feuillantines (one of Chartres's few gastronomic restaurants) rarely falters and very often soars. Try the superb house-made terrine with tangy cornichons to start, followed by duck risotto topped with caramelized shallots or beef ravioli perfumed with lemongrass and smoked tea. **Known for:** unique gastronomic dishes; outdoor garden; great prices. ⑤ *Average main: €21* ⊠ *4 rue du Bourg* ☎ *02–37–30–22–21* ⊗ *Closed Sun. and Mon.*

FRENCH
Fodor's Choice
★

$$$ ▦ **Best Western Le Grand Monarque.** On Chartres's main square, not far from the cathedral, this converted coaching inn warmly evokes the 19th century; many guest rooms are outfitted with brick walls, attractive antiques, lush drapes, and modern bathrooms (the best are in a separate turn-of-the-20th-century building overlooking a garden, while the most atmospheric are tucked away in the attic).

HOTEL

19

Pros: old-fashioned charm; spa and fitness center offering beauty treatments and massage; Michelin-starred restaurant on-site. **Cons:** best rooms are in an annex; uphill walk to cathedral; some decor is worn. $ *Rooms from: €175 ⊠ 22 pl. des Épars, Île de Nantes* ☎ *02–37–18–15–15* ⊕ *www.bw-grand-monarque.com* ⇥ *50 rooms, 5 suites* ⏍ *No meals.*

DISNEYLAND PARIS

38 km (24 miles) east of Paris via A4.

Disneyland Paris is probably not what you've traveled to France for. But if you have a child in tow, the promise of a day with Mickey might get you through an afternoon at Versailles or Fontainebleau. If you're a dyed-in-the-wool Disney fan, you'll also want to make a beeline here to see how the park has been molded to suit European tastes (Disney's "Imagineers" call it their most lovingly detailed one, and it simultaneously feels both decidedly foreign and eerily familiar). And if you've never experienced this particular form of Disney showmanship before, you may want to put in an appearance simply to find out what all the fuss is about.

GETTING HERE AND AROUND

Take the RER-A from central Paris (stations at Étoile, Auber, Les Halles, Gare de Lyon, and Nation) to Marne-la-Vallée–Chessy—the *gare* there is 100 yards from the Disneyland entrance; trains operate every 10–30 minutes, depending on the time of day (40 mins, €7.50). High-speed TGV train service (⊕ *www.tgv.com*) links Disneyland to Lille, Lyon, Brussels, and London (via Lille and the Channel Tunnel). Disneyland's hotel complex also offers a shuttle bus service connecting it with the Orly and Charles de Gaulle airports; in each case the trip takes about 45 minutes and tickets cost €20.

Visitor Information Disneyland Paris Reservations Office. ☎ *01–60–30–60–90, 407/939–7675 in the U.S.* ⊕ *www.disneylandparis.com.*

EXPLORING

FAMILY   **Disneyland Paris.** A slightly downsized version of its United States
Fodor's Choice   counterpart, Disneyland Paris is nevertheless a spectacular sight,
★   created with an acute attention to detail. **Disneyland Park,** as the original theme park is styled, consists of five "lands": Main Street U.S.A., Frontierland, Adventureland, Fantasyland, and Discoveryland. The central theme of each land is relentlessly echoed in every detail, from attractions to restaurant menus to souvenirs. In **Main Street U.S.A,** tots adore Alice's Curious Labyrinth, Peter Pan's Flight, and especially the whirling Mad Hatter's Teacups, while everyone loves the afternoon parades, with huge floats swarming with all of Disney's most beloved characters—just make sure to stake your place along Main Street in advance for a good spot.

Top attractions at **Frontierland** are the chilling Phantom Manor, haunted by holographic ghosts, and the thrilling runaway mine train of Big Thunder Mountain, a roller coaster that plunges wildly through floods and avalanches in a setting meant to evoke Utah's Monument Valley. Whiffs of Arabia, Africa, and the Caribbean give **Adventureland** its exotic cachet; the spicy meals and snacks served here rank among the best food in the park. Don't miss Pirates of the Caribbean, an exciting mise-en-scène populated by lifelike animatronic figures, or Indiana Jones and the Temple of Doom, a rapid-fire ride that re-creates some of this hapless hero's most exciting moments.

Fantasyland charms the youngest parkgoers with familiar cartoon characters from such classic Disney films as *Snow White, Pinocchio, Dumbo, Alice in Wonderland,* and *Peter Pan.* The focal point of Fantasyland, and indeed Disneyland Paris, is Le Château de la Belle au Bois Dormant (Sleeping Beauty's Castle), a 140-foot, bubblegum-pink structure topped with 16 blue- and gold-tipped turrets. **Discoveryland** is a high-tech, futuristic eye-popper. Robots on roller skates welcome you on your way to Star Tours, a pitching, plunging, sense-confounding ride based on the *Star Wars* films; and another robot, the staggeringly realistic 9-Eye, hosts a simulated space journey in Le Visionarium.

The older the child, the more they will enjoy **Walt Disney Studios,** a cinematically driven area next to the Disneyland Park, where many of the newer Disney character–themed rides can be found. It's divided into four "production zones," giving visitors insight into different parts of the production process, including Animation Couryard, where Disney artists demonstrate the various phases of character animation, and Production Courtyard, where you can go on a behind-the-scenes Studio Tram tour of location sites, movie props, studio interiors, and costumes, ending with a visit to Catastrophe Canyon in the heart of a film shoot. ⊠ *Marne-la-Vallée* ☎ *01–64–74–40–00* ⊕ *www.disneylandparis. com* 🎫 *€90, 3-day Passport €174; includes admission to all individual attractions within Disneyland or Walt Disney Studios; tickets for Walt Disney Studios are also valid for admission to Disneyland during last 3 opening hrs of same day.*

19

WHERE TO STAY

$$$$
HOTEL
🏨 **Sequoia Lodge.** Ranging from superluxe to just barely affordable, Disneyland Paris has 5,000 rooms throughout several hotels, but your best bet on all counts may be the Sequoia Lodge—a grand recreation of an American mountain lodge, just a few minutes' walk from the theme park. **Pros:** package deals include admission to theme park; cozy, secluded feel; great pools. **Cons:** restaurants a bit ho-hum; many rooms do not have lake view; prices can flutuate. ⑤ *Rooms from: €300* ⊠ *Marne-la-Vallée* ☎ *01–60–30–60–90, 407/939–7675 in the U.S.* ⊕ *www.disneylandparis.com* 🛏 *1,020 rooms* ⦿ *No meals.*

NIGHTLIFE AND PERFORMING ARTS

Disney Village. Nocturnal entertainment outside the park centers on Disney Village, a vast pleasure mall designed by American architect Frank Gehry. Homesick kids who've had enough croque monsieurs will be happy to hear that vintage American-style restaurants—a diner, a deli, and a steak house among them—dominate the food scene here. One highlight within Disney Village is **Buffalo Bill's Wild West Show**, a two-hour dinner extravaganza with a menu of sausage, spareribs, and chili. The entertainment component includes performances by a talented troupe of stunt riders, bronco busters, tribal dancers, and musicians; plus some 50 horses, a dozen buffalo, a bull, and an Annie Oakley–style sharpshooter, with a golden-maned "Buffalo Bill" as emcee. A re-creation of a show that dazzled Parisians 100 years ago, it's corny but great fun. Tickets for shows, which start nightly at 6:30 and 9:30, cost €65–€80. ⊠ *Marne-la-Vallée* ⊕ *www.disneylandparis.com.*

UNDERSTANDING PARIS

VOCABULARY

VOCABULARY

One of the trickiest French sounds to pronounce is the nasal final n sound (whether or not the n is actually the last letter of the word). You should try to pronounce it as a sort of nasal grunt—as in "huh." The vowel that precedes the n will govern the vowel sound of the word, and in this list we precede the final n with an h to remind you to be nasal.

Another problem sound is the ubiquitous but untransliterable eu, as in bleu (blue) or deux (two), and the very similar sound in je (I), ce (this), and de (of). The closest equivalent might be the vowel sound in "put," but rounded. The famous rolled r is a glottal sound. Consonants at the ends of words are usually silent; when the following word begins with a vowel, however, the two are run together by sounding the consonant. There are two forms of "you" in French: vous (formal and plural) and tu (a singular, personal form). When addressing an adult you don't know, vous is always best.

ENGLISH	PRONUNCIATION	FRENCH

BASICS

ENGLISH	PRONUNCIATION	FRENCH
Yes/no	wee/nohn	Oui/non
Please	seel voo play	S'il vous plaît
Thank you	mair- **see**	Merci
You're welcome	deh ree- **ehn**	De rien
Excuse me, sorry	pahr- **don**	Pardon
Good morning/ afternoon	bohn- **zhoor**	Bonjour
Good evening	bohn- **swahr**	Bonsoir
Good-bye	o ruh- **vwahr**	Au revoir
Mr. (Sir)	muh- **syuh**	Monsieur
Mrs. (Ma'am)	ma- **dam**	Madame
Miss	mad-mwa- **zel**	Mademoiselle
Pleased to meet you	ohn-shahn- **tay**	Enchanté(e)
How are you?	kuh-mahn-tahl-ay **voo**	Comment allez-vous?
Very well, thanks	tray bee-ehn, mair- **see**	Très bien, merci
And you?	ay voo?	Et vous?

NUMBERS

one	uhn	un
two	deuh	deux
three	twah	trois
four	**kaht**-ruh	quatre
five	sank	cinq

ENGLISH	PRONUNCIATION	FRENCH
six	seess	six
seven	set	sept
eight	wheat	huit
nine	nuf	neuf
ten	deess	dix
eleven	ohnz	onze
twelve	dooz	douze
thirteen	trehz	treize
fourteen	kah- **torz**	quatorze
fifteen	kanz	quinze
sixteen	sez	seize
seventeen	deez- **set**	dix-sept
eighteen	deez- **wheat**	dix-huit
nineteen	deez- **nuf**	dix-neuf
twenty	vehn	vingt
twenty-one	vehnt-ay- **uhn**	vingt-et-un
thirty	trahnt	trente
forty	ka- **rahnt**	quarante
fifty	sang- **kahnt**	cinquante
sixty	swa- **sahnt**	soixante
seventy	swa-sahnt- **deess**	soixante-dix
eighty	kaht-ruh- **vehn**	quatre-vingts
ninety	kaht-ruh-vehn- **deess**	quatre-vingt-dix
one hundred	sahn	cent
one thousand	meel	mille

COLORS

black	nwahr	noir
blue	bleuh	bleu
brown	bruhn/mar- **rohn**	brun/marron
green	vair	vert
orange	o- **rahnj**	orange
pink	rose	rose
red	rouge	rouge

ENGLISH	PRONUNCIATION	FRENCH
violet	vee-o- **let**	violette
white	blahnk	blanc
yellow	zhone	jaune

DAYS OF THE WEEK

Sunday	dee- **mahnsh**	dimanche
Monday	luhn- **dee**	lundi
Tuesday	mahr- **dee**	mardi
Wednesday	mair-kruh- **dee**	mercredi
Thursday	zhuh- **dee**	jeudi
Friday	vawn-druh- **dee**	vendredi
Saturday	sahm- **dee**	samedi

MONTHS

January	zhahn-vee- **ay**	janvier
February	feh-vree- **ay**	février
March	marce	mars
April	a- **vreel**	avril
May	meh	mai
June	zhwehn	juin
July	zhwee- **ay**	juillet
August	ah- **oo**	août
September	sep- **tahm**-bruh	septembre
October	awk- **to**-bruh	octobre
November	no- **vahm**-bruh	novembre
December	day- **sahm**-bruh	décembre

USEFUL PHRASES

Do you speak English?	par-lay **voo** ahn- **glay**	Parlez-vous anglais?
I don't speak ...	zhuh nuh parl pah ...	Je ne parle pas ...
French	frahn- **say**	français
I don't understand	zhuh nuh kohm- **prahn** pah	Je ne comprends pas
I understand	zhuh kohm- **prahn**	Je comprends
I don't know	zhuh nuh say **pah**	Je ne sais pas

ENGLISH	PRONUNCIATION	FRENCH
I'm American/ British	zhuh sweez a-may-ree- **kehn** /ahn- **glay**	Je suis américain/ anglais
What's your name?	ko-mahn vooz a-pell-ay- **voo**	Comment vous appelez-vous?
My name is ...	zhuh ma- **pell** ...	Je m'appelle ...
What time is it?	kel air eh- **teel**	Quelle heure est-il?
How?	ko- **mahn**	Comment?
When?	kahn	Quand?
Yesterday	yair	Hier
Today	o-zhoor- **dwee**	Aujourd'hui
Tomorrow	duh- **mehn**	Demain
Tonight	suh **swahr**	Ce soir
What?	kwah	Quoi?
What is it?	kess-kuh- **say**	Qu'est-ce que c'est?
Why?	poor- **kwa**	Pourquoi?
Who?	kee	Qui?
Where is ...	oo ay	Où est ...
the train station?	la gar	la gare?
the subway station?	la sta- **syon** duh may- **tro**	la station de métro?
the bus stop?	la-ray duh booss	l'arrêt de bus?
the post office?	la post	la poste?
the bank?	la bahnk	la banque?
the ... hotel?	lo- **tel**	l'hôtel ...?
the store?	luh ma-ga- **zehn**	le magasin?
the cashier?	la **kess**	la caisse?
the ... museum?	luh mew- **zay**	le musée ...?
the hospital?	lo-pee- **tahl**	l'hôpital?
the elevator?	la-sahn- **seuhr**	l'ascenseur?
the telephone?	luh tay-lay- **phone**	le téléphone?
Where are the ...	oo sohn lay	Où sont les ...
restrooms?	twah- **let**	toilettes?
(men/women)	(**oh**-mm/ **fah**-mm)	(hommes/femmes)
Here/there	ee- **see** /la	Ici/là

ENGLISH	PRONUNCIATION	FRENCH
Left/right	a goash/a draht	A gauche/à droite
Straight ahead	too drwah	Tout droit
Is it near/far?	say pray/lwehn	C'est près/loin?
I'd like ...	zhuh voo- **dray**	Je voudrais ...
a room	ewn **shahm**-bruh	une chambre
the key	la clay	la clé
a newspaper	uhn zhoor- **nahl**	un journal
a stamp	uhn **tam**-bruh	un timbre
I'd like to buy ...	zhuh voo- **dray** **ahsh**-tay	Je voudrais acheter ...
cigarettes	day see-ga- **ret**	des cigarettes
matches	days a-loo- **met**	des allumettes
soap	dew sah- **vohn**	du savon
city map	uhn plahn de **veel**	un plan de ville
road map	ewn cart roo-tee- **air**	une carte routière
magazine	ewn reh- **vu**	une revue
envelopes	dayz ahn-veh- **lope**	des enveloppes
writing paper	dew pa-pee- **ay** a **let**-ruh	du papier à lettres
postcard	ewn cart pos- **tal**	une carte postale
How much is it?	say comb-bee- **ehn**	C'est combien?
A little/a lot	uhn peuh/bo- **koo**	Un peu/beaucoup
More/less	plu/mwehn	Plus/moins
Enough/too (much)	a-say/tro	Assez/trop
I am ill/sick	zhuh swee ma- **lahd**	Je suis malade
Call a ...	a-play uhn	Appelez un ...
doctor	dohk- **tehr**	docteur
Help!	o suh- **koor**	Au secours!
Stop!	a-reh- **tay**	Arrêtez!
Fire!	o fuh	Au feu!
Caution!/Look out!	a-tahn-see- **ohn**	Attention!

ENGLISH	PRONUNCIATION	FRENCH

DINING OUT

A bottle of ...	ewn boo- **tay** duh	une bouteille de ...
A cup of ...	ewn tass duh	une tasse de ...
A glass of ...	uhn vair duh	un verre de ...
Bill/check	la-dee-see- **ohn**	l'addition
Bread	dew panh	du pain
Breakfast	luh puh- **tee** day-zhuh- **nay**	le petit-déjeuner
Butter	dew burr	du beurre
Cheers!	ah **vo**-truh sahn- **tay**	A votre santé!
Cocktail/aperitif	uhn ah-pay-ree- **teef**	un apéritif
Dinner	luh dee- **nay**	le dîner
Dish of the day	luh plah dew **zhoor**	le plat du jour
Enjoy!	bohn a-pay- **tee**	Bon appétit!
Fixed-price menu	luh may- **new**	le menu
Fork	ewn four- **shet**	une fourchette
I am diabetic	zhuh swee dee-ah-bay- **teek**	Je suis diabétique
I am vegetarian	zhuh swee vay-zhay-ta-ree- **en**	Je suis végétarien(ne)
I cannot eat ...	zhuh nuh puh pah mahn- **jay** deh	Je ne peux pas manger de ...
I'd like to order	zhuh voo- **dray** ko-mahn- **day**	Je voudrais commander
Is service/the tip included?	ess kuh luh sair- **veess** ay comb- **pree**	Est-ce que le service est compris?
It's good/bad	say bohn/mo- **vay**	C'est bon/mauvais
It's hot/cold	say sho/frwah	C'est chaud/froid
Knife	uhn koo- **toe**	un couteau
Lunch	luh day-zhuh- **nay**	le déjeuner
Menu	la cart	la carte
Napkin	ewn sair-vee- **et**	une serviette
Pepper	dew **pwah**-vruh	du poivre
Plate	ewn a-see- **et**	une assiette
Please give me ...	doe-nay- **mwah**	Donnez-moi ...

ENGLISH	PRONUNCIATION	FRENCH
Salt	dew sell	du sel
Spoon	ewn kwee- **air**	une cuillère
Sugar	dew **sook**-ruh	du sucre
Waiter!/Waitress!	muh- **syuh** / mad-mwa- **zel**	Monsieur!/ Mademoiselle!
Wine list	la cart day vehn	la carte des vins

MENU GUIDE

FRENCH	ENGLISH

GENERAL DINING

FRENCH	ENGLISH
Entrée	Appetizer/Starter
Garniture au choix	Choice of vegetable side
Plat du jour	Dish of the day
Selon arrivage	When available
Supplément/En sus	Extra charge
Sur commande	Made to order

PETIT DÉJEUNER (BREAKFAST)

FRENCH	ENGLISH
Confiture	Jam
Miel	Honey
Oeuf à la coque	Boiled egg
Oeufs sur le plat	Fried eggs
Oeufs brouillés	Scrambled eggs
Tartine	Bread with butter

POISSONS/FRUITS DE MER (FISH/SEAFOOD)

FRENCH	ENGLISH
Anchois	Anchovies
Bar	Bass
Brandade de morue	Creamed salt cod
Brochet	Pike
Cabillaud/Morue	Fresh cod
Calmar	Squid
Coquilles St-Jacques	Scallops
Crevettes	Shrimp
Daurade	Sea bream

FRENCH	ENGLISH
Ecrevisses	Prawns/Crayfish
Harengs	Herring
Homard	Lobster
Huîtres	Oysters
Langoustine	Prawn/Lobster
Lotte	Monkfish
Moules	Mussels
Palourdes	Clams
Saumon	Salmon
Thon	Tuna
Truite	Trout

VIANDE (MEAT)

Agneau	Lamb
Boeuf	Beef
Boudin	Sausage
Boulettes de viande	Meatballs
Brochettes	Kebabs
Cassoulet	Casserole of white beans, meat
Cervelle	Brains
Chateaubriand	Double fillet steak
Choucroute garnie	Sausages with sauerkraut
Côtelettes	Chops
Côte/Côte de boeuf	Rib/T-bone steak
Cuisses de grenouilles	Frogs' legs
Entrecôte	Rib or rib-eye steak
Épaule	Shoulder
Escalope	Cutlet
Foie	Liver
Gigot	Leg
Porc	Pork
Ris de veau	Veal sweetbreads
Rognons	Kidneys
Saucisses	Sausages

FRENCH	ENGLISH
Selle	Saddle
Tournedos	Tenderloin of T-bone steak
Veau	Veal

METHODS OF PREPARATION

A point	Medium
A l'étouffée	Stewed
Au four	Baked
Ballotine	Boned, stuffed, and rolled
Bien cuit	Well-done
Bleu	Very rare
Frit	Fried
Grillé	Grilled
Rôti	Roast
Saignant	Rare

VOLAILLES/GIBIER (POULTRY/GAME)

Blanc de volaille	Chicken breast
Canard/Caneton	Duck/Duckling
Cerf/Chevreuil	Venison (red/roe)
Coq au vin	Chicken stewed in red wine
Dinde/Dindonneau	Turkey/Young turkey
Faisan	Pheasant
Lapin/Lièvre	Rabbit/Wild hare
Oie	Goose
Pintade/Pintadeau	Guinea fowl/Young guinea fowl
Poulet/Poussin	Chicken/Spring chicken

LÉGUMES (VEGETABLES)

Artichaut	Artichoke
Asperge	Asparagus
Aubergine	Eggplant
Carottes	Carrots
Champignons	Mushrooms
Chou-fleur	Cauliflower
Chou (rouge)	Cabbage (red)

FRENCH	ENGLISH
Laitue	Lettuce
Oignons	Onions
Petits pois	Peas
Pomme de terre	Potato
Tomates	Tomatoes

FRUITS/NOIX (FRUITS/NUTS)

Abricot	Apricot
Amandes	Almonds
Ananas	Pineapple
Cassis	Black currants
Cerises	Cherries
Citron/Citron vert	Lemon/Lime
Fraises	Strawberries
Framboises	Raspberries
Pamplemousse	Grapefruit
Pêche	Peach
Poire	Pear
Pomme	Apple
Prunes/Pruneaux	Plums/Prunes
Raisins/Raisins secs	Grapes/Raisins

DESSERTS

Coupe (glacée)	Sundae
Crème Chantilly	Whipped cream
Gâteau au chocolat	Chocolate cake
Glace	Ice cream
Tarte tatin	Caramelized apple tart
Tourte	Layer cake

DRINKS

A l'eau	With water
Avec des glaçons	On the rocks
Bière	Beer
Blonde/brune	Light/dark
Café noir/crème	Black coffee/with steamed milk

FRENCH	ENGLISH
Chocolat chaud	Hot chocolate
Eau-de-vie	Brandy
Eau minérale	Mineral water
Gazeuse/non gazeuse	Carbonated/still
Jus de ...	.. juice
Lait	Milk
Sec	Straight or dry
Thé	Tea
Au lait/au citron	With milk/lemon
Vin	Wine
Blanc	White
Doux	Sweet
Léger	Light
Brut	Very dry
Rouge	Red

TRAVEL SMART
PARIS

GETTING HERE AND AROUND

Addresses in Paris are fairly straightforward: there's the number, the street name, and the zip code designating one of Paris's 20 *arrondissements* (districts); for instance, in Paris 75010, the last two digits ("10") indicate that the address is in the 10e. The large 16e arrondissement has two numbers assigned to it: 75016 and 75116. ⇨ *For the layout of Paris's arrondissements, see the What's Where map in the Experience chapter.*

The arrondissements are laid out in a spiral, beginning from the area around the Louvre (1er arrondissement), then moving clockwise through the Marais, the Latin Quarter, St-Germain, and then out from the city center to the outskirts to Ménilmontant/Père-Lachaise (20e arrondissement). Occasionally you may see an address with a number plus *bis*—for instance, 20 bis, rue Vavin. This indicates the next entrance or door down from 20 rue Vavin. Note that in France you enter a building on the ground floor, or *rez-de-chaussée* (RC or 0), and go up one floor to the first floor, or *premier étage*. General address terms used in this book are *av.* (avenue), *bd.* (boulevard), *carrefour* (crossway), *cours* (promenade), *passage* (passageway), *pl.* (place), *quai* (quay/wharf/pier), *rue* (street), and *sq.* (square).

▌ AIR TRAVEL

Flying time to Paris is about 7 hours from New York, 8 hours from Chicago, and 11 hours from Los Angeles. Flying time from London to Paris is 1½ hours.

The French are notoriously stringent about security, particularly for international flights. Don't be surprised by the armed security officers patrolling the airports, and be prepared for very long check-in lines. Peak travel times in France are between mid-July and September, during the Christmas–New Year's holidays in late December and early January, and during the February school break. Through these periods airports are especially crowded, so allow plenty of extra time. Never leave your luggage unattended, even for a moment. Unattended bags are considered a security risk and may be destroyed.

Airline and Airport Links.com. Airline and Airport Links.com has links to many of the world's airlines and airports. ⊕ *www.airlineandairportlinks.com.*

Airline Security Issues Transportation Security Administration. ⊕ *www.tsa.gov.*

AIRPORTS

The major airports are Charles de Gaulle (CDG, also known as Roissy), 26 km (16 miles) northeast of Paris, and Orly (ORY), 16 km (10 miles) south of Paris. Both are easily accessible from the city. Whether you take a car or bus to travel from Paris to the airport on your departure, always allot an extra hour because of the often horrendous traffic tie-ups in the airports themselves (especially in peak seasons and at peak times). Free light-rail connections (Orlyval and CDGval), available between the major terminals, are one option for avoiding some of the traffic mess, but still give yourself enough time to navigate these busy airports.

Airport Information Charles de Gaulle/Roissy and Orly. ☎ *3950 (press "0" for service in English) €0.35 per minute, 0033/1–70–36–39–50 outside of France* ⊕ *www.adp.fr.*

GROUND TRANSPORTATION

By bus from CDG/Roissy: Roissybus, operated by the RATP (Paris Transit Authority), runs between Charles de Gaulle (T1, T2A, C, E, F, and T3) and the Opéra every 15 minutes (though the wait can be far longer) from 6 am to 8:45 pm and then every 20 minutes until 12:30 am; the cost is €12. The trip takes about 60 minutes in regular traffic, about 90 minutes at rush hour.

By coach from CDG/Roissy: Le Bus Direct, formerly known as the Air France bus, is a shuttle service in comfortable coaches equipped with Wi-Fi and USB ports. Buy your tickets online or onboard (€1 supplement). Line 2 goes from the airport to Paris's Étoile/Champs-Élysées, Porte Maillot, Trocadéro, Tour Eiffel, and La Motte-Piquet métro stations from 5:15 am to 11 pm, leaving every 30 minutes; journey time is about an hour in normal traffic. Tickets cost €17 one way save €6 if you buy a return ticket). Line 4 goes to Montparnasse and the Gare de Lyon from 6 am to 10 pm. Buses run every 30 minutes and cost €17; count on a trip of about 50–80 minutes. To reach the Arrivals-level bus station between the two terminals, passengers arriving in Terminal 1 need to take Exit 32; Terminals 2A, 2C, and 2D go to Exit C10; 2E and 2F use Exit E8 or E9. From Terminal 2G, take the free shuttle bus N2 to Terminal 2E/F. There's a 15%–25% discount on any of these buses for parties of four or more if you buy online. At the time of this update, Terminal 2B is closed for a major renovation.

A number of van companies, such as SuperShuttle Paris, serve both Charles de Gaulle and Orly airports. Prices arc sct, so there are no surprises even if traffic is a snail-pace nightmare. To make a reservation, call or reserve online at least one week in advance, and an air-conditioned van with a bilingual chauffeur will be waiting for you. Confirm the day before. The shared van service costs a third of their exclusive non-stop option but picks up other passengers, which adds at least 20 minutes to the trip.

By taxi from CDG/Roissy: Taxis are the most convenient way into Paris but certainly not the fastest during peak times. At best, the ride takes 30 minutes, but it can hit 90 minutes during rush hour. At least the once-unpredictable fares are now fixed in either direction; count on a flat rate of €50 (Left Bank) and €55 (Right Bank). Share a ride with Taxis G7 Sharing (*see Taxi Travel,*) and save as much as $20.

Taxis G7 also offers Familycabs with baby car seats and boosters. ParisGreenCar is an eco-friendly alternative (€79 flat rate) with an energy-efficient fleet of hybrid taxis; they make a €0.50 charitable donation with each booking. Whichever company you use, only take an official taxi from designated areas outside the terminal; they will have an illuminated roof sign and a meter. Additionally, Uber and other ride-hailing apps service CDG and they're usually cheaper.

By train from CDG/Roissy: The cheapest—and often the fastest—way into Paris from CDG is via the RER-B Line, the hybrid rapid transit-suburban train, which runs from 5 am to 11 pm daily. The free CDGVal lightrail connects each airport terminal (except 2G) to the Roissypôle RER station in 6 minutes. For Terminal 2G, take the free N2 "navette" shuttle bus outside Terminal 2F. Trains to central Paris (Les Halles, Gare du Nord, St-Michel, Luxembourg) depart every 10 to 20 minutes. The fare (including métro connection) is €10.30, and journey time is about 35 minutes to Les Halles. If you're catching a flight, be sure to check www.ratp.fr or a transport app for delays (they can be frequent).

By bus from Orly: RATP's Orlybus leaves every 10 to 20 minutes for the Denfert-Rochereau métro station in Montparnasse from Exit L in Orly South and Exit D in Orly West. The cost is €8.30. The cheapest bus is the RATP city bus 183, which shuttles you from métro Porte de Choisy (Line 7) to Orly South (Gate C, stop 4) for just €2. It departs every 30 minutes from 6 am to 12:20 am (frequency may be reduced on Sunday and holidays); travel time is about 45 to 60 minutes.

By coach from Orly: Le Bus Direct's Line 1, formerly the Air France bus, runs from Orly to Montparnasse, La Motte-Piquet, Tour Eiffel, Trocadéro, and Étoile/Champs-Élysées every 20 to 30 minutes from 5:50 am to 11:30 pm. The fare is €12 (discounts available online on a return ticket and for group travel) and

TRAVEL TO CENTRAL PARIS

Via	CDG	Orly
Taxi	30 mins–60 mins; €50–€55	25 mins–40 mins; €30–€35
Bus	60 mins–90 mins; €12	45 mins–60 mins; €2–€8.30
Coach	50 mins–80 mins; €17	45 mins–60 mins; €12
RER	35 mins; €10.30	35 mins; €6.35–€13.25

journey time is between 45 and 60 minutes, depending on traffic. To find the bus, take Exit L, stop 3 from Orly South or Exit D, stop 5 from Orly West. Private van companies also provide shuttle service.

By taxi from Orly: You'll find taxi stands at Orly South at Exit L and at Orly West at Exit B.(look for signs)). A cab to Paris costs a flat rate in either direction of €30 (Left Bank) and €35 (Right Bank); plan on 25–40 minutes in normal traffic. Uber and other ride-hailing apps service Orly.

By train from Orly: The cheapest way to get into Paris by train is to take the Go C shuttle bus ("*Paris par le train*") from Exit C, stop 5 at Orly South or Exit D, stop 7 at Orly West to the train station RER-C Pont de Rungis–Aéroport d'Orly. Trains to Paris leave every 15 to 20 minutes. Buy tickets at the automatic machines; the combined fare is €6.35 and journey time is about 35 minutes. Another slightly faster option is to take the Orlyval monorail, which runs from both Orly terminals to the Antony RER-B daily every 5 to 8 minutes from 6 am to 11:35 pm. Passengers arriving in the South Terminal should use the automatic machines or Orlyval counter at Exits K; take Exit A if you've arrived in the West Terminal. The fare to Paris is €13.25 including the RER transfer.

■ TIP→ A Paris-Visite pass allows you unlimited public transportation over 1, 2, 3, or 5 consecutive days. Prices start at €27.80 with airport travel. See https://en.parisinfo.com/what-to-see-in-paris/paris-pass.

TRANSFERS BETWEEN AIRPORTS

To travel between Paris's airports, there are several options. The RER-B goes from CDG to Paris St-Michel–Notre-Dame where you transfer to the RER-C to Orly West. Travel time is about 60 to 80 minutes, and tickets cost €16.15. Le Bus Direct's ' Line 3 shuttle also runs between the airports for €21 one way, every 20–30 minutes; the trip takes about 75 minutes in normal traffic. Taxis are available but expensive: from €70 to €110, depending on traffic.

Contacts Le Bus Direct. ☎ 08–10–81–20–01 €0.12 per min ⊕ www.lebusdirect.com. **Paris-GreenCar.** ☎ 08–92–69–69–00 €0.40 per min ⊕ www.parisgreencar.com. **RATP.** ☎ 3246 €0.80 per min ⊕ www.ratp.fr. **SuperShuttle Paris.** ☎ 08–11–70–78–12 €0.06 per min. ⊕ www.supershuttle.fr.

FLIGHTS

As one of the premier destinations in the world, Paris is serviced by a great many international carriers and a surprisingly large number of U.S.-based airlines. Air France (which partners with Delta) is the French flag carrier and offers numerous direct flights (often several per day) between Paris's Charles de Gaulle Airport and New York City's JFK Airport; Newark, New Jersey; Washington's Dulles Airport; and the cities of Boston, Atlanta, Miami, Chicago, Houston, Seattle, San Francisco, and Los Angeles. Most other North American cities are served through Air France's partnership with Delta via connecting flights. United Airlines has nonstop flights to Paris from Chicago, New York, and San Francisco. American Airlines offers nonstop service from numerous cities, including New York

City's JFK, Boston, Chicago, Dallas/Fort Worth, and Miami. Low-cost upstart Norwegian has shaken up the market with cheaper fares from a growing list of U.S. cities. In Canada, Air France, Air Canada, and Air Transat are the leading choices for travel from Toronto and Montréal (in peak season departures are often daily). From London, Air France and British Airways offer up to 15 flights per day in peak season. In addition, direct routes link Manchester, Edinburgh, and Southampton with Paris. Many carriers including Ryanair, easyJet, CityJet, Flybe, Aer Lingus, Lufthansa, and KLM offer direct service from Paris to Dublin, Birmingham, London, Glasgow, Zurich, Copenhagen, Madrid, Marrakech, Prague, Brussels, and other cities. Tickets are available online only and need to be booked well in advance to get the best prices—a one-way ticket from Paris to Dublin could cost €40 or less, for example. Be aware that low-cost airlines (and some major carriers) charge extra for baggage, whch can sometimes double the ticket price.

▌ BICYCLE TRAVEL

Cycling is a terrific way to see the city—and work off the extra calories from all those rich pastries you've sampled. With an extensive system of dedicated bike lanes, cycling in Paris has never been easier. There are many bike-rental services and tours available, and Paris was a world leader in 2007 when the city launched Velib', a 24/7 self-service, bike-rental program. A new service provider began tearing up and replacing 1,200 docking stations across the city (and adding 200 more) in late 2017. After some bumps, Velib' Métropole got off the ground in 2018 with a new generation of bikes that are sleeker and lighter. And for those too tired to pedal, 30% of the new bikes have an electric option (they are aqua blue; regular bikes are light green) clocking a top speed of 25 kph (15 mph). Just as Parisians were getting used to the new system, a flood of Chinese-made "dockless"

lightweight rental bikes began wreaking havoc. You order the bikes via an app on your phone and unlock them by scanning a barcode. The problem? With no dedicated parking spots, users were leaving the bikes with names like GoBee, Mobike, Obike, and Ofo literally everywhere. Many of them ended up in twisted heaps on already crowded sidewalks or at the bottom of the Seine. Extensive vandalism prompted GoBee to pull out of two other French cities in 2018, and the future for the renegade cycles in Paris seemed hardly secure. While you may occasionally see a Velib' with a deliberately punctured tire or a seat twisted off, city cyclists and visitors alike have embraced the service, copied in many cities worldwide, as a hassle-free alternative to public transportation. There are two ways to rent a Velib': sign up on the website or buy a ticket from a machine at each docking station (major credit cards accepted). First, select the amount of time you wish to rent (€5 per day, up to 3 rentals; €15 per week, unlimited rentals), then tap the code you're given on the bike's keypad to unlock it. The idea is to take short rides; the first 30 minutes are free, after that it costs €1 per 30 minutes for a regular bike, €2 for an electric bike. If you're staying in Paris for more than a week, check out the subscription options on the website.

Information Vélib'. ☎ 01–76–49–12–34 ⊕ www.velib-metropole.fr.

▌ BOAT TRAVEL

Ferries linking France and the United Kingdom cross the Channel in about 90 minutes; popular routes connect Boulogne and Folkestone, Le Havre, and Portsmouth, and—the most booked passage—Calais and Dover. P&O European Ferries alone has 23 sailings a day between Calais and Dover. A company called Direct Ferries groups the websites for several operators to make reservations more streamlined.

The driving distance from Calais to Paris is 290 km (180 miles). The fastest routes to Paris from each port are via N43, A26, and A1 from Calais and the Channel Tunnel; and via N1 from Boulogne.

Information Direct Ferries. ☎ 08–92–23–08–58 €0.45 per min ⊕ www.directferries.fr. **P&O European Ferries.** ☎ 03–66–74–03–25 ⊕ www.poferries.com.

▋ BUS TRAVEL

ARRIVING AND DEPARTING PARIS

The excellent national train service in France means that long-distance bus service in the country is practically nonexistent; regional buses are found where train service is spotty. Local bus information to the rare rural areas where trains do not go can be obtained from the SNCF (see Train Travel).

The largest international bus operator here is Eurolines, whose main terminal is in the Parisian suburb of Bagnolet (a ½-hour métro ride from central Paris, at the end of métro Line 3). It runs to more than 600 cities in Europe. The price of a round-trip bus ticket can be as much as 50% cheaper than taking a train or plane, so if you have the time and the energy, this is a good way to cut the cost of travel.

Eurolines provides bus service from London's Victoria Coach Station, via the Dover–Calais ferry, to Paris's Porte de Bagnolet. There's at least four trips a day—more in summer— between 8:30 am and 10:30 pm. Travel time is about seven hours. Fares start at €38 round-trip. The company also offers a discounted "mini-pass" between two European capitals, plus a 15-day pass (€225–€320), and a 30-day pass (€340–€425). Check the Eurolines website for special discounts or incentives. The earlier you buy your ticket, the cheaper it will be. Reservations for international bus trips are essential.

IN PARIS

With dedicated bus lanes now in place throughout the city—allowing buses and taxis to whiz past other traffic mired in tedious jams—taking the bus is an appealing option. Although nothing can beat the métro for speed, buses—eco-friendly electric and diesel-electric hybrids—offer great city views, and air-conditioning is a nice perk on sweltering August days.

Paris buses are green and white; the route number and destination are marked in front, and major stopping places are noted along the sides. Glass-covered bus shelters contain timetables, and route maps, and most have electronic boards telling you how long you'll wait for your ride; note that buses at stops servicing multiple lines must be hailed. Smaller stops are designated simply by a pole bearing bus numbers.

Today more than 350 bus routes thread throughout Paris, reaching virtually every nook and cranny of the city. On weekdays and Saturday, buses run every 5 to 10 minutes, but you'll have to wait 15 to 20 minutes on Sunday and holidays. One ticket will take you anywhere within the city and is valid for one bus transfer within 90 minutes.

Most routes operate from 6:30 am to 10:30 pm, some until 12:30 am. After 12:30 am you must take either the métro, which begins shutting down at 12:40 am Sunday through Thursday and 2:15 am on Friday, Saturday, and on major holidays, or one of the Noctilien lines (indicated by a separate signal at bus stops). Using the same tickets as the métro and regular buses, 48 Noctilien buses operate every 15 to 60 minutes (12:30 am–5:30 am) between Châtelet, major train stations, and various nearby suburbs; you can hail them at any point on their route.

A map of the bus system is on the flip side of every métro map, in all métro stations, and at all bus stops. Maps are also found in each bus; a free map is available at RER stations and tourist offices, or download the RATP app on iTunes or www.ratp.fr. An onboard electronic display announces the name of the next stop. To get off, press one of the red buttons mounted on the silver poles that run the length of the bus, and the *arrêt demandé* (stop requested) light directly behind the driver will light up. Use the middle or rear door to exit.

The Balabus—an orange-and-white public bus that runs on Sunday and holidays from 1:30 pm to 8:30 pm, April through September—gives an eye-catching 50-minute tour around the major sights. You can use your Paris-Visite or Mobilis pass *(see Métro Travel)*, or one to three bus tickets, depending on how far you ride. The route runs from La Défense to the Gare de Lyon.

The city has expanded its modern tram system with several lines linking the city with its outer suburbs; line T3 (with extensions 3a and 3b) ring Paris from the southern edge at Pont du Garigliano to Porte de la Chapelle in the north. One ticket is good for the entire line.

Trams and buses take the same tickets as the métro. When buying tickets, your best bet is a *carnet* of 10 tickets, available for €14.90 at any métro station. A single ticket can be bought on board for €1.90 (exact change appreciated). If you have individual tickets or Paris-Visite passes, you should be prepared to validate your ticket in the gray machines at the entrance of the vehicle. You can also buy tickets in some bar–tabac cafés.

Bus Information Eurolines. ☎ 08–92–89–90–91 €0.35 per min, 0033/0033–141–86–2421 from abroad ⊕ www.eurolines.fr. **Noctilien.** ⊕ www.ratp.fr/en/getting-around-night/its-easy-get-around-night. **RATP.** ☎ 3246 €0.80 per min ⊕ www.ratp.fr.

▍CAR TRAVEL

We can't say it too many times: unless you have a special, compelling reason, do yourself a favor and **avoid driving in Paris.** But if you've decided to do it anyway,

there are some things to know. France's roads are classified into five types; they are numbered and have letter prefixes: *A* (*autoroute*, expressways), *N* (*route nationale*), *D* (*route départmentale*), and the smaller *C* or *V*. There are excellent links between Paris and most French cities. When trying to get around Ile-de-France, it's often difficult to avoid Paris—just try to steer clear of rush hours (7–9:30 and 4:30–7:30). A *péage* (toll) must be paid on most expressways outside Ile-de-France: the rate varies but can be steep. Certain booths allow you to pay with a credit card.

The major ring road encircling Paris is called the *périphérique,* with the *périphérique intérieur* going counterclockwise around the city, and the *périphérique extérieur,* or the outside ring, going clockwise; maximum speed is 70 kph (43 mph). Up to five lanes wide, the périphérique is a major highway from which 30 *portes* (gates) connect Paris to the major highways of France. The names of these highways function on the same principle as the métro, with the final destination as the determining point in the direction you must take.

Heading north, look for Porte de la Chapelle (direction Lille and Charles de Gaulle Airport); east, for Porte de Bagnolet (direction Metz and Nancy); south, for Porte d'Orléans (direction Lyon and Bordeaux); and west, for Porte d'Auteuil (direction Rouen and Chartres) or Porte de St-Cloud (Boulogne-Billancourt).

For short jaunts, you could use the car-sharing service Autolib', a zero-emissions fleet of nearly 4,000 small electric cars docked at 1,100 stations in and around Paris. (Service is limited to within the Ile-de-France.) To rent one, all you need is an international drivers' license (or a European drivers' license), passport, and credit card. The process takes about 10 minutes at stations on the street or you can sign up online. You can reserve a car and a parking spot wherever you're going. See www.autolib.eu.

GASOLINE

There are gas stations throughout the city, but they can be difficult to spot; you will often find them in the underground tunnels that cross the city and in larger parking garages. Gas is expensive and prices vary enormously, ranging from about €1.40 to €1.90 per liter. If you're on your way out of Paris, save money by waiting until you've left the city to fill up. All gas stations accept credit cards.

PARKING

Finding parking in Paris is tough.If you must have a car, at least paying to park it is easy, if expensive. Metered parking in the capital costs €4 an hour for arrondissements 1–11 and €2.40 for arrondissements 12–20, Monday to Saturday from 9 am to 8 pm, with a six-hour limit for visitors. Look for the nearest dark green ticket machine *horodateur* and enter your license plate number to begin, then choose the amount of time you want, and insert your card (no cash or coins). Place the green receipt on the passenger side of the dashboard. You can also download the PMobile app and pay on your phone (www.pmobile.paris.fr). Parking tickets are expensive, and there's no shortage of blue-uniformed parking police doling them out. An often cheaper alternative is finding a lot or underground garage—look for the blue signs with a white "P"; rates in the city center start at about €3.60 an hour, or €20 per day, while outside of the center you'll pay €10 to €15 per day. Parkings de Paris (www.parkingsdeparis.com) lets you reserve and prepay a spot in more than 100 city car parks (see other options at www.parisinfo.com). Happily, you can park for free on Sunday and national holidays; sadly, the city stopped the popular practice of free street parking in August.

ROAD CONDITIONS

Chaotic traffic is a way of life in Paris. Some streets in the city center can seem impossibly narrow; street signs are often hard to spot; jaded city drivers often make erratic, last-minute maneuvers without signaling; and motorcycles often weave around traffic. Priority is given to drivers coming from the right, so watch for drivers barreling out of small streets on your right. A move by City Hall cutting the speed limit in much of the capital to 30 kph (18.6 mph) drew scoffs from annoyed drivers, but they'd better get used to it—by 2020 some 85% of city streets will be subject to the lower limit. Watch out for cyclists in 30 kph zones; they are permitted to pedal against traffic on one-way streets. Traffic lights are placed to the left and right of crosswalks, not above, so they may be blocked from view by vehicles ahead of you.

There are a few major roundabouts at the most congested intersections, notably at L'Étoile (around the Arc de Triomphe), Place de la Bastille, and Place de la Concorde; stick to the outer lane to make your exit. The *périphériques* (ring roads) are generally easier to use. Quays that parallel the Seine are no longer open to cars, causing even more traffic jams on the roads above. Electronic signs on the périphériques and highways post traffic conditions: *fluide* (clear) or *bouchon* (jammed).

Some important traffic terms and signs to note: *sortie* (exit), *sens unique* (one way), *stationnement interdit* (no parking), *impasse* (dead end). Blue rectangular signs indicate a highway; triangles carry illustrations of a particular traffic hazard; speed limits are indicated in a circle, with the maximum speed circled in red.

RULES OF THE ROAD

You must always carry vehicle registration documents and your personal identification. The French police are entitled to stop you at will to verify your ID and your car—such spot checks are frequent, especially at peak holiday times. In France you drive on the right and give priority to drivers coming from the right (this rule is called *priorité à droite*).

The driver and all passengers in vehicles must wear seat belts, and children under 12 may not travel in the front seat.

Children under 10 need to be in a car seat or specific child-restraining device, always in the back seat. Speed limits are designated by the type of road you're driving on: 130 kph (80 mph) or 110 kph (70 mph) on highways (*autoroutes*), 90 kph (55 mph) on divided roads (*routes nationales*), 50 kph (30 mph) on departmental roads (*routes*), and 35 kph (22 mph) in some cities and towns (*villes et villages*). These limits are reduced on some roadways by as much as 20 kph (12 mph) in rainy, snowy, and foggy conditions. Drivers are expected to know these limits, so signs are generally posted only when there are exceptions to the rules. Right-hand turns are not allowed on a red light.

The use of headsets and handheld cellular phones while driving is forbidden (even if you are only holding them); the penalty is a €135 fine. Alcohol laws are also quite tough—there is a 0.05% blood alcohol limit (a lower limit than in the United States), which drops to 0.02% for drivers who've been licensed for fewer than three years.

▌ MÉTRO TRAVEL

Taking the métro is the most efficient way to get around Paris. Métro stations are recognizable either by a large yellow "M" within a circle or by the distinctive curly green Art Nouveau railings and archway bearing the full title (*Métropolitain*).

Sixteen métro and five RER (Réseau Express Régional, or the Regional Express Network) lines crisscross Paris and the suburbs, and you are seldom more than 500 yards from the nearest station. The métro network connects at several points in Paris with the RER, the commuter trains that go from the city center to the suburbs. RER trains crossing Paris on their way from suburb to suburb can be great time-savers because they make only a few stops in the city (you can use the same tickets for the métro and the RER within Paris).

It's essential to know the name of the last station on the line you take, as this name appears on all signs. A connection (you can make as many as you like on one ticket) is called a *correspondance*. At junction stations, illuminated orange signs bearing the name of the line terminus appear over the correct corridors for each correspondence. Illuminated blue signs marked *sortie* indicate the station exit. Note that tickets are valid only inside the gates, or *limites*.

Access to métro and RER platforms is through an automatic ticket barrier. Slide your ticket in and pick it up as it pops out. **Keep your ticket during your journey**; you'll need it to leave the RER system and in case you run into any green-clad ticket inspectors, who will impose a hefty fine if you can't produce your ticket (they even accept credit cards!).

Métro service starts at 5:30 am and continues until the last trains reach their terminus at 1:15 am) Sunday through Thursday, and until 2:15 am on Friday, Saturday, and some national holidays. Some lines and stations in Paris can be dodgy late at night, in particular Lines 2 and 13, and the mazelike stations at Les Halles and République, so don't travel alone. But in general, the biggest risk on the métro is posed by the nimble Parisian pickpockets, so keep an eye on your wallet and pricey gadgets.

All métro tickets and passes are valid not only for the métro but also for all RER, tram, and bus travel within Paris. Métro tickets cost €1.90 each; a *carnet* (10 tickets for €14.90) is a better value. The *Carte Navigo* system is the daily, monthly, and weekly subscription plan, with reusable cards available at automatic ticket machines and ticket windows. (Note that at many stations your only option is to use the machines; they accept bills or cards with electronic chips). Get a Navigo Découverte card for €5 plus the subscription you choose: unlimited travel for one day (€7.50), for one week (€22.80) or one month (€75.20, beginning the first of the month). Be sure to sign your name and immediately attach a passport-size photo (there are photo booths in larger métro stations.). The card allows you to swipe through the turnstiles and can be kept for years; just recharge it at any purple kiosk in the métro stations. If that seems like too much hassle, buy a Mobilis (one day) or Paris-Visite (up to five days) pass for unlimited travel across the regional RATP network; both are valid starting any day of the week. Mobilis costs €7.50. Paris-Visite—which also gives you discounts on a few museums and attractions—costs €12 (one day) to €38.35 (five days).

■TIP→ For itineraries, maps, and real-time tips on delays and closings, download the RATP transit system's Vianavigo or Citymapper for a trove of handy info like which end of the métro platform gets you closest to your exit on the other end of your journey.

Métro Information RATP. ☎ 3246 €0.80 per min ⊕ www.ratp.fr.

TICKET/PASS	PRICE
Single Fare	€1.90
Daily Mobilis Pass	€7.50
Paris-Visite One-Day Pass	€12
10-Ticket Carnet	€14.90
Paris-Visite Two-Day Pass	€19.50
Paris-Visite Three-Day Pass	€26.65
Paris-Visite Five-Day Pass	€38.35
Pass Navigo Découverte Weekly	€22.80
Pass Navigo Découverte Monthly	€75.20

▌ TAXI TRAVEL

Taxi rates are based on location and time. Monday to Saturday, daytime rates (10 am–5 pm) within Paris are €1.06 per km (½ mile); nighttime rates (5 pm–midnight) are €1.27 per km. On Sunday, you'll pay €1.58 per km from midnight to 7 am and €1.30 from 7 am to midnight within Paris.

Thanks to competition from ride-hailing services like Uber, the once unpredictable rates that official taxes charged to and from the airports into Paris are now fixed, and drivers are obligated to accept credit cards. Pay a flat €50 to and from Charles de Gaulle/Roissy for the Right Bank, €55 for the Left Bank; to and from Orly, pay €30 for Left Bank and €35 for Right Bank. There's a basic hire charge of €2.60 for all rides (excluding flat fares), and a minimum fare of €7. Waiting time is charged at €35 per hour. The easiest way to get a taxi is to ask your hotel or a restaurant to call one for you (you may be charged a reservation supplement of €4–€7). Order one yourself with the handy app by Taxi G7, or find a taxi stand, which is marked by a square, dark-blue sign with a white "T" in the middle. ■TIP→ A taxi is available when the roof sign is lighted green and taken when it's lighted red. It's customary, but not obligatory, to tip up to 5% (See Tipping in Essentials.).

Uber and other ride-sharing services you order via an app on your smartphone have reshaped the transportation landscape in Paris, making rides easier to get and usually cheaper. Plus, the cash-free system—the app is linked to your credit card—makes using them a breeze. They remain controversial and extremely unpopular with traditional taxi drivers who resent the competition. Despite legal challenges, they have been allowed to operate with restrictions. The Uber app works worldwide, wherever the service is available, including to and from both CDG and Orly airports, though you'll need to ensure your smartphone works upon arrival in order to use it. Other options include Chauffeur Privé and Taxify. Download the apps to compare prices before you book.

Taxi Companies Alpha Taxis. ☎ 01-45-85-85-85 ⊕ www.alphataxis.fr. **Taxis G7.** ☎ 01-41-27-66-99 for service in English, 3607 €0.15 per min ⊕ www.taxisg7.fr.

▌TRAIN TRAVEL

The SNCF, France's rail system, is fast, punctual, comfortable, and comprehensive—when it's not on strike. There are various options: local trains, overnight trains with sleeping accommodations, and the high-speed TGVs (or Trains à Grande Vitesse), which average 320 kph.

The TGVs, the fastest way to get around the country, operate between Paris and Lille/Calais, Paris and Lyon/Switzerland/Provence, Paris and Angers/Nantes, Paris and Tours/Poitiers/Bordeaux, Paris and Brussels, and Paris and Amsterdam. TGVs also go direct to Avignon, Marseille, and Nice.

Paris has six international rail stations: Gare du Nord (northern France, northern Europe, and England via Calais or Boulogne); Gare St-Lazare (Normandy, and England via Dieppe); Gare de l'Est (Strasbourg, Luxembourg, Basel, southern Germany, and central Europe); Gare de Lyon (Lyon, Marseille, Provence, Geneva, and Italy); Gare d'Austerlitz (Loire Valley, central France, and overnight to Nice and Spain); and Gare Montparnasse (Brittany, Aquitaine, TGV-Atlantique service to the west and southwest of France, Spain). Smoking is prohibited on all trains in France.

The country has two classes of train service: *première* (first class) or *deuxième* (second). First-class seats have 50% more legroom and nicer upholstery than those in second class, and the first-class cars tend to be quieter. First-class seats on the TGV also have power sockets for computer connections and individual reading lights, but fares can cost nearly twice as much as those for second-class seats.

Fares are cheaper if you avoid traveling at peak times of day (and around holidays and weekends) and purchase tickets three months (or at least 15 days) in advance; for the best prices check the SNCF website for deals, including discounted (*billet Prem's*), or find your destination among the last-minute offers listed under the TGVPop section.

Reserving online is the easiest way to book your trip, but you can call for train information or reserve tickets in any Paris station, irrespective of destination, and you can access the multilingual computerized schedule information network at any Paris station, and buy your tickets there. Go to the Grandes Lignes counter for travel within France and to the Billets Internationaux desk if you're heading out of the country.

If you plan to travel outside Paris by train, consider purchasing a France Rail Pass through Rail Europe; it allows for 1, 2, 3, 4, 5, 6, 7, 8, 9, or 15 days of unlimited train travel in a one-month period. If you travel solo for three days, first class will run you $282 and second class $227; eight days costs $465 for first class and $396 for second class. In both first and second class, two or more people traveling together can save 15% on each fare with a Saver Pass, and children often can travel free.

France is one of 28 countries where you can use Eurail passes, which provide unlimited train travel for a set amount of time. If you plan to rack up the miles, get a Global Pass; it's valid for rail travel in first- or second-class in all member nations for periods ranging from $580 (first class) for five days to $2,029 (first class) for three months. The Two Country Pass covers rail travel in and between pairs of bordering countries over a two-month period; a France–Italy pass costs $396 for four days of travel in first class and $645 for 10 days.

In addition to standard Eurail passes, there is the Eurail youth pass (for those age 27 and under), the Eurail Saver Pass (which gives a discount for two to five people traveling together), and the Eurail flexi pass (which allows a certain number of travel days within a flexible period). ▌TIP➔ A select few European train stations sell a limited number of Eurail passes, but they cost more—so buy yours at home before you leave for France; purchase through the Eurail website or through travel agents.

Another option for those traveling extensively on the French SNCF network is to buy one of the various discount rail cards available to children, youths 12–27, families, and seniors (those over 60). You pay a fee of up to €60 for the card (renewable each year) but then you can save up to 50% on tickets.

■TIP➔ A rail pass does not guarantee you a seat on the train. You need to book seats ahead even if you have a pass.

Seat reservations are required on TGVs but not on the regional TER network. So if you're traveling by TER, be sure to board early during busy travel periods, especially in July and August, to ensure you get a seat. The trains are notoriously overbooked, and even a first-class ticket may not guarantee you a seat. Note that you need a reservation for sleeping accommodations.

Train Information Rail Europe. ☎ 800/622-8600 in the U.S. and Canada, 847/916-1028 ⊕ www.raileurope.com. **SNCF.** ☎ 3635 €0.40 per min ⊕ www.oui.sncf. **TGV.** ☎ 3635 €0.40 per min ⊕ www.tgv.com.

THE CHANNEL TUNNEL
Short of flying, taking the Channel Tunnel is the fastest way to cross the English Channel: 35 minutes from Folkestone to Calais, 60 minutes from motorway to motorway, or two hours and 15 minutes from London's St. Pancras Station to Paris's Gare du Nord, with stops in Ebbsfleet (UK), Ashford (UK), Calais, and Lille. The Belgian border is just a short drive northeast of Calais. High-speed Eurostar trains use the same tunnels to connect London's St. Pancras Station directly with Midi Station in Brussels in around two hours.

There's three categories of travel and a vast range of prices for Eurostar—round-trip tickets range from €620 for business class (with access to the Philippe Starck–designed Première Class lounge and a three-course Raymond Blanc meal) to €56 for the most basic ticket. Booking early can save you a bundle. Last-minute tickets can cost more than flying.

It's a good idea to make a reservation if you're traveling with your car on a Chunnel train; vehicles without reservations, if they can get on at all, are charged 20% extra.

Channel Tunnel Information Eurostar. ☎ 01–70–70–60–88 in France, 646/934–6454 from the U.S. ⊕ www.eurostar.com. **Eurotunnel.** ☎ 08–10–63–03–04 €0.06 per min ⊕ www.eurotunnel.com.

ESSENTIALS

▌ COMMUNICATIONS

INTERNET AND WI-FI

Getting online in Paris is rarely a problem because free or pay-as-you-go Wi-Fi (pronounced *wee-fee*) is widely available. Many hotels offer business services with Internet access or high-speed wireless access; and most accommodations offer in-room Wi-Fi at no extra charge. Moreover, Paris has made a big push in going wireless in recent years with 260 sites furnished by the city where you can connect for free in parks, squares (like the Centre Pompidou plaza), and libraries; look for the "Paris Wi-Fi" logo. Access is free and unlimited for anyone (select the Paris_ Wi-Fi network and launch your browser). Many cafés offer free Wi-Fi , but verify before ordering a drink. McDonald's has free Wi-Fi spaces (sometimes disabled during peak dining hours), as do the 56 Starbucks outlets. Note that you may pick up a signal for "Free Wi-Fi," but this is the name of a French Internet provider, and you have to pay to use it. To charge your devices, don't forget to bring along an adapter with a European-style plug.

PHONES

The good news is that with Wi-Fi widely available, you should be able to Skype, Facetime, or WhatsApp for free (remember to turn off your Data Roaming). This means you can avoid using the phone in your hotel and hefty surcharges for international calls. If you still want to use the phone, you could save money by picking up a prepaid calling card *carte télépho-nique* sold at some cafés with a "Tabac" sign. Be sure to ask for one that works with a landline *ligne fixe*. To use it, you enter a code on the back of the card Mobile phones *(below)*, while expensive, are still usually cheaper than making international calls from your hotel. If you're staying in an apartment rental, note that most telecom operators in France offer an all-in-one service, with Internet, TV, and a landline with free local and international calls, for an low monthly rate of about €40. (Be sure to check first before you start dialing abroad.)

The country code for France is 33. The first two digits of French numbers are a prefix determined by zone: Paris and Ile-de-France, 01; the northwest, 02; the northeast, 03; the southeast, 04; and the southwest, 05. Note that it's often cheaper to call between 9 pm and 9 am. Pay close attention to numbers beginning with 08: some—but not all—are toll-free (when you dial one with a fee attached, a recorded message will tell you how much it will cost to proceed with the call, from €0.6 to €0.80 or more per minute). Numbers beginning with 09, connected to DSL and Internet lines, are generally free when calling in France. Numbers that begin with 06 and 07 are reserved for cell phones.

When dialing France from abroad, you should drop the initial 0 from the telephone number (all numbers listed in this book include the initial 0, which is used for calling *from within* France). To call a number in Paris from the United States, dial 00–33 plus the phone number, but minus the initial 0 listed for the specific number in Paris. In other words, the local number for the Louvre is 01–40–20–51–51. To call this number from New York City, dial 00–33–1–40–20–51–51. To call this number from within Paris, dial 01–40–20–51–51.

CALLING OUTSIDE FRANCE

To make an international call out of France, dial 00 then dial the country code (1 for the United States and Canada, 44 for the United Kingdom) and the area code (minus any initial 0) and number.

To call with the help of an AT&T international operator, dial the toll-free number 08–00–99–00 plus the last two digits of the country code. Dial 08–00–99–00–11 for the United States and

Canada, 08–00–99–00–44 for the United Kingdom.

CALLING WITHIN FRANCE

For telephone information in France, you need to call one of the dozen or so six-digit *renseignement* numbers that begin with 118. (For Les Pages Jaunes—the French Yellow Pages—you dial 118–008; €2.99 per minute.)

Since all local numbers in Paris and the Ile-de-France begin with a 01, you must dial the full 10-digit number, including the initial 0.

MOBILE PHONES

Cell phones are called *portables* in France, and using yours can be an expensive proposition. Figuring out how to make affordable calls can take some research. The easiest, if not the cheapest, way is to sign up for an international plan with your service provider at home. Check to see if your phone is unlocked and works on the global-standard GSM network (AT&T and T-Mobile are on this network; Verizon and Sprint are not). Prices vary greatly: AT&T offers a flat rate plan ($10 per day in 2018) for unlimited calls and texts; others charge up to $1.50 minute for calls and $0.50 for texts. U.S.-based Cellular Abroad and other services will sell you an international SIM card or rent you an iPhone with unlimited calling for $10 a day or $150 for three weeks.

If you plan to make a lot of local calls, another option is to buy a cheap phone once you arrive in France (or bring an old phone that is unlocked) and pick up a prepaid SIM card. You can get one with a French phone number, making it easy to get call-backs. It pays to shop around. Le France Mobile caters to English-speaking visitors but charges higher prices than other local providers. SFR, for example, offers €15 pre-paid cards with unlimited calling in France and to the United States, plus 15G of data. Lycamobile has many pre-paid calling/data combinations such as €9.99 for unlimited international calls and 200 mb of data.

■ TIP➜ If you travel internationally often and your cell phone provider's international plan is too pricey, save one of your old mobile phones or buy a cheap one online; ask your provider to unlock it for you, and take it with you as a travel phone, buying a new SIM card with pay-as-you-go service in each destination.

Contacts **Cellular Abroad.** ☎ *00800/36–23–33–33 in France, 800/287–5072 in the U.S. and Canada* ⊕ *www.cellularabroad.com.* **Le French Mobile.** ☎ *01–74–95–95–00* ⊕ *www.lefrench-mobile.com.* **Lycamobile.** ☎ *866/277–3221 in the U.S. and Canada, 01/77–72–22–23 in France* ⊕ *www.lycamobile.us.* **SFR.** ☎ *1026 English helpline in France* ⊕ *www.sfr.fr.*

■ CUSTOMS AND DUTIES

You're always allowed to bring goods of a certain value back home without having to pay any duty or import tax. But there's a limit on the amount of tobacco and liquor you can return with duty-free, and some countries have separate limits for perfumes; for exact quotas, check with your customs department. The values of so-called duty-free goods are included in these amounts. When you shop abroad, save all your receipts, as customs inspectors may ask to see them as well as the items you purchased. If the total value of your goods is more than the duty-free limit, you'll have to pay a tax (most often a flat percentage) on the value of everything beyond that limit.

If you're coming from outside the European Union (EU), you may import the following duty-free: 200 cigarettes or 100 cigarillos or 50 cigars or 250 grams of tobacco or a mix of these products; 2 liters of wine and 1 liter of alcohol (like spirits) over 22% volume or 2 liters of dessert or sparkling wine not exceeding 22%; gold (except personal jewelry) up to 500 grams; other goods with a total value of €430 per adult (€90 for ages 15 and under).

If you're arriving from an EU country, you may import the following goods for

LOCAL DO'S AND TABOOS

CUSTOMS OF THE COUNTRY

The French like to look at people (that's half the point of cafés and fashion), so you might as well get used to it—it's as natural here as breathing. They'll look at your shoes or your watch, check out what you're wearing or reading. What they will not do is maintain steady eye contact or smile. If a stranger of the opposite sex smiles at you, it's best to do as the French do and return only a blank look before turning away. If you smile back, you might find yourself in a Pepé Le Pew–type situation.

Visitors' exuberance—and accompanying loud voices—may cause discreet Parisians to raise their eyebrows or give a deep chesty sigh. They're not being rude, but they're telling you that they think you are. Be aware of your surroundings and lower your voice accordingly, especially in churches, museums, restaurants, theaters, cinemas, and the métro.

When entering and leaving a shop, say hello and good-bye to the staff. A simple *bonjour, monsieur/madame*, and *au revoir, merci* are considered a virtual necessity for politeness. Other basic pleasantries in French include *bonne journée* (have a nice day); *bonne soirée* (have a nice evening); *enchanté* (nice to meet you); *s'il vous plaît* (please); and *je vous en prie* (you're welcome). When asking for directions or other help, be sure to preface your request with a polite *bonjour, monsieur/madame* before you say *excusez-moi r.*

GREETINGS

When meeting someone for the first time, whether in a social or a professional setting, it's appropriate to shake hands. Other than that, the French like to kiss. For the Parisians, it's two *bisous*, which are more like air kisses with your cheeks touching lightly—don't actually smack your lips onto the person's face!

OUT ON THE TOWN

When visiting a French home, don't expect to be invited into the kitchen or taken on a house tour. The French have a very definite sense of personal space, and you'll be escorted to what are considered the guest areas. If you're invited to dinner, be sure to bring a gift, such as wine, flowers, or chocolates.

Table manners are often considered a litmus test of your character or upbringing. When dining out, note that the French fill wineglasses only half full—it's considered bad manners to fill it to the brim. They never serve themselves before serving the rest of the table. During a meal, keep both hands above the table, and keep your elbows off the table. Bread is broken, never cut, and is placed next to the plate, never on the plate. When slicing a cheese, don't cut off the point (or "nose"). Coffee or tea is ordered after dessert, not with dessert. (In fact, coffee and tea usually aren't ordered with any courses during meals, except breakfast.) Eating on the street is generally frowned on—though with the onslaught of Starbucks you can sometimes see people drinking coffee on the go.

LANGUAGE

One of the best ways to avoid being an Ugly American is to learn a bit of the local language. Parisians may appear prickly at first to English-speaking visitors, but it usually helps if you make an effort to speak some French. A simple, friendly *bonjour* will do, as will asking if the person you're greeting speaks English (*parlez-vous anglais?*).

personal consumption: 800 cigarettes, 400 cigarillos, 200 cigars, or 1 kilogram of tobacco; for alcohol, 90 liters of wine, 110 liters of beer, 20 liters of alcohol less than 22% volume, or 10 liters of spirits over 22%.

PETS

Any pet coming to France must have all standard vaccinations and a recent rabies shots (no less than 21 days before departure), and an International Standards Organization (ISO) compatible microchip. Be sure to have all paperwork on hand at the airport—including the bilingual *"Certificat Vétérinaire vers l'UE"* (EU veterinary certificate), as customs officials will inspect the animal in question. The form can be downloaded from the Animal and Plant Health Inspection Service website (⊕ *www.aphis.usda.gov*).

Information in Paris Direction des Douanes. ☎ 01–72–40–78–50 ⊕ ee.france.fr.

U.S. Information U.S. Customs and Border Protection. ⊕ www.cbp.gov.

▌ELECTRICITY

The electrical current in Paris is 220 volts, 50 cycles alternating current (AC); and electrical outlets take Continental-type plugs, with two round prongs. So you may need to use both an adapter (which enables you to plug your appliance into the different style of socket) and a converter (which allows it to run on the different voltage). Most laptops and mobile phone chargers are dual voltage (i.e., they operate equally well on 110 and 220 volts), so require only an adapter. These days the same is true of many small appliances, though be wary of hair dryers. Always check labels and manufacturer instructions to be sure. Don't use 110-volt outlets marked "For Shavers Only" for high-wattage appliances such as hair dryers.

▌EMERGENCIES

The French National Health Care system (*Sécurité Sociale*) has been organized to provide fully equipped, fully staffed hospitals within 30 minutes of every resident in Paris. A sign of a white cross in a blue box appears on all hospitals. This book does not list the major Paris hospitals, as the French government prefers that an emergency operator assign you the best and most convenient option. Note that if you're able to walk into a hospital emergency room by yourself, you are often considered "low priority," and the wait can be extremely long. So if time is of the essence, it's best to call 112—the French equivalent of 911. Be sure to check with your insurance company before going abroad to verify that you are covered for medical care in other countries.

In a less urgent situation, do what the French do and call SOS Médecins or SOS Dentaire services; like magic, often in less than an hour, a certified, experienced doctor or dentist arrives at the door, armed with an old leather case filled with the essentials for diagnosis and treatment (at an average cost of €65). The doctor or dentist may or may not be bilingual, but, at worst, will have a rudimentary understanding of English. This is a very helpful 24-hour service to use for common symptoms of benign illnesses that need to be treated quickly for comfort, such as high fever, toothache, or upset stomachs (a late-night digestive consequence of eating like the French).

The American Hospital (which also has a dental unit) and the Institut Hospitalier Franco-Britannique (formerly the Hertford British Hospital) both have 24-hour emergency hotlines with bilingual doctors and nurses who can provide advice. For small problems, go to a pharmacy, marked by a green neon cross. Pharmacists are authorized to administer first aid and recommend over-the-counter drugs, and they can be very helpful in advising you in English or sending you to the nearest English-speaking pharmacist.

Call the police (112 or 17) if there has been a crime or an act of violence. On the street, some French phrases that may be needed in an emergency are *Au secours!* (Help!), *urgence* (emergency), *samu* (ambulance), *pompiers* (firemen), *poste de police* (police station), *médecin* (doctor), and *hôpital* (hospital). A hotline of note is SOS Help for English-language crisis information, open daily 3 pm–11 pm.

If you need a 24-hour pharmacy, there's a comprehensive list on the Tourist Office's website, www.parisinfo.com (at the date of this update, the link in English is en.parisinfo.com/practical-paris/useful-info/health-in-paris).

Doctor and Dentist Referrals SOS Dentaire. ☎ *01–43–37–51–00* ⊕ *www.sos-dentaire.com.* **SOS Médecin.** ☎ *01–47–07–77–77, 3624 €0.15 per min* ⊕ *www.sosmedecins.fr.*

Foreign Embassies U.S. Embassy Consular Section. ☒ *4 av. Gabriel, 8e, Champs-Élysées* ☎ *01–43–12–22–22 , appointments required (online form) except for lost or stolen passports and emergencies, in which case press "0" when you hear the automated message* ⊕ *fr.usembassy.gov* Ⓜ *Concorde.*

General Emergency Contacts Ambulance. ☎ *15.* **Fire Department.** ☎ *18.* **General emergency services for police, fire, and ambulance (like 911).** ☎ *112.* **Police.** ☎ *112, 17.*

Hospitals and Clinics The American Hospital. ☒ *63 bd. Victor-Hugo, Neuilly-sur-Seine* ☎ *01–46–41–25–25* ⊕ *www.american-hospital. org.* **Institut Hospitalier Franco-Britannique.** ☒ *3 rue Barbès, or 4 rue Kléber, Levallois-Perret* ☎ *01–47–59–59–59* ⊕ *www.ihfb.org/en.*

Hotline SOS Help. ☎ *01–46–21–46–46* ⊕ *www.soshelpline.org.*

Pharmacies Pharmacie des Arts. ☒ *106 bd. Montparnasse, 14e, Montparnasse* ☎ *01–43–35–44–88.* **Pharmacie Internationale.** ☒ *5 pl. Pigalle, 9e, Montmartre* ☎ *01–48–78–38–12* ⊕ *pharmacieinternationale.pharminfo.fr.*

Pharmacie du Drugstore des Champs-Elysées. ☒ *Galerie des Champs, 133 av. des Champs-Élysées, 8e, Champs-Élysées* ☎ *01–47–20–39–25* ⊕ *www.pharmaciedrugstore-champselysees.com.* **Pharmacie Matignon.** ☒ *1 av. Matignon, at Rond-Point des Champs-Élysées, 8e, Champs-Élysées* ☎ *01–43–59–86–55* ⊕ *www.pharmaciematignon.com.*

▮ HOLIDAYS

With 11 national holidays (*jours feriés*) and five weeks of paid vacation, the French have their share of repose. In May there's a holiday nearly every week, so be prepared for stores, banks, and post offices to shut their doors for days at a time. If a holiday falls on a Tuesday or Thursday, many businesses *font le pont* (make the bridge) and close on that Monday or Friday as well. Some exchange booths in tourist areas, small grocery stores, restaurants, cafés, and bakeries usually remain open. Bastille Day (July 14) is observed in true French form. Celebrations begin on the evening of the 13th, when city firefighters open the doors to their stations, often classed as historical monuments, to host their much-acclaimed all-night balls and finish the next day with the annual military parade and air show.

Note that these dates are for the calendar year 2019: January 1 (New Year's Day); April 21–22 (Easter Sunday–Monday); May 1 (Labor Day); May 8 (VE Day); May 30 (Ascension Day); June 10 (Pentecost Monday); July 14 (Bastille Day); August 15 (Assumption Day); November 1 (All Saints' Day); November 11 (Armistice Day); December 25 (Christmas).

▮ HOURS OF OPERATION

On weekdays banks are generally open 9–5, with a lunchtime closure from 12:30 to 2 (note that the Banque de France is an exception, operating 9:30–12:30 and 2–4); some banks are also open Saturday 9–5. In general, government offices and businesses are open 9–5. *See Mail, below, for post office hours.*

Most museums are closed one day a week (typically Monday or Tuesday) and on a handful of national holidays. Generally, museums and national monuments are open from 10 to 5 or 6. A few close for lunch (noon–2) and are open only in the afternoon on Sunday. Many of the large museums have one *nocturne* (nighttime) opening per week, when they welcome visitors until 9:30 or 10. Pharmacies are generally open Monday to Saturday 8:30–8; when they're closed, they will (or should) post on the door the area pharmacies that are open on Sundays and 24 hours..

Generally, large shops are open from 9 or 10 to 7 or 8 Monday to Saturday and remain open through lunchtime. Many of the large department stores stay open later on Thursday. Smaller shops and many supermarkets often open earlier (8 am) but take a lengthy lunch break (1–3) and generally close around 8 pm; small food shops are often open Sunday morning 9–1. There is typically a small corner grocery store that stays open late, usually until 11, handy if you're in a bind for basic necessities like diapers, bread, cheese, or fruit. Note that prices are substantially higher in such outlets than in the larger supermarkets. Not all stores stay open on Sunday, except in the Marais. The Bastille, the Quartier Latin, the Champs-Élysées, Ile St-Louis, and the Ile de la Cité also have shops that open Sunday. Keep in mind, though, that many small shops close from mid-July to the end of August.

▮ MAIL

Post offices, or PTT, are scattered throughout every arrondissement and are recognizable by a yellow "La Poste" sign. They're usually open weekdays 8–7 and Saturday 8–noon. Airmail (*prioritaire*) letters or postcards usually take at least four days to reach North America. When shipping home antiques or art, request assistance from the dealer, who can usually handle the customs paperwork for you or recommend a licensed shipping company.

Airmail letters and postcards to the United States and Canada cost €1.30 for 20 grams, and €2.600 for 50–100 grams. Stamps can be bought in post offices and some cafés displaying a red "Tabac" sign.

SHIPPING PACKAGES

Sending overnight mail from Paris is relatively easy. Besides DHL, Federal Express, and UPS, the French post office has an overnight mail service called Chronopost that has special prepaid boxes for international use (and also boxes specifically made to mail wine). All agencies listed can be used as drop-off points, and all have information in English.

Express Services DHL. ✉ *23 rue Feydeau, 2e, Grands Boulevards* ☎ *08–25–10–00–80* €*0.18 per min* ⊕ *www.dhl.com.* **Federal Express.** ✉ *63 bd. Haussmann, 8e, Louvre* ☎ *08–20–12–38–00* €*0.12 per minute* ⊕ *www.fedex.com/fr.* **UPS.** ✉ *Office Depot, 168 rue du Faubourg St-Honoré, 8e, Grands Boulevards* ☎ *08–21–23–38–77* €*0.12 per min* ⊕ *www.ups.com.*

▮ MONEY

Although a stay in Paris is far from cheap, you can find plenty of affordable places to eat and shop, particularly if you avoid the obvious tourist traps. Prices tend to reflect the standing of an area in the eyes of Parisians; the touristy area where value is most difficult to find is the 8e arrondissement, on and around the Champs-Élysées. Places where you can generally be certain to shop, eat, and stay without overpaying include the St-Michel/Sorbonne area on the Rive Gauche; the mazelike streets around Les Halles and Le Marais in central Paris; in Montparnasse south of the boulevard; and in the Bastille, République, and Belleville areas of eastern Paris.

In cafés, bars, and some restaurants you can save money by eating or drinking at the counter instead of sitting at a table. Two prices are listed—*au comptoir* (at the counter) and *à salle* (at a table)—and sometimes a third for the terrace. A cup of coffee, standing at a bar, costs from €2; if you sit, it will cost €2.50 to €7. A glass of beer costs from €3 standing and from €4 to €7 sitting; a soft drink costs between €3 and €5. A ham sandwich will cost between €3.50 and €6.

Expect to pay €8 to €15 for a short taxi ride, less if you take Uber or another service that operates as a ride-hailing app. Museum entry is usually between €7 and €12, though there are hours or days of the week when admission is reduced or free. If you plan on museum hopping, it might be better value to pick up a Paris Museum Pass valid for two, four, or six consecutive days; these cost €448, €62, and €74, respectively.

Prices throughout this guide are given for adults. Substantially reduced fees are almost always available for children, students, and senior citizens.

ATMS AND BANKS

Your own bank will probably charge a fee for using ATMs (*guichets*) abroad; the foreign bank you use may also charge a fee. Nevertheless, you can usually get a better exchange rate at ATMs than at currency exchange offices, which are a disappearing breed. And taking out money as you need it is a safer option than carrying around a large amount of cash. Be sure to know your withdrawal limit before taking out cash, and note that French ATMs sometimes restrict how much money you can take out, regardless of your bank balance.

Although ATMs are plentiful, you may have to hunt around for Cirrus and Plus locations (they can be looked up online at ⊕ *www.mastercard.ca/atm-locator. html* and ⊕ *www.visa.com/atmlocator*, respectively). Note, too, that you may have better luck with ATMs if you're using a debit card that doubles as a Visa or MasterCard.

The largest bank in France, BNP Paribas, has agreements with both Barclay's and Bank of America, among others, that allow no-fee withdrawals between affiliated ATMs, typically a savings of $5 per transaction. Check with your local bank to see if it has an agreement with a French bank.

■ TIP➡ To get cash at ATMs in Paris, your PIN must be four digits long. If yours has five or more, remember to change it before you leave. If you're having trouble remembering your PIN, do not try more than twice, because at the third attempt the machine will eat your card, and it may take time for the bank to retrieve your card..

CREDIT CARDS

It's a good idea to inform your credit-card company before you travel, especially if you don't go abroad very often. Otherwise, the credit-card company might put a hold on your card owing to unusual activity—not a good thing halfway through your trip. Record all your credit-card numbers, plus the phone numbers to call if your cards are lost or stolen, in a safe place (but not your wallet or purse!), so you're prepared should something go wrong. Some travelers also like to leave a USB key with this information plus scanned passport pages with a trusted family member back home. Both MasterCard and Visa have general numbers you can call if your card is lost, but you're better off dialing the number of your issuing bank, since MasterCard and Visa generally just transfer you to your bank anyway; your bank's number is usually printed on your card. Take note: American Express is not as widely accepted in France, so it's wise to have a back-up card.

If you plan to use your credit card for cash advances, you'll need to apply for a PIN at least two weeks before your trip. Although it's usually cheaper (and safer) to use a credit card abroad for large purchases (so you can cancel payments or be reimbursed if there's a problem), some credit-card companies *and* the banks that issue them add substantial percentages to all foreign transactions, whether they're in a foreign currency or not. Check on these fees before leaving home, so there won't be any surprises when you get the bill.

■TIP→ Before you charge something, ask the merchant whether he or she plans to do a dynamic currency conversion (DCC). In such a transaction the credit-card processor (shop, restaurant, or hotel, not Visa or MasterCard) converts the currency and charges you in dollars. In most cases you'll pay the merchant a 3% fee for this service in addition to any credit-card company and issuing-bank foreign-transaction surcharges.

Reporting Lost Cards American Express. ☎ 800/528-4800 in the U.S. and Canada, 01-47-77-70-00 ⊕ www.americanexpress. com. **MasterCard.** ☎ 800/627-8372 in the U.S. and Canada, 08-00-90-13-87 ⊕ www. mastercard.com. **Visa.** ☎ 800/847-2911 in the U.S. and Canada, 08-00-90-11-79 ⊕ www. visa.com.

CURRENCY AND EXCHANGE

In 2002 the single European Union (EU) currency—the euro—became the official currency of the 19 of 28 member countries participating in the Eurozone (with the notable exceptions of Great Britain, Denmark, Norway, and Sweden). The euro system has eight coins: 1 and 2 euros, plus 1, 2, 5, 10, 20, and 50 cents. All coins have one side that has the value of the euro on it, whereas the opposite side is adorned with each country's own unique national symbol. (Be aware that, because of their high nickel content, euro coins can pose problems for people with an allergic sensitivity to the metal.) There are also seven colorful notes: 5, 10, 20, 50, 100, 200, and 500 euros. Notes have the principal architectural styles from antiquity onward on one side and the map and the flag of Europe on the other and are the same for all countries. If you happen to have brought some rumpled old francs from home on this trip, you may as well frame them and hang them on the wall for posterity, not prosperity:

the Banque de France stopped exchanging francs in 2012.

At this writing, €1 equaled approximately US$1.23 and $1.56 Canadian.

The easiest way to get euros is through ever-present ATMs. ATM rates are excellent because they are based on wholesale rates offered only by major banks. Whenever possible, it's best to use machines that are protected by a door and not directly on the street; don't speak to people in line, and always cover your hand when entering your code in case there is a hidden camera. ■TIP→ It's a good idea to bring some euros with you from home so you don't have to wait in line at the airport. At exchange booths always confirm the rate with the teller before changing money. You won't do as well at exchange booths in airports or rail and bus stations, in hotels, in restaurants, or in stores. French banks only exchange the money of their own clients.

■ PACKING

You'll notice it right away: in Paris the women dress well to go shopping, to go to the cinema, to have a drink; the men look good when they're sipping an espresso. Admittedly, you may see them wearing the latest athletic clothes now, even when they're not doing something *sportif*—but we're not talking gray hoodies. Embroidered designs, quilted materials, animal prints, sparkles: leave it to the French to create a style that's comfy chic. If you want to blend in, don't wear shorts, sweats, or sneakers.

Be sure to bring rain gear, a comfortable pair of walking shoes, and a sweater or pashmina for cool churches and museums. You can never tell about the weather, so it's prudent to have a small, foldable umbrella. If you'd like to scrutinize the stained glass in churches, bring a pair of small binoculars. An additional note: if you're the kind of person who likes a washcloth in the bathroom, bring your own; you won't find one in Paris hotels.

▮ PASSPORTS AND VISAS

All citizens of Canada and the United States, even infants, need a valid passport to enter France for stays of up to 90 days. If you lose your passport, call the nearest embassy or consulate and the local police immediately.

▮ RESTROOMS

Use of public toilet facilities in cafés and bars is usually reserved for customers, so you may need to buy a little something first. Bathrooms are often downstairs and can be unisex, which may mean walking by a men's urinal to reach the cubicle. Turkish-style toilets—holes in the ground with porcelain pads for your feet—are now fortunately scarce. In certain cafés the lights will not come on in the bathroom until the cubicle door is locked. These lights work on a timer to save electricity. Simply press the button again if the lights go out, or move and a sensor will switch it back on. Clean public toilets are available in fast-food chains, department stores, and public parks. Paris also has 400 *sanisettes,* or public toilet units, located around the city; 150 in hot spots are open 24/7; 220 others are open 6 am to 10:50 pm, and 30 more from 6 am to 1 am. They are free and generally as proper as one could expect, because they self-clean after every use. Some public restroom charge €0.50 to €1.50—but when you gotta go, you gotta pay.

There are restroom attendants in train and métro stations, so always bring some coins to the bathroom. Attendants in restaurants and clubs are in charge of cleaning the bathrooms and perhaps handing you a clean towel; slip some small change into the prominently placed saucer.

▮ SAFETY

Paris is as safe as any big city can be, but you should always remain streetwise and alert. Certain neighborhoods are more seedy than dangerous, thanks to the night trade that goes on around Les Halles and St-Denis and on Boulevard de Clichy in Pigalle. Some off-the-beaten-path neighborhoods (particularly the outlying suburban communities) may warrant extra precaution. When in doubt, stick to the boulevards and well-lighted, populated streets; keep in mind, however, that the Champs-Élysées, Notre-Dame, and Louvre areas are a haven for pickpockets.

The métro is quite safe overall, though some lines and stations, in particular Lines 2 and 13, get dodgy late at night, so try not to travel alone, memorize the time of the last métro train to your station, ride in the first car by the conductor, and just use common sense. If you're worried, spend the money on a taxi. Pickpocketing is the main problem, day or night. Be wary of anyone crowding you unnecessarily, distracting you, or leaning into you. As much as possible, try to blend in and speak softly (as the French do). Pickpockets often work in groups—and they move fast; on the métro they usually strike just before a stop so that they can leap off the train as it pulls into the station. Be especially careful if taking the RER from Charles de Gaulle/Roissy airport into town; disoriented or jet-lagged travelers are vulnerable to sticky fingers.

Pickpockets love bling and won't miss the opportunity to yank off a necklace or follow a tourist wearing a flashy girl's-best-friend on her finger. They often target purses, smartphones, and laptop bags, so keep your valuables on your person. It's also wise to distribute your cash, credit cards, IDs, and other valuables between a deep front pocket, an inside jacket or vest pocket, and a hidden money pouch. Don't reach for the money pouch once you're in public. If someone holding a map, even a well-dressed woman, asks for directions, go against your helpful American nature and keep walking. Also be wary of the "ring trick" when a passerby suddenly stops in front of you to pick a gold ring off the ground and then offers to sell it to you.

A tremendous number of protest demonstrations are held in Paris—scarcely a week goes by without some kind of march or public gathering. Most are peaceful, but it's best to avoid them. The CRS (French riot police) carefully guard all major demonstrations, directing traffic and preventing violence. They are armed and use tear gas when and if they see fit.

Report any thefts or other problems to the police as soon as possible (note that *officiers* wear a badge indicating what languages they speak). There are three or four police stations in every arrondissement in Paris and one police station in every train station; go to the one in the area where the event occurred. In the case of pickpocketing or other theft, the police will give you a *Déclaration de Perte ou de Vol* (receipt for theft or loss). Police reports must be made in person, and the process is helped along by the S.A.V.E. assistance system for foreign victims—a multilingual software program that files your complaint (and provides you with a receipt) in English. You can also pre-file an incident of theft report in French online at ⊕ *www.pre-plainte-en-ligne. gouv.fr*; this saves time on the paperwork, although a visit in person to the police station will still be necessary. Valuables are usually unrecoverable, but identity documents have been known to resurface. You may need your receipt of theft or loss to replace stolen train and plane tickets or passports; the receipts may also be useful for filing insurance claims.

Although women traveling alone sometimes encounter troublesome comments and the like, *dragueurs* (men who flirt, sometimes *way*too much) are a dying breed in this increasingly politically correct world. Note that smiling automatically out of politeness is not part of French culture and can be quickly misinterpreted. If you encounter a problem, don't be afraid to show your irritation. Completely ignoring the dragueur should be discouragement enough; if the hassling

doesn't let up, don't hesitate to move quickly away.

■TIP➜ A few words of advice: leave your jewelry at home, and make sure that smartphones and tablets stay out of sight. Don't talk to strangers. If someone approaches asking you to take a photo, sign a petition, or provide directions, just keep walking.

▌TAXES

Taxes must be included in affixed prices in France. Prices in restaurants and hotels must by law include taxes and service charges. ■TIP➜ If these appear as additional items on your bill, you should complain. There is, however, one exception: don't be shocked to find the *taxe de séjour* (tourist tax) on your hotel tab when you check out. Ranging from €0.22 (for campers) to €4.40 per person per day, it is applied to all types of lodging. Even if you prepaid your accommodation online through a third-party travel website, you'll still have to cough up the coins.

The standard rate of the V.A.T. (value-added tax, known in France as T.V.A.) is now 20%. A lower rate applies to restaurant food (10%), pharmacy goods, and books, but it can be as high as 33% for certain luxury items. The V.A.T. for services (restaurants, theaters, etc.) is not refundable, but foreigners are often entitled to a V.A.T. refund on goods they buy. To qualify for one, you must have bought more than €175 worth on the same day in the same participating store (look for the "Tax-Free" sticker on the door) and have stayed three months or less in the EU at the time of purchase. The system is now simpler to obtain under the revised PABLO system: Participating retailers will provide you with a computer-generated PABLO Value-Added Tax (V.A.T.) refund form containing a barcode and the PABLO logo. You then scan the code before checking in at the airport for your outbound flight. The PABLO machines at CDG and Orly provide service in English and can credit the refunded amount directly to your bank account or credit card.

At the airport, be sure to have your passport, your ticket, and your PABLO form for items purchased. Go to the La Détaxe/tax refund machine, scan the form's barcode and you'll receive a message *"OK bordereau validé"* ("OK, form valid") with a green screen (a red screen will give further instructions). An electronic confirmation will be sent directly to the retailer for your reimbursement to be processed. Remember, this must be done BEFORE checking-in your luggage.

▌ TIME

The time difference between New York and Paris is six hours (so when it's 1 pm in New York, it's 7 pm in Paris). The time difference between London and Paris is one hour (so 1 pm in London is 2 pm in Paris). Note that Daylight Saving Time is different in Europe and North America: European clocks change one week earlier in the fall and three weeks later in the spring.

The European format for abbreviating dates is day/month/year, so 7/5/19 means May 7, not July 5.

▌ TIPPING

Although Americans may have been voted the world's worst tourists, they are the heavyweight champions when it comes to tipping. In France, this is not a cultural norm. Bills in bars and restaurants must by law include service (despite what entrepreneurial servers may tell you), so tipping isn't required. Waiters are paid well; it is polite, however, to round your bill with small change unless you're dissatisfied. The amount varies—from €0.20 for a beer to €1–€3 after a meal. In expensive restaurants, it's common to leave an additional 5%–10% on the table.

With taxi drivers, round up for shorter trips and add up to 5% of the tab for longer ones. Tip hairdressers 10%. In some

theaters and hotels cloakroom attendants may expect nothing (watch for signs that say *pourboire interdit*—tipping forbidden; otherwise, give them €1).

If you stay more than two or three days in a hotel, leave something for the chambermaid—about €1–€2 per day; if the chambermaid also does pressing or laundering for you, give her an extra €1.50–€2 on top of the bill. Expect to pay €2 (€1 in a moderately priced hotel) to the person who carries your bags or hails a taxi for you. In hotels providing room service, give €1–€2 to the waiter (unless breakfast is routinely served in your room). If the concierge has been helpful, leave a tip of €5–€20 depending on the service.

Museum guides should get €1–€1.50 after a tour. For other kinds of tours, tip the guide or leader 10% of the tour cost. It's standard practice to tip long-distance bus drivers about €2 after an excursion, too.

TIPPING GUIDELINES FOR PARIS	
Bellhop	€1–€2, depending on the level of the hotel
Hotel Concierge	€5–€20 if he or she performs a service for you
Hotel Doorman	€1–€2 if he helps you get a cab
Hotel Maid	€1–€2 a day (either daily or at the end of your stay, in cash)
Hotel Room-Service Waiter	€1–€2 per delivery, even if a service charge has been added
Taxi Driver	5% is considered a good tip
Tour Guide	10% of the cost of the tour (but museum guides, €1–€1.50 after a tour)
Valet Parking Attendant	€1–€2, but only when you get your car
Waiter	Round up for small bills, €1–€3 for meals, 5%–10% in expensive restaurants
Restroom Attendant	Restroom attendants in more expensive restaurants expect small change or €1

■ TOURS

Guided tours are a good option when you don't want to do it all yourself. A knowledgeable guide can take you places that you might never discover on your own, and you may be pushed to see more than you would have otherwise. Tours aren't for everyone, but they can be just the thing for trips to places where making travel arrangements is difficult or time-consuming (particularly when you don't speak the language). Whenever you book a guided tour, find out what's included and what isn't. In most cases prices in tour brochures don't include fees and taxes, plus you'll be expected to tip your guide (in cash) at the end of the tour.

BIKE AND SEGWAY TOURS

A number of companies organize bike tours around Paris and its environs (Versailles, Chantilly, and Fontainebleau); these always include bikes, helmets, and an English-speaking guide. Costs start at around €35 for a half day; reservations are recommended.

Fat Tire Tours Paris is the best-known Anglophone group; they are now a multiple-tour outfit and have a nighttime cycling trip that includes a boat cruise on the Seine; Segway tours are also available. Paris à Vélo, C'est Sympa! offers tours that take pedal pushers through the heart of Paris or around outlying arrondissements.

Information Fat Tire Tours Paris. ⊠ 24 rue Edgar Faure, 15e ☎ 01-82-88-80-96, 866/614-6218 in the U.S. and Canada ⊕ www. fattiretours.com/paris. **Paris à Vélo, C'est Sympa!** ⊠ 22 rue Alphonse Baudin, 11e ☎ 01-48-87-60-01 ⊕ https://parisvelosympa. fr/paris-a-velo-cest-sympa.

BOAT TOURS

Several boat-tour companies operate Seine cruises that include sightseeing and, in some cases, dining. Batobus offers a convenient way to travel between all major sites along the river, including Notre-Dame, the Louvre, and the Eiffel Tower. A ticket for one day of unlimited hop-on/hop-off travel costs €17. One-hour Bateaux Parisiens sightseeing cruises cost €15 and depart from the Eiffel Tower every 30 minutes from 10 to 10, April to September; themed dinner and lunch cruises start at €69 and €59, respectively. Canauxrama organizes leisurely tours year-round in flat-bottom barges along the Seine and the Canal St-Martin in eastern Paris. There are four daily departures from April to October (less during the rest of the year); trips cost €18 and last about 2½ hours, with commentary in French and English. Compagnie des Bateaux-Mouches runs a tight ship 12 months of the year. Tickets for the 70-minute Seine tour cost €13.50; lunch cruises are €60, and dinner cruises start at €75. Other year-round operators include Paris Canal, which offers 2½-hour trips with live bilingual commentary between the Musée d'Orsay and the Parc de La Villette (€14; €59 dinner cruise)

Information Bateaux Parisiens. ⊠ Port de la Bourdonnais, 7e ☎ 08-25-01-01-01 ⊕ www. bateauxparisiens.com. **Batobus.** ⊠ Port de la Bourdonnais, 7e ☎ 08-25-05-01-01 €0.15 per min ⊕ www.batobus.com. **Canauxrama.** ⊠ Bassin de la Villette, 13 quai de la Loire, 19e ☎ 01-42-39-15-00 ⊕ www.canauxrama.com. **Compagnie des Bateaux-Mouches.** ⊠ Port de la Conférence, 8e ☎ 01-42-25-96-10 ⊕ www.bateaux-mouches.fr. **Paris Canal.** ⊠ Paris Canal, Bassin de la Villette, 21 quai de la Loire, 19e ☎ 01-42-40-96-97 ⊕ www. pariscanal.com.

BUS TOURS

Pariscityvision.com runs a broad assortment of tours and day trips starting at €15. Buses are equipped with headsets that provide commentary in more than a dozen languages, and there are special recordings for children. Paris Open Tour' offers hop-on/hop-off tours in a London-style double-decker bus with English or French commentary via individual headsets; you can catch one at any of the 50 pickup points on its four lines. Passes cost €33 (1 day), €37 (2 days), or €41 (3 days). More hop-on/hop-off tours aboard double-decker buses are available through Big Bus Paris; it has more than 11 stops, and a one-day ticket costs €31.50. Low-cost Foxity has two main departures, from Notre-Dame and Opéra; a two-hour outing with headphone commentary costs €17. By day or night, Foxity takes visitors around most of central Paris and offers handicap access. For an inexpensive, commentary-free alternative, try a regular Parisian bus. The Montmartrobus (€1.90) runs from the Anvers métro station to the top of Montmartre's winding streets. April through September on Sunday and holidays.,.

Information Big Bus Tours. ⊠ *17 quai de Grenelle, 15e* ☎ *01-53-95-39-53* ⊕ *eng. bigbustours.com/paris/home.html.* **Foxity.** ⊠ *5 av. de l'Opera, 9e* ☎ *01-42-96-07-97* ⊕ *www. foxity.com.* **Open Tour Paris.** ⊠ *13 rue Auber, 9e* ☎ *01-42-66-56-56* ⊕ *www.paris.opentour. com/en.* **Pariscityvision.com.** ⊠ *2 rue des Pyramides, 1er* ☎ *01-44-55-61-00* ⊕ *www. pariscityvision.com.* **RATP.** ☎ *3246 €0.80 per min* ⊕ *www.ratp.fr.*

MINIBUS AND CAR TOURS

Pariscityvision.com runs minibus excursions with a multilingual guide to places like Mont St-Michel and the Loire Valley (check the website for promos and prices). Paris Trip and Paris Major Limousine organize tours of Paris and environs by limousine, Mercedes, or minibus (for 4–15 passengers) for a minimum of four hours. Chauffeurs are bilingual. Prices range from €68 to €999, depending on the type of vehicle and the distance covered. Another four-wheel option is 4 Roues sous 1 Parapluie: take the Unknown Paris tour (90 minutes, €60) and discover the city's best-kept secrets in an old-school Citroën 2CV (France's answer to the Volkswagen Beetle), or try a ride around the Champs-Élysées (45 minutes, €30). With 20-odd options available in this iconic car, you can leave the driving to others and just enjoy being a tourist.

Information 4 Rues sous 1 Parapluie. ⊠ *22 rue Bernard Dimey, 18e* ☎ *01-58-59-27-82* ⊕ *www.4roues-sous-1parapluie.com.* **Paris Major Limousine.** ⊠ *199 bd. Malesherbes, 17e* ☎ *01-44-52-50-00* ⊕ *www.1st-limousine-services.com.* **Paris Trip.** ⊠ *41 av. de la Bourdonnais, 7e* ☎ *01-86-21-96-91* ⊕ *www. paris-trip.com.* **Pariscityvision.com.** ⊠ *2 rue des Pyramides, 1er* ☎ *01-44-55-61-00* ⊕ *www.pariscityvision.com.*

SPECIAL-INTEREST AND WALKING TOURS

Has it been a while since Art History 101? Paris Muse can help guide you through the city's museums; with its staff of art historians (all native English-speakers) you can crack the da Vinci code or gain a new understanding of hell in front of Rodin's sculpted gates. Rates start at €70, including museum admission.

If you'd like a bit of guidance flexing your own artistic muscles, take a themed photography tour with Photo Tours in Paris. Run by Randy Harris, these relaxed excursions are perfect for first-time visitors and anyone hoping to improve their photographic skills. Expect to pay $165 for a daytime tour, $275 for the evening version.

Sign up with Chic Shopping Paris to smoothly navigate the city's retail scene. Tours, which start at €100, include Chic Consignment (focusing on vintage–secondhand places), Très Teens, and Unique Boutiques; itineraries can also be tailor-made to fit your interests.

Edible Paris, the brainchild of food writer Rosa Jackson, is a customized service for vacationing gastronomes. Submit a wish list of your interests and guidelines for your tastes, and you'll receive a personalized itinerary, maps, and restaurant reservations on request. Prices start around €300 for three hours.

Paris by Mouth—the most popular English-language website about eating and drinking in the city—offers tasting tours led by local food writers. Three-hour outings, which run every day of the week, are available for up to eight people (€110 per person). Private tours and larger group tours are available upon request; you can also add on a wine tasting, shared lunch, or baguette-making class.

Paris Walks offers a wide selection of tours, some year-round, that range from neighborhood visits and museum jaunts to themed tours such as Hemingway's Paris. The guides are knowledgeable, taking you into less trammeled streets and divulging interesting stories about even the most unprepossessing spots. A two-hour group tour costs €15, and you don't have to reserve.

For a more intimate experience, Context Paris offers specialized in-depth tours of the city's art and architecture led by English-speaking architects and art historians; tours aimed at foodies are also available. Prices range from €117 per person for a three-hour group tour to around €500 for a private tour.

Black Paris Tours explores the places made famous by African American musicians, writers, artists, and political exiles. Options include a 5½-hour walking-bus-métro tour (€125) that provides first-time visitors with a city orientation and a primer on the history of African Americans in Paris.

Interesting walking tours are also available from the Centre des Monuments Nationaux; check the website or look for listings in the weekly magazine *L'Officiel des Spectacles,* which covers them under the heading "Conférences" (most tours are in French, unless otherwise noted).

If you are as interested in the locals as in the sights per se, you can't go wrong with Paris Greeters (*Parisien d'un Jour*). English-speaking resident volunteers take groups of up to six visitors out for a stroll, providing an insider's look at Parisian life along the way. Best of all, the experience is free, though donations are always welcome.

Information Black Paris Tours. ☎ *06–62–68–03–96* ⊕ *www.blackparistour.com.* **Centre des monuments nationaux.** ⊠ *Bureau des Visites/Conférences, Hôtel de Sully, 62 rue St-Antoine, 4e* ☎ *01–44–61–20–00* ⊕ *www.monuments-nationaux.fr.* **Chic Shopping Paris.** ⊕ *www.chicshoppingparis.com.* **Context Paris.** ☎ *800/691–6036 U.S. office* ⊕ *www.contexttravel.com.* **Edible Paris.** ⊕ *www.edible-paris.com.* **Paris by Mouth.** ⊕ *www.parisbymouth.com.* **Paris Greeters.** ⊕ *www.greeters.paris.* **Paris Muse.** ☎ *06–73–77–33–52* ⊕ *www.parismuse.com.* **Paris Photo Tours.** ☎ *06–40–14–84–49* ⊕ *www.parisphototours.com.* **Paris Walks.** ⊠ *12 passage Meunier, St-Denis* ☎ *01–48–09–21–40* ⊕ *www.pariswalks.com.*

❚ VISITOR INFORMATION

The regional tourism board—with multiple Arrivals-level kiosks at both Charles de Gaulle and Orly airports—can provide you with maps, brochures, and more the moment you touch down. Once you're in Paris, you can turn to the civic tourist information office. The main one is centrally located on Rue des Pyramides (near the Opéra), and four branch offices are stationed at the city's most popular tourist sights. Most are open daily; the Gare de Lyon and Gare de l'Est branches, however, are open Monday through Saturday only. These tourism bureaus have friendly, efficient, multilingual staff. You can gather info on special events, local transit, hotels, tours, excursions, and discount passes. You can also purchase museum passes and the coveted passports for Versailles, which enable you to avoid additional lines at the château. Extra kiosks pop up in the summer by Notre-Dame, Hotel de Ville, the Champs-Élysées, and Bastille.

Local Tourism Information Office du Tourisme de la Ville de Paris Anvers. ⊠ *Across from 72 bd. Rochechouart, 18e, Montmartre* ⊕ *www.parisinfo.com* Ⓜ *Anvers.* **Office du Tourisme de la Ville de Paris Gare de l'Est.** ⊠ *Facing platform 1 and 2, Pl. du 11 novembre 1918, 10e, Canal St-Martin* ⊕ *www.parisinfo.com* Ⓜ *Gare de l'Est.* **Office du Tourisme de la Ville de Paris Gare de**

Lyon. ✉ *Hall 1, facing L & M platforms, 20 bd. Diderot, 12e, Bastille* ⊕ *www.parisinfo.com* Ⓜ *Gare de Lyon.* **Office du Tourisme de la Ville de Paris Gare du Nord.** ✉ *Under glass ceiling at Ile de France section, 18 rue de Dunkerque, 10e, Stalingrad* ⊕ *www.parisinfo. com* Ⓜ *Gare du Nord.* **Office du Tourisme de la Ville de Paris Pyramides.** ✉ *25 rue des Pyramides, 1er, Louvre* ⊕ *www.parisinfo.com* Ⓜ *Pyramides.* **Visit Paris Region.** ⊕ *www. visitparisregion.com.*

ONLINE RESOURCES

Besides the official tourist office websites ⊕ *en.parisinfo.com* and ⊕ *www.visit-parisregion.com*, there are several other helpful government-sponsored sites. The Paris mayor's office site, ⊕ *www.paris.fr*, covers all kinds of public cultural attractions, student resources, parks, markets, and more. On the French Ministry of Culture's site, ⊕ *www.culture.fr*, you can search by theme (contemporary art, cinema, music, theater, etc.) or by region (Paris is in Ile-de-France). The Réunion des Musées Nationaux hosts a group site, ⊕ *www.rmn.fr*, that provides visitor info and exhibition updates for 20 member museums; most are in Paris proper, including the Louvre, the Musée Rodin, and the Musée d'Orsay. Bonjour Paris ⊕ *www.bonjourparis.com* keeps tabs on what's hot around town.

A useful website for checking Paris addresses is the phone and address directory, Les Pages Jaunes (⊕ *www.pages-jaunes.fr*). Input a specific address, and you get not just a street map but a photo as well.

The team at Paris by Mouth (⊕ *parisby-mouth.com*) dishes on the local food scene with help from expat writers like Alexander Lobrano. Also check Lobrano's site (⊕ *www.hungryforparis.com*) for his latest Hungry for Paris & France dining reviews and favorite Paris food links. Secrets of Paris (⊕ *www.secretsofparis. com*) has a free online newsletter with tips on dining, nightlife, accommodations, and sightseeing off the beaten path.

Though not entirely dedicated to Paris, France Today (⊕ *www.francetoday.com*) and The Local (⊕ *www.thelocal.fr*) often cover Paris-related news, arts events, and restaurants.

There are all sorts of Paris-related blogs that can be great sources of information and travel inspiration. Some of our favorites are Do it in Paris (⊕ *www.doitinparis. com*), and My Little Paris ⊕ *www.mylit-tleparis.com* bilingual sites focused on fashion, shopping, dining, and fun activities; and the Hip Paris Blog (⊕ *hipparis. com*), which combines a trendy array of Parisian pics with insight into food, arts, and local living. Professional pastry-chef-turned-author David Lebovitz left California to live (and write exquisitely about) the sweet life in Paris on his blog at ⊕ *www.davidlebovitz.com.*

INDEX

ABOUT OUR WRITERS

 Journalist and photographer **Linda Hervieux** has explored most corners of Paris since moving to the City of Light in 2004. Her writing has appeared in the *New York Times*, the *International Herald Tribune*, and the *New York Daily News*, among others. For Fodor's she has scoped out more than 100 museums and galleries and spent countless hours in her favorite: the mighty Musée du Louvre, where she studied art history. Her website is ⊕ *www.lindahervieux.com*. She updated the Experience, Around the Louvre, Side Trips From Paris, and Travel Smart chapters this edition.

 When writer-editor **Jennifer Ladonne** decided it was time to leave her longtime home of Manhattan, there was only one place to go: Paris. Her insatiable curiosity—which earned her a reputation in New York for knowing just the right place to go for just the right anything—has found the perfect home in the inexhaustible streets of Paris. An avid cook and wine lover, she's a frequent contributor on food, culture, and travel and a monthly columnist for the magazine *France Today*. Whether you're looking for the best neighborhood bistros or the perfect little black dress, she's the person to ask, as we did for our Where to Eat, Shopping, Where to Stay, and Nightlife chapters.

 A life-long urban explorer, journalist and photo editor **Virginia Power** has been strolling the streets of Paris for the past 25 years. She has written and reported on a variety of subjects—culture, politics, sports, social issues—for *Newsweek*, *Paris* Magazine, and other publications. Writing for Fodor's has brought her back to doing what she does best: wandering, discovering, and enjoying what Paris has to offer. This edition, she updated the Montparnasse and St-Germain-des-Prés neighborhood chapters.

 Jack Vermee is a Canadian university lecturer, film critic, screenwriter, film festival programmer, and freelance writer/editor who happily exchanged nature for culture by moving from Vancouver to Paris six years ago. Starting in the pre-video days of the early 1980s, when he first visited the city to watch classic films at the old Cinémathèque Française, he has carried on a shameless love affair with *la ville-lumière* and its innumerable charms. He suspects the love affair will never run its course—with 6,100 city streets to explore and new adventures just around the next corner, how could it? Jack brought his knowledge to the following neighborhood chapters: Les Grands Boulevards, Montmartre, the Marais, Eastern Paris, Western Paris, Around the Eiffel Tower, Champs-Élysées, Ile St-Lous and Ile de la Cité, and the Latin Quarter. You can reach him at *jvermee@gmail.com*.

Paris Métro and RER